# ROAD ATLAS

# 2023 BIG EASY TO R BRITAIN

C000089029

www.philips-maps.co.uk

First published in 2020 by Philip's
a division of Octopus Publishing Group Ltd
www.octopusbooks.co.uk
Carmelite House, 50 Victoria Embankment
London EC4Y 0DZ
An Hachette UK Company
www.hachette.co.uk

Third edition 2022
Second impression 2022

ISBN 978-1-84907-596-1

Cartography by Philip's
Copyright © 2022 Philip's

This product includes mapping data licensed from Ordnance Survey®, with the permission of the Controller of Her Majesty's Stationery Office. © Crown copyright 2022. All rights reserved. Licence number 100011710

Information for National Parks, Areas of Outstanding Natural Beauty, National Trails and Country Parks in Wales supplied by the Countryside Council for Wales.

Information for National Parks, Areas of Outstanding Natural Beauty, National Trails and Country Parks in England supplied by Natural England. Data for Regional Parks, Long Distance Footpaths and Country Parks in Scotland provided by Scottish Natural Heritage.

Gaelic name forms used in the Western Isles provided by Comhairle nan Eilean.

Data for the National Nature Reserves in England provided by Natural England. Data for the National Nature Reserves in Wales provided by Countryside Council for Wales. Darparwyd data'n ymwneud â Gwarchodfeydd Natur Cenedlaethol Cymru gan Gyngor Cefn Gwlad Cymru.

Information on the location of National Nature Reserves in Scotland was provided by Scottish Natural Heritage.

Data for National Scenic Areas in Scotland provided by the Scottish Executive Office. Crown copyright material is reproduced with the permission of the Controller of HMSO and the Queen's Printer for Scotland. Licence number C02W0003960.

Printed in China

*Data from Nielsen Total Consumer Market 2020 weeks 27–39

MIX
Paper from
responsible sources
FSC® C016973
www.fsc.org

# CONTENTS

**II** **Key to map symbols**

**III** **Restricted motorway junctions**

**IV** **Route planning maps**

**XIV** **Distances and journey times**

**1** **Key to road map pages**

**2** **Road maps of Britain**

**161** **Urban approach maps**

  **161** Bristol *approaches*
  **162** Birmingham *approaches*
  **164** Cardiff *approaches*
  **165** Edinburgh *approaches*
  **166** Glasgow *approaches*
  **167** Leeds *approaches*
  **168** London *approaches*
  **172** Liverpool *approaches*
  **173** Manchester *approaches*
  **174** Newcastle *approaches*

**175** **Town plans**

  **175** Aberdeen, Ayr, Bath
  **176** Birmingham, Blackpool, Bournemouth
  **177** Bradford, Brighton, Bristol
  **178** Bury St Edmunds, Cambridge, Canterbury, Cardiff
  **179** Carlisle, Chelmsford, Cheltenham, Chester
  **180** Chichester, Colchester, Coventry, Derby
  **181** Dorchester, Dumfries, Dundee, Durham
  **182** Edinburgh, Exeter, Gloucester
  **183** Glasgow, Grimsby, Harrogate
  **184** Hull, Inverness, Ipswich, Kendal
  **185** King's Lynn, Leeds, Lancaster
  **186** London
  **188** Leicester, Lincoln, Liverpool
  **189** Llandudno, Llanelli, Luton, Macclesfield
  **190** Manchester, Maidstone, Merthyr Tydfil
  **191** Middlesbrough, Milton Keynes, Newcastle upon Tyne, Newport
  **192** Newquay, Northampton, Norwich, Nottingham
  **193** Oxford, Perth, Peterborough, Plymouth
  **194** Poole, Portsmouth, Preston, Reading
  **195** St Andrews, Salisbury, Scarborough, Shrewsbury
  **196** Sheffield, Stoke-on-Trent (Hanley), Southampton
  **197** Southend-on-Sea, Stirling, Stratford-upon-Avon, Sunderland
  **198** Swansea, Swindon, Taunton, Telford
  **199** Torquay, Truro, Winchester, Windsor
  **200** Wolverhampton, Worcester, Wrexham, York

**201** **Index to road maps of Britain**

Inside back cover: **County and unitary authority boundaries**

# Road map symbols

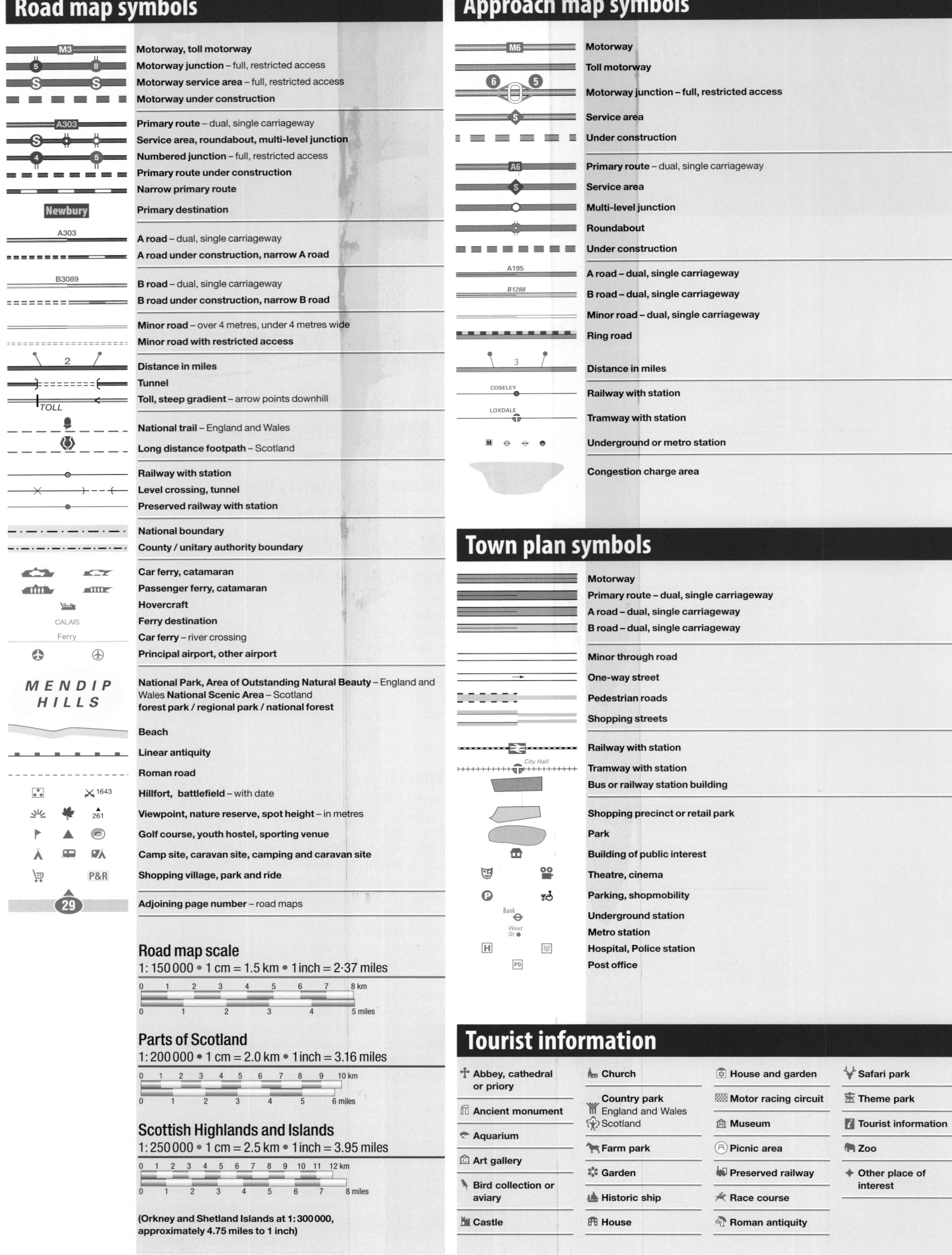

Motorway, toll motorway
Motorway junction – full, restricted access
Motorway service area – full, restricted access
Motorway under construction

Primary route – dual, single carriageway
Service area, roundabout, multi-level junction
Numbered junction – full, restricted access
Primary route under construction
Narrow primary route
Primary destination

Newbury

A road – dual, single carriageway
A road under construction, narrow A road

B road – dual, single carriageway
B road under construction, narrow B road

Minor road – over 4 metres, under 4 metres wide
Minor road with restricted access

Distance in miles
Tunnel
Toll, steep gradient – arrow points downhill

National trail – England and Wales
Long distance footpath – Scotland

Railway with station
Level crossing, tunnel
Preserved railway with station

National boundary
County / unitary authority boundary

Car ferry, catamaran
Passenger ferry, catamaran
Hovercraft
Ferry destination
Car ferry – river crossing
Principal airport, other airport

MENDIP HILLS

National Park, Area of Outstanding Natural Beauty – England and Wales National Scenic Area – Scotland
forest park / regional park / national forest

Beach
Linear antiquity
Roman road
Hillfort, battlefield – with date
Viewpoint, nature reserve, spot height – in metres
Golf course, youth hostel, sporting venue
Camp site, caravan site, camping and caravan site
Shopping village, park and ride

Adjoining page number – road maps

## Road map scale
1: 150 000 • 1 cm = 1.5 km • 1 inch = 2·37 miles

## Parts of Scotland
1: 200 000 • 1 cm = 2.0 km • 1 inch = 3.16 miles

## Scottish Highlands and Islands
1: 250 000 • 1 cm = 2.5 km • 1 inch = 3.95 miles

(Orkney and Shetland Islands at 1: 300 000, approximately 4.75 miles to 1 inch)

# Approach map symbols

Motorway
Toll motorway
Motorway junction – full, restricted access
Service area
Under construction

Primary route – dual, single carriageway
Service area
Multi-level junction
Roundabout
Under construction

A road – dual, single carriageway
B road – dual, single carriageway
Minor road – dual, single carriageway
Ring road

Distance in miles
COSELEY    Railway with station
LOXDALE    Tramway with station
Underground or metro station
Congestion charge area

# Town plan symbols

Motorway
Primary route – dual, single carriageway
A road – dual, single carriageway
B road – dual, single carriageway

Minor through road
One-way street
Pedestrian roads
Shopping streets

Railway with station
City Hall    Tramway with station
Bus or railway station building

Shopping precinct or retail park
Park
Building of public interest
Theatre, cinema
Parking, shopmobility
Bank    Underground station
West St    Metro station
Hospital, Police station
Post office

# Tourist information

Abbey, cathedral or priory
Ancient monument
Aquarium
Art gallery
Bird collection or aviary
Castle

Church
Country park England and Wales Scotland
Farm park
Garden
Historic ship
House

House and garden
Motor racing circuit
Museum
Picnic area
Preserved railway
Race course
Roman antiquity

Safari park
Theme park
Tourist information
Zoo
Other place of interest

# Restricted motorway junctions

| M1 | Northbound | Southbound |
|---|---|---|
| 2 | No exit | No access |
| 4 | No exit | No access |
| 6A | No exit. Access from M25 only | No access. Exit to M25 only |
| 7 | No exit. Access from A414 only | No access. Exit to A414 only |
| 17 | No access. Exit to M45 only | No exit. Access from M45 only |
| 19 | No exit to A14 | No access from A14 |
| 21A | No access | No access |
| 23A | | Exit to A42 only |
| 24A | No exit | No access |
| 35A | No access | No exit |
| 43 | No access. Exit to M621 only | No exit. Access from M621 only |
| 48 | No exit to A1(M) southbound | |

| M3 | Eastbound | Westbound |
|---|---|---|
| 8 | No exit | No access |
| 10 | No access | No exit |
| 13 | No access to M27 eastbound | |
| 14 | No exit | No access |

| M4 | Eastbound | Westbound |
|---|---|---|
| 1 | Exit to A4 eastbound only | Access from A4 westbound only |
| 2 | Access from A4 eastbound only | Access from A4 westbound only |
| 21 | No exit | No access |
| 23 | No access | No exit |
| 25 | No exit | No access |
| 25A | No exit | No access |
| 29 | No exit | No access |
| 38 | | No access |
| 39 | No exit or access | No access |
| 41 | No access | No exit |
| 41A | No exit | No access |
| 42 | Access from A483 only | Exit to A483 only |

| M5 | Northbound | Southbound |
|---|---|---|
| 10 | No exit | No access |
| 11A | No access from A417 eastbound | No exit to A417 westbound |

| M6 | Northbound | Southbound |
|---|---|---|
| 3A | No access. | No exit. Access from M6 eastbound only |
| 4A | No exit. Access from M42 southbound only | No access. Exit to M42 only |
| 5 | No access | No exit |
| 10A | No access. Exit to M54 only | No exit. Access from M54 only |
| 11A | No exit. Access from M6 Toll only | No access. Exit to M6 Toll only |
| 20 | No exit to M56 eastbound | No access from M56 westbound |
| 24 | No exit | No access |
| 25 | No access | No exit |
| 30 | No exit. Access from M61 northbound only | No access. Exit to M61 southbound only |
| 31A | No access | No exit |
| 45 | No access | No exit |

| M6 Toll | Northbound | Southbound |
|---|---|---|
| T1 | | No exit |
| T2 | No exit, no access | No access |
| T5 | No exit | No access |
| T7 | No access | No exit |
| T8 | No access | No exit |

| M8 | Eastbound | Westbound |
|---|---|---|
| 6 | No exit | No access |
| 6A | No access | No exit |
| 7 | No Access | No exit |
| 7A | No exit. Access from A725 northbound only | No access. Exit to A725 southbound only |
| 8 | No exit to M73 northbound | No access from M73 southbound |
| 9 | No access | No exit |
| 13 | No exit southbound | Access from M73 southbound only |

| 14 | No access | No exit |
|---|---|---|
| 16 | No exit | No access |
| 17 | No exit | |
| 18 | | No exit |
| 19 | No exit to A814 eastbound | No access from A814 westbound |
| 20 | No exit | No access |
| 21 | No access from M74 | No exit |
| 22 | No exit. Access from M77 only | No access. Exit to M77 only |
| 23 | No exit | No access |
| 25 | Exit to A739 northbound only. Access from A739 southbound only | |
| 25A | No exit | No access |
| 28 | No exit | No access |
| 28A | No exit | No access |
| 29A | No exit | No access |

| M9 | Eastbound | Westbound |
|---|---|---|
| 2 | No access | No exit |
| 3 | No exit | No access |
| 6 | No access | No exit |
| 8 | No exit | No access |

| M11 | Northbound | Southbound |
|---|---|---|
| 4 | No exit | No access |
| 5 | No access | No exit |
| 8A | No access | No exit |
| 9 | No access | No exit |
| 13 | No access | No exit |
| 14 | No exit to A428 westbound | No access. Access from A14 westbound only |

| M20 | Eastbound | Westbound |
|---|---|---|
| 2 | No access | No exit |
| 3 | No exit. Access from M26 eastbound only | No access. Exit to M26 westbound only |
| 10 | No access | No exit |
| 11A | No access | No exit |

| M23 | Northbound | Southbound |
|---|---|---|
| 7 | No exit to A23 southbound | No access from A23 northbound |
| 10A | No exit | No access |

| M25 | Clockwise | Anticlockwise |
|---|---|---|
| 5 | No exit to M26 eastbound | No access from M26 westbound |
| 19 | No access | No exit |
| 21 | No exit to M1 southbound. Access from M1 southbound only | No exit to M1 southbound. Access from M1 southbound only |
| 31 | No exit | No access |

| M27 | Eastbound | Westbound |
|---|---|---|
| 10 | No exit | No access |
| 12 | No access | No exit |

| M40 | Eastbound | Westbound |
|---|---|---|
| 3 | No exit | No access |
| 7 | No exit | No access |
| 8 | No exit | No access |
| 13 | No exit | No access |
| 14 | No access | No exit |
| 16 | No access | No exit |

| M42 | Northbound | Southbound |
|---|---|---|
| 1 | No exit | No access |
| 7 | No access. Exit to M6 northbound only | No exit. Access from M6 northbound only |
| 7A | No access. Exit to M6 southbound only | No exit |
| 8 | No exit. Access from M6 southbound only | Exit to M6 northbound only. Access from M6 southbound only |

| M45 | Eastbound | Westbound |
|---|---|---|
| M1 J17 | Access to M1 southbound only | No access from M1 southbound |
| With A45 | No access | No exit |

| M48 | Eastbound | Westbound |
|---|---|---|
| M4 J21 | No exit to M4 westbound | No access from M4 eastbound |
| M4 J23 | No access from M4 westbound | No exit to M4 eastbound |

| M49 | Southbound | Northbound |
|---|---|---|
| 18A | No exit to M5 northbound | No access from M5 southbound |

| M53 | Northbound | Southbound |
|---|---|---|
| 11 | Exit to M56 eastbound only. Access from M56 westbound only | Exit to M56 eastbnd only. Access from M56 westbound only |

| M56 | Eastbound | Westbound |
|---|---|---|
| 2 | No exit | No access |
| 3 | No access | No exit |
| 4 | No exit | No access |
| 7 | | No access |
| 8 | No exit or access | No exit |
| 9 | No access from M6 northbound | No access to M6 southbound |
| 15 | No exit to M53 | No access from M53 northbound |

| M57 | Northbound | Southbound |
|---|---|---|
| 3 | No exit | No access |
| 5 | No exit | No access |

| M58 | Eastbound | Westbound |
|---|---|---|
| 1 | No exit | No access |

| M60 | Clockwise | Anticlockwise |
|---|---|---|
| 2 | No exit | No access |
| 3 | No exit to A34 northbound | No exit to A34 northbound |
| 4 | No access from M56 | No exit to M56 |
| 5 | No exit to A5103 southbound | No exit to A5103 northbound |
| 14 | No exit | No access |
| 16 | No exit | No access |
| 20 | No access | No exit |
| 22 | | No access |
| 25 | No access | |
| 26 | | No exit or access |
| 27 | No exit | No access |

| M61 | Northbound | Southbound |
|---|---|---|
| 2 | No access from A580 eastbound | No exit to A580 westbound |
| 3 | No access from A580 eastbound. No access from A666 southbound | No exit to A580 westbound |
| M6 J30 | No exit to M6 southbound | No access from M6 northbound |

| M62 | Eastbound | Westbound |
|---|---|---|
| 23 | No access | No exit |

| M65 | Eastbound | Westbound |
|---|---|---|
| 9 | No access | No exit |
| 11 | No exit | No access |

| M66 | Northbound | Southbound |
|---|---|---|
| 1 | No access | No exit |

| M67 | Eastbound | Westbound |
|---|---|---|
| 1A | No access | No exit |
| 2 | No exit | No access |

| M69 | Northbound | Southbound |
|---|---|---|
| 2 | No exit | No access |

| M73 | Northbound | Southbound |
|---|---|---|
| 2 | No access from M8 eastbound | No exit to M8 westbound |

| M74 | Northbound | Southbound |
|---|---|---|
| 3 | No access | No exit |
| 3A | No exit | No access |
| 7 | No exit | No access |
| 9 | No exit or access | |
| 10 | | No exit |
| 11 | No exit | No access |
| 12 | No access | No exit |

| M77 | Northbound | Southbound |
|---|---|---|
| 4 | No exit | No access |
| 6 | No exit | No access |
| 7 | No exit | |
| 8 | No access | No access |

| M80 | Northbound | Southbound |
|---|---|---|
| 4A | No access | No exit |
| 6A | No exit | No access |
| 8 | Exit to M876 northbound only. | Access from M876 southbound only. No exit |

| M90 | Northbound | Southbound |
|---|---|---|
| 1 | Access from A90 northbound only | No access. Exit to A90 southbound only |
| 2A | No access | No exit |
| 7 | No exit | No access |
| 8 | No access | No exit |
| 10 | No access from A912 | No exit to A912 |

| M180 | Eastbound | Westbound |
|---|---|---|
| 1 | No access | No exit |

| M621 | Eastbound | Westbound |
|---|---|---|
| 2A | No exit | No access |
| 4 | No exit | No access |
| 5 | No exit | No access |
| 6 | No access | No exit |

| M876 | Northbound | Southbound |
|---|---|---|
| 2 | No access | No exit |

| A1(M) | Northbound | Southbound |
|---|---|---|
| 2 | No access | No exit |
| 3 | | No access |
| 5 | No exit | No exit, no access |
| 14 | No access | No exit |
| 40 | No access | No exit |
| 43 | No exit. Access from M1 only | No access. Exit to M1 only |
| 57 | No access | No exit |
| 65 | No access | No exit |

| A3(M) | Northbound | Southbound |
|---|---|---|
| 1 | No exit | No access |
| 4 | No access | No exit |

| A38(M) with Victoria Rd, (Park Circus) Birmingham | | |
|---|---|---|
| Northbound | No exit | |
| Southbound | No access | |

| A48(M) | Northbound | Southbound |
|---|---|---|
| M4 Junc 29 | Exit to M4 eastbound only | Access from M4 westbound only |
| 29A | Access from A48 eastbound only | Exit to A48 westbound only |

| A57(M) | Eastbound | Westbound |
|---|---|---|
| With A5103 | No access | No exit |
| With A34 | No access | No exit |

| A58(M) | | Southbound |
|---|---|---|
| With Park Lane and Westgate, Leeds | | No access |

| A64(M) | | Eastbound | Westbound |
|---|---|---|---|
| With A58 Clay Pit Lane, Leeds | | No access from A58 | No exit to A58 |

| A74(M) | Northbound | Southbound |
|---|---|---|
| 18 | No access | No exit |
| 22 | | No exit to A75 |

| A194(M) | Northbound | Southbound |
|---|---|---|
| A1(M) J65 Gateshead Western Bypass | Access from A1(M) northbound only | Exit to A1(M) southbound only |

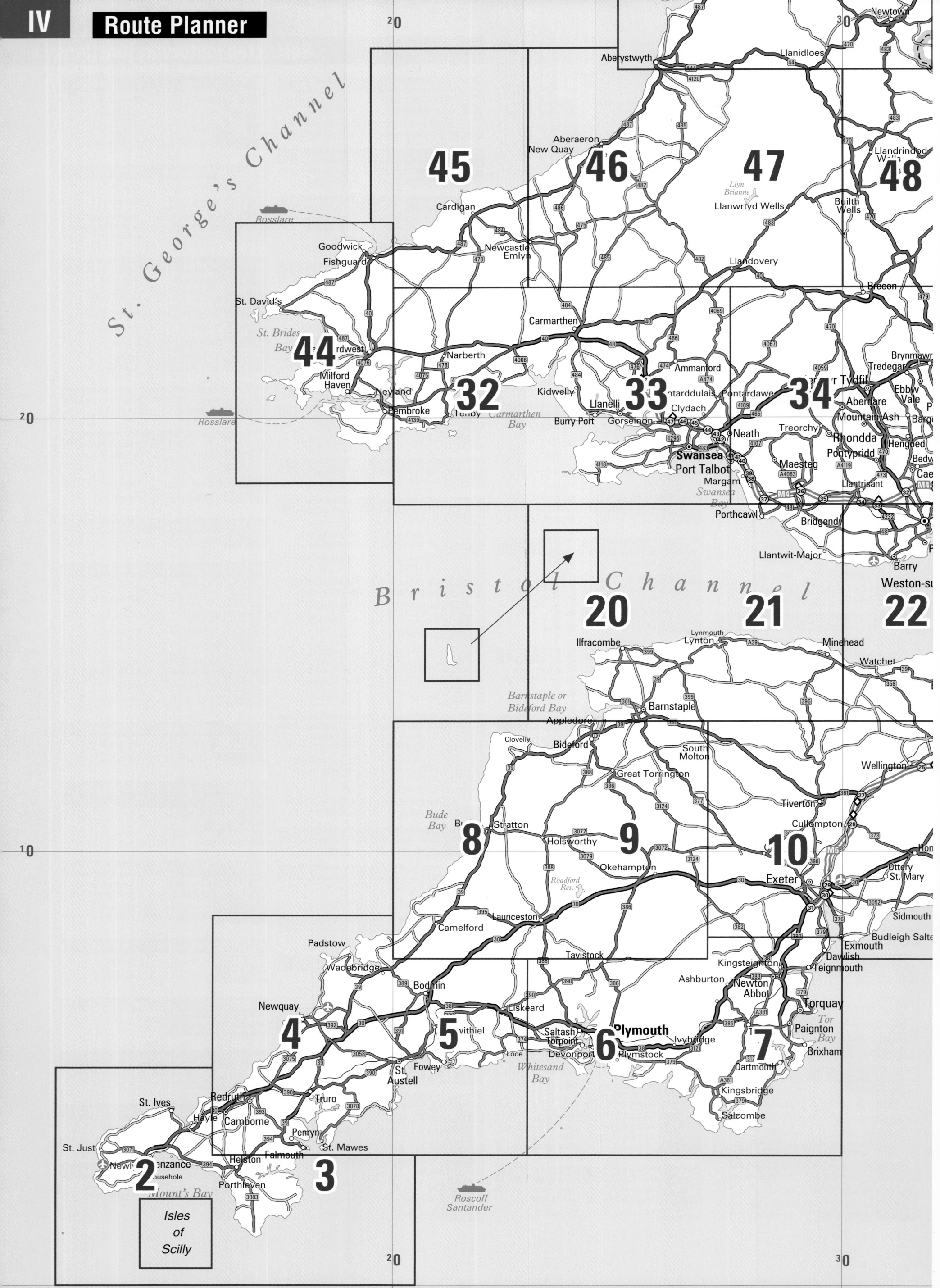

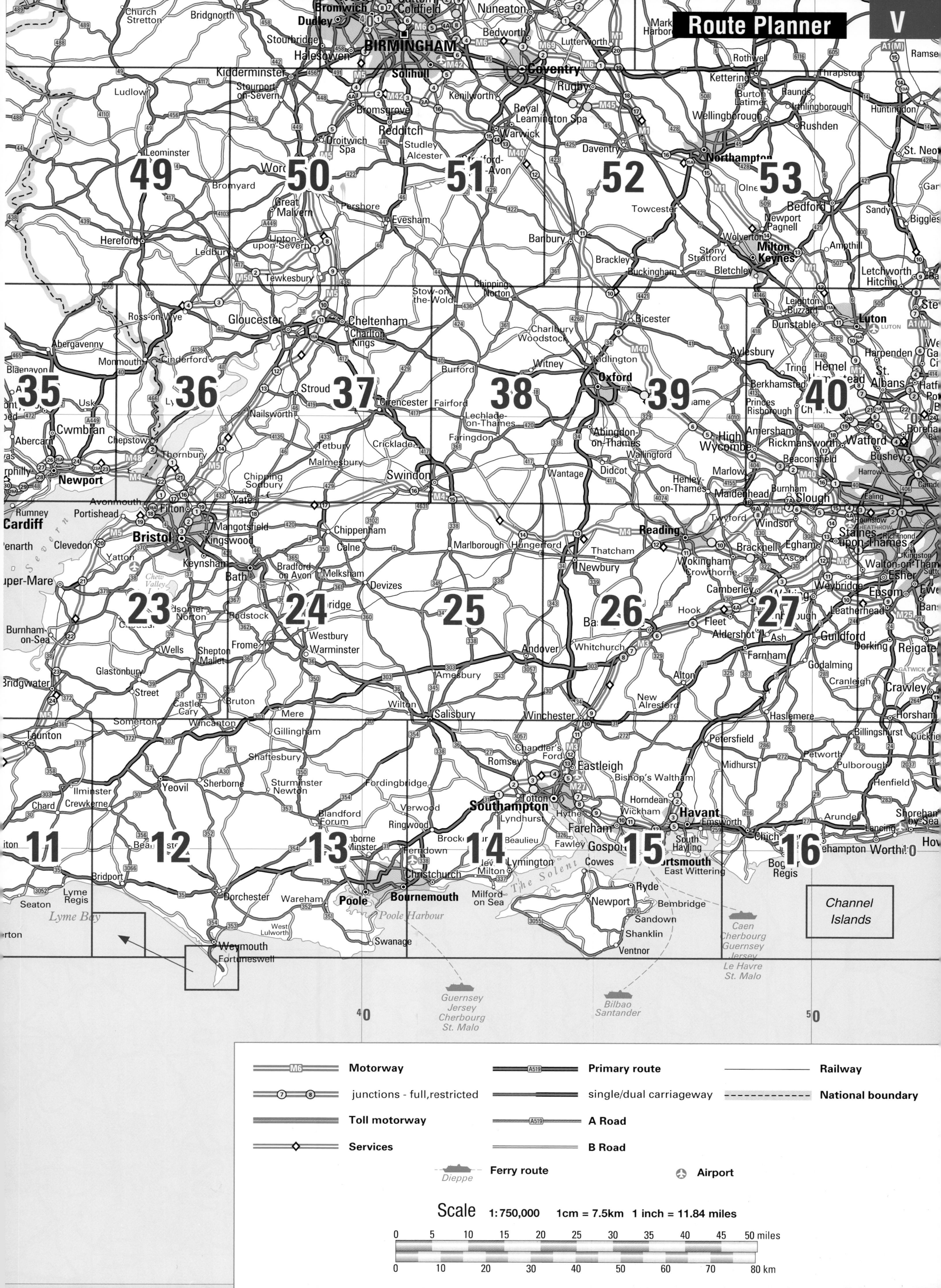

**Legend**

| | |
|---|---|
| Motorway | Primary route |
| junctions - full, restricted | single/dual carriageway |
| Toll motorway | A Road |
| Services | B Road |
| Ferry route | Airport |
| Railway | |
| National boundary | |

Scale   1:750 000   1cm = 7.5km   1 inch = 11.84 miles

0  5  10  15  20  25  30  35  40  45  50 miles

0  10  20  30  40  50  60  70  80 km

Channel Islands

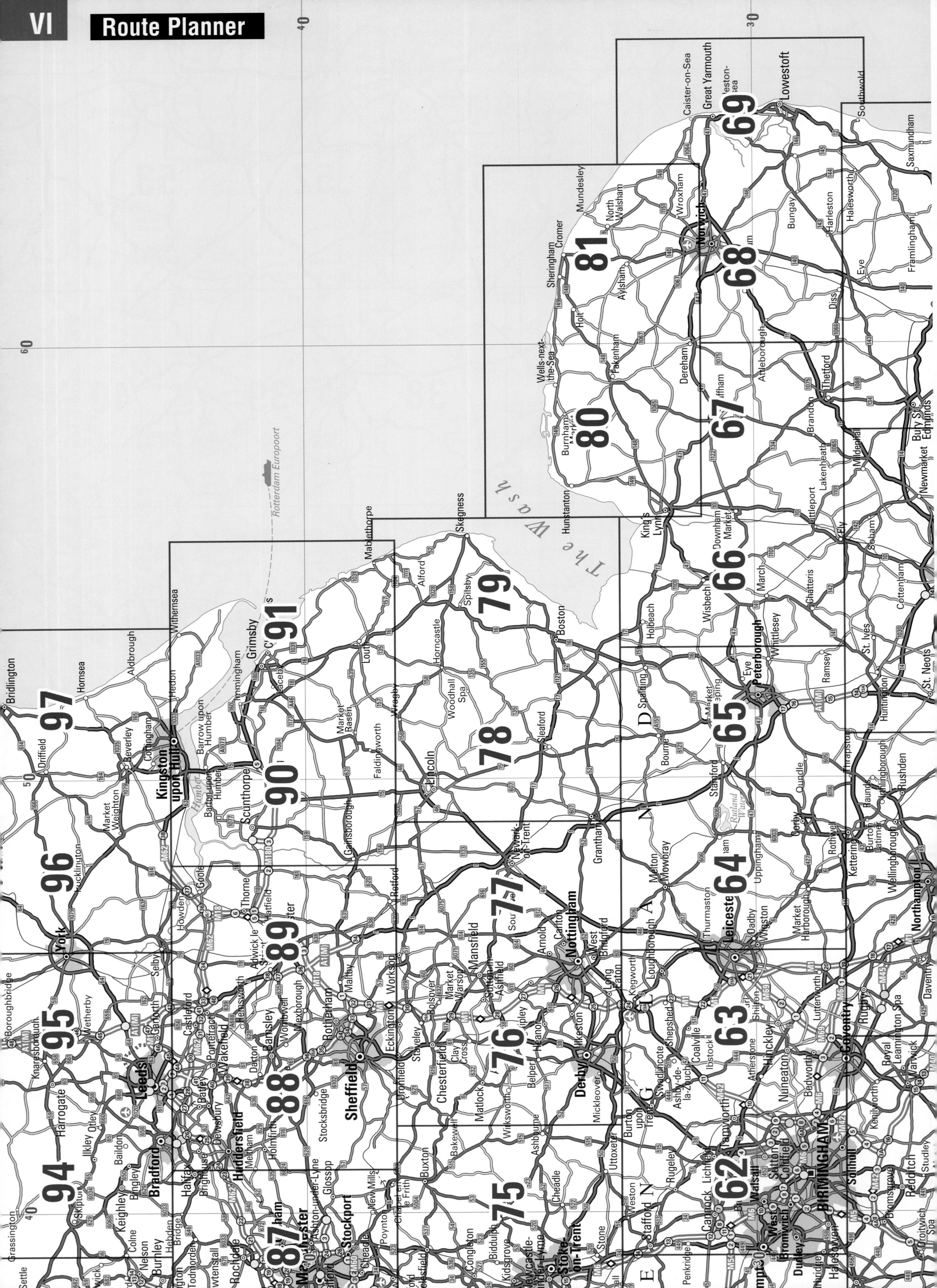

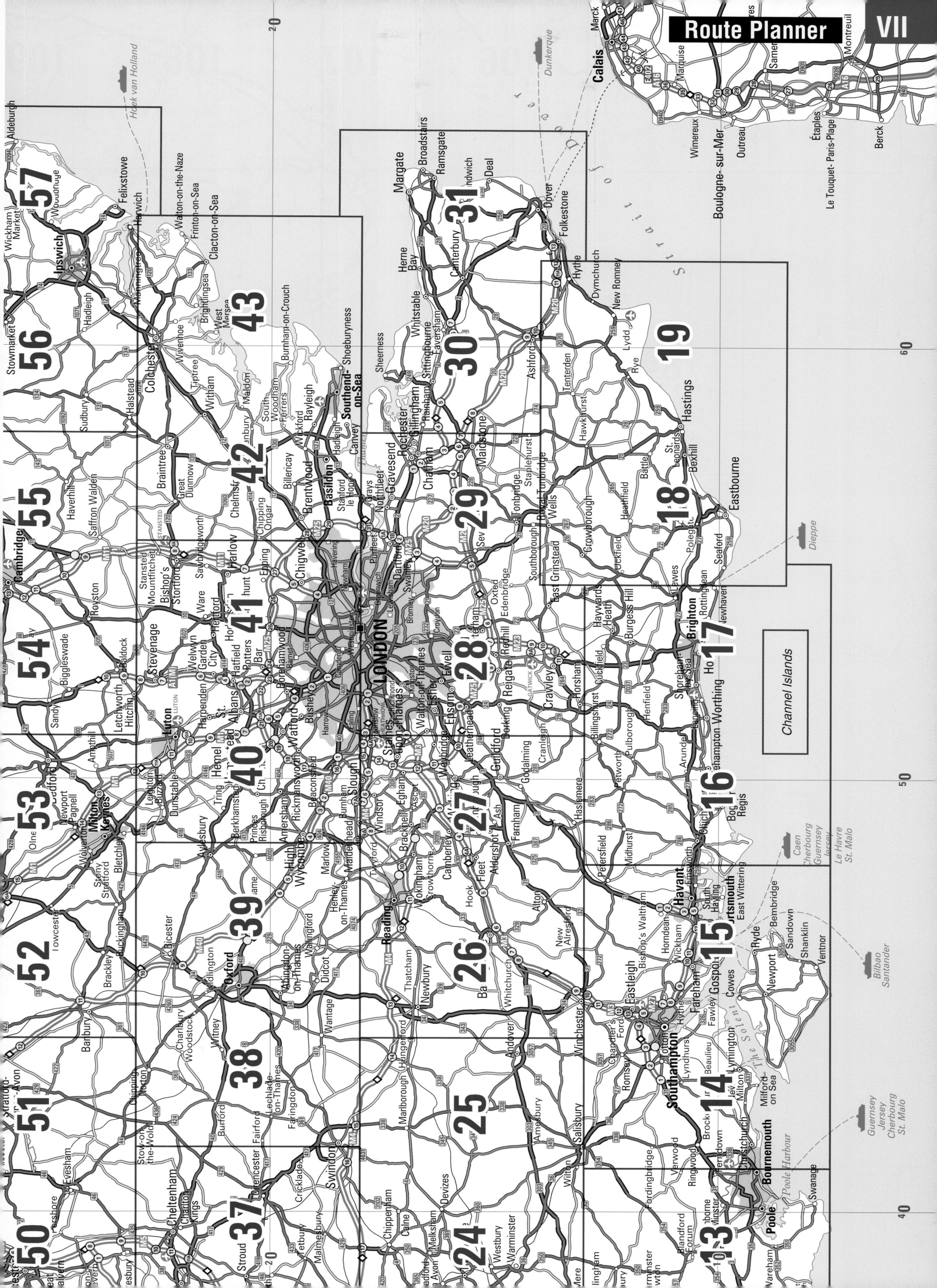

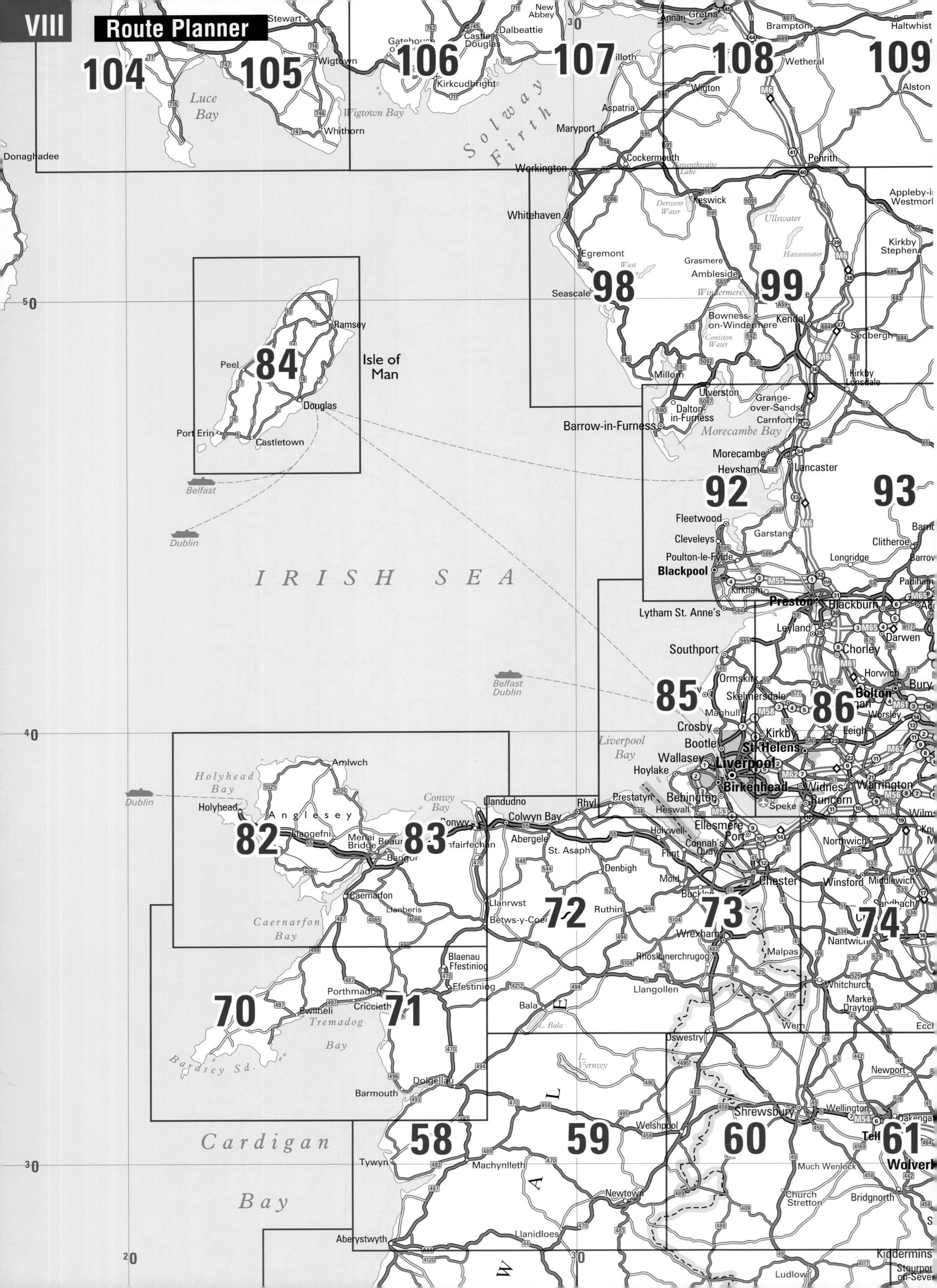

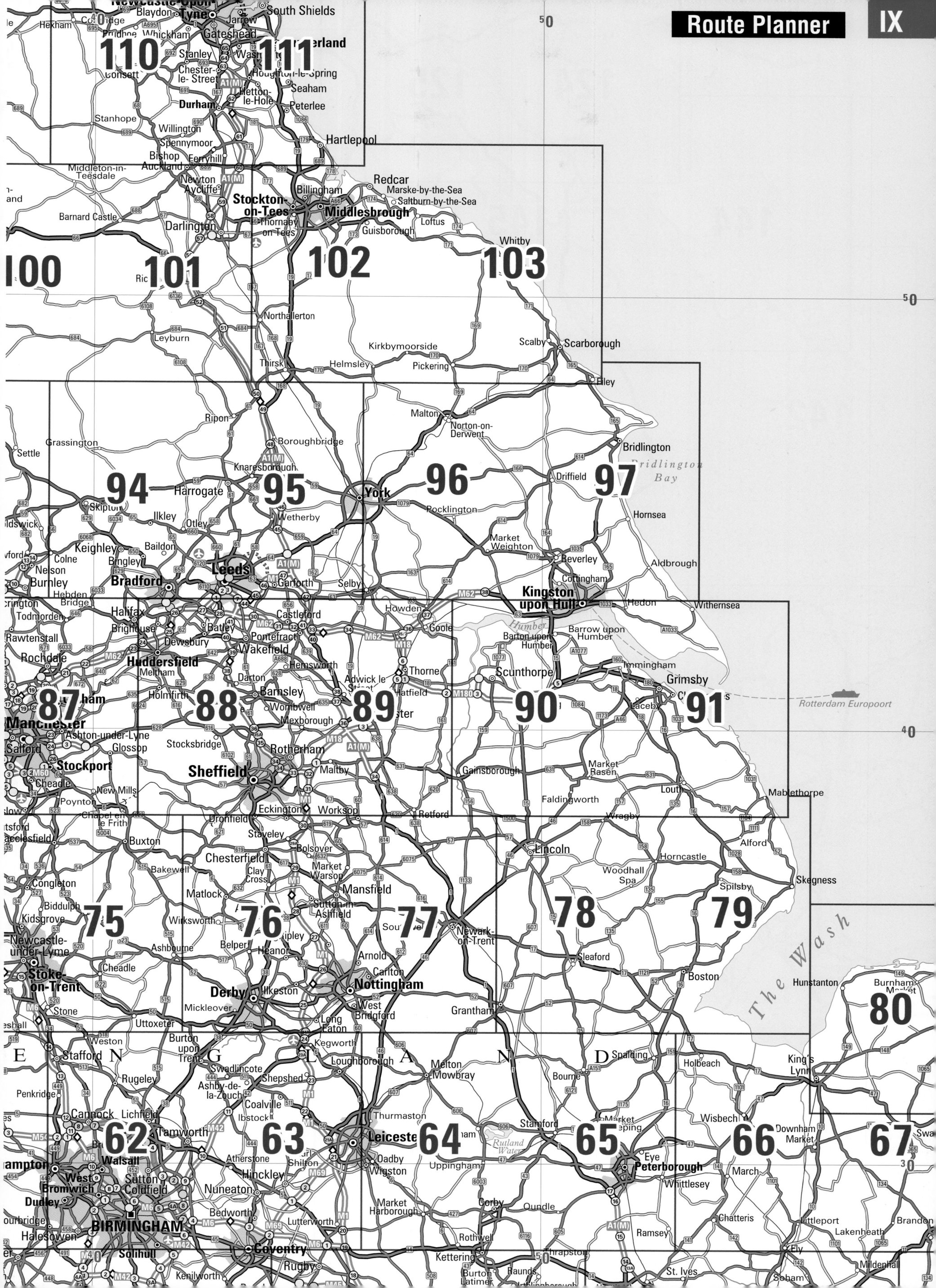

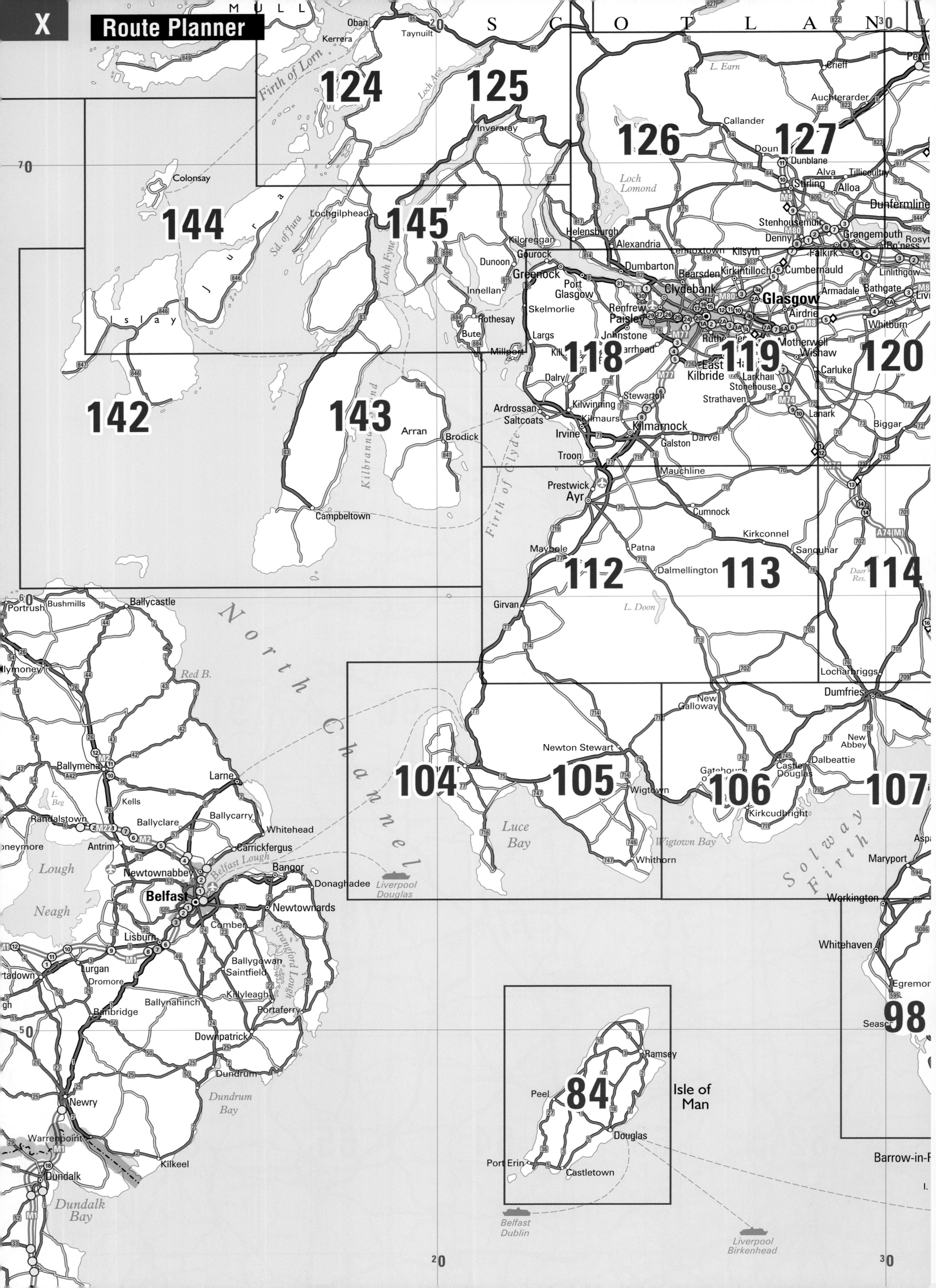

**Route Planner**

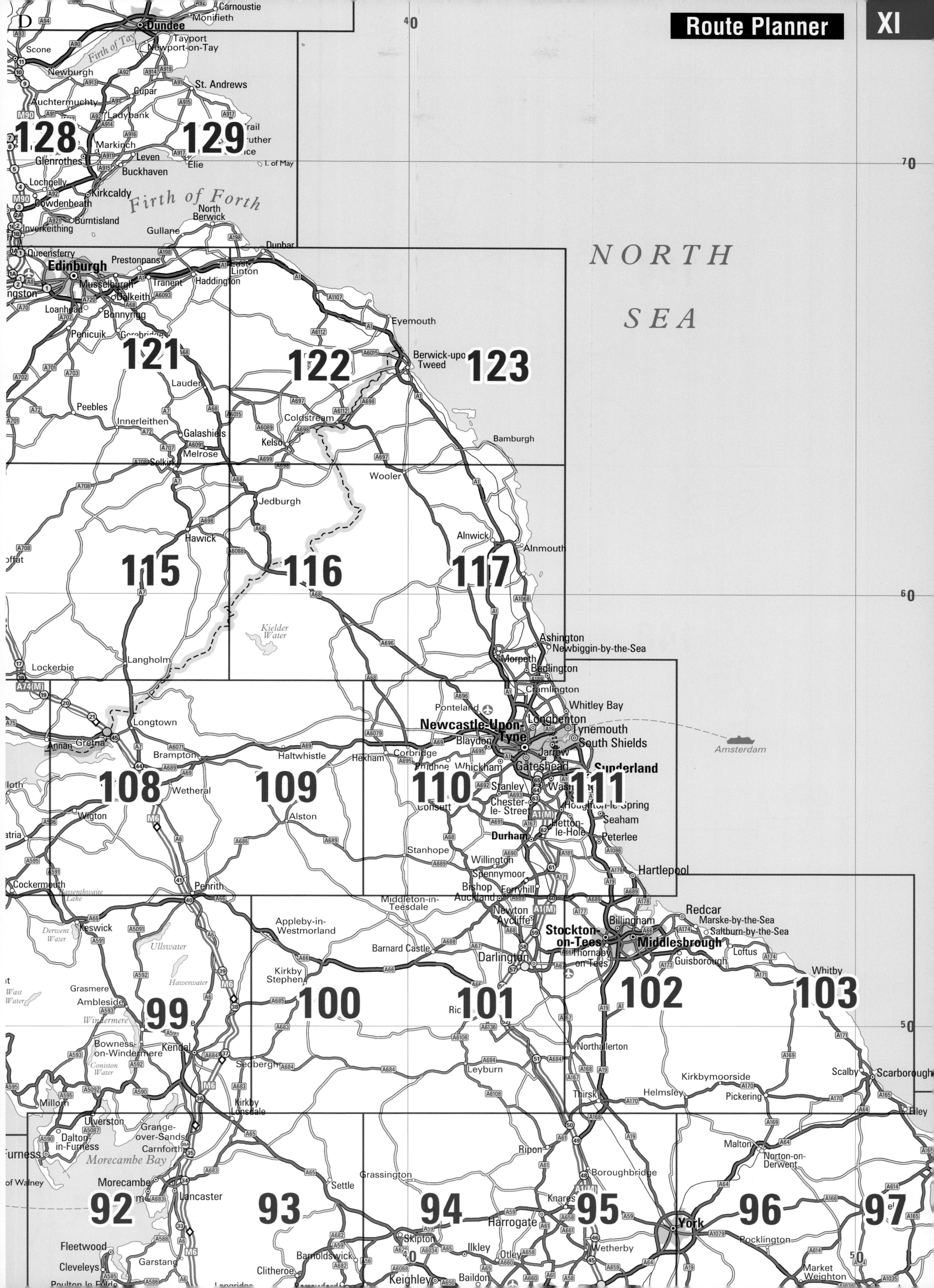

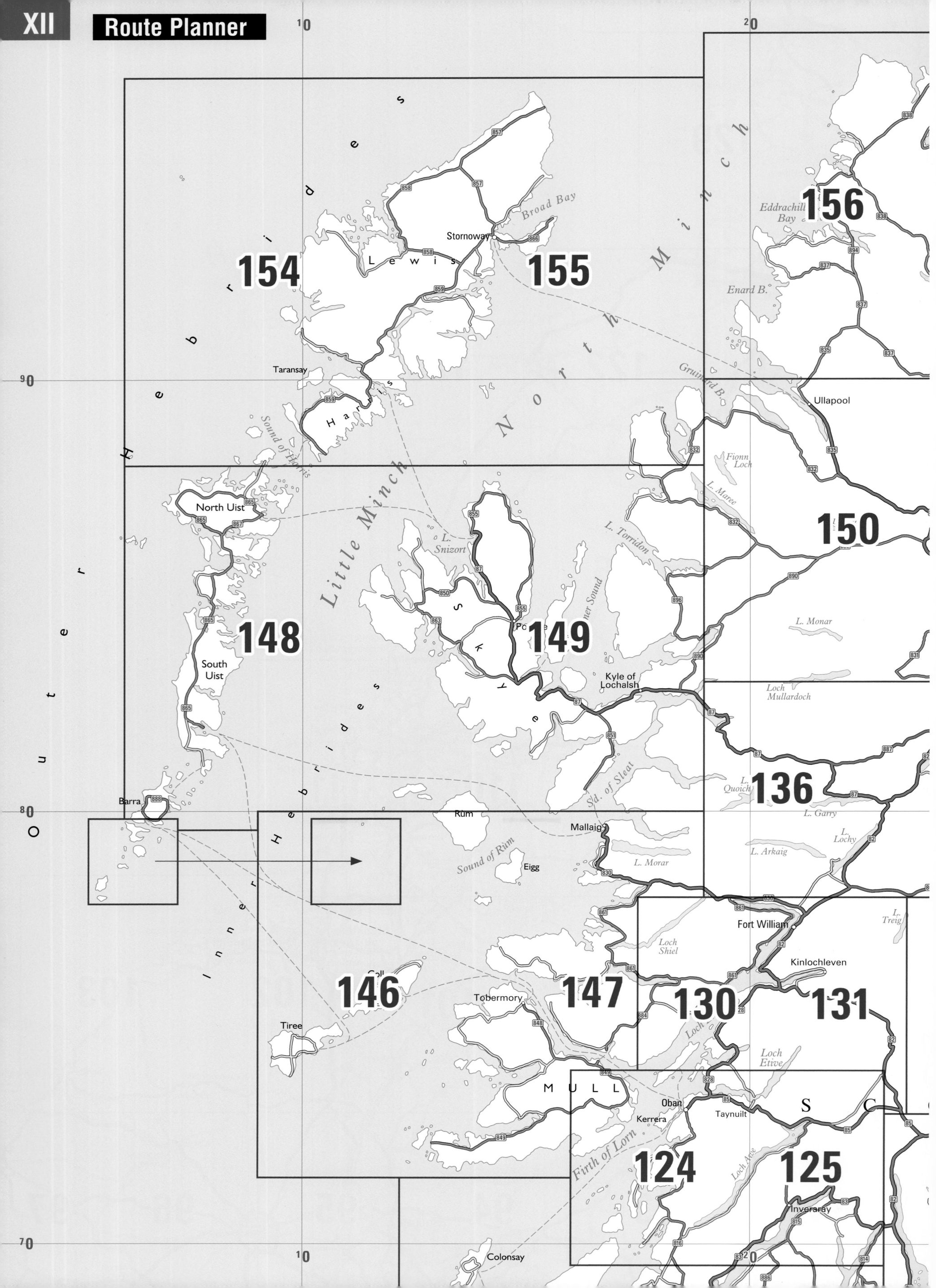

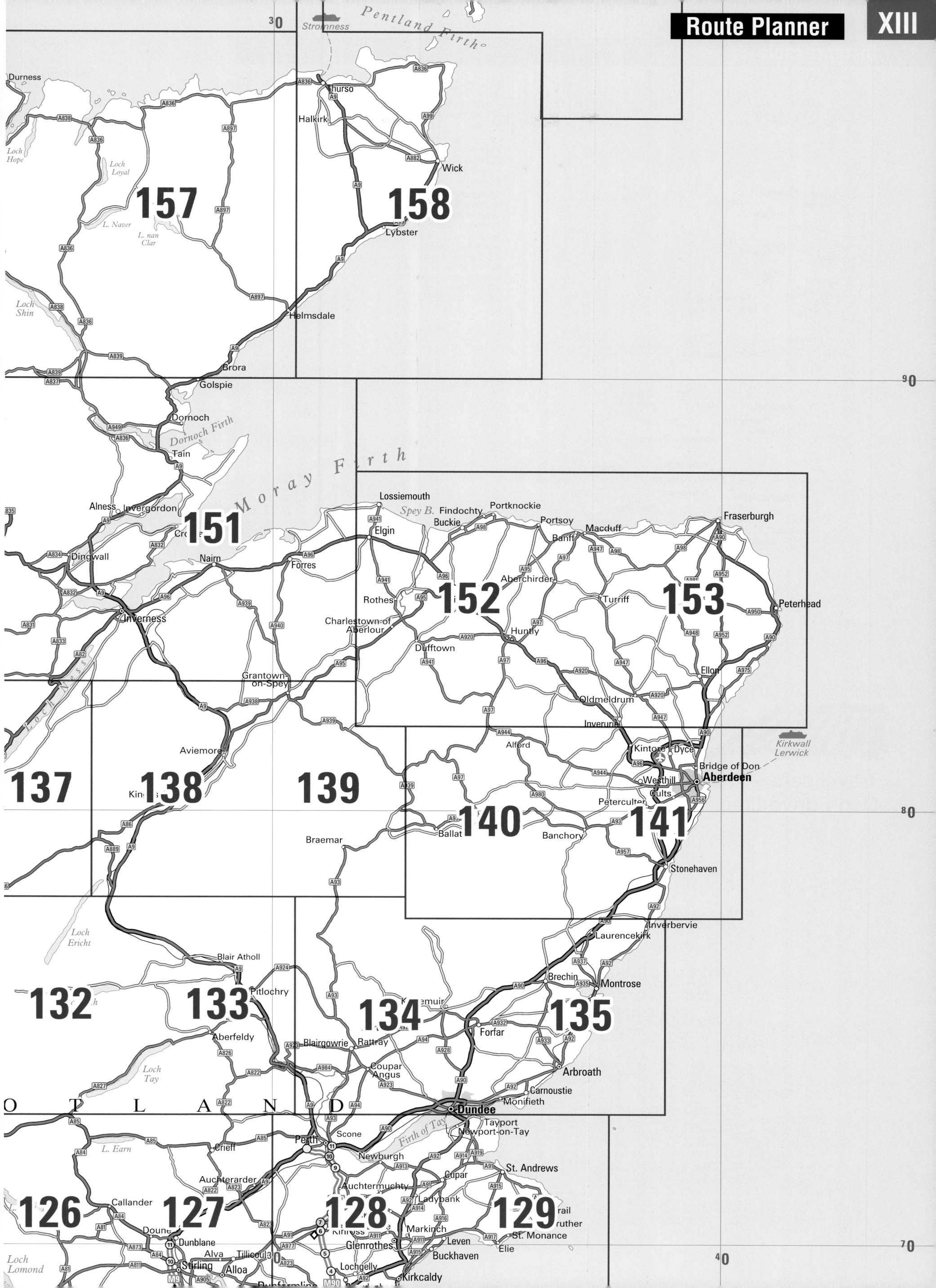

# Distance table

## How to use this table

Distances are shown in miles and kilometres with estimated journey times in hours and minutes.

For example: the distance between Dover and Fishguard is 331 miles or 533 kilometres with an estimated journey time of 6 hours, 20 minutes.

Estimated driving times are based on an average speed of 60mph on Motorways and 40mph on other roads. Drivers should allow extra time when driving at peak periods or through areas likely to be congested.

Supporting

**THINK!**

## Travel safe – Don't drive tired

---

The distance table is a triangular chart. For each pair of places the three stacked figures give: miles, kilometres, and the estimated journey time (hours : minutes).

Places (read along the diagonal):

London · Aberdeen · Aberystwyth · Ayr · Berwick-upon-Tweed · Birmingham · Blackpool · Bournemouth · Braemar · Brighton · Bristol · Cambridge · Cardiff · Carlisle · Doncaster · Dover · Dundee · Edinburgh · Exeter · Fishguard · Fort William · Glasgow · Gloucester · Great Yarmouth · Harwich · Holyhead · Inverness · John o' Groats · Kingston upon Hull · Kyle of Lochalsh · Land's End · Leeds · Leicester · Lincoln · Liverpool · Manchester · Newcastle upon Tyne · Norwich · Nottingham · Oban · Oxford · Plymouth · Portsmouth · Sheffield · Shrewsbury · Southampton · Stranraer · Swansea · York

Selected readings from the chart:

| From | To | Miles | Km | Time |
|---|---|---|---|---|
| Dover | Fishguard | 331 | 533 | 6:20 |
| London | Aberdeen | 517 | 832 | 11:20 |
| London | Aberystwyth | 445 | 716 | 8:40 |
| Aberdeen | Aberystwyth | 211 | 340 | 4:40 |
| London | Ayr | 317 | 510 | 7:20 |
| London | Birmingham | 117 | 188 | 2:50 |
| London | Blackpool | 226 | 364 | 4:30 |
| Dover | Dundee | 523 | 842 | 9:10 |
| Dover | Edinburgh | 462 | 744 | 8:10 |
| Dover | Exeter | 248 | 399 | 4:40 |
| Dover | Fort William | 596 | 959 | 11:00 |

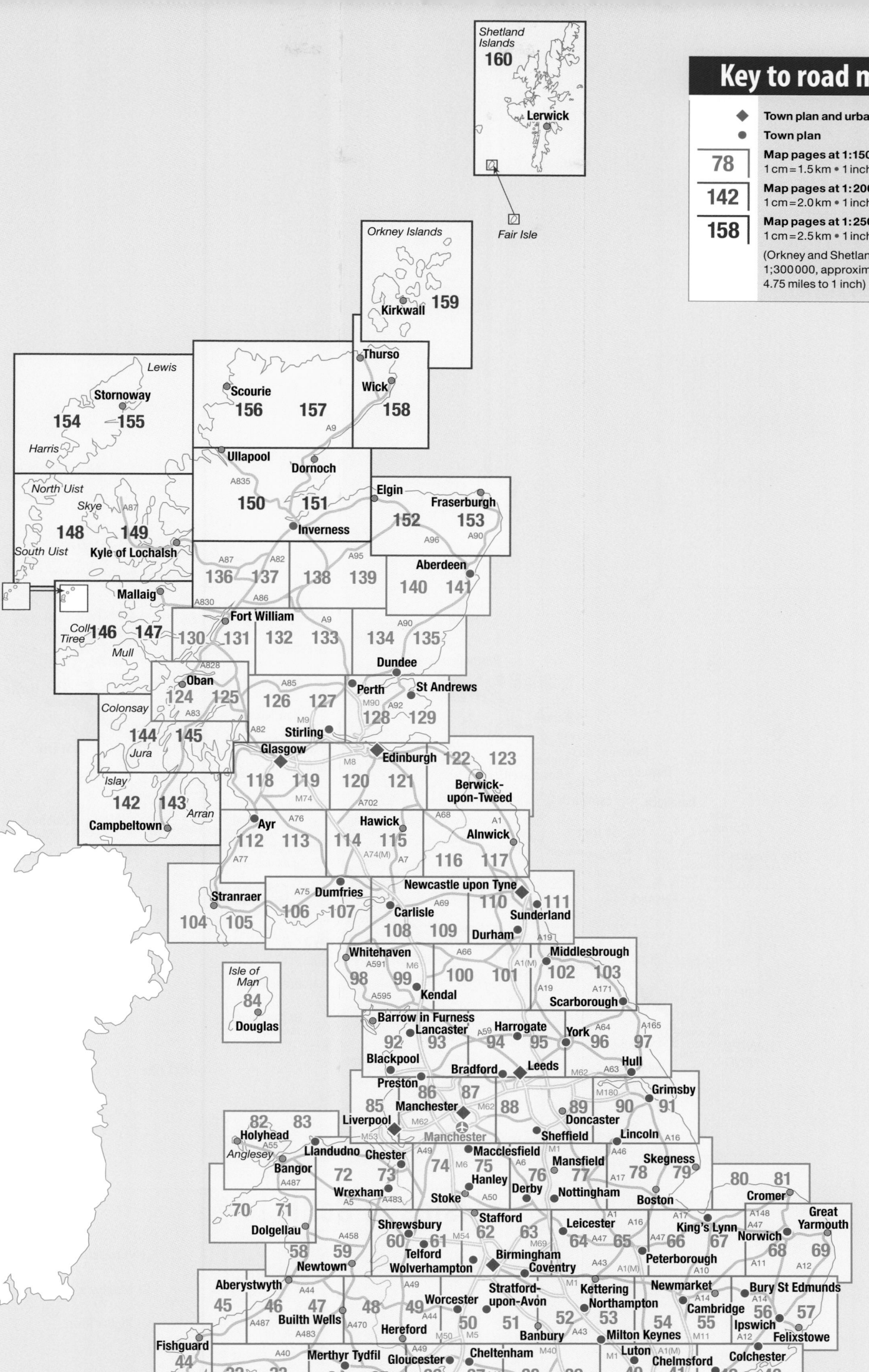

## Key to road map pages

◆ Town plan and urban approach map
● Town plan

**78** Map pages at 1:150000
1 cm = 1.5 km • 1 inch = 2.37 miles

**142** Map pages at 1:200000
1 cm = 2.0 km • 1 inch = 3.16 miles

**158** Map pages at 1:250000
1 cm = 2.5 km • 1 inch = 3.95 miles
(Orkney and Shetland Islands at
1;300000, approximately
4.75 miles to 1 inch)

Shetland Islands **160**
Lerwick

Orkney Islands
Kirkwall **159**

Fair Isle

Lewis
Stornoway
**154** **155**
Harris

Thurso
Scourie **156** **157** Wick **158**

North Uist
Skye A87
**148** **149**
South Uist Kyle of Lochalsh

Ullapool **150** Dornoch **151**
A835

Elgin Fraserburgh
**152** **153**
A96 A90

Inverness

Aberdeen
**136** **137** **138** **139** **140** **141**
A87 A82 A95 A90

Mallaig
A830 A86
Fort William
Coll **146** **147** **130** **131** **132** **133** A9 **134** **135**
Tiree A90

Mull
A828 Dundee
Oban A85 Perth St Andrews
**124** **125** **126** **127** **128** **129**
Colonsay A83 M90 A92
M9
Stirling
**144** **145** A82 Glasgow Edinburgh **122** **123**
Jura **118** **119** **120** **121**
M8 Berwick-upon-Tweed
Islay M74
**142** **143** A702
Arran Ayr A76 Hawick Alnwick
Campbeltown **112** **113** **114** **115** **116** **117**
A77 A74(M) A7 A68 A1

Stranraer A75 Dumfries Newcastle upon Tyne
**104** **105** **106** **107** Carlisle **108** **109** A69 **110** **111** Sunderland
Durham A19
Whitehaven Middlesbrough
A591 A66 A1(M) **102** **103**
**98** **99** **100** **101** Scarborough
A595 Kendal A19 A171

Isle of Barrow in Furness Harrogate York A64 A165
Man **92** Lancaster **93** **94** **95** **96** **97**
**84** A59 Hull
Douglas Blackpool Bradford Leeds
Preston **86** **87** **88** M62 A63
M62 **85** Manchester **89** **90** Grimsby **91**
Liverpool Sheffield Doncaster M180
Holyhead **82** **83** M62 Manchester A46 Lincoln A16
A55 Llandudno Chester Macclesfield Mansfield Skegness
Anglesey Bangor **72** **73** **74** **75** **76** **77** **78** **79** **80** **81**
A487 Wrexham Hanley Derby Nottingham A17 Cromer A148
**70** **71** A5 Stoke A50 Boston A47 A47
Dolgellau A483 Stafford A1 Leicester A16 King's Lynn Norwich Great
Shrewsbury **62** **63** **64** **65** **66** **67** **68** Yarmouth
**58** **59** **60** **61** Telford M54 Birmingham M69 A47 Peterborough A10 A11 **69** A12
Newtown Wolverhampton Coventry A43 A1(M) Newmarket Bury St Edmunds
Aberystwyth A49 Stratford-upon-Avon Kettering A14 A14
**45** **46** **47** **48** **49** Worcester **50** **51** **52** Northampton **53** **54** **55** Cambridge **56** **57**
A44 A487 Builth Wells A44 Banbury Milton Keynes M11 A12 Ipswich Felixstowe
Fishguard A483 Hereford A43
**44** A40 Merthyr Tydfil Gloucester Cheltenham M40 Luton Colchester
Pembroke **32** **33** **34** **35** **36** **37** **38** **39** **40** **41** **42** **43**
Llanelli Newport Swindon Oxford A34 M40 Chelmsford Southend-on-Sea
Swansea M4 A470 A40 Reading London Heathrow
**20** **21** **22** **23** **24** **25** **26** **27** **28** **29** **30** **31**
Lundy Ilfracombe Cardiff Bristol Bath Newbury Windsor Croydon Canterbury
Bideford M5 A37 Salisbury Southampton M3 Gatwick Maidstone Dover
**8** **9** **10** **11** **12** **13** **14** **15** **16** **17** **18** **19**
A39 Taunton Dorchester Poole Portsmouth Winchester Ashford
A386 A303 Chichester Lewes Brighton A259
Exeter Weymouth
Newquay Plymouth A35 Bournemouth Isle of Wight
**4** **5** A38 **6** **7**
Truro Torquay
Penzance
**2** **3**
Isles of A30
Scilly

Alderney

Channel Islands
Guernsey

Jersey

## Isles of Scilly

St Helens
White Island
KING CHARLES CASTLE
St Martin's
Bryher
47
CROMWELL'S CASTLE
New Grimsby
Higher Town
Bryher
Tresco
TRESCO ABBEY GARDENS
Samson
Crow Sound
Eastern Isles
The Road
BANT'S CARN
Newford
INNISIDGEN CAIRNS
North West Passage
51
Maypole
Hugh Town
St Mary's
A3110
ST MARY'S
Old Town
GARRISON WALLS
Broad Sound
Annet
Smith Sound
St Mary's Sound
PENZANCE (Mar-Nov)
Gugh
St Agnes
St Agnes

CORNWALL

The Carracks
Clodgy Pt.
Godrevy Island
Navax Pt.
Portrea
TEHIDY CORN
Gurnard's Head
Zennor
Halsetown
St Ives Bay
Godrevy Pt.
Roscroggan
Godrevy
TATE ST IVES
The Island
St Ives
SOUTH WEST COAST PATH
Gwithian
BARBARA HEPWORTH MUSEUM
Kehelland
A30
A3047
247
Carbis Bay
B3306
Roseworthy
Porthmeor
Towednack
A3074
Phillack
TREVITHICK COTTAGE
SHIRE & CARN
Cripplesease
Lelant
Connor Downs
Morvah
PARADISE PARK
Copperhouse
Barripper
Bojewyan
252
Nancledra
Hayle
Carnhell Green
Higher Boscaswell
CHYSAUSTER ANCIENT VILLAGE
Canon's Town
Praze-an-Beeble
Pendeen
SW
Newmill
St Erth
Fraddam
Trewellard
B3311
Leedstown
Crow
GEEVOR TIN MINE MUSEUM
Ludgvan
B3301
Townshend
B3303
Botallack
Carnyorth
B3318
Crowlas
Relubbus
Drym
Cape Cornwall
A3071
TRENGWAINTON
Madron
P&R
Gulval
GODOLPHIN HOUSE
St Just
6
Heamoor
A30
Trescowe
Godolphin Cross
The Brisons
Newbridge
PENZANCE
St Hilary
Nance
BALLOWALL BARROW
Chyandour
A394
Bosavern
224
Sancreed
Marazion
St Michael's Mount
Goldsithney
Germoe
Crown
Kelynack
CARN EUNY ANCIENT VILLAGE
Res.
Penzance
St Michael's Mount
Perranuthnoe
Ashton
Sithney
LAND'S END
Tredavoe
Newlyn Art Gallery
SOUTH WEST COAST PATH
Breage
Brane
Lower Drift
Newlyn
Praa Sands
A394
Whitesand Bay
8
Crows-an-wra
Catchall
Paul
Cudden Pt.
Rinsey
12
Sennen Cove
B3283
Kerris
Mousehole
MOUNT'S BAY
Longships
St Buryan
Trewoofe
St Clement's Island
Trewavas Hd.
Porthleven
Sennen
LAND'S END
B3315
Lamorna
SOUTH WEST COAST PATH
The Loe
LAND'S END
Polgigga
Boskenna
Gunwall
Porthcurno
B3315
TREGIFFIAN BURIAL CHAMBER
Lamorna Cove
ISLES OF SCILLY (Mar-Nov)
Porthleven Sands
Treen
TELEGRAPH MUSEUM PORTHCURNO
St Levan
MINACK OPEN AIR THEATRE
Gwennap Hd.
Runnel Stone

0  1  2  3  4  5  6 miles
0 1 2 3 4 5 6 7 8 9 10km

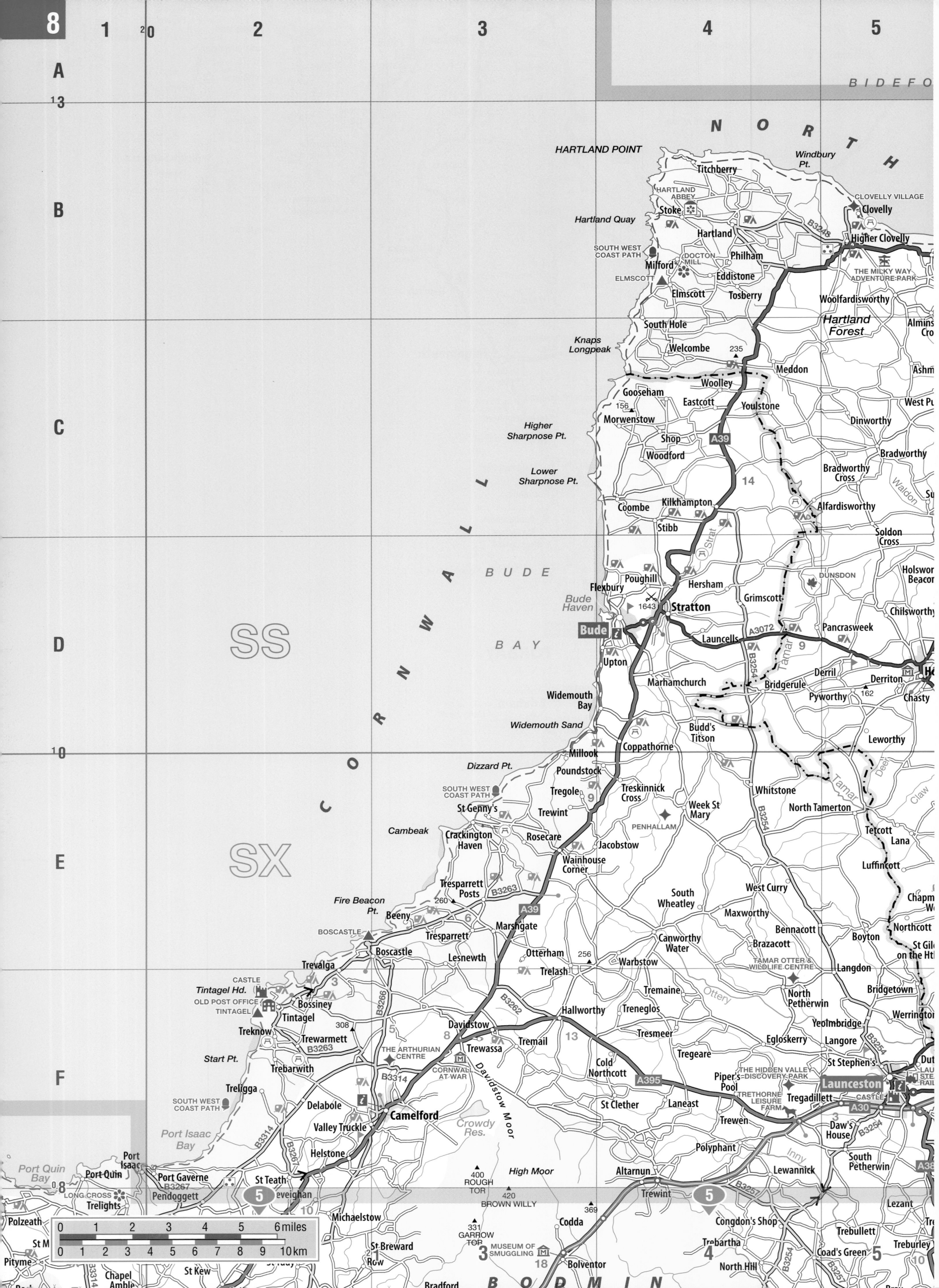

1  2  3  4  5

A

BIDEFO

B

NORTH

HARTLAND POINT
Titchberry
Windbury Pt.
HARTLAND ABBEY
Stoke
CLOVELLY VILLAGE
Clovelly
Hartland Quay
Hartland
Higher Clovelly
Philham
THE MILKY WAY
ADVENTURE PARK
SOUTH WEST
COAST PATH
DOCTON
MILL
Milford
Eddistone
Woolfardisworthy
ELMSCOTT
Elmscott
Tosberry
Hartland
Forest
South Hole
Almins
Cro

C

Knaps
Longpeak
Welcombe
235
Meddon
Woolley
Youlstone
Ashm
Higher
Sharpnose Pt.
Gooseham
Eastcott
West P
156
Morwenstow
A39
Dinworthy
Shop
Bradworthy
Lower
Sharpnose Pt.
Woodford
14
Bradworthy
Cross
Coombe
Kilkhampton
Alfardisworthy
Soldon
Cross
Stibb
DUNSDON
Holsw
Beacor

D

BUDE
Poughill
Flexbury
Hersham
Grimscott
Chilsworthy
Bude
Haven
1643
Stratton
Bude
Launcells
A3072
Pancrasweek
Launceston
Derril
Derriton
Upton
Marhamchurch
Bridgerule
Pyworthy
162
Chasty
Widemouth
Bay
A3254
Budd's
Leworthy
Widemouth Sand
Coppathorne
Titson

SS

CORNWALL
BUDE
BAY

E

Millook
Dizzard Pt.
Poundstock
Whitstone
SOUTH WEST
COAST PATH
Tregole
9
Treskinnick
Cross
Week St
Mary
North Tamerton
Tetcott
St Genny's
Trewint
PENHALLAM
Lana
Cambeak
Crackington
Haven
Rosecare
Jacobstow
Luffincott
Tresparrett
Posts
Wainhouse
Corner
South
Wheatley
West Curry
Chapm
Wa
Fire Beacon
Pt.
260
B3263
Maxworthy
Northcott
Beeny
6
Marshgate
Canworthy
Water
Bennacott
Boyton
St Gil
on the Ht
BOSCASTLE
Tresparrett
Otterham
Brazacott
TAMAR OTTER &
WILDLIFE CENTRE
Langdon
Trevalga
Boscastle
Lesnewth
256
Warbstow
Bridgetown

SX

F

CASTLE
Tintagel Hd.
Trelash
Tremaine
North
Petherwin
Werrington
OLD POST OFFICE
TINTAGEL
3
Bossiney
B3266
Hallworthy
Treneglos
Tresmeer
Tregeare
Tintagel
308
B3262
Davidstow
13
Yeolmbridge
Treknow
5
Trewassa
Tremail
Langore
Trewarmett
8
Egloskerry
B3263
THE ARTHURIAN
CENTRE
Trewassa
St Stephen's
Start Pt.
CORNWALL
AT WAR
Cold
Northcott
PIPER'S
DISCOVERY PARK
Dut
Trebarwith
B3314
Davidstow Moor
A395
Laneast
Launceston
LAU
RAIL
Treligga
Delabole
St Clether
Trewen
Tregadillett
CASTLE
SOUTH WEST
COAST PATH
Valley Truckle
Camelford
Crowdy
Res.
Daw's
House
A30
Polyphant
Port Isaac
Bay
Helstone
Polyphant
Port Quin
Bay
High Moor
Altarnun
South
Petherwin
Port Quin
Port
Isaac
St Teath
400
ROUGH
TOR
Lewannick
A3
LONG CROSS
Pendoggett
eveighan
Trewint
Lezant
Trelights
10
Michaelstow
420
BROWN WILLY
369
Congdon's Shop
Trebullett
Polzeath
St Breward
331
GARROW
TOR
MUSEUM OF
SMUGGLING
Codda
Trebartha
Coad's Green
Treburley
St M
Row
3
18
North Hill
Pityme
BODMIN
Bolventor
St Kew
Bradford
Chapel
Amble

0  1  2  3  4  5  6 miles
0  1  2  3  4  5  6  7  8  9  10km

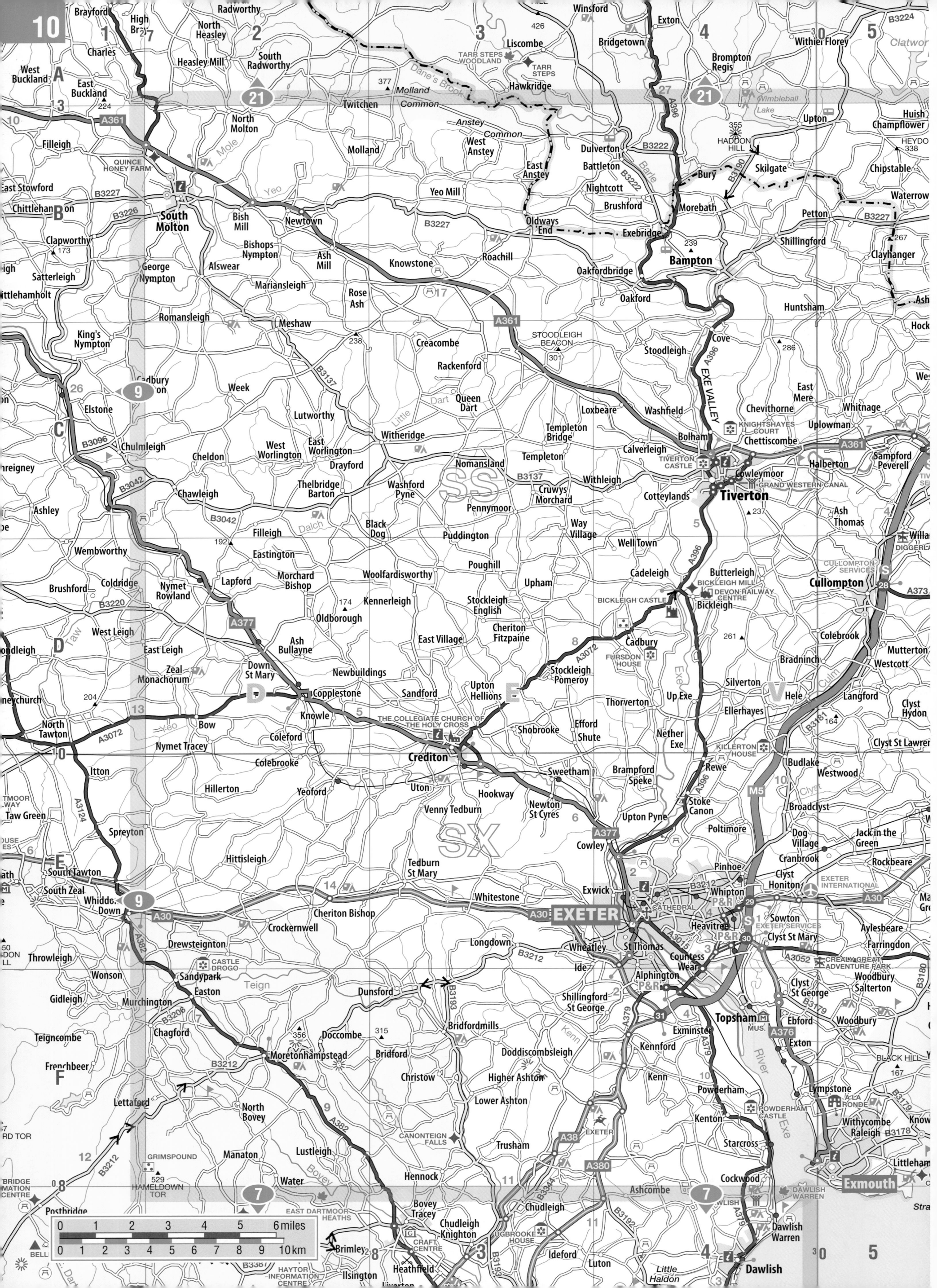

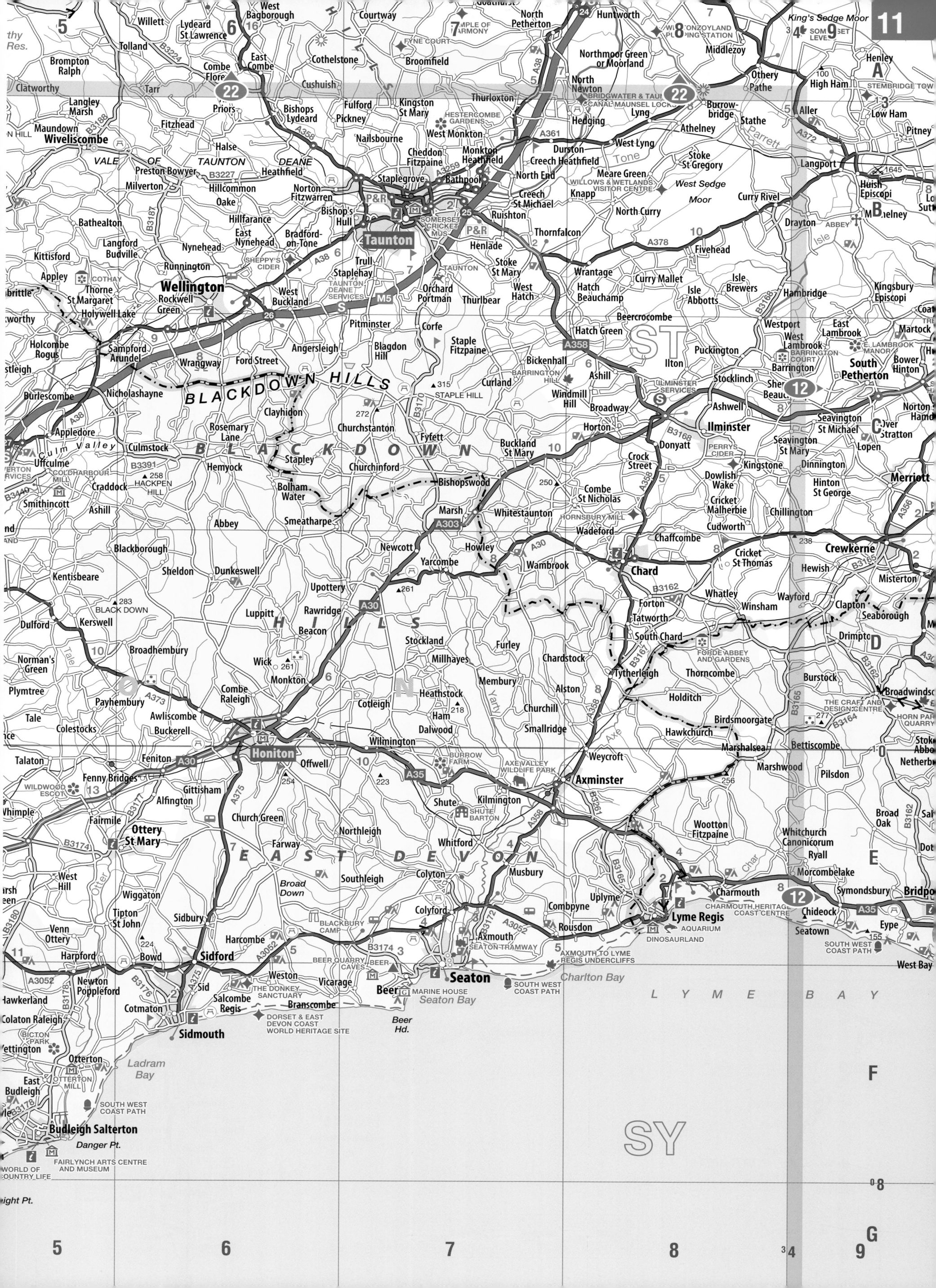

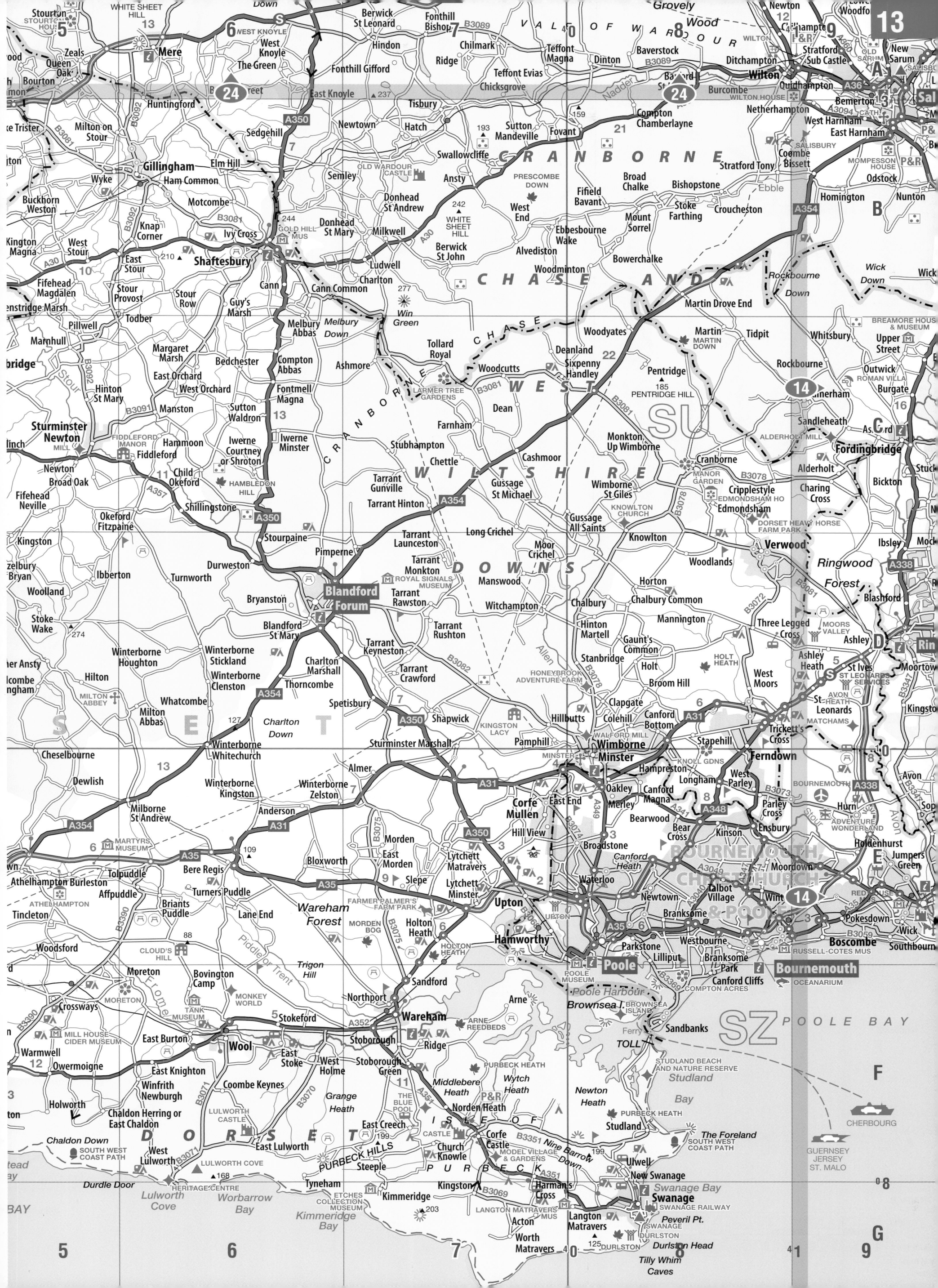

A

¹8

B

**LUNDY**

North West Point

North East Point

LUNDY MARINE NATURE RESERVE

C

142

South West Point

Surf Point

ILFRACOMBE BIDEFORD (April-Oct)

¹5
²2

²1
¹4

D

SS

E

NORTH DEVON

LUNDY (April-Oct)

HELE CORN MILL

Combe Martin Bay

Rillage Pt.

Ilfracombe  ILFRACOMBE MUSEUM  WATERMOUTH CASTLE.  Trentishoe

Bull Pt.  206  Hele  Girt Down  349  Heale

Rockham Bay  Lee  Berrynarbor  Combe Martin  BAF

Mortehoe  Whitestone  Slade  A361  B3230  Sterridge  10  WILDLIFE & DINOSAUR PARK

Morte Point  269  A3123  A399  Kentisbury

Woolacombe  Trimstone  Berry  Berry Down Cross  Patchole

MORTE BAY  B3343  210  Cheglinch  Down  Kentisbury Ford

Woolacombe Sand  Dean  Bittadon  East Down  EXMOOR ZOO

SOUTH WEST COAST PATH  West Down  Churchill  Arlington

Pickwell  North Buckland  A361  A39  ARLINGTON COURT

Baggy Pt.  Putsborough  Nethercott  Halsinger  Milltown  Loxhore  Knightacott

Croyde Bay  Georgeham  Darracott  Muddiford  11

Croyde  158  Knowle  Marwood  Guineaford  Shirwell  Brat

B3231  Lobb  Pippacott  MARWOOD  Kingsheanton  198  Shirwell Cross  Flem

Saunton  14  HILL GARDENS  Prixford  BROOMHILL  Stoke Rivers

ELLIOT GALLERY  Braunton  Heanton Punchardon  Ashford  Goodleigh  Gunn

Saunton Sands  Wrafton  Chivenor  Burridge

TOLL  A361  Pilton  Barnstaple  Westcott

Braunton Burrows  Taw  MUSEUM OF BARNSTAPLE & NORTH DEVON  We Buckl

LUNDY (April-Oct)  Fremington  Yelland  Bickington  P&R  Newport  Landkey

B3233  Bickleton  A39  Bishops  Swimbridge  Newland

BIDEFORD BAY  NORTH DEVON MARITIME MUSEUM  Instow  Tawton  Swimbridge

Northam Burrows  7  9

9  Appledore

Westward Ho!  Northam  A386  Westleigh  TAPELEY PARK GDNS  Horwood  Newton  Herner  Col ton

Orchard Hill  Westcott  Tracey  Ensis  COBBATON COMBAT

THE BIG SHEEP  4  3  Bideford  Eastleigh  4  5 ton

Titchb  BURTON ART GALL & MUS  Woodtown  Hiscott  Chapelton

CLOVELLY VILLAGE  Abbotsham  East-the-Water  A39  Handy

F

13

0  1  2  3  4  5  6 miles

0  1  2  3  4  5  6  7  8  9  10km

MÔR HAFREN
BRISTOL CHANNEL

SS

EXMOOR FOREST

EXMOOR FOREST NATIONAL PARK

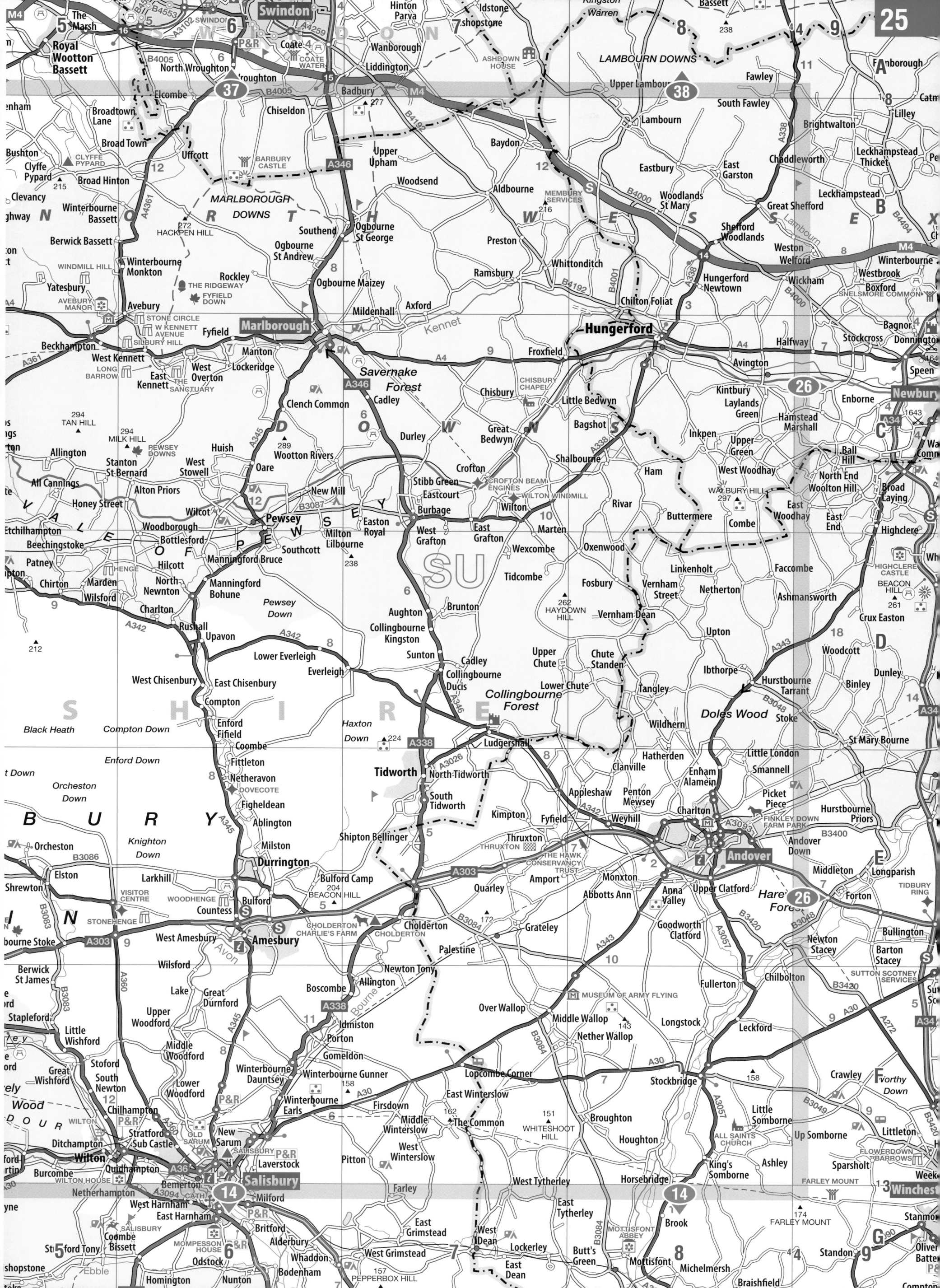

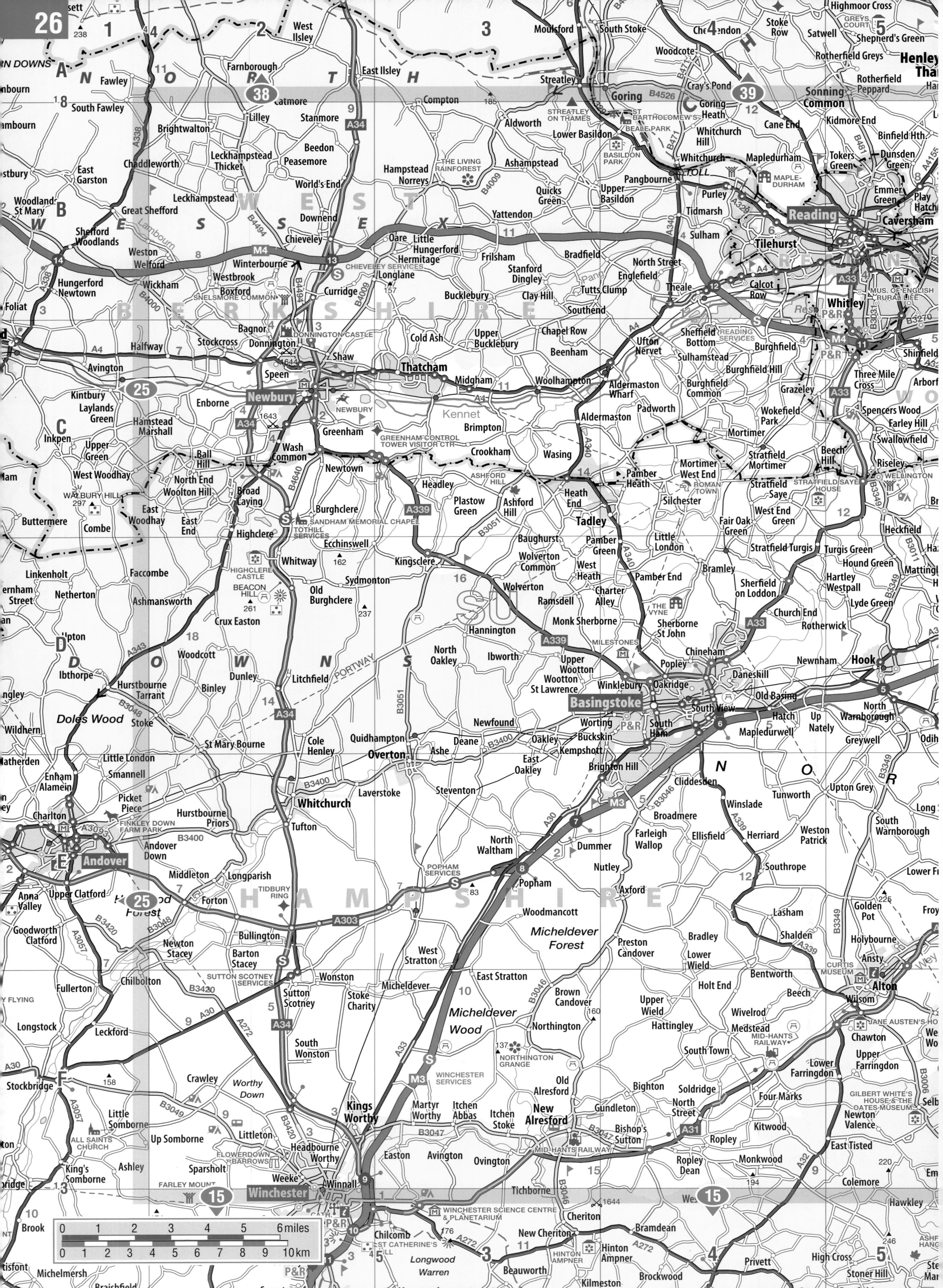

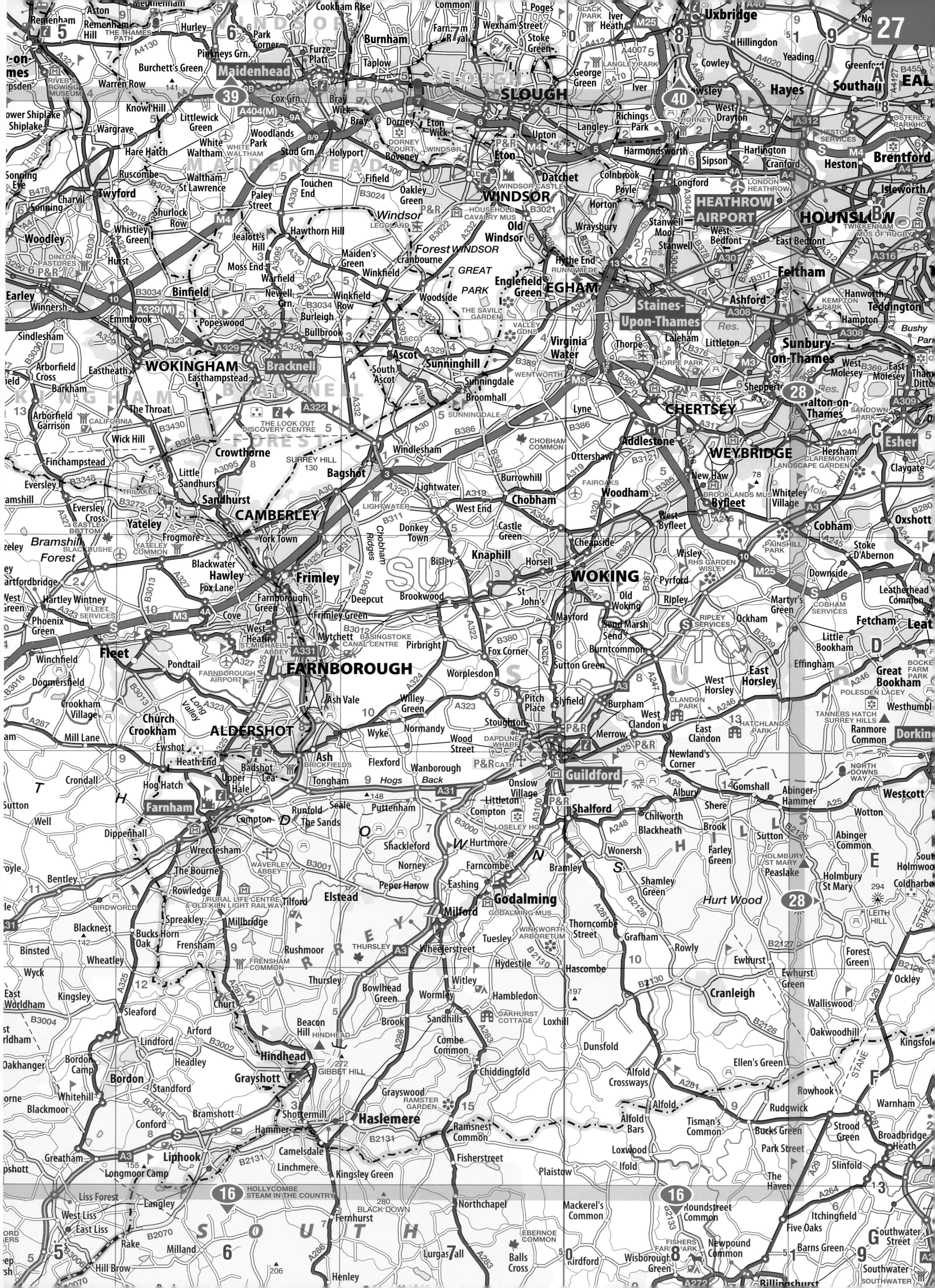

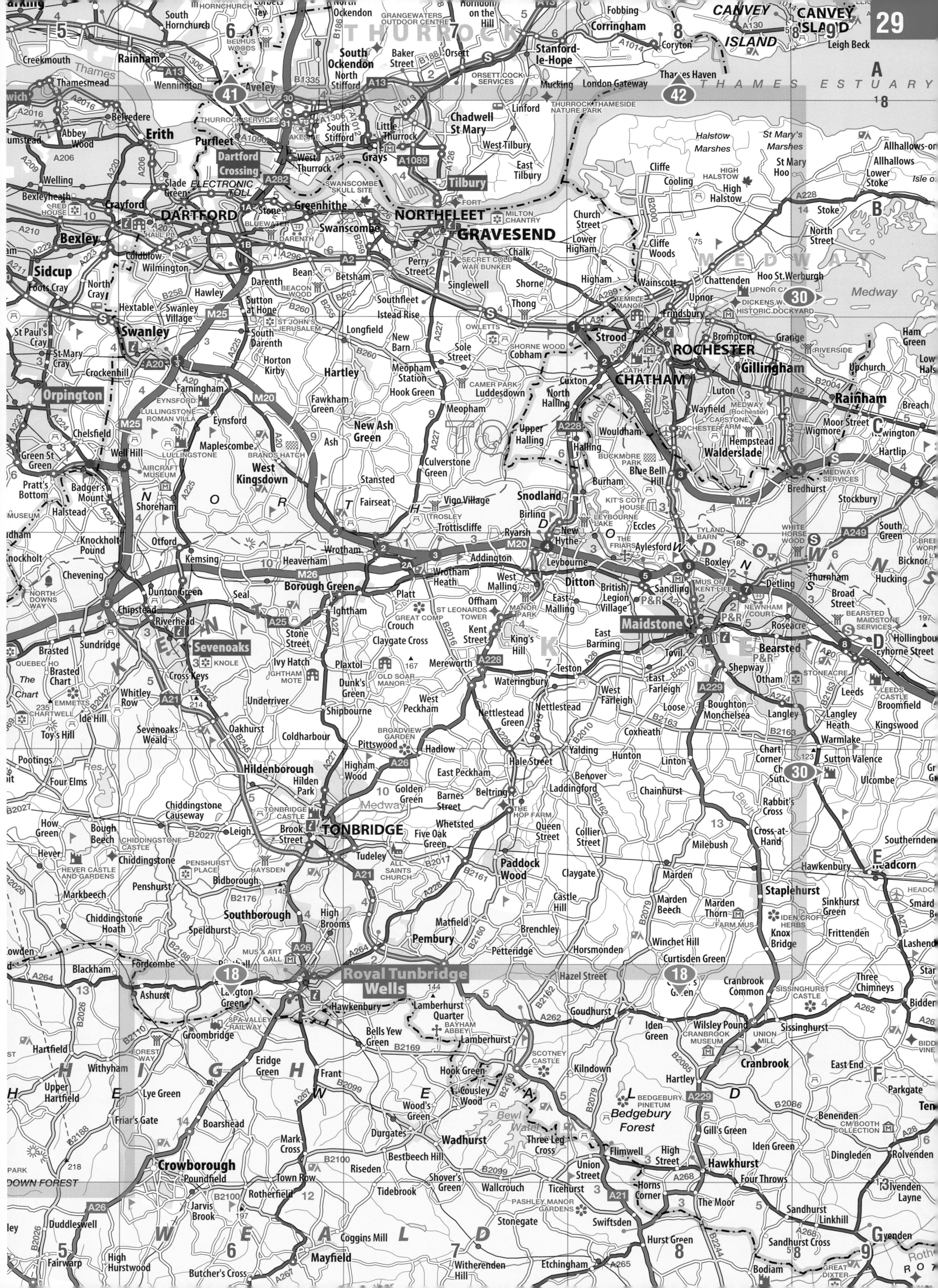

5  6  7  8  ⁶5 9

A

¹8

B

TURNER
CONTEMPORARY
THE SHELL GROTTO
**Margate**
Cliftonville
Foreness Pt.
Westgate on Sea
Kingsgate
DREAMLAND
B2052
Northdown
NORTH
RECULVER
RECULVER TOWERS
AND ROMAN FORT
Minnis Bay
FORELAND
LIGHTHOUSE
Reculver
Hillborough
Birchington
St Peter's
NE BAY
Beltinge
A299
QUEX HOUSE
Isle of Thanet
A255
Northwood
BROADSTAIRS
iffe
Greenhill
Broomfield
St Nicholas
at Wade
Acol
SPITFIRE AND
HURRICANE MEM
DICKENS HOUSE MUSEUM
Herne
11
A299
B2190
A256
Dumpton
Hoath
Boyden
Gate
Sarre
A299
WINDMILL
Manston
Newington
Calcott
Chislet
Upstreet
A253
Monkton
15
Way
Cliffsend
Ramsgate
9
Broadoak
Hersden
A28
Grove
STODMARSH
West Stourmouth
Minster
Way
Cliffsend
Pegwell
SANDWICH &
PEGWELL BAY
MARITIME MUSEUM
Sturry
Westbere
Preston
East Stourmouth
Westmarsh
Ware
St. AUGUSTINE'S
CROSS
Pegwell
Bay
C
Fordwich
Stodmarsh
Elmstone
Hoaden
RICHBOROUGH
CASTLE
A256
P&R
Canterbury
Wickhambreux
Ickham
AMPHITHEATRE
Great Stonar
Sandwich
Bay
A257
ST. AUGUSTINE'S ABBEY
Littlebourne
11
Wingham
Guilton
Ash
Sandwich
ROYAL ST. GEORGE'S
HOWLETTS WILD
ANIMAL PARK
WINGHAM
WILDLIFE
PARK
Marshborough
TOLL
TR
P&R
Bramling
Staple
Woodnesborough
Stone Cross
A2
Bekesbourne
Goodnestone
Gore
Worth
Patrixbourne
GOODNESTONE PARK
Eastry
Ham
MARITIME AND
LOCAL HISTORY MUSEUM
Bridge
Adisham
Chillenden
Knowlton
Finglesham
Betteshanger
Sholden
THE
DOWNS
D
Lower
Hardres
Aylesham
Nonington
Easole Street
Betteshanger
Northbourne
DEAL
Bishopsbourne
Kingston
Snowdown
Tilmanstone
Elvington
Great
Mongeham
DEAL CASTLE
Upper Hardres
Court
Womenswold
9
Ripple
Walmer
Barham
Barfreston
EAST KENT
RL'Y
Sutton
WALMER CASTLE
AND GARDENS
Derringstone
Woolage
Green
Eythorne
East
Studdal
Ringwould
Kingsdown
ngham
A2
Coxhill
Shepherdswell
West
Langdon
Martin
A258
Denton
7
Coldred
A256
East
Langdon
Martin Mill
Wingmore
Selsted
Lydden
Whitfield
Guston
St Margaret's at Cliffe
Elham
LYDDEN
TEMPLE EWELL
Ewell
Minnis
8
West
Cliffe
THE BAY MUSEUM
E
odes
Ottinge
Swingfield
Street
ST JOHN'S
COMMANDERY
Temple
Ewell
3
THE PINES
GARDEN
St Margaret's Bay
10
Swingfield
Minnis
CRABBLE
CORN MILL
Buckland
A2
SOUTH
FORELAND
Lyminge
Densole
Drellingore
Alkham
ROMAN PAINTED
HOUSE
WHITE
CLIFFS
Etchinghill
Hawkinge
West
Hougham
Maxton
Farthingloe
CASTLE & HELLFIRE CORNER
CALAIS
DUNKERQUE
borough
Paddlesworth
A20
DOVER
CHANNEL
TUNNEL
Newington
Capel le
Ferne
B2011
Aycliff
DE BRADELEI
WHARF
11A
12
13
EAST CLIFF &
WARREN
SAMPHIRE
HOE
Cheriton
ELHAM VALLEY
RLY MUS
Folkestone
East Wear
Bay
Saltwood
Sandgate
CLIFF LIFT
F
Hythe
19
CHANNEL
G
arsh

5  6  7  8  ⁶5 9

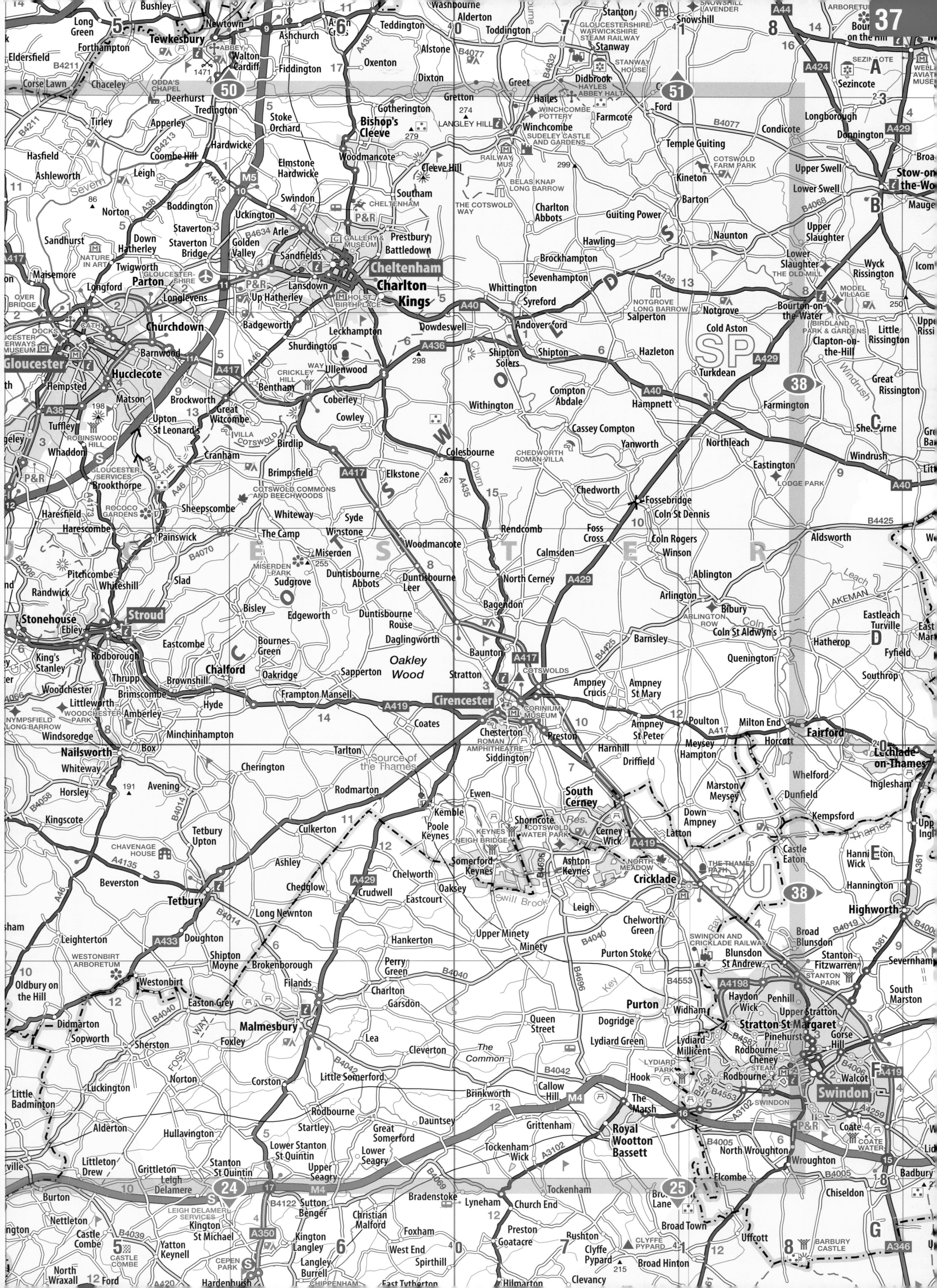

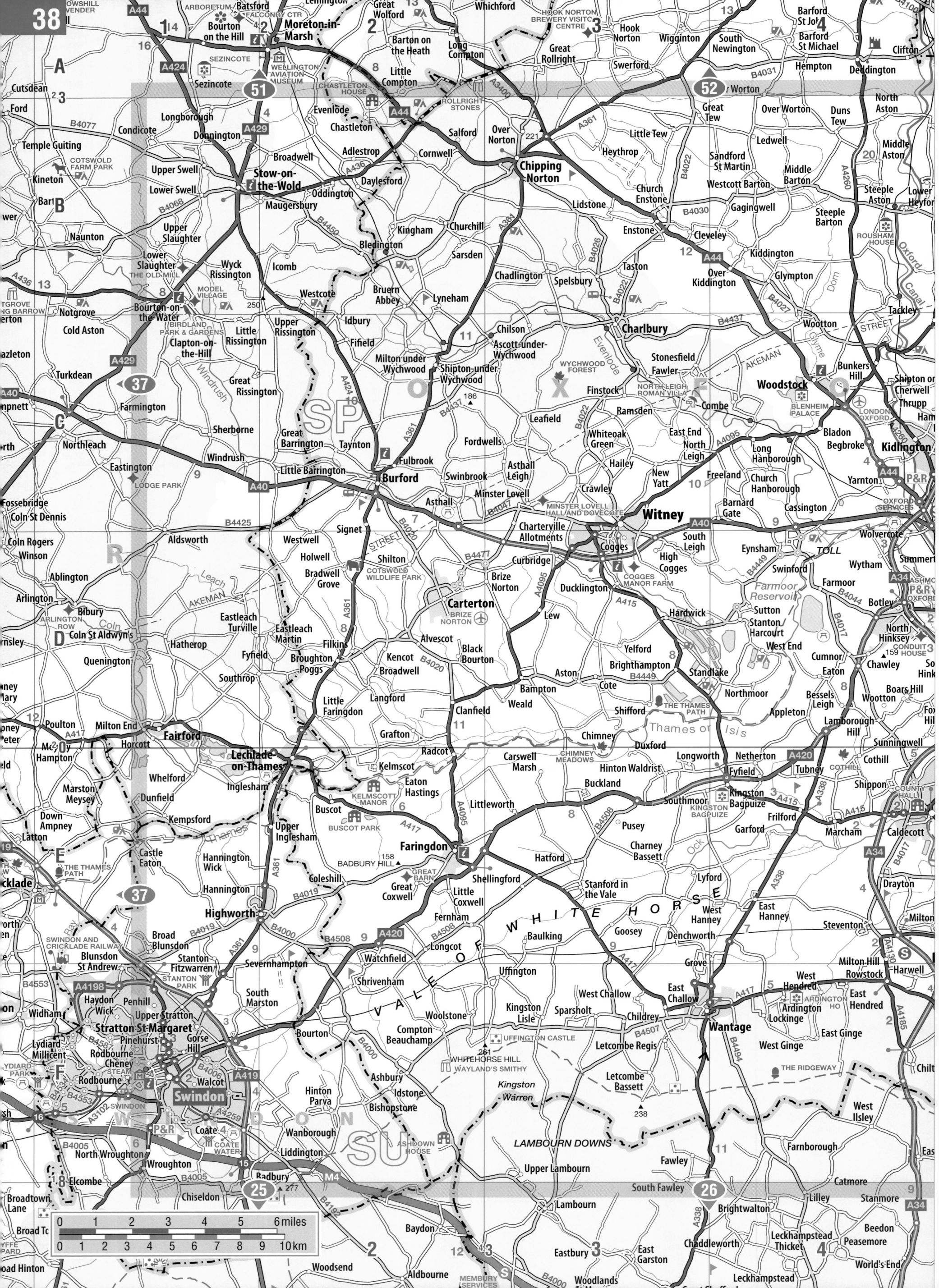

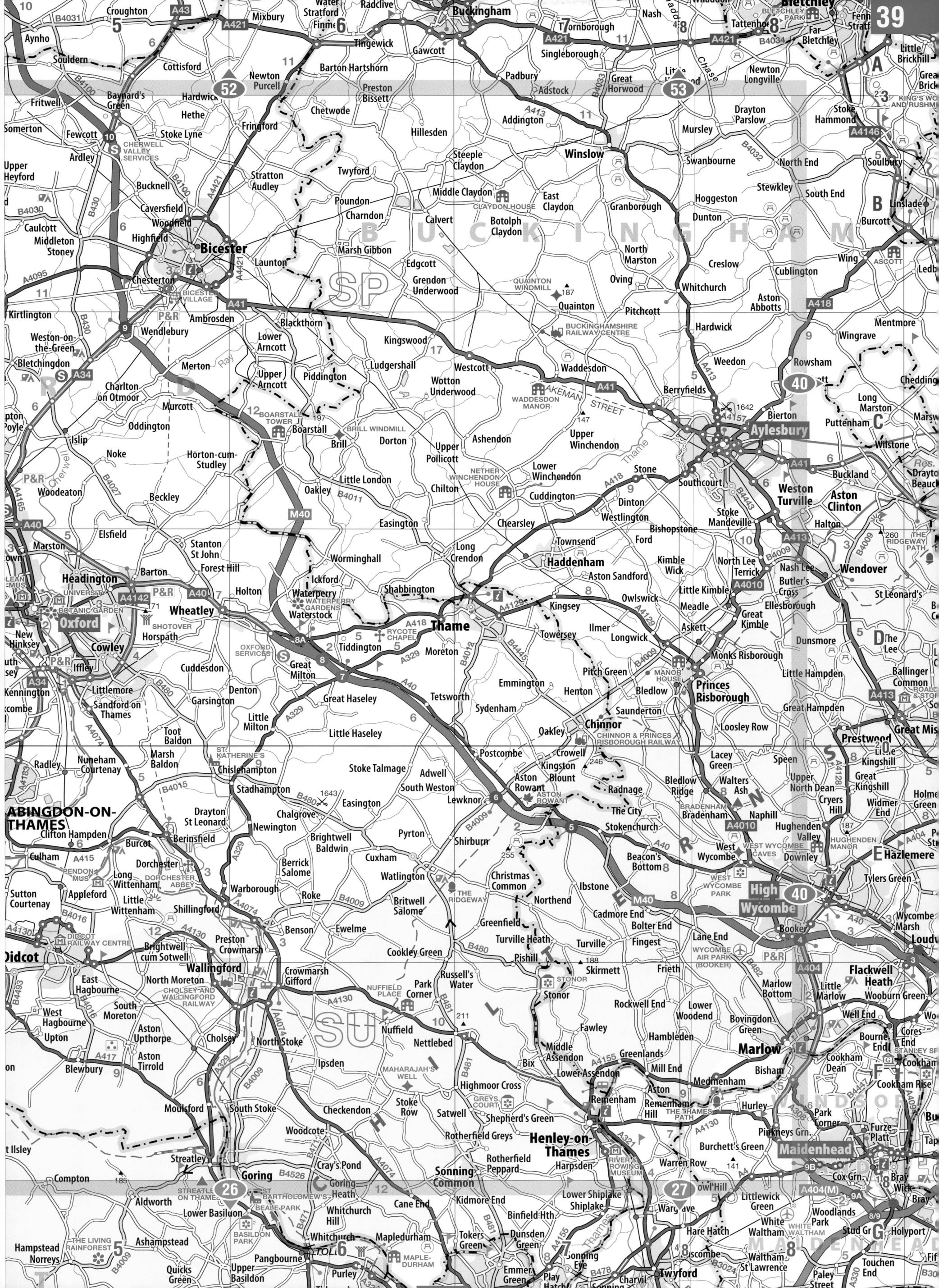

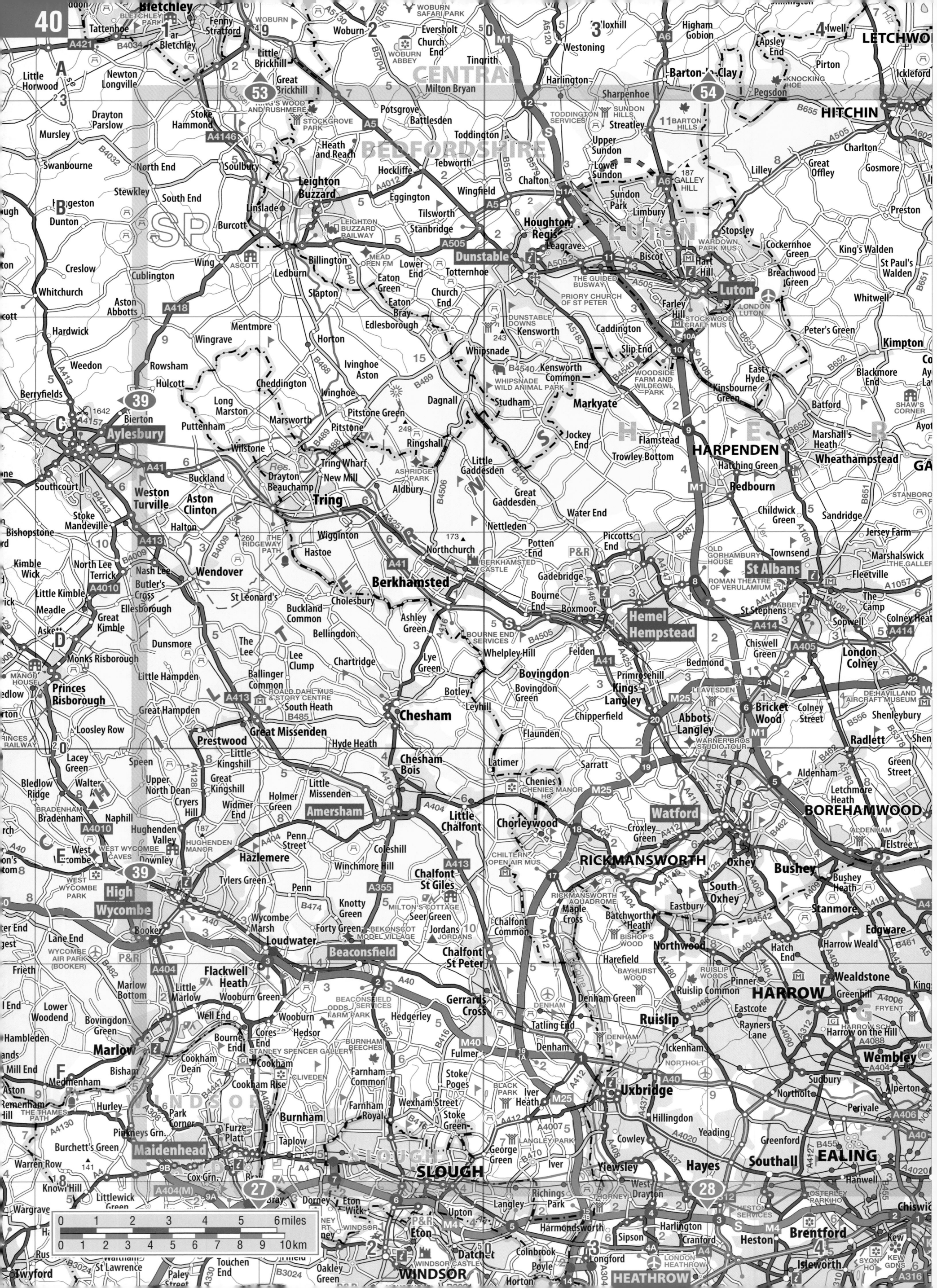

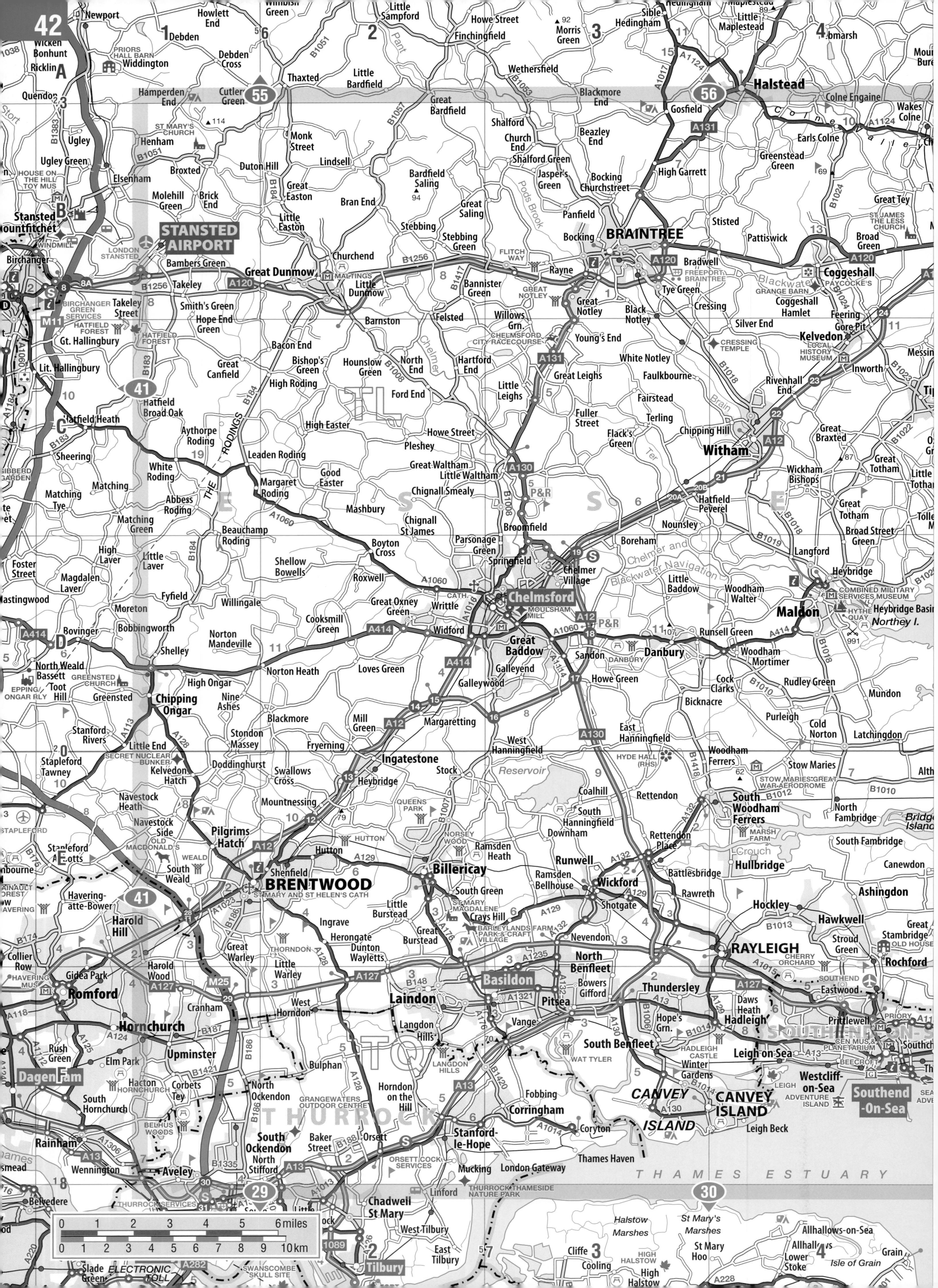

Stour
Bures
5
Little
Horkesley
Wormingford
0
Nayland
Roxted
Boxted
Boxted
Cross
Boxted
Heath
Langham
Dedham
Heath
St Mary's
A12
6
Dedham
Brantham
Cattawade
Upper Street
BRIDGE
COTTAGE
Stour
Valley
7
Holbrook
Bay
Harkstead
Shop
Corner
2
Shotley
Gate
8
Stour
HARWICH
RESERVE
43
AMUSE

Mistley
Towers
Mistley
Lawford
Manningtree
Wrabness
Parkeston
Upper
Dovercourt
Dovercourt
HARWICH
REDOUBT
FORT
A

Bradfield
Bradfield Heath
12
A120
57
2 3
HOEK VAN HOLLAND

Ardleigh
Horsley
Cross
Horsleycross
Street
Wix
Little
Oakley

appel
Fordham
West
Bergholt
Mile End
Parsons
Heath
Fox
Street
Crockleford
Heath
Great
Bromley
Little
Bromley
Stone's
Green
Great
Oakley
Horsey
Island
The Naze

Eight
Ash Green
Fordstreet
Aldham
Highwoods
St Botolph's
Priory
7
Colchester
A133
Elmstead
Market
Little
Bentley
Tendring
Green
Beaumont
HAMFORD
WATER
MARITIME
MUSEUM
B

Marks
Tey
Lexden
26
27
Beacon End
Stanway
25
Shrub
End
Abbey
Field
Old Heath
Maypole
Green
Blackheath
Hare Green
Balls
Green
BETH
CHATTO
GDNS
14
Wivenhoe
Cross
Frating
Green
9
Tendring
Thorpe
Green
Thorpe-
le-Soken
Kirby-
le-Soken
Walton-on-
the-Naze

2
Copford
Green
Easthorpe
Hardy's Green
Heckfordbridge
Layer de
la Haye
BOURNE
MILL
Wivenhoe
Rowhedge
Great
Bentley
Aingers
Green
Weeley
Weeley
Heath
11
Kirby
Cross
Frinton-on-Sea

Smythe's
Green
Birch
Birch
Green
Malting
Green
Fingringhoe
Alresford
Row Heath
Little
Clacton
Great
Holland

Layer
Marney
LAYER MARNEY
TOWER
Layer
Breton
Abberton
Reservoir
Abberton
Langenhoe
Thorrington
St Osyth
Heath
A133
CLACTON
VILLAGE
HOLLAND
HAVEN

otree
Paternoster
Heath
Great
Wigborough
Peldon
Brightlingsea
St Osyth
PRIORY
St Osyth
Little
Clacton
Holland-on-Sea

Salcott
COLCHESTER
ZOO
Mersea Island
East Mersea
CUDMORE
GROVE
Point Clear
Great
Clacton
Clacton-On-Sea
C

Tolleshunt
D'Arcy
BLACKWATER
ESTUARY
Blue Row
COLNE ESTUARY
Jaywick
shunt
ajor
B1023
West Mersea
MERSEA ISLAND MUSEUM
Colne Pt.

Goldhanger
The Nass
Virley Channel

Blackwater
Osea I.
Sales Pt.
ST PETERS
ON THE WALL
Bradwell
Waterside
TM
D

Ramsey
Island
St Lawrence
Bradwell
on Sea

Steeple
Tillingham
DENGIE
B1021

Asheldham
Dengie
2 0

Mayland
Ray
Sand

Southminster
B1018
B1010
4
Stoneyhills
MANGAPPS RAILWAY MUS
Montsale
Deal Hall

Ostend
Burnham-
on-Crouch
MUS
Foulness Sand
Foulness Pt.
TR
E

Creaksea
Crouch
Courtsend

Paglesham
Churchend
WALLASEA
WETLANDS
Churchend

Ballards
Gore
Paglesham
Eastend
Potton
Island
FOULNESS
ISLAND

Barling
Havengore
Island
M A P L I N   S A N D S

Little
Wakering
Great Wakering
Bournes
Green
B1017
North
Shoebury
F
59
A13
E LIFE
ENTURE
B1016
Thorpe Bay
Shoeburyness
Cambridge
Town
Shoeburyness
1 8

30
G
5
6
7
8

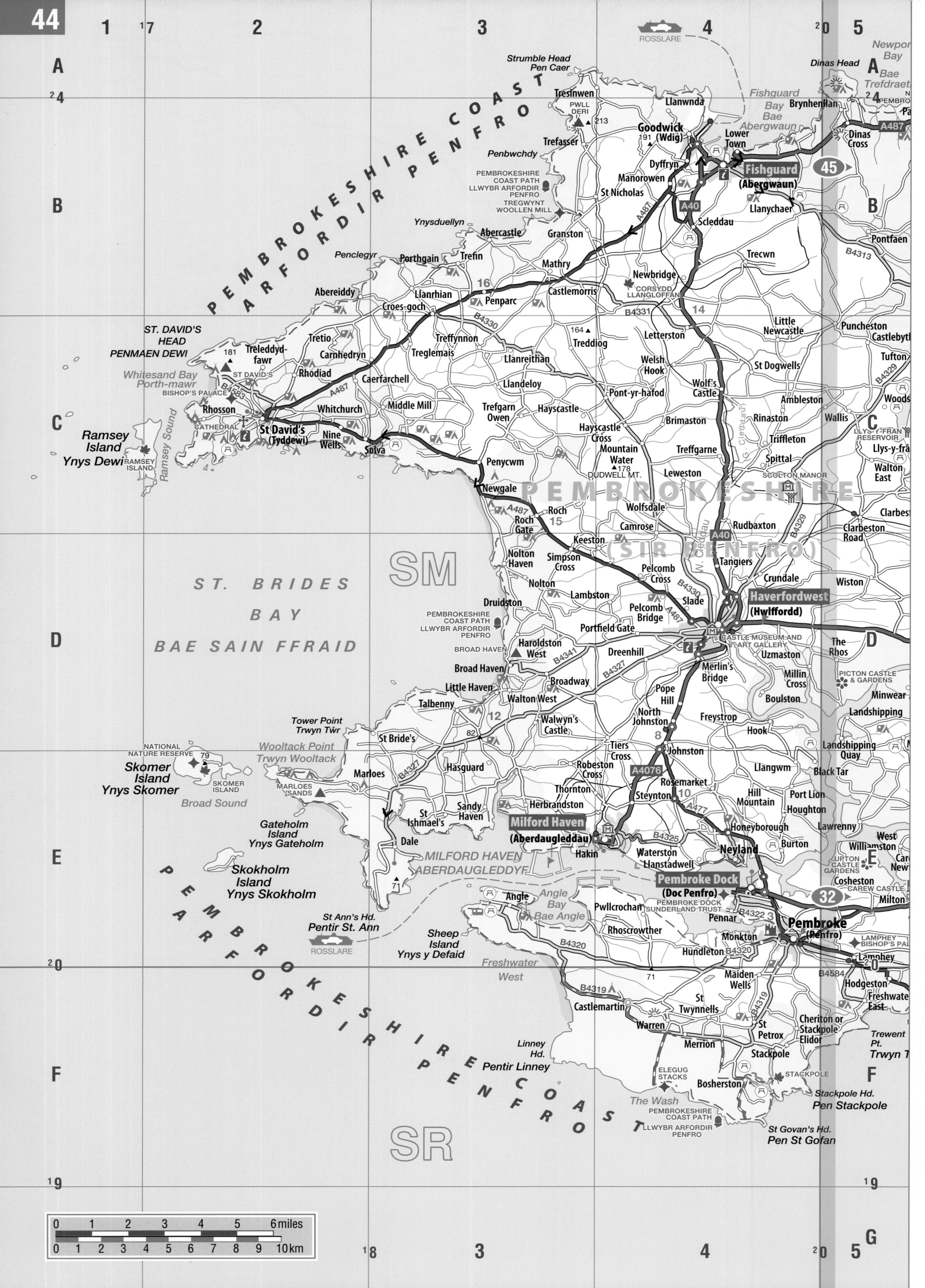

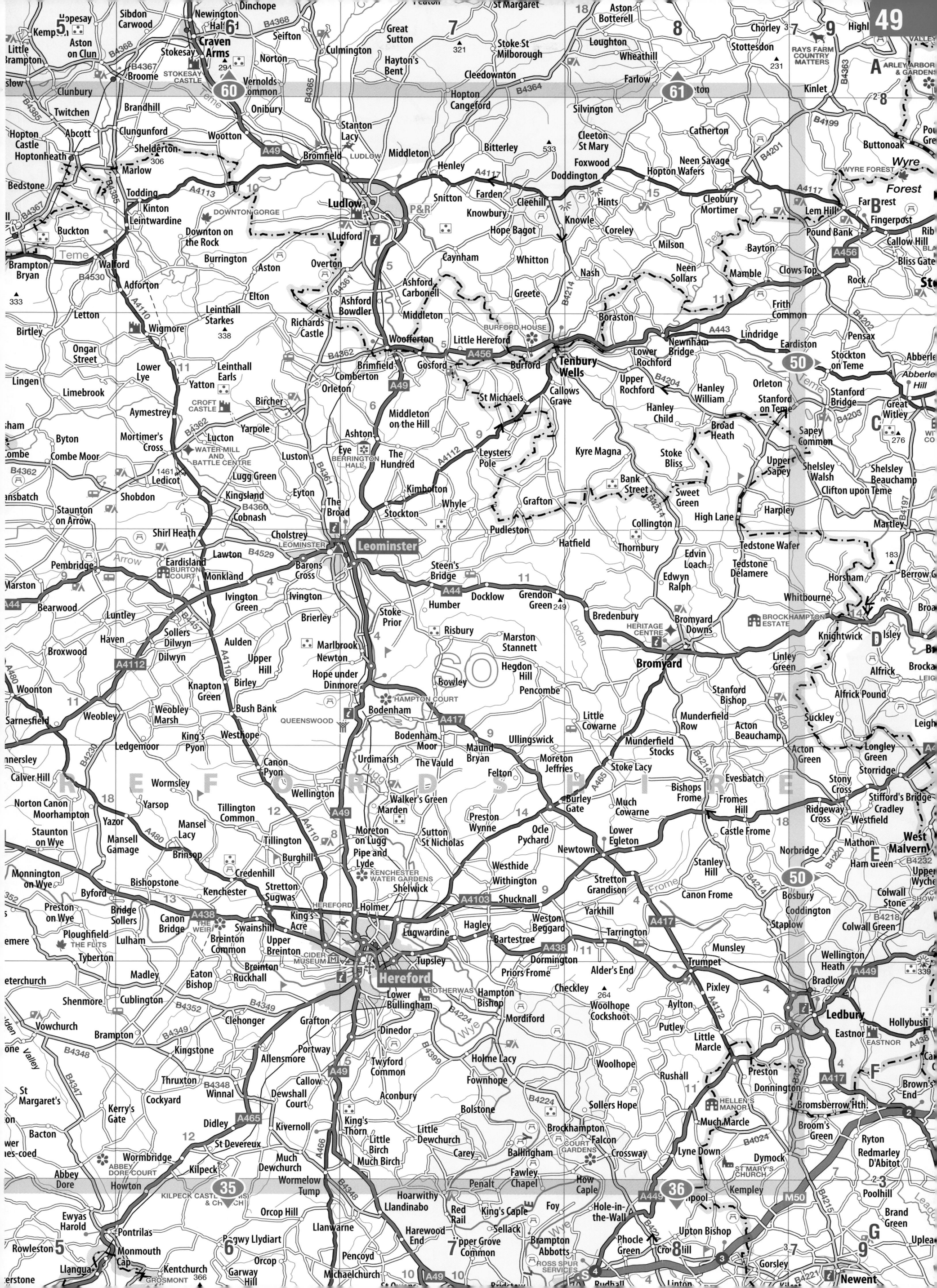

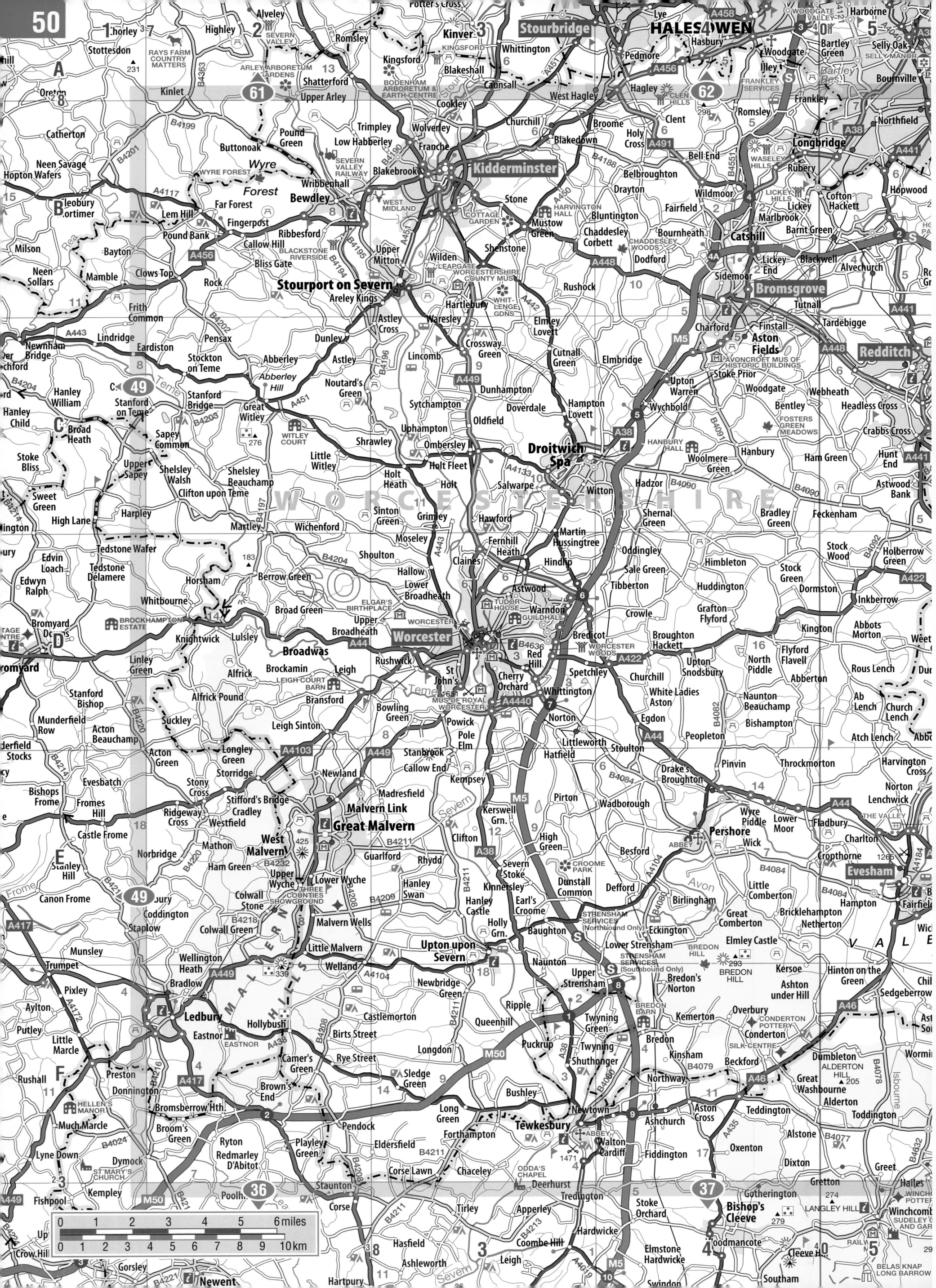

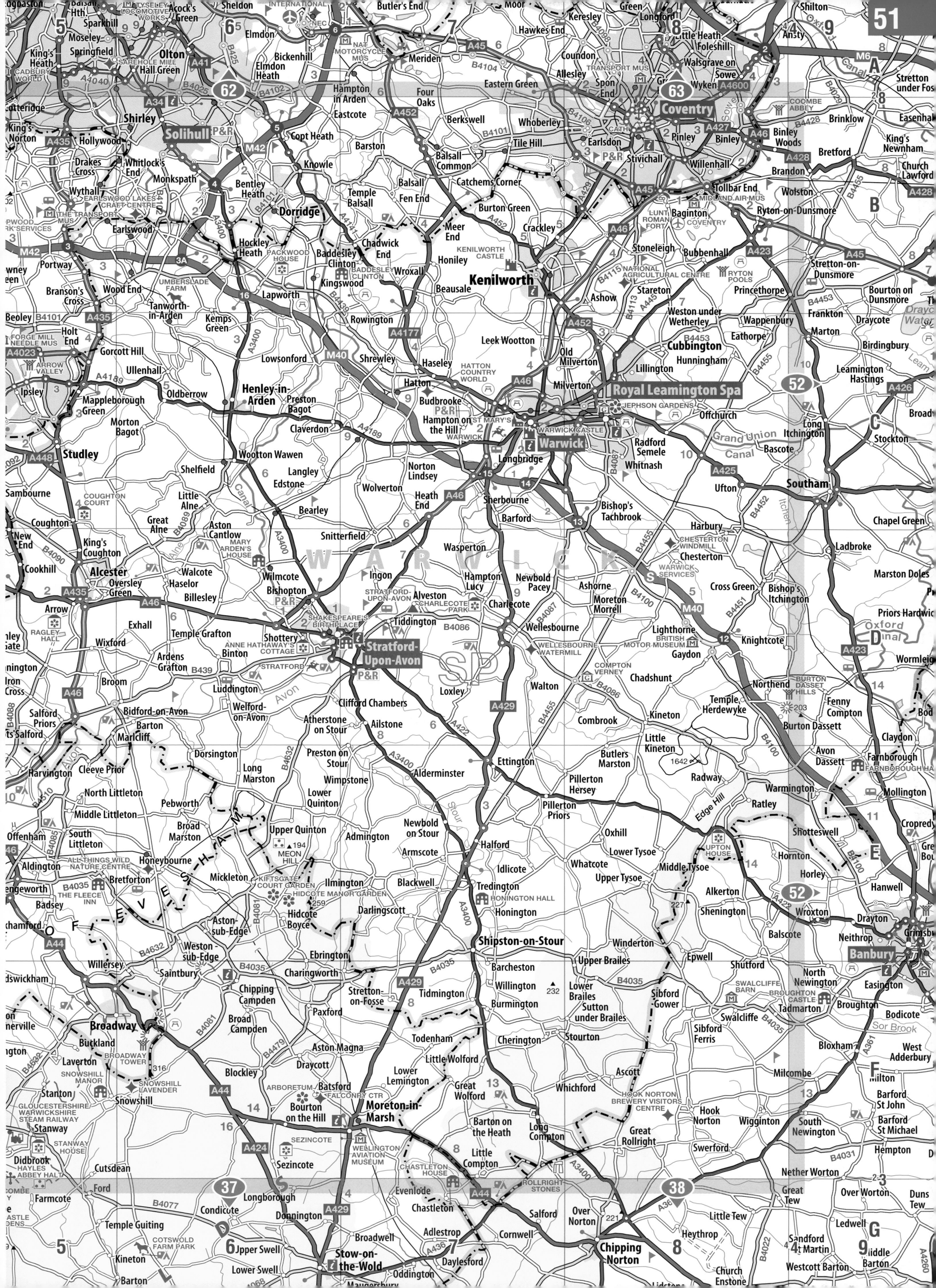

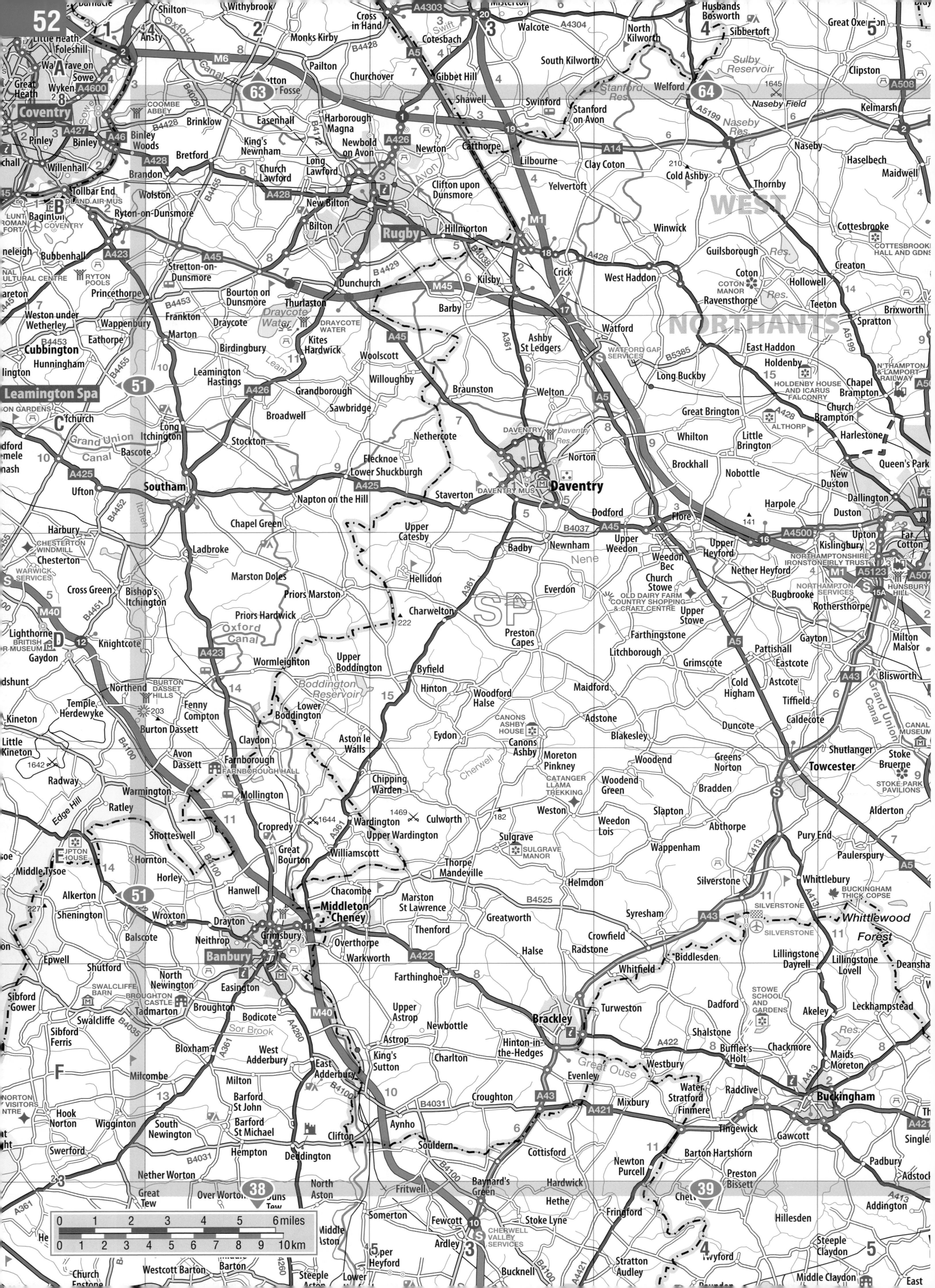

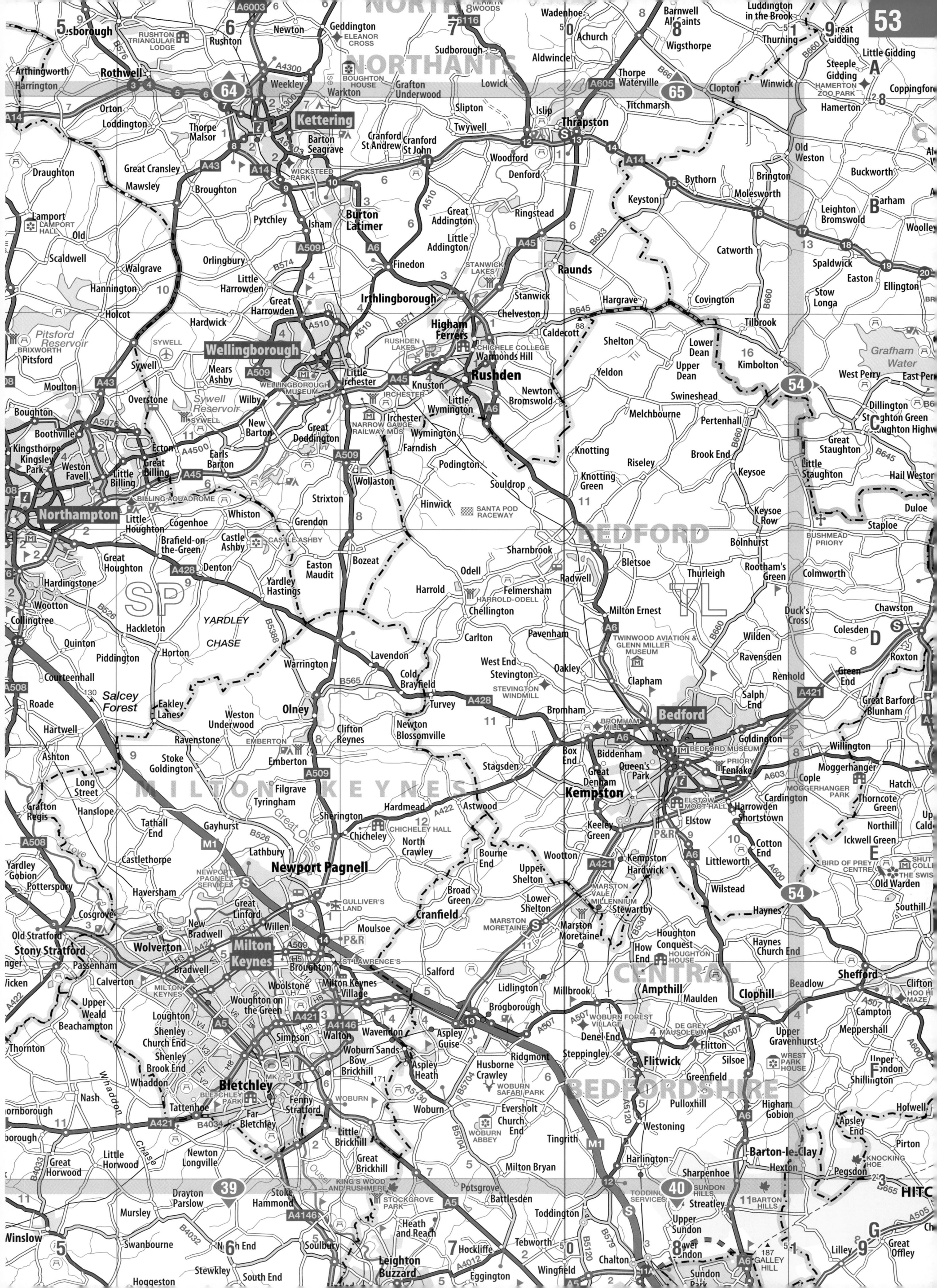

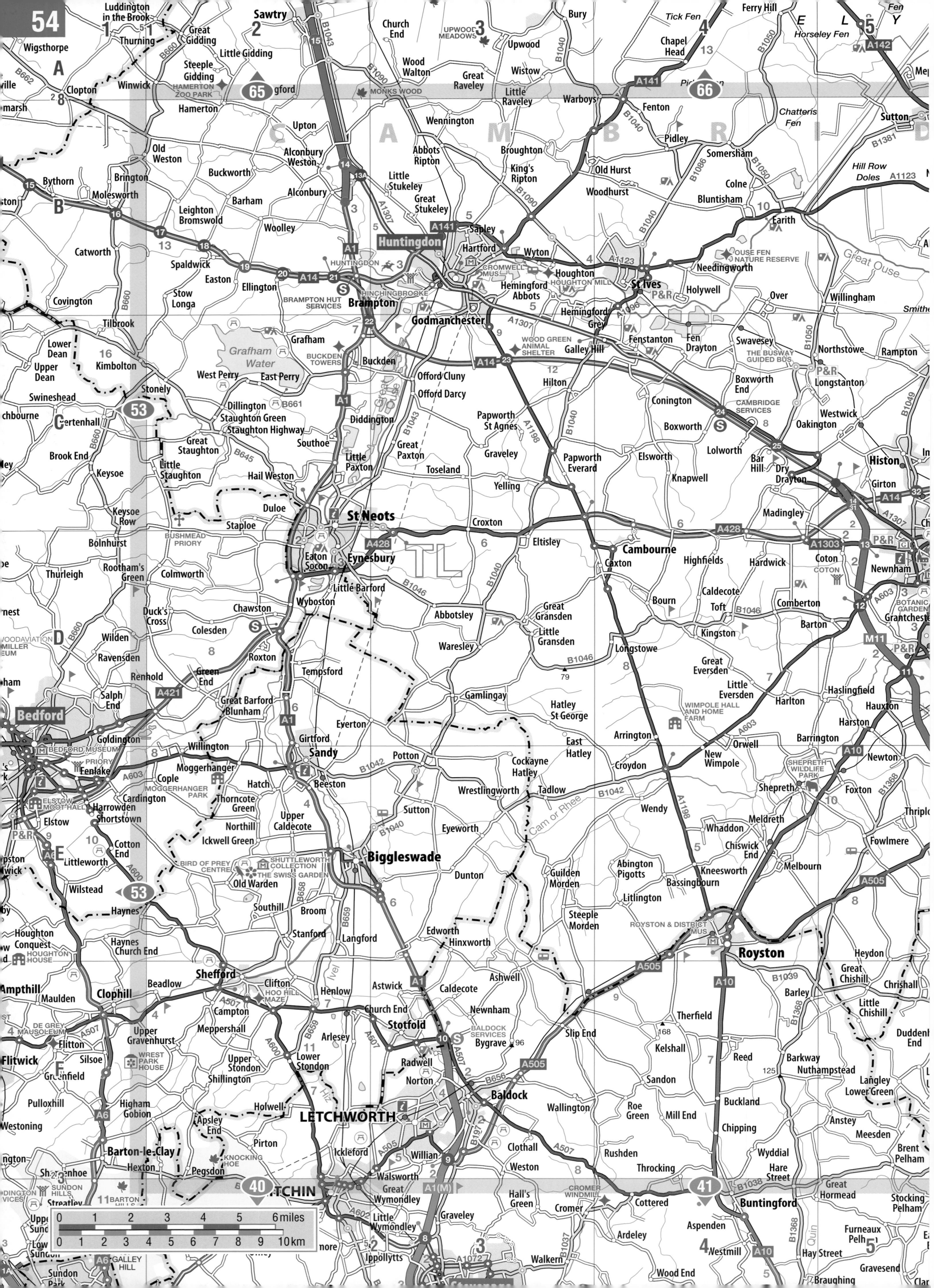

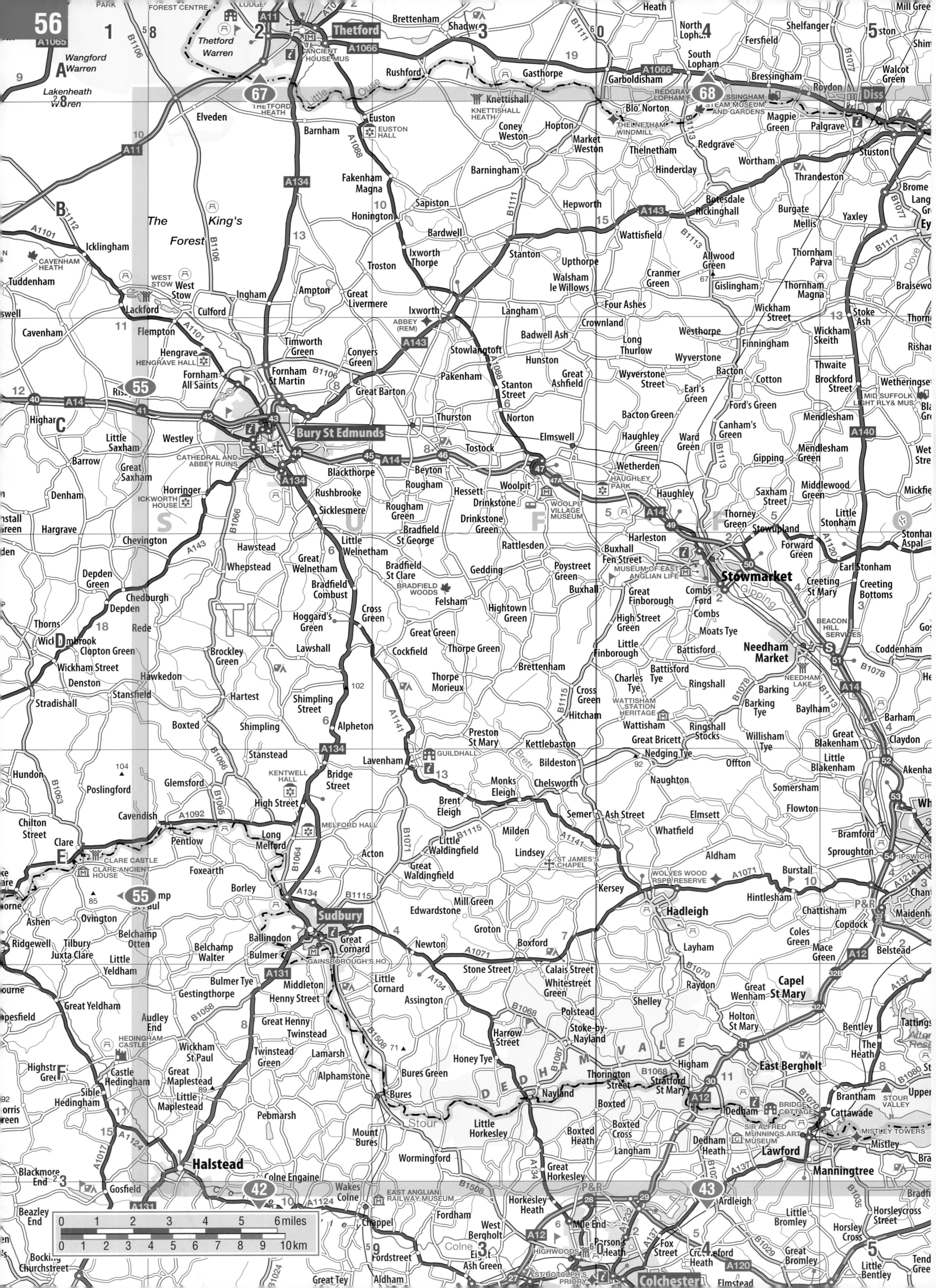

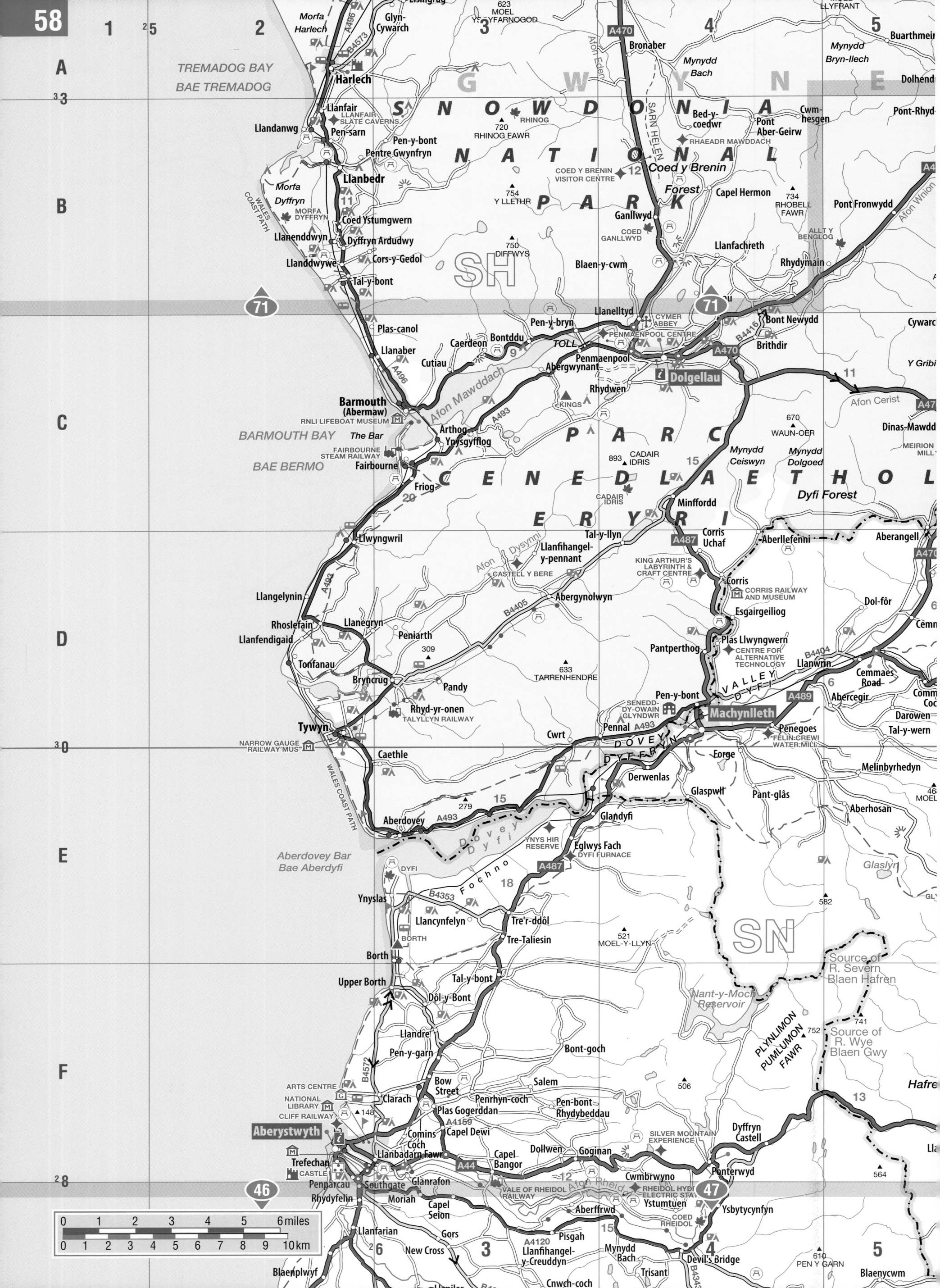

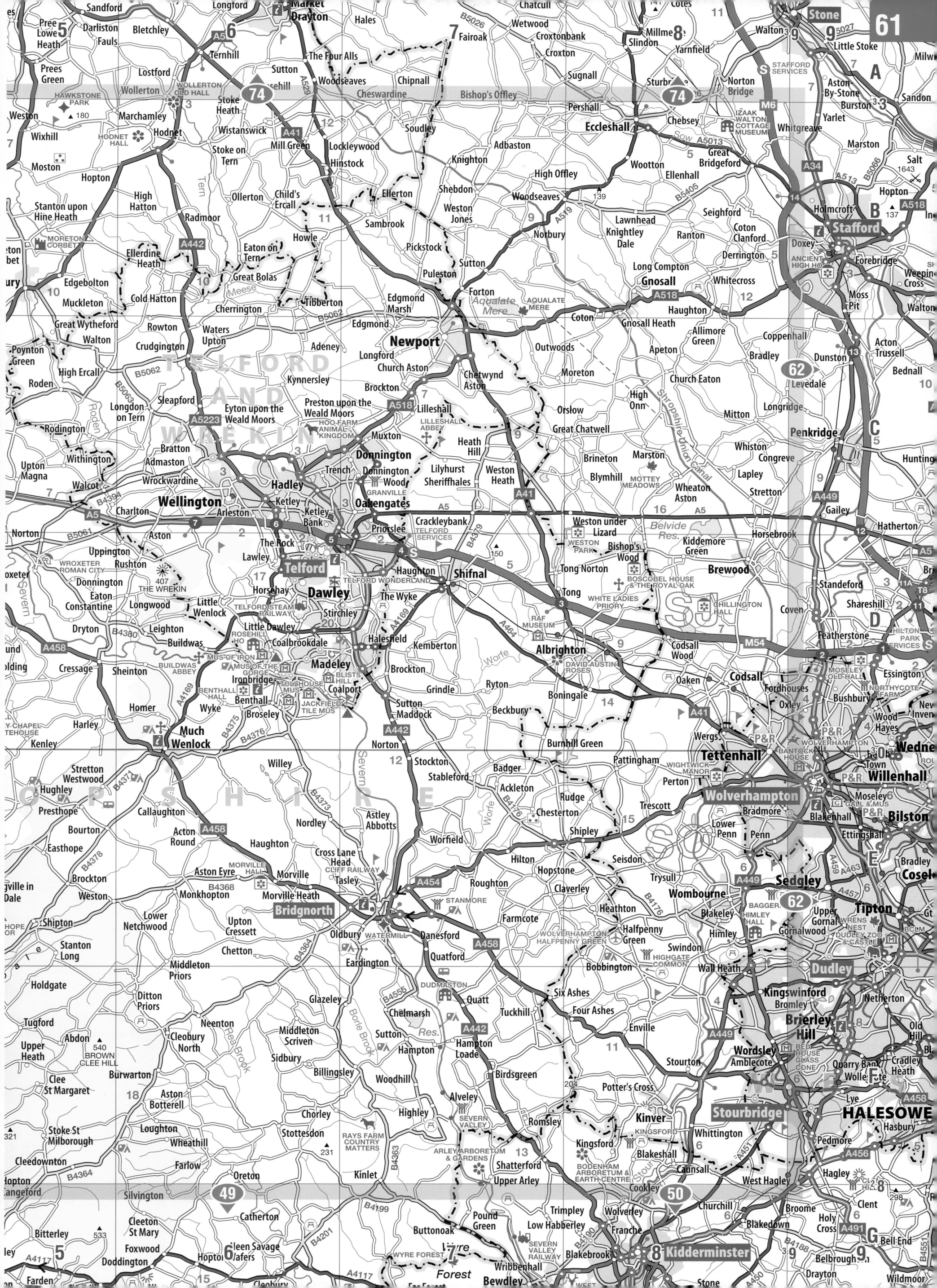

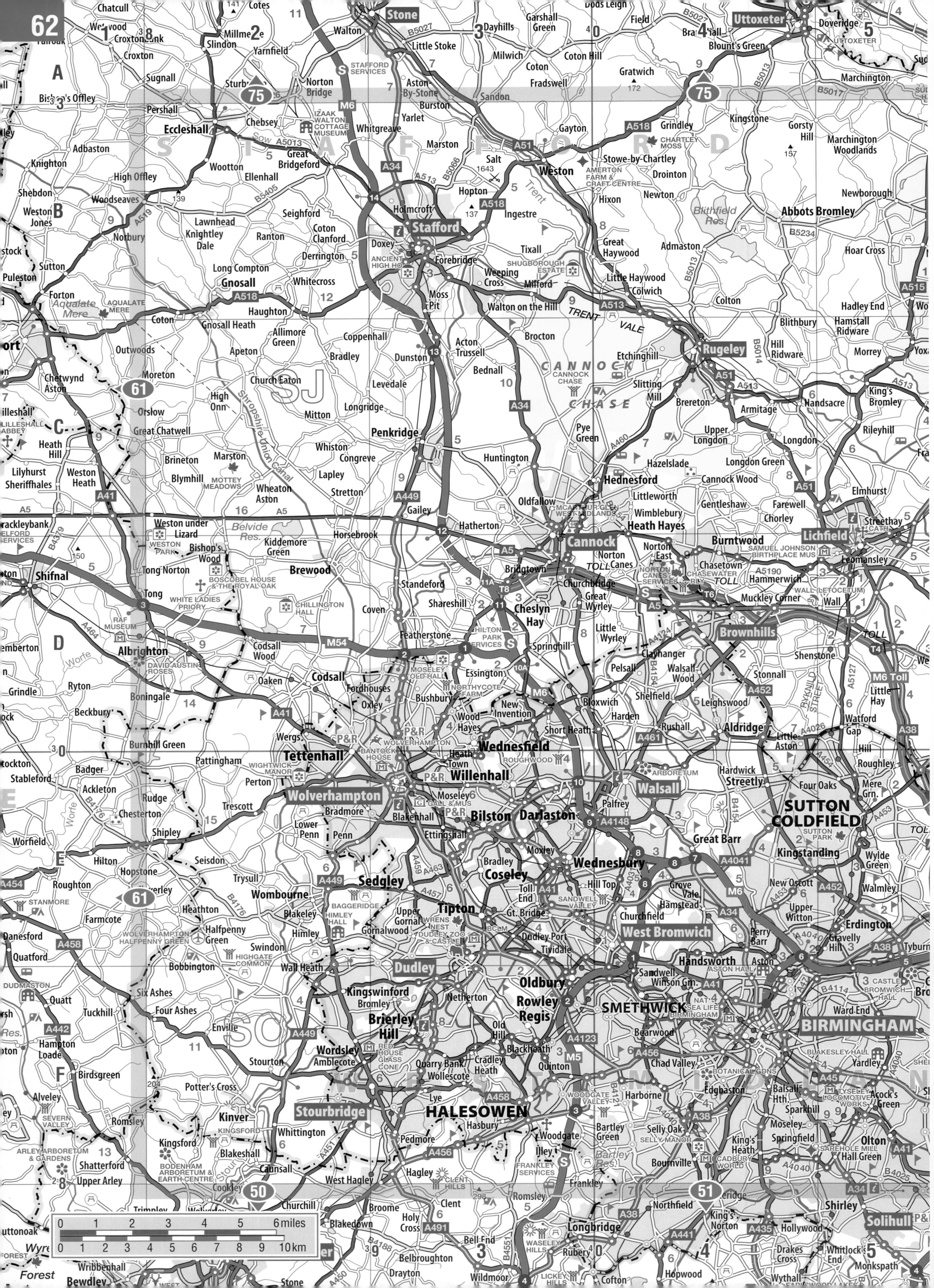

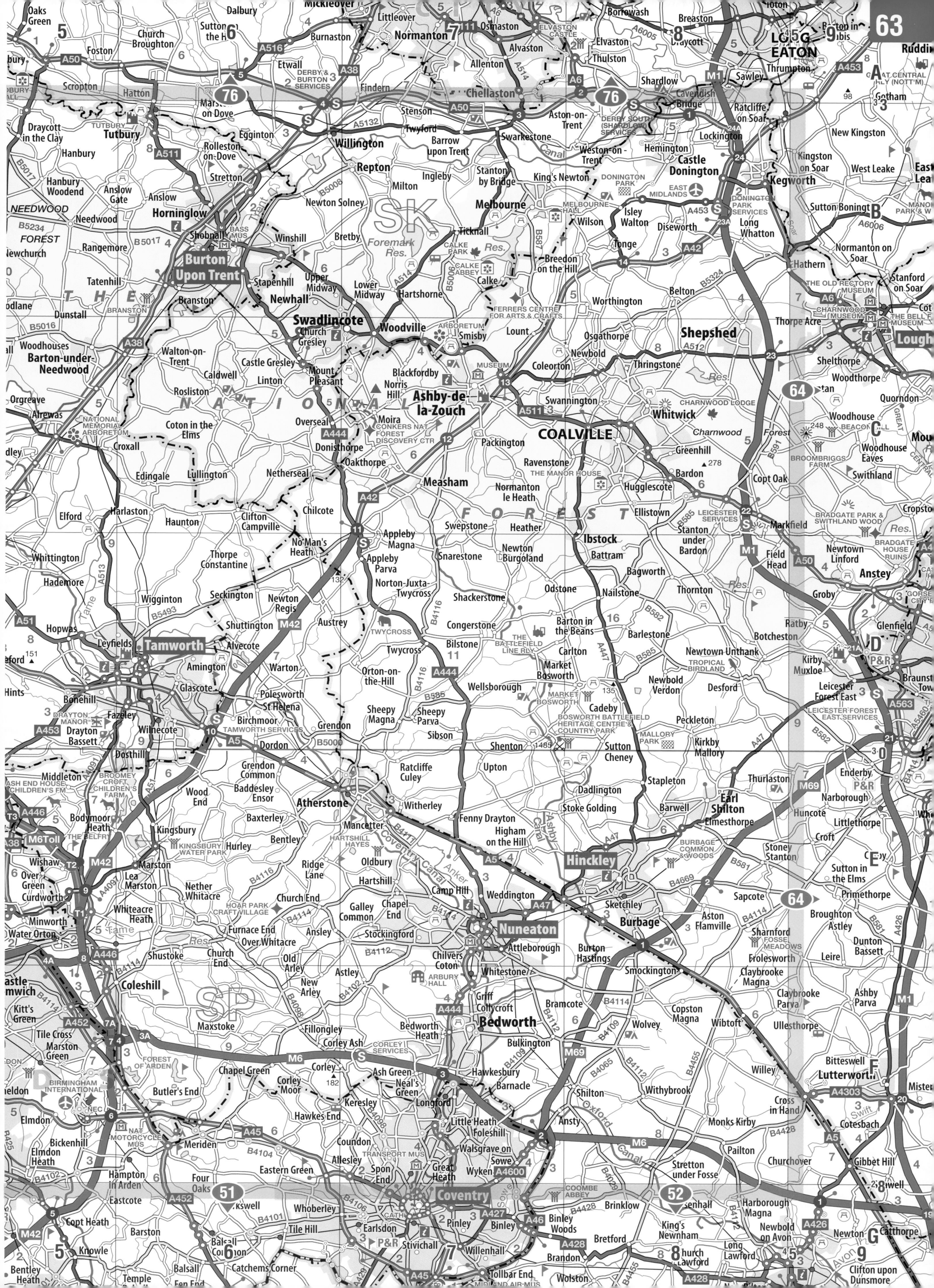

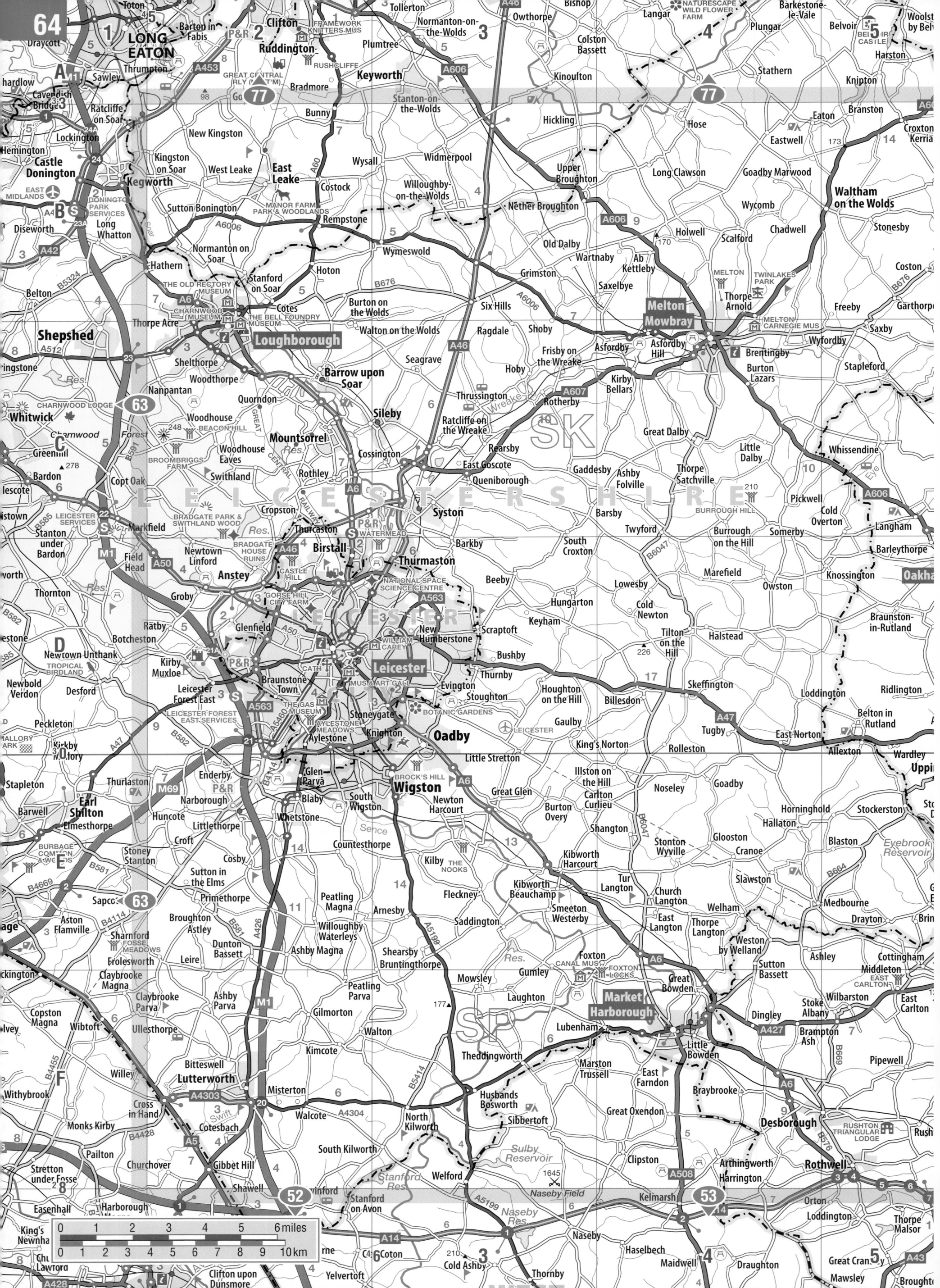

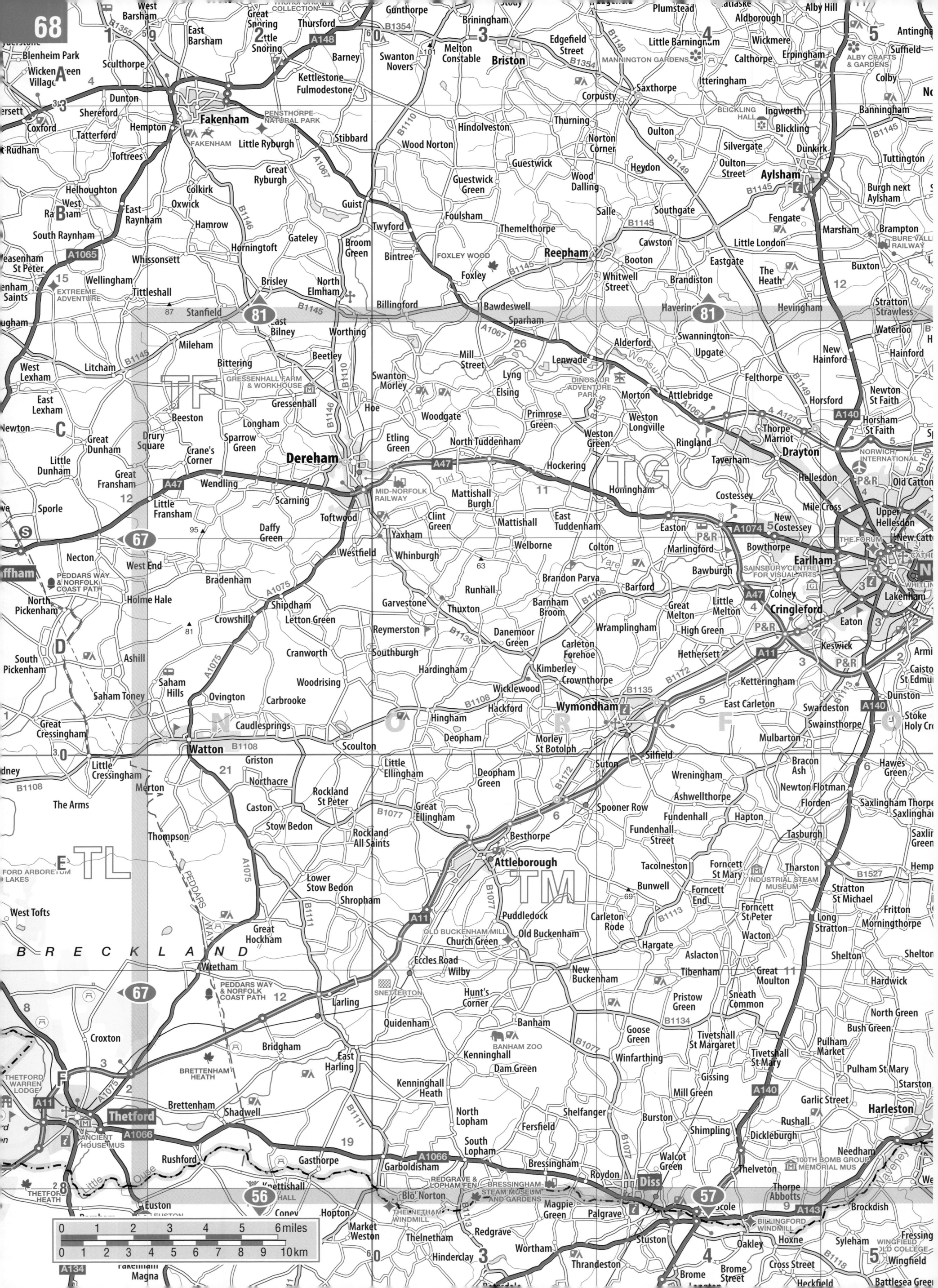

A

³6

*Malltraeth Bay*
*Bae Malltraeth*
**Newborough**
*Forest*
ANGLESEY
MODEL
VILLAGE
*Llanddwyn I.*
**Ynys Llanddwyn**
*The Bar*
CAS
REGIMENTAL
*Abermenai*
*Pt.*
**Trwyn**
**Abermenai**

**C A E R N A R F O N**
AIRWORLD
AVIATION MUSEUM
**Morfa Dinlle**
**Dinas Dinlle**
Ffrw
**Llandwrog**
GLYNLLIFO
14

B

**B A Y**

**B A E**

**Pontllyfni**

**C A E R N A R F O N**

**Aberdesach**

82
**Clynnog-fawr**
Tain

*Gyrn-goch*
**Capel Uchaf**

**Bryn-yr-eryr**
509
BWLCH
MAWR
Up
Clyn
522
GYRN DDU
**Trefor**

SH

LLEYN
564
YR EIFL
**Llanaelhaearn**
**Pen-sarn**
B4417
6
**Llithfaen**

Wales Coast Path

C

*Carreg Ddu*
*Porth*
*Dinllaen*
**Pistyll**
**Llwyndyrys**
**Pencaenewydd**

**Morfa Nefyn**
**Nefyn**
LLEYN MARITIME
MUSEUM
**Fron**
**Llangybi**
**Edern**
Tan-y-
graig
B4354
**Llanarmon**
**Rhos-fawr**
**Y Ffôr**
**Chwilog**
B4417
**Glanrhyd**
PENARTH FAWR
MEDIEVAL HOUSE
**Rhos-y-llan**
CORS
GEIRCH
**Boduan**
7
A497
**Tudweiliog**
**Llannor**
**Abererch**
L
**Dinas**
**Efailnewydd**
HAVEN
14
**Garnfadryn**
**Rhyd-y-**
**clafdy**
**Denio**
**Pwllheli**

D

*Porth Golmon*
Y
N
**Bryn-mawr**
**Llaniestyn**
B4415
**Penrhos**
7
**South Beach**
*Carreg yr Imbill*
**Pen-y-graig**
**Rhedyn**
**Llangwnnadl**
P
**Sarn**
**Meyllteyrn**
B4413
**Llanbedrog**
*Penrhyn Mawr*
E
N
**Botwnnog**
**Mynytho**
*Trwyn Llanbedrog*
**Ty-hen**
**Pen-y-**
**groeslon**
**Bryncroes**
**Nanhoron**
R
**Methlem**
**Llandegwning**
**Rhydlios**
H
St Tudwal's
Road
304
MYNYDD
RHIW
PLAS-YN-
RHIW
**Llangian**
A499
Angorfa St Tudwal
**Rhoshirwaun**
**Llawrdref**
**Bellaf**
**Capel Carmel**
**Abersoch**
**Rhiw**
191
B4413
**Llanengan**
*Porth Neigwl or*
*Hell's Mouth*
**Sarn Bach**
St Tudwal's Island East
**Ynys St Tudwal Dwyrain**
**Uwchmynydd**
**Bwlchtocyn**
**Aberdaron**
**Marchroes**
St Tudwal's Island West
**Ynys St Tudwal Gorllewin**

E

*Bardsey Sound*
*Swnt Enlli*
**Bodermid**
**Cilan Uchaf**
*Pen-y-cil*
*Trwyn Cilan*
167
YNYS ENLLI
**Bardsey**
**Island**
**Ynys Enlli**
L L E Y N

³1

F

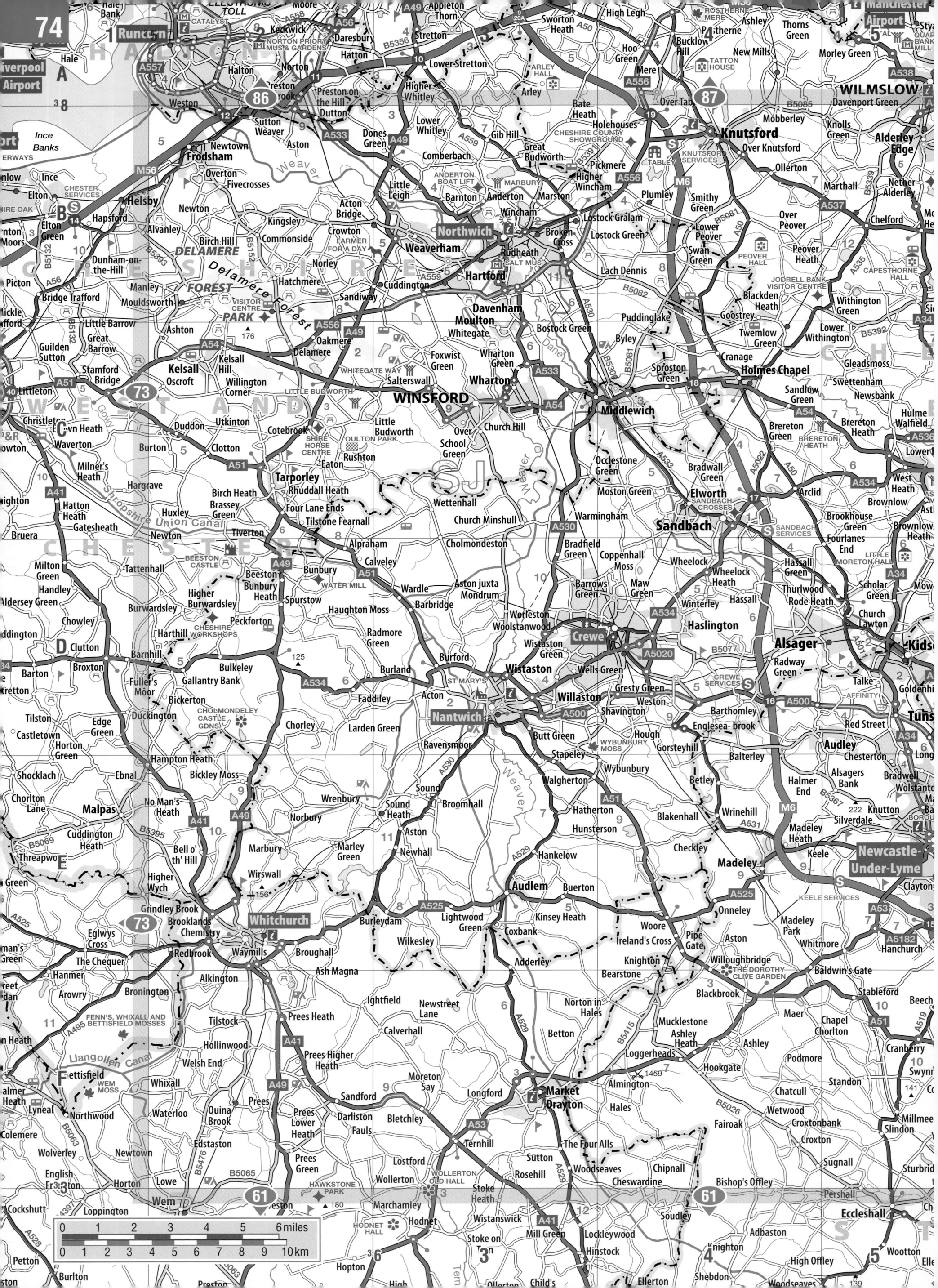

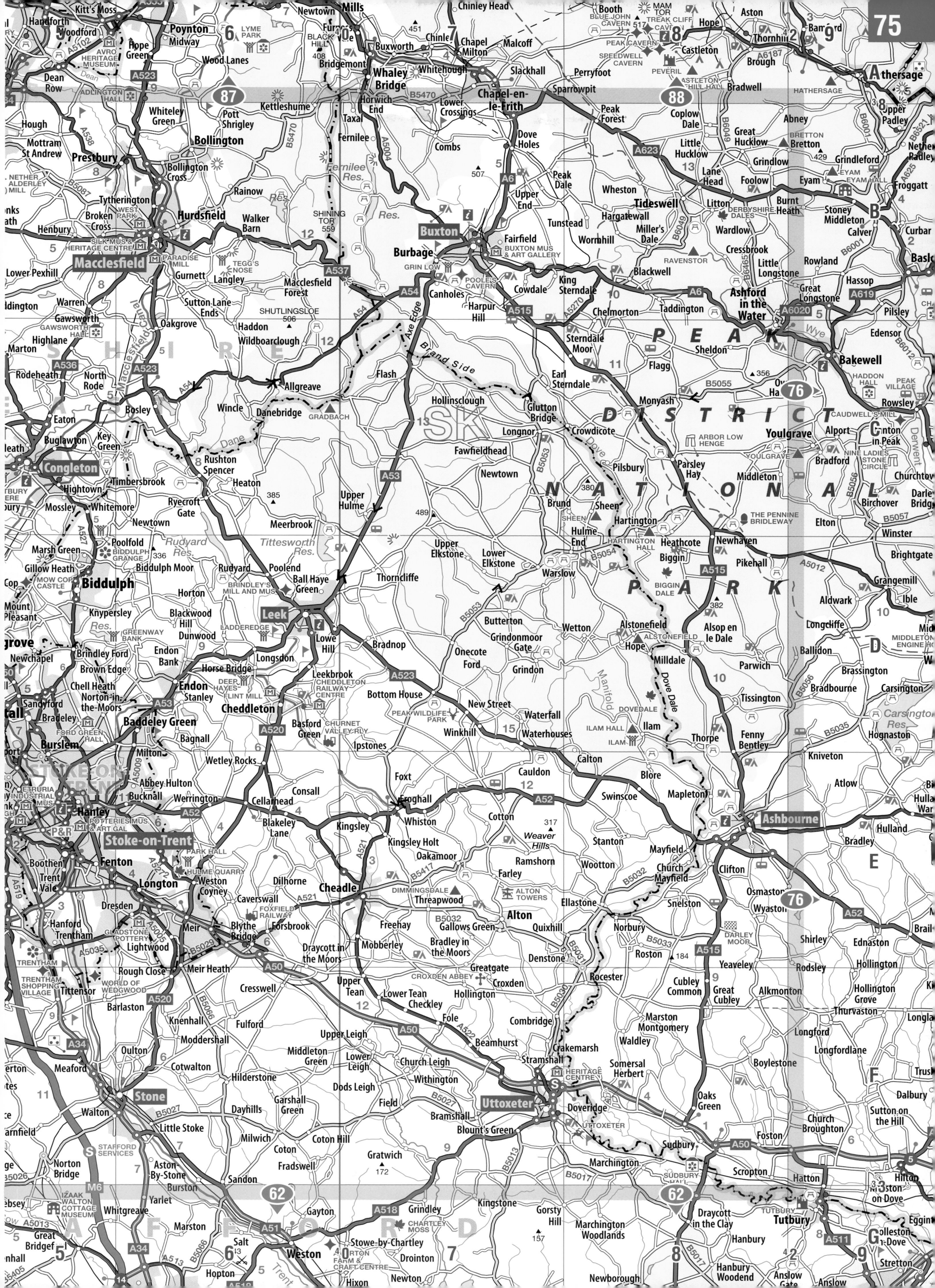

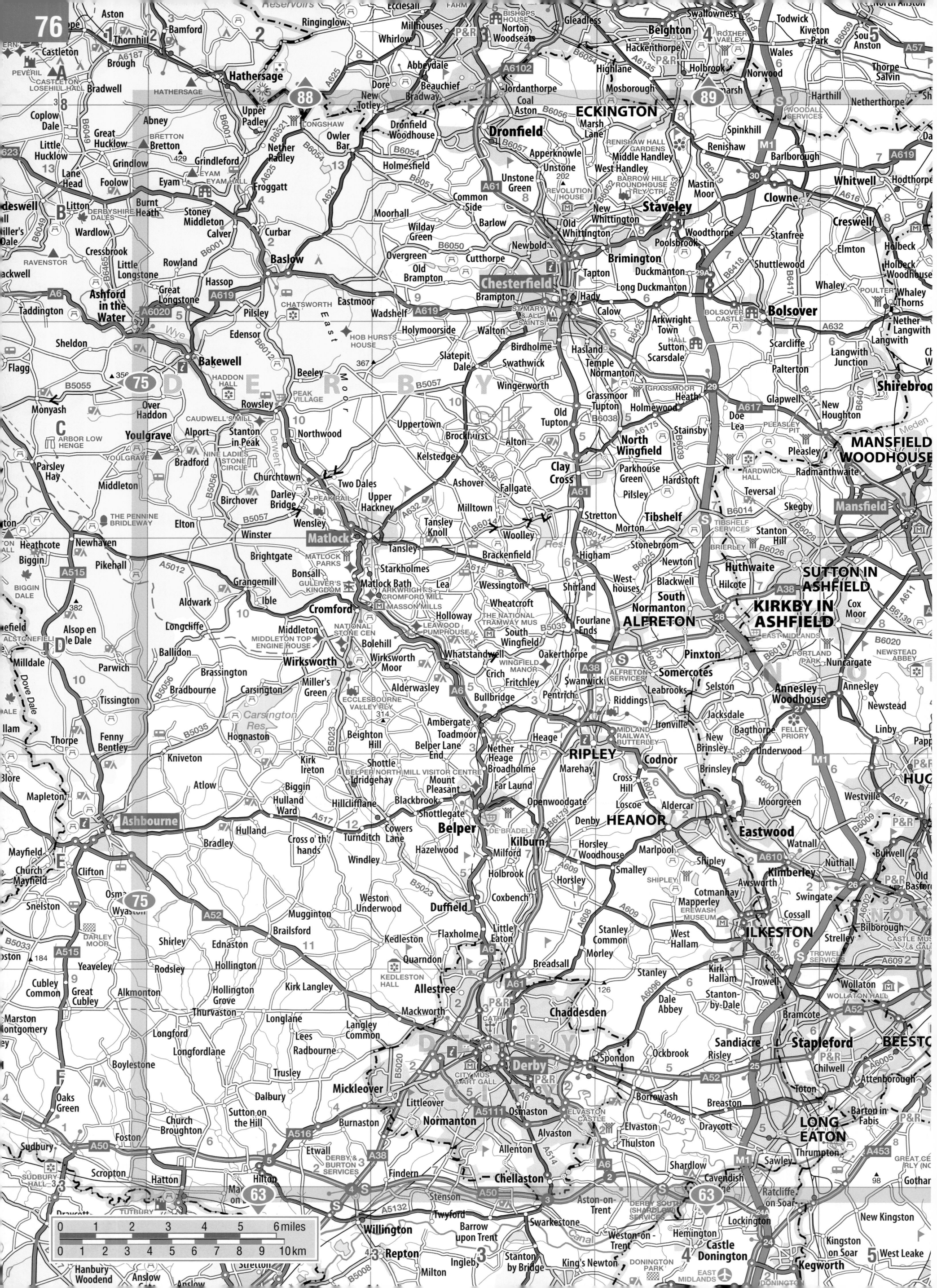

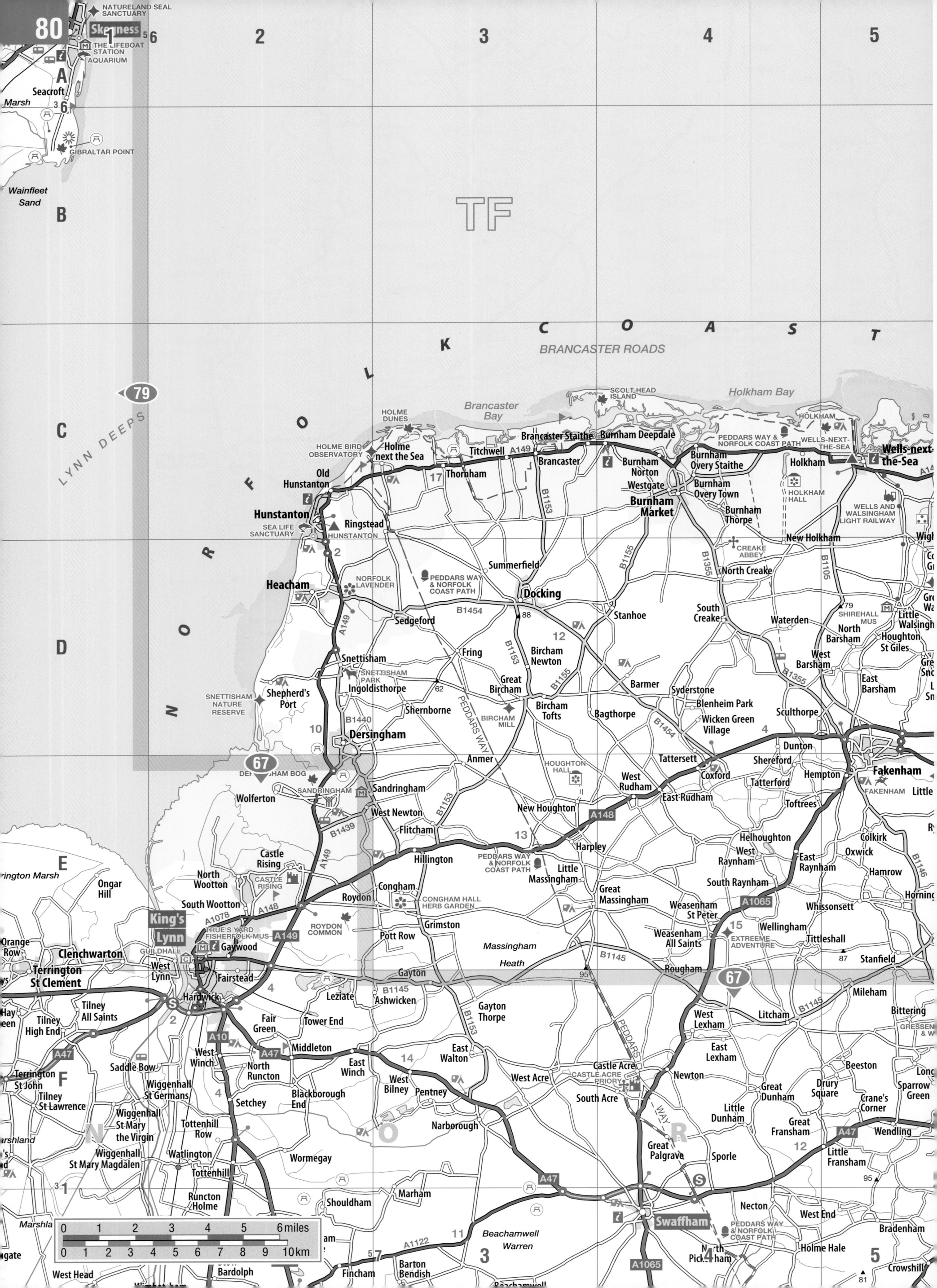

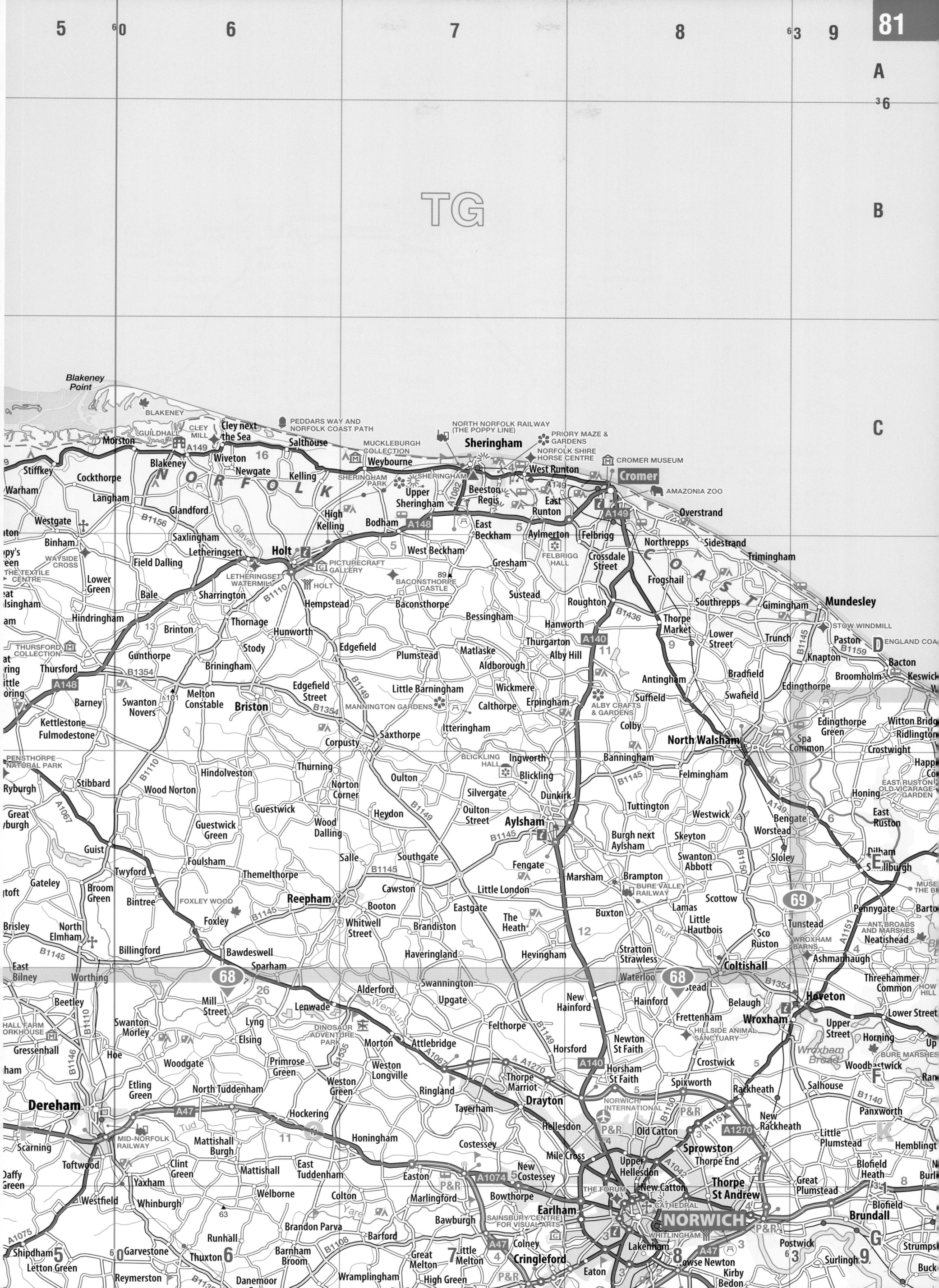

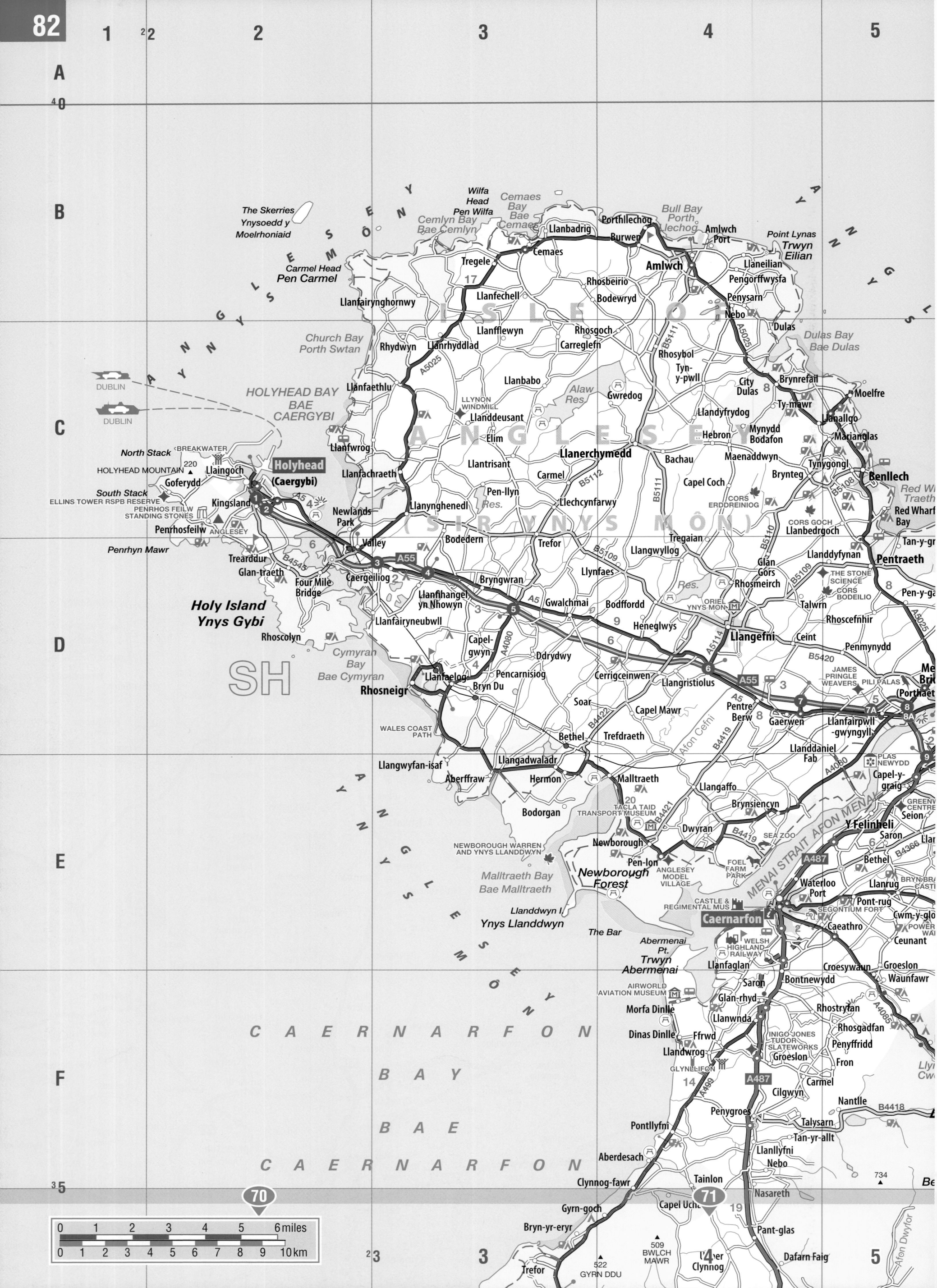

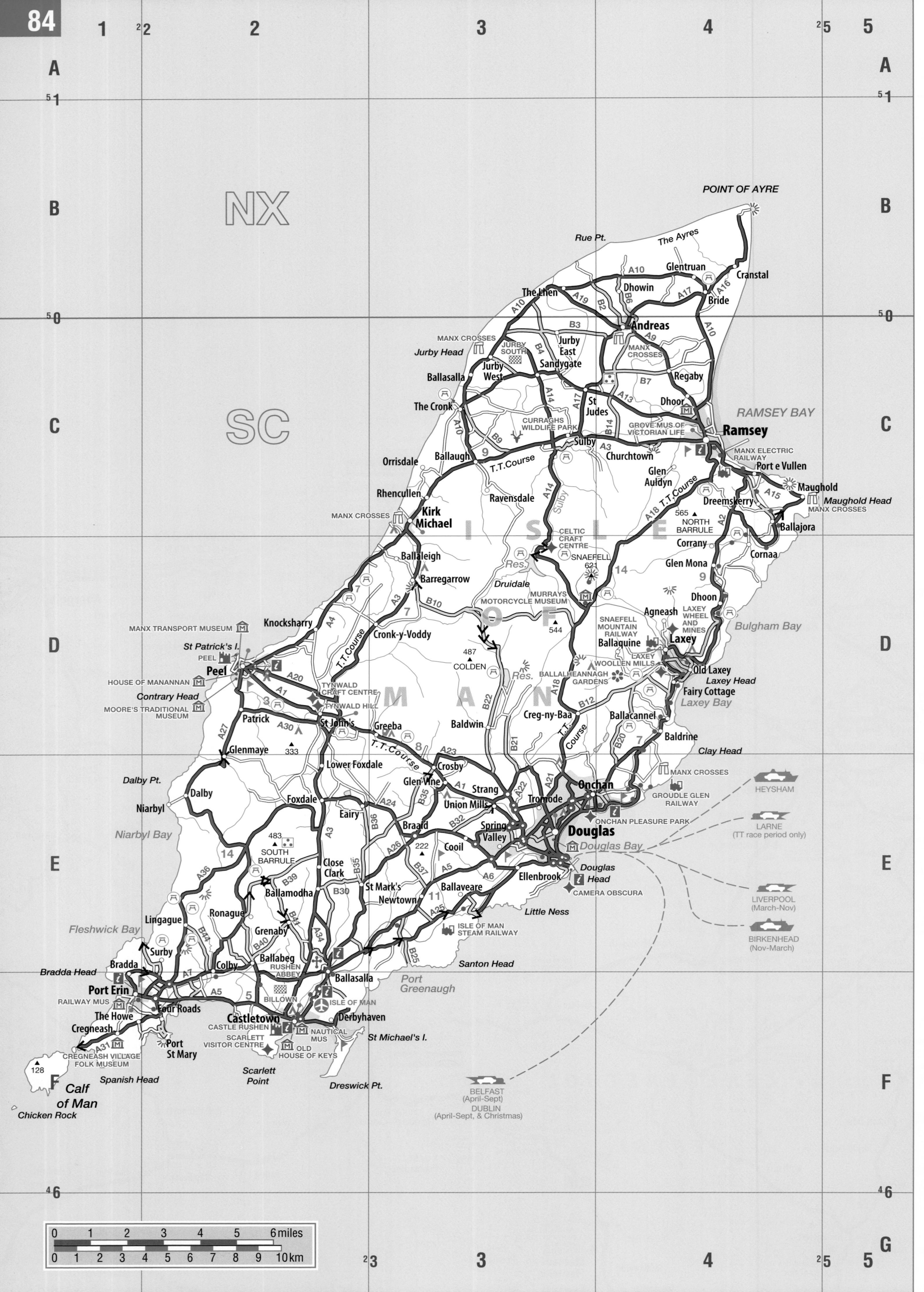

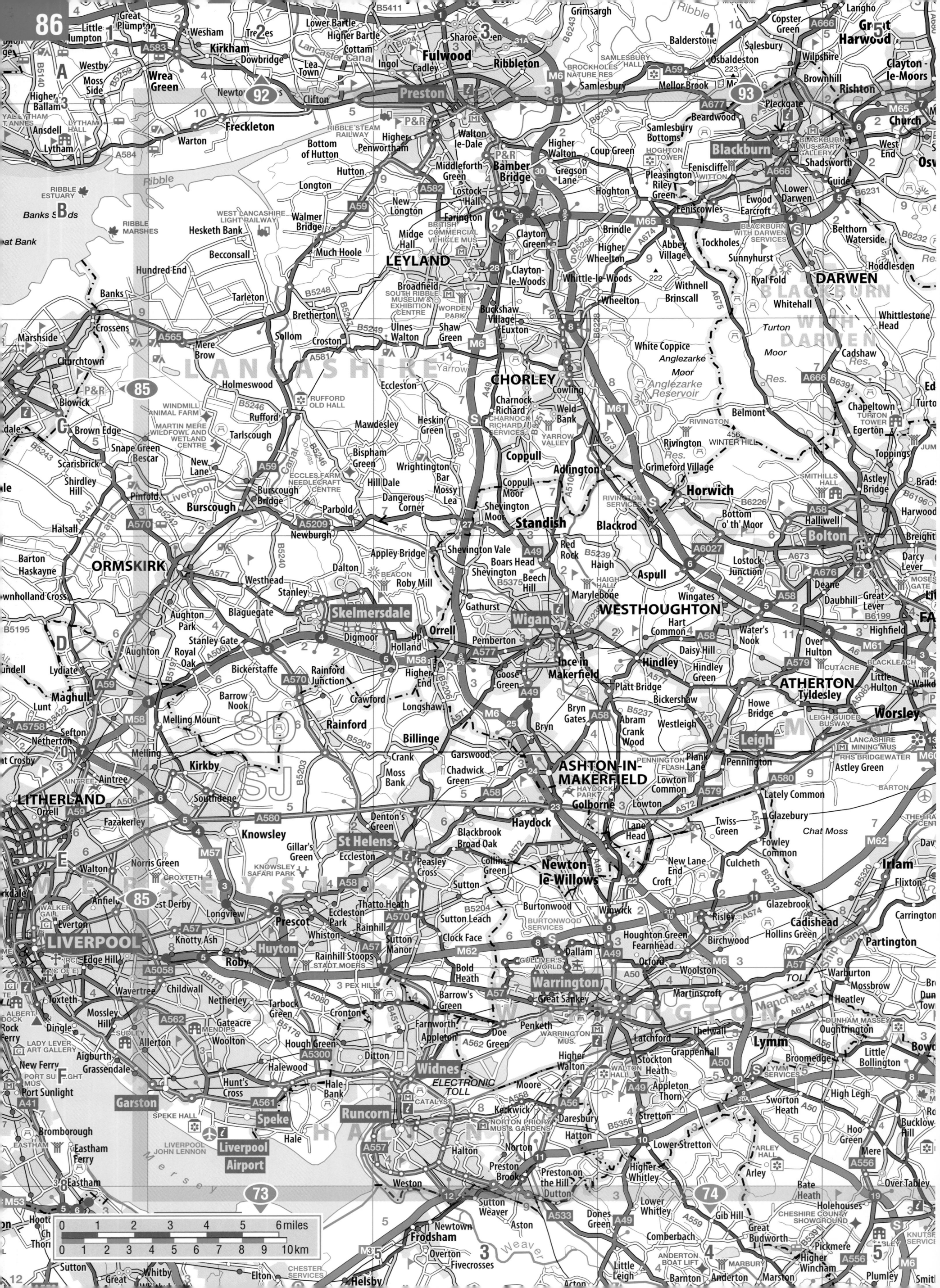

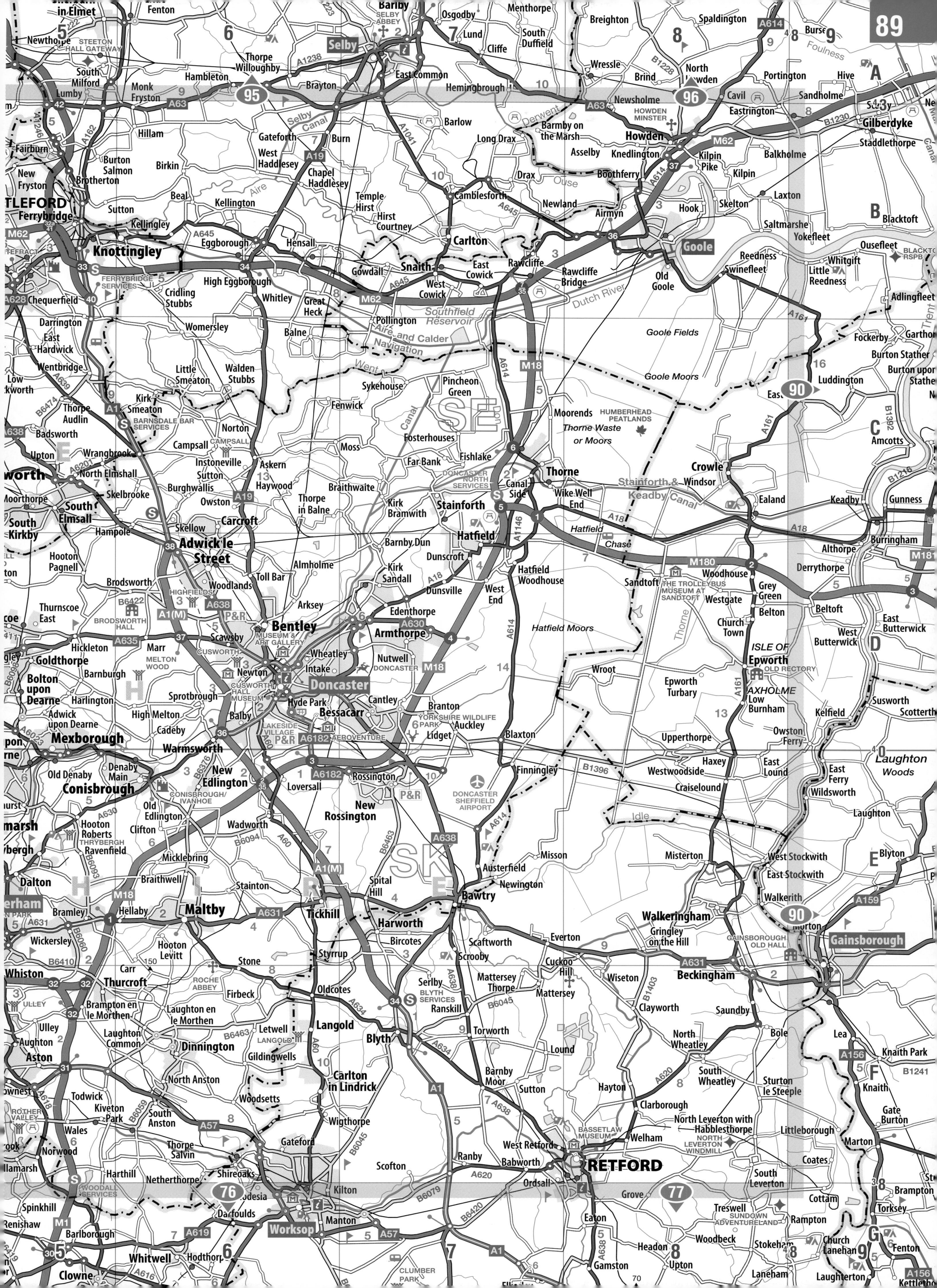

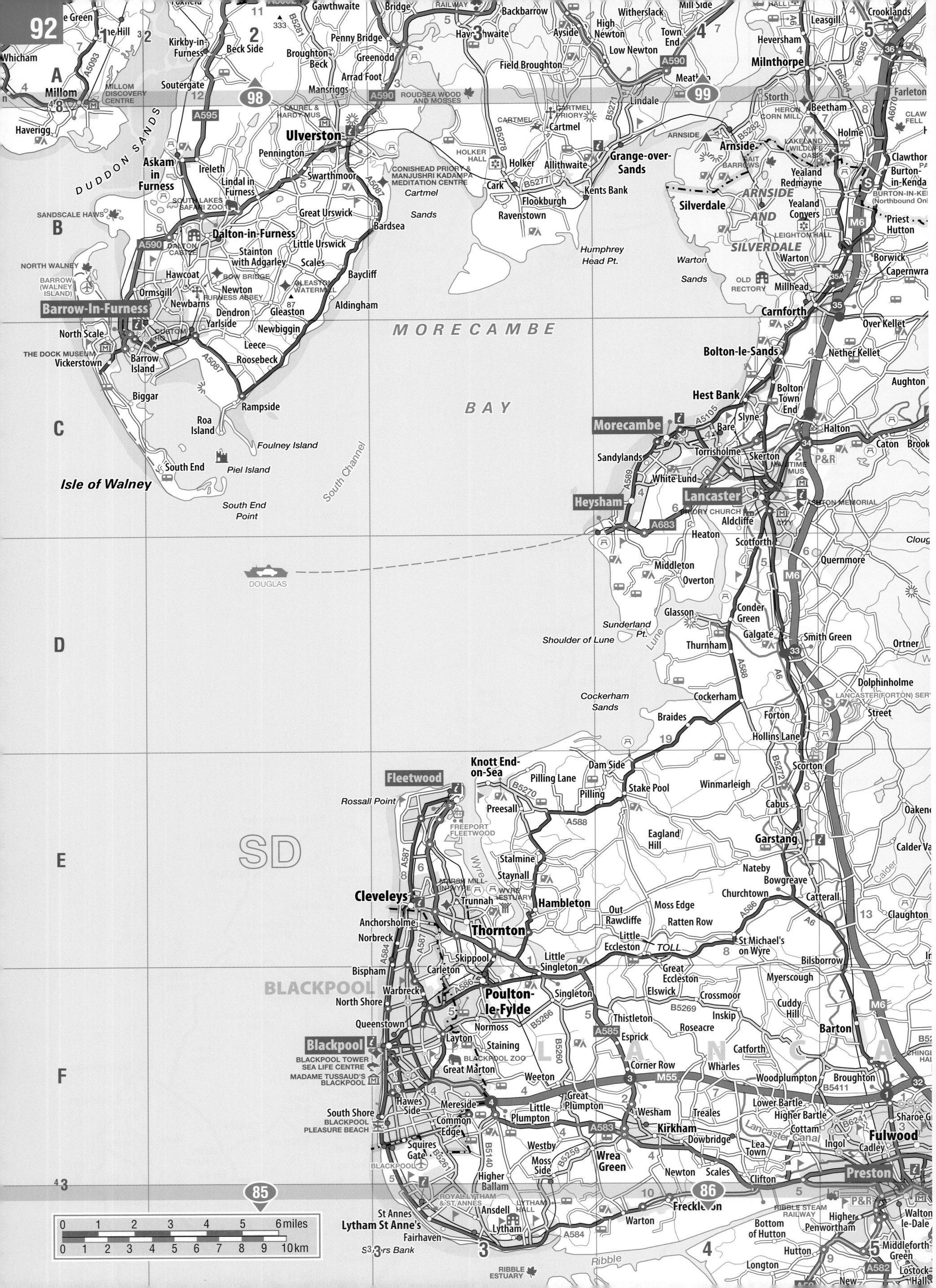

A

B

C

D

E

F

G

5
6
7
8
9

**Filey**
Filey Brigg
Filey Bay
Primrose Valley
Hunmanby Moor
Reighton Sands
Reighton Gap
**Hunmanby**
Reighton
Speeton
Buckton
Bempton
**FLAMBOROUGH HEAD**
Grindale
**Flamborough**

Yons Nab
CLEVELAND WAY
Eastfield
B126
Gristhorpe
A1039
Folkton
Muston
Staxton
A1039
Flixton
103
Willerby
PLAYDALE FARM PARK
Ganton
Potter Brompton
Fordon
Wold Newton
Burton Fleming
Foxholes
Butterwick
Weaverthorpe
Lutton
Octon
Thwing
15
Octon Cross Roads
Langtoft
Cottam
Rudston
B1253
Boynton
Bessingby
Carnaby
Haisthorpe
Thornholme
Kilham
BURTON AGNES HALL
BURTON AGNES MANOR HOUSE
Burton Agnes
Ruston Parva
12
Harpham
Lowthorpe
Garton-on-the-Wolds
**Nafferton**
A166
Elmswell
Little Driffield
**Driffield**
Kelleythorpe
Kirkburn
Southburn
Wansford
Skerne
Brigham
Foston on the Wolds
B1249
Driffield Canal
Church End
North Frodingham
Rotsea
**Hutton Cranswick**
Hutton
Watton
Burshill
Hempholme
Baswick Steer
Kilnwick
Lund
Beswick
Lockington
13
A164
Thorpe
Scorborough
Aike
Arram
Watton Beck
Leven Canal
**Leven**
Hull
Eske
Leconfield
Etton
6
Routh
A1035
Tickton
Cherry Burton
Long Riston
Arnold
**Beverley**
Molescroft
BEVERLEY
Bishop Burton
A1079
Walkington
Weel
Meaux
Skirlaugh
Woodmansey
BEVERLEY FRIARY
MINSTER
Wawne
Bentley
6
A1174
4
Thearne
Dunswell
Skidby
Little Weighton
SKIDBY WINDMILL
**Cottingham**
Inglemire
**Bransholme**
Sutton on Hull
A1033
A165
Epplewort
Riplingham
Willerby
Newland
Sculcoates
Stoneferry
Sutton Ings
Summergangs
WILBERFORCE HOUSE
Kirk Ella
90
West Ella
Anlaby
A1105
Marfleet
A1033
Hessle
Swanland
B1231
Northfi
A63
**KINGSTON UPON HULL**
THE DEEP
STREETLIFE
FERENS ART GALLERY
TOLL
HUMBER BR
North Ferriby
Paull
Haven Side
FORT PAULL
Thorngumbald
Ryehill

**Bridlington**
PRIORY
BAYLE MUSEUM
West Hill
Hilderthorpe
P&R
OLD PENNY MEMORIES
SEWERBY HALL AND GARDENS
BONDVILLE MODEL VILLAGE
**Sewerby**
B1255
B1259
B1229
10
A165
B1253

**BRIDLINGTON BAY**
Fraisthorpe
BRIDLINGTON BIRDS OF PREY & ANIMAL PARK
A614
Gransmoor
Barmston
Great Kelk
Lissett
14
Gembling
Ulrome
A165
16
SKIPSEA CASTLE
Beeford
Skipsea Brough
**Skipsea**
B1249
Dunnington
B1242
Bewholme
Atwick
North Cliff
Brandesburton
Seaton
**Hornsea**
Hornsea Mere
HORNSEA MUSEUM
HORNSEA FREEPORT
Hornsea Bridge
Catwick
Sigglesthorne
Goxhill
Rolston
Rise
Little Hatfield
Mappleton
Great Hatfield
Great Cowden
Withernwick
New Ellerby
B1242
**Aldbrough**
Marton
West Newton
East Newton
17
Old Ellerby
Flinton
BURTON CONSTABLE HALL
Garton
Swine
Coniston
Thirtleby
Sproatley
Humbleton
Fitling
Hilston
Grimston
Ganstead
B1238
Lelley
Elstronwick
Owstwick
Tunstall
Bilton
B1240
Preston
West End
Burton Pidsea
North End
**Roos**
91
Waxholme
Salt End
**Hedon**
Burstwick
B1362
Camerton
Halsham
Rimswell
**Withernse**
Owthorne
B1242
A1033
Paull
Camerton
Halsham
Keyingham
18

TA

53
9
48
53
9d
43

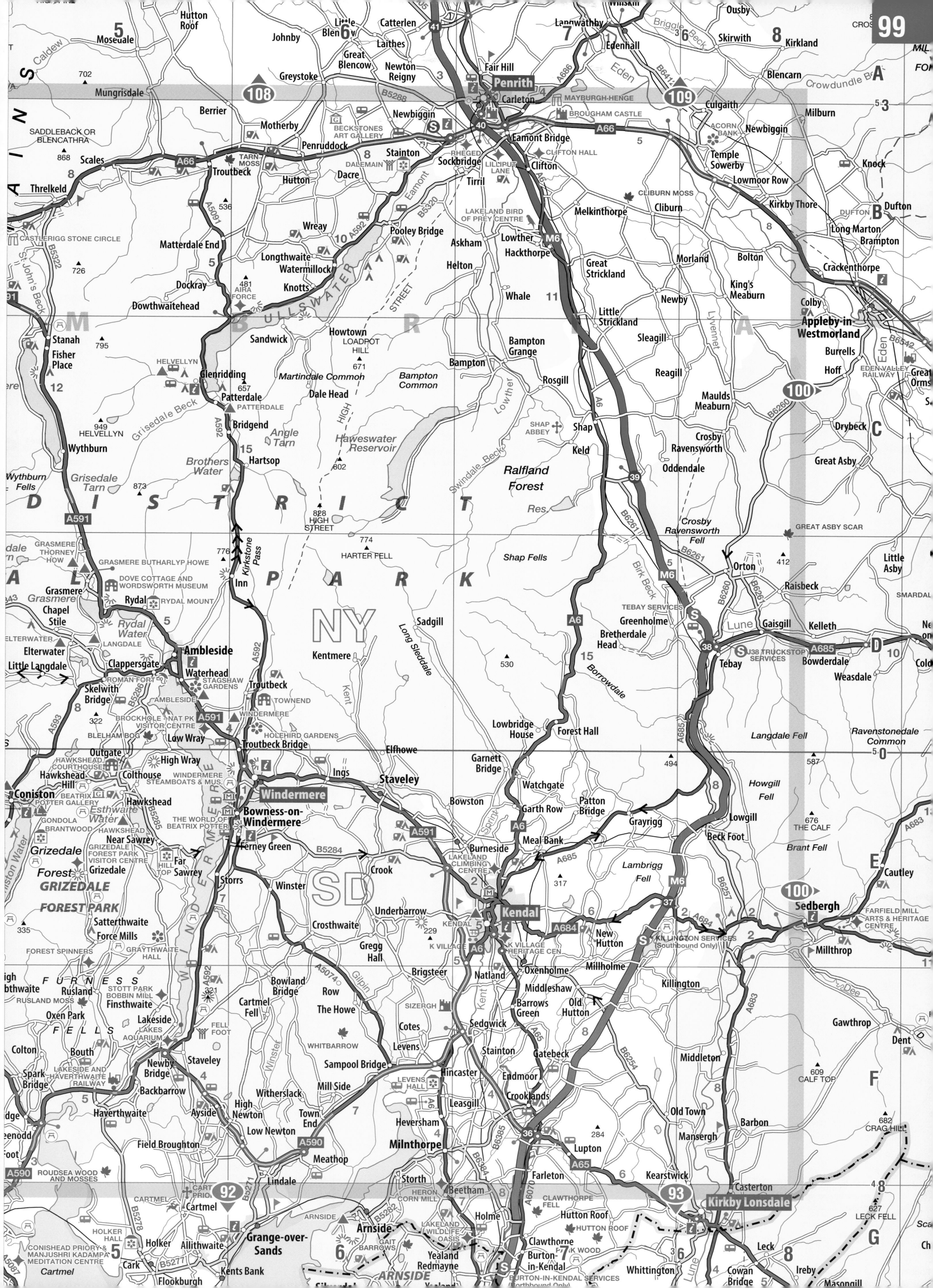

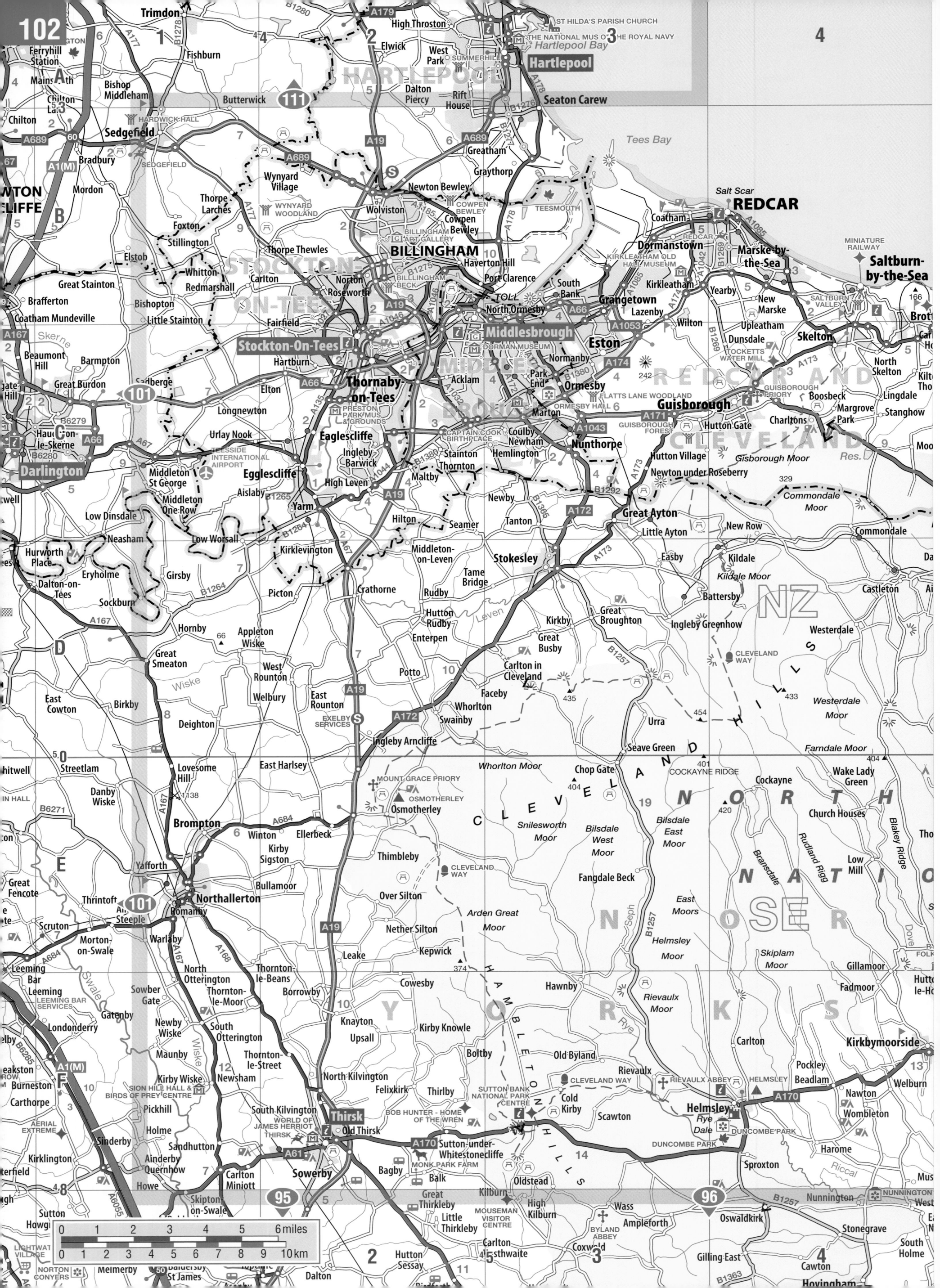

NZ OV

SE

TA

NW

| | | | | | | | | | | |
|---|---|---|---|---|---|---|---|---|---|---|

**Stranraer**

CARLETON CSTLE
112
Colmonell
B734 265
Knockdolian
Heronsford
Glen Tig
Balkiss
Ballantrae
Ballantrae Bay
Downan Pt.
Auchencrosh
439 BENERAIRD
A77
BELFAST
LARNE
Mark
Glen App
257
17
Milleur Pt.
Penwhirn Res.
Corsewall Pt.
Portencalzie
Barnhills
North Cairn
South Cairn
Corsewall
Cairnryan
B738
Loch Connell
Kirkcolm
Braid Fell
Dounan Bay
Mains of Airies
Ervie
A77
B798
Low Salchrie
The Wig
LOCH RYAN
Innermessan
Auchmant
Knocknain
Leswalt
Slouchnawen Bay
Craigencross
A718
A751
Black Loch
CASTLE KENNEDY GARDENS
White Loch
Glenstockadale
Aird
Castle Kennedy
Broadsea Bay
CASTLE OF ST-JOHN VISITORS CENTRE
Soulseat Loch
STRANRAER MUSEUM
Knockglass
Black Hd.
Lochans
Mark
B7077
Dunskey Ho.
182
A77
LITTLE WHEELS
Awhirk
Torrs War
Portpatrick
Stoneykirk
A716
B7084
Port of Spittal Bay
B7042
Luce Sa
Cairngarroch
KIRKMADRINE STONES
Sandhead
Cairngarroch Bay
Sandhead Bay
Money Hd.
Clachanmore
Hole Stone Bay
Ardwell
Ardwell Mains
Chapel Rossan
Ardwell Pt.
Logan Mains
10
LOGAN BOTANIC GARDEN
Balgowan Pt.
Mull of Logan
LOGAN FISH POND MARINE LIFE CENTRE
Port Nessock or Port Logan Bay
Port Logan
Cairnywellan Hd.
B7065
A716
Clanyard Bay
Low Clanyard
Drumm
Laggantalluch Hd.
Kirkmaiden
Crammag Hd.
164
Damnaglaur
B7041
Cairngaan
Ma
Port Kemin

| 0 | 1 | 2 | 3 | 4 | 5 | 6 miles |
|---|---|---|---|---|---|---|
| 0 | 1 2 3 4 5 6 7 8 9 | 10km |

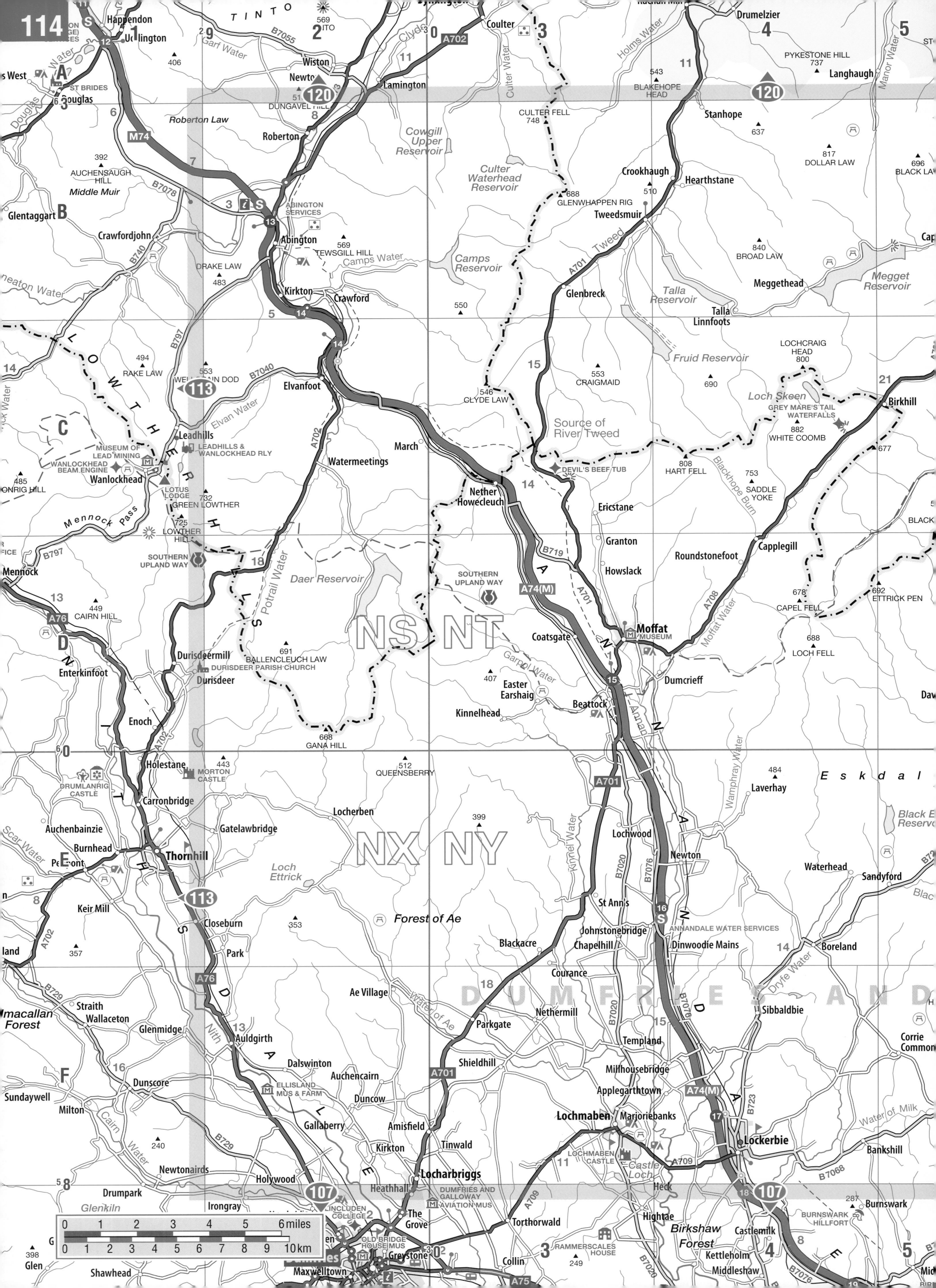

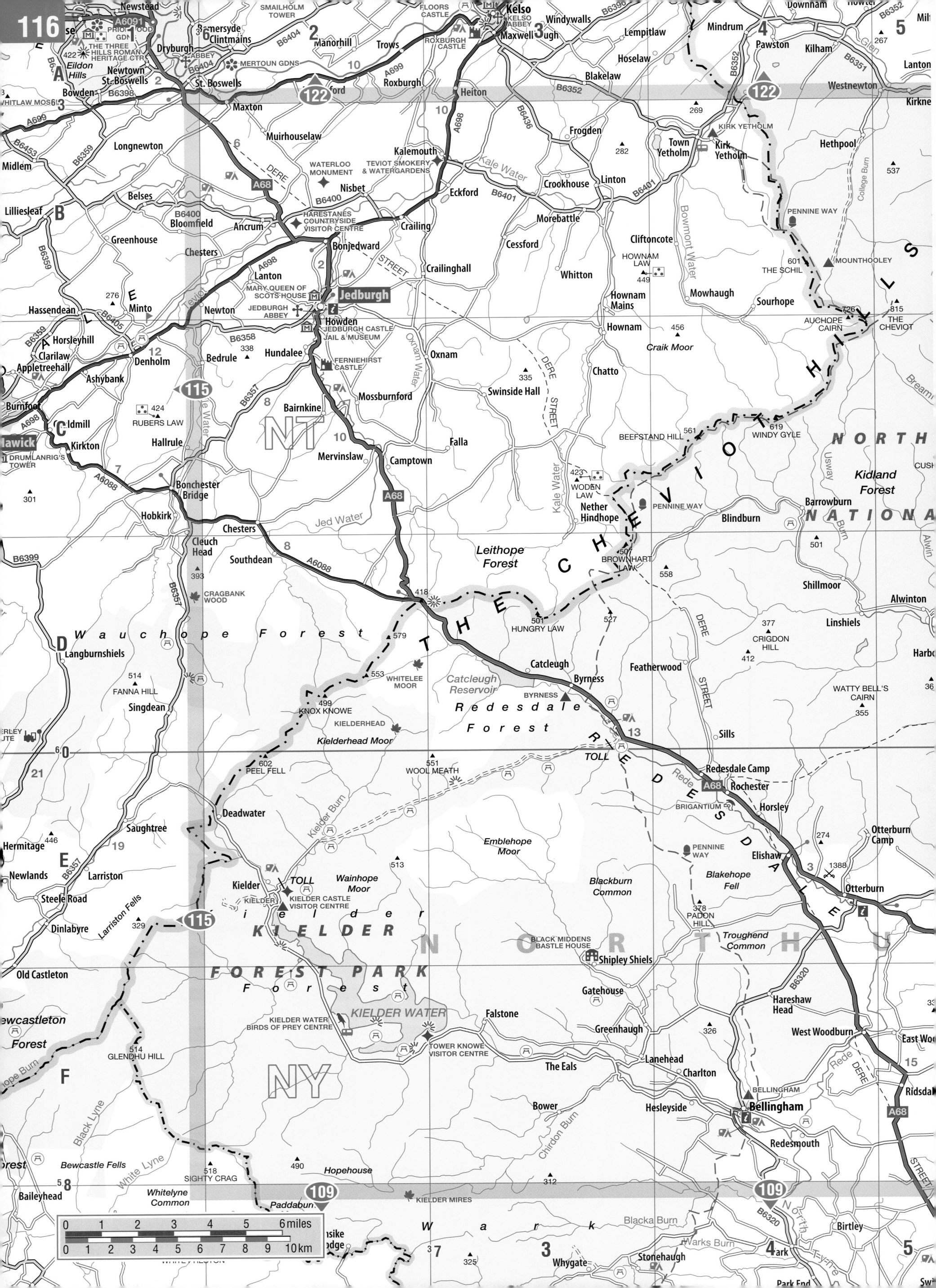

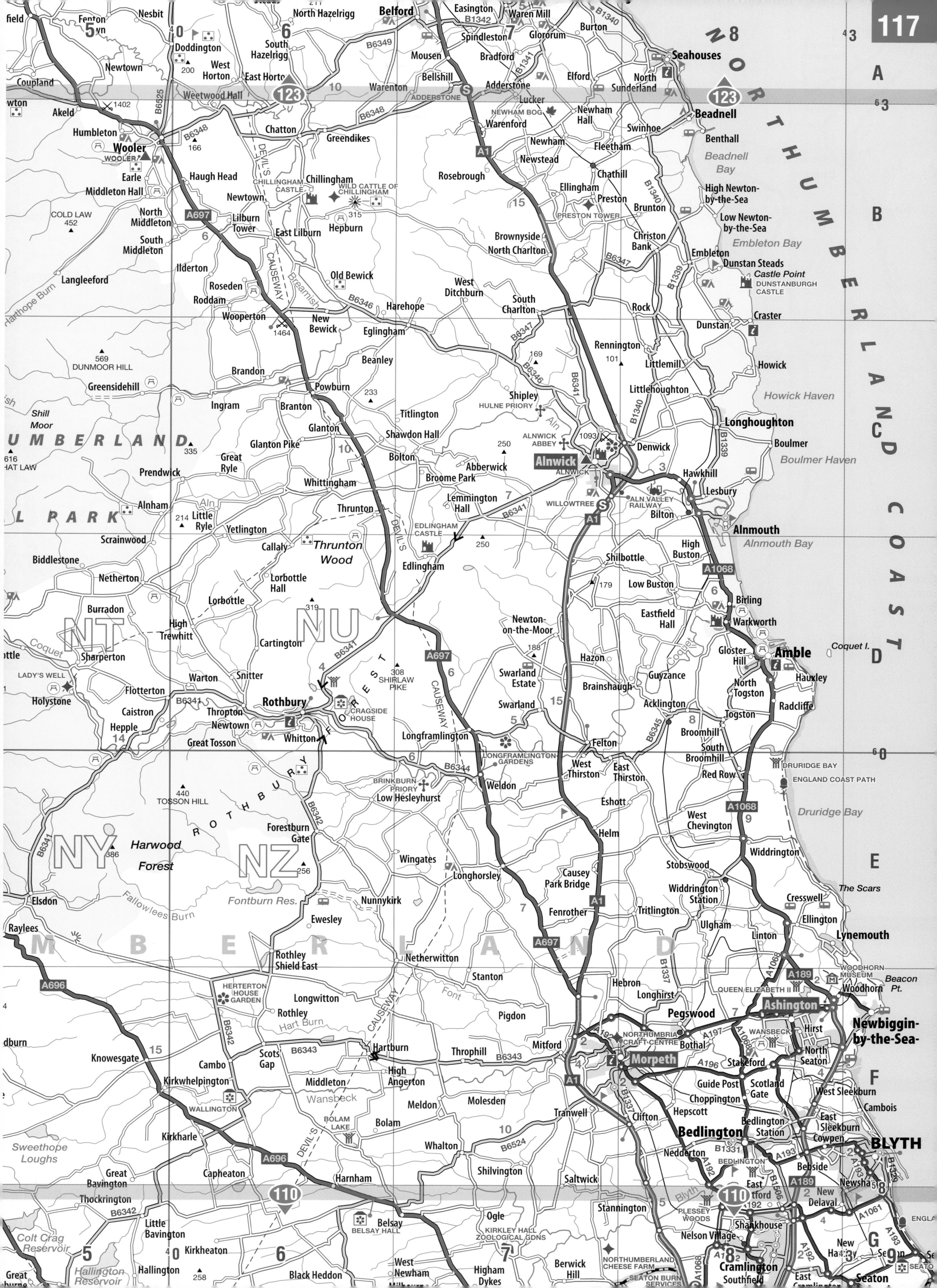

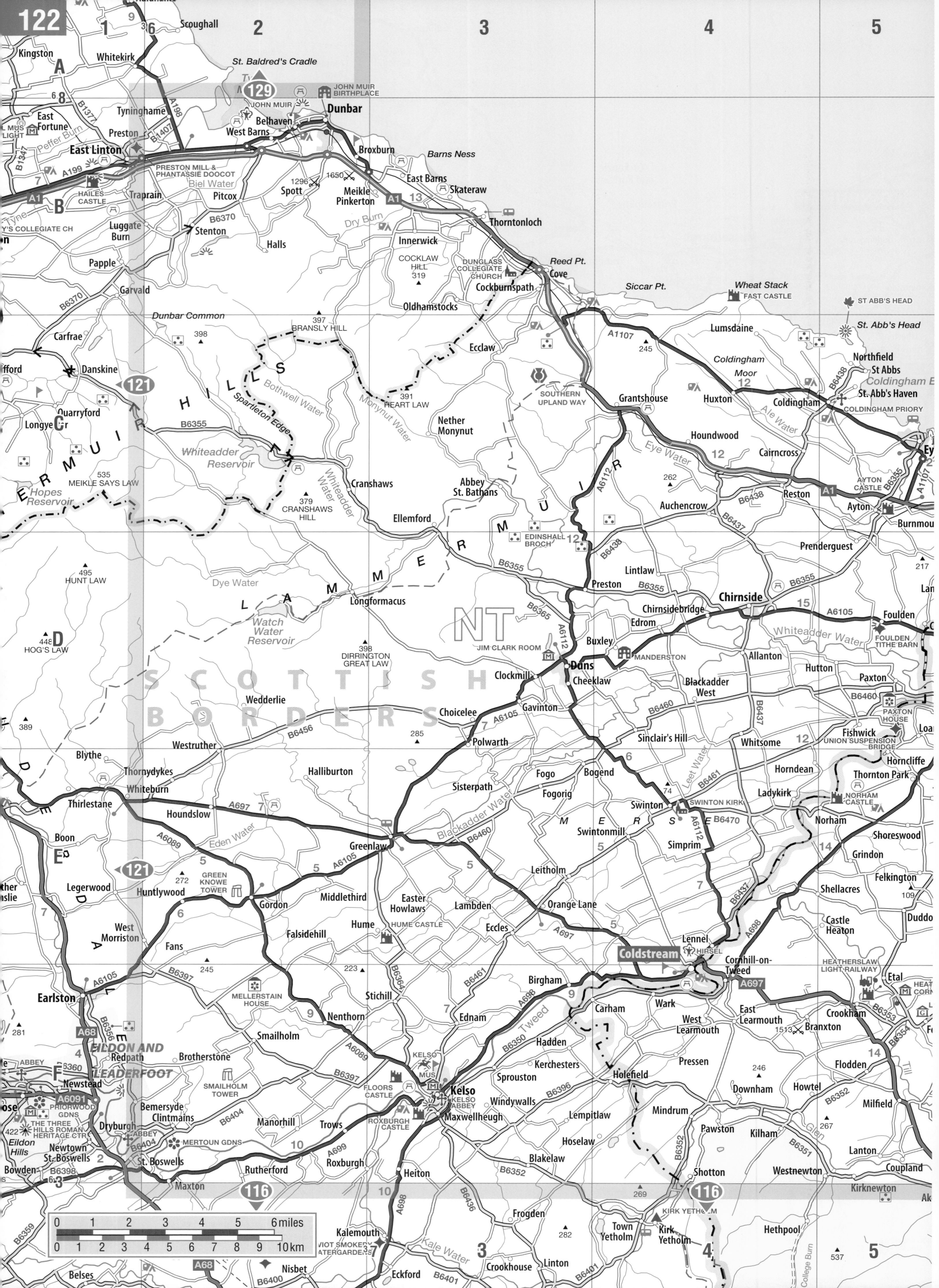

5 40 6 7 8 43 9

A

6 8

B

C

*Bay*

D

🏛 EYEMOUTH MUSEUM
emouth

th

5

*Lamberton*
*Beach*

amberton

lappers

1333 ✂

Highfields

**Berwick-Upon-Tweed**
BERWICK-UPON-TWEED
BARRACKS & MAIN GUARD

B6461

East
Ord

BERWICK
Tweedmouth

Spittal

Prior
Park

A698

nend
*Tweed*

A1167

*Redshin Cove*

108 ▲

Murton

Thornton

Scremerston

West Allerdean

Shoresdean

Cheswick

Ancroft

B6354

Goswick

Berrington

Haggerston

South Low

A1

North Low

Bowsden

82

12

Barmoor
Castle

Barmoor
Lane End

B6353

West
Kyloe

Lowick

Buckton

*Kyloe
Hills*

East
Kyloe

Fenwick

HERSLAW
NMILL

LADY WATERFORD HALL

B6353

rd

157 ▲

Kimmerston

Fenton
Town

Nesbit

Holburn

Hetton
Steads

211 ▲

North Hazelrigg

Detchant

Middleton

**Belford**

B6349

Doddington

200 ▲

South
Horton

East Horton

West
Horton

Newtown

Weetwood Hall

B6525

1402

Humbleton

B6348

**117**

Chatton

Greendikes

B6348

Wooler

WOOLER ▲

166 ▲

5 40 6

Earle

Haugh Head

Middleton Hall

Chillingham

CHILLINGHAM
CASTLE

WILD CATTLE OF
CHILLINGHAM ✹

Newtown

NU

N
O
R
T
H
U
M
B
E
R
L
A
N
D

C
O
A
S
T

LINDISFARNE 🍁

*Emmanuel Hd.*

**Holy Island
(Lindisfarne)**

Holy
Island

LINDISFARNE CASTLE 🏰

*Causeway
Holy
Island
Sands*

*Castle Pt.*

🏛 HERITAGE
CENTRE

LINDISFARNE
PRIORY

Beal

Fenham

*Guile
Pt.*

Elwick

Ross

*Budle
Bay*

*Farne
Islands*

*Staple Sound*

BAMBURGH
CASTLE

FARNE ISLANDS 🍁

*Inner Sound*

Budle

BAMBURGH
CASTLE

**Bamburgh**

Easington
B1342

Waren Mill 5

Glororum

Burton

B1340

Spindlestone

Mousen

Bradford

Bellshill

Warenton

ADDERSTONE

S

B1341

Adderstone

Lucker

Elford

Bead

**117**

Seahouses

North
Sunderland

i

NEWHAM BOG 🍁

Newham
Hall

Newham

Warenford

Swinhoe

Benthall

A1

Newstead

Fleetham

*Beadnell
Bay*

E

F

6 3

G

43 9

5 40 6 7 8 43 9

Rosebrough

Chathill

Ellingham

Preston

High Newton-
by-the-Sea

15

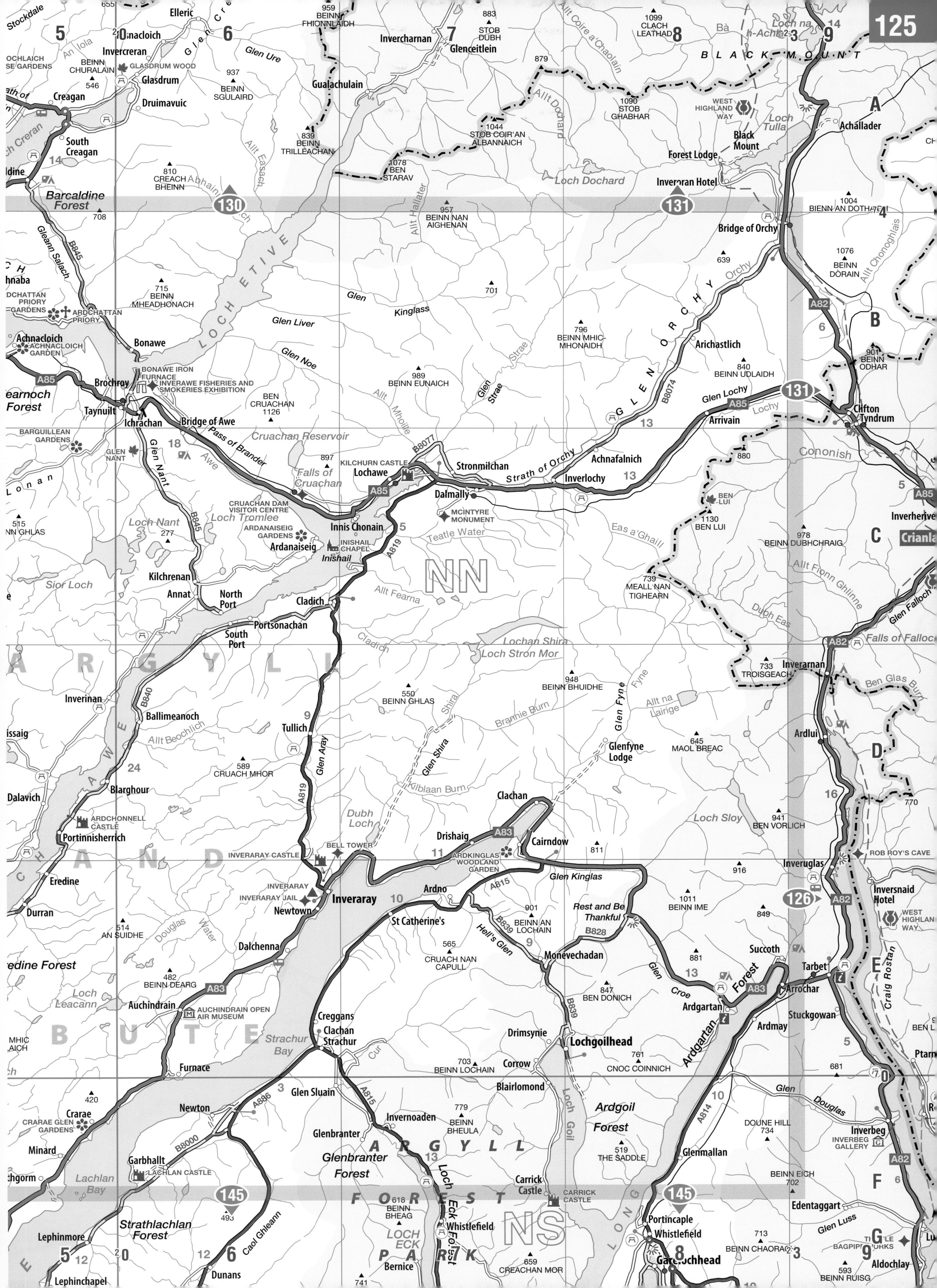

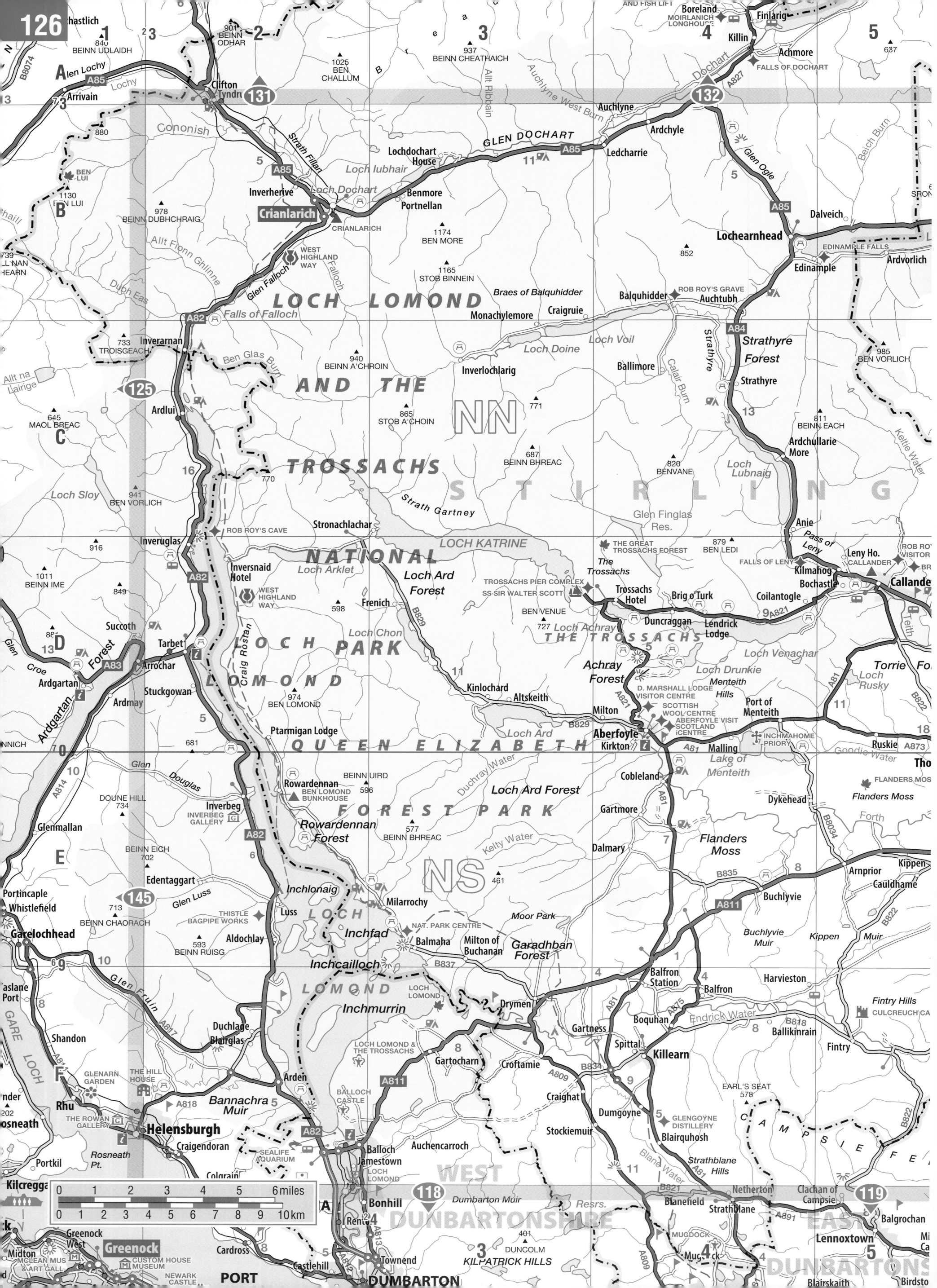

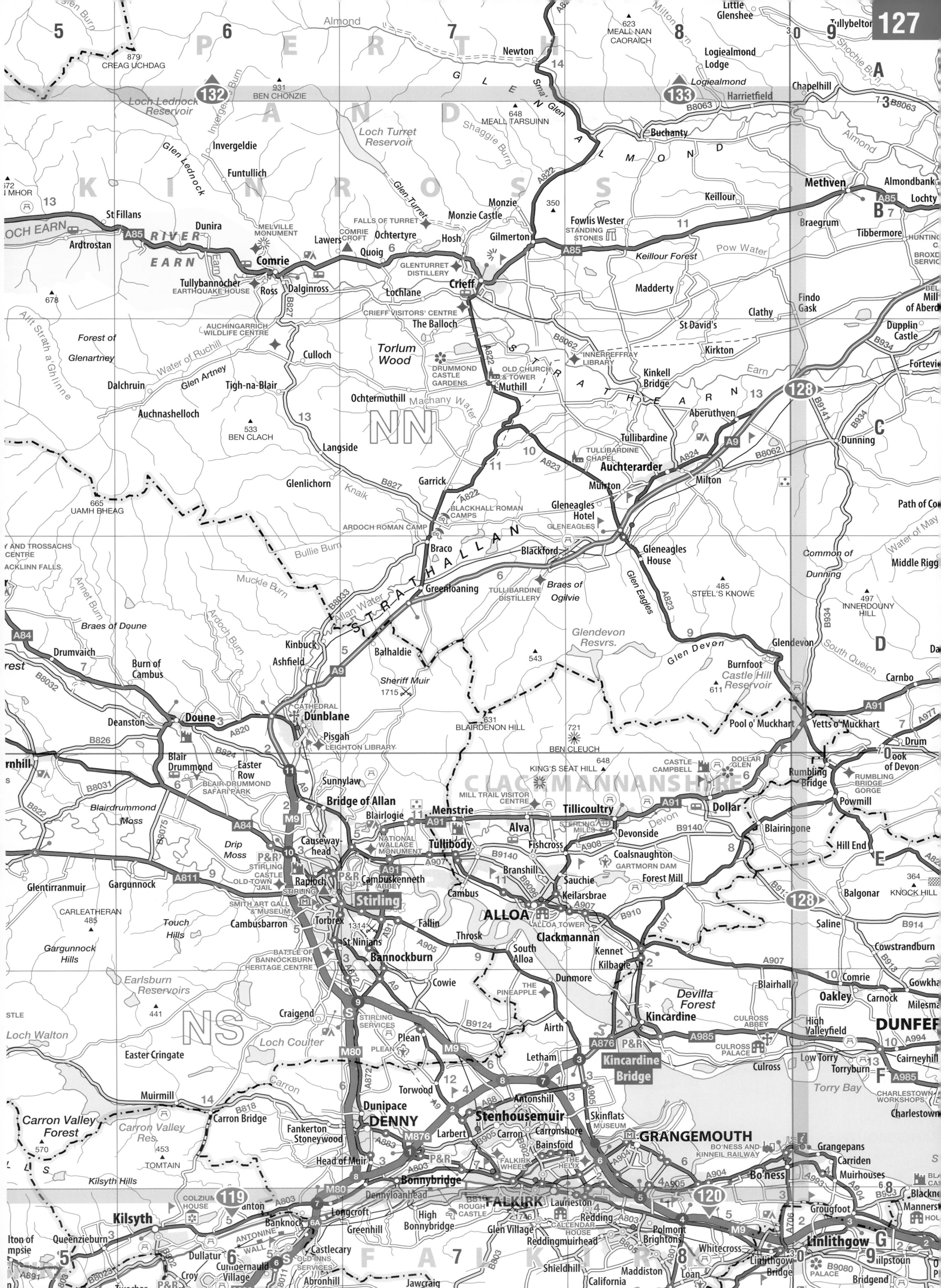

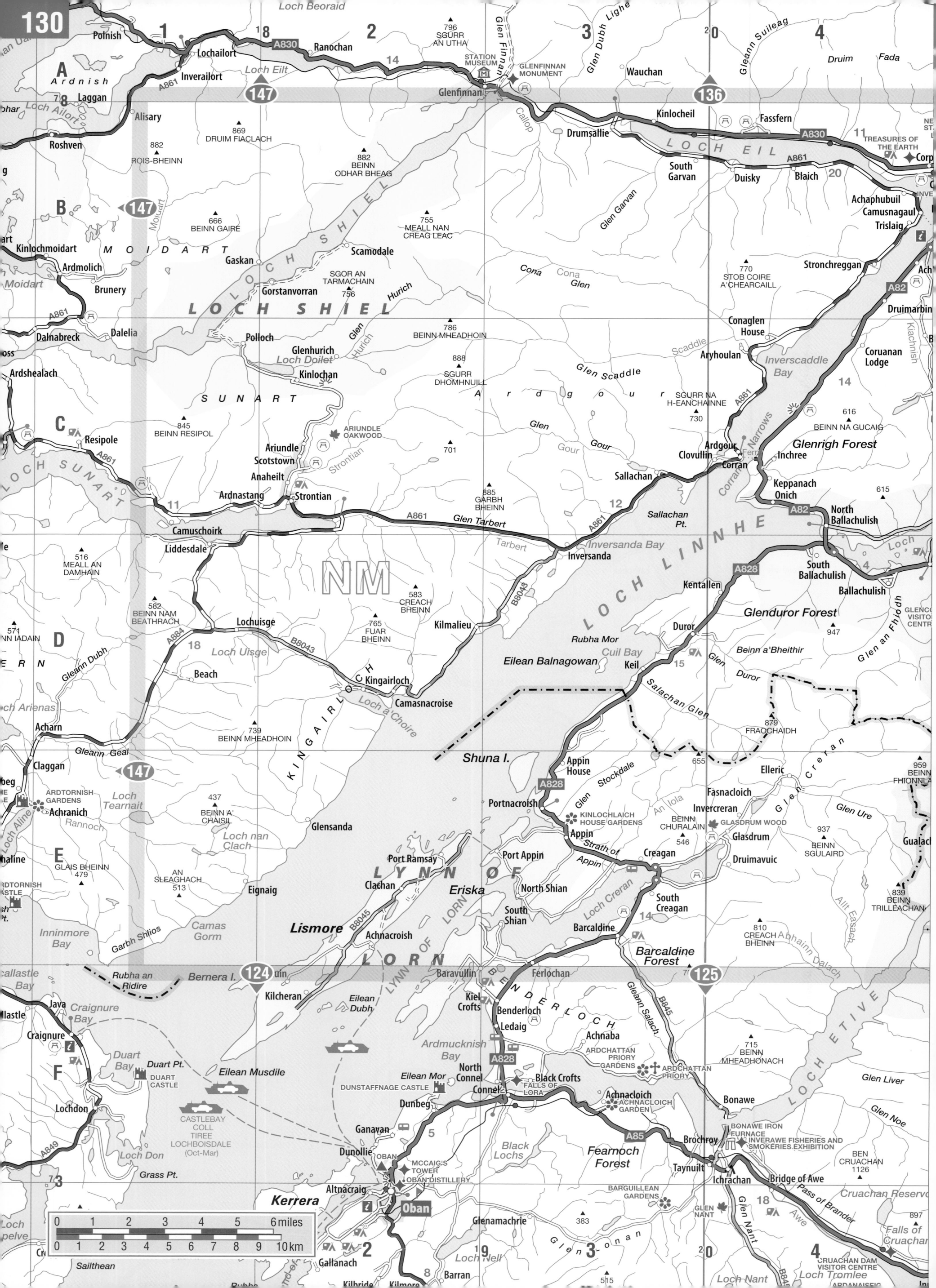

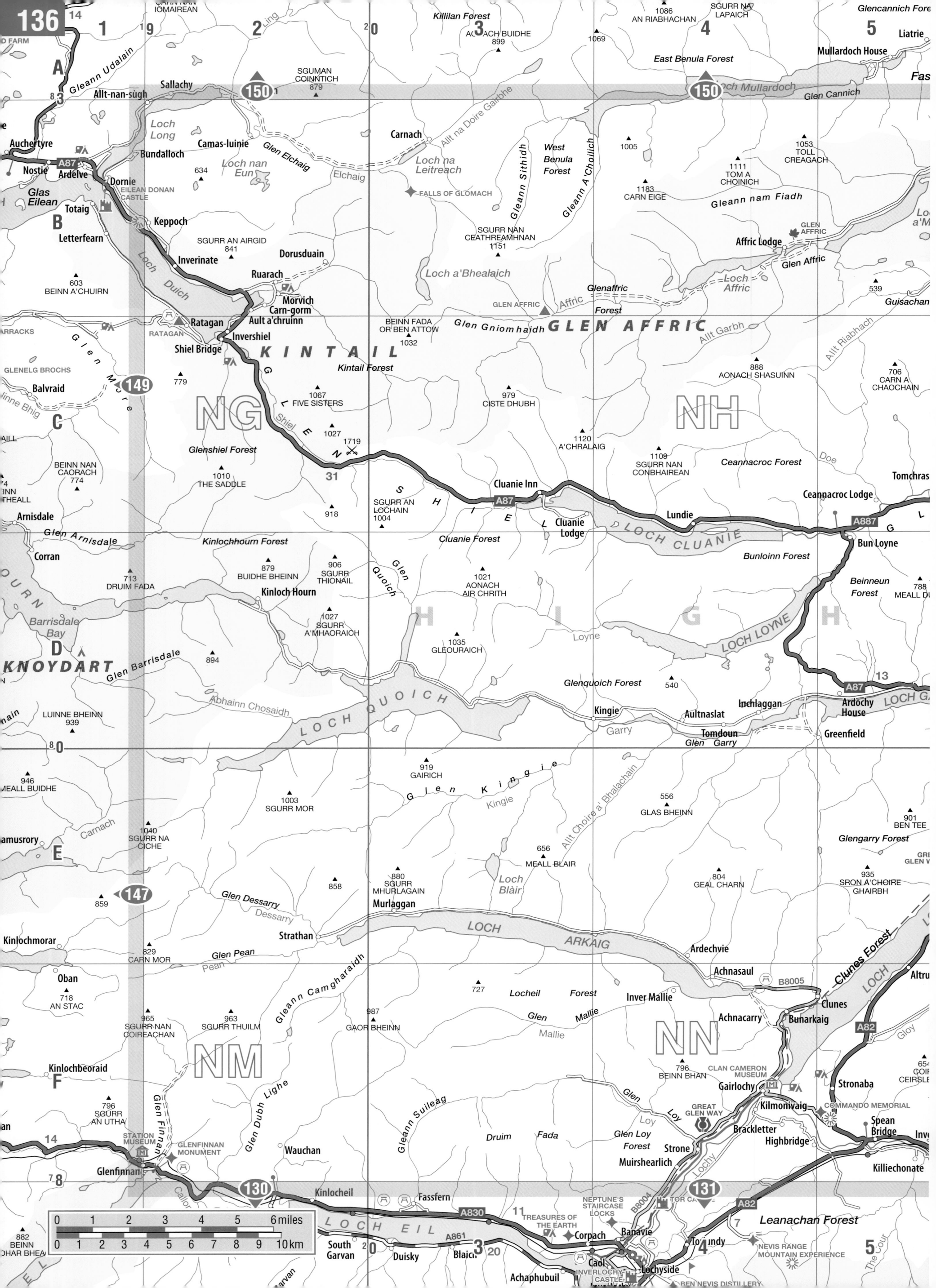

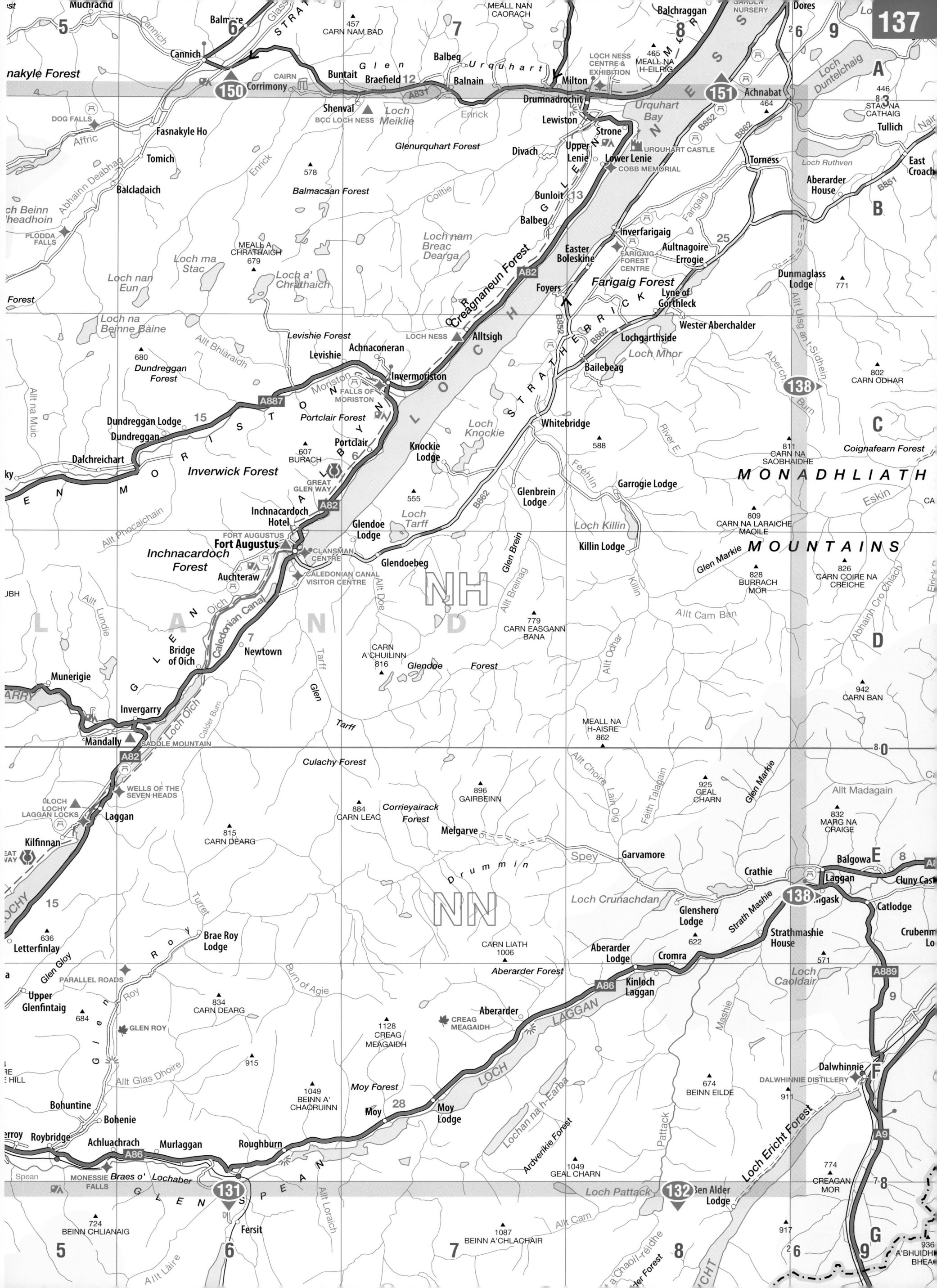

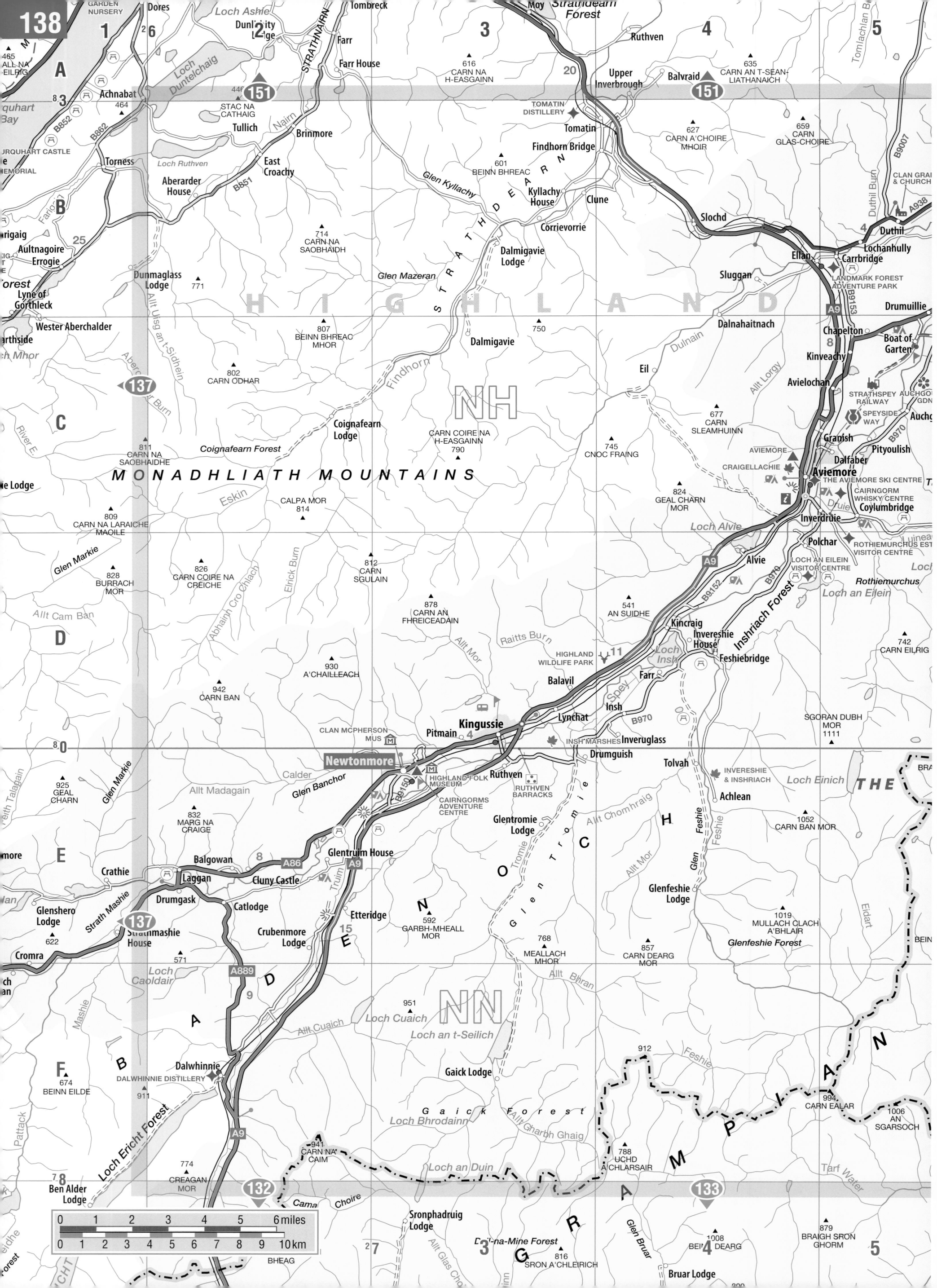

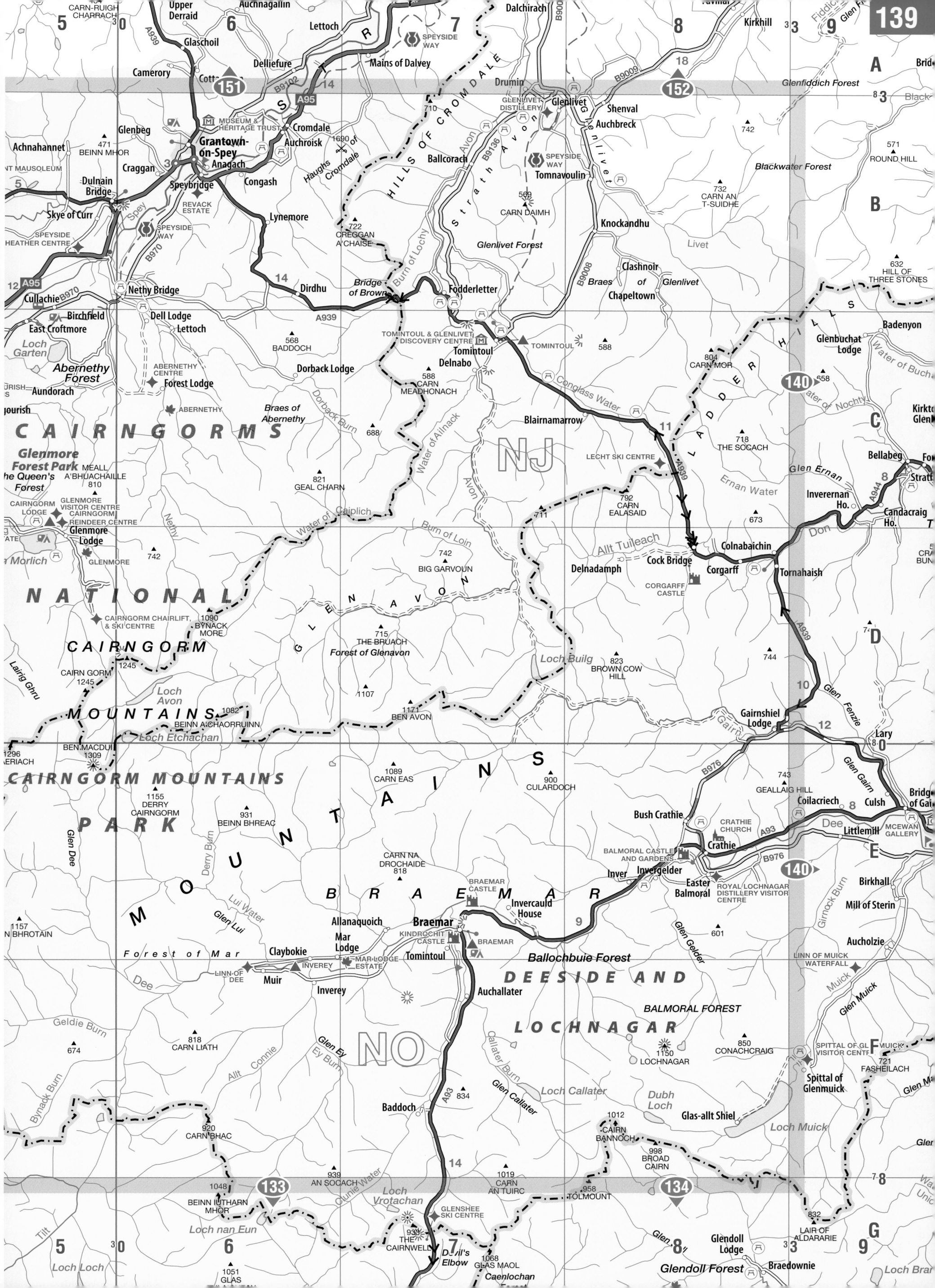

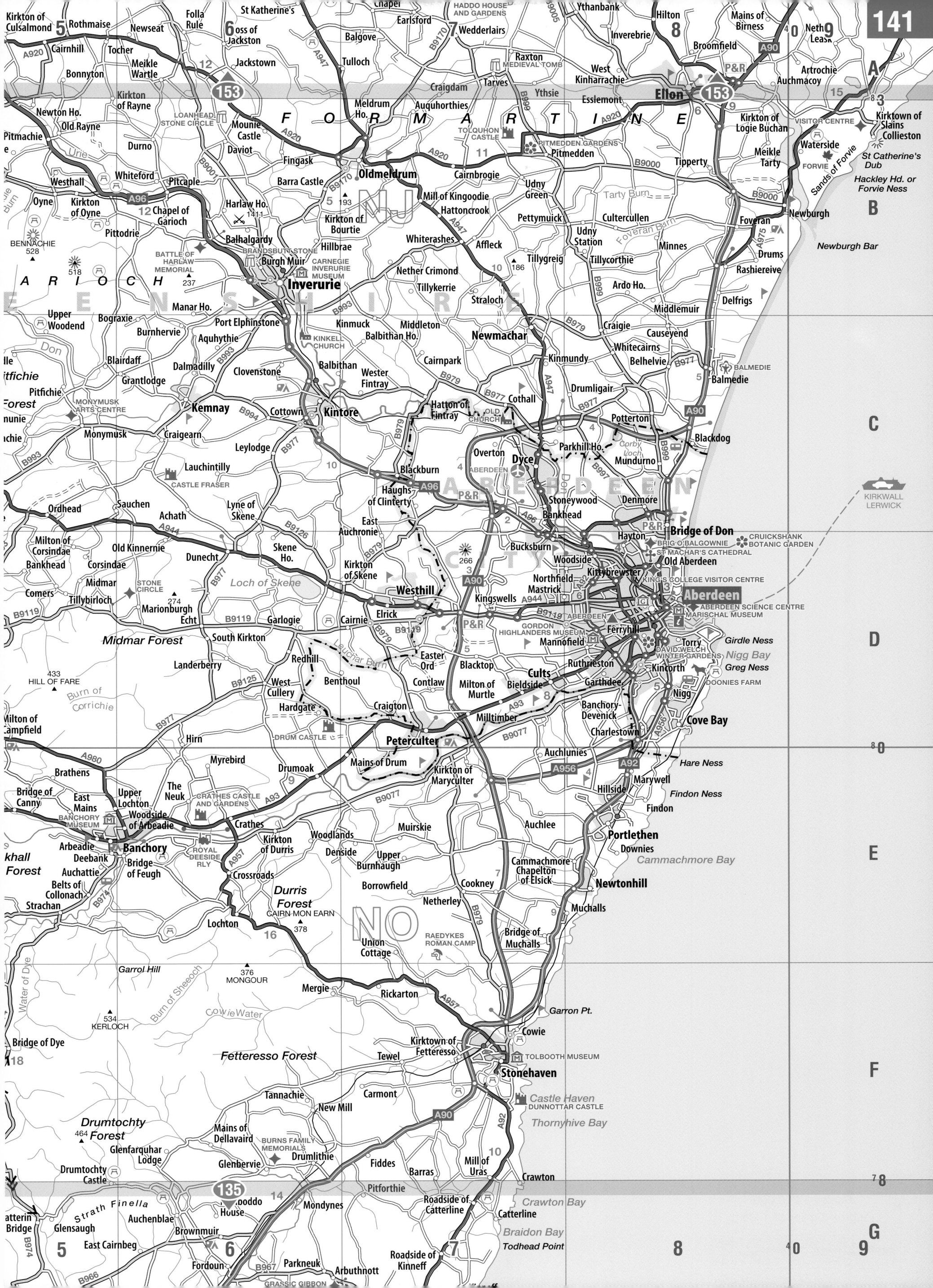

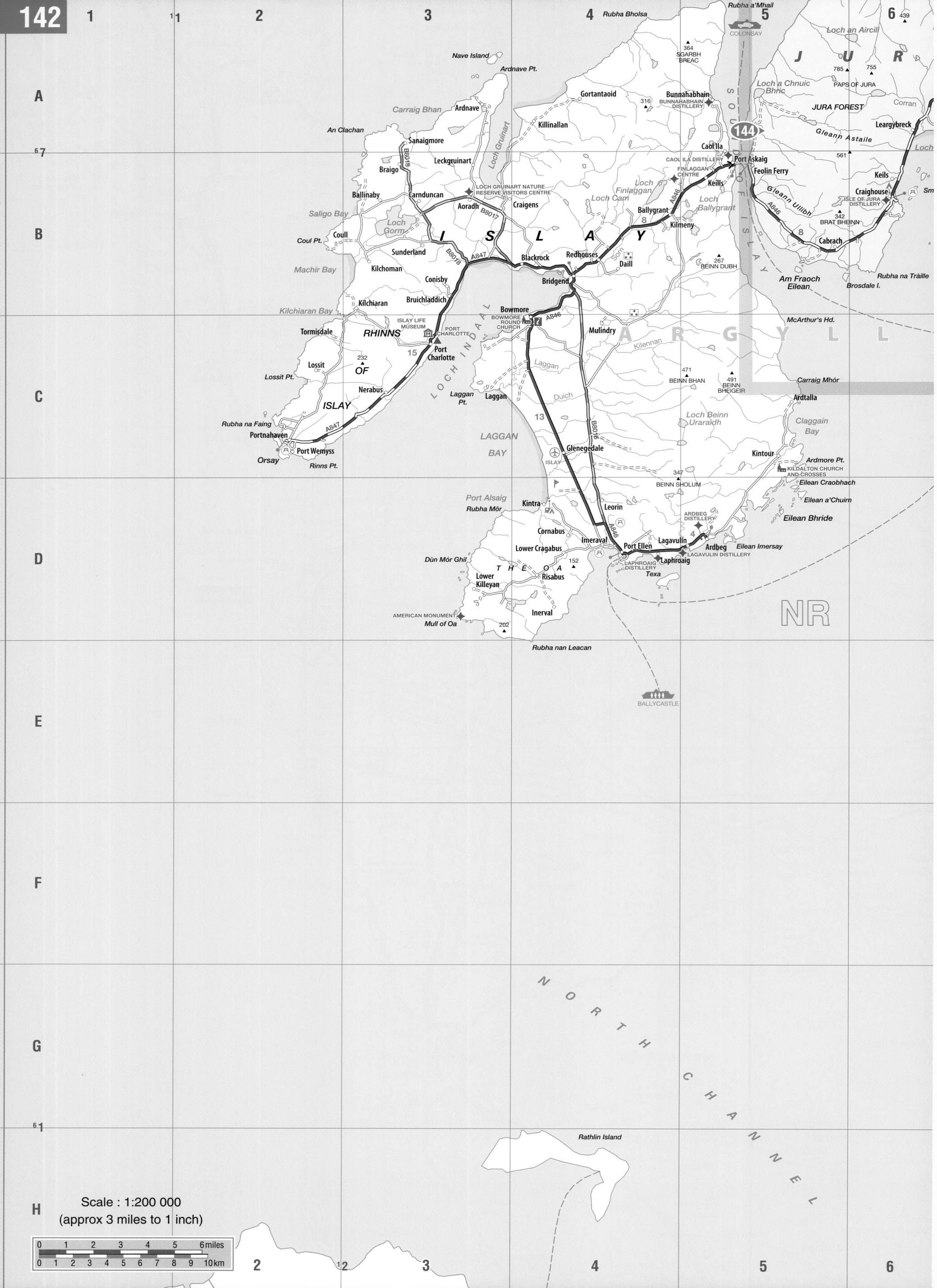

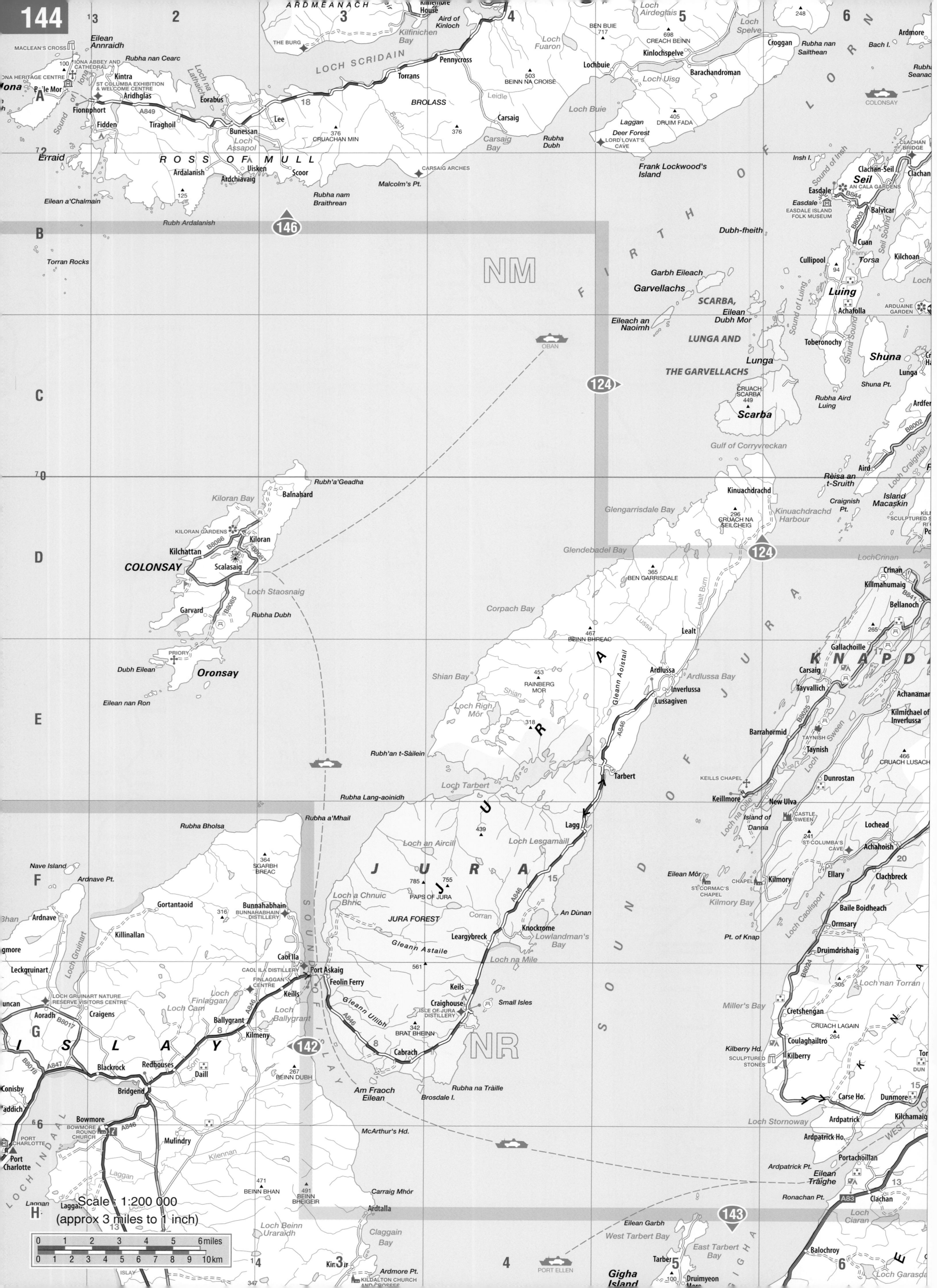

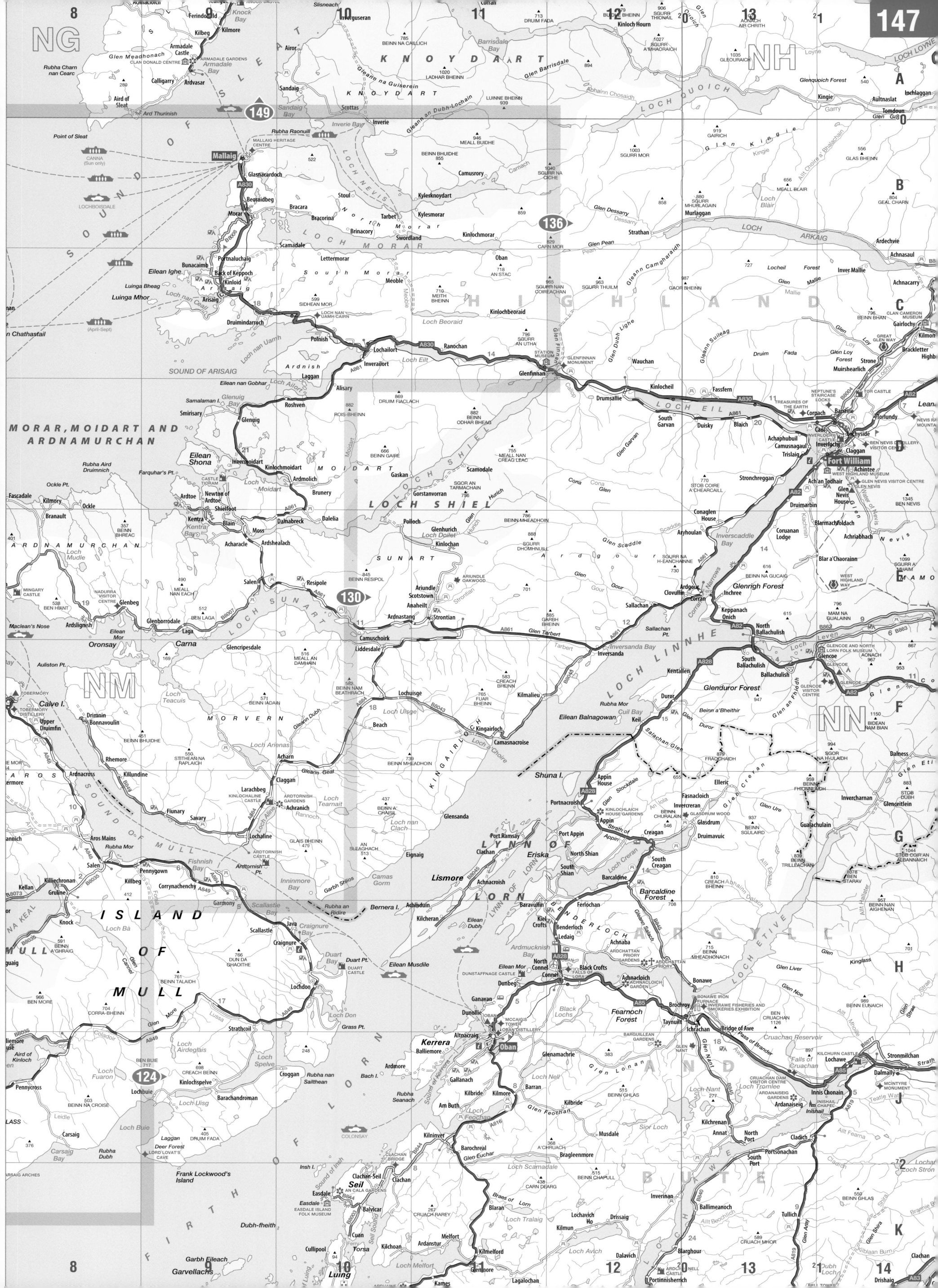

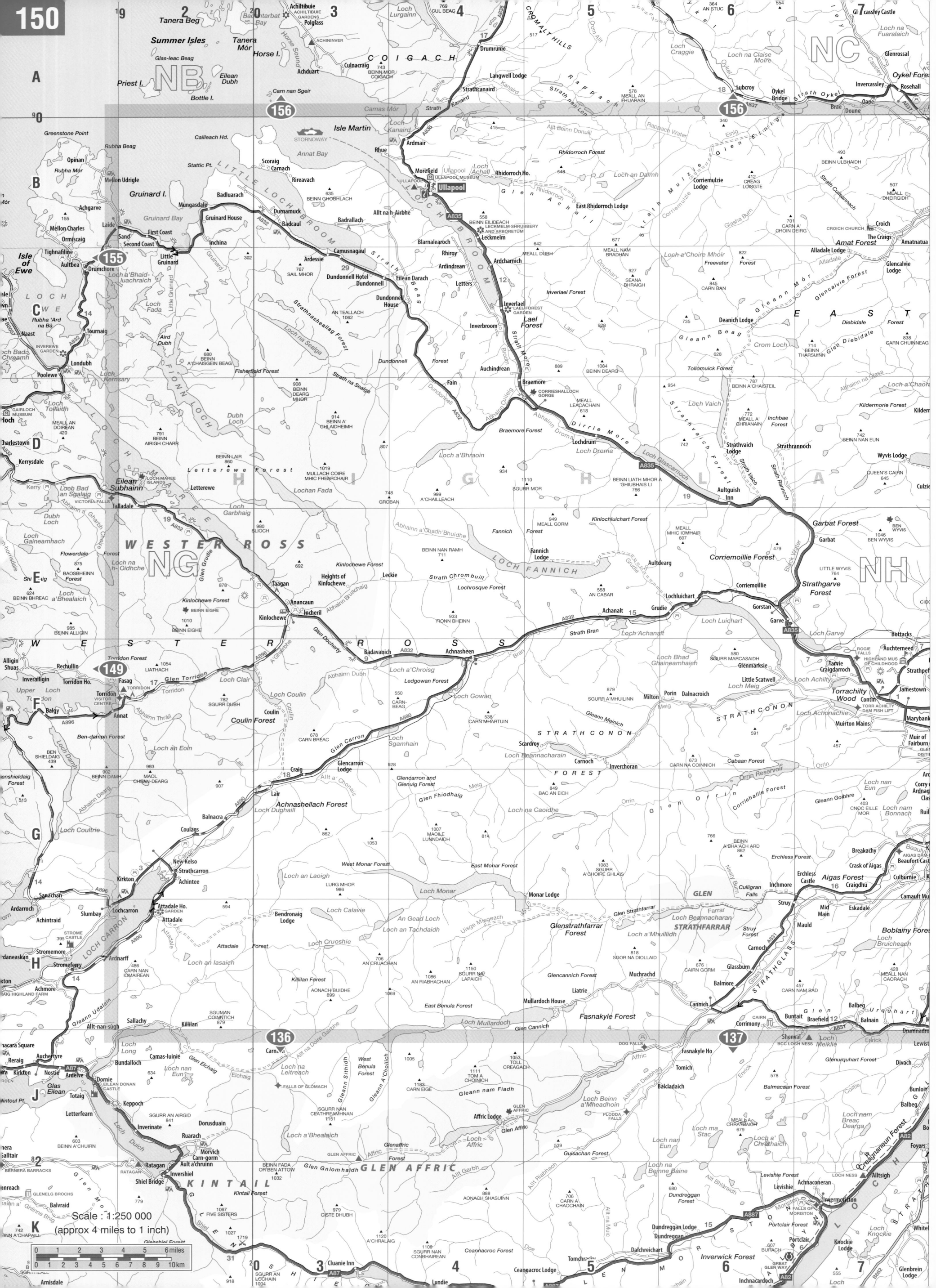

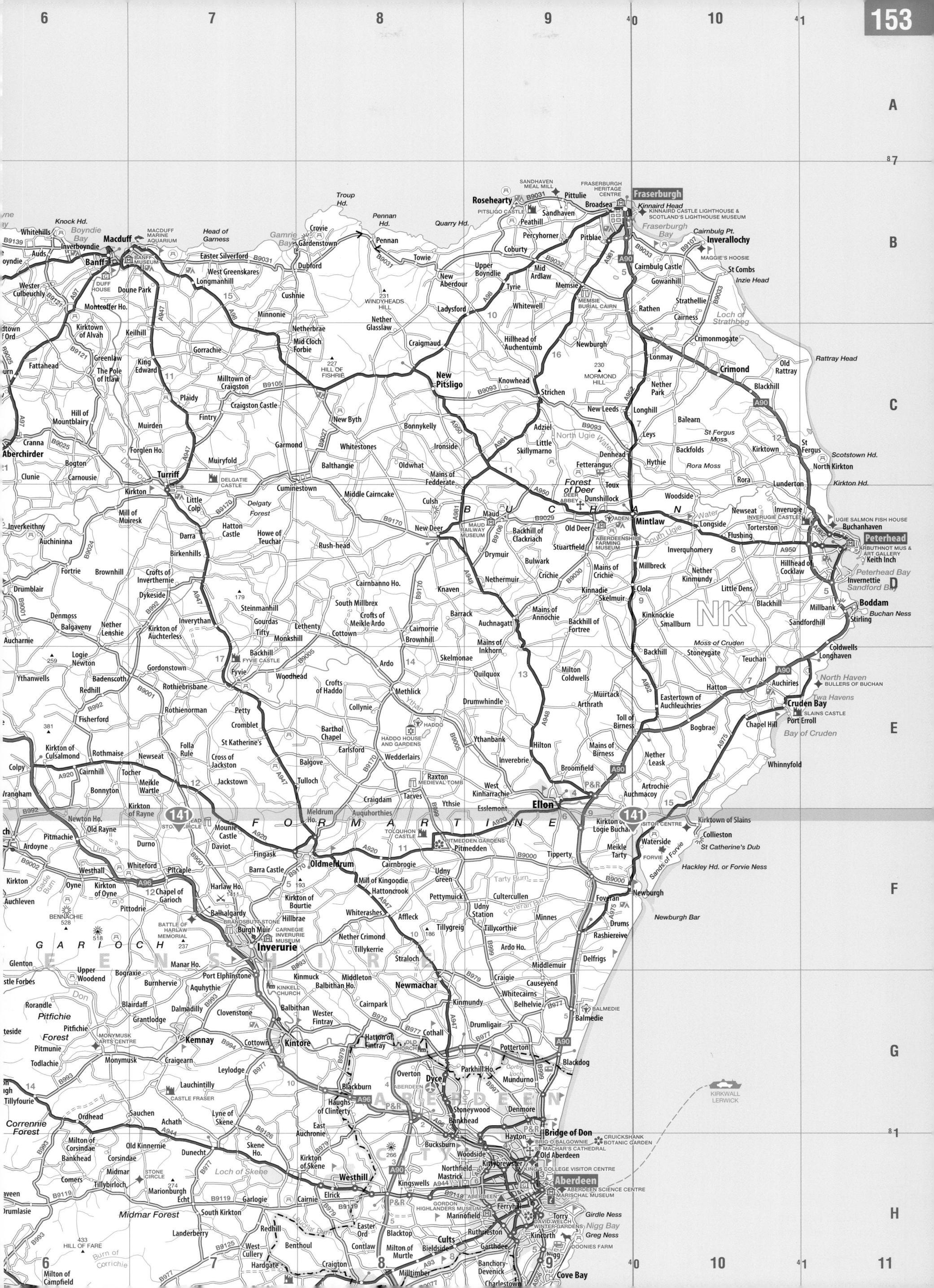

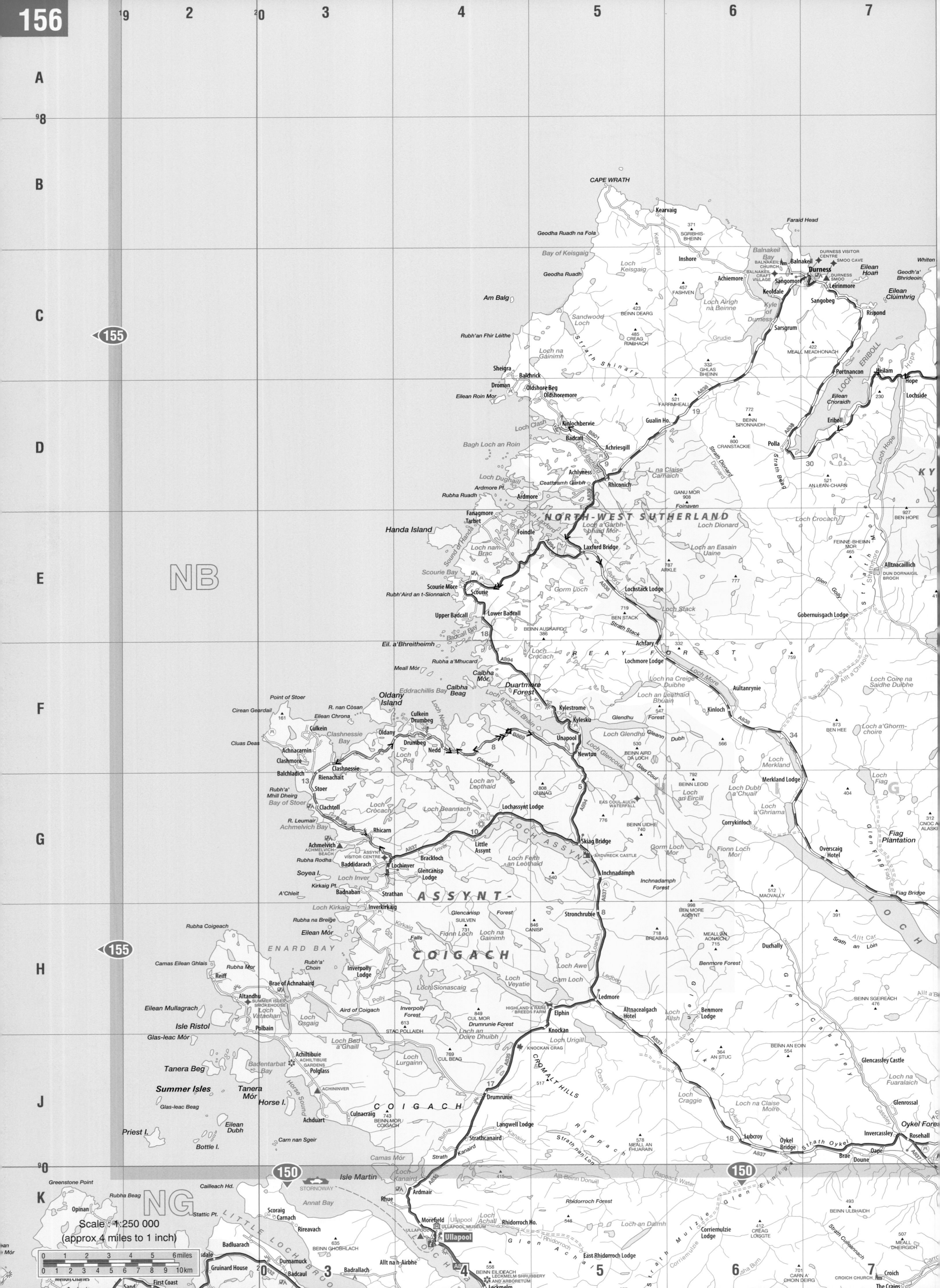

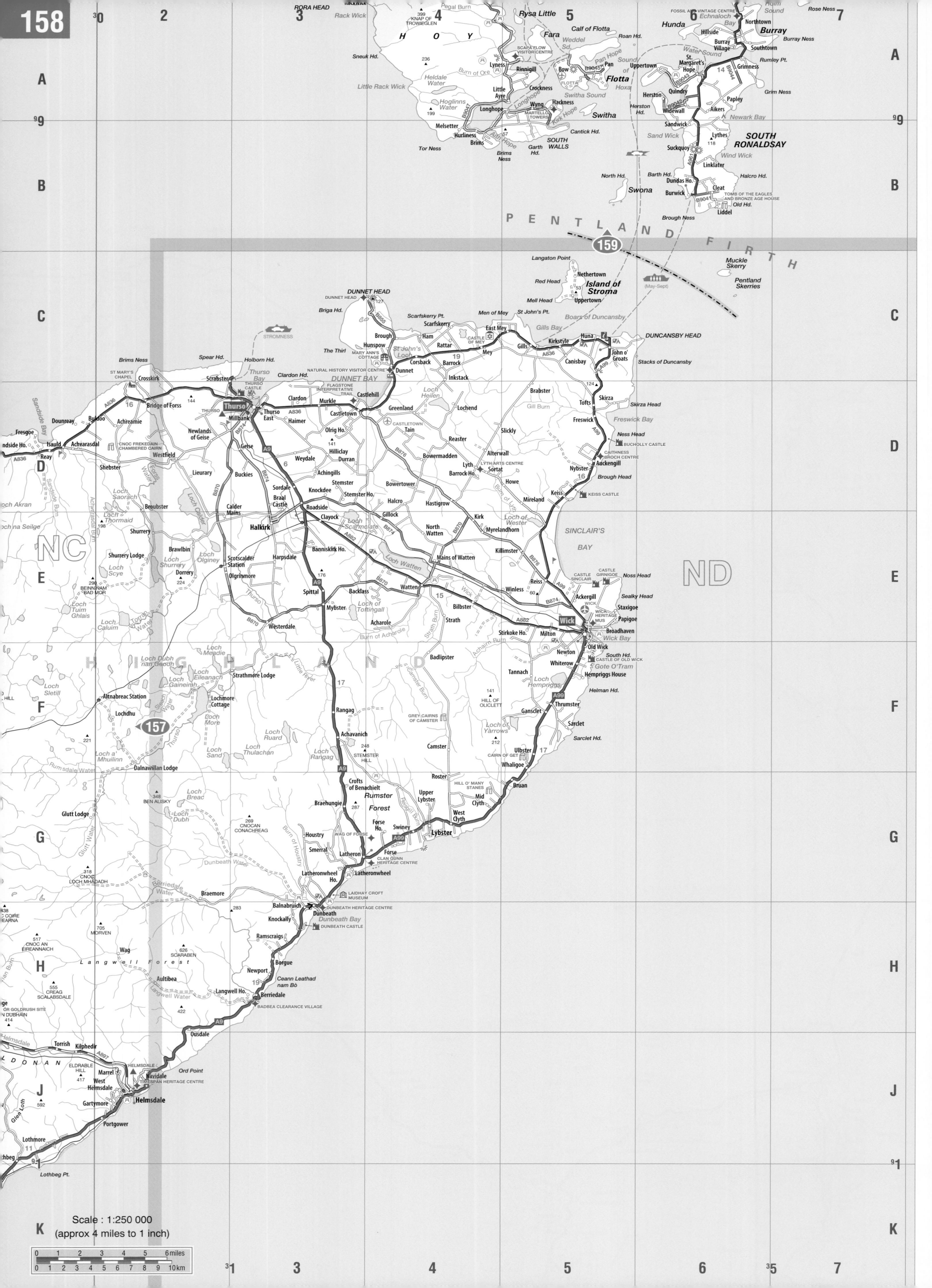

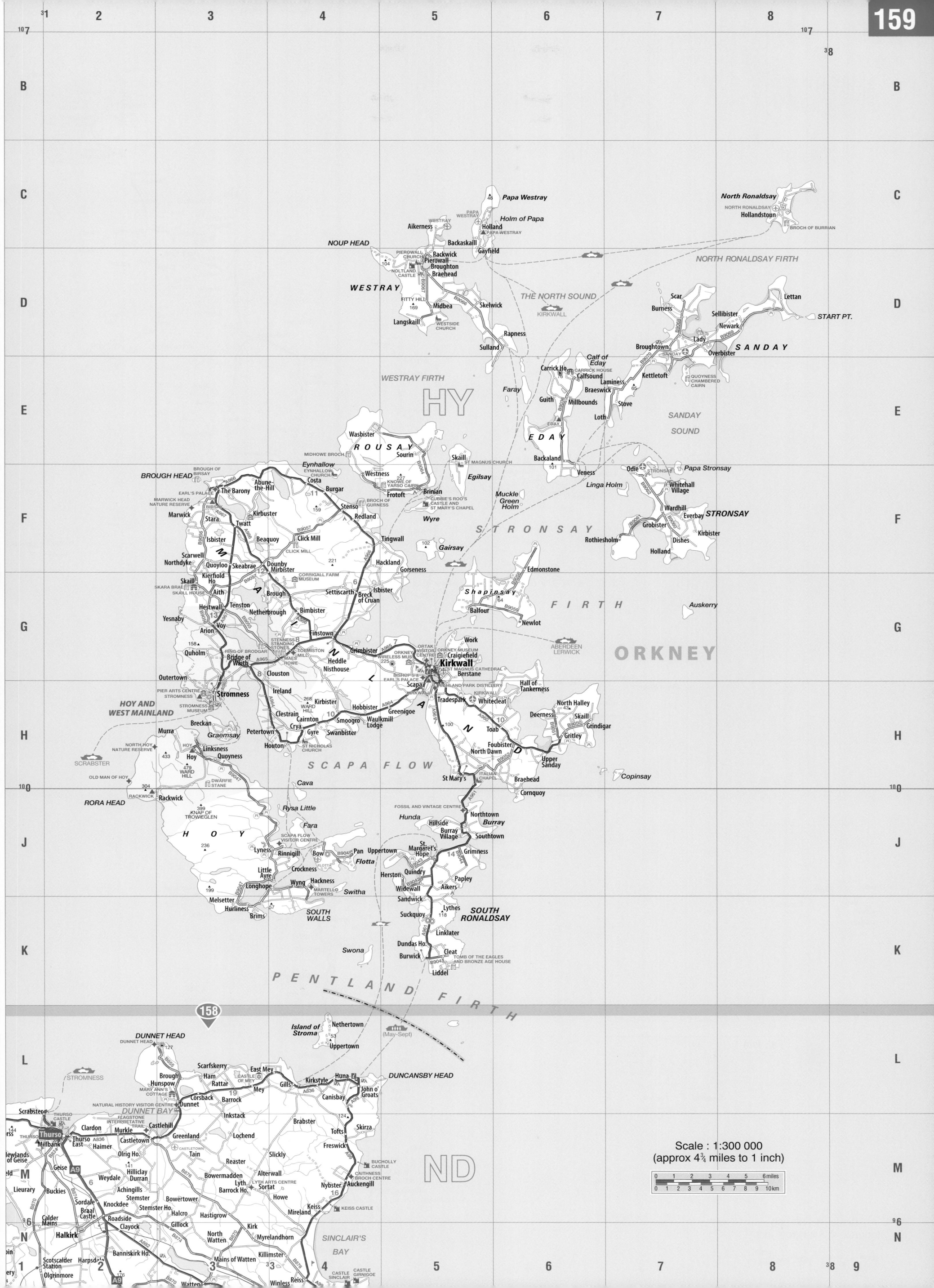

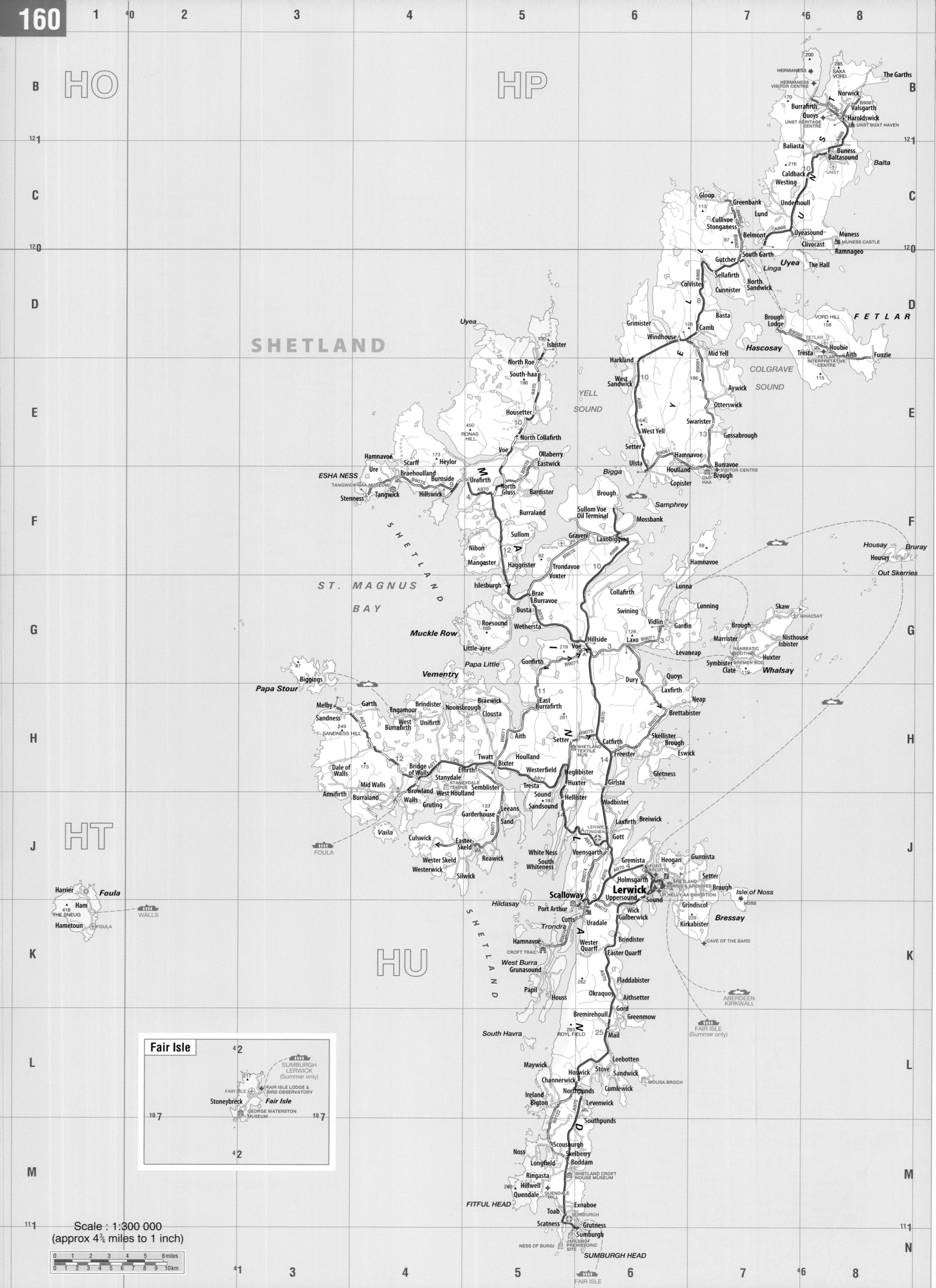

SHETLAND

ST. MAGNUS BAY

YELL SOUND

COLGRAVE SOUND

FETLAR

ESHA NESS

FITFUL HEAD

SUMBURGH HEAD

**Fair Isle**

Stoneybreck

*Fair Isle*

SUMBURGH LERWICK (Summer only)

FAIR ISLE LODGE & BIRD OBSERVATORY

GEORGE WATERSTON MUSEUM

Scale : 1:300 000
(approx 4¾ miles to 1 inch)

0  1  2  3  4  5  6miles
0  1  2  3  4  5  6  7  8  9  10km

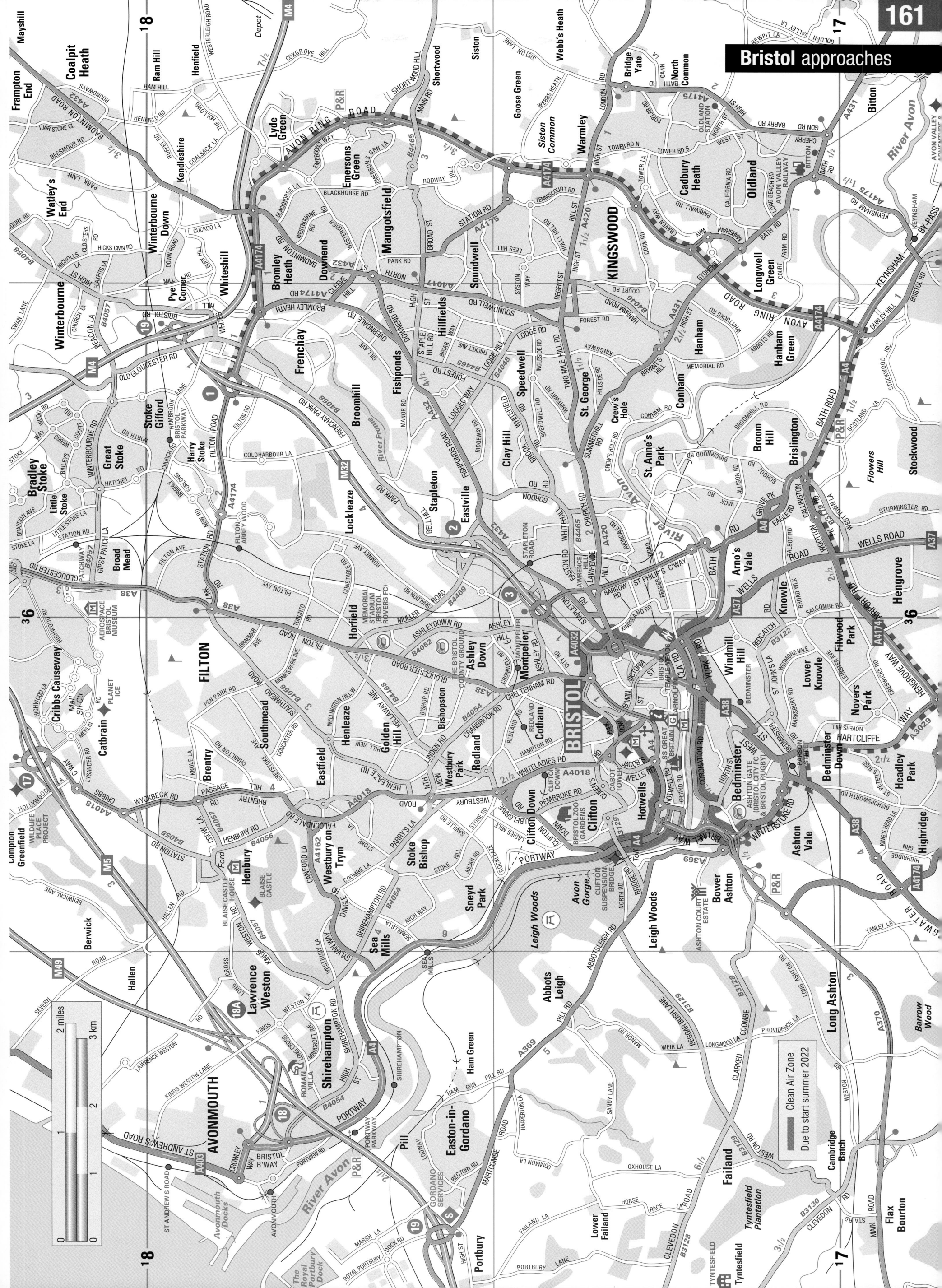

Clean Air Zone
Due to start summer 2022

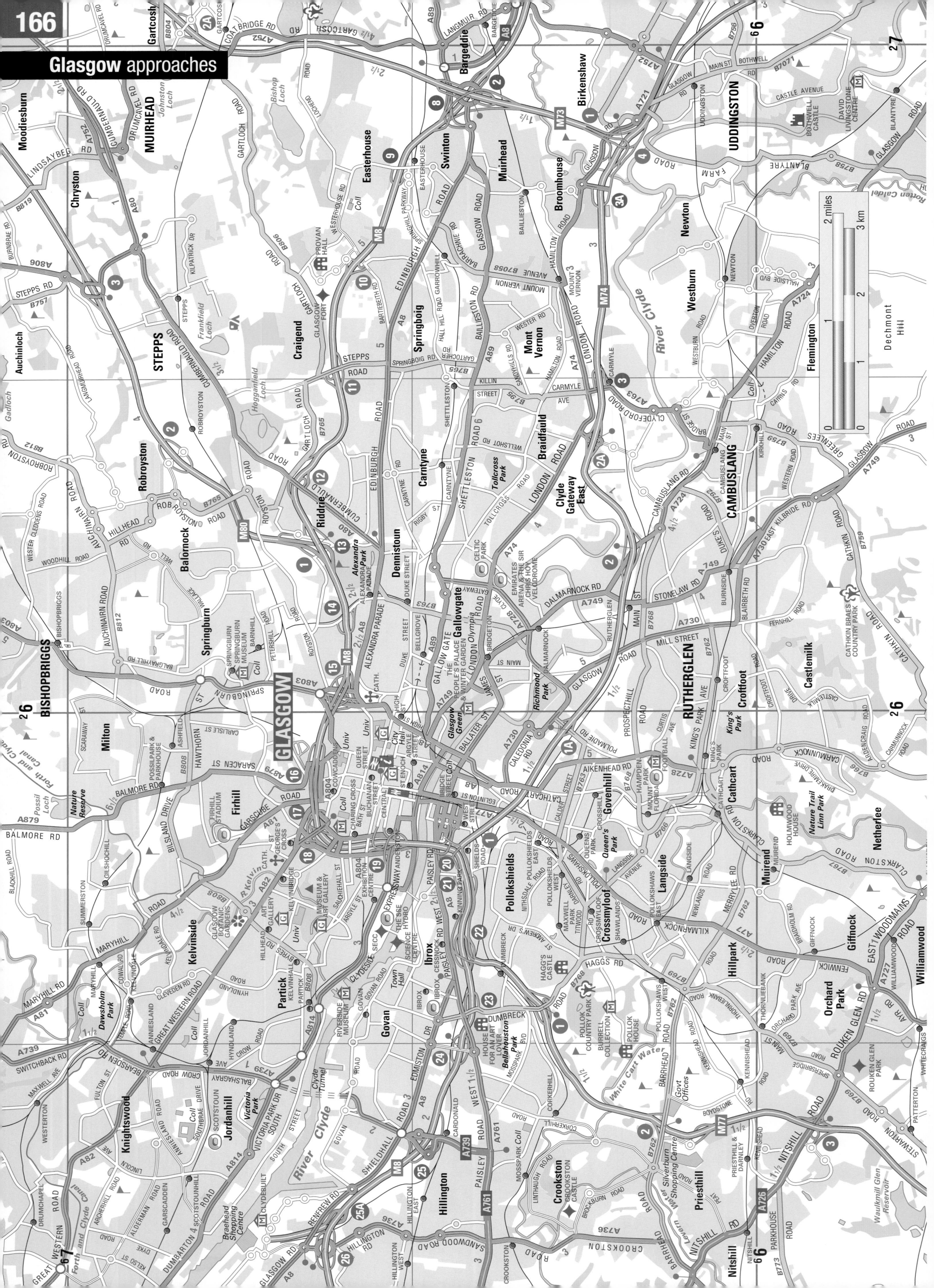

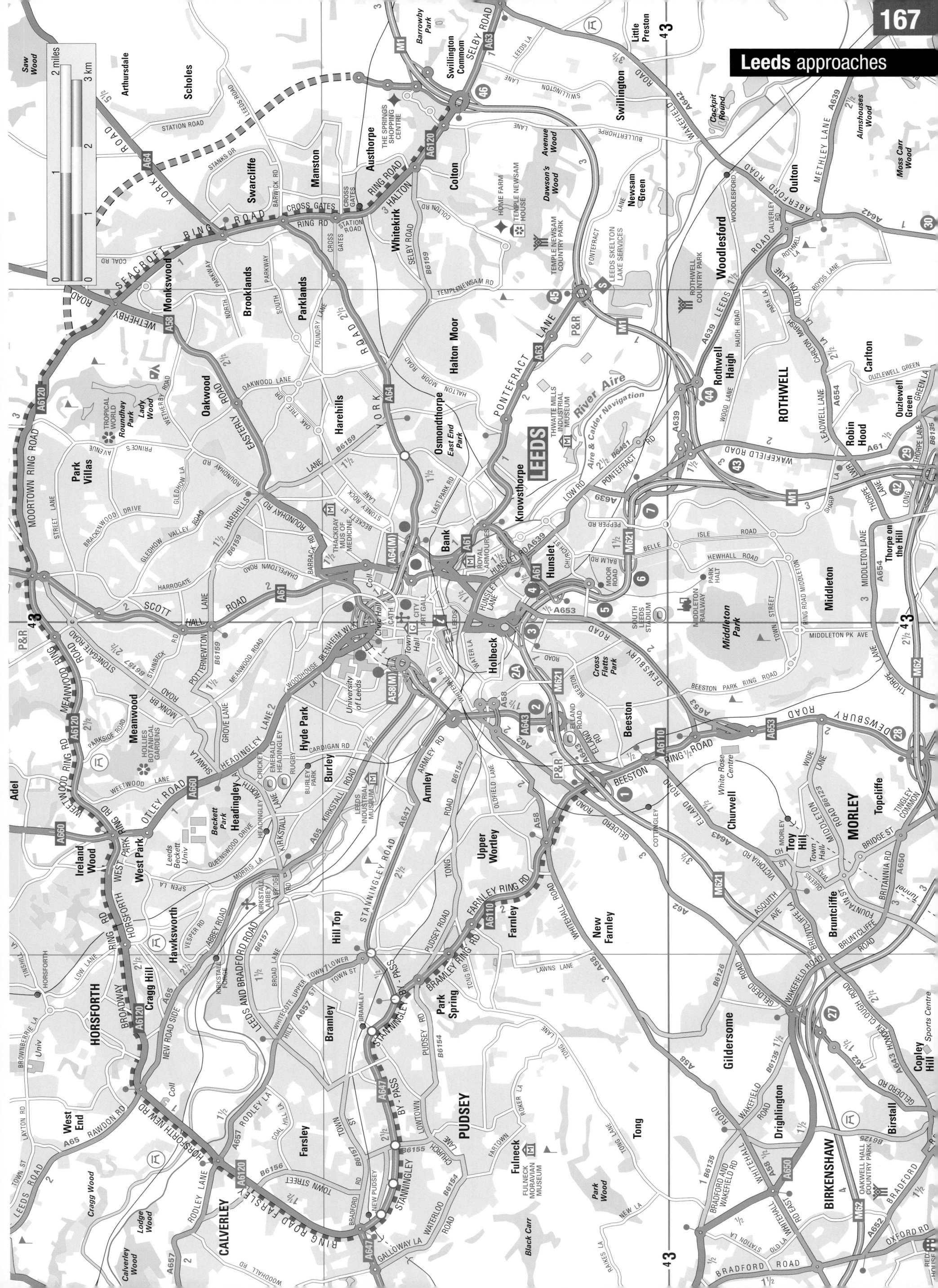

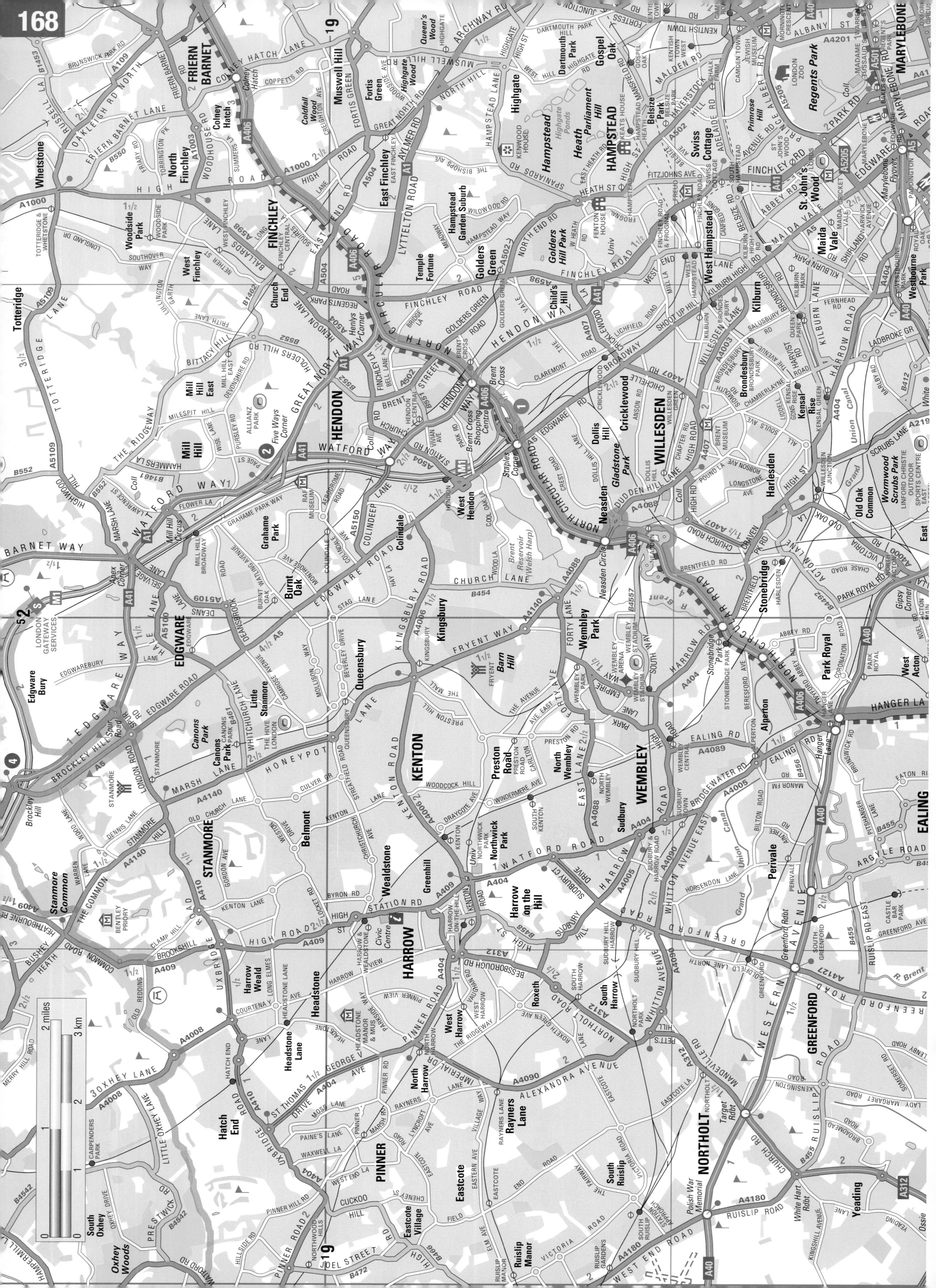

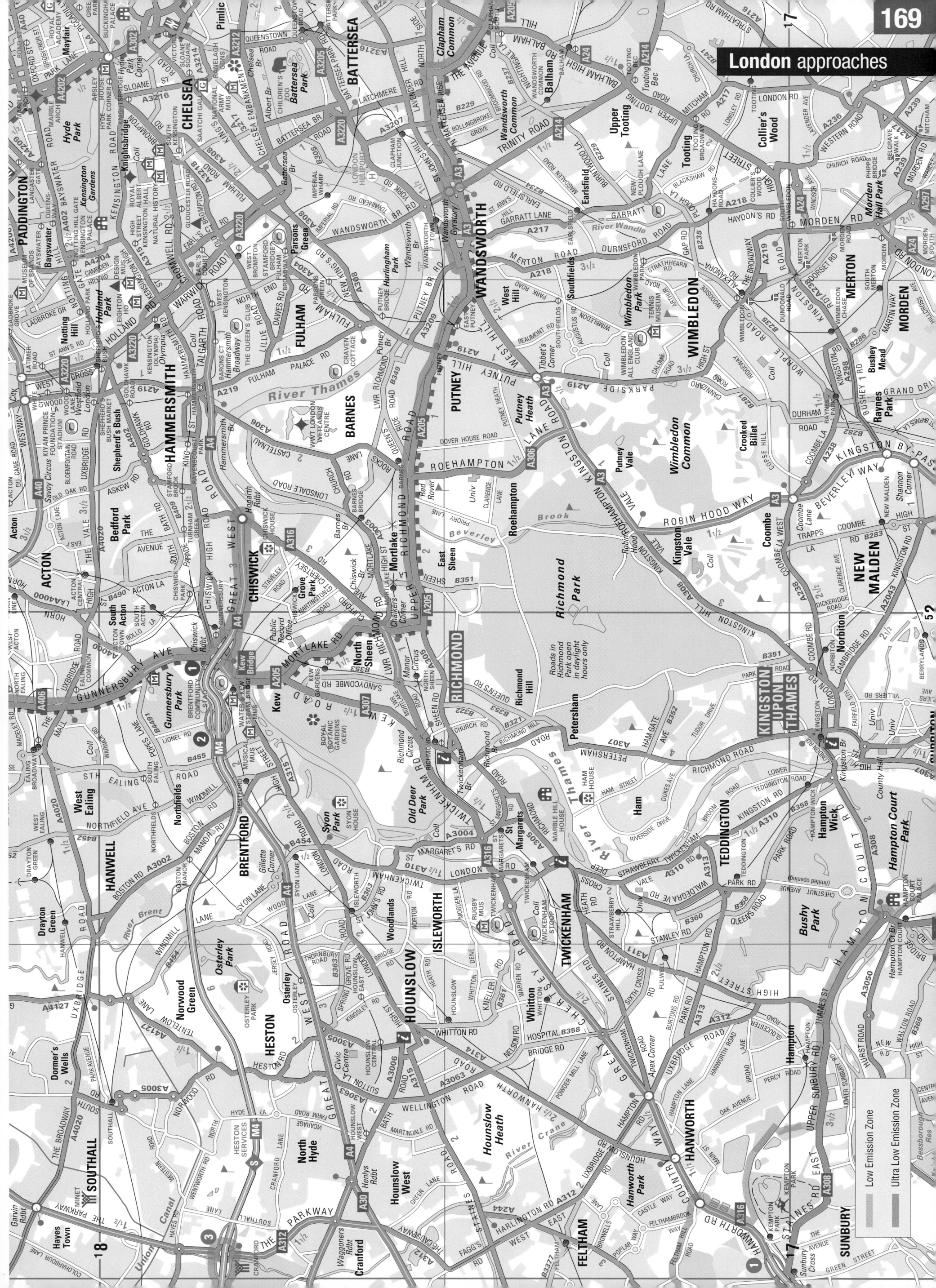

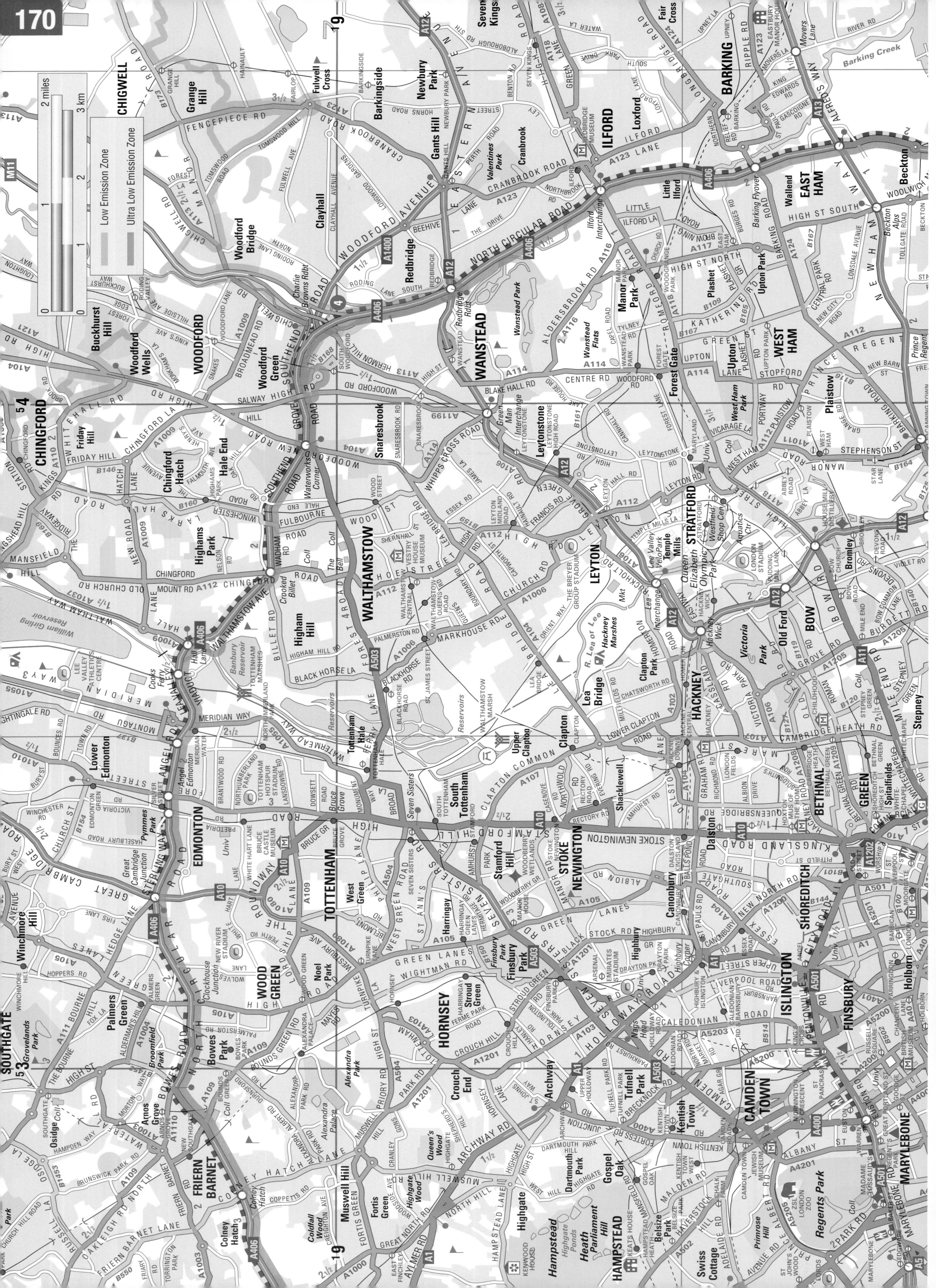

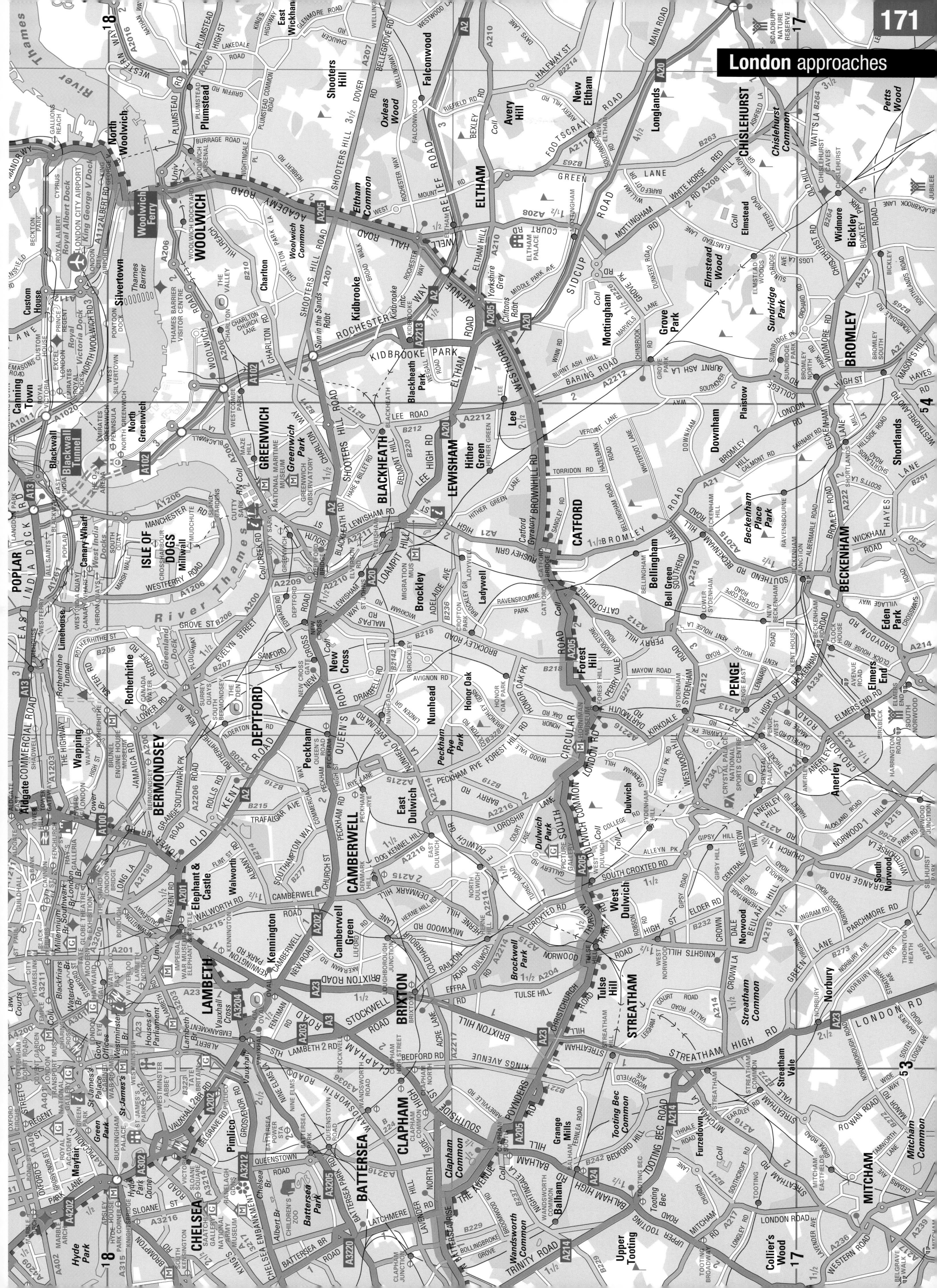

# Town plan symbols

| | |
|---|---|
| | Motorway |
| | Primary route – dual, single carriageway |
| | A road – dual, single carriageway |
| | B road – dual, single carriageway |

| | |
|---|---|
| | Minor through road |
| | One-way street |
| | Pedestrian roads |
| | Shopping streets |

| | |
|---|---|
| | Railway with station |
| | Tramway with station |
| | Underground or Metro station |

| | |
|---|---|
| H | Hospital |
| P | Parking |
| | Police, Post Office |
| | Shopmobility |
| ▲ | Youth hostel |

| | |
|---|---|
| | Bus or railway station building |
| | Shopping precinct or retail park |
| | Park |
| | Congestion charge zone |

| | |
|---|---|
| ✝ | Abbey or cathedral |
| | Ancient monument |
| | Aquarium |
| G | Art gallery |
| | Bird collection or aviary |
| | Building of interest |
| | Castle |
| | Church of interest |
| | Cinema |
| | Garden |
| | Historic ship |
| | House |
| | House and garden |
| M | Museum |
| | Preserved railway |
| | Roman antiquity |
| | Safari park |
| | Theatre |
| i | Tourist information |
| | Zoo |
| ✦ | Other place of interest |

## Aberdeen

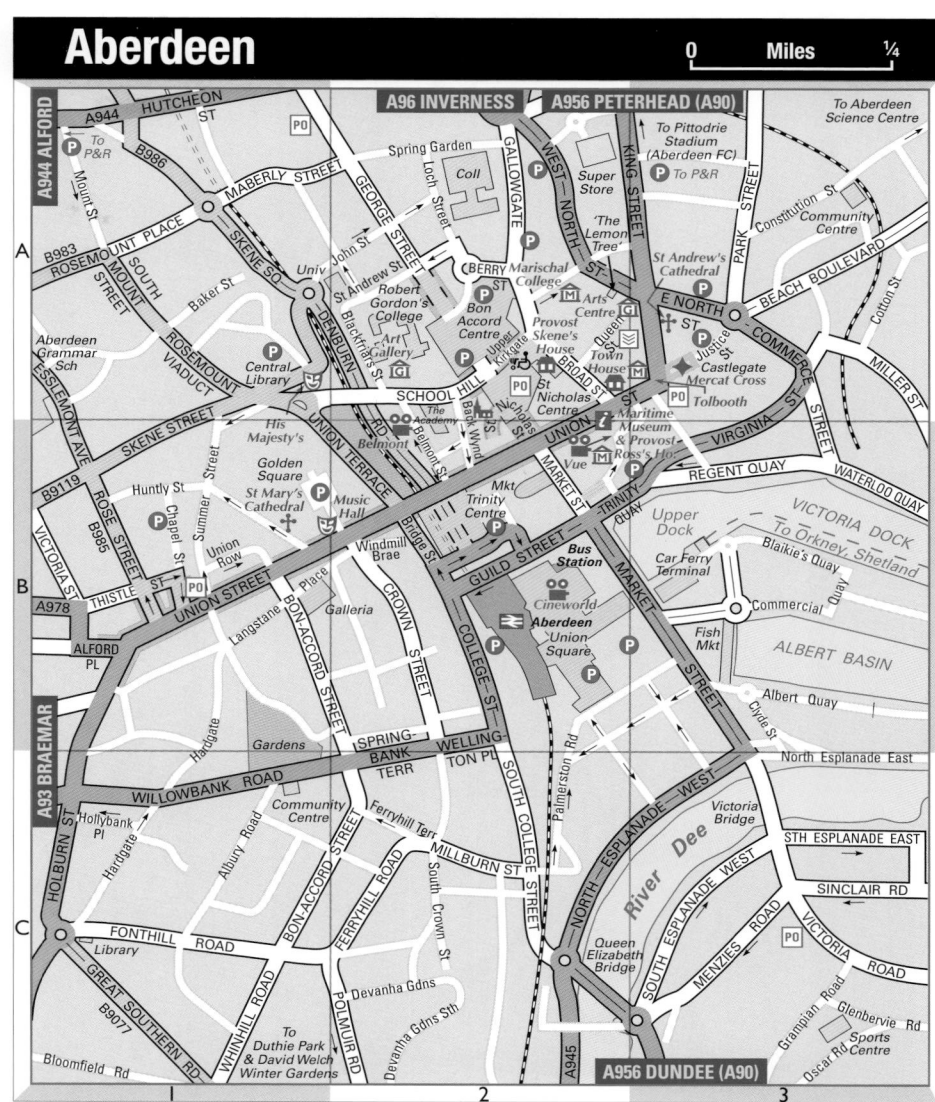

## Ayr

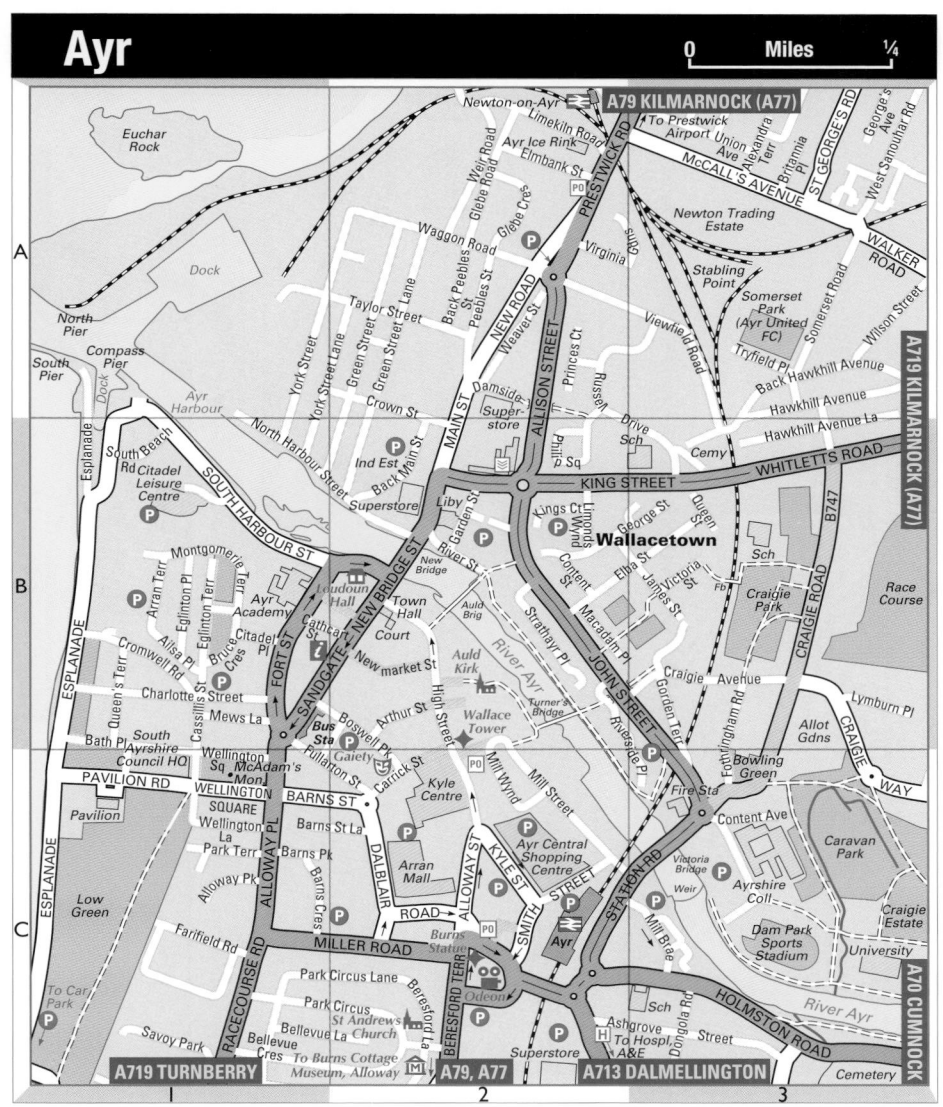

## Bath

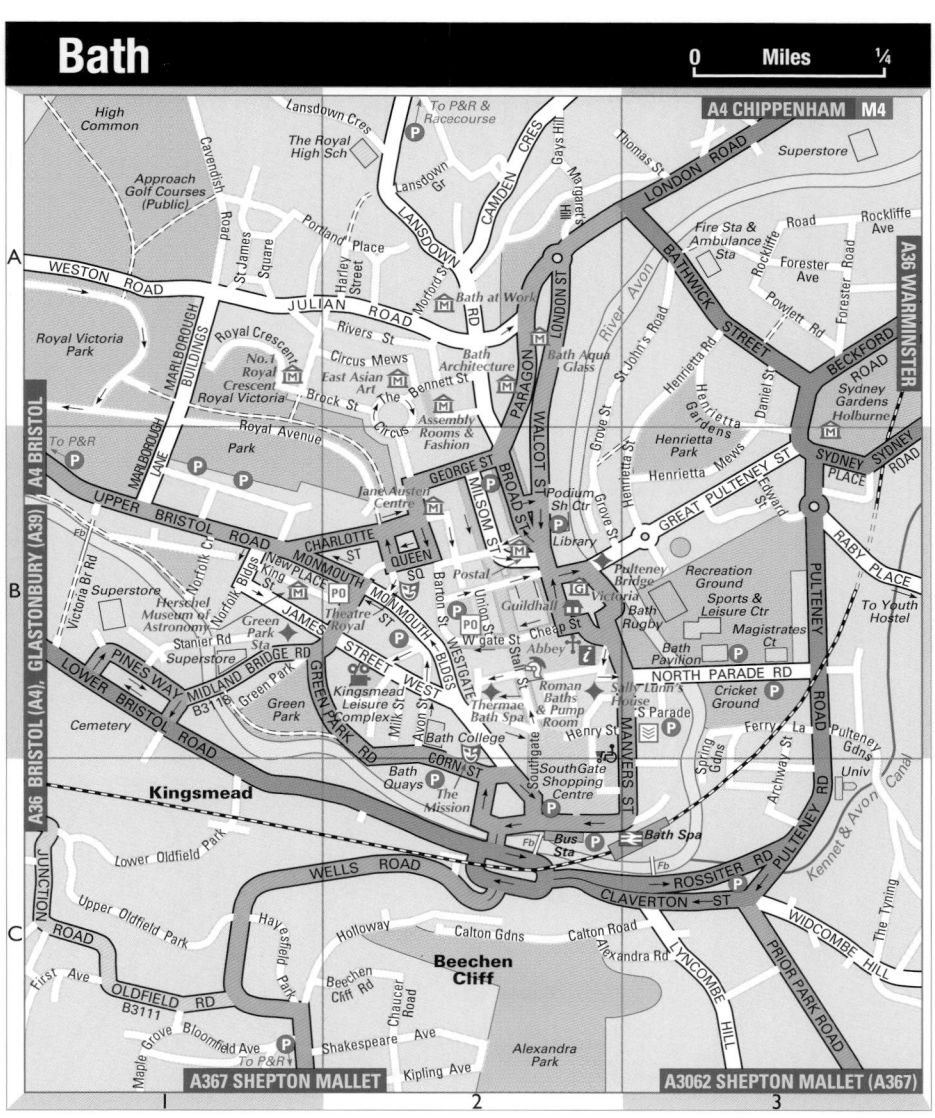

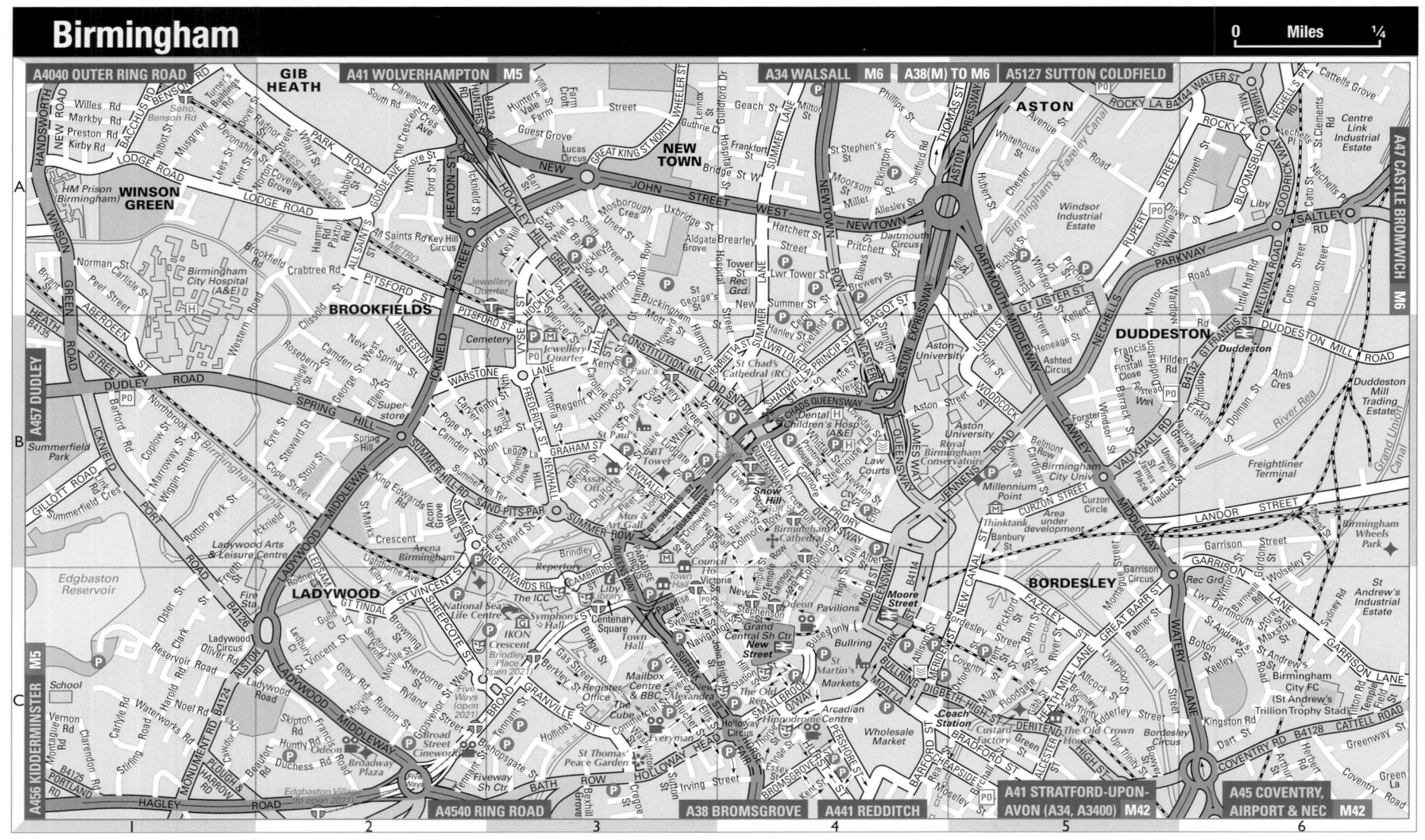

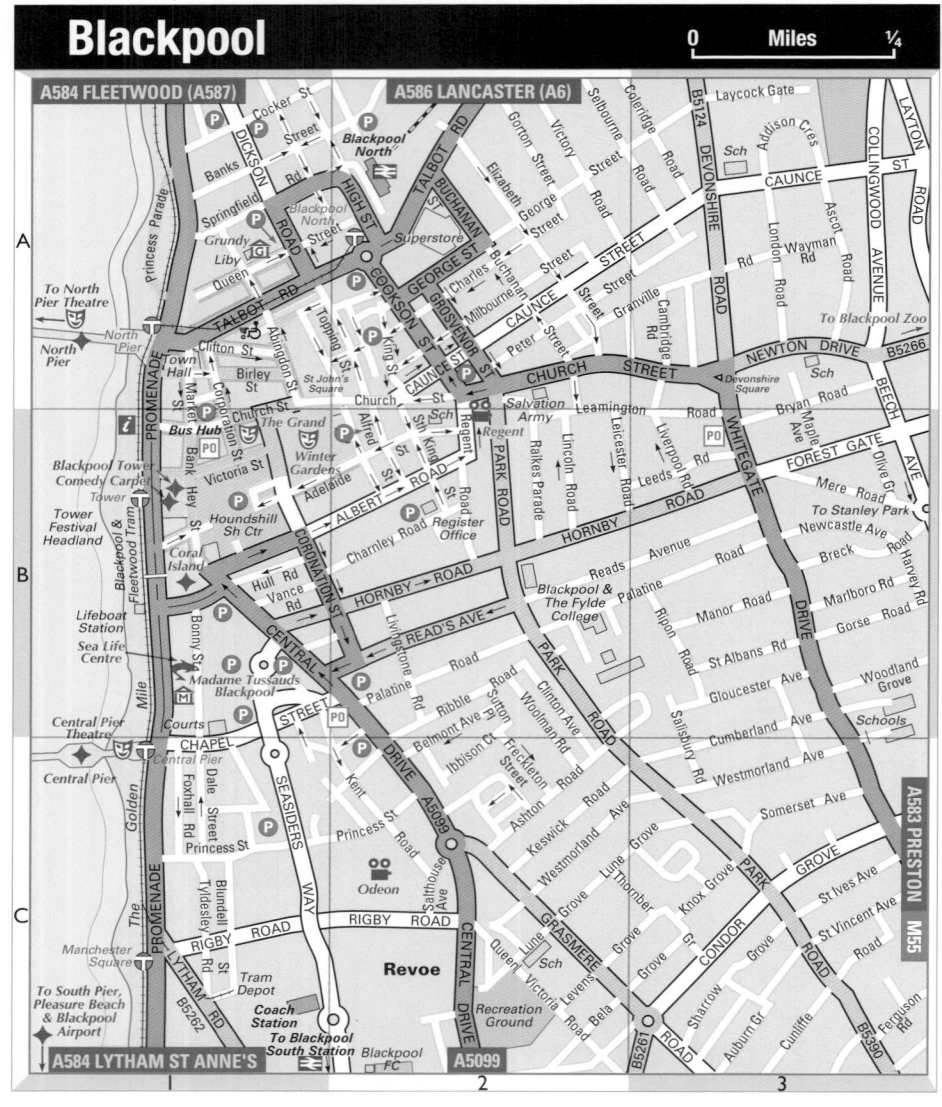

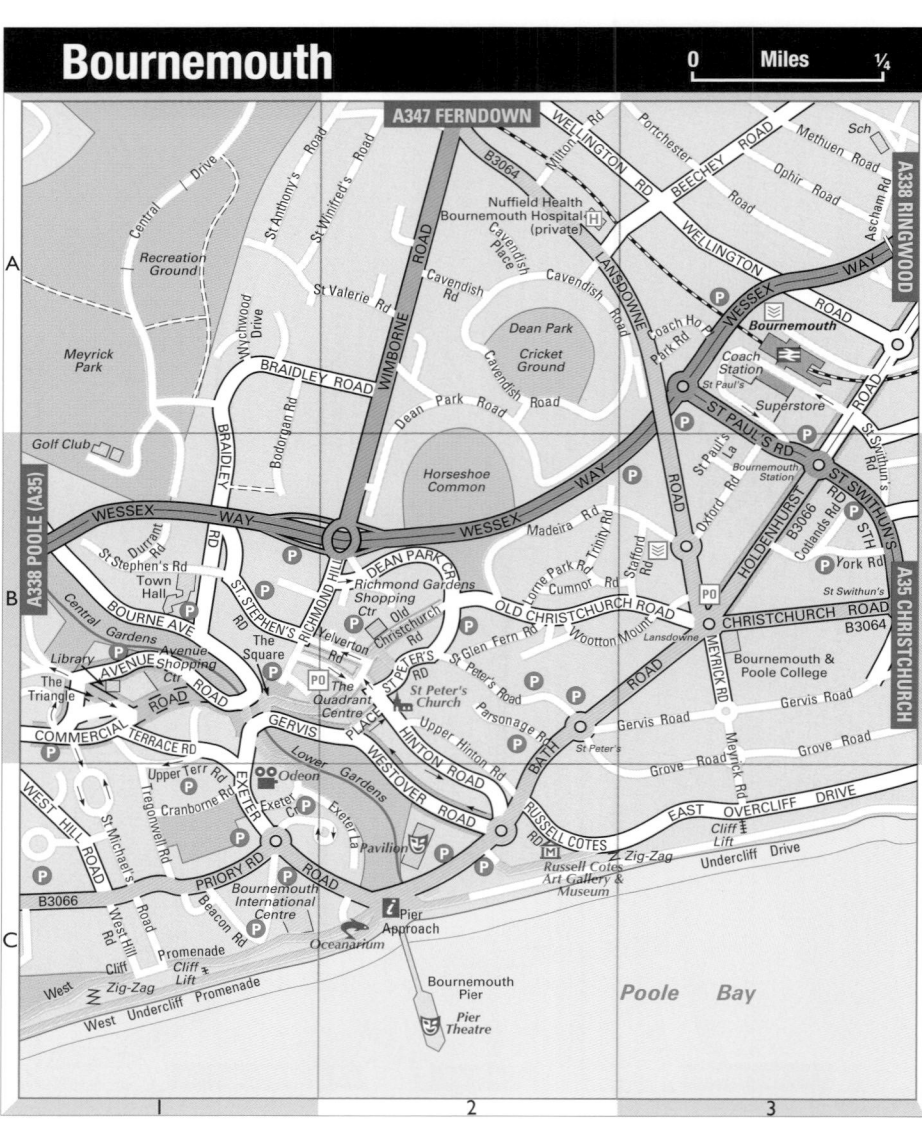

# Bradford

0 — Miles — ¼

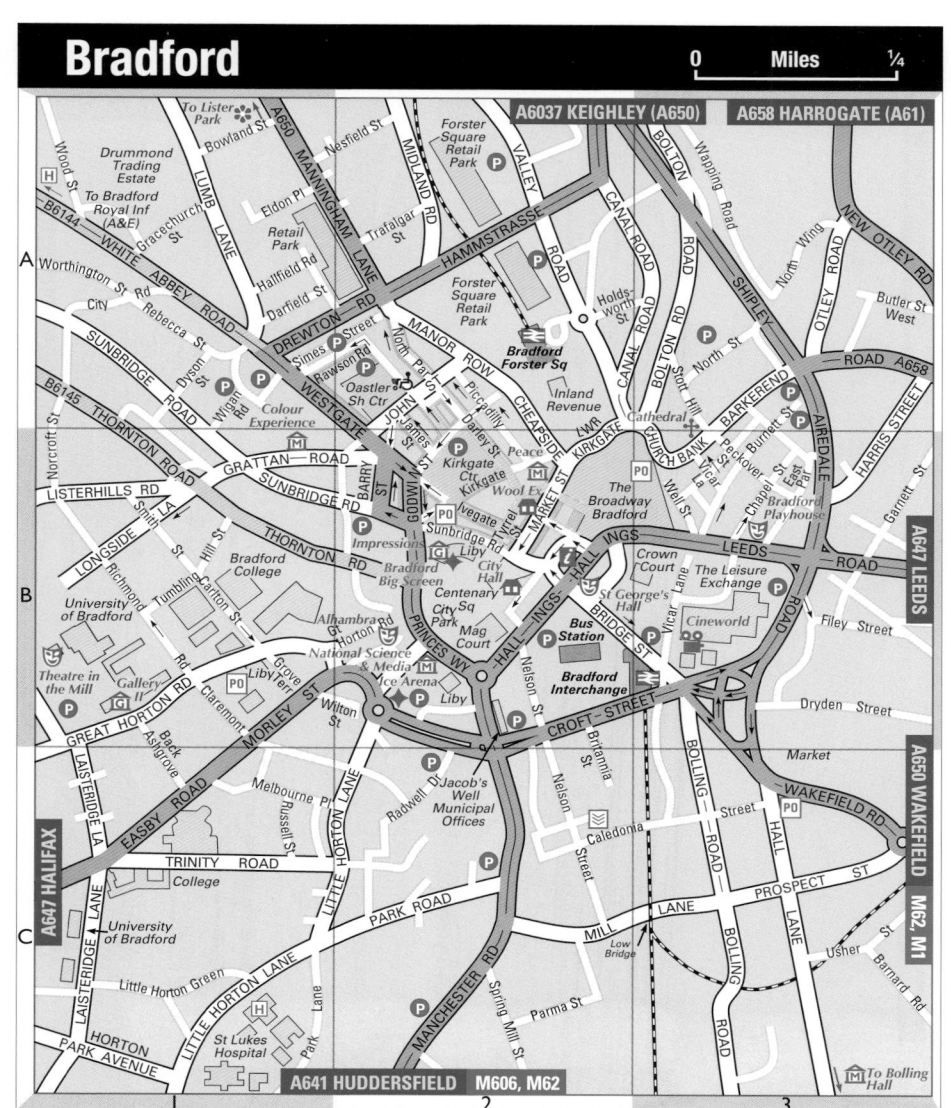

# Brighton

0 — Miles — ¼

# Bristol

0 — Miles — ¼

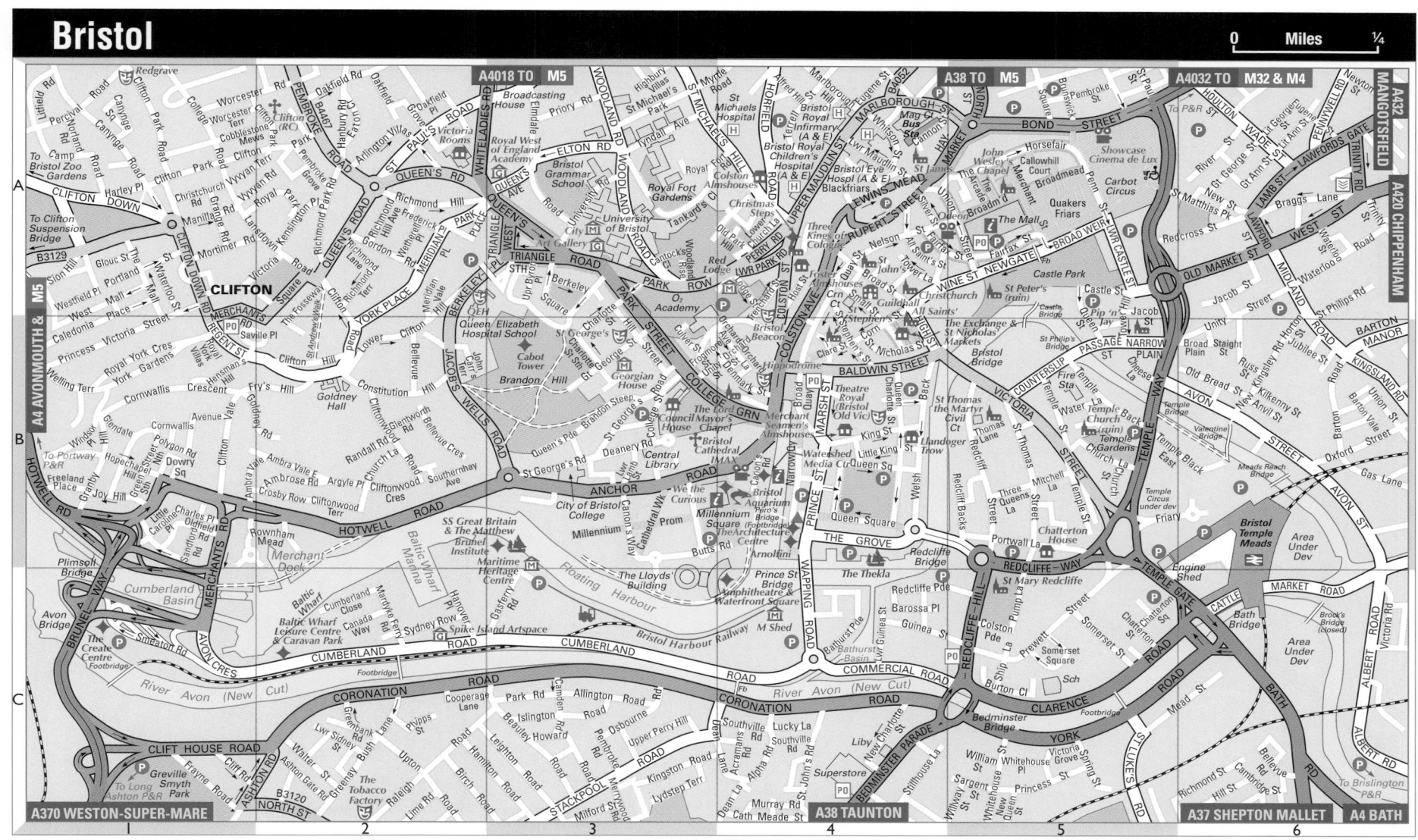

# Bury St Edmunds

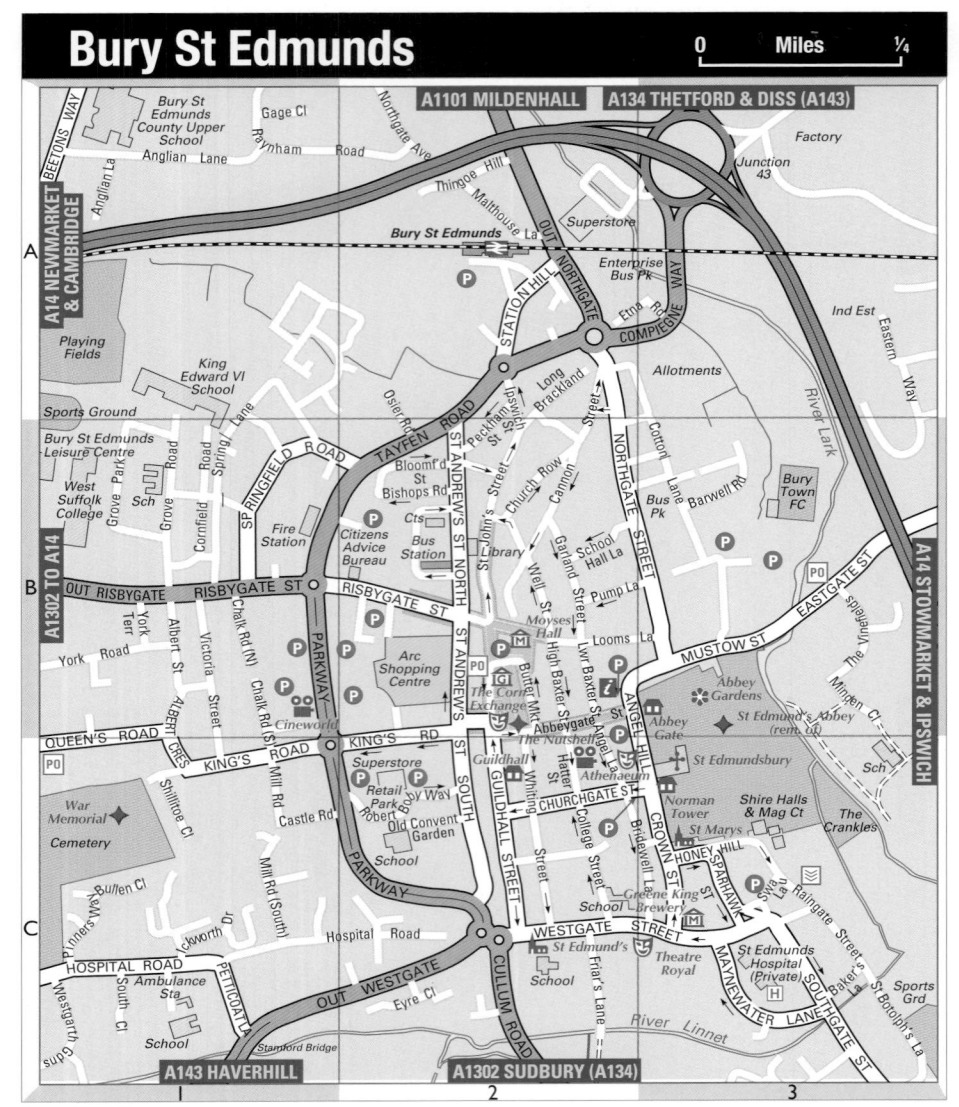

# Cambridge

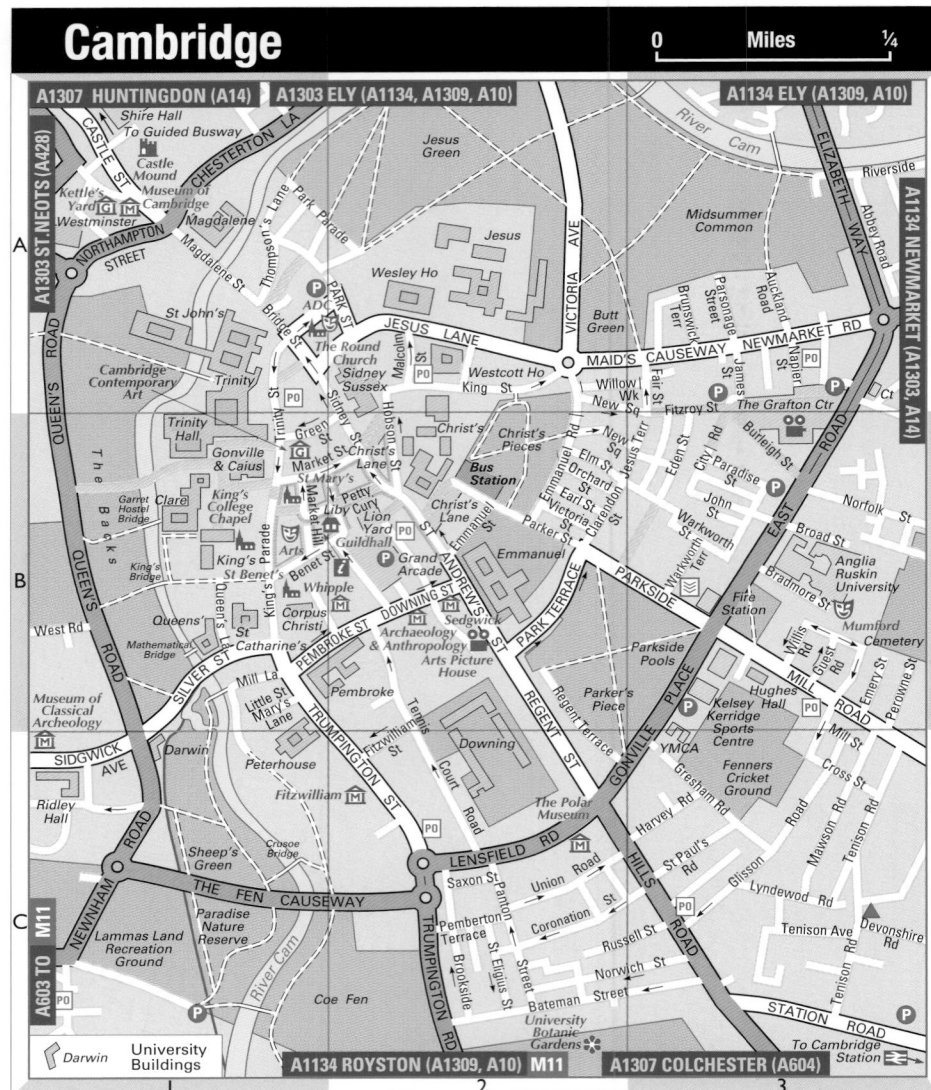

# Canterbury

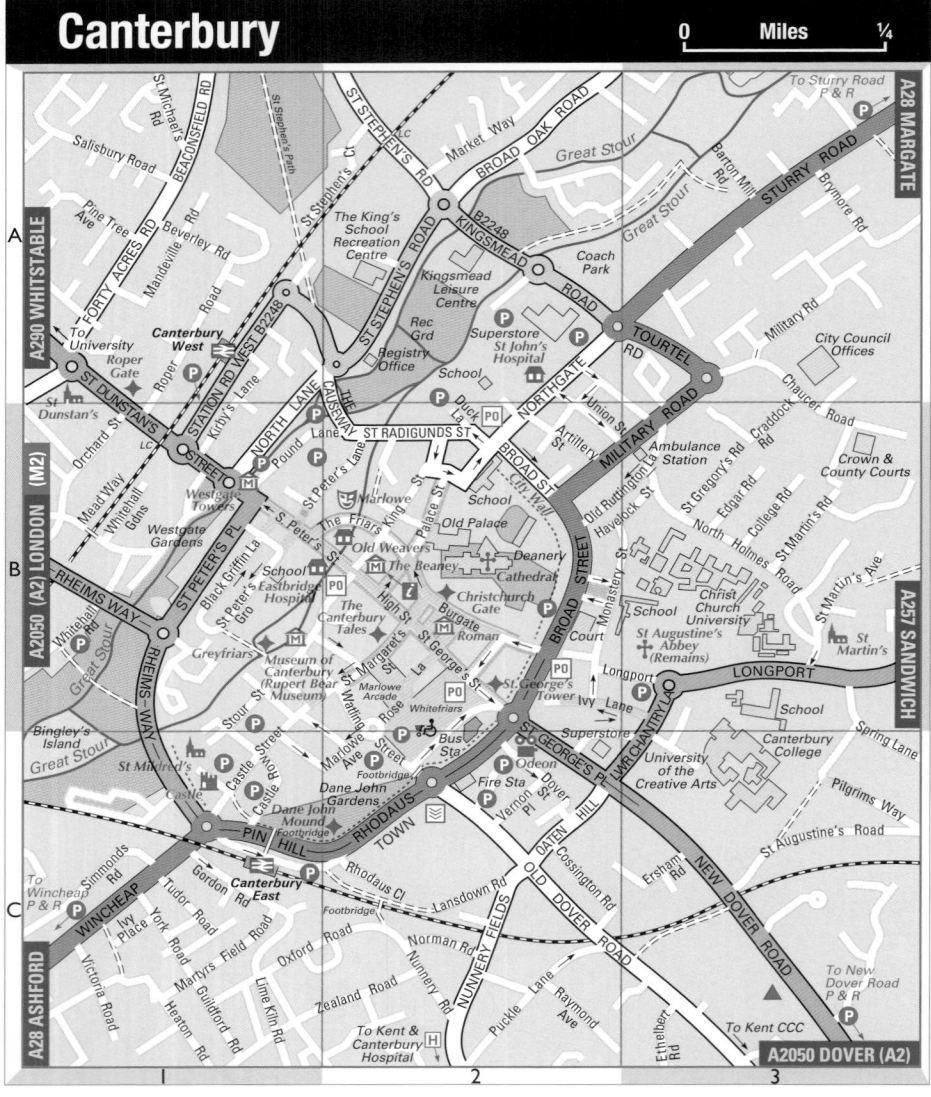

# Cardiff / Caerdydd

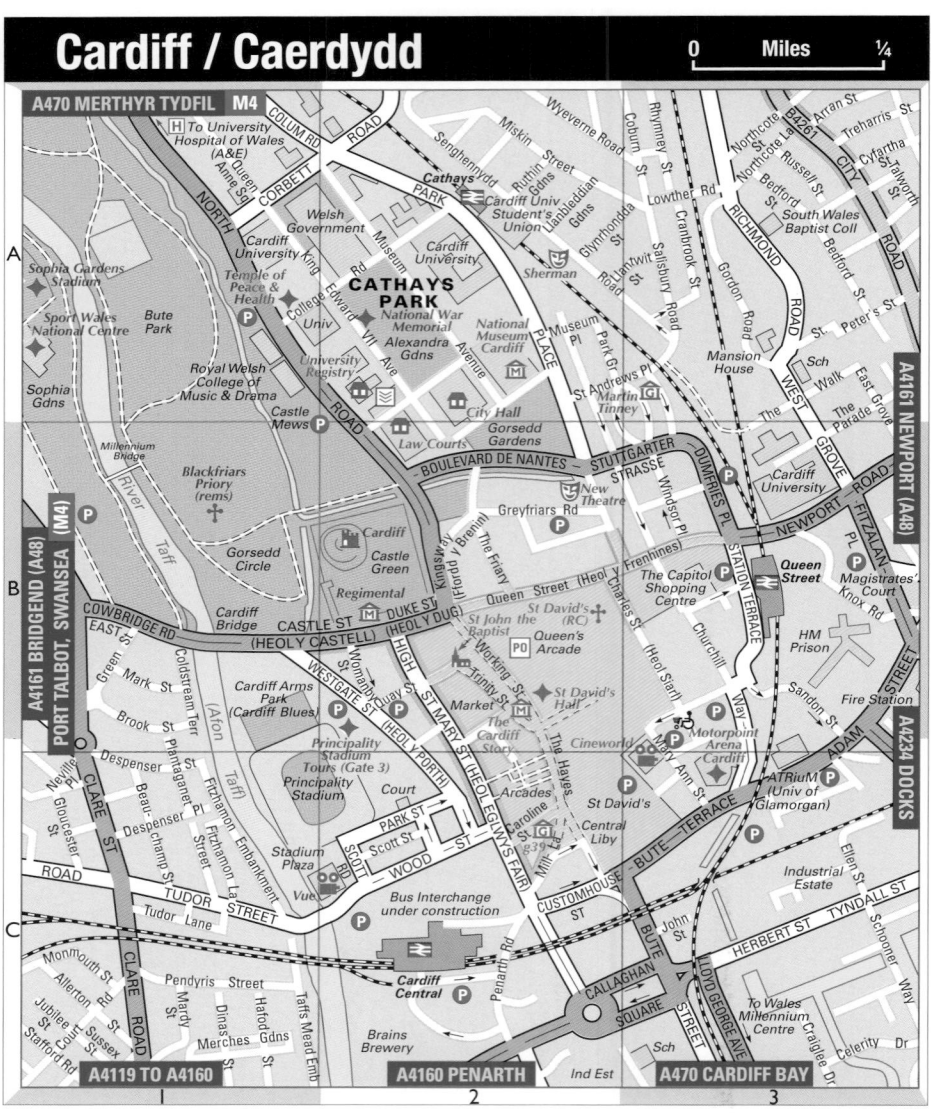

# Carlisle

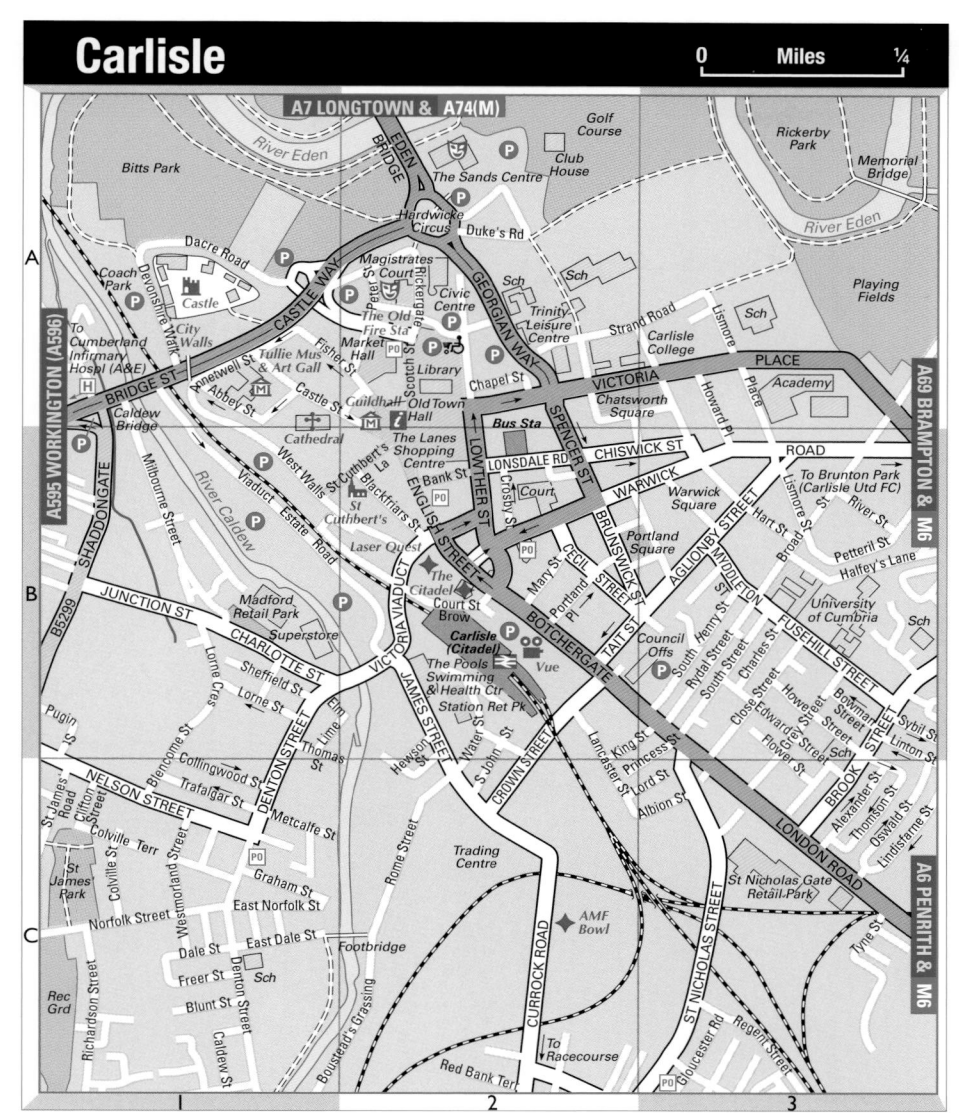

# Chelmsford

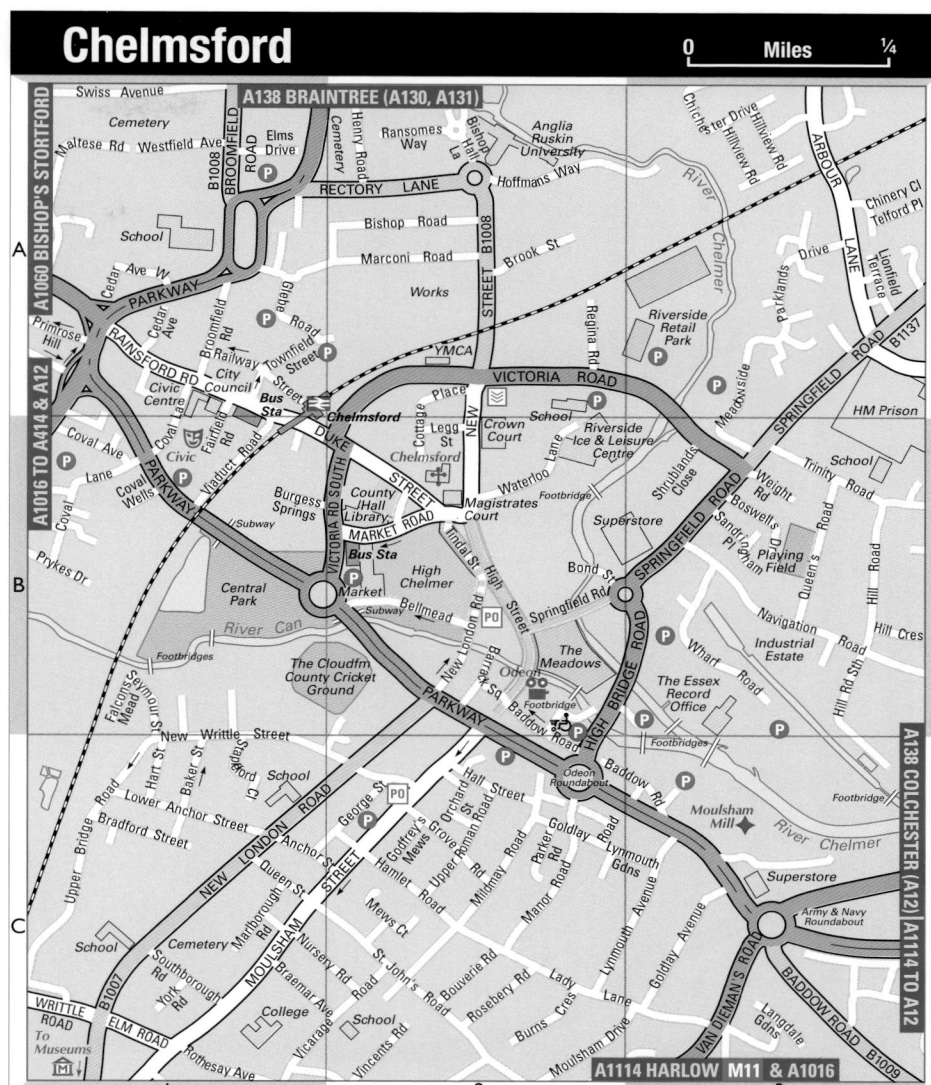

# Cheltenham

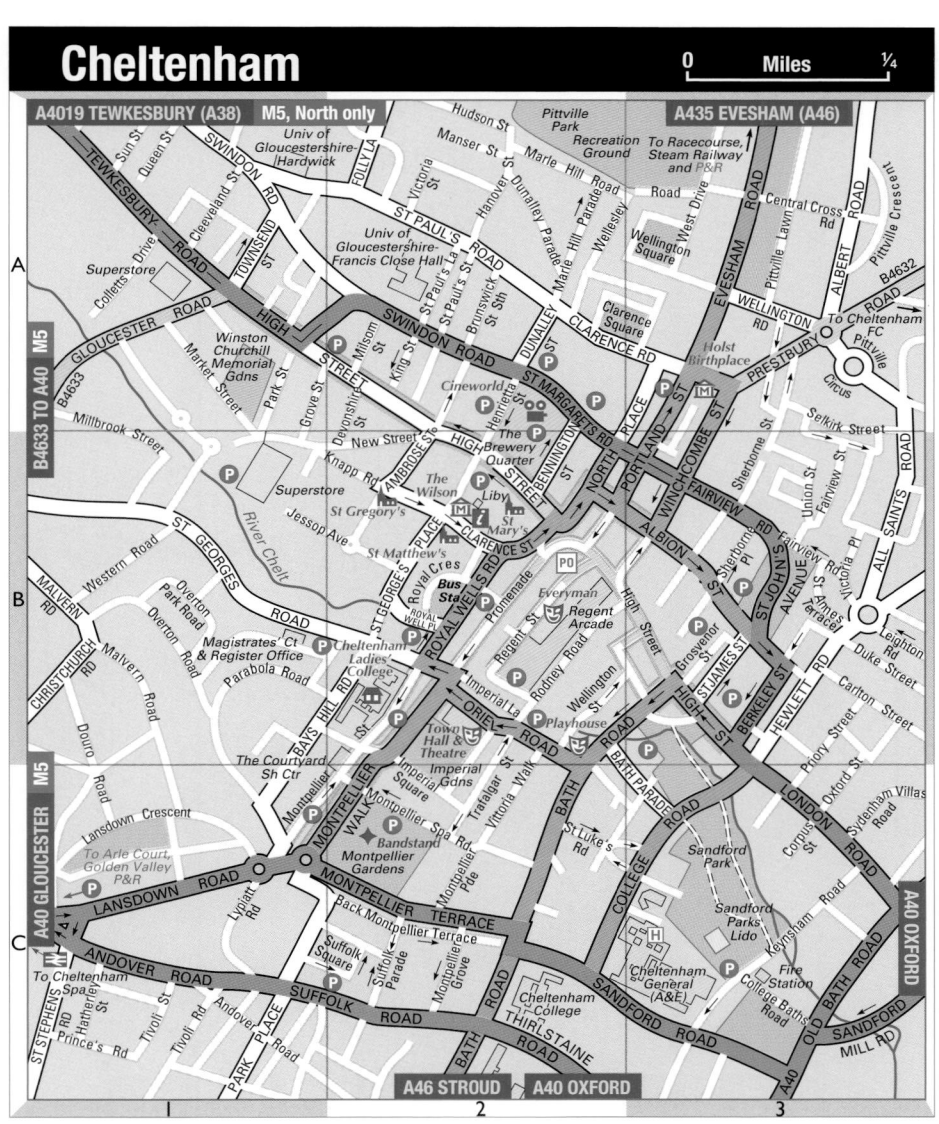

# Chester

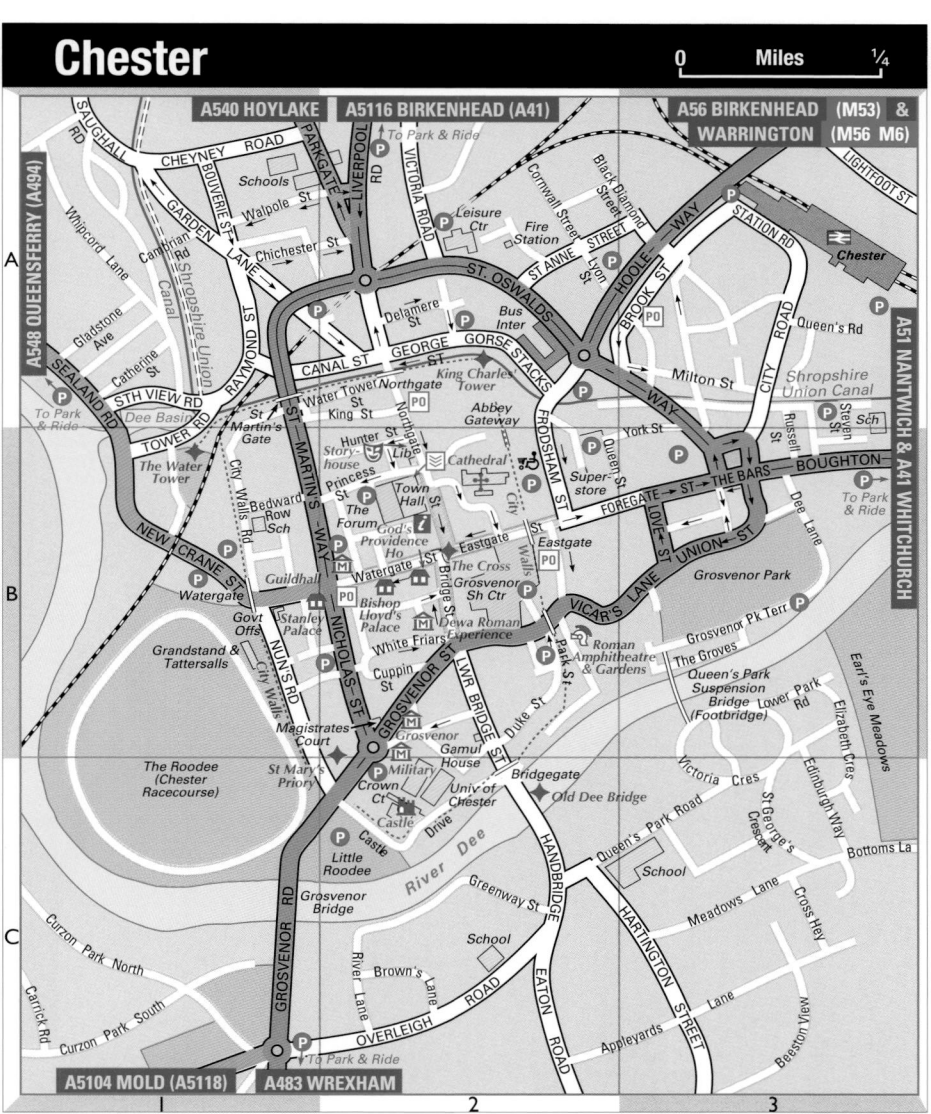

# Chichester

0   Miles   ¼

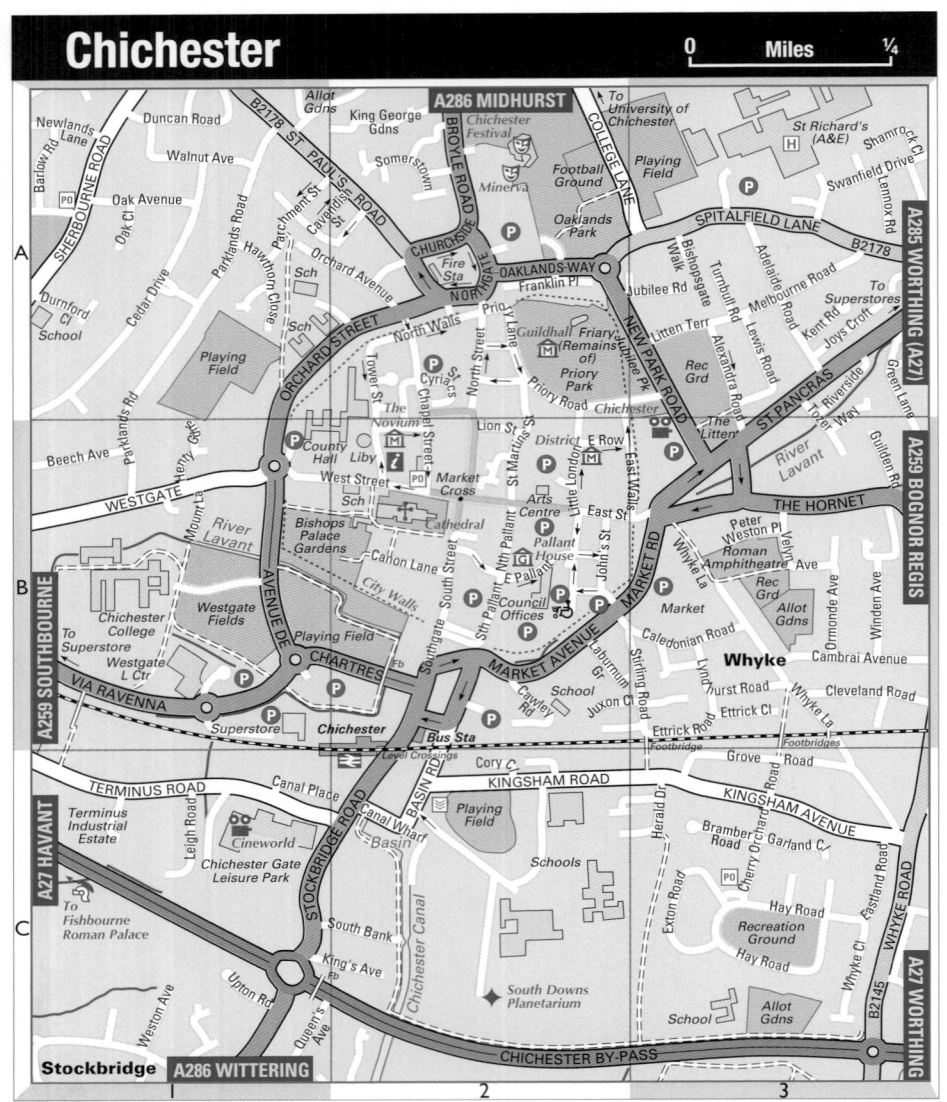

# Colchester

0   Miles   ¼

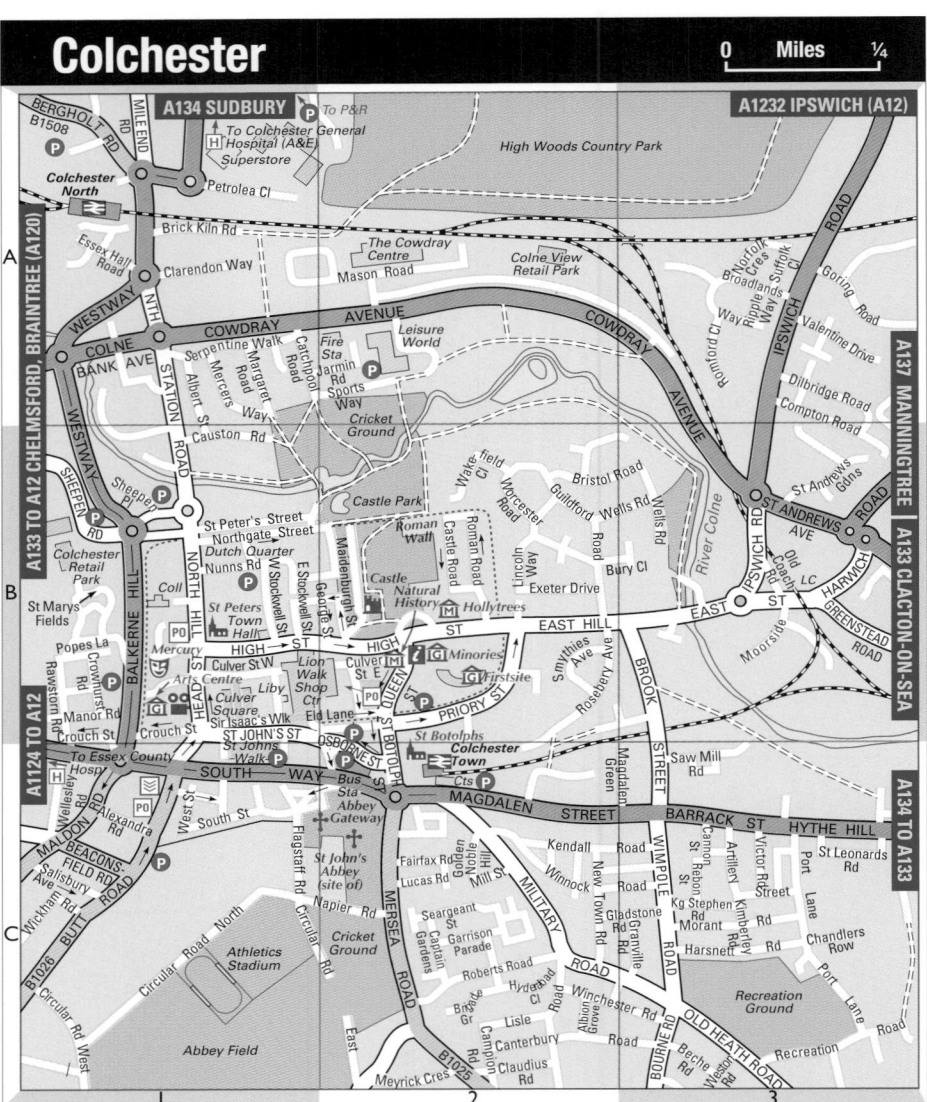

# Coventry

0   Miles   ¼

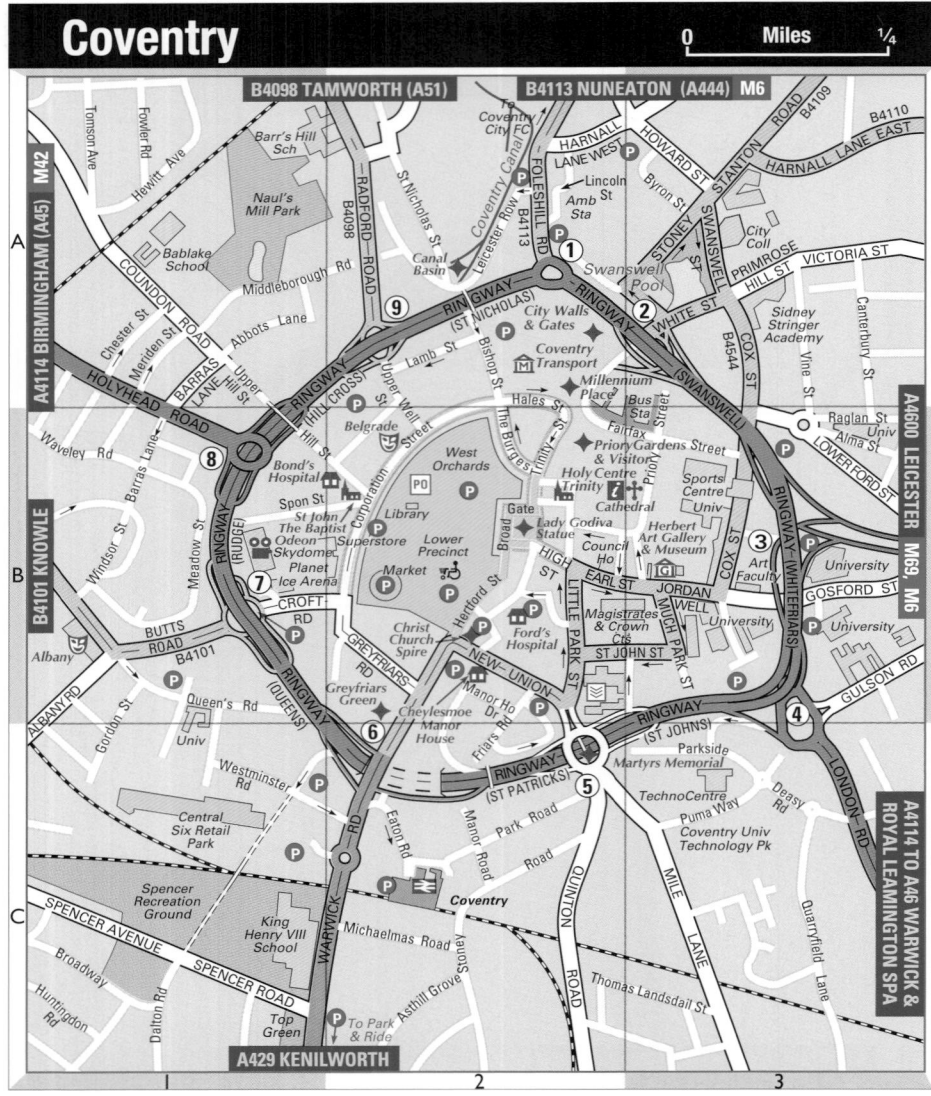

# Derby

0   Miles   ¼

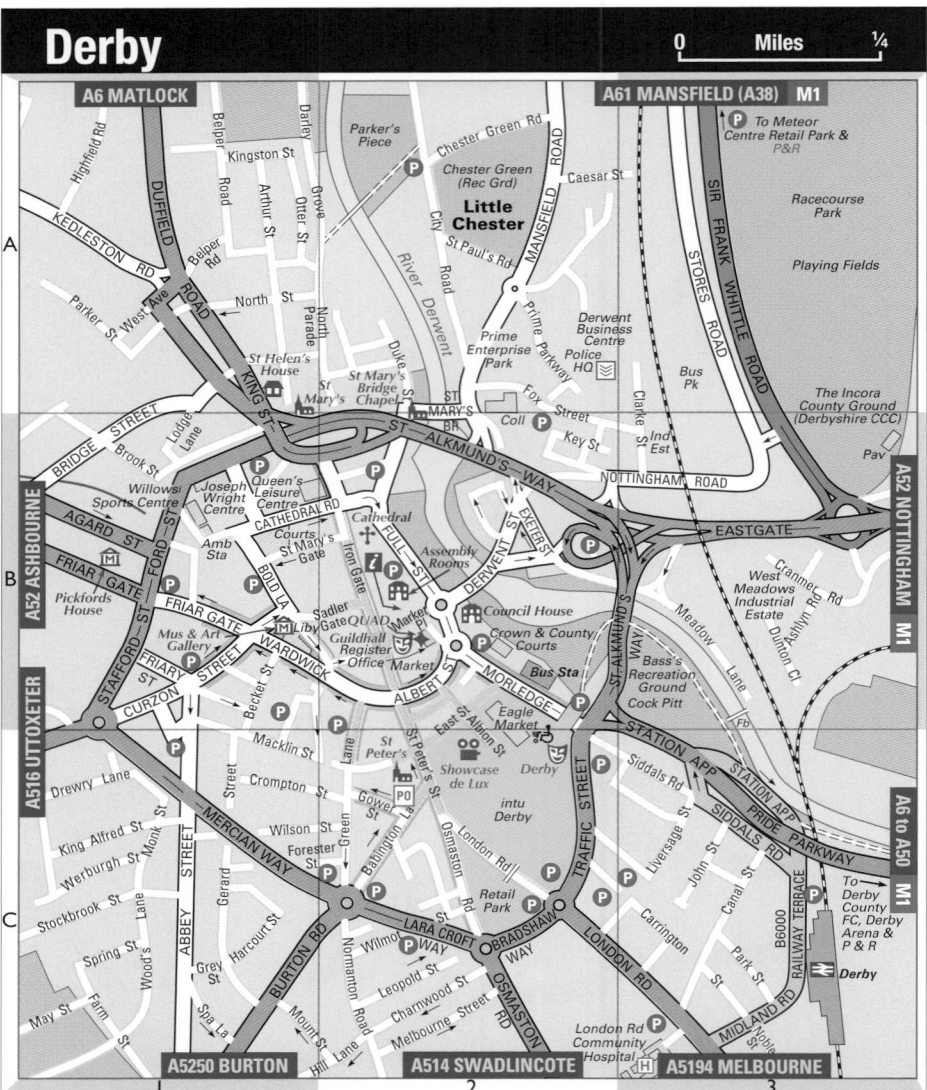

# Dorchester

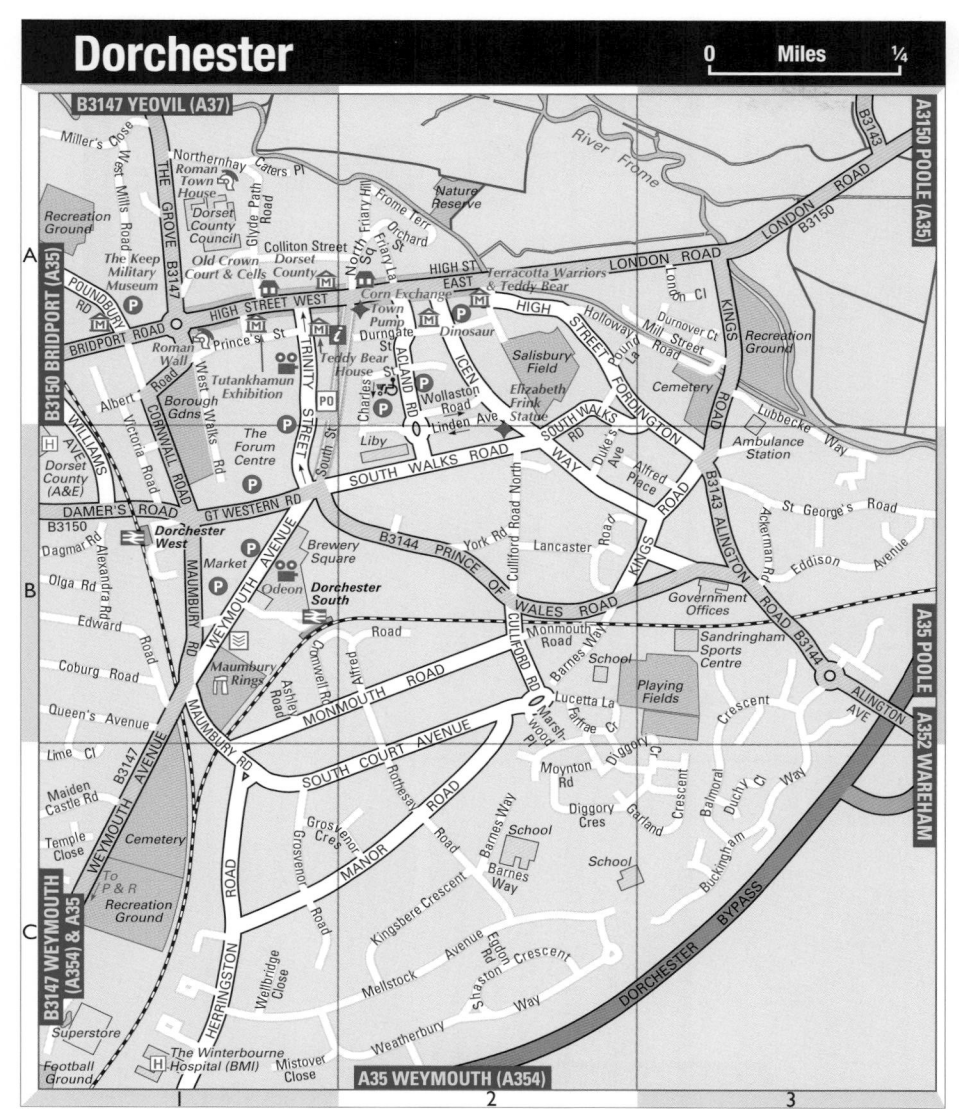

# Dumfries

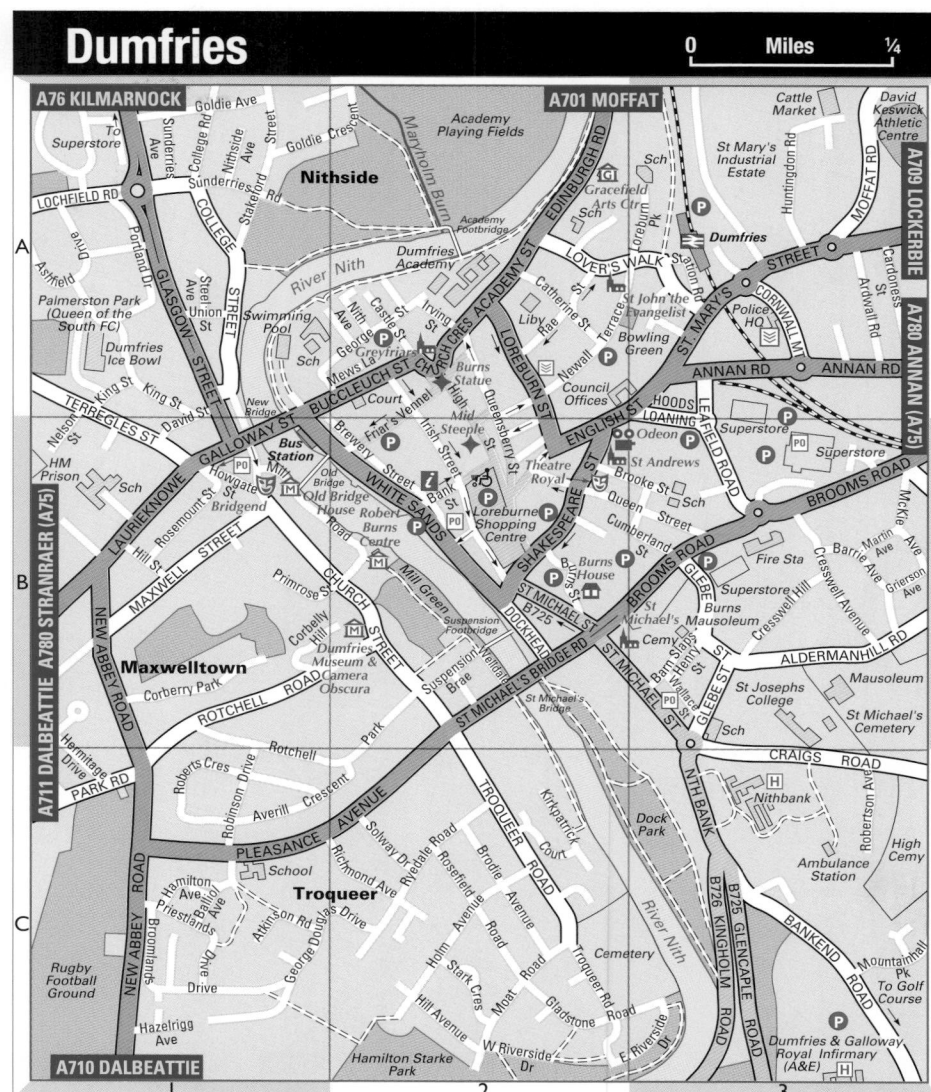

# Dundee

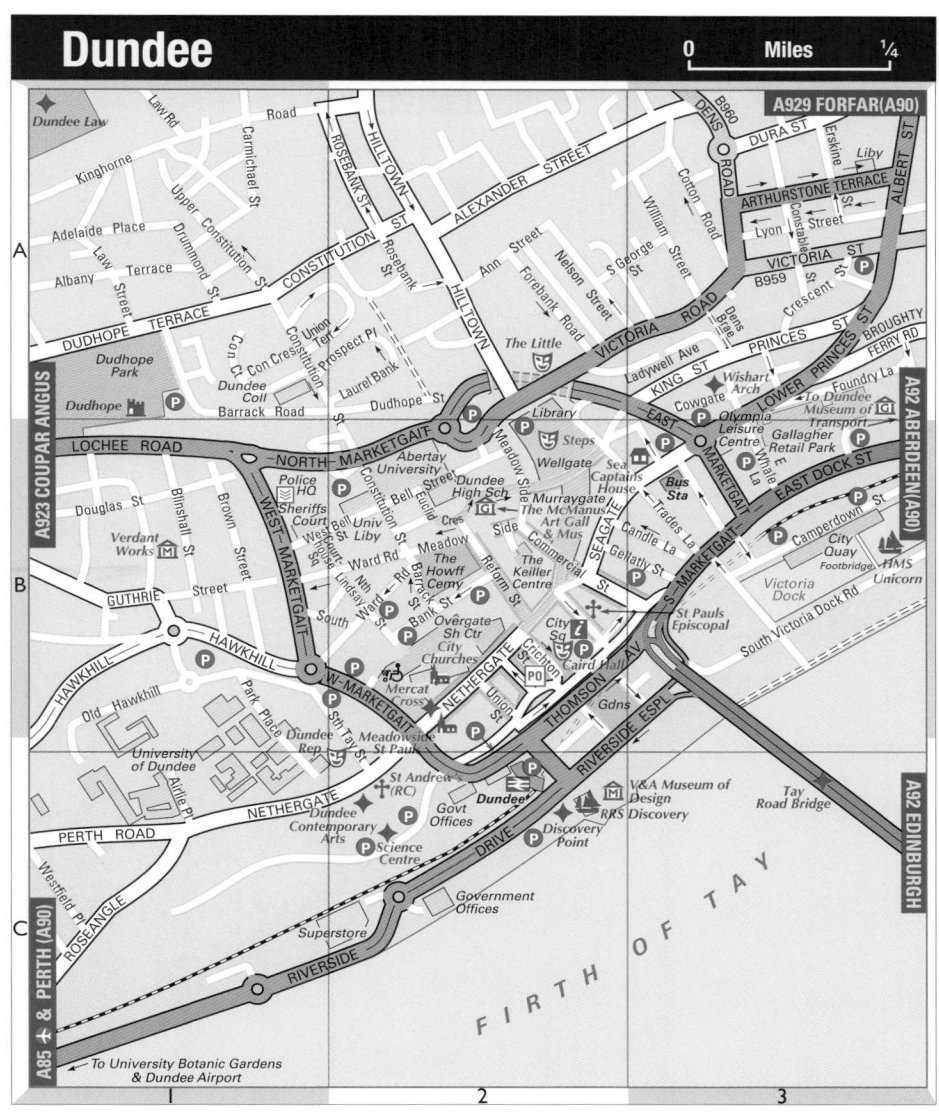

# Durham

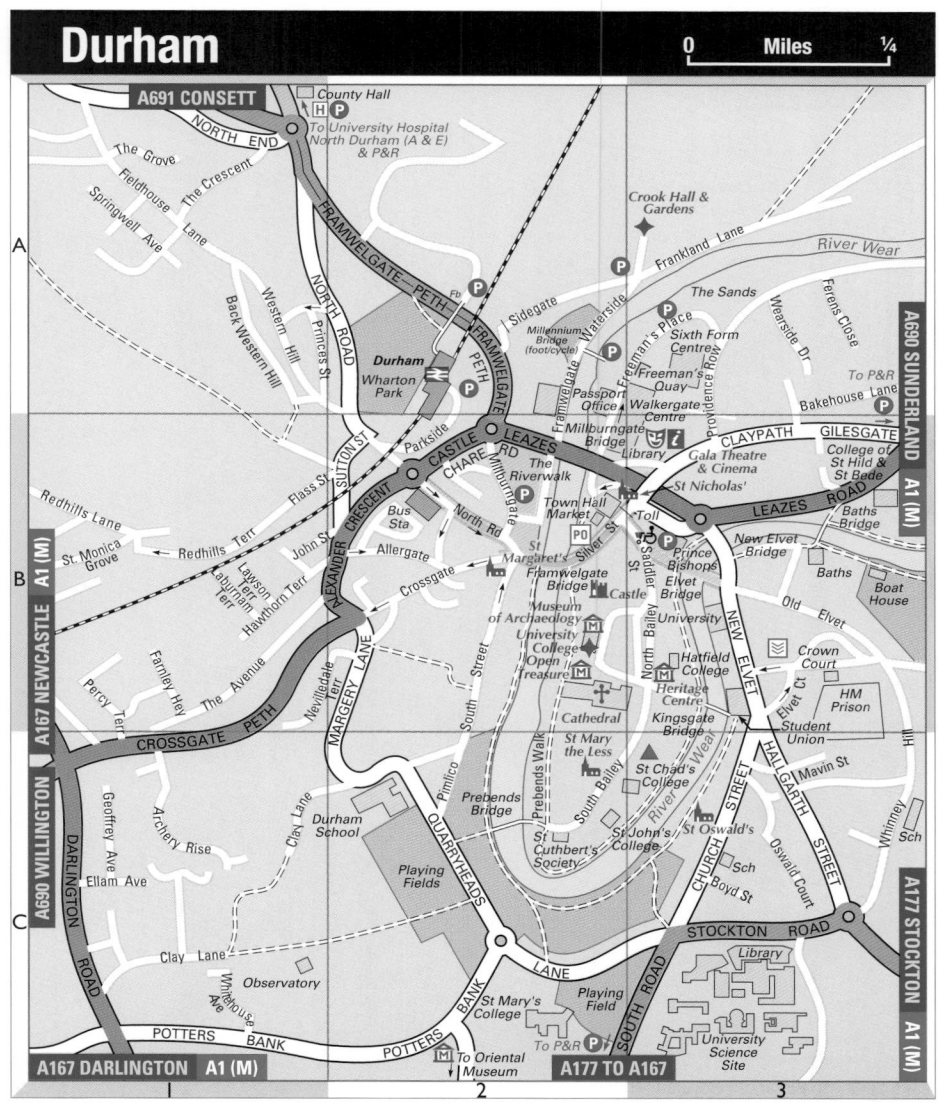

# Edinburgh

0   Miles   ¼

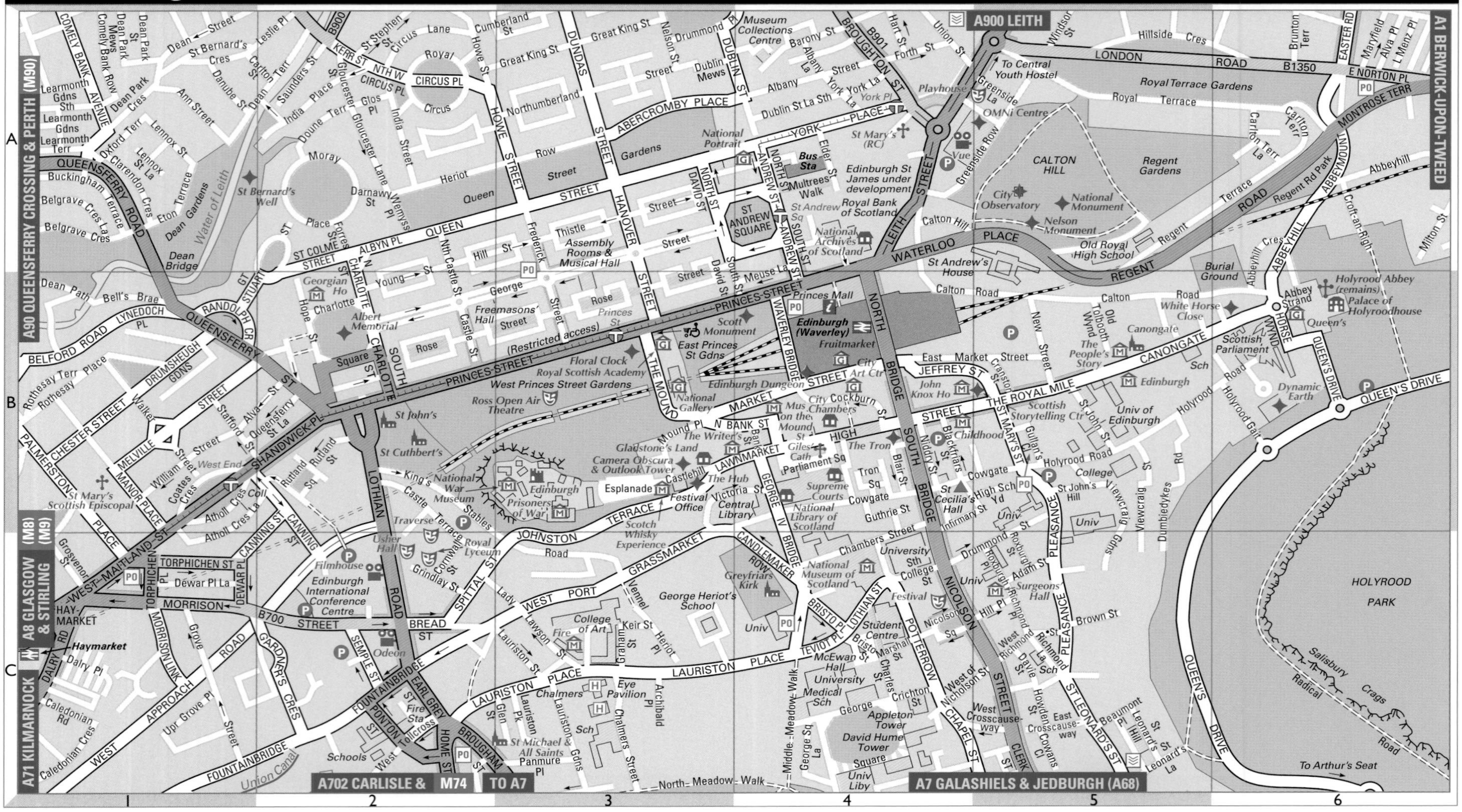

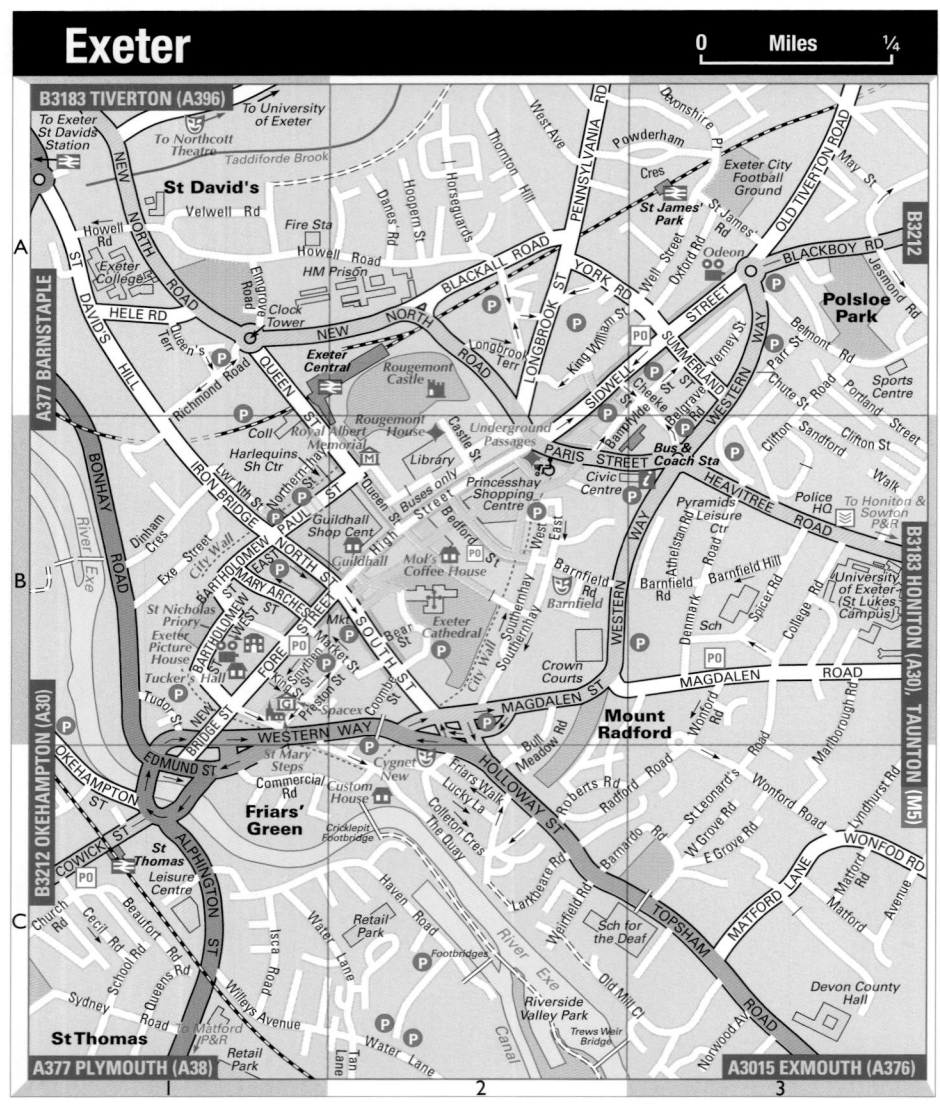

# Exeter

0   Miles   ¼

# Gloucester

0   Miles   ¼

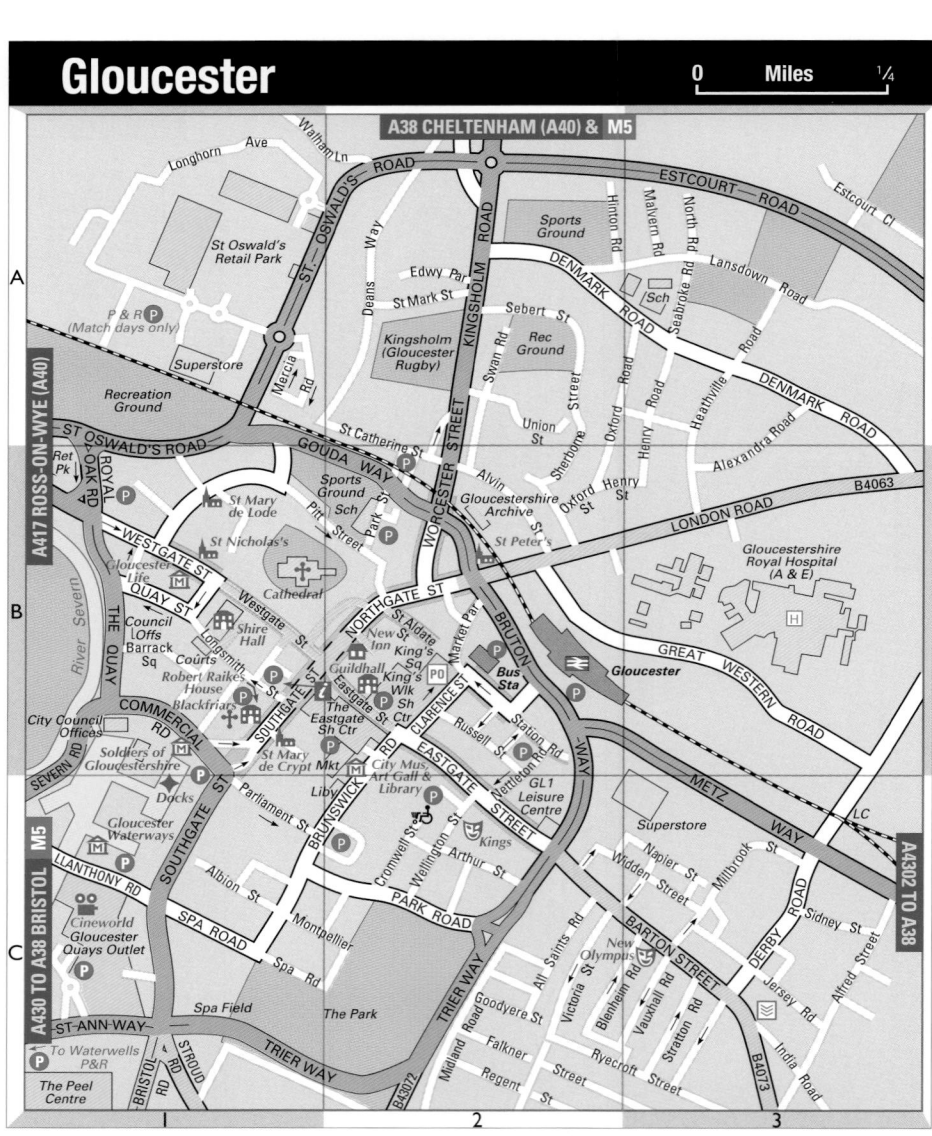

# Glasgow

0  Miles  ¼

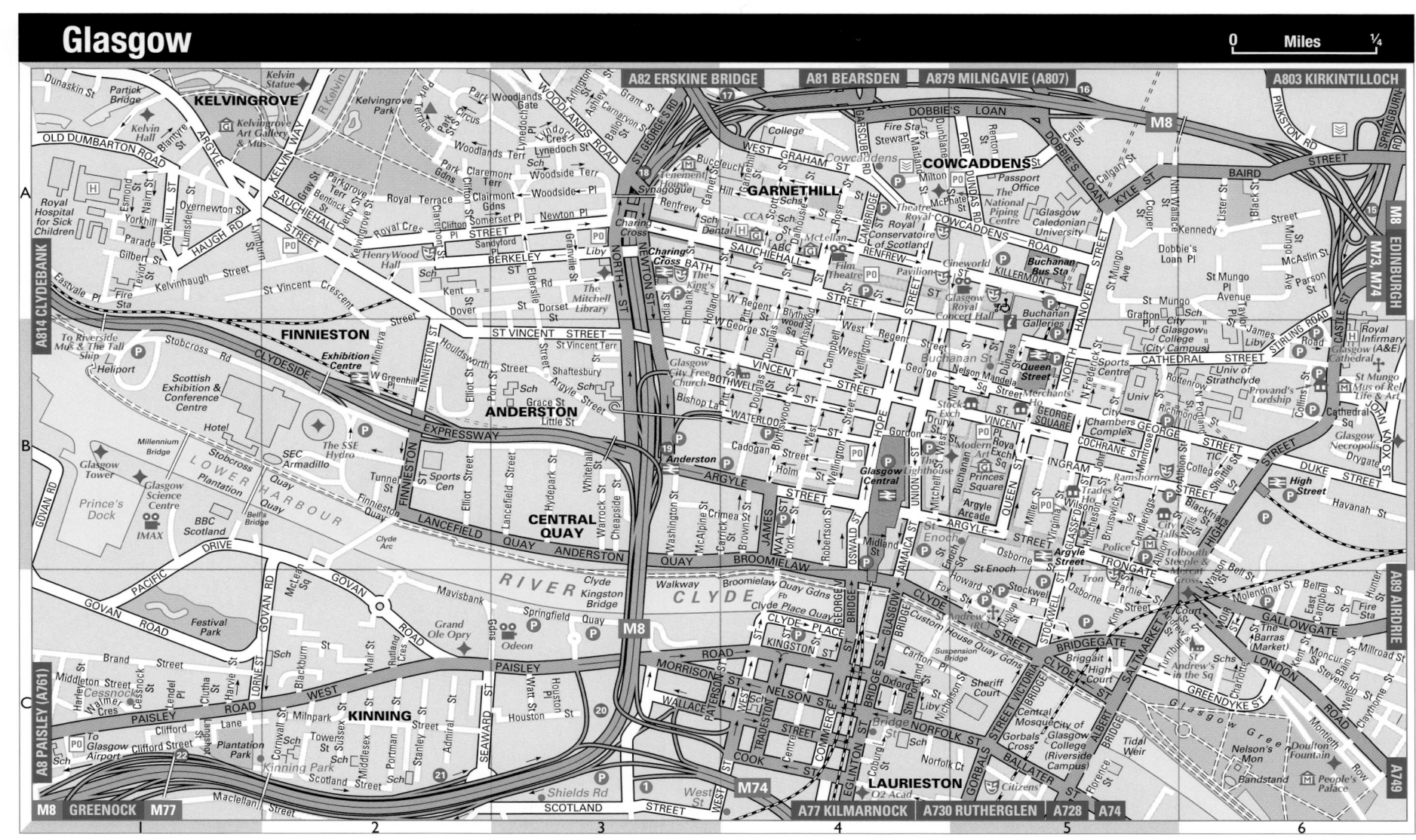

# Grimsby

0  Miles  ¼

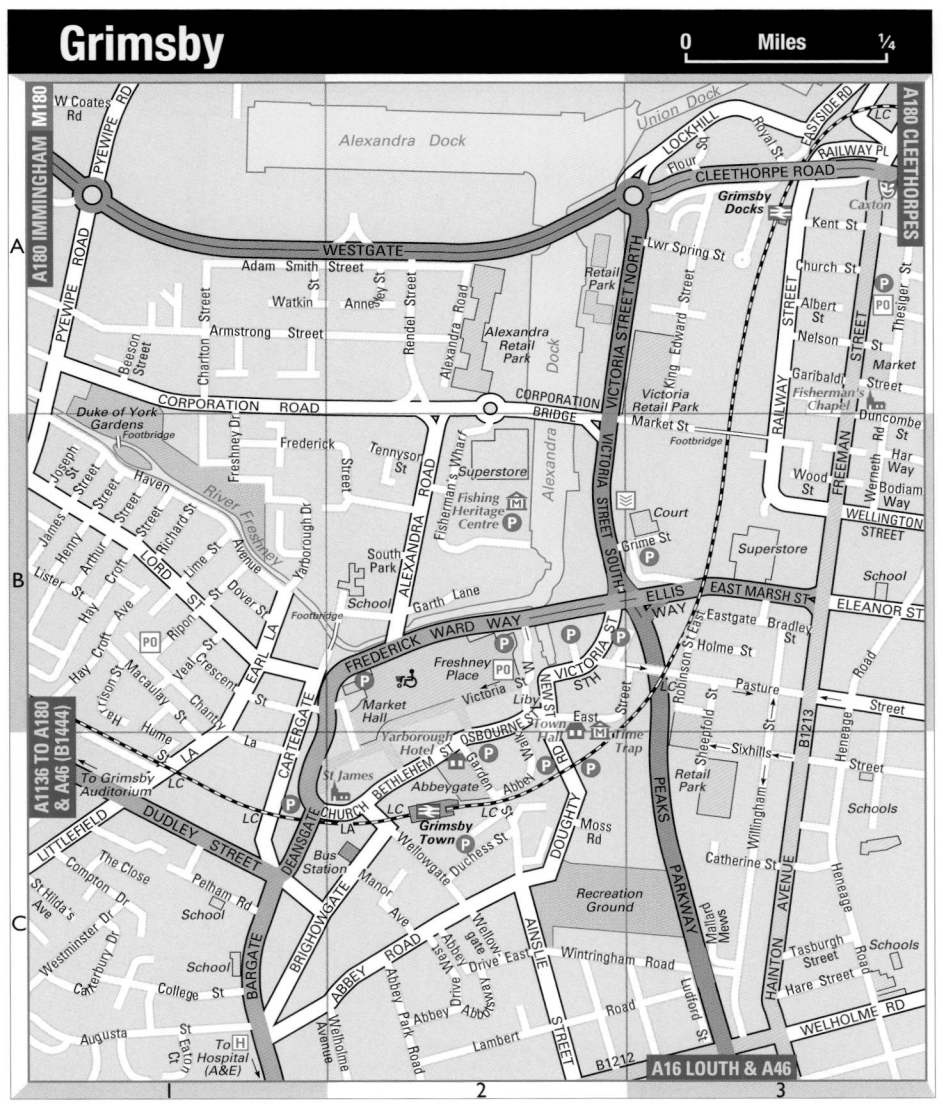

# Harrogate

0  Miles  ¼

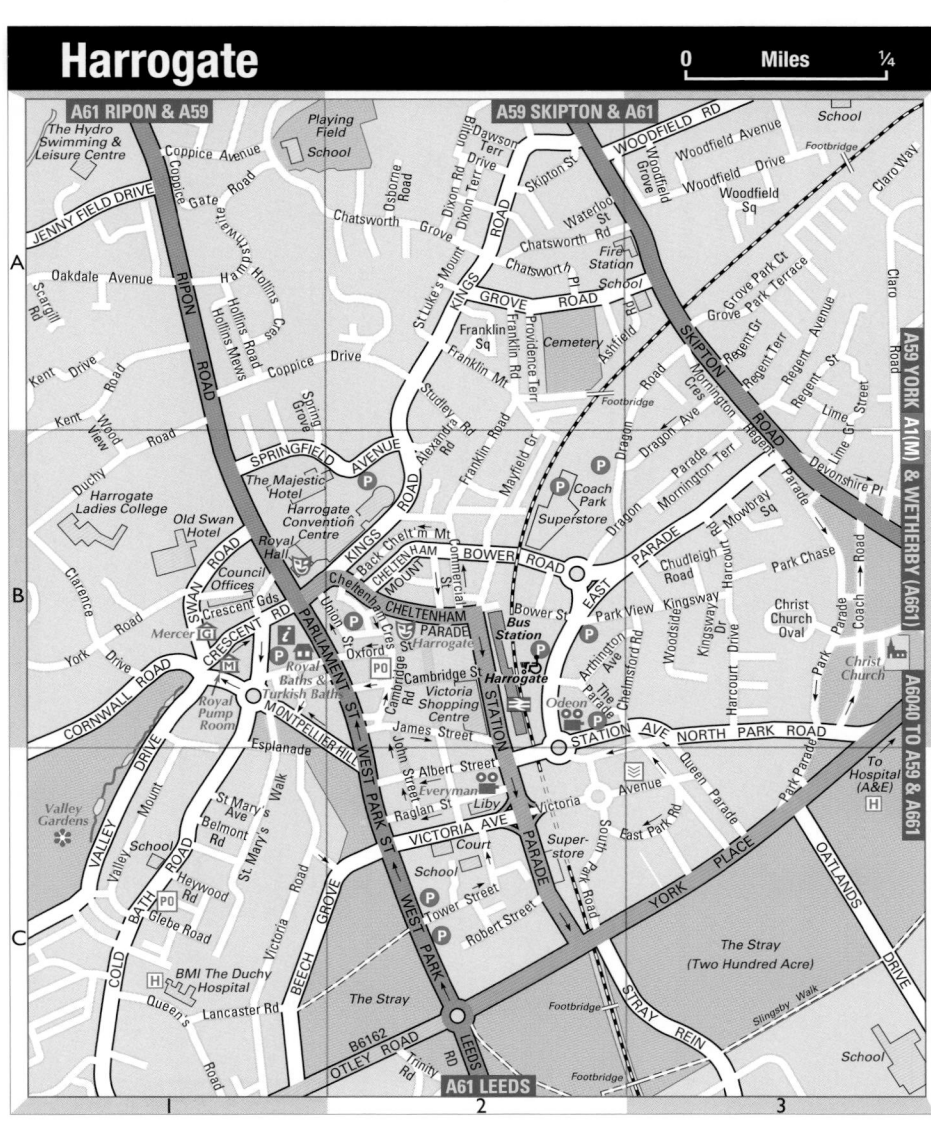

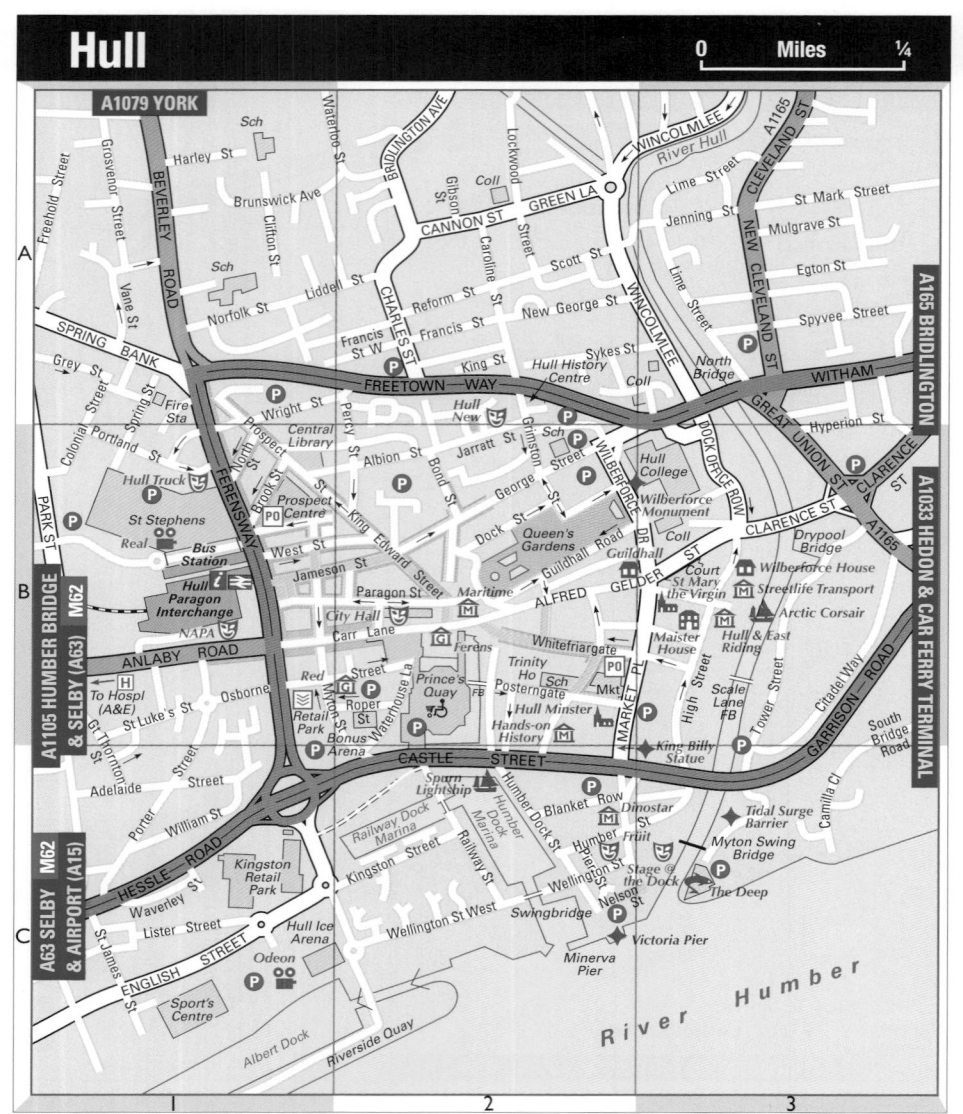

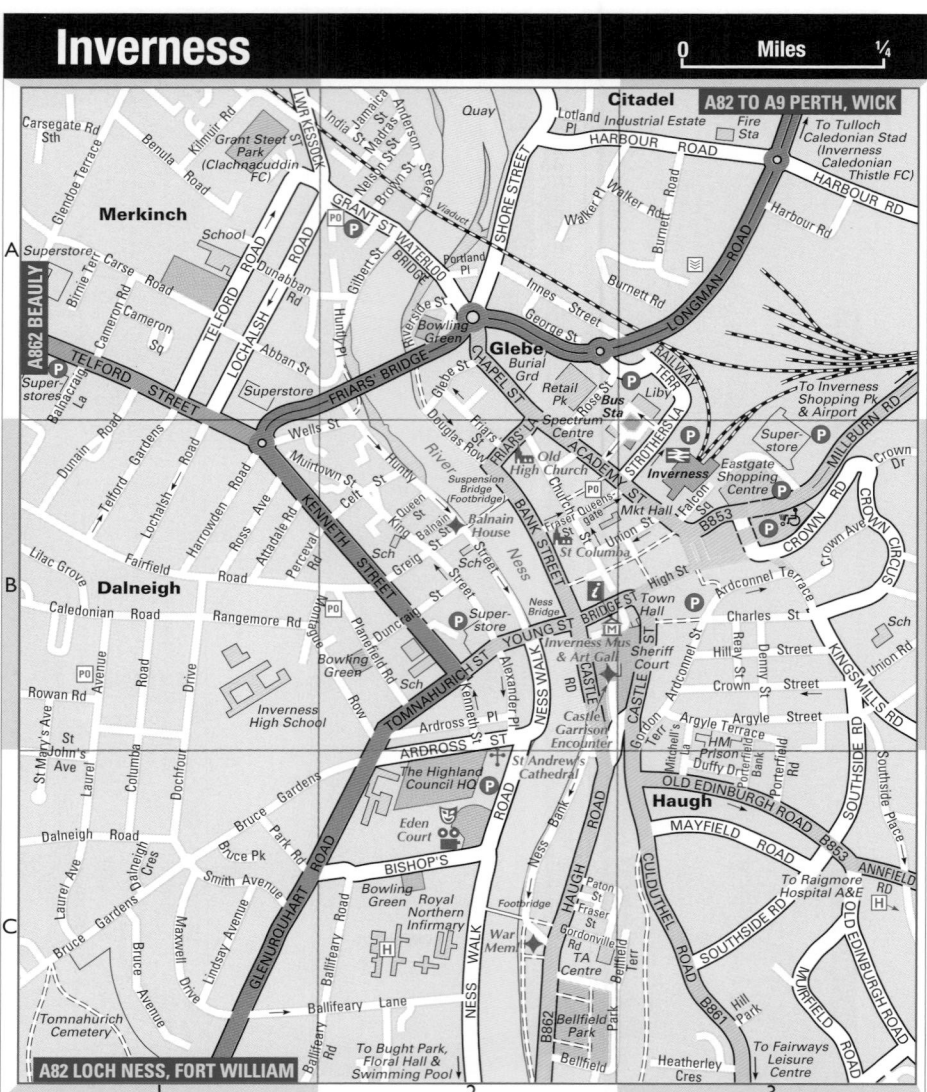

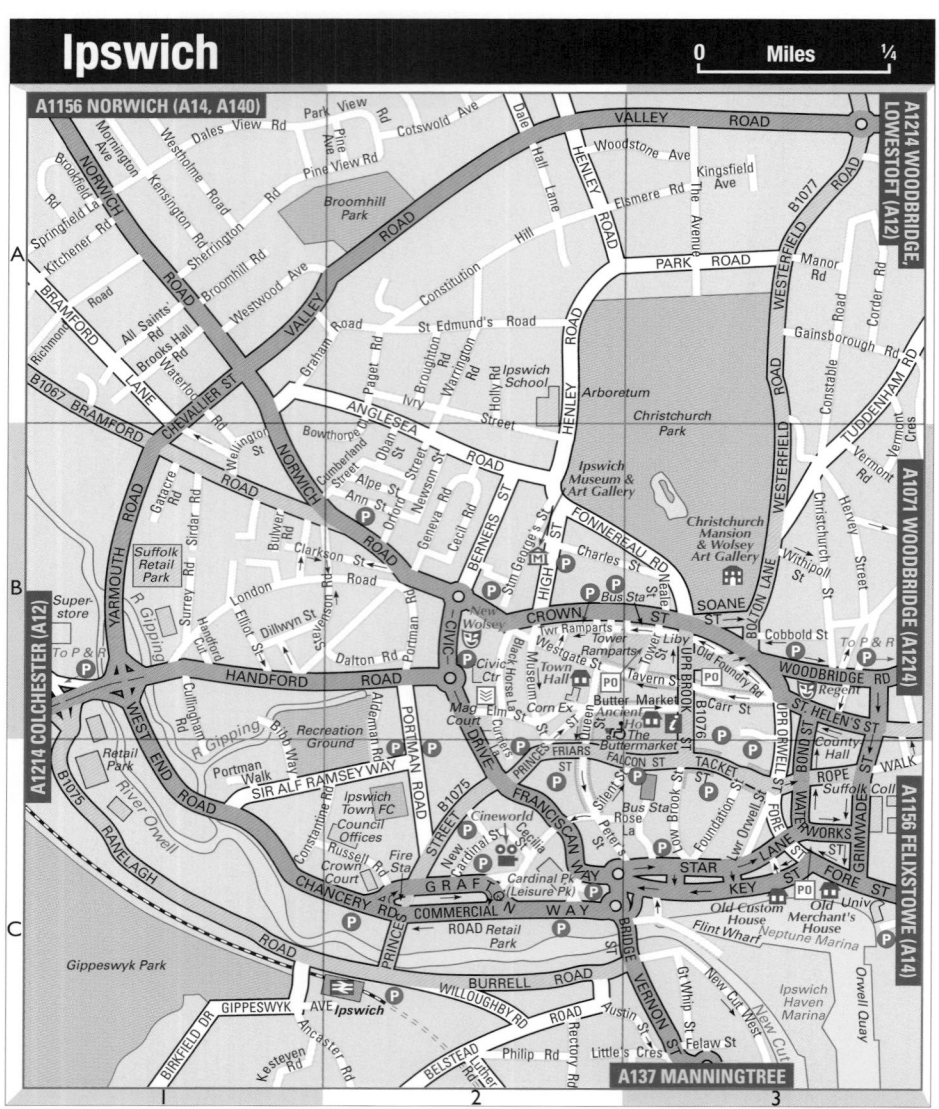

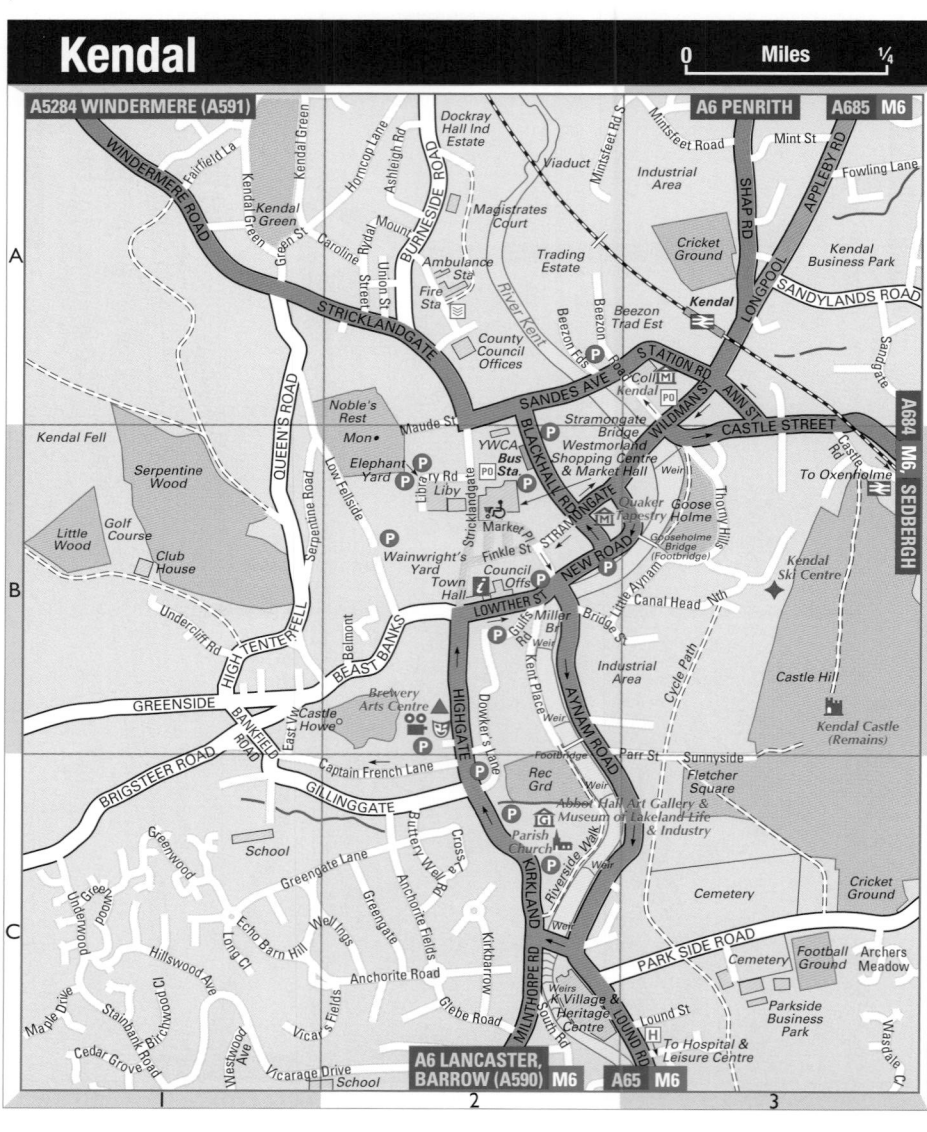

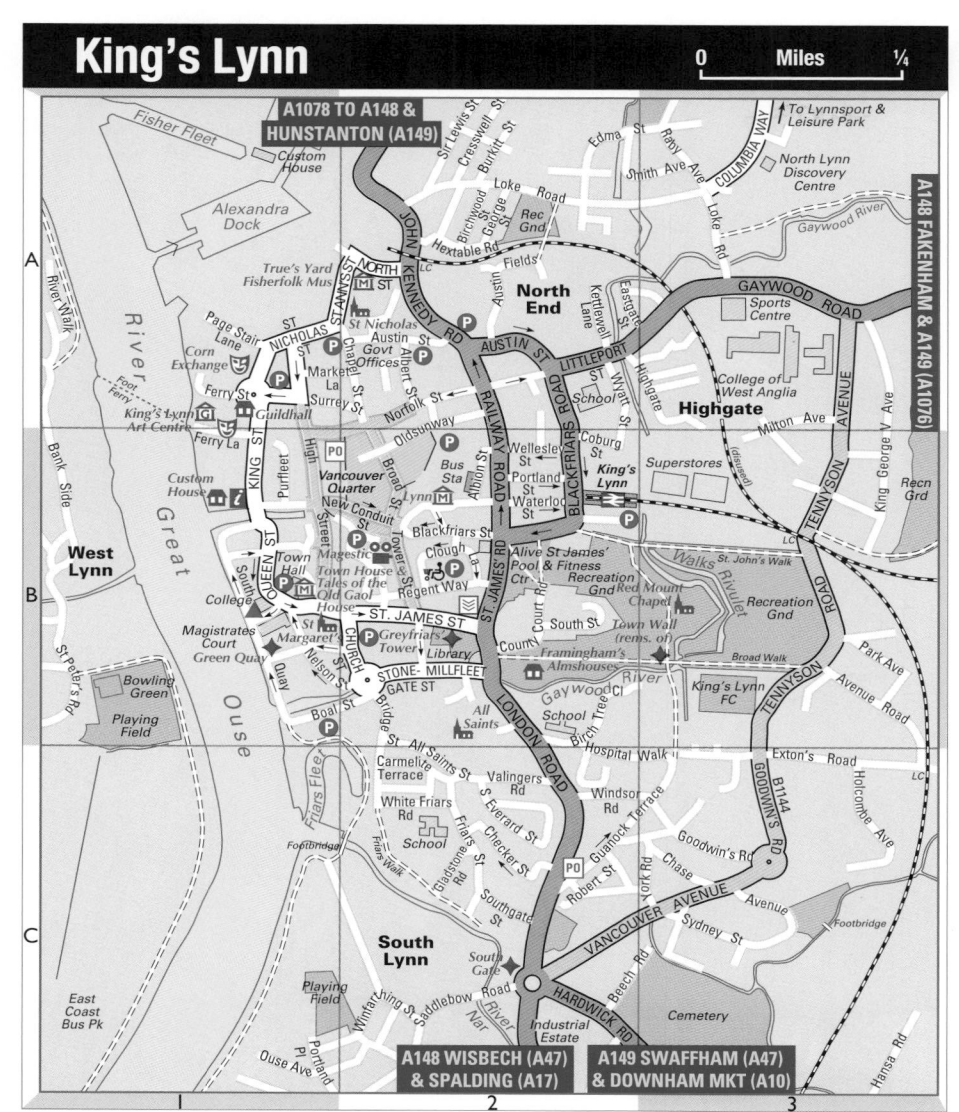

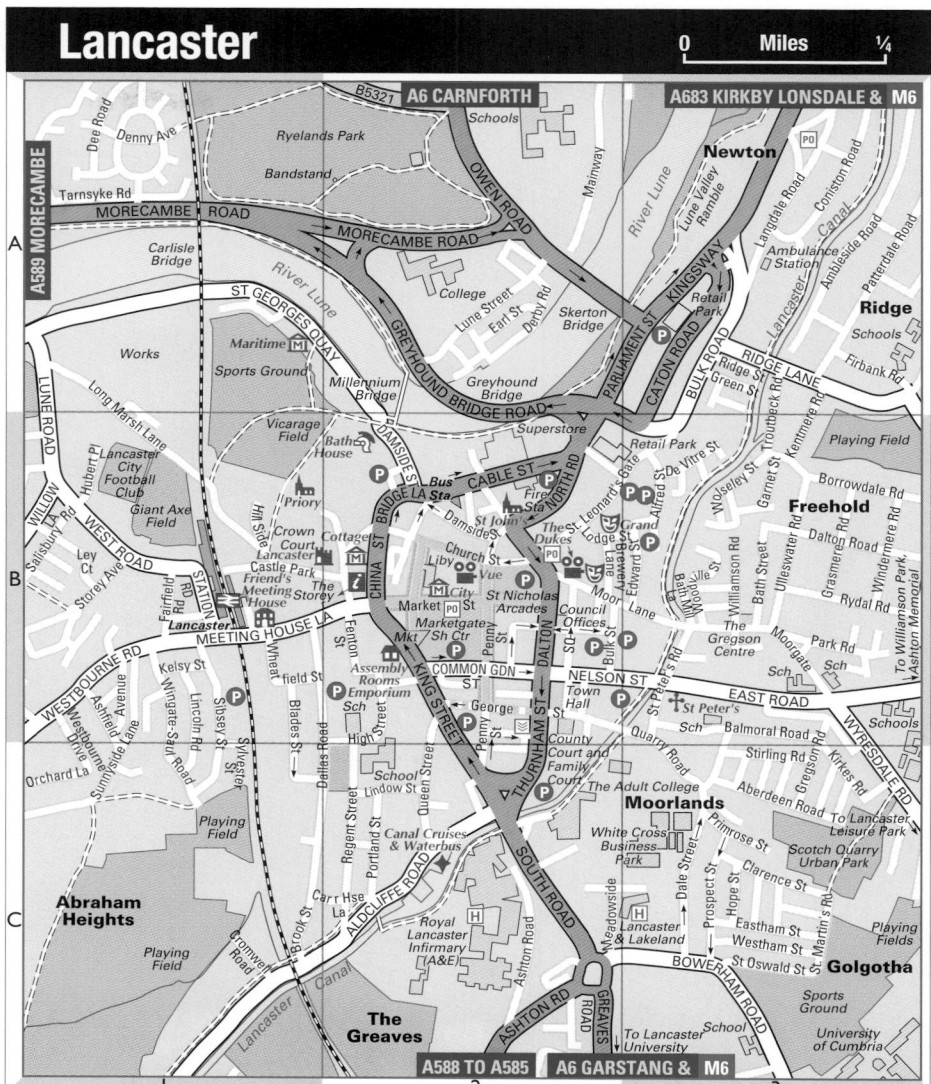

## King's Lynn

## Lancaster

## Leeds

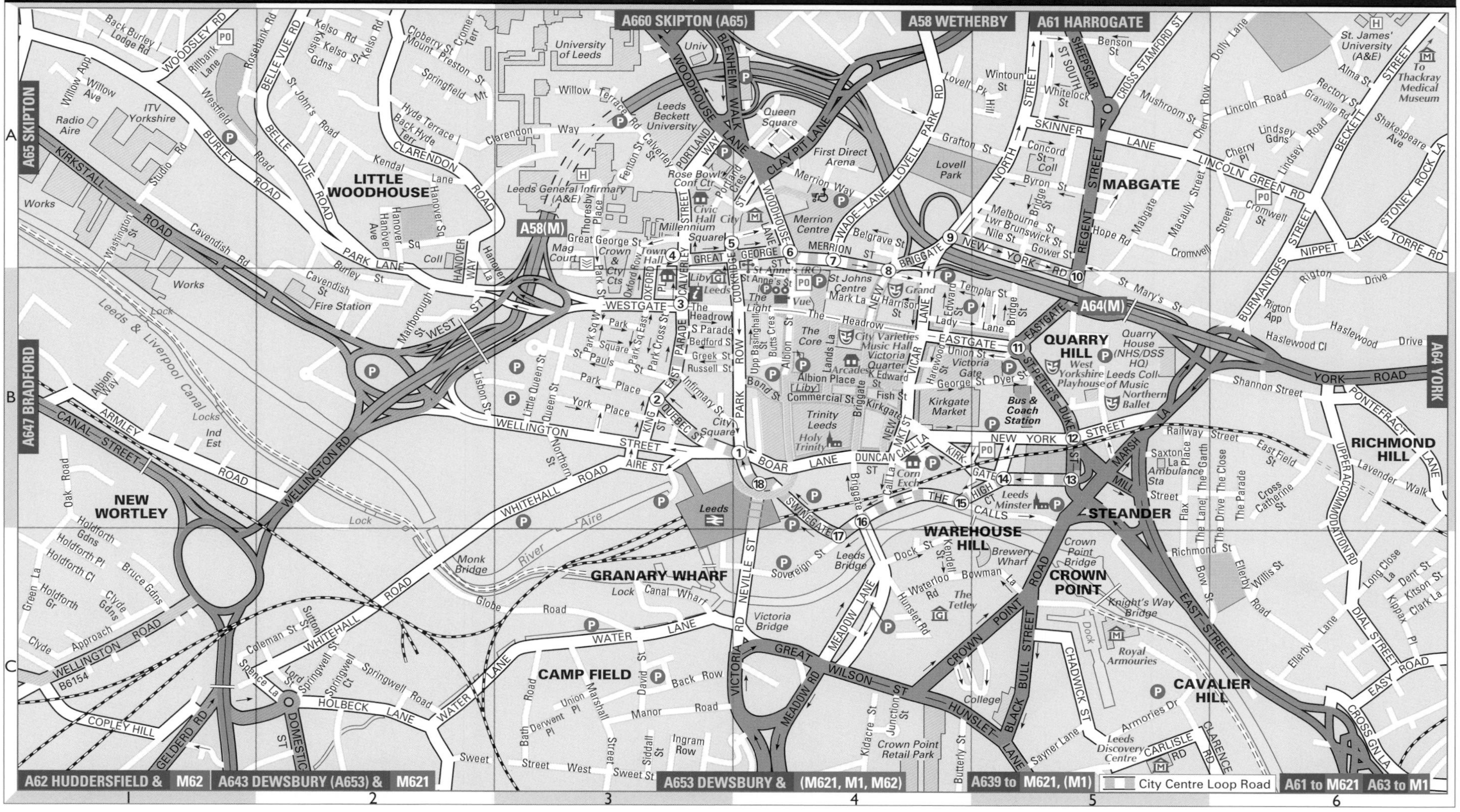

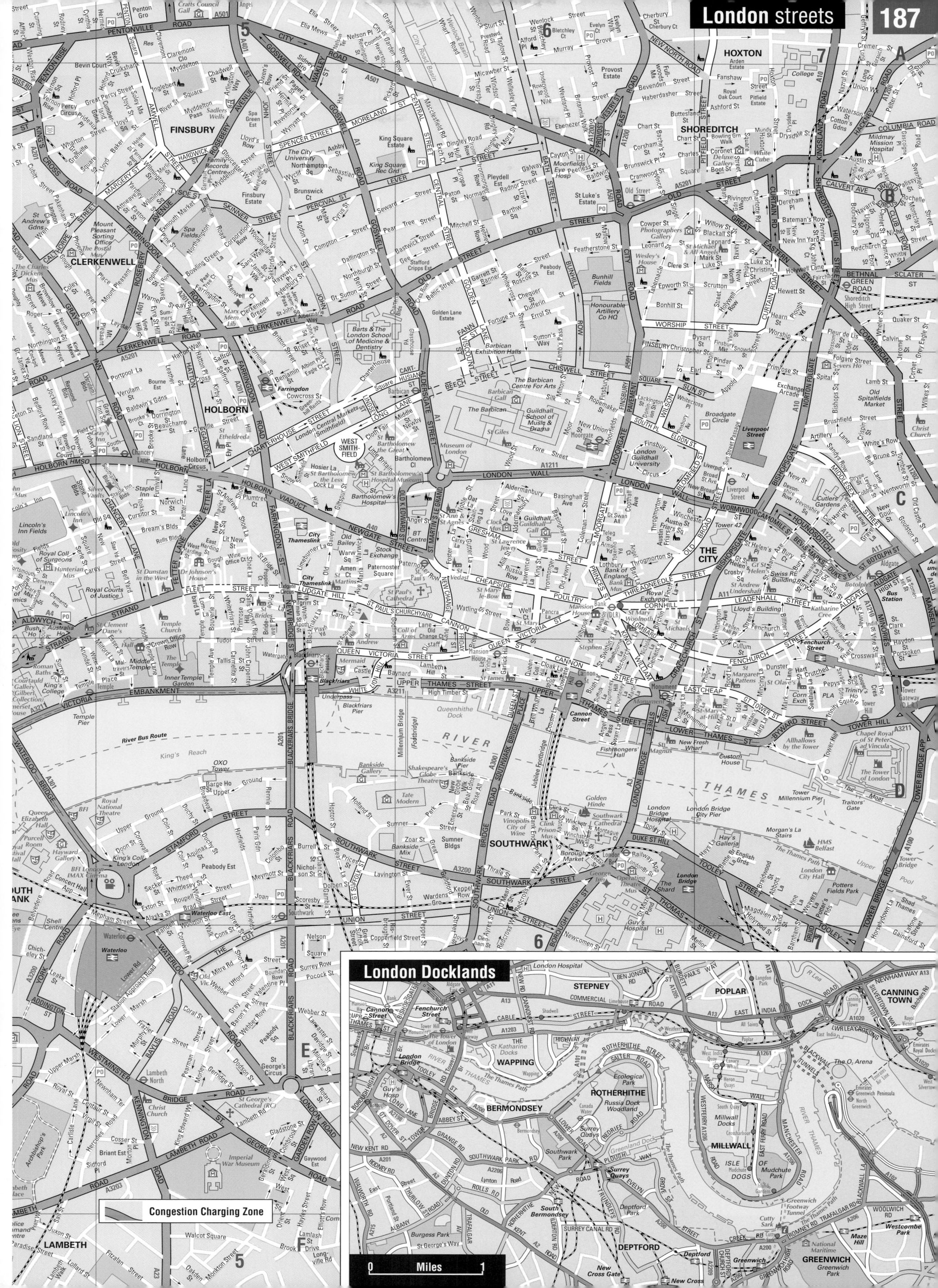

Congestion Charging Zone

**London Docklands**

0  Miles  1

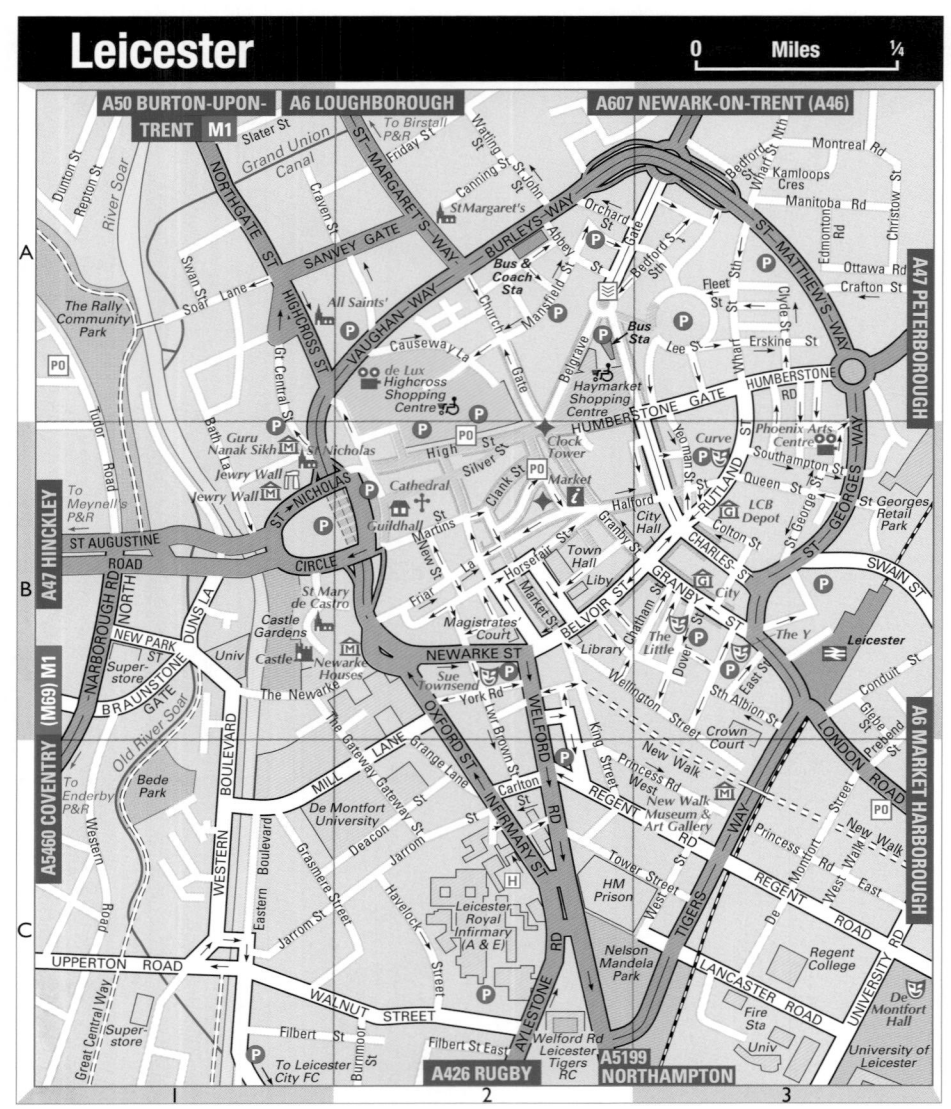

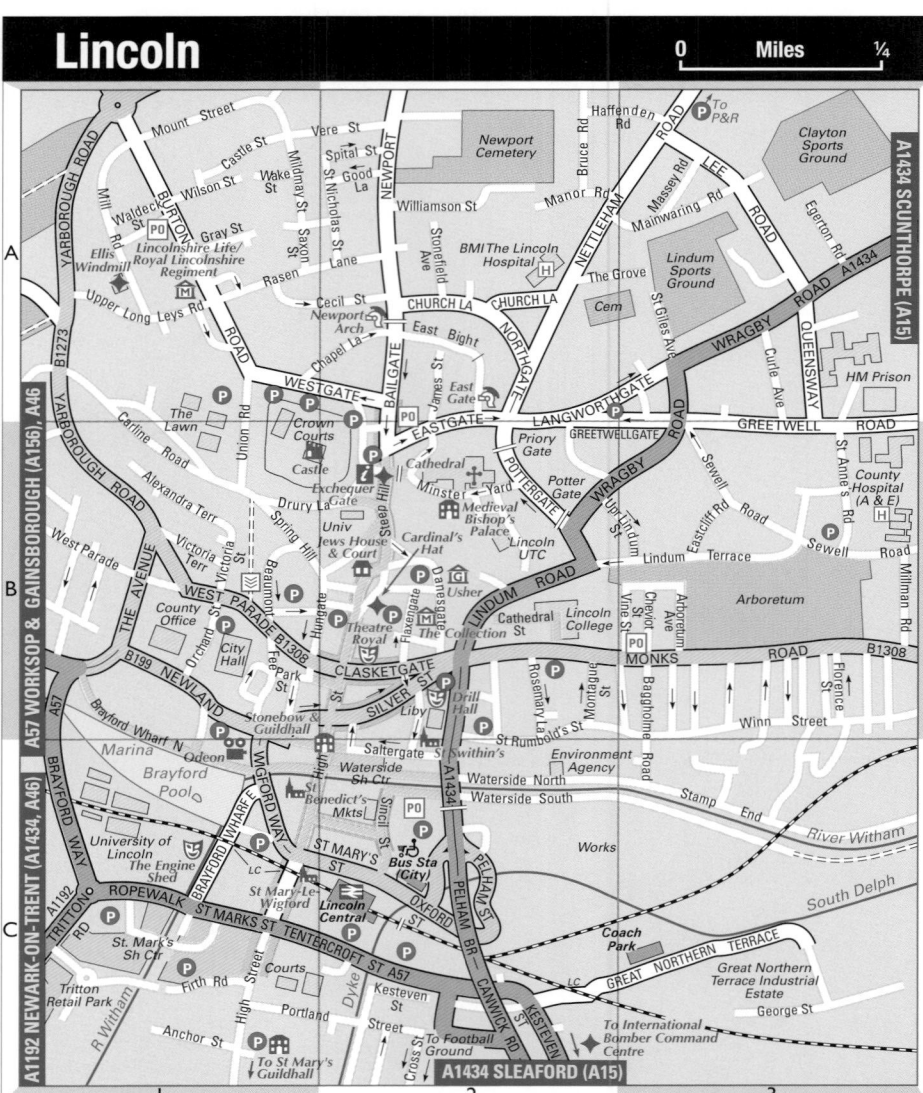

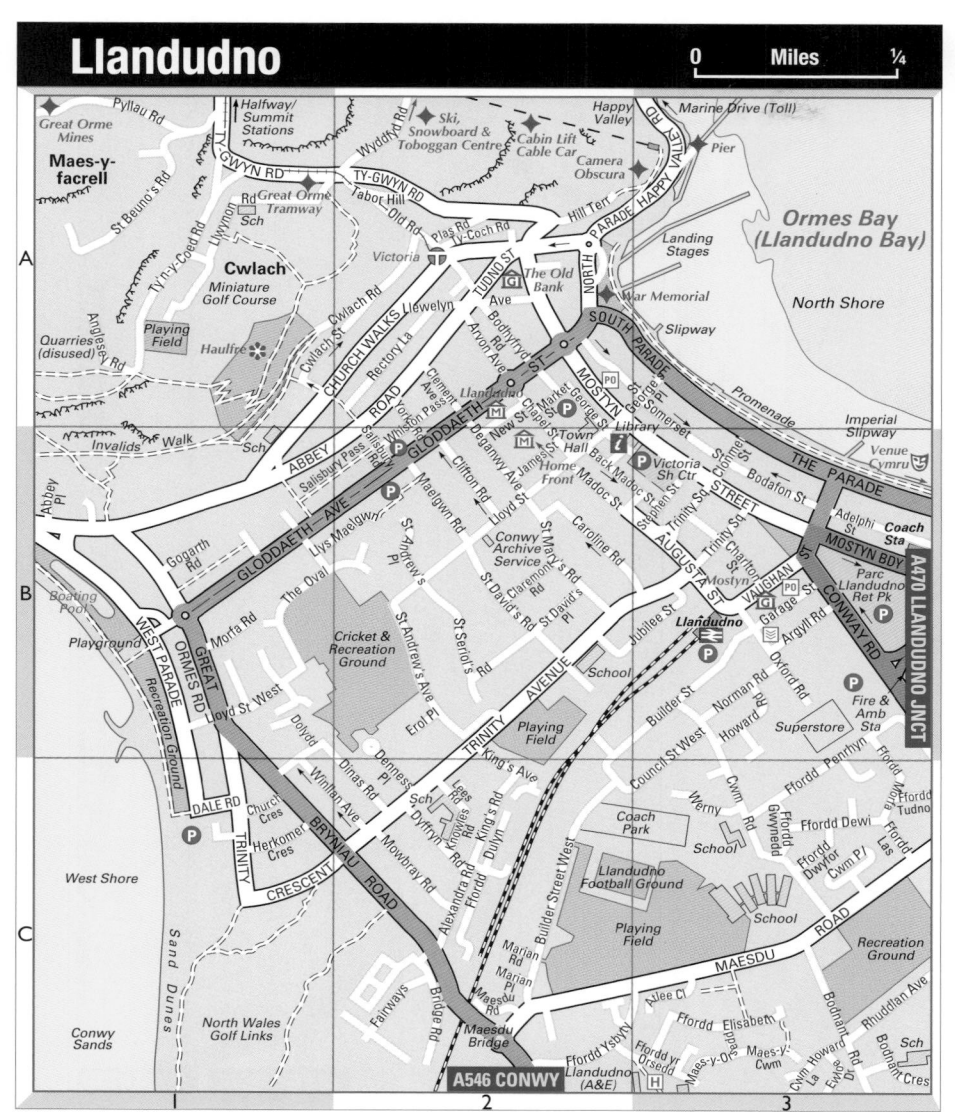

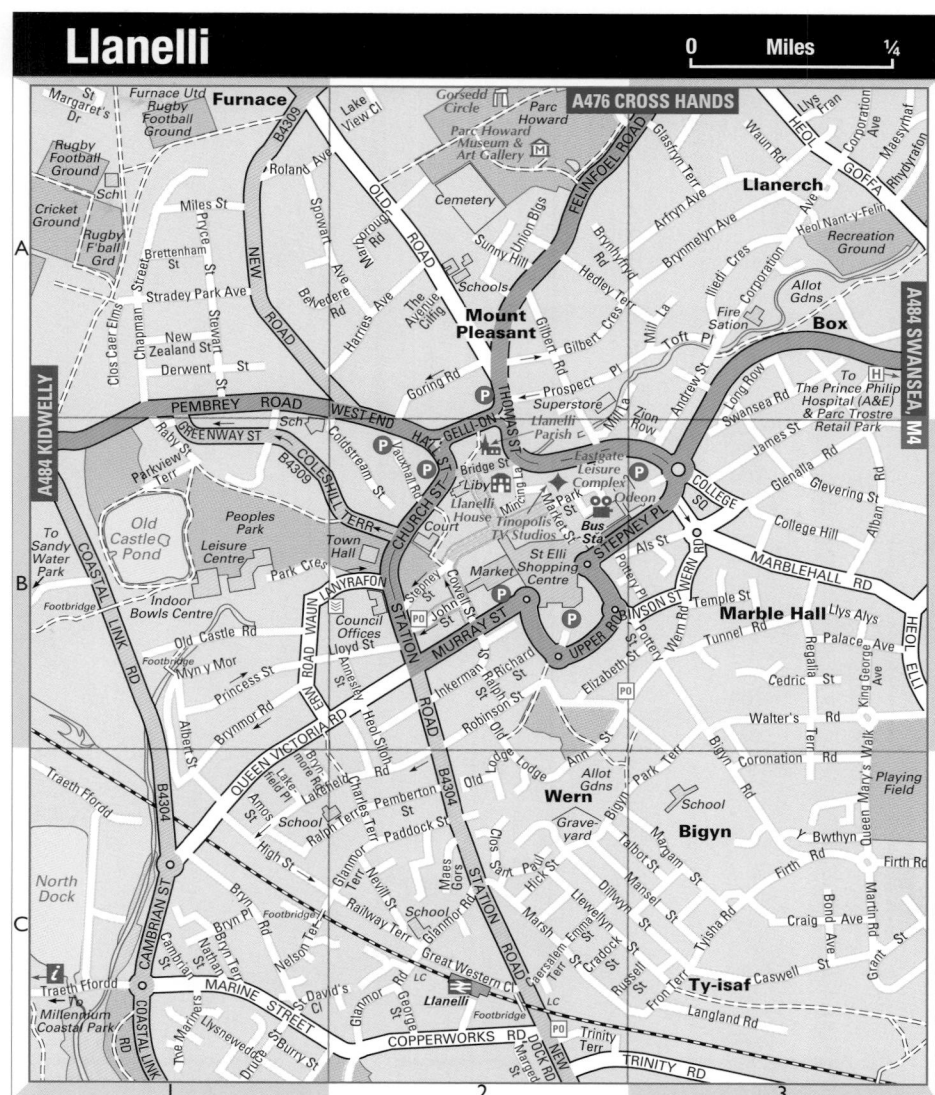

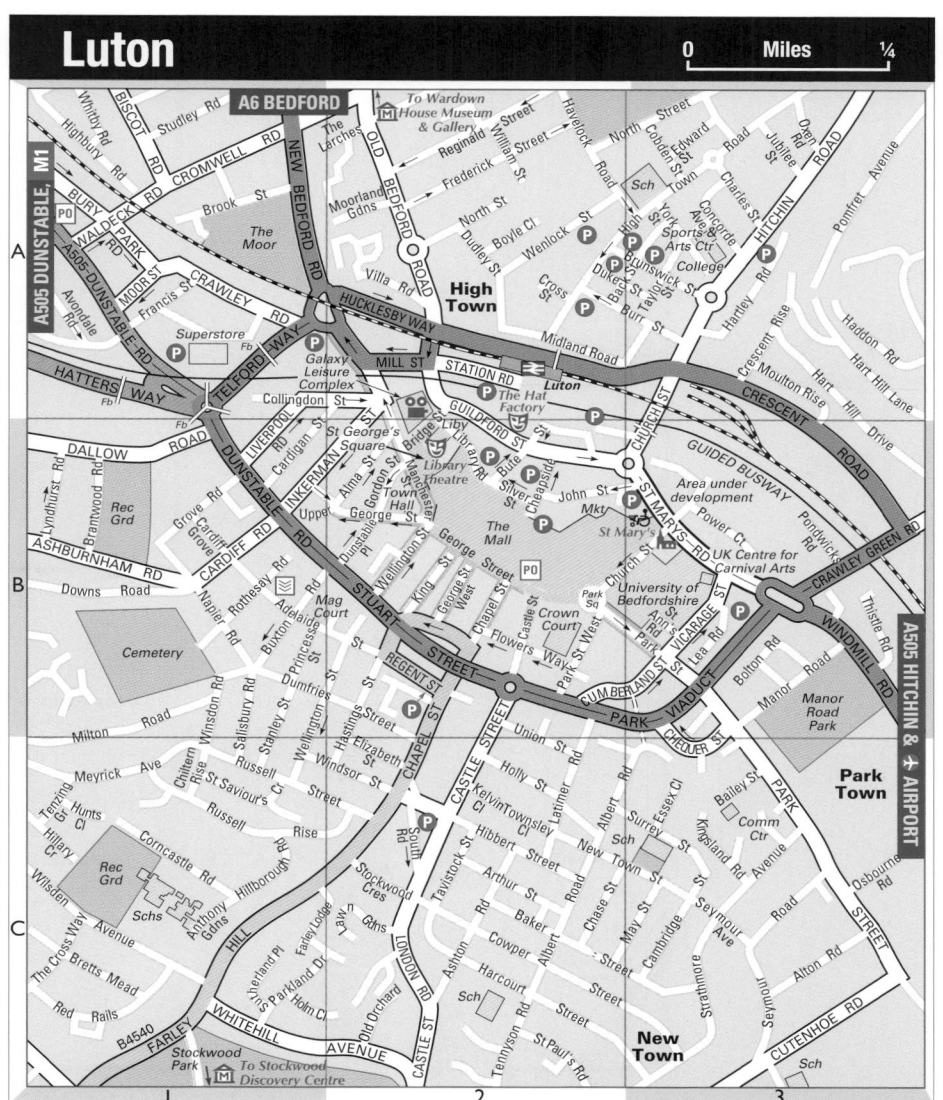

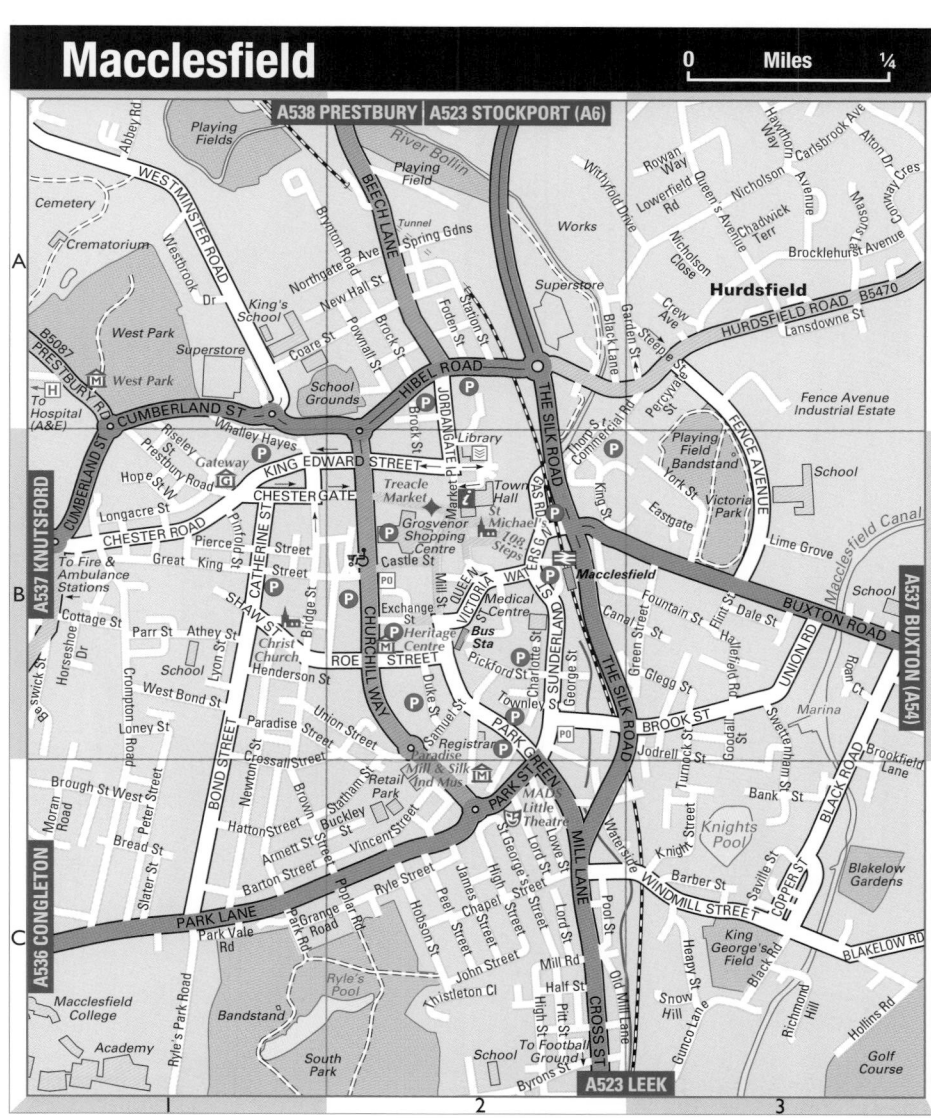

## Manchester

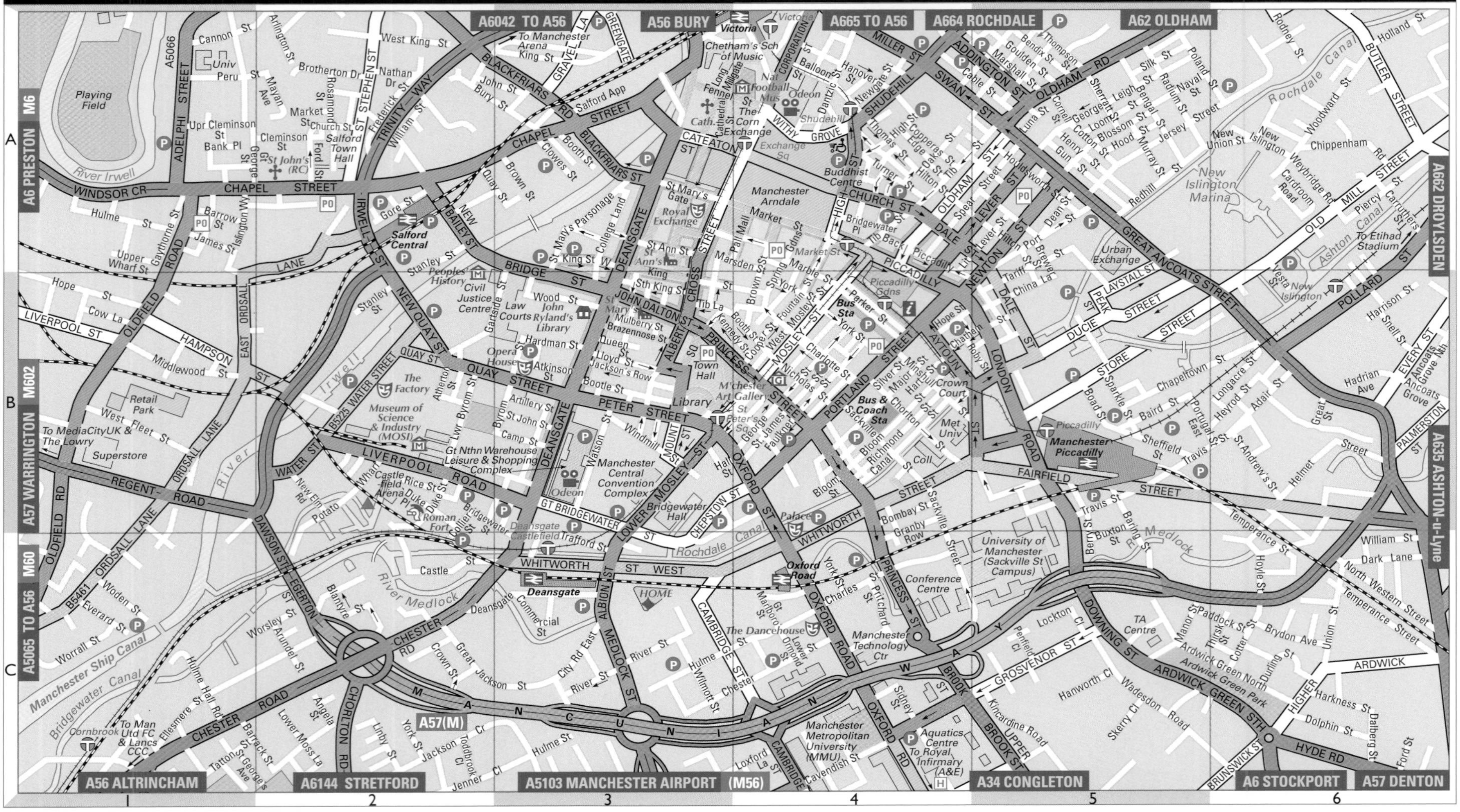

0     Miles     ¼

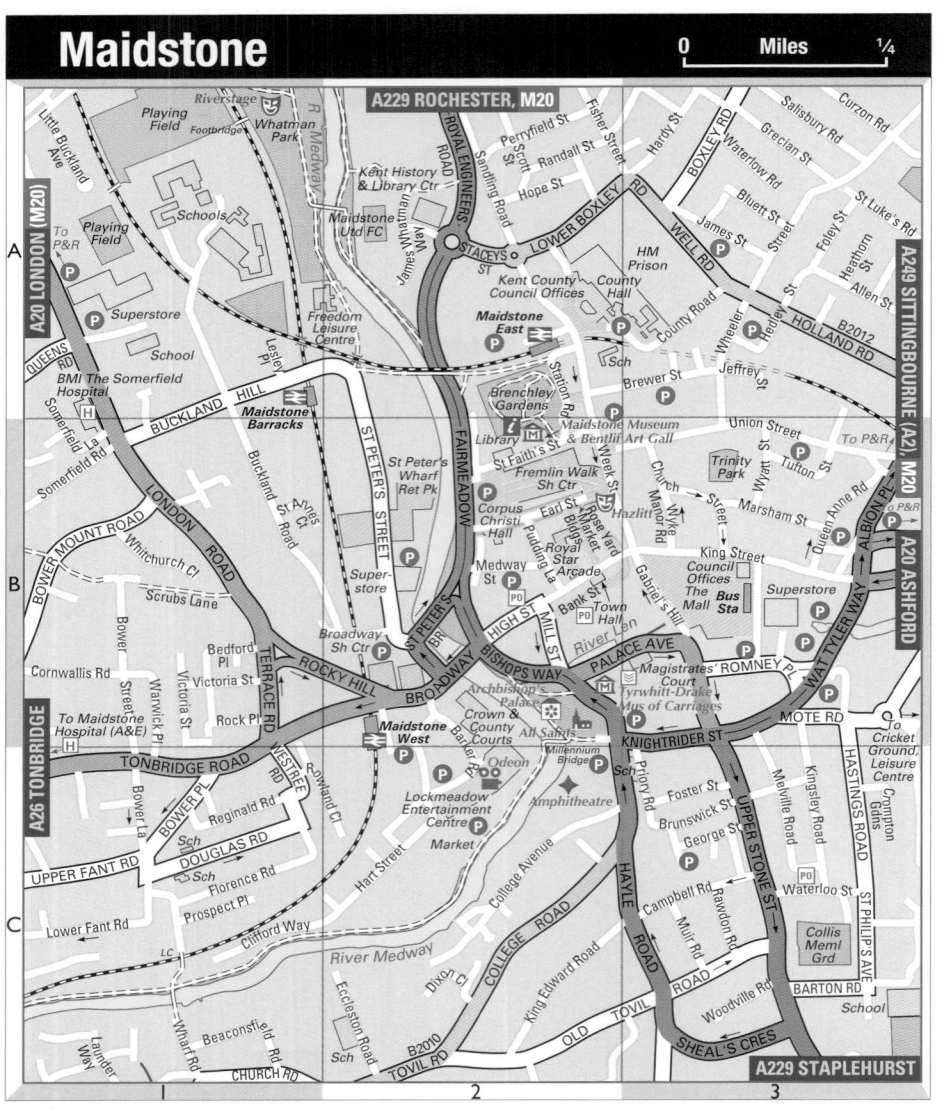

## Maidstone

0     Miles     ¼

## Merthyr Tydfil / Merthyr Tudful

0     Miles     ¼

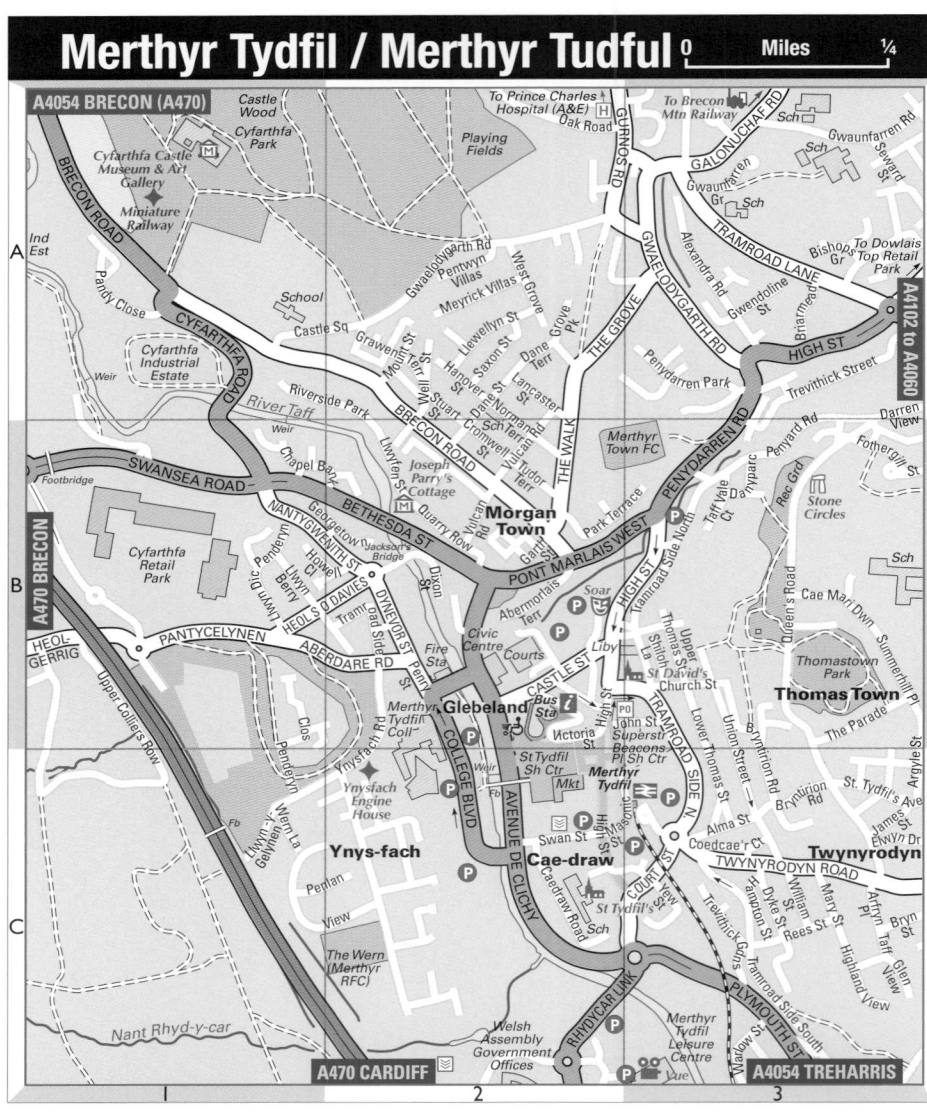

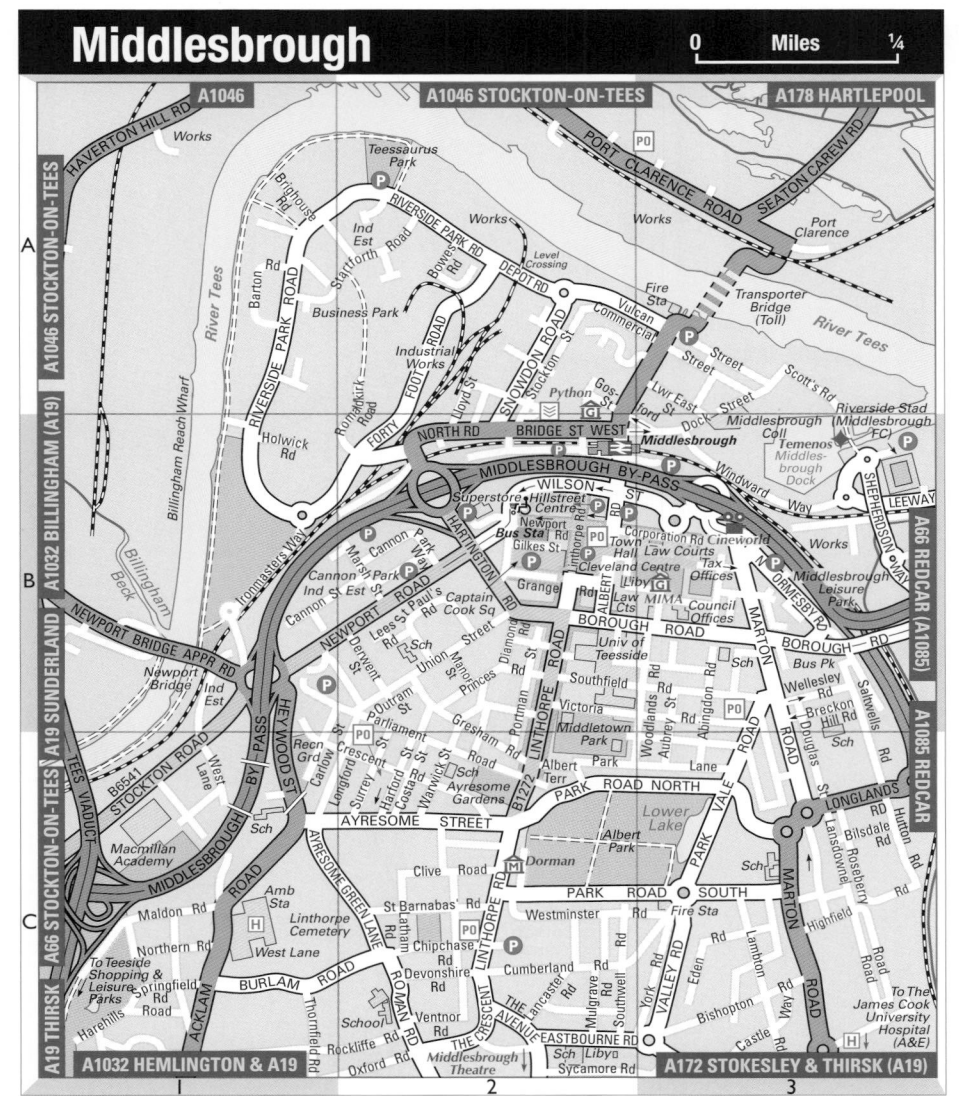

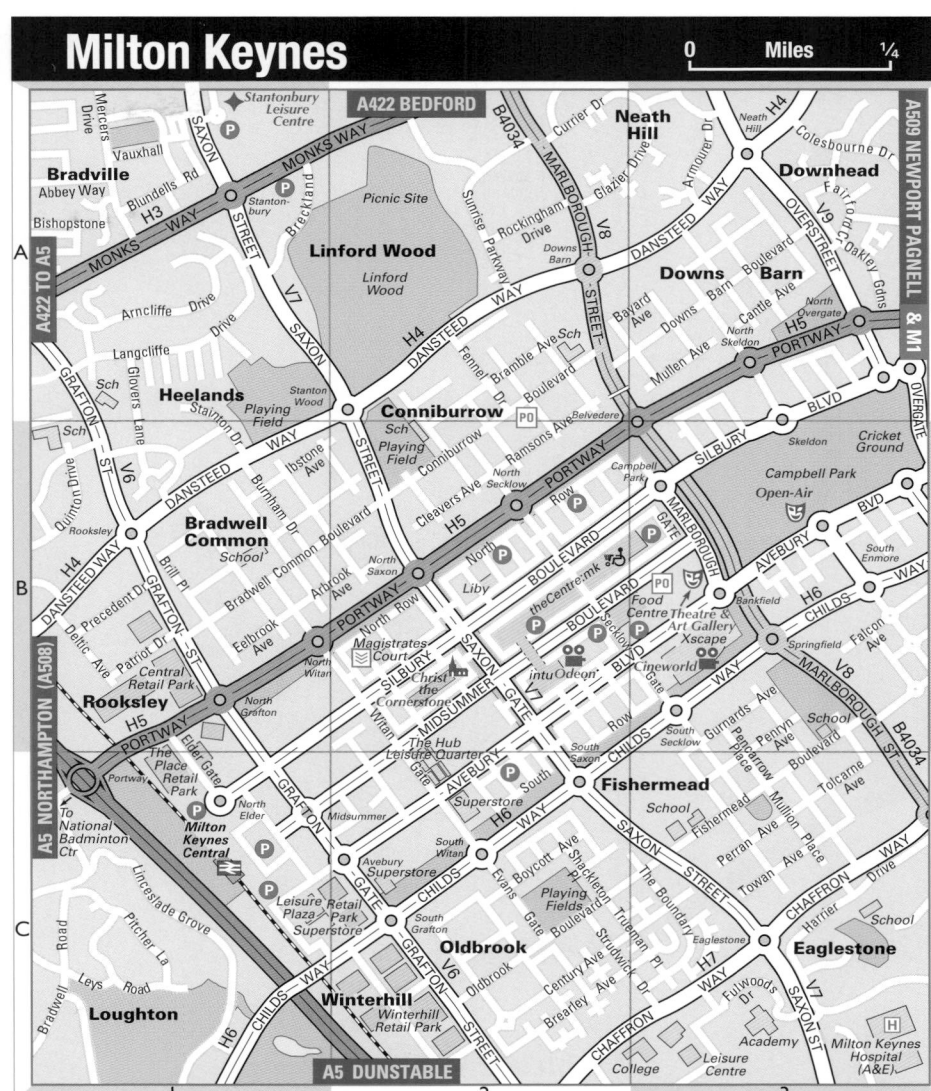

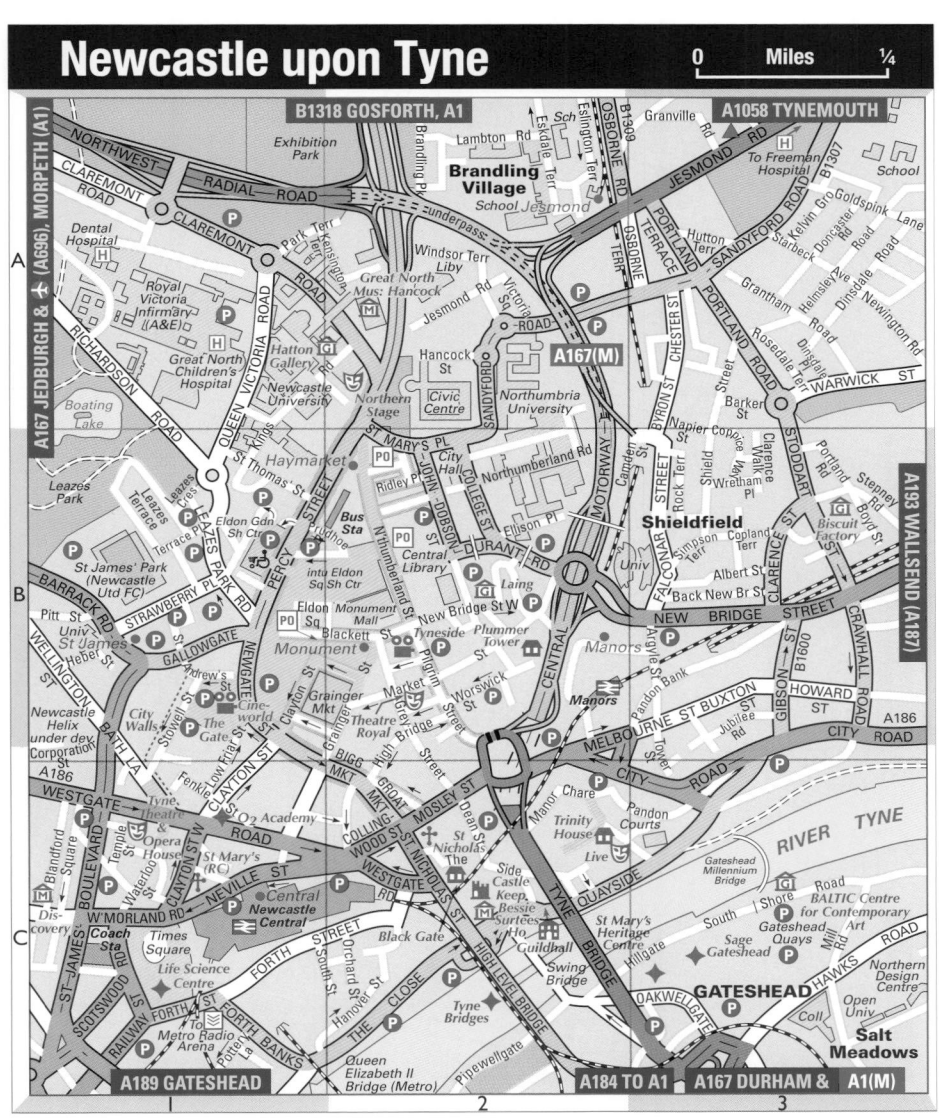

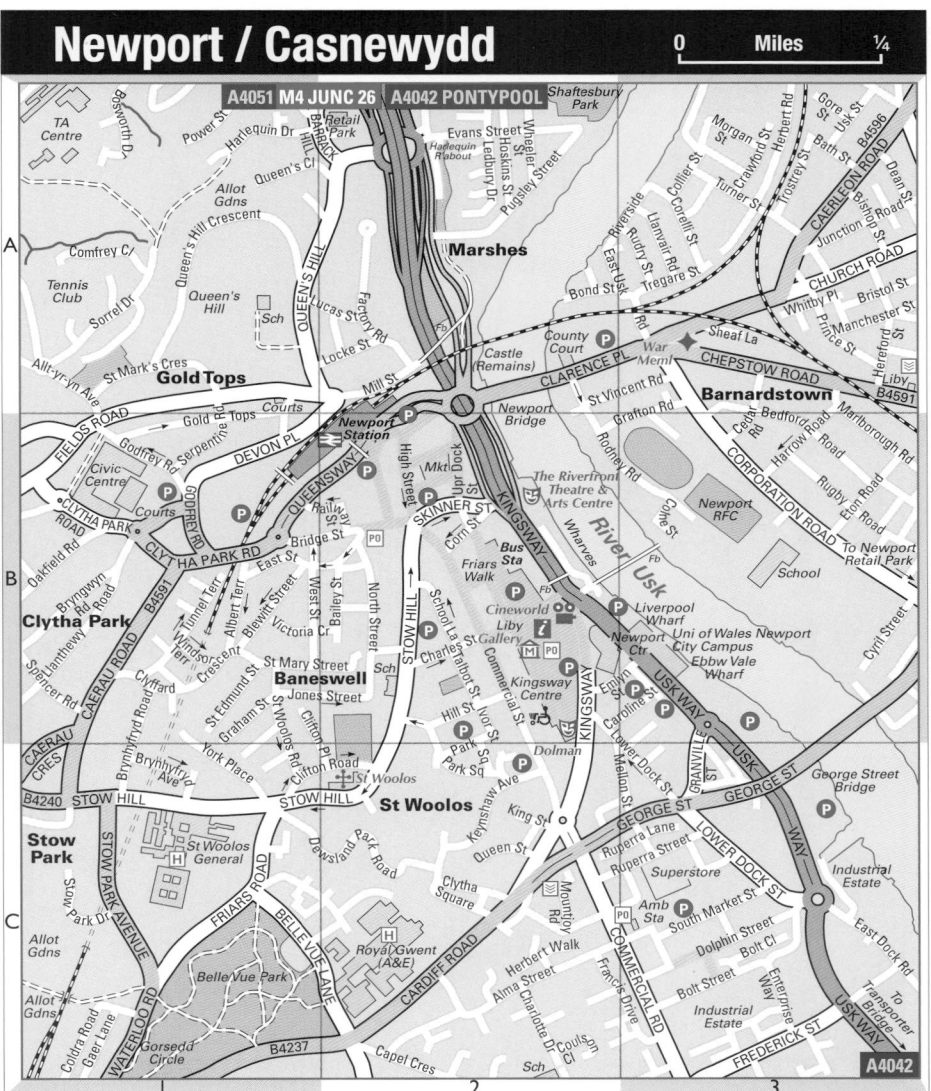

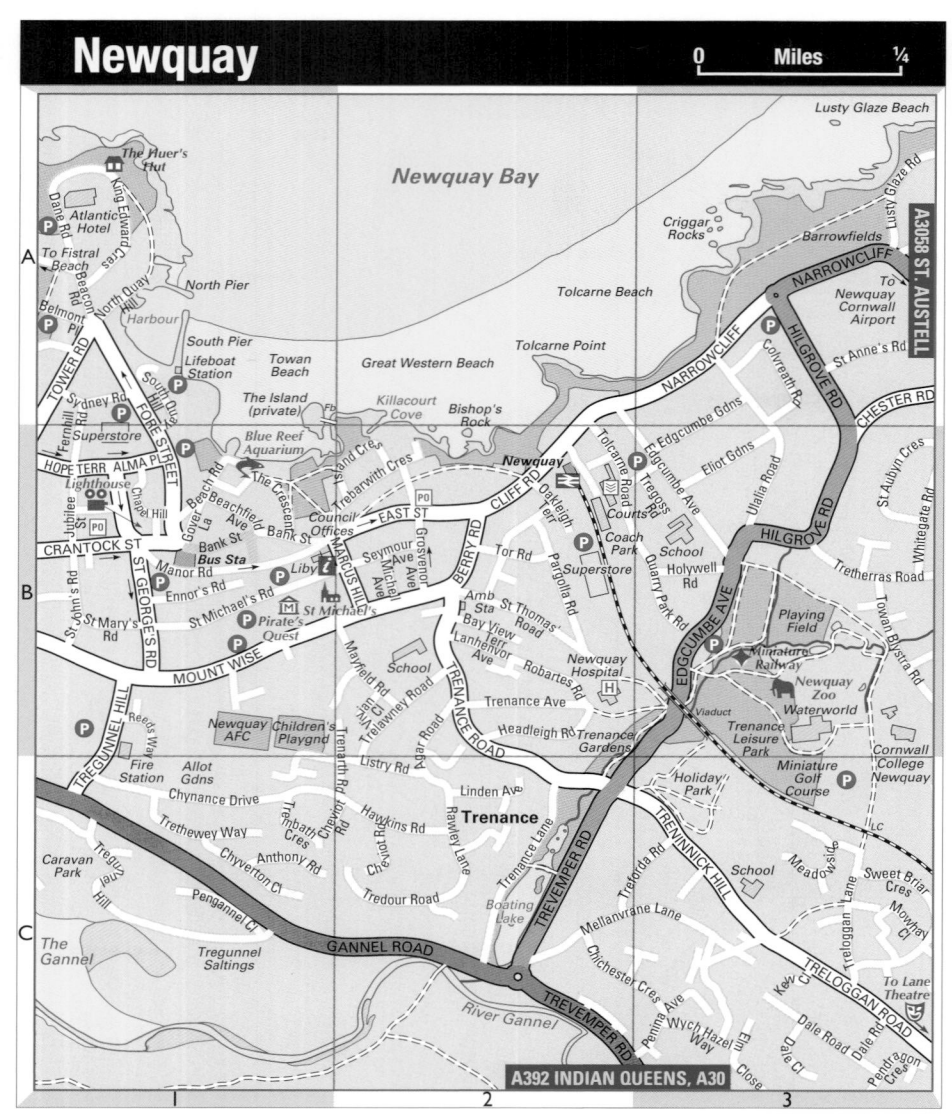

## Newquay

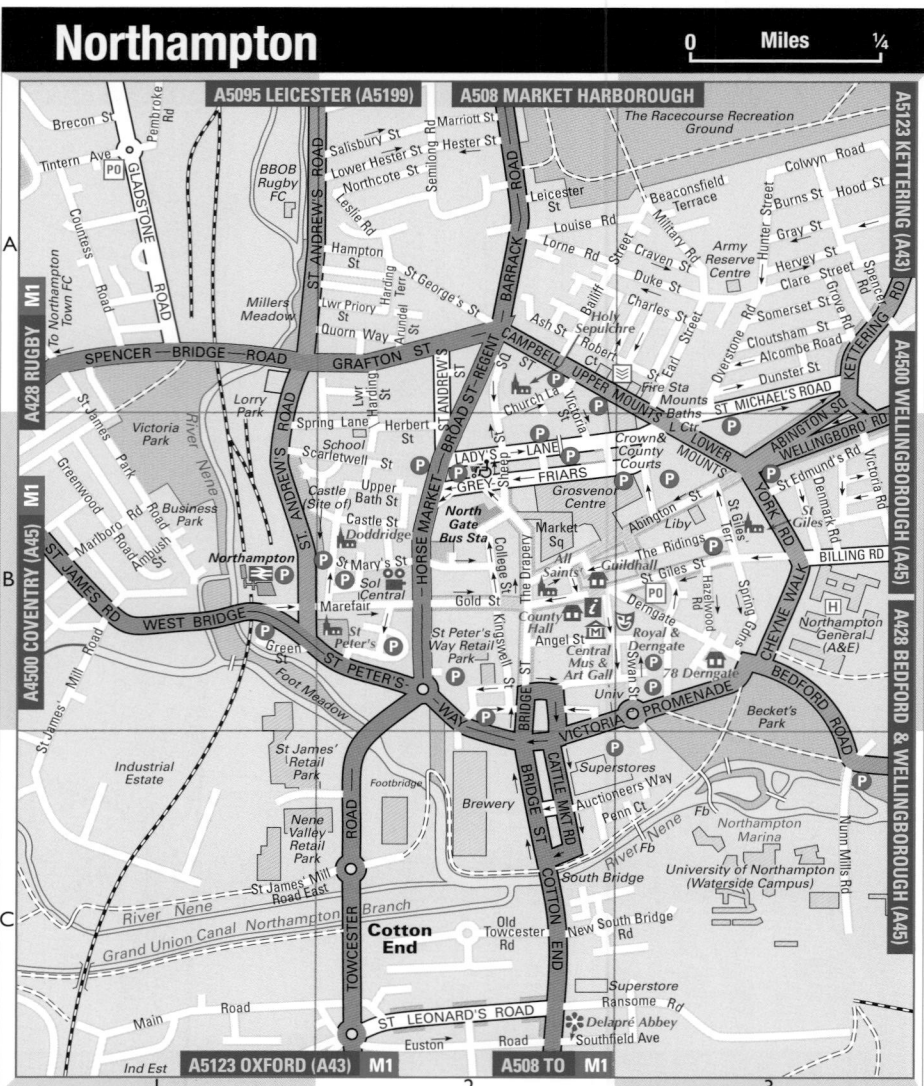

## Northampton

## Norwich

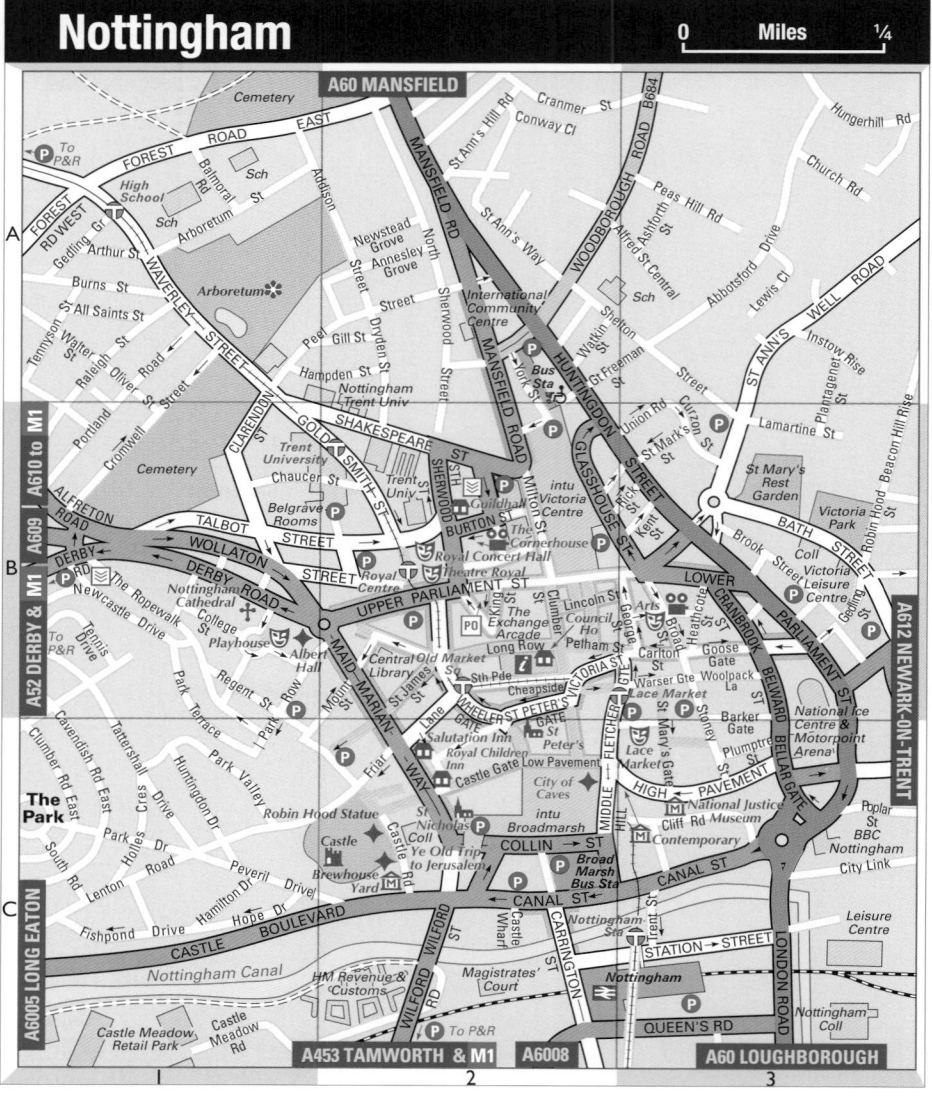

## Nottingham

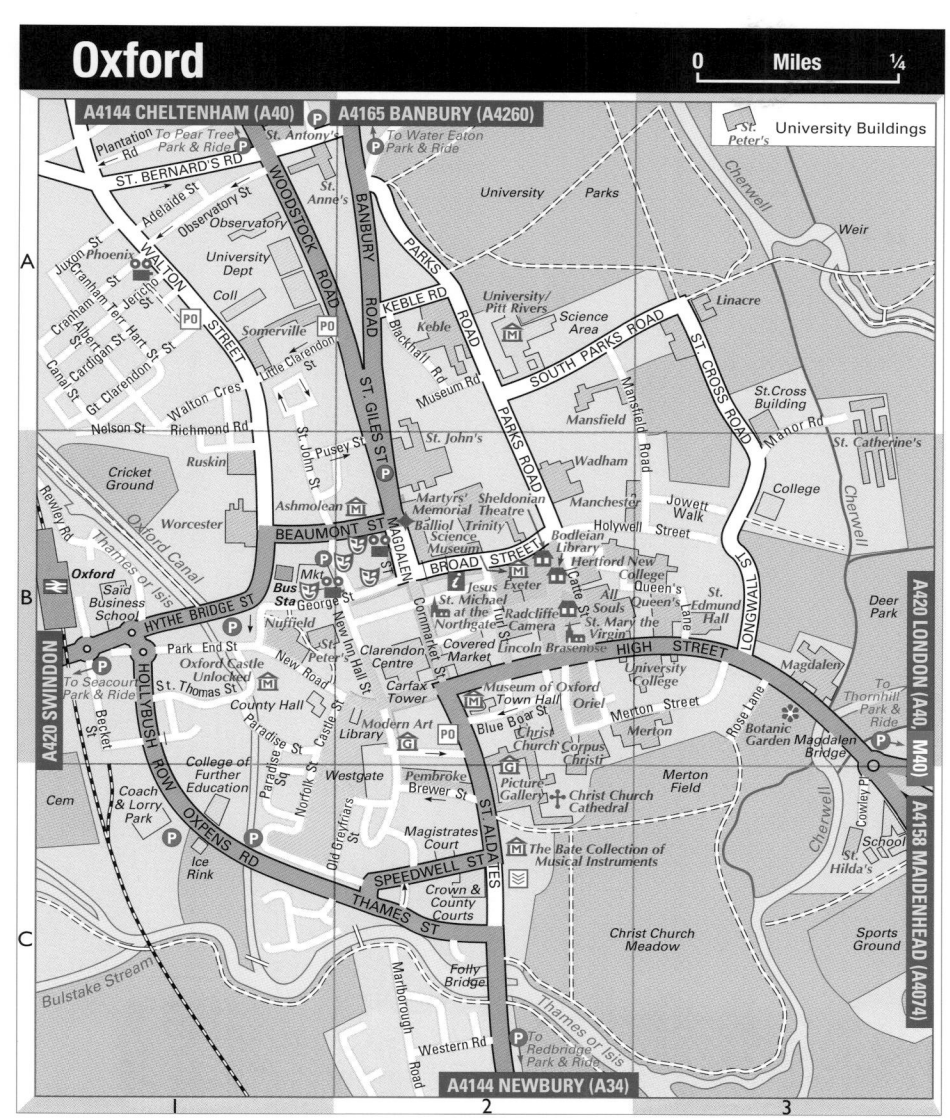

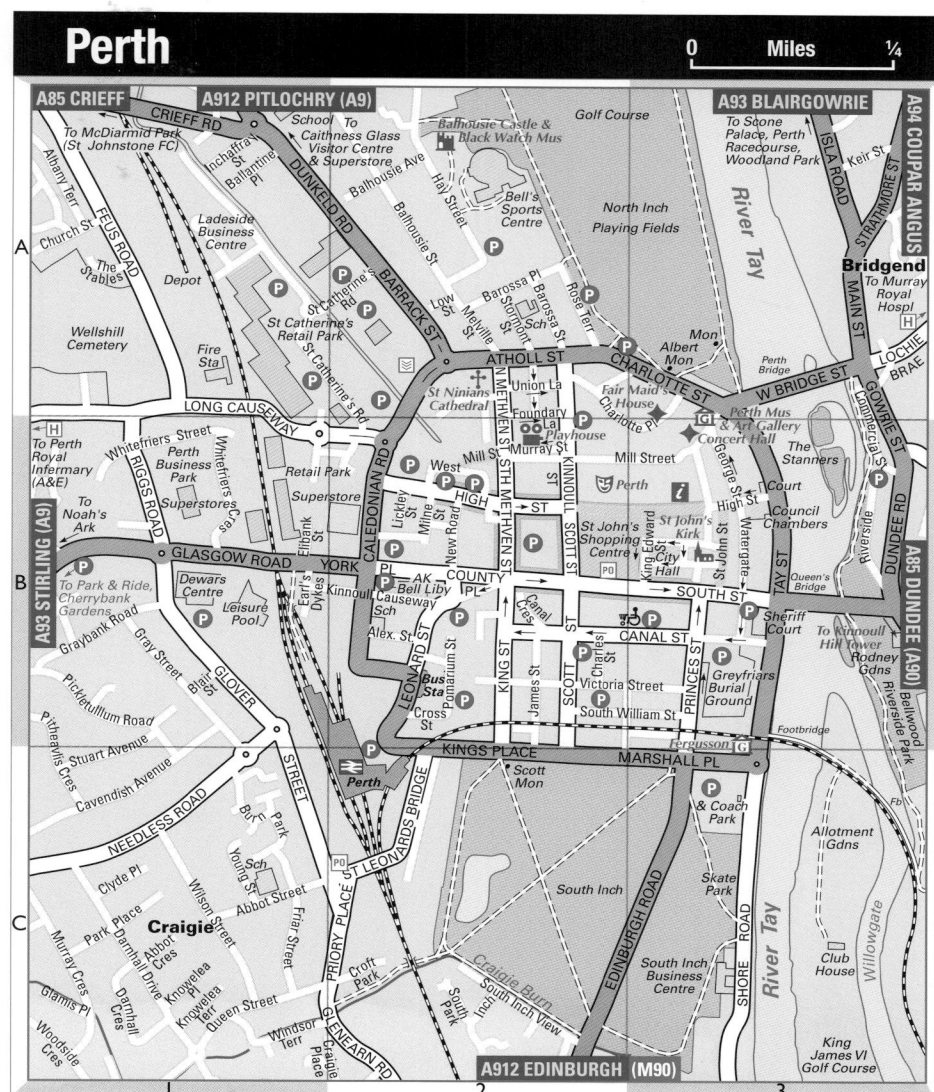

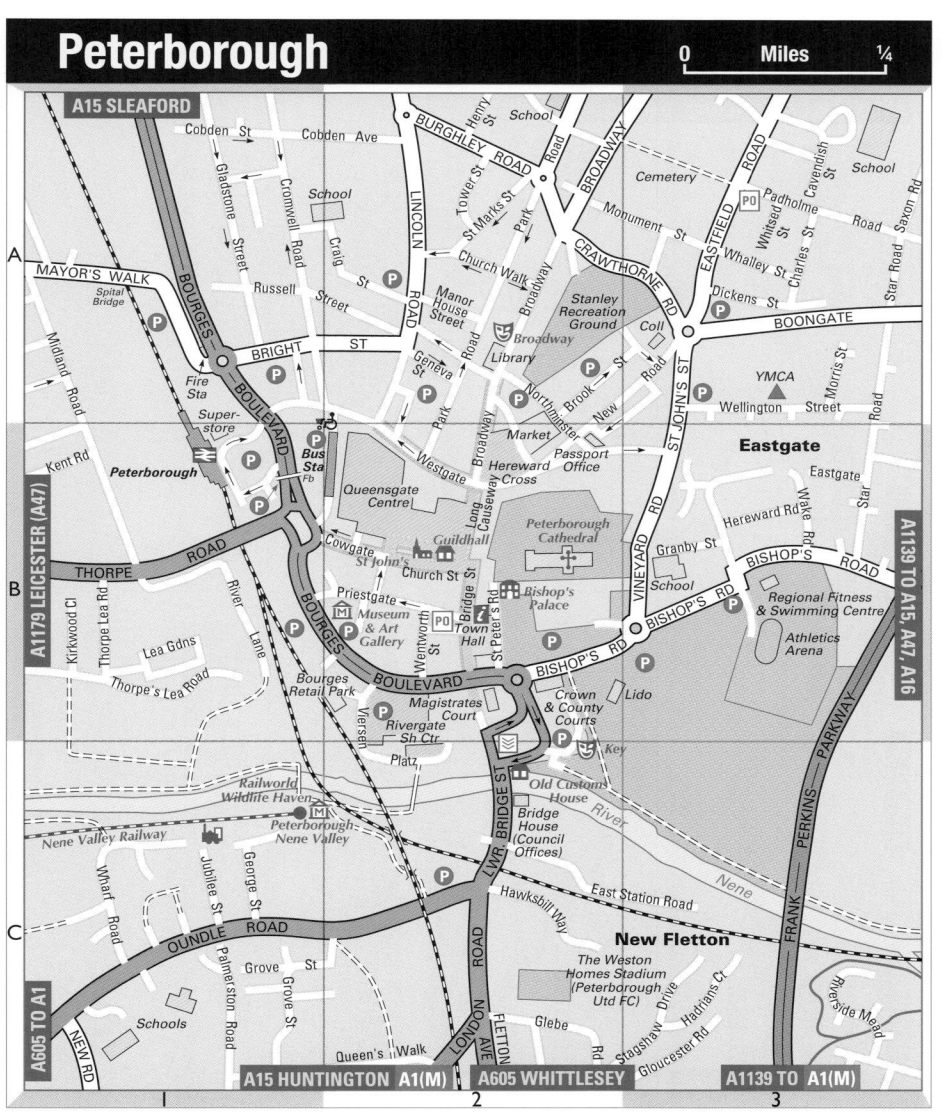

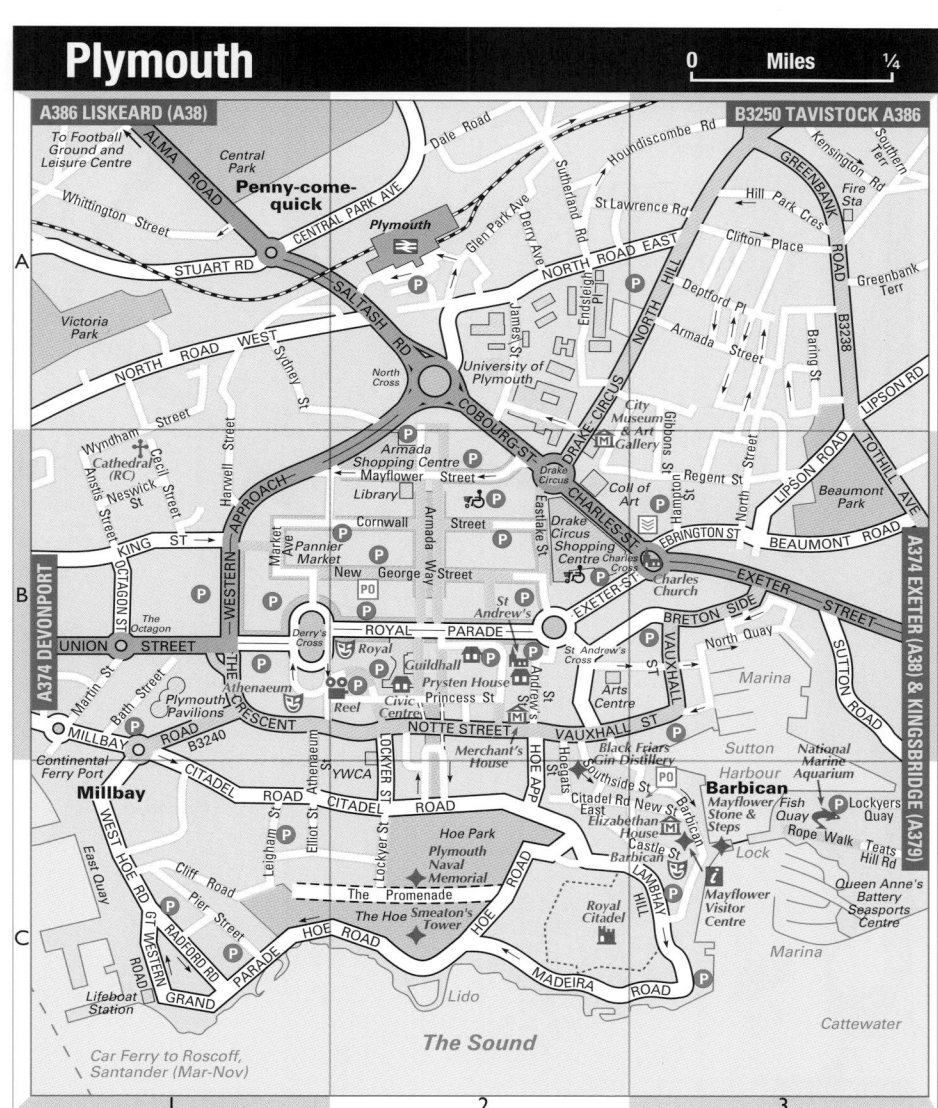

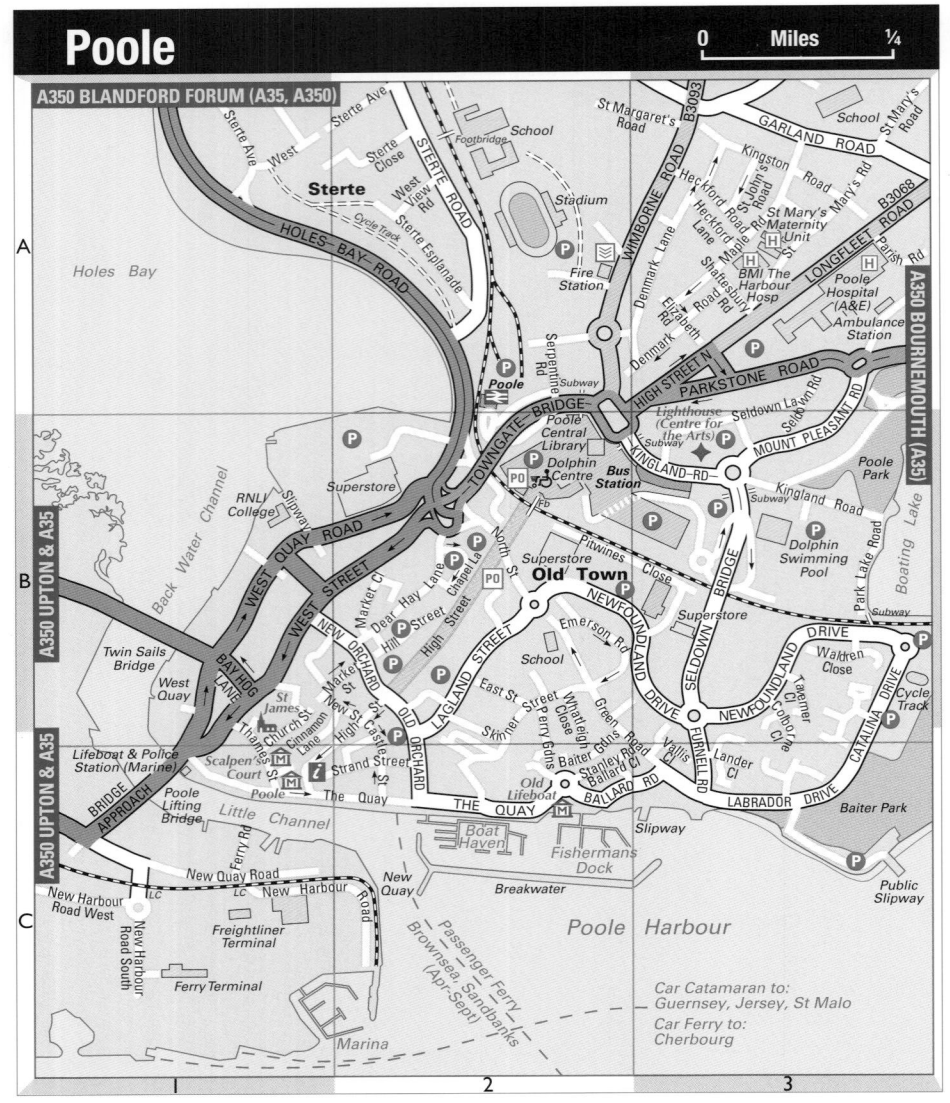

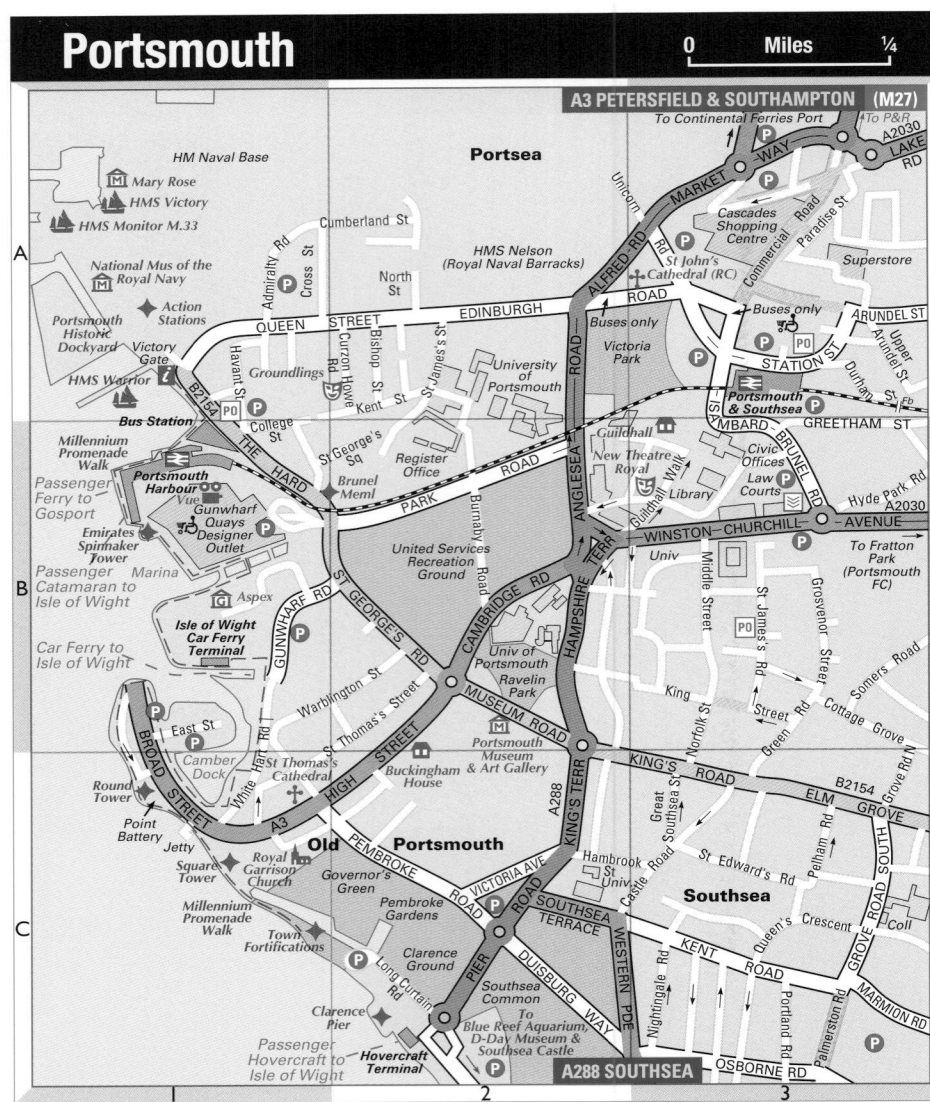

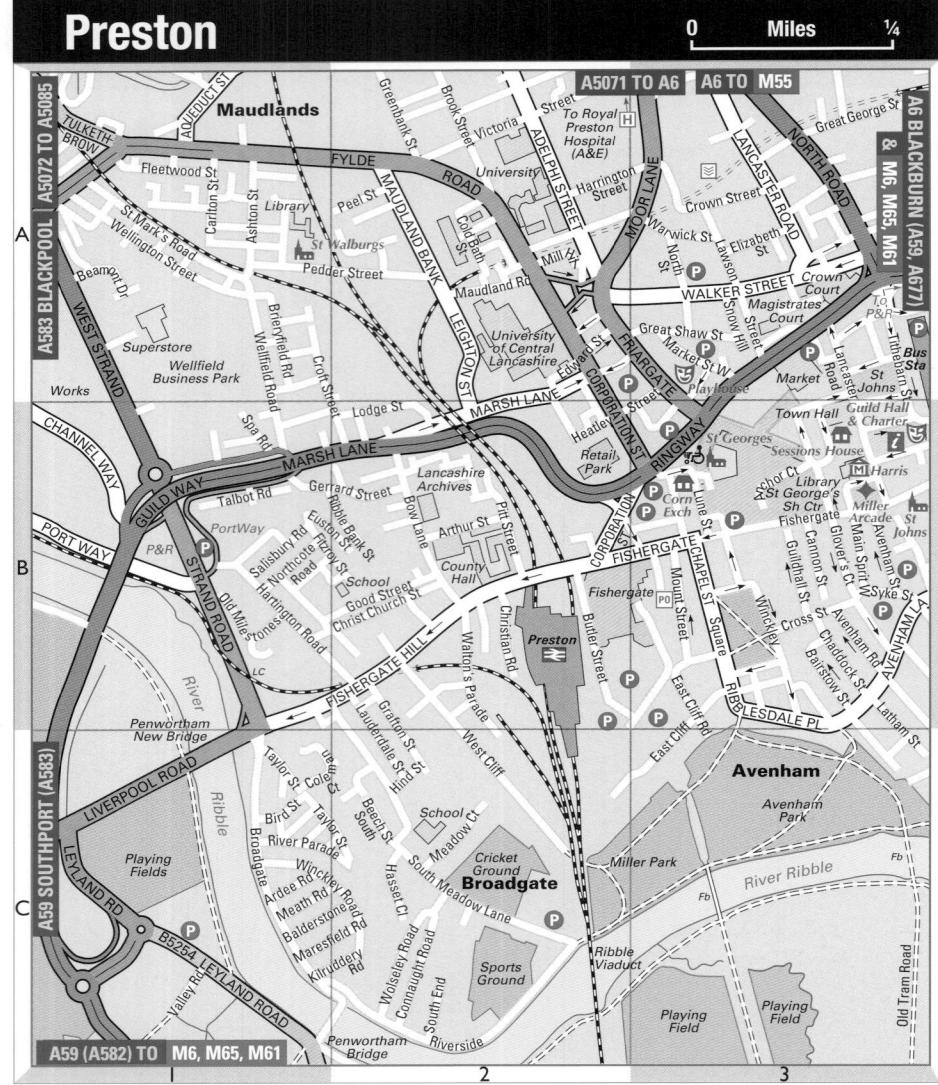

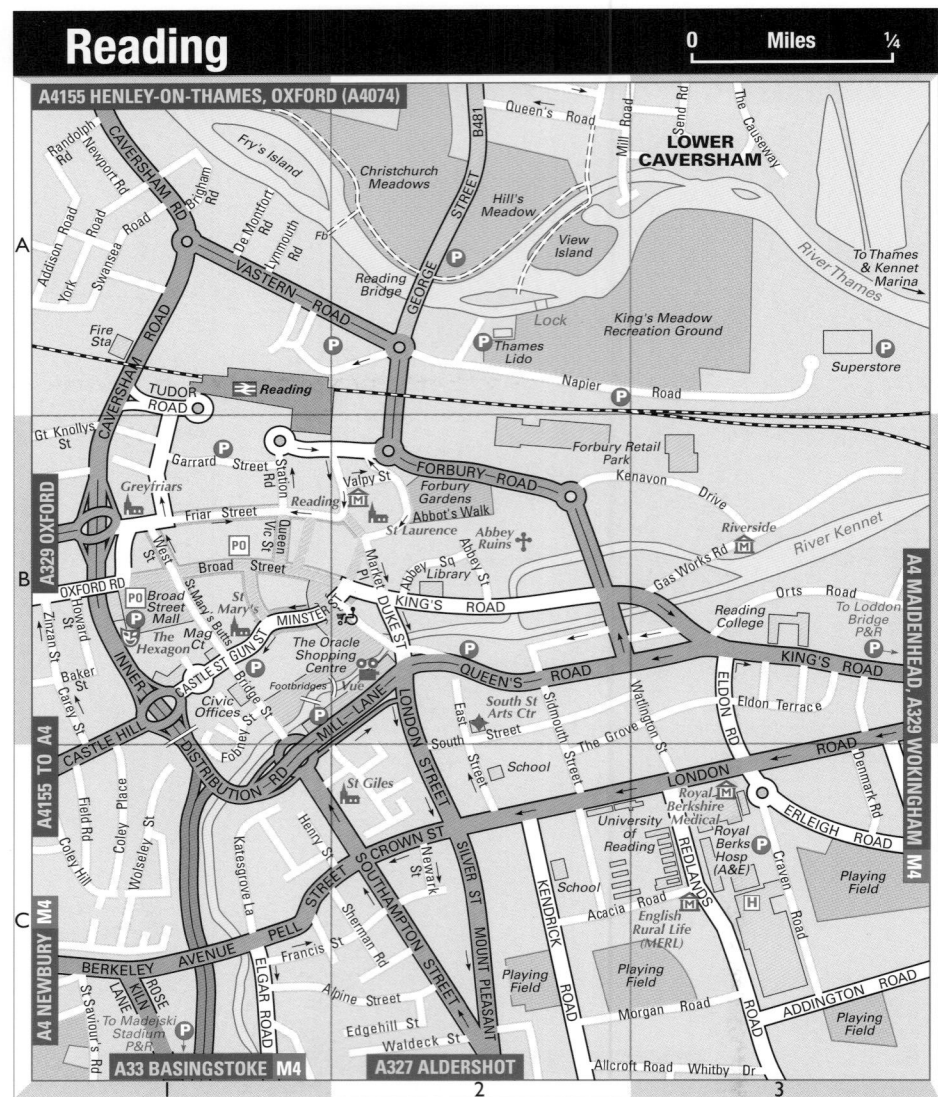

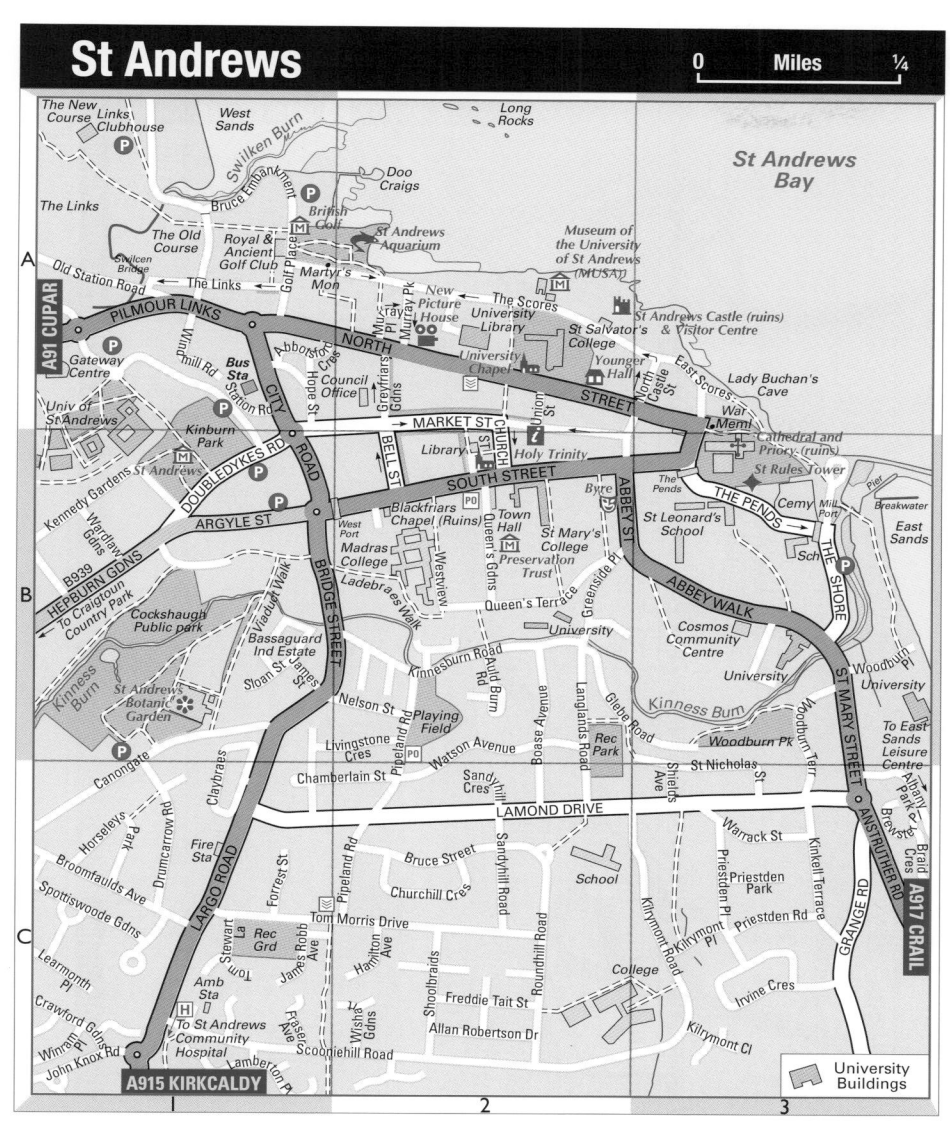

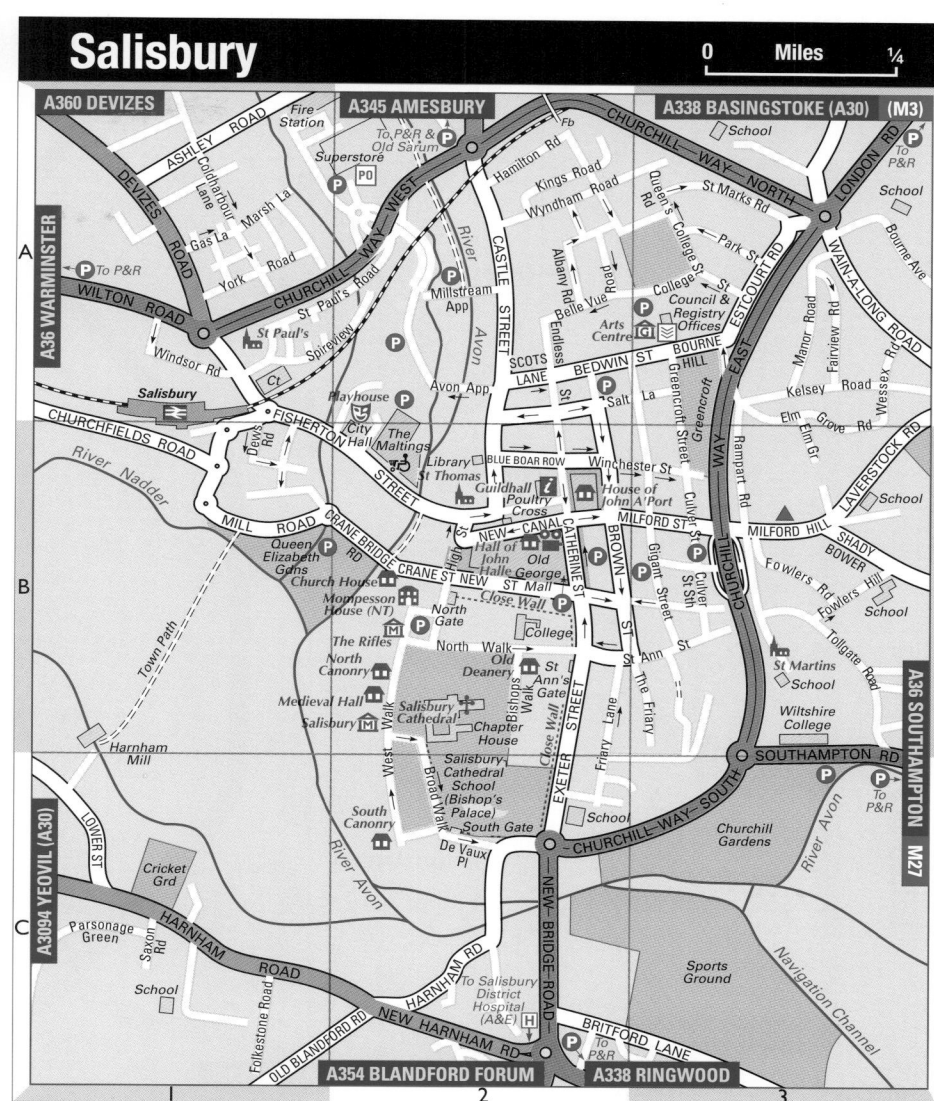

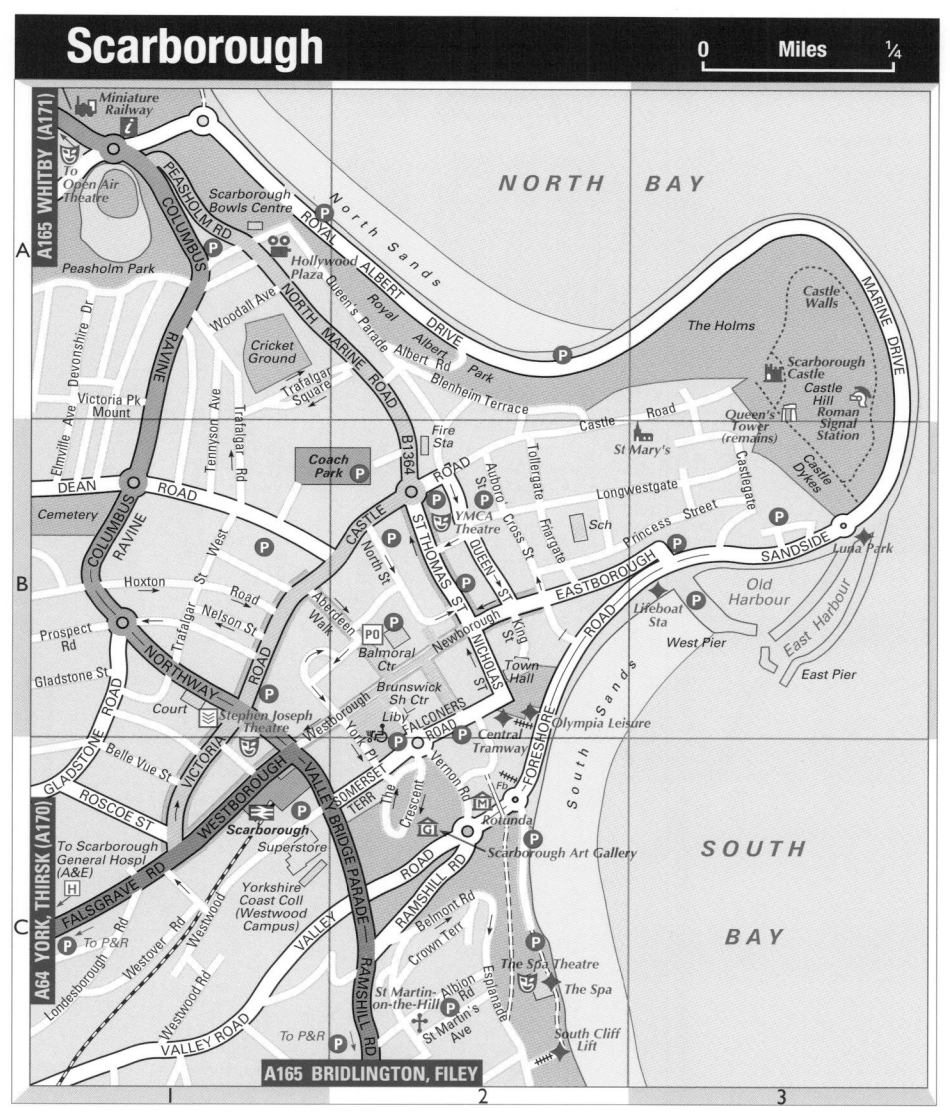

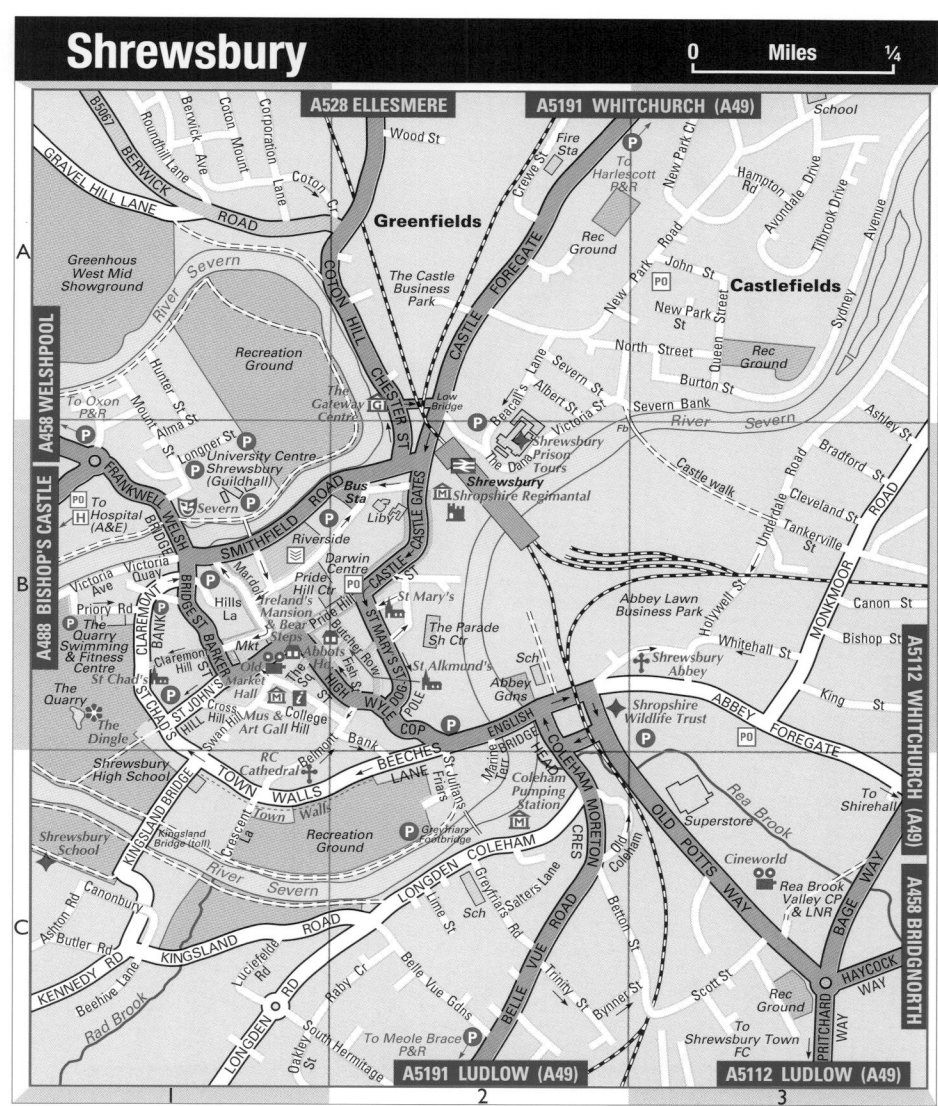

## Sheffield

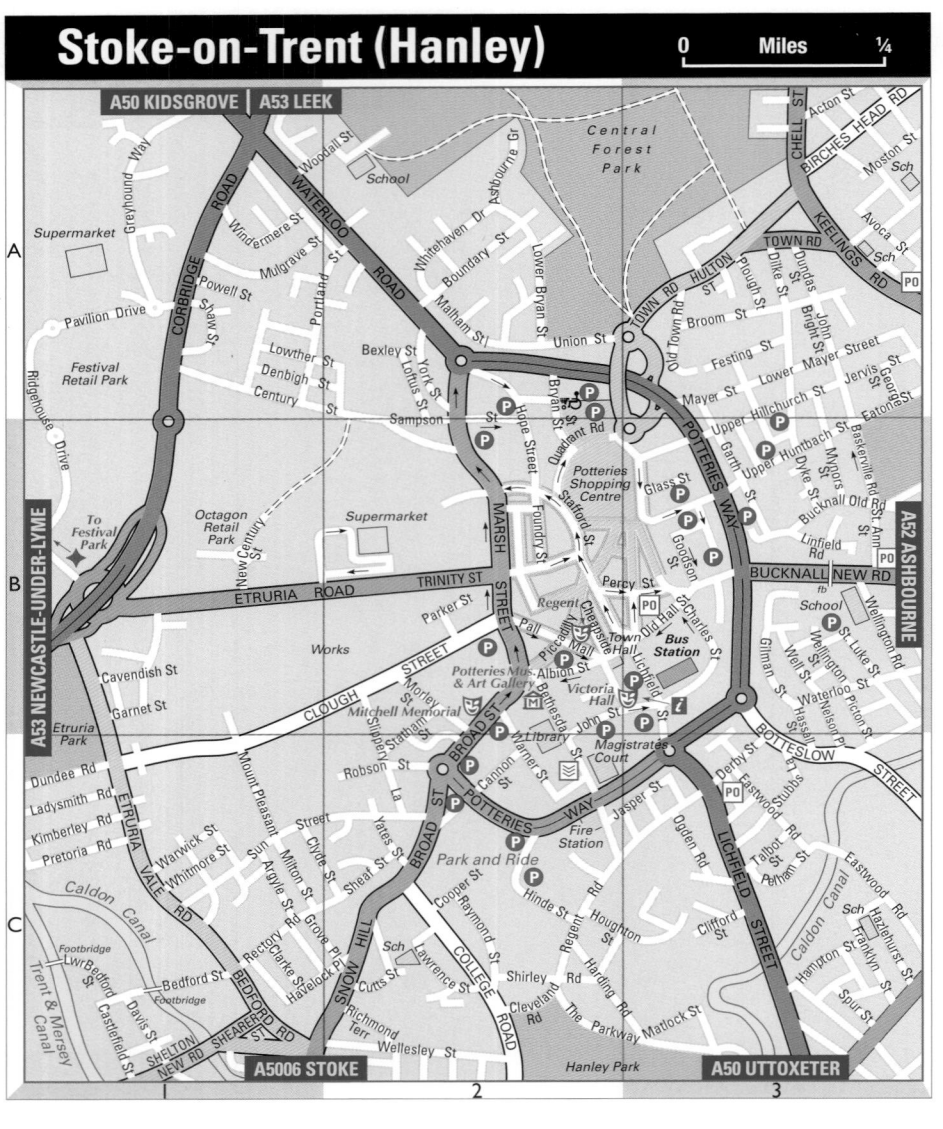

## Stoke-on-Trent (Hanley)

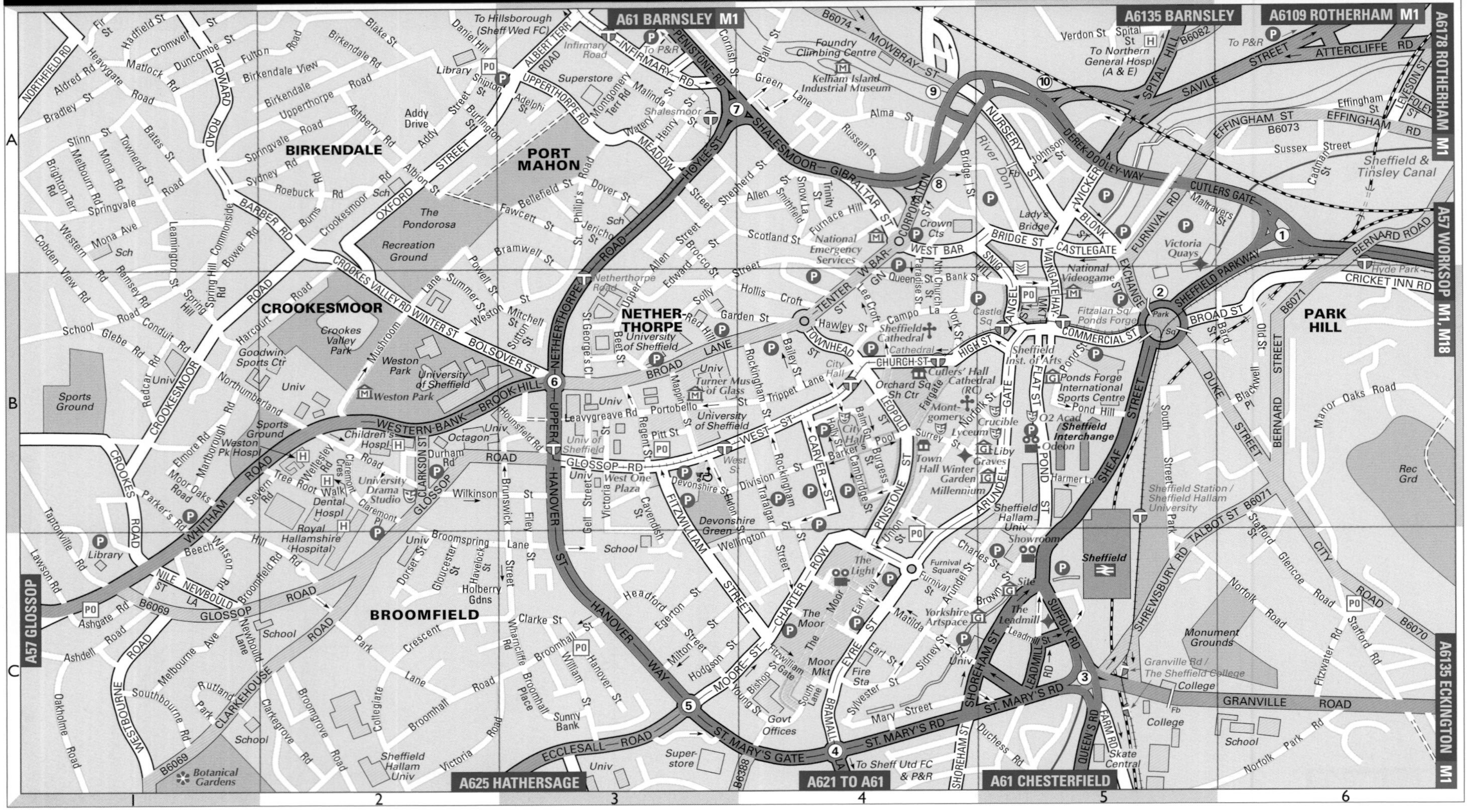

## Southampton

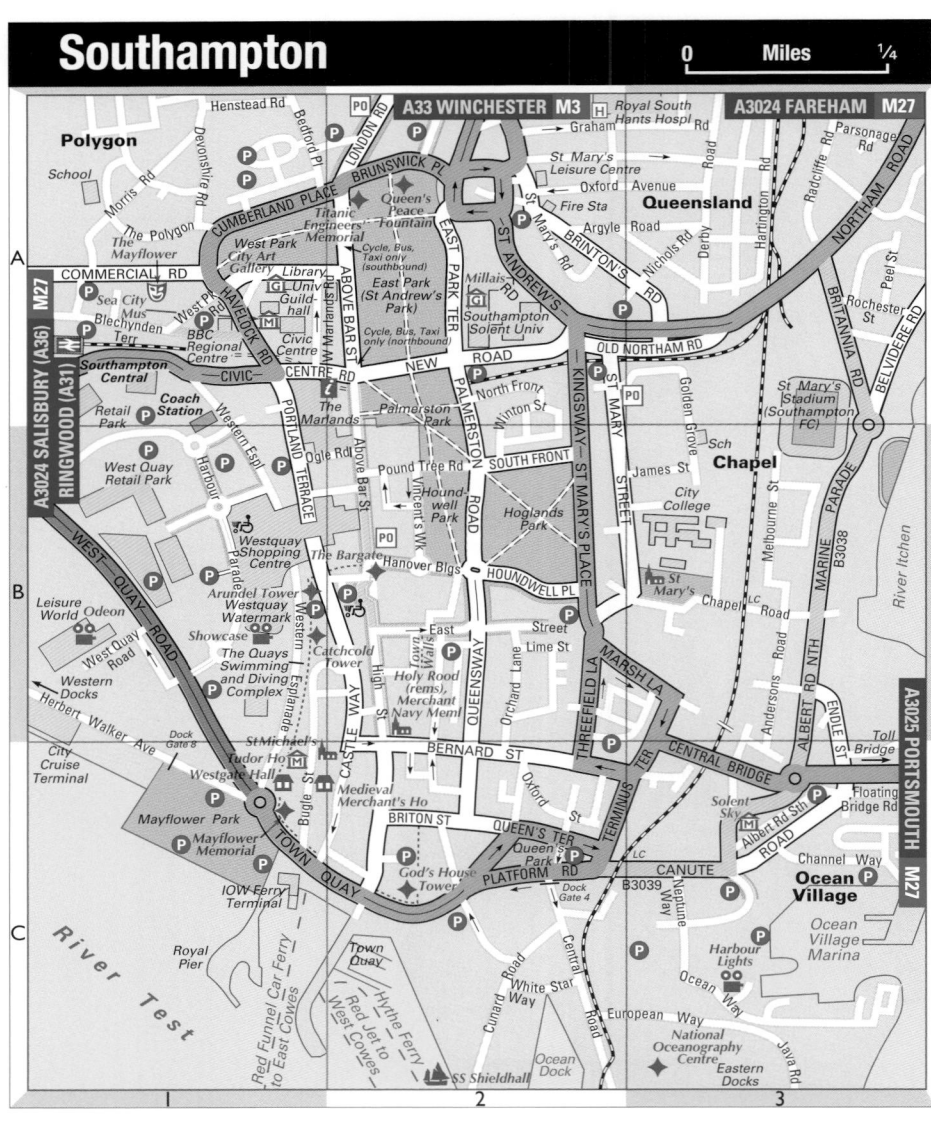

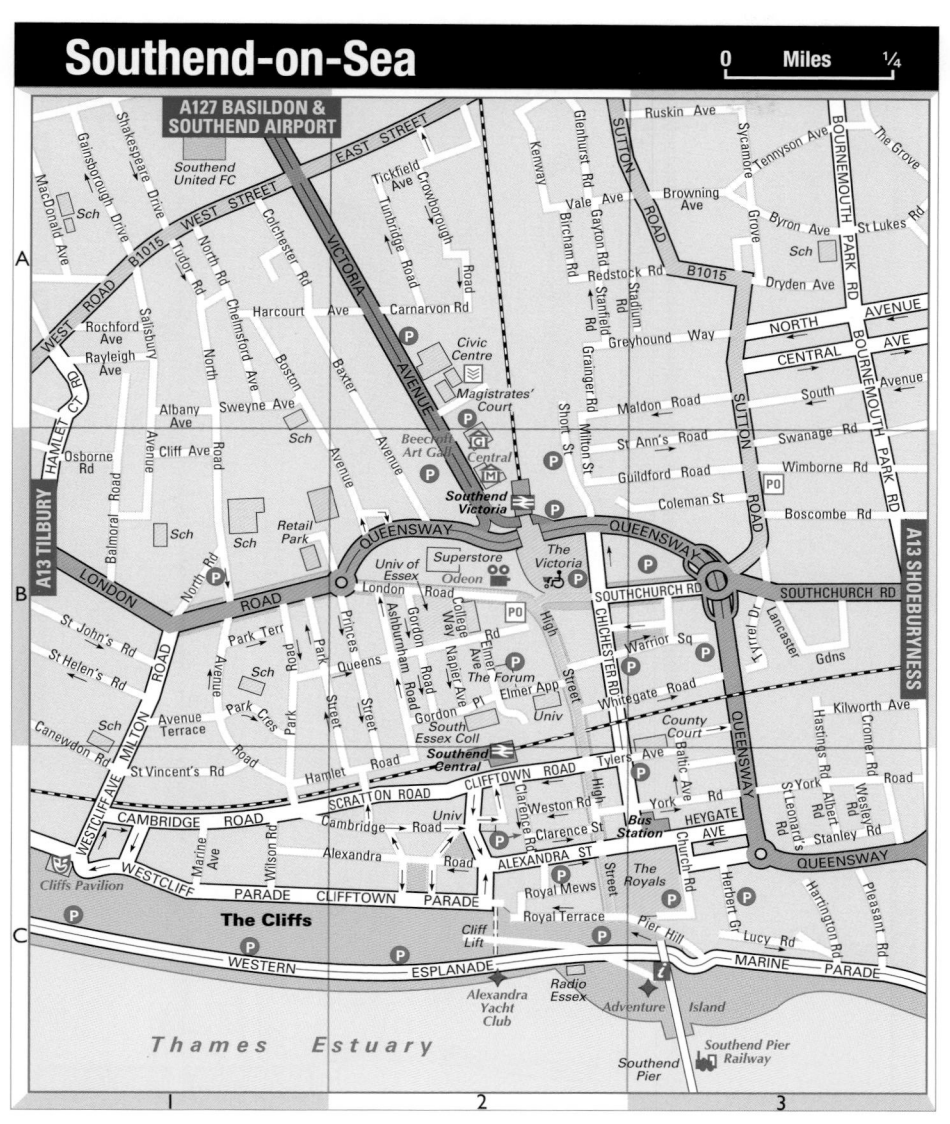

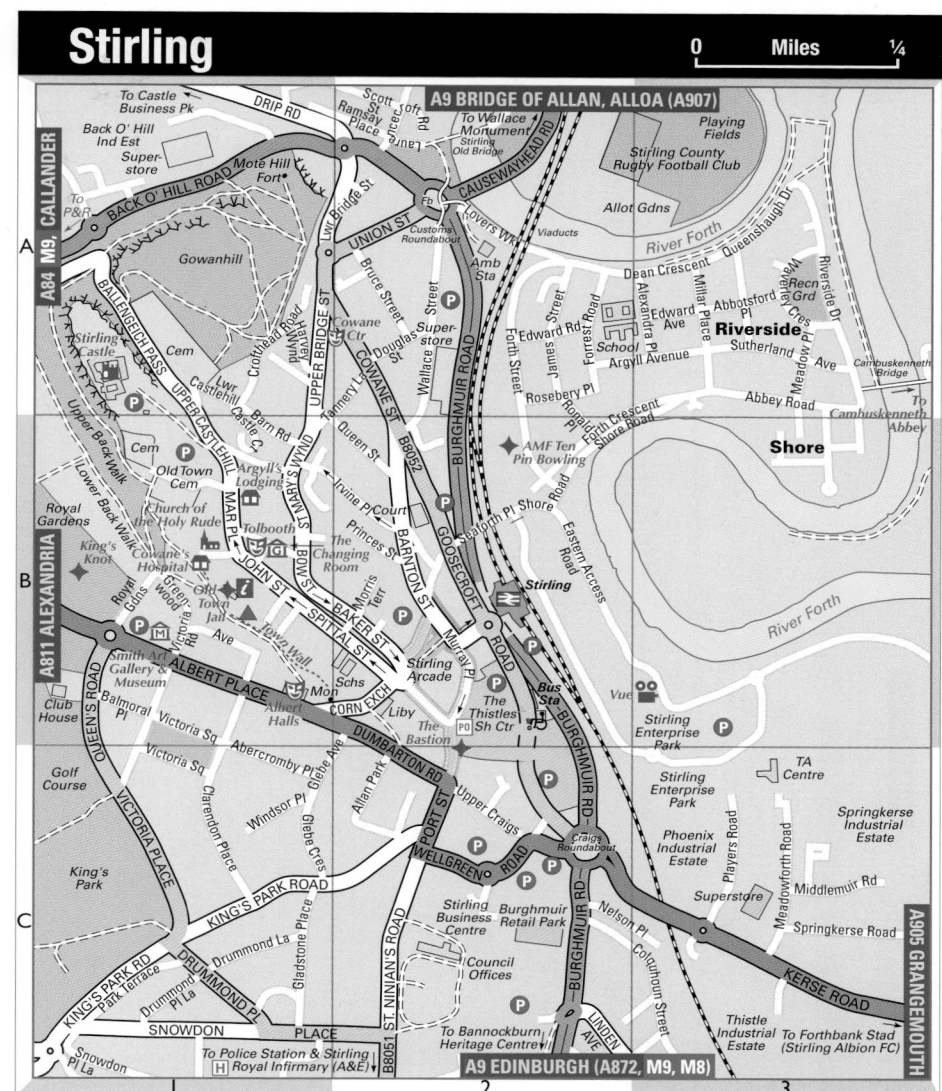

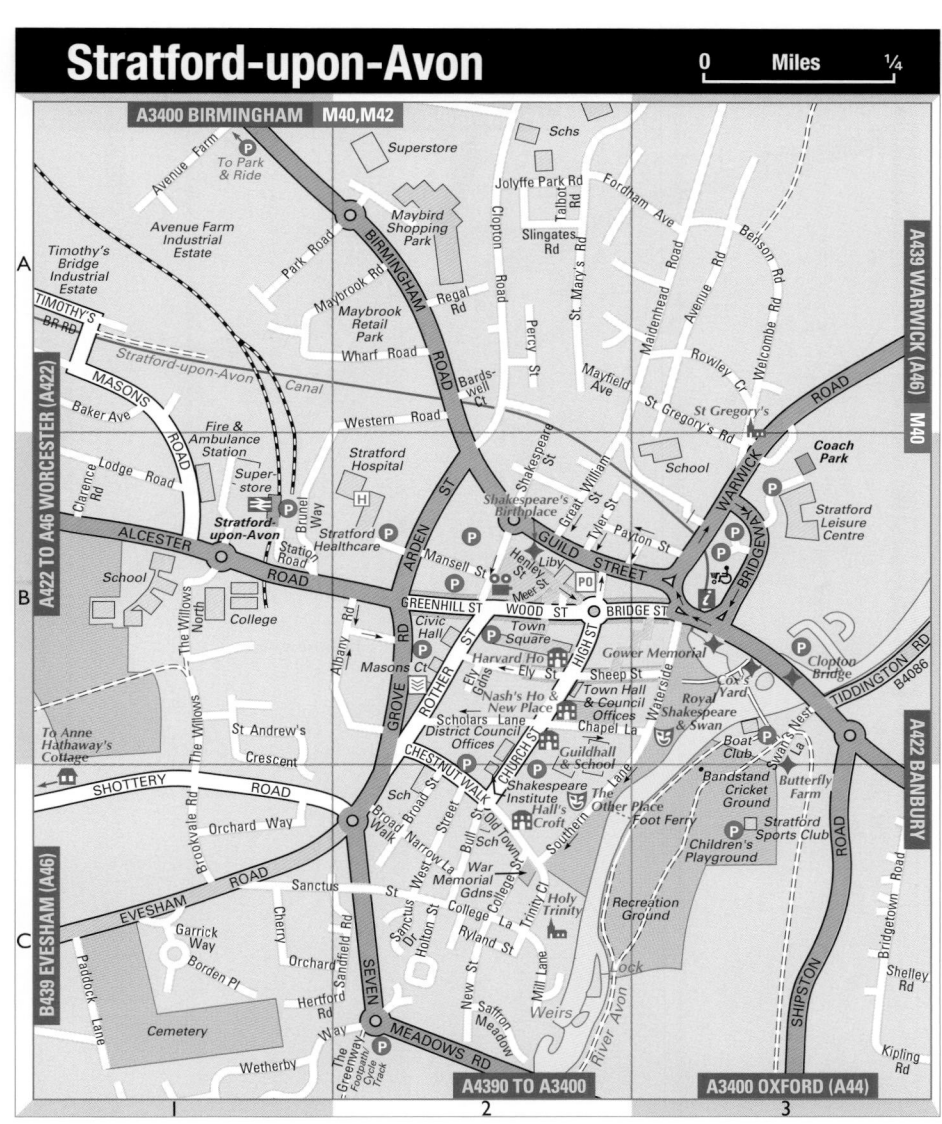

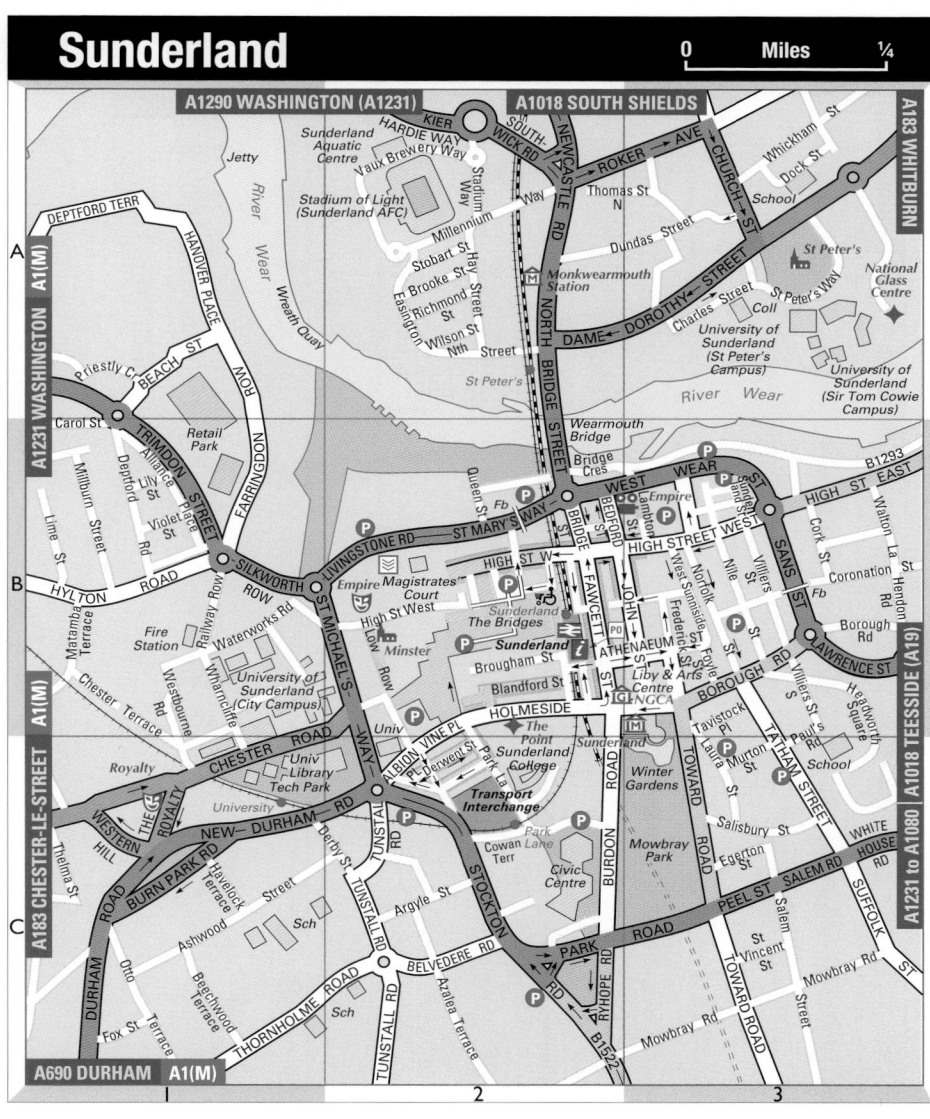

## Swansea / Abertawe

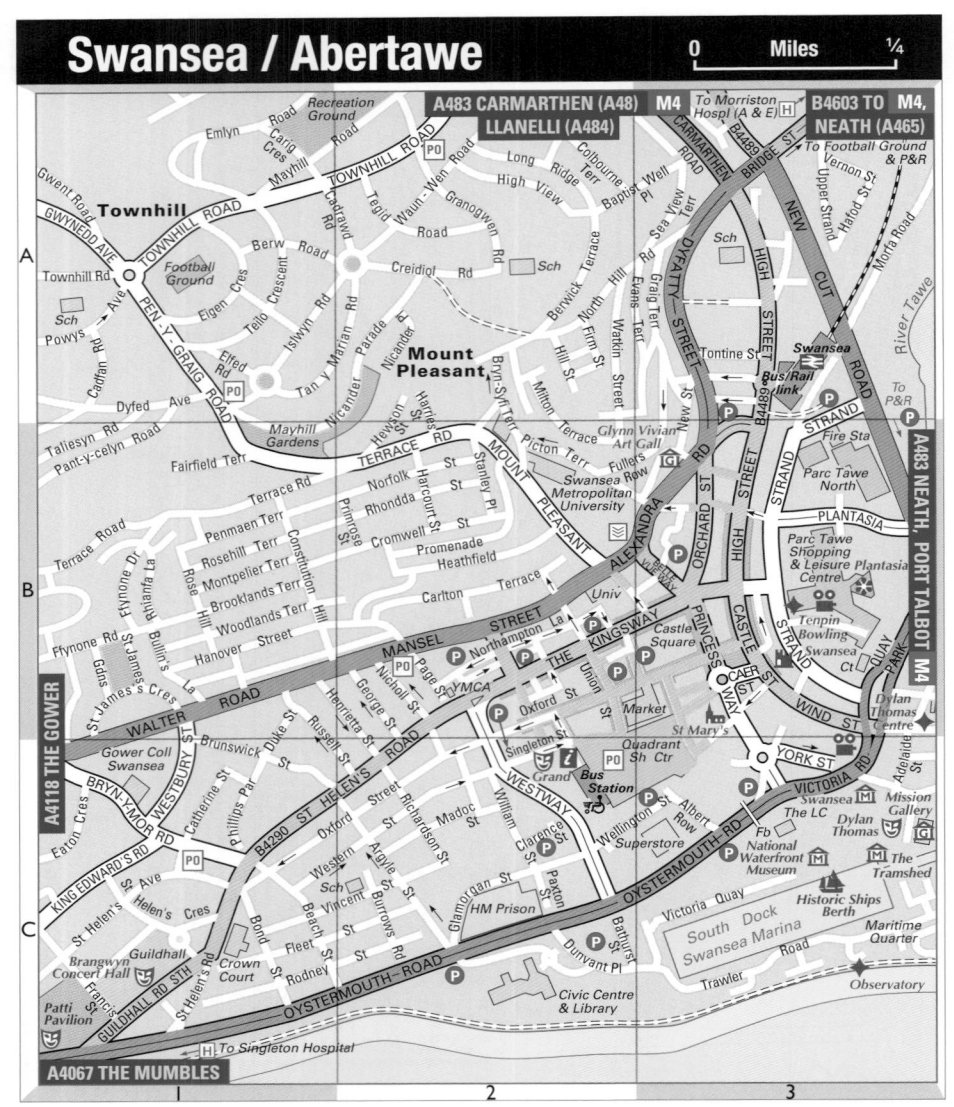

## Swindon

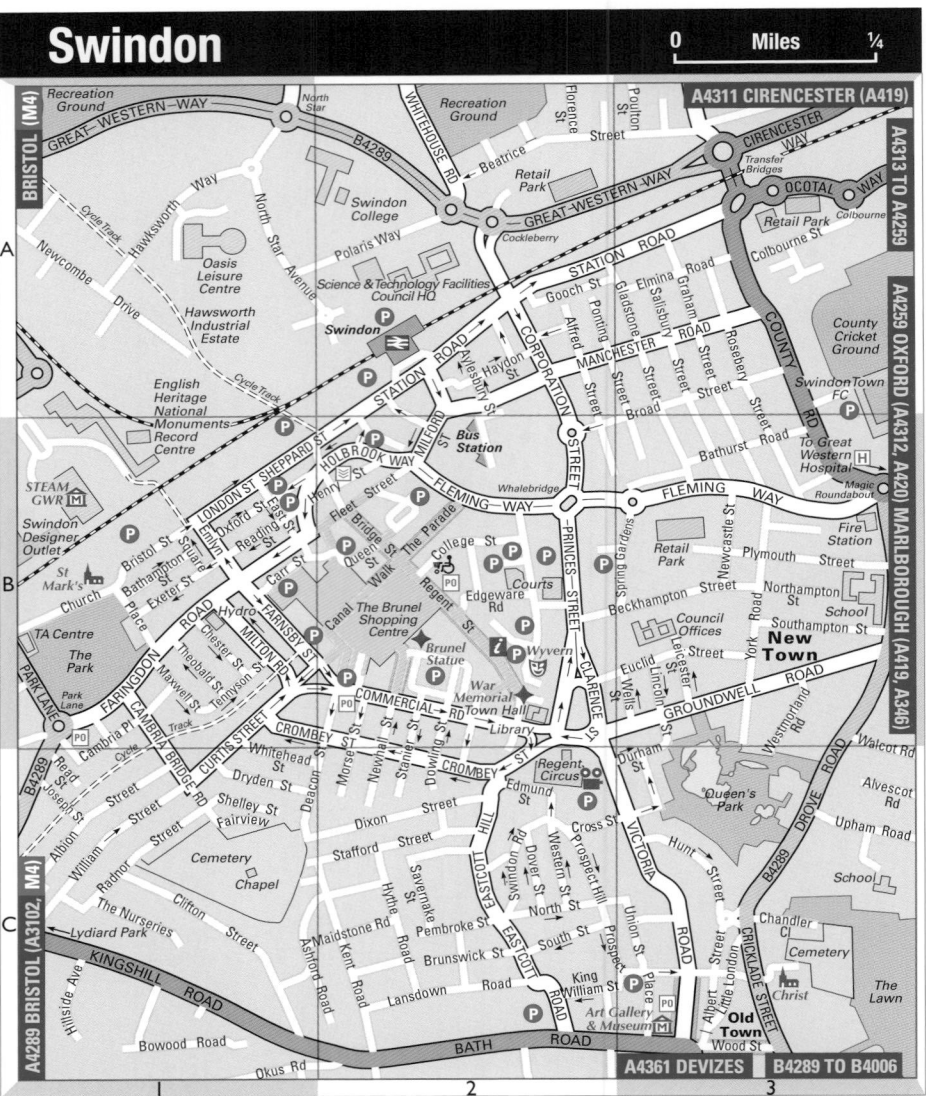

## Taunton

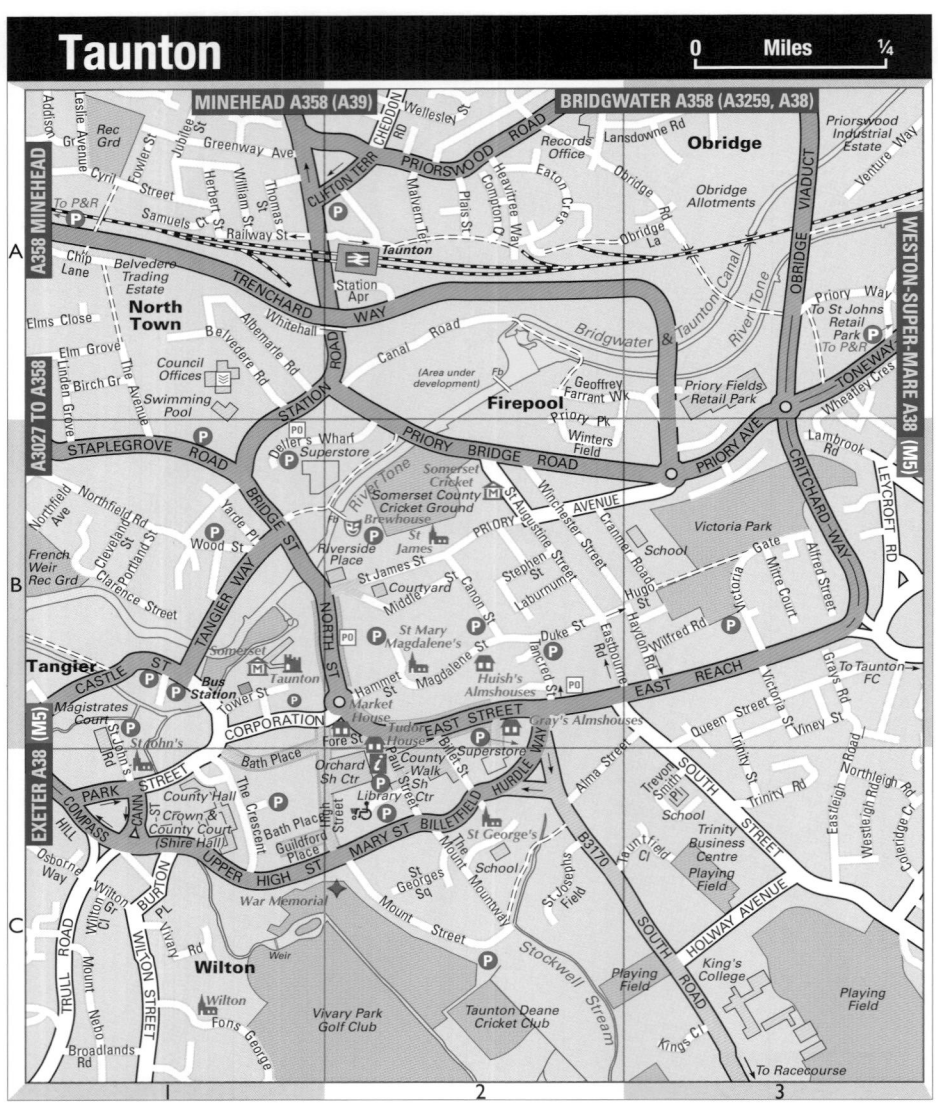

## Telford

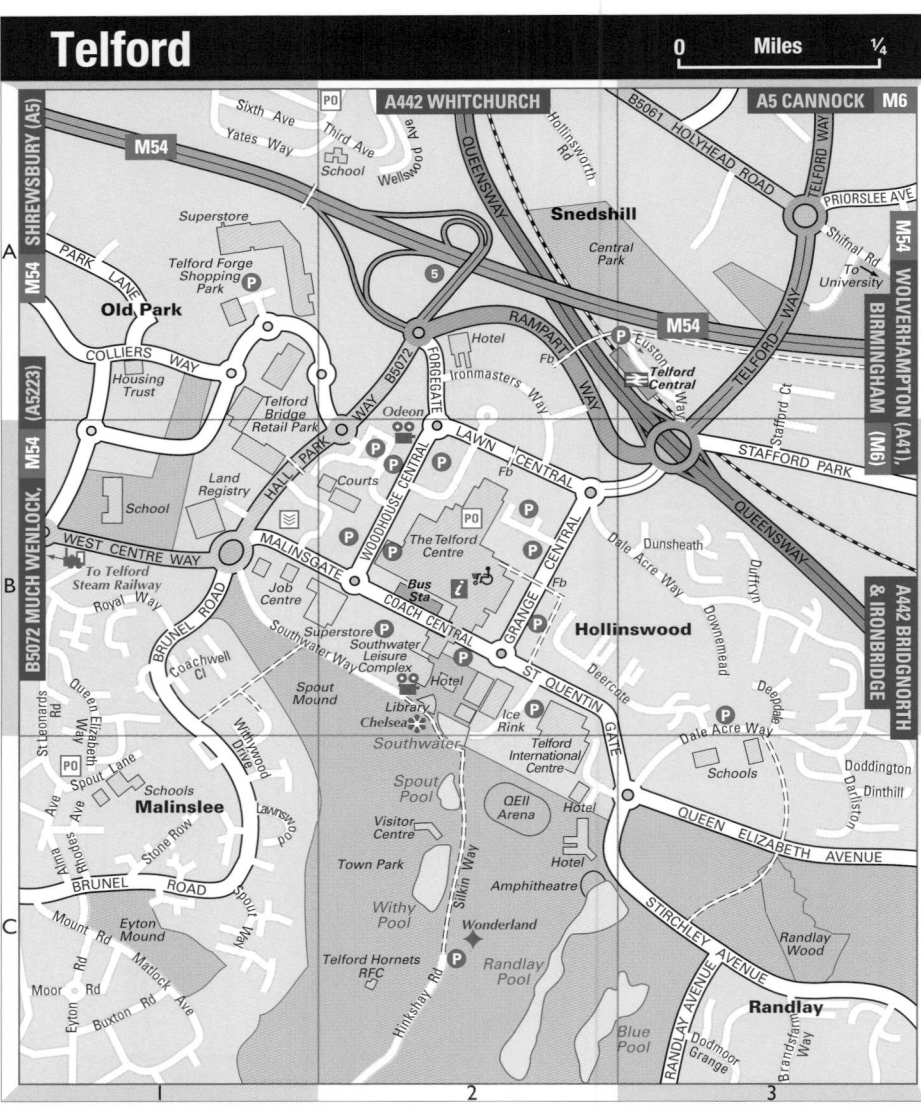

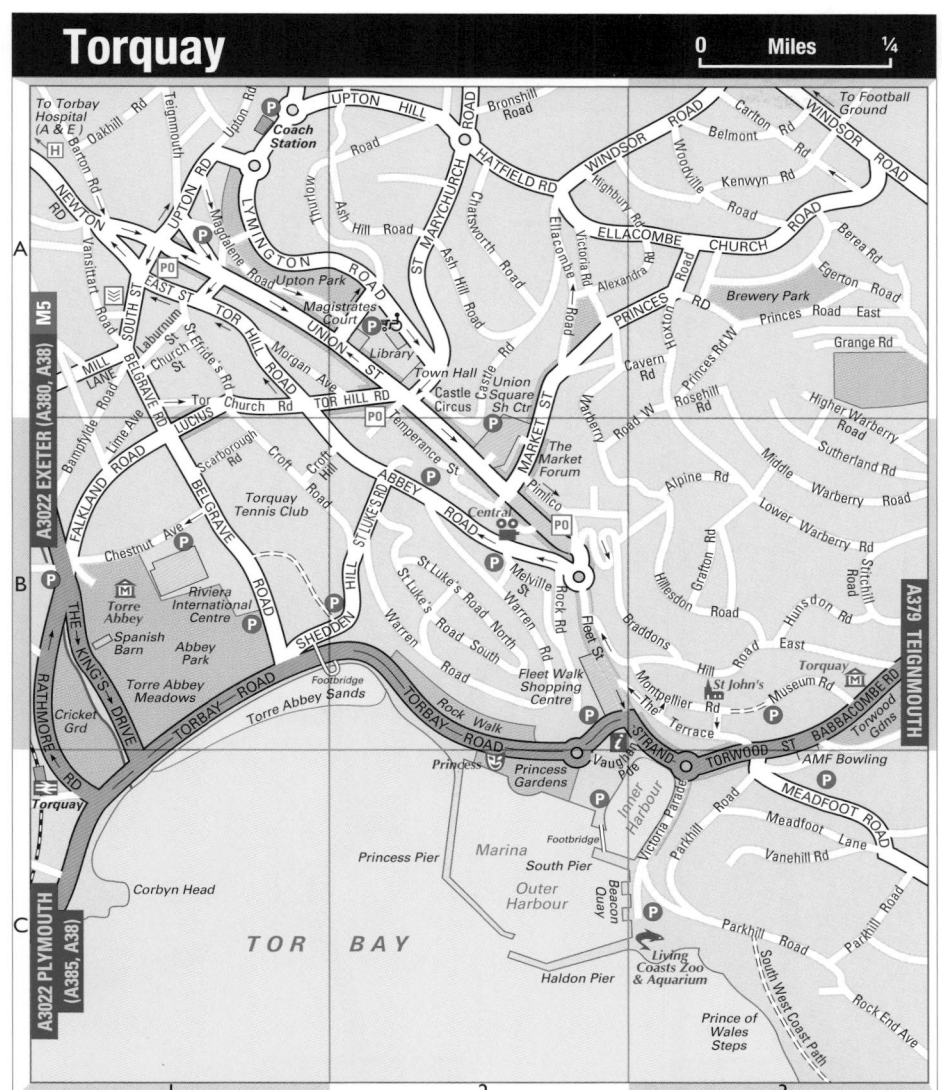

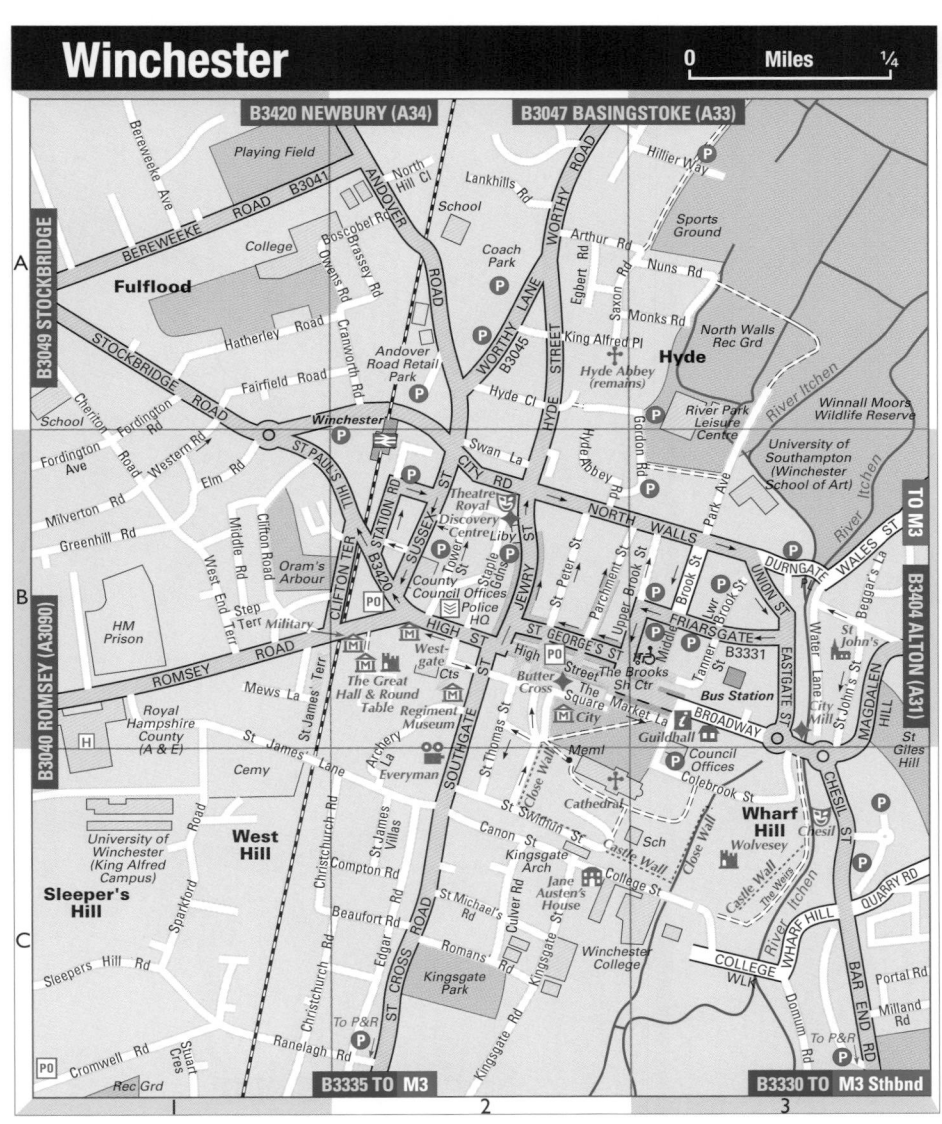

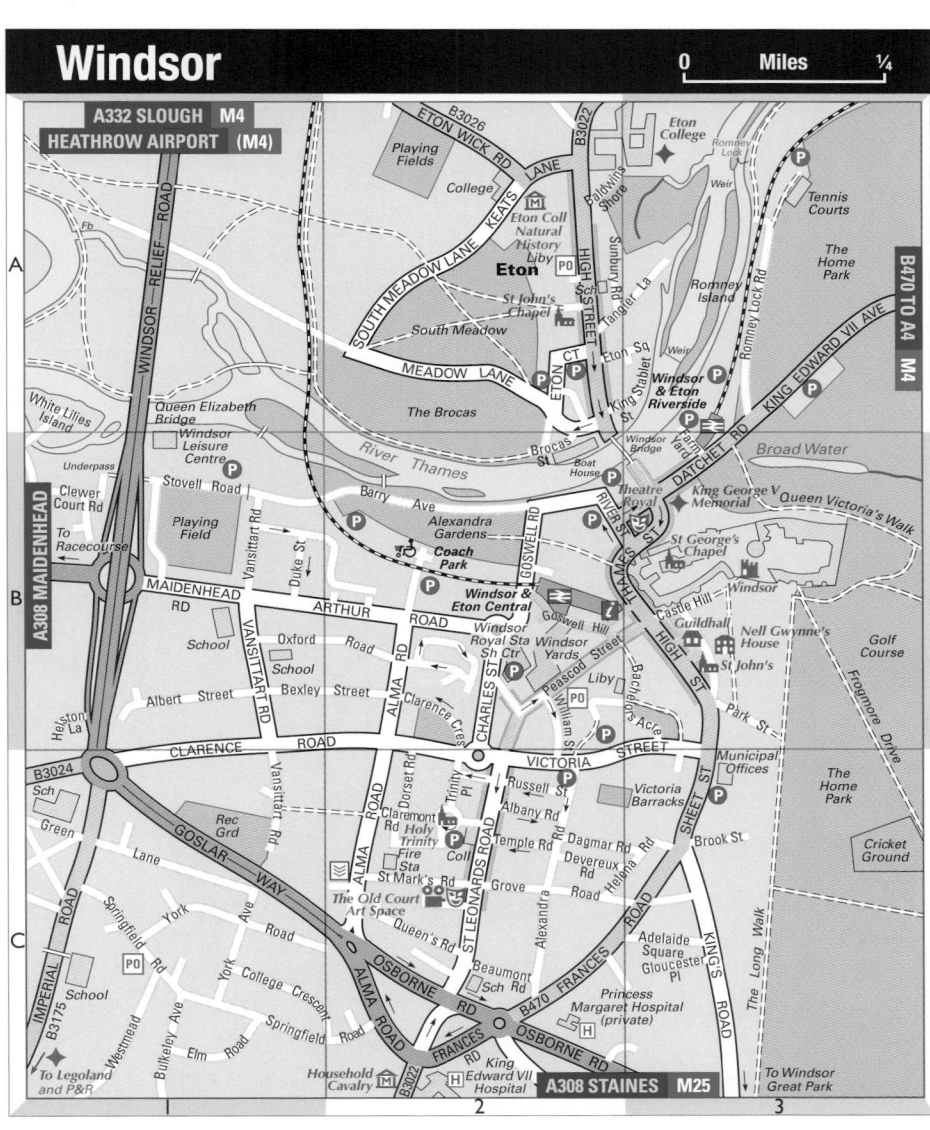

## Wolverhampton

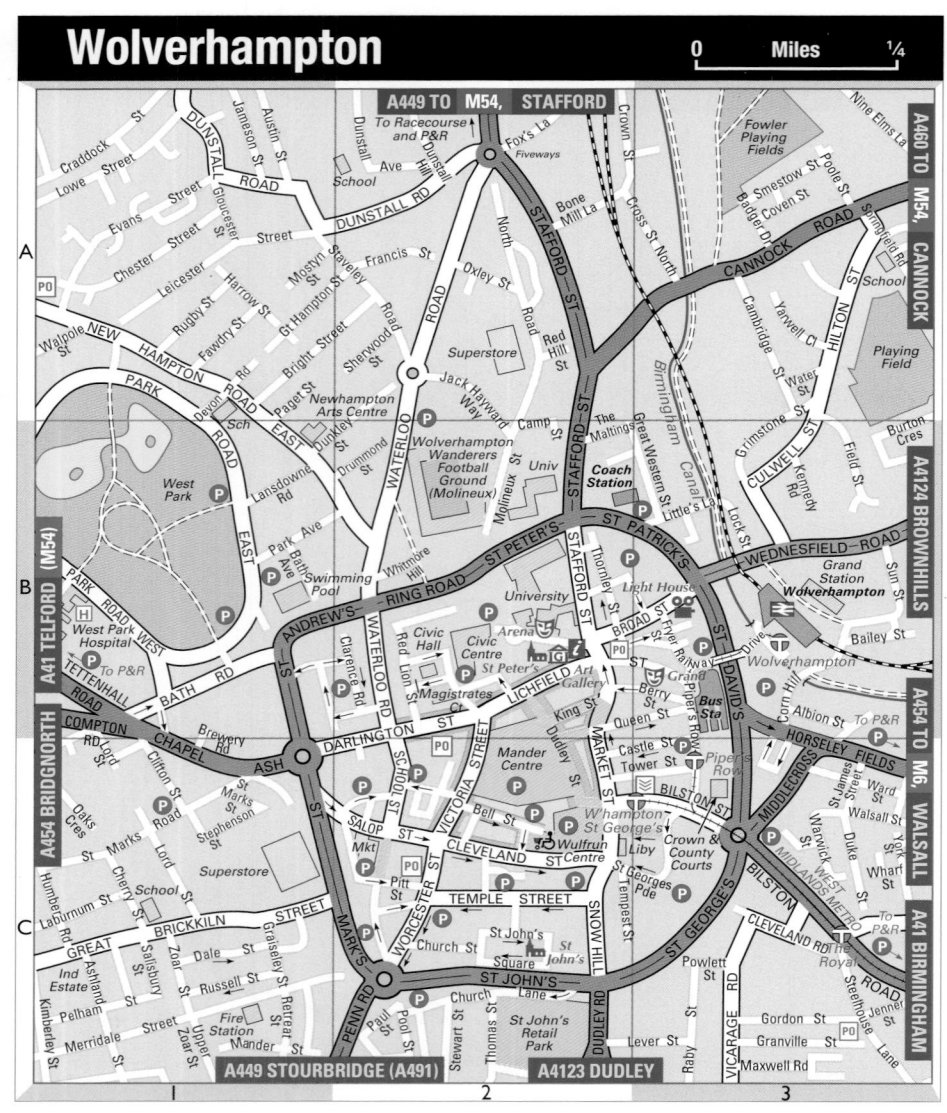

## Worcester

## Wrexham / Wrecsam

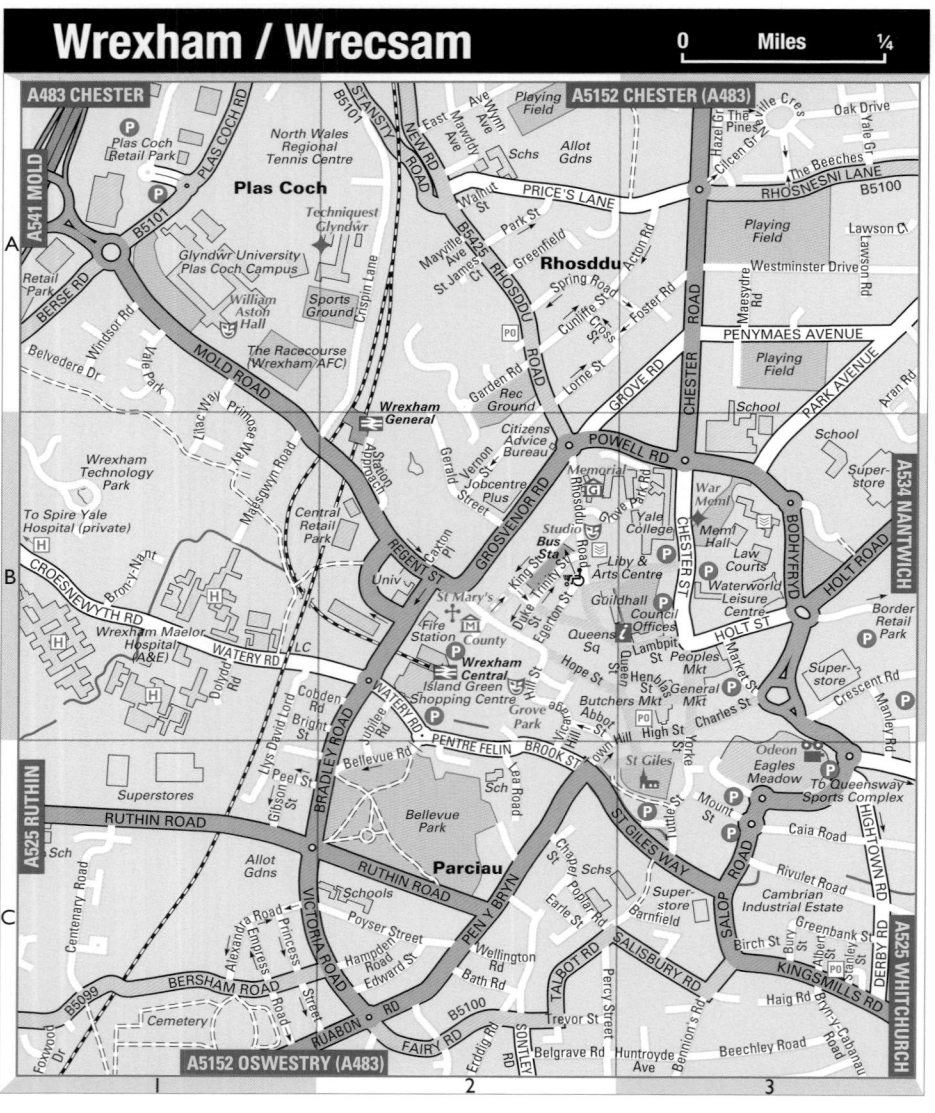

## York

## Abbreviations used in the index

| | |
|---|---|
| Aberdeen | **Aberdeen City** |
| Aberds | **Aberdeenshire** |
| Ald | **Alderney** |
| Anglesey | **Isle of Anglesey** |
| Angus | **Angus** |
| Argyll | **Argyll and Bute** |
| Bath | **Bath and North East Somerset** |
| BCP | **Bournemouth, Christchurch and Poole** |
| Bedford | **Bedford** |
| Blackburn | **Blackburn with Darwen** |
| Blackpool | **Blackpool** |
| Bl Gwent | **Blaenau Gwent** |
| Borders | **Scottish Borders** |
| Brack | **Bracknell** |
| Bridgend | **Bridgend** |
| Brighton | **City of Brighton and Hove** |
| Bristol | **City and County of Bristol** |
| Bucks | **Buckinghamshire** |
| Caerph | **Caerphilly** |
| Cambs | **Cambridgeshire** |
| Cardiff | **Cardiff** |
| Carms | **Carmarthenshire** |
| C Beds | **Central Bedfordshire** |
| Ceredig | **Ceredigion** |
| Ches E | **Cheshire East** |
| Ches W | **Cheshire West and Chester** |
| Clack | **Clackmannanshire** |
| Conwy | **Conwy** |
| Corn | **Cornwall** |
| Cumb | **Cumbria** |
| Darl | **Darlington** |
| Denb | **Denbighshire** |
| Derby | **City of Derby** |
| Derbys | **Derbyshire** |
| Devon | **Devon** |
| Dorset | **Dorset** |
| Dumfries | **Dumfries and Galloway** |
| Dundee | **Dundee City** |
| Durham | **Durham** |
| E Ayrs | **East Ayrshire** |
| Edin | **City of Edinburgh** |
| E Dunb | **East Dunbartonshire** |
| E Loth | **East Lothian** |
| E Renf | **East Renfrewshire** |
| Essex | **Essex** |
| E Sus | **East Sussex** |
| E Yorks | **East Riding of Yorkshire** |
| Falk | **Falkirk** |
| Fife | **Fife** |
| Flint | **Flintshire** |
| Glasgow | **City of Glasgow** |
| Glos | **Gloucestershire** |
| Gtr Man | **Greater Manchester** |

| | |
|---|---|
| Guern | **Guernsey** |
| Gwyn | **Gwynedd** |
| Halton | **Halton** |
| Hants | **Hampshire** |
| Hereford | **Herefordshire** |
| Herts | **Hertfordshire** |
| Highld | **Highland** |
| Hrtlpl | **Hartlepool** |
| Hull | **Hull** |
| Invclyd | **Inverclyde** |
| IoM | **Isle of Man** |
| IoW | **Isle of Wight** |
| Jersey | **Jersey** |
| Kent | **Kent** |
| Lancs | **Lancashire** |
| Leicester | **City of Leicester** |
| Leics | **Leicestershire** |
| Lincs | **Lincolnshire** |
| London | **Greater London** |
| Luton | **Luton** |
| Mbro | **Middlesbrough** |
| Medway | **Medway** |
| Mers | **Merseyside** |
| Midloth | **Midlothian** |
| M Keynes | **Milton Keynes** |
| Mon | **Monmouthshire** |
| Moray | **Moray** |
| M Tydf | **Merthyr Tydfil** |
| N Ayrs | **North Ayrshire** |
| Neath | **Neath Port Talbot** |
| NE Lincs | **North East Lincolnshire** |
| Newport | **City and County of Newport** |
| N Lanark | **North Lanarkshire** |
| N Lincs | **North Lincolnshire** |
| N Nhants | **North Northamptonshire** |
| Norf | **Norfolk** |
| Northumb | **Northumberland** |
| Nottingham | **City of Nottingham** |
| Notts | **Nottinghamshire** |
| N Som | **North Somerset** |
| N Yorks | **North Yorkshire** |
| Orkney | **Orkney** |
| Oxon | **Oxfordshire** |
| Pboro | **Peterborough** |
| Pembs | **Pembrokeshire** |
| Perth | **Perth and Kinross** |
| Plym | **Plymouth** |
| Powys | **Powys** |
| Ptsmth | **Portsmouth** |
| Reading | **Reading** |
| Redcar | **Redcar and Cleveland** |
| Renfs | **Renfrewshire** |
| Rhondda | **Rhondda Cynon Taff** |
| Rutland | **Rutland** |

| | |
|---|---|
| S Ayrs | **South Ayrshire** |
| Scilly | **Scilly** |
| S Glos | **South Gloucestershire** |
| Shetland | **Shetland** |
| Shrops | **Shropshire** |
| S Lanark | **South Lanarkshire** |
| Slough | **Slough** |
| Som | **Somerset** |
| Soton | **Southampton** |
| Southend | **Southend-on-Sea** |
| Staffs | **Staffordshire** |
| Stirling | **Stirling** |
| Stockton | **Stockton-on-Tees** |
| Stoke | **Stoke-on-Trent** |
| Suff | **Suffolk** |
| Sur | **Surrey** |
| Swansea | **Swansea** |
| Swindon | **Swindon** |
| S Yorks | **South Yorkshire** |
| T&W | **Tyne and Wear** |
| Telford | **Telford and Wrekin** |
| Thurrock | **Thurrock** |
| Torbay | **Torbay** |
| Torf | **Torfaen** |
| V Glam | **The Vale of Glamorgan** |
| Warks | **Warwickshire** |
| Warr | **Warrington** |
| W Berks | **West Berkshire** |
| W Dunb | **West Dunbartonshire** |
| Wilts | **Wiltshire** |
| Windsor | **Windsor and Maidenhead** |
| W Isles | **Western Isles** |
| W Loth | **West Lothian** |
| W Mid | **West Midlands** |
| W Nhants | **West Northamptonshire** |
| Wokingham | **Wokingham** |
| Worcs | **Worcestershire** |
| Wrex | **Wrexham** |
| W Sus | **West Sussex** |
| W Yorks | **West Yorkshire** |
| York | **City of York** |

## How to use the index

Example

**Charlton Mackerell** Som **12** B3

- grid square
- page number
- county or unitary authority

---

# A

Abbas Combe . . . .12 B5
Abberley . . . . . . . .50 C2
Abberton
  Essex . . . . . . . . . .43 C6
  Worcs . . . . . . . . .50 D4
Abberwick . . . . . .117 C7
Abbess Roding . . .42 C1
Abbey . . . . . . . . . . .11 C6
Abbey-cwm-hir . .48 B2
Abbeydale . . . . . . .88 F4
Abbey Dore . . . . .49 F5
Abbey Field . . . . . .43 B5
Abbey Hulton . . . .75 E6
Abbey
  St Bathans . . . . .122 C3
Abbeystead . . . . . .93 D5
Abbey Town . . . . .107 D8
Abbey Village . . . .86 B4
Abbey Wood . . . . .29 B5
Abbots Bickington .9 C5
Abbots Bromley . .62 B4
Abbotsbury . . . . . .12 F3
Abbotsham . . . . . . .9 B6
Abbotskerswell . . .7 C6
Abbots Langley . . .40 D3
Abbots Leigh . . . . .23 B7
Abbotsley . . . . . . .54 D3
Abbots Morton . . .50 D5
Abbots Ripton . . . .54 B3
Abbots Salford . . .51 D5
Abbotswood . . . . .14 B4
Abbotts Ann . . . . . .25 E8
Abcott . . . . . . . . . .49 B5
Abdon . . . . . . . . . .61 F5
Aber . . . . . . . . . . . .46 E3
Aberaeron . . . . . . .46 C3
Aberaman . . . . . . .34 D4
Aberangell . . . . . . .58 C5
Aber-Arad . . . . . . .46 F2
Aberarder . . . . . . .137 F7
Aberarder
  House . . . . . . . . .138 B2
Aberarder
  Lodge . . . . . . . . .137 F8
Aberargie . . . . . . .128 C3
Aberarth . . . . . . . .46 C3
Aberavon . . . . . . . .33 E8
Aber-banc . . . . . . .46 E2
Aberbeeg . . . . . . . .35 D6
Abercanaid . . . . . .34 D4
Abercarn . . . . . . . .35 E6
Abercastle . . . . . . .44 B3
Abercegir . . . . . . . .58 D5
Aberchirder . . . . .152 C6
Aber Cowarch . . . .59 C5
Abercraf . . . . . . . . .34 C2
Abercrombie . . . . .129 D7
Abercych . . . . . . . .45 E4
Abercynafon . . . . .34 C4
Abercynon . . . . . . .34 E4
Aberdalgie . . . . . . .128 B2
Aberdâr
  = Aberdare . . . . .34 D3
Aberdare
  = Aberdâr . . . . . .34 D3
Aberdaron . . . . . . .70 E2
Aberdaugleddau
  = Milford Haven . .44 E4

Aberdeen . . . . . . .141 D8
Aberdesach . . . . . .82 F4
Aberdour . . . . . . . .128 F3
Aberdovey . . . . . . .58 E3
Aberdulais . . . . . . .34 D1
Aberedw . . . . . . . . .48 E2
Abereiddy . . . . . . .44 B2
Abererch . . . . . . . .70 D4
Aberfan . . . . . . . . .34 D4
Aberfeldy . . . . . . .133 E6
Aberffraw . . . . . . . .82 E3
Aberffrwd . . . . . . .47 B5
Aberford . . . . . . . .95 F7
Aberfoyle . . . . . . .126 D4
Abergavenny
  = Y Fenni . . . . . .35 C6
Abergele . . . . . . . .72 B3
Aber-Giâr . . . . . . . .46 E4
Abergorlech . . . . .46 F4
Abergwaun
  = Fishguard . . . . .44 B4
Abergwesyn . . . . .47 D7
Abergwili . . . . . . . .33 B5
Abergwynant . . . . .58 C3
Aber-gwynfi . . . . . .34 E2
Abergwyngregyn . .83 D6
Abergynolwyn . . . .58 D3
Aberhafesp . . . . . .59 E7
Aberhonddu
  = Brecon . . . . . . .34 B4
Aberhosan . . . . . . .58 E5
Aberkenfig . . . . . . .34 F2
Aberlady . . . . . . . .129 F6
Aberlemno . . . . . .135 D5
Aberllefenni . . . . .58 D4
Abermagwr . . . . . .47 B5
Abermaw
  = Barmouth . . . . .58 C3
Abermeurig . . . . . .46 D4
Abermule . . . . . . . .59 E8
Abernaint . . . . . . . .59 B8
Abernant . . . . . . . .32 B4
Abernethy . . . . . . .128 C3
Abernyte . . . . . . . .134 F2
Aberpennar
  = Mountain Ash . .34 E4
Aberporth . . . . . . .45 D4
Aber-Rhiwlech . . . .59 B6
Abersoch . . . . . . . .70 E4
Abersychan . . . . . .35 D6
Abertawe
  = Swansea . . . . . .33 E7
Aberteifi
  = Cardigan . . . . . .45 E3
Aberthin . . . . . . . . .22 B2
Abertillery
  = Abertyleri . . . . .35 D6
Abertridwr
  Caerph . . . . . . . . .35 F5
  Powys . . . . . . . . .59 C7
Abertyleri
  = Abertillery . . . . .35 D6
Abertysswg . . . . . .35 D5
Aberuthven . . . . . .127 C8
Aber-Village . . . . . .35 B5
Aberyscir . . . . . . . .34 B3
Aberystwyth . . . . .58 F2
Abhainn Suidhe .154 G5
Abingdon-
  on-Thames . . . . . .38 E4

Abinger Common .28 E2
Abinger Hammer .27 E8
Abington . . . . . . . .114 B2
Abington Pigotts .54 E4
Ab Kettleby . . . . . .64 B4
Ab Lench . . . . . . . .50 D5
Ablington
  Glos . . . . . . . . . . .37 D8
  Wilts . . . . . . . . . .25 E6
Abney . . . . . . . . . . .75 B8
Aboyne . . . . . . . . .140 E4
Abram . . . . . . . . . .86 D4
Abriachan . . . . . . .151 H8
Abridge . . . . . . . . .41 E7
Abson . . . . . . . . . . .24 B2
Abthorpe . . . . . . . .52 E4
Abune-the-Hill . . .159 F3
Aby . . . . . . . . . . . . .79 B7
Acaster Malbis . . .95 E8
Acaster Selby . . . .95 E8
Accrington . . . . . . .87 B5
Acha . . . . . . . . . . .146 F4
Achabraid . . . . . . .145 E7
Achachork . . . . . .149 D9
Achafolla . . . . . . . .124 D3
Achagary . . . . . . . .157 D10
Achahoish . . . . . . .144 F6
Achalader . . . . . . .133 E8
Achallader . . . . . . .131 E7
Acha Mor . . . . . . .155 E8
Achanalt . . . . . . . .150 E5
Achanamara . . . . .144 E6
Achandunie . . . . . .151 D9
Ach'an Todhair . . .130 B4
Achany . . . . . . . . .157 J8
Achaphubuil . . . . .130 B4
Acharacle . . . . . . .147 E9
Acharn
  Highld . . . . . . . . .147 F10
  Perth . . . . . . . . . .132 E4
Acharole . . . . . . . .158 E4
Achath . . . . . . . . . .141 C6
Achavanich . . . . . .158 F3
Achavraat . . . . . . .151 G12
Achddu . . . . . . . . . .33 D5
Achduart . . . . . . . .156 J3
Achentoul . . . . . . .157 F11
Achfary . . . . . . . . .156 F5
Achgarve . . . . . . . .155 H13
Achiemore
  Highld . . . . . . . . .156 C6
  Highld . . . . . . . . .157 D11
A'Chill . . . . . . . . . .148 H7
Achiltibuie . . . . . .156 J3
Achina . . . . . . . . . .157 C10
Achinduich . . . . . .157 J8
Achinduin . . . . . . .124 B4
Achingills . . . . . . .158 D3
Achintee
  Highld . . . . . . . . .131 B5
  Highld . . . . . . . . .150 G2
Achintraid . . . . . . .149 E13
Achlean . . . . . . . . .138 E4
Achleck . . . . . . . . .146 G7
Achluachrach . . . .137 F5
Achlyness . . . . . . .156 D5
Achmelvich . . . . . .156 G3
Achmore
  Highld . . . . . . . . .149 E13
  Stirling . . . . . . . .132 F2

Achnaba
  Argyll . . . . . . . . .124 B5
  Argyll . . . . . . . . .145 E8
Achnabat . . . . . . .151 H8
Achnacarnin . . . . .156 F3
Achnacarry . . . . . .136 F4
Achnacloich
  Argyll . . . . . . . . .125 B5
  Highld . . . . . . . . .149 H10
Achnaconeran . . . .137 C7
Achnacraig . . . . . .146 G7
Achnacroish . . . . .130 E2
Achnadrish . . . . . .146 F7
Achnafalnich . . . . .125 C8
Achnagarron . . . . .151 E9
Achnaha . . . . . . . .146 E7
Achnahanat . . . . .151 B8
Achnahannet . . . . .139 B5
Achnairn . . . . . . . .157 H8
Achnaluachrach .157 J9
Achnasaul . . . . . . .136 F4
Achnasheen . . . . .150 F4
Achosnich . . . . . . .146 E7
Achranich . . . . . . .147 G10
Achreamie . . . . . .157 C13
Achriabhach . . . . .131 C5
Achriesgill . . . . . .156 D5
Achrimsdale . . . . .157 J12
Achtoty . . . . . . . . .157 C9
Achurch . . . . . . . . .65 F7
Achuvoldrach . . . .157 D8
Achvaich . . . . . . . .151 B10
Achvarasdal . . . . .157 C12
Ackergill . . . . . . . .158 E5
Acklam
  Mbro . . . . . . . . . .102 C2
  N Yorks . . . . . . . .96 C3
Ackleton . . . . . . . .61 E7
Acklington . . . . . .117 D8
Ackton . . . . . . . . . .88 B5
Ackworth
  Moor Top . . . . . .88 C5
Acle . . . . . . . . . . . .69 C7
Acock's Green . . .62 F5
Acol . . . . . . . . . . . .31 C7
Acomb
  Northumb . . . . . .110 C2
  York . . . . . . . . . . .95 D8
Aconbury . . . . . . . .49 F7
Acre . . . . . . . . . . . .87 B5
Acrefair . . . . . . . . .73 E6
Acre Street . . . . . .15 E8
Acton
  Ches E . . . . . . . . .74 D3
  Dorset . . . . . . . . .13 G7
  London . . . . . . . .41 F5
  Shrops . . . . . . . . .60 F3
  Suff . . . . . . . . . . .56 E2
  Wrex . . . . . . . . . .73 D7
Acton
  Beauchamp . . . .49 D8
Acton Bridge . . . .74 B2
Acton Burnell . . . .60 D5
Acton Green . . . . .49 D8
Acton Pigott . . . . .60 D5
Acton Round . . . . .61 E6
Acton Scott . . . . . .60 F4
Acton Trussell . . . .62 C3
Acton Turville . . . .37 F5
Adbaston . . . . . . . .61 B7
Adber . . . . . . . . . . .12 B3

Adderley . . . . . . . .74 E3
Adderstone . . . . .123 F7
Addiewell . . . . . . .120 C2
Addingham . . . . . .94 E3
Addington
  Bucks . . . . . . . . .39 B7
  Kent . . . . . . . . . .29 D7
  London . . . . . . . .28 C4
Addinston . . . . . . .121 D8
Addiscombe . . . . .28 C4
Addlestone . . . . . .27 C8
Addlethorpe . . . . .79 C8
Adel . . . . . . . . . . . .95 F5
Adeney . . . . . . . . .61 C7
Adfa . . . . . . . . . . . .59 D7
Adforton . . . . . . . .49 B6
Adisham . . . . . . . . .31 D6
Adlestrop . . . . . . . .38 B2
Adlingfleet . . . . . .90 B2
Adlington . . . . . . . .86 C4
Admaston
  Staffs . . . . . . . . . .62 B4
  Telford . . . . . . . .61 C6
Admington . . . . . . .51 E7
Adstock . . . . . . . . .52 F5
Adstone . . . . . . . . .52 D3
Adversane . . . . . . .16 B4
Advie . . . . . . . . . . .152 E1
Adwalton . . . . . . . .88 B3
Adwell . . . . . . . . . .39 E6
Adwick le Street . .89 D6
Adwick upon
  Dearne . . . . . . . .89 D5
Adziel . . . . . . . . . .153 C9
Ae Village . . . . . . .114 F2
Affleck . . . . . . . . .141 B7
Affpuddle . . . . . . .13 E6
Affric Lodge . . . . .136 B4
Afon-wen . . . . . . . .72 B5
Afton . . . . . . . . . . .14 F4
Agglethorpe . . . . .101 F5
Agneash . . . . . . . . .84 D4
Aigburth . . . . . . . .85 F4
Aiginis . . . . . . . . . .155 D9
Aike . . . . . . . . . . . .97 E6
Aikerness . . . . . . .159 C5
Aikers . . . . . . . . . .159 J5
Aiketgate . . . . . . .108 E4
Aikton . . . . . . . . . .108 D2
Ailey . . . . . . . . . . . .48 E5
Ailstone . . . . . . . . .51 D7
Ailsworth . . . . . . . .65 E8
Ainderby
  Quernhow . . . . .102 F1
Ainderby
  Steeple . . . . . . .101 E8
Aingers Green . . .43 B7
Ainsdale . . . . . . . .85 C4
Ainsdale-on-Sea 85 C4
Ainstable . . . . . . .108 E5
Ainsworth . . . . . . .87 C5
Ainthorpe . . . . . . .103 D5
Aintree . . . . . . . . . .85 E4
Aird
  Argyll . . . . . . . . .124 E3
  Dumfries . . . . . .104 C4
  Highld . . . . . . . .149 A12
  W Isles . . . . . . . .155 D10
Aird a Mhachair 148 D2
Aird a' Mhulaidh 154 F6
Aird Asaig . . . . . .154 G6

Aird Dhail . . . . . .155 A9
Airdens . . . . . . . . .151 B9
Aird Mhidhinis .148 H2
Aird Mhighe
  W Isles . . . . . . . .154 H6
  W Isles . . . . . . . .154 J5
Aird Mhor . . . . . .148 H2
Aird of Sleat . . . .149 H10
Airdrie . . . . . . . . .119 C7
Aird Thunga . . . . .155 D9
Airdtorrisdale . . .157 C9
Aird Uig . . . . . . . .154 D5
Aird a
  Bhruaich . . . . . .154 F7
Airieland . . . . . . . .106 D4
Airmyn . . . . . . . . . .89 B8
Airntully . . . . . . . .133 F7
Airor . . . . . . . . . . .149 H12
Airth . . . . . . . . . . .127 F7
Airton . . . . . . . . . . .94 D2
Airyhassen . . . . . .105 E7
Aisby
  Lincs . . . . . . . . . .78 F3
  Lincs . . . . . . . . . .90 E2
Aisgernis . . . . . . .148 F2
Aiskew . . . . . . . . .101 F7
Aislaby
  N Yorks . . . . . . .103 D6
  N Yorks . . . . . . .103 F5
  Stockton . . . . . .102 C2
Aisthorpe . . . . . . .78 A2
Aith
  Orkney . . . . . . . .159 G3
  Shetland . . . . . . .160 D8
  Shetland . . . . . . .160 H5
Aithsetter . . . . . . .160 K6
Aitkenhead . . . . . .112 D3
Aitnoch . . . . . . . . .151 H12
Akeld . . . . . . . . . .117 B5
Akeley . . . . . . . . . .52 F5
Akenham . . . . . . . .56 E5
Albaston . . . . . . . . .6 B2
Alberbury . . . . . . .60 C3
Albourne . . . . . . . .17 C6
Albrighton
  Shrops . . . . . . . . .60 C4
  Shrops . . . . . . . . .62 D2
Alburgh . . . . . . . . .69 F5
Albury
  Herts . . . . . . . . . .41 B7
  Sur . . . . . . . . . . . .27 E8
Albury End . . . . . .41 B7
Alby Hill . . . . . . . .81 D7
Alcaig . . . . . . . . . .151 F8
Alcaston . . . . . . . .60 F4
Alcester . . . . . . . . .51 D5
Alciston . . . . . . . . .18 E2
Alcombe
  Som . . . . . . . . . . .21 E8
  Wilts . . . . . . . . . .24 C3
Alconbury . . . . . . .54 B2
Alconbury
  Weston . . . . . . . .54 B2
Aldbar Castle . . . .135 D5
Aldborough
  Norf . . . . . . . . . . .81 D7
  N Yorks . . . . . . . .95 C7
Aldbourne . . . . . . .25 B7
Aldbrough . . . . . . .97 F8
Aldbrough
  St John . . . . . . .101 C7

Aldbury . . . . . . . . .40 C2
Aldcliffe . . . . . . . . .92 C4
Aldclune . . . . . . . .133 C6
Aldeburgh . . . . . . .57 D8
Aldeby . . . . . . . . . .69 E7
Aldenham . . . . . . .40 E4
Alderbury . . . . . . .14 B2
Aldercar . . . . . . . . .76 E4
Alderford . . . . . . . .68 C4
Alderholt . . . . . . . .14 C2
Alderley . . . . . . . . .36 E4
Alderley Edge . . . .74 B5
Aldermaston . . . . .26 C3
Aldermaston
  Wharf . . . . . . . . .26 C4
Alderminster . . . . .51 E7
Alder's End . . . . . .49 E8
Aldersey Green . . .73 D8
Aldershot . . . . . . .27 D6
Alderton
  Glos . . . . . . . . . . .50 F5
  Shrops . . . . . . . . .60 B4
  Suff . . . . . . . . . . .57 E7
  Wilts . . . . . . . . . .37 F5
  W Nhants . . . . . . .52 E5
Alderwasley . . . . .76 D3
Aldfield . . . . . . . . .95 C5
Aldford . . . . . . . . .73 D8
Aldham
  Essex . . . . . . . . . .43 B5
  Suff . . . . . . . . . . .56 E4
Aldie . . . . . . . . . .151 C10
Aldingbourne . . . .16 D3
Aldingham . . . . . . .92 B2
Aldington
  Kent . . . . . . . . . . .19 B7
  Worcs . . . . . . . . .51 E5
Aldochlay . . . . . . .126 E2
Aldreth . . . . . . . . .54 B5
Aldridge . . . . . . . . .62 D4
Aldringham . . . . . .57 C8
Aldsworth . . . . . . .38 C1
Aldunie . . . . . . . . .140 B2
Aldwark
  Derbys . . . . . . . . .76 D2
  N Yorks . . . . . . . .95 C7
Aldwick . . . . . . . . .16 E3
Aldwincle . . . . . . .65 F7
Aldworth . . . . . . . .26 B3
Alexandria . . . . . .118 B3
Alfardisworthy . . . .8 C4
Alfington . . . . . . . .11 E6
Alfold . . . . . . . . . . .27 F8
Alfold Bars . . . . . .27 F8
Alfold Crossways .27 F8
Alford
  Aberds . . . . . . . .140 C4
  Lincs . . . . . . . . . .79 B7
  Som . . . . . . . . . . .23 F8
Alfreton . . . . . . . . .76 D4
Alfrick . . . . . . . . . .50 D2
Alfrick Pound . . . .50 D2
Algaltraig . . . . . . .145 F9
Algarkirk . . . . . . . .79 F5
Alhampton . . . . . . .23 F8
Aline Lodge . . . . .154 F6
Alisary . . . . . . . . .147 D10
Alkborough . . . . . .90 B2
Alkerton . . . . . . . . .51 E8

Alkham . . . . . . . . . .31 E6
Alkington . . . . . . . .74 F2
Alkmonton . . . . . . .75 F8
Alladale Lodge . .150 C7
Allaleigh . . . . . . . . .7 D5
Allanaquoich . . . .139 E7
Allangrange
  Mains . . . . . . . . .151 F9
Allanton
  Borders . . . . . . .122 D4
  N Lanark . . . . . . .119 D8
Allathasdal . . . . . .148 H1
All Cannings . . . . .25 C5
Allendale Town . .109 D8
Allenheads . . . . . .109 E8
Allensford . . . . . .110 D3
Allens Green . . . . .41 C7
Allensmore . . . . . .49 F6
Allenton . . . . . . . . .76 F3
Aller . . . . . . . . . . . .12 B2
Allerby . . . . . . . . .107 F7
Allerford . . . . . . . .21 E8
Allerston . . . . . . . .103 F6
Allerthorpe . . . . . .96 E3
Allerton
  Mers . . . . . . . . . .86 F2
  W Yorks . . . . . . . .94 F4
Allerton Bywater .88 B5
Allerton
  Mauleverer . . . . .95 D7
Allesley . . . . . . . . .63 F7
Allestree . . . . . . . .76 F3
Allet . . . . . . . . . . . . .3 B6
Allexton . . . . . . . . .64 D5
Allgreave . . . . . . . .75 C6
Allhallows . . . . . . .30 B2
Allhallows-on-
  Sea . . . . . . . . . . .30 B2
Alligin Shuas . . . .149 C13
Allimore Green . . .62 C2
Allington
  Lincs . . . . . . . . . .77 E8
  Wilts . . . . . . . . . .25 C5
  Wilts . . . . . . . . . .25 F7
Allithwaite . . . . . . .92 B3
Alloa . . . . . . . . . . .127 E7
Allonby . . . . . . . . .107 E7
Alloway . . . . . . . . .112 C3
All Saints South
  Elmham . . . . . . .69 F6
All Stretton . . . . . .60 E4
Allt . . . . . . . . . . . . .33 D6
Alltforgan . . . . . . .59 B6
Alltmawr . . . . . . . .48 E2
Alltnacaillich . . . .156 E7
Allt na h-Airbhe 150 B4
Allt-nan-sùgh . . .136 B2
Alltsigh . . . . . . . . .137 C7
Alltwalis . . . . . . . . .46 F3
Alltwen . . . . . . . . .33 D8
Alltyblaca . . . . . . .46 E4
Allwood Green . . .56 B4
Almeley . . . . . . . . .48 D5
Almer . . . . . . . . . . .13 E7
Almholme . . . . . . .89 D6
Almington . . . . . . .74 F4
Alminstone Cross . .8 B5
Almondbank . . . . .128 B2
Almondbury . . . . . .88 C2
Almondsbury . . . . .36 F3

Alne . . . . . . . . . . . .95 C7
Alness . . . . . . . . . .151 E9
Alnham . . . . . . . . .117 C5
Alnmouth . . . . . . .117 C8
Alnwick . . . . . . . . .117 C7
Alperton . . . . . . . . .40 F4
Alphamstone . . . . .56 F2
Alpheton . . . . . . . .56 D2
Alphington . . . . . . .10 E4
Alport . . . . . . . . . . .76 C2
Alpraham . . . . . . . .74 D2
Alresford . . . . . . . .43 B6
Alrewas . . . . . . . . .63 C5
Alsager . . . . . . . . .74 D4
Alsagers Bank . . . .74 E5
Alsop en le Dale . .75 D8
Alston
  Cumb . . . . . . . . .109 E7
  Devon . . . . . . . . .11 D8
Alstone . . . . . . . . . .50 F4
Alstonefield . . . . . .75 D8
Alswear . . . . . . . . .10 B2
Altandhu . . . . . . . .156 H2
Altanduin . . . . . . .157 G11
Altarnun . . . . . . . . .8 F4
Altass . . . . . . . . . .156 J7
Alterwall . . . . . . . .158 D4
Altham . . . . . . . . . .93 F7
Althorne . . . . . . . . .43 E5
Althorpe . . . . . . . . .90 D2
Alticry . . . . . . . . . .105 D6
Altnabreac
  Station . . . . . . . .157 E13
Altnacealgach
  Hotel . . . . . . . . .156 H5
Altnacraig . . . . . . .124 C4
Altnafeadh . . . . . .131 D6
Altnaharra . . . . . .157 F8
Altofts . . . . . . . . . .88 B4
Alton
  Derbys . . . . . . . . .76 C3
  Hants . . . . . . . . . .26 F5
  Staffs . . . . . . . . . .75 E7
Alton Pancras . . . .12 D5
Alton Priors . . . . . .25 C6
Altrincham . . . . . . .87 F5
Altrua . . . . . . . . . .136 F5
Altskeith . . . . . . . .126 D3
Altyre House . . . .151 F13
Alva . . . . . . . . . . . .127 E7
Alvanley . . . . . . . . .73 B8
Alvaston . . . . . . . . .76 F3
Alvechurch . . . . . .50 B5
Alvecote . . . . . . . .63 D6
Alvediston . . . . . . .13 B7
Alveley . . . . . . . . . .61 F7
Alverdiscott . . . . . .9 B7
Alverstoke . . . . . . .15 E7
Alverstone . . . . . . .15 F6
Alverton . . . . . . . . .77 E7
Alves . . . . . . . . . . .152 B1
Alvescot . . . . . . . . .38 D2
Alveston
  S Glos . . . . . . . . .36 F3
  Warks . . . . . . . . .51 D7
Alvie . . . . . . . . . . .138 D4
Alvingham . . . . . . .91 E7
Alvington . . . . . . . .36 D3

**Abb–Alv**

Alwalton....65 E8
Alweston....12 C4
Alwinton....116 D5
Alwoodley....95 E5
Alyth....134 E2
Amatnatua....150 B7
Am Baile....148 G2
Ambergate....76 D3
Amber Hill....78 E5
Amberley
  Glos....37 D5
  W Sus....16 C4
Amble....117 D8
Amblecote....62 F2
Ambler Thorn....87 B8
Ambleside....99 D5
Ambleston....44 C5
Ambrosden....39 C6
Am Buth....124 C4
Amcotts....90 C2
Amersham....40 E2
Amesbury....25 E6
Amington....63 D6
Amisfield....114 F2
Amlwch....82 B4
Amlwch Port....82 B4
Ammanford
  =Rhydaman....33 C7
Amod....143 E8
Amotherby....96 B3
Ampfield....14 B5
Ampleforth....95 B8
Ampney Crucis....37 D7
Ampney St Mary....37 D7
Ampney St Peter....37 D7
Amport....25 E7
Ampthill....53 F8
Ampton....56 B2
Amroth....32 D2
Amulree....133 F5
Anagach....139 B6
Anaheilt....130 C2
Anancaun....150 E3
An Caol....149 C11
Ancaster....78 E2
Anchor....59 F8
Anchorsholme....92 E3
An Cnoc....155 D9
Ancroft....123 E5
Ancrum....116 B2
Anderby....79 B8
Anderson....13 E6
Anderton....74 B3
Andover....25 E8
Andover Down....25 E8
Andoversford....37 C7
Andreas....84 C4
Anfield....85 E4
Angersleigh....11 C6
Angle....44 E3
An Gleann Ur....155 D9
Angmering....16 D4
Angram
  N Yorks....95 E8
  N Yorks....100 E3
Anie....126 C4
Ankerville....151 D11
Anlaby....90 B4
Anmer....80 E3
Annan....107 C8
Annat
  Argyll....125 C6
  Highld....149 C13
Anna Valley....25 E8
Annbank....112 B4
Annesley....76 D5
Annesley
  Woodhouse....76 D4
Annfield Plain....110 D4
Annifirth....160 J3
Annitsford....111 B5
Annscroft....60 D4
Ansdell....85 B4
Ansford....23 F8
Ansley....63 E6
Anslow....63 B6
Anslow Gate....63 B6
Anstey
  Herts....54 F5
  Leics....64 D2
Anstruther
  Easter....129 D7
Anstruther
  Wester....129 D7
Ansty
  Hants....26 E5
  Warks....63 F7
  Wilts....13 B7
  W Sus....17 B6
Anthill Common....15 C7
Anthorn....107 D8
Antingham....81 D8
An t-Ob
  =Leverburgh....154 J5
Anton's Gowt....79 E5
Antonshill....127 F7
Antony....5 D8
Anwick....78 D4
Anwoth....106 D2
Aoradh....142 B3
Apes Hall....67 E5
Apethorpe....65 E7
Apeton....62 C2
Apley....78 B4
Apperknowle....76 B3
Apperley....37 B5
Apperley Bridge....94 F4
Appersett....100 E3
Appin....130 E3
Appin House....130 E3
Appleby....90 C3
Appleby-in-
  Westmorland....100 B1
Appleby Magna....63 D7
Appleby Parva....63 D7
Applecross....149 D12
Applecross
  House....149 D12
Appledore
  Devon....11 C5
  Devon....20 F3
  Kent....19 C6
Appledore Heath....19 B6
Appleford....39 E5
Applegarthtown....114 F4

Appleshaw....25 E8
Applethwaite....98 B4
Appleton
  Halton....86 F3
  Oxon....38 D4
Appleton-
  le-Moors....103 F5
Appleton-
  le-Street....96 B3
Appleton Roebuck....95 E8
Appleton Thorn....86 F4
Appleton Wiske....102 D1
Appletreehall....115 C8
Appletreewick....94 C3
Appley....11 B5
Appley Bridge....86 D3
Apse Heath....15 F6
Apsley End....54 F2
Apuldram....16 D2
Aquhythie....141 C6
Arabella....151 D11
Arbeadie....141 E5
Arberth
  =Narberth....32 C2
Arbirlot....135 E6
Arborfield....27 C5
Arborfield Cross....27 C5
Arborfield
  Garrison....27 C5
Arbourthorne....88 F4
Arbroath....135 E6
Arbuthnott....135 B7
Archiestown....152 D2
Arclid....74 C4
Ardachu....157 J9
Ardalanish....146 K6
Ardanaiseig....125 C6
Ardaneaskan....149 E13
Ardanstur....124 D4
Ardargie House
  Hotel....128 C2
Ardarroch....149 E13
Ardbeg
  Argyll....142 D5
  Argyll....145 E10
Ardcharnich....150 C4
Ardchiavaig....146 K6
Ardchullarie
  More....126 C4
Ardchyle....126 B4
Arddleen....60 C2
Ardechive....136 E4
Ardeley....41 B6
Ardelve....149 F13
Arden....126 F2
Ardens Grafton....51 D6
Ardentinny....145 E10
Ardentraive....145 F9
Ardeonaig....132 F3
Ardersier....151 F10
Ardessie....150 C3
Ardfern....124 E4
Ardgartan....125 E8
Ardgay....151 B8
Ardgour....130 C4
Ardheslaig....149 C12
Ardiecow....152 B5
Ardindrean....150 C4
Ardingly....17 B7
Ardington....38 F4
Ardlair....140 B4
Ardlamont
  House....145 G8
Ardleigh....43 B6
Ardler....134 E2
Ardley....39 B5
Ardlui....126 C2
Ardlussa....144 E5
Ardmair....150 B4
Ardmay....125 E8
Ardminish....143 D7
Ardmolich....147 D10
Ardmore
  Argyll....124 C3
  Highld....151 C10
  Highld....156 D5
Ardnacross....147 G8
Ardnadam....145 F10
Ardnagrask....151 G8
Ardnarff....149 E13
Ardnastang....130 C2
Ardnave....142 A3
Ardno....125 E7
Ardo....153 E8
Ardoch....133 F7
Ardochy House....136 D5
Ardoyne....141 B5
Ardpatrick....144 H6
Ardpatrick
  House....144 H6
Ardpeaton....145 E11
Ardrishaig....145 E7
Ardross
  Fife....129 D7
  Highld....151 D9
Ardross Castle....151 D9
Ardrossan....118 E2
Ardshealach....147 E9
Ardsley....88 D4
Ardslignish....147 E8
Ardtalla....142 C5
Ardtalnaig....132 F4
Ardtoe....147 D9
Ardtrostan....127 B5
Arduaine....124 D3
Ardullie....151 E9
Ardvasar....149 H11
Ardverikie....137 F7
Ardvorlich....126 B5
Ardwell....104 E5
Ardwell Mains....104 E5
Ardwick....87 E6
Areley Kings....50 B3
Arford....27 F6
Argoed
  Caerph....35 E5
  Powys....47 C8
Arichamish....124 E5
Arichastlich....125 B8
Aridhglas....146 J6
Arileod....146 F4
Arinacrinachd....149 C12
Arinagour....146 F5
Arion....159 G3
Arisaig....147 C9

Ariundle....130 C2
Arkendale....95 C6
Arkesden....55 F5
Arkholme....93 B5
Arkleby....107 E8
Arkle Town....101 D5
Arkley....41 E5
Arksey....89 D6
Arkwright Town....76 B4
Arle....37 B6
Arlecdon....98 C2
Arlesey....54 F2
Arleston....61 C6
Arley....86 F4
Arlingham....36 C4
Arlington
  Devon....20 E5
  E Sus....18 E2
  Glos....37 D8
Armadale
  Highld....157 C10
  W Loth....120 C2
Armadale
  Castle....149 H11
Armathwaite....108 E5
Arminghall....69 D5
Armitage....62 C4
Armley....95 F5
Armscote....51 E7
Armthorpe....89 D7
Arnabost....146 F5
Arncliffe....94 B2
Arncroach....129 D7
Arne....13 F7
Arnesby....64 E3
Arngask....128 C3
Arnisdale....149 G13
Arnish....149 D10
Arniston Engine....121 C6
Arnol....155 C8
Arnold
  E Yorks....97 E7
  Notts....77 E5
Arnprior....126 E5
Arnside....92 B4
Aros Mains....147 G8
Arowry....73 F8
Arpafeelie....151 F9
Arrad Foot....99 F5
Arram....97 E6
Arrathorne....101 E7
Arreton....15 F6
Arrington....54 D4
Arrivain....125 B8
Arrochar....125 E8
Arrow....51 D5
Arthington....95 E5
Arthingworth....64 F4
Arthog....58 C3
Arthrath....153 E9
Arthurstone....134 E2
Artrochie....153 E10
Arundel....16 D4
Aryhoulan....130 C4
Asby....98 B2
Ascog....145 G10
Ascot....27 C7
Ascott....51 F8
Ascott-under-
  Wychwood....38 C3
Asenby....95 B6
Asfordby....64 C4
Asfordby Hill....64 C4
Asgarby
  Lincs....78 E4
  Lincs....79 C6
Ash
  Kent....29 C6
  Kent....31 D6
  Som....12 B2
  Sur....27 D6
Ashampstead....26 B3
Ashbocking....57 D5
Ashbourne....75 E8
Ashbrittle....11 B5
Ash Bullayne....10 D2
Ashburton....7 C5
Ashbury
  Devon....9 E7
  Oxon....38 F2
Ashby....90 D3
Ashby by Partney....79 C7
Ashby cum Fenby....91 D6
Ashby de la
  Launde....78 D3
Ashby-de-
  la-Zouch....63 C7
Ashby Folville....64 C4
Ashby Magna....64 E2
Ashby Parva....64 F2
Ashby Puerorum....79 B6
Ashby St Ledgers....52 C3
Ashby St Mary....69 D6
Ashchurch....50 F4
Ashcombe....7 B7
Ashcott....23 F6
Ashdon....55 E6
Ashe....26 E3
Asheldham....43 D5
Ashen....55 E8
Ashendon....39 C7
Ashfield
  Carms....33 B7
  Stirling....127 D6
  Suff....57 C6
Ashfield Green....57 B6
Ashfold
  Crossways....17 B6
Ashford
  Devon....20 F4
  Hants....14 C2
  Kent....30 E4
  Sur....27 B8
Ashford Bowdler....49 B7
Ashford
  Carbonell....49 B7
Ashford Hill....26 C3
Ashford in the
  Water....75 C8
Ashgill....119 E7
Ash Green....63 F7
Ashill
  Devon....11 C5
  Norf....67 D8
  Som....11 C8
Ashingdon....42 E4
Ashington
  Northumb....117 F8

Ashington continued
  Som....12 B3
  W Sus....16 C5
Ashintully
  Castle....133 C8
Ashkirk....115 B7
Ashlett....15 D5
Ashleworth....37 B5
Ashley
  Cambs....55 C7
  Ches E....87 F5
  Devon....9 C8
  Dorset....14 D2
  Glos....37 E6
  Hants....14 E3
  Hants....25 F8
  N Nhants....64 E4
  Staffs....74 F4
Ashley Green....40 D2
Ashley Heath
  Dorset....14 D2
  Staffs....74 F4
Ash Magna....74 F2
Ashmanhaugh....69 B6
Ashmansworth....26 D2
Ashmansworthy....8 C5
Ashmore....13 C7
Ashorne....51 D8
Ashover....76 C3
Ashow....51 B8
Ashprington....7 D6
Ash Priors....11 B6
Ashreigney....9 C8
Ash Street....56 E4
Ash Thomas....10 C5
Ashton
  Ches W....74 C2
  Corn....2 D5
  Hants....15 C6
  Hereford....49 C7
  Invclyd....118 B2
  N Nhants....65 F7
  N Nhants....53 E5
Ashton Common....24 D3
Ashton-in-
  Makerfield....86 E3
Ashton Keynes....37 E7
Ashton under Hill....50 F4
Ashton-
  under-Lyne....87 E7
Ashton upon
  Mersey....87 E5
Ashurst
  Hants....14 C4
  Kent....18 B2
  W Sus....17 C5
Ashurstwood....28 F5
Ashwater....9 E5
Ashwell
  Herts....54 F3
  Rutland....65 C5
  Som....11 C8
Ashwellthorpe....68 E4
Ashwick....23 E8
Ashwicken....67 C7
Ashybank....115 C8
Askam in Furness.92 B2
Askern....89 C6
Askerswell....12 E3
Askett....39 D8
Askham
  Cumb....99 B7
  Notts....77 B7
Askham Bryan....95 E8
Askham Richard....95 E8
Asknish....145 D8
Askrigg....100 E4
Askwith....94 E4
Aslackby....78 F3
Aslacton....68 E4
Aslockton....77 F7
Asloun....140 C4
Aspatria....107 E8
Aspenden....41 B6
Asperton....79 F5
Aspley Guise....53 F7
Aspley Heath....53 F7
Aspull....86 D4
Asselby....89 B8
Asserby....79 B7
Assington....56 F3
Assynt House....151 E8
Astbury....74 C5
Astcote....52 D4
Asterley....60 D3
Asterton....60 E3
Asthall....38 C2
Asthall Leigh....38 C3
Astley
  Shrops....60 C5
  Warks....63 F7
  Worcs....50 C2
Astley Abbotts....61 E7
Astley Bridge....86 C5
Astley Cross....50 C3
Astley Green....86 E5
Aston
  Ches E....74 E3
  Ches W....74 B2
  Derbys....88 F2
  Hereford....49 B6
  Herts....41 B5
  Oxon....38 D3
  Shrops....60 B5
  S Yorks....89 F5
  Telford....61 D6
  W Mid....62 F4
  Wokingham....39 F7
Aston Abbotts....39 B8
Aston Botterell....61 F6
Aston-by-Stone....75 F6
Aston Cantlow....51 D6
Aston Clinton....40 C1
Aston Crews....36 B3
Aston Cross....50 F4
Aston End....41 B5
Aston Eyre....61 E6
Aston Fields....50 C4
Aston Flamville....63 E8
Aston Ingham....36 B3
Aston juxta
  Mondrum....74 D3
Aston le Walls....52 D2
Aston Magna....51 F6

Aston Munslow....60 F5
Aston on Clun....60 F3
Aston-on-Trent....63 B8
Aston Rogers....60 D3
Aston Rowant....39 E7
Aston Sandford....39 D7
Aston Somerville....50 F5
Aston Subedge....51 E6
Aston Tirrold....39 F5
Aston Upthorpe....39 F5
Astrop....52 F3
Astwick....54 F3
Astwood
  M Keynes....53 E7
  Worcs....50 D3
Astwood Bank....50 C5
Aswarby....78 F3
Aswardby....79 B6
Atcham....60 D5
Atch Lench....50 D5
Athelhampton....13 E5
Athelington....57 B6
Athelney....11 B8
Athelstaneford....121 B8
Atherington....9 B7
Atherstone....63 E7
Atherstone on
  Stour....51 D7
Atherton....86 D4
Atley Hill....101 D7
Atlow....76 E2
Attadale....150 H2
Attadale House....150 H2
Attenborough....76 F5
Atterby....90 E3
Attercliffe....88 F4
Attleborough
  Norf....68 E3
  Warks....63 E7
Attlebridge....68 C4
Atwick....97 D7
Atworth....24 C3
Auberrow....49 E6
Auchagallon....143 E9
Auchallater....139 F7
Auchareoch....143 F10
Aucharnie....153 D6
Auchattie....141 E5
Auchavan....134 C1
Auchbreck....139 B8
Auchenback....118 D5
Auchenbainzie....113 E8
Auchenblae....135 B7
Auchenbrack....113 E7
Auchenbreck....145 E9
Auchencairn
  Dumfries....106 D4
  Dumfries....114 E2
  N Ayrs....143 F11
Auchencrow....122 C4
Auchendinny....121 C5
Auchengray....120 D2
Auchenhalrig....152 B3
Auchenheath....119 E8
Auchenlochan....145 F8
Auchenmalg....105 D6
Auchensoul....112 E2
Auchentiber....118 E3
Auchertyre....149 F13
Auchgourish....138 C5
Auchincarroch....126 F3
Auchindrain....125 E6
Auchindrean....150 C4
Auchininna....153 D6
Auchinleck....113 B5
Auchinloch....119 B6
Auchinroath....152 C2
Auchintoul....140 C4
Auchiries....153 E10
Auchlee....141 E7
Auchleven....140 B5
Auchlochan....119 F8
Auchlossan....140 D4
Auchlunies....141 E7
Auchlyne....126 B4
Auchmacoy....153 E9
Auchmair....140 B2
Auchmantle....105 C5
Auchmillan....112 B5
Auchmithie....135 E6
Auchmuirbridge....128 D4
Auchmull....135 B5
Auchnacree....134 C4
Auchnagallin....151 H13
Auchnagatt....153 D9
Auchnaha....145 E8
Auchnashelloch 127 C6
Aucholzie....140 E2
Auchrannie....134 D2
Auchroisk....139 B6
Auchronie....140 F3
Auchterarder....127 C8
Auchteraw....137 D6
Auchterderran....128 E4
Auchterhouse....134 F3
Auchtermuchty....128 C4
Auchterneed....150 F7
Auchtertool....128 E4
Auchtertyre....152 C1
Auchtubh....126 B4
Auckengill....158 D5
Auckley....89 D7
Audenshaw....87 E7
Audlem....74 E3
Audley....74 D4
Audley End....56 F2
Auds....153 B6
Aughton
  E Yorks....96 F3
  Lancs....85 D4
  Lancs....93 C5
  S Yorks....89 F5
  Wilts....25 D7
Aughton Park....86 D2
Auldearn....151 F12
Aulden....49 D6
Auldgirth....114 F2
Auldhame....129 F7
Auldhouse....119 D6
Ault a'chruinn....136 B2
Aultanrynie....156 F6
Aultbea....155 J13
Aultdearg....150 E5
Aultgrishan....155 J12
Aultguish Inn....150 D6
Aultibea....157 G13
Aultiphurst....157 C11
Aultmore....152 C4

Aultnagoire....137 B8
Aultnamain Inn....151 C9
Aultnaslat....136 D4
Aulton....140 B5
Aundorach....139 C5
Aunsby....78 F3
Auquhorthies....141 B7
Aust....36 F2
Austendike....66 B2
Austerfield....89 E7
Austrey....63 D6
Austwick....93 C7
Authorpe....91 F8
Authorpe Row....79 B8
Avebury....25 C6
Aveley....42 F1
Avening....37 E5
Averham....77 D7
Aveton Gifford....6 E4
Avielochan....138 C5
Aviemore....138 C4
Avington
  Hants....26 F3
  W Berks....25 C8
Avoch....151 F10
Avon....14 E2
Avonbridge....120 B2
Avon Dassett....52 E2
Avonmouth....23 B7
Avonwick....6 D5
Awbridge....14 B4
Awhirk....104 D4
Awkley....36 F2
Awliscombe....11 D6
Awre....36 D4
Awsworth....76 E4
Axbridge....23 D6
Axford
  Hants....26 E4
  Wilts....25 B7
Axminster....11 E7
Axmouth....11 E7
Axton....85 F2
Aycliff....31 E7
Aycliffe....101 B7
Aydon....110 C3
Aylburton....36 D3
Ayle....109 E7
Aylesbeare....10 E5
Aylesbury....39 C8
Aylesby....91 D6
Aylesford....29 D8
Aylesham....31 D6
Aylestone....64 D2
Aylmerton....81 D7
Aylsham....81 E7
Aylton....49 F8
Aymestrey....49 C6
Aynho....52 F3
Ayot St Lawrence 40 C4
Ayot St Peter....41 C5
Ayr....112 B3
Aysgarth....101 F5
Ayside....99 F5
Ayston....65 D5
Aythorpe Roding.42 C1
Ayton....122 C5
Aywick....160 E7
Azerley....95 B5

**B**

Babbacombe....7 C7
Babbinswood....73 F7
Babcary....12 B3
Babel....47 F7
Babell....73 B5
Babraham....55 D6
Babworth....89 F7
Bac....155 C9
Bachau....82 C4
Backaland....159 E6
Backaskaill....159 C5
Backbarrow....99 F5
Backe....32 C3
Backfolds....153 C10
Backford....73 B8
Backford Cross....73 B7
Backhill
  Aberds....153 E7
  Aberds....153 E10
Backhill of
  Clackriach....153 D9
Backhill of
  Fortree....153 D9
Backhill of
  Trustach....140 E5
Backies....157 J11
Backlass....158 E4
Back of
  Keppoch....147 C9
Back Rogerton....113 B5
Backwell....23 C6
Backworth....111 B6
Bacon End....42 C2
Baconsthorpe....81 D7
Bacton
  Hereford....49 F5
  Norf....81 D9
  Suff....56 C4
Bacton Green....56 C4
Bacup....87 B6
Badachro....149 A12
Badanloch
  Lodge....157 F10
Badavanich....150 F4
Badbury....38 F1
Badby....52 D3
Badcall....156 D5
Badcaul....150 B3
Baddeley Green....75 D6
Baddesley
  Clinton....51 B6
Baddesley Ensor....63 E6
Baddidarach....156 G3
Baddock....151 F10
Baddoch....139 F7
Baddock....151 F10
Badenscoth....153 E7
Badenyon....140 C2
Badger....61 E7
Badger's Mount....29 C5
Badgeworth....37 C6
Badgworth....23 D5
Badicaul....149 F12
Badingham....57 C7
Badlesmere....30 D4
Badlipster....158 F4

Badluarach....150 B2
Badminton....37 F5
Badnaban....156 G3
Badninish....151 B10
Badrallach....150 B3
Badsey....51 E5
Badshot Lea....27 E6
Badsworth....89 C5
Badwell Ash....56 C3
Bae Colwyn
  =Colwyn Bay....83 D8
Bag Enderby....79 B6
Bagendon....37 D7
Bagh a Chaisteil
  =Castlebay....148 J1
Baghasdal....148 G2
Bagh Mor....148 C3
Bagh
  Shiarabhagh....148 H2
Bagillt....73 B6
Baginton....51 B8
Baglan....33 E8
Bagley....60 B4
Bagnall....75 D6
Bagnor....26 C2
Bagshot
  Sur....27 C7
  Wilts....25 C8
Bagthorpe
  Norf....80 D3
  Notts....76 D4
Bagworth....63 D8
Bagwy Llydiart....35 B8
Baildon....94 F4
Baile....154 J4
Baile Ailein....155 E7
Baile a
  Mhanaich....148 C2
Baile an Truiseil 155 B8
Bailebeag....137 C8
Baile Boidheach 144 F6
Baile Glas....148 C3
Baile Mhartainn 148 A2
Baile Mhic Phail 148 A3
Baile Mor
  Argyll....146 J5
  W Isles....148 B2
Baile na Creige 148 H1
Baile nan
  Cailleach....148 C2
Baile Raghaill....148 A2
Bailesward....152 E4
Baileyhead....108 B5
Bailiesward....152 E4
Baillieston....119 C6
Bail'lochdrach....148 C3
Bail Uachdraich 148 B3
Bail'Ur
  Tholastaidh....155 C10
Bainbridge....100 E4
Bainsford....127 F7
Bainshole....152 E6
Bainton
  E Yorks....97 D5
  Pboro....65 D7
Bairnkine....116 C2
Baker's End....41 C6
Baker Street....42 F2
Bakewell....76 C2
Bala
  =Y Bala....72 F3
Balachuirn....149 D10
Balavil....138 D3
Balbeg
  Highld....137 B7
  Highld....150 H7
Balbeggie....128 B3
Balbithan....141 C6
Balbithan House 141 C7
Balblair
  Highld....151 B8
  Highld....151 E10
Balby....89 D6
Balchladich....156 F3
Balchraggan
  Highld....151 G11
  Highld....151 H8
Balchrick....156 D4
Balchrystie....129 D6
Balcombe....28 F4
Balcombe Lane....28 F4
Balcomie....129 C8
Balcurvie....128 D5
Baldersby....95 B6
Baldersby
  St James....95 B6
Balderstone....93 F6
Balderton
  Ches W....73 C7
  Notts....77 D8
Baldhu....3 B6
Baldinnie....129 C6
Baldock....54 F3
Baldovie....134 F4
Baldrine....84 D4
Baldslow....18 D4
Baldwin....84 D3
Baldwinholme....108 D3
Baldwin's Gate....74 E4
Bale....81 D6
Balearn....153 C10
Balemartine....146 G2
Balephuil....146 G2
Balerno....120 C4
Balevullin....146 G2
Balfield....135 C5
Balfour....159 G5
Balfron....126 F4
Balfron Station....126 F4
Balgaveny....153 D6
Balgavies....135 D5
Balgonar....128 E2
Balgove....153 E8
Balgowan....138 E2
Balgown....149 B8
Balgrochan....119 B6
Balgy....149 C13
Balhaldie....127 D7
Balhalgardy....141 B6
Balham....28 B3
Balhary....134 E2
Baliasta....160 C8
Baligill....157 C11
Balintore
  Angus....134 D2
  Highld....151 D11
Balintraid....151 D10
Balk....102 F2
Balkeerie....134 E3
Balkemback....134 F3
Balkholme....89 B8
Ball....60 B3
Ballabeg....84 E2
Ballacannel....84 D3
Ballachulish....130 D4
Ballajora....84 C4
Ballaleigh....84 D3
Ballantrae....104 A4
Ballaugh....84 C3
Ballechin....133 D6
Balleigh....151 C10
Ballencrieff....121 B7
Ballentoul....133 C5
Ball Haye Green....75 D6
Ball Hill....26 C2
Ballidon....76 D2
Balliemore
  Argyll....124 C4
  Argyll....145 E9
Ballikinrain....126 F4
Ballimeanoch....125 D6
Ballimore
  Argyll....145 E8
  Stirling....126 C4
Ballinaby....142 B3
Ballindean....128 B4
Ballingdon....56 E2
Ballinger
  Common....40 D2
Ballingham....49 F7
Ballingry....128 E3
Ballinlick....133 E6
Ballinluig....133 D6
Ballintuim....133 D8
Balloch
  Angus....134 D3
  Highld....151 G10
  N Lanark....119 B7
  W Dunb....126 F2
Ballochan....140 E4
Ballochford....152 E3
Ballochmorrie....112 F2
Balls Cross....16 B3
Balls Green....43 B6
Ballygown....146 G7
Ballygrant....142 B4
Ballyhaugh....146 F4
Balmacara....149 F13
Balmacara
  Square....149 F13
Balmaclellan....106 B3
Balmacneil....133 D6
Balmacqueen....149 A9
Balmae....106 E3
Balmaha....126 E3
Balmalcolm....128 D5
Balmeanach....149 D10
Balmedie....141 C8
Balmer Heath....73 F8
Balmerino....129 B5
Balmerlawn....14 D4
Balmichael....143 E10
Balmirmer....135 F5
Balmore
  Highld....149 D7
  Highld....150 H6
  Highld....151 G11
  Perth....133 D6
Balmule....128 F4
Balmullo....129 B6
Balmungie....151 F10
Balnaboth....134 C3
Balnabruaich....151 E10
Balnabruich....158 H3
Balnacoil....157 H11
Balnacra....150 G2
Balnafoich....151 H9
Balnagall....151 C11
Balnaguard....133 D6
Balnahard
  Argyll....144 D3
  Argyll....146 J7
Balnain....150 H7
Balnakeil....156 C6
Balnaknock....149 B9
Balnapaling....151 E10
Balne....89 C6
Balochroy....143 C8
Balone....129 C6
Balornock....119 C6
Balquharn....133 D6
Balquhidder....126 B4
Balsall....51 B7
Balsall Common....51 B7
Balsall Heath....62 F4
Balscott....51 E8
Balsham....55 D6
Baltasound....160 C8
Balterley....74 D4
Baltersan....105 C8
Balthangie....153 C8
Baltonsborough....23 F7
Balvaird....151 F8
Balvicar....124 D3
Balvraid
  Highld....149 G13
  Highld....151 H11
Bamber Bridge....86 B3
Bambers Green....42 B1
Bamburgh....123 F7
Bamff....134 D2
Bamford
  Derbys....88 F3
  Gtr Man....87 C6
Bampton
  Cumb....99 C7
  Devon....10 B4
  Oxon....38 D3
Bampton
  Grange....99 C7
Banavie....131 B5
Banbury....52 E2
Bancffosfelen....33 C5
Banchory....141 E5

Banchory-
  Devenick....141 D8
Bancycapel....33 C5
Bancyfelin....32 C4
Bancyffordd....46 F3
Bandirran....134 F2
Banff....153 B6
Bangor....83 D5
Bangor-is-y-coed
  =Bangor-on-Dee .73 E7
Bangor-on-Dee
  =Bangor-is-y-coed .73 E7
Banham....68 F3
Bank....14 D3
Bankend....107 C7
Bankfoot....133 F7
Bankglen....113 C6
Bankhead
  Aberds....141 C7
  Aberds....141 D6
Bank Newton....94 D2
Banknock....119 B7
Banks
  Cumb....109 C5
  Lancs....85 B4
Bankshill....114 F4
Bank Street....49 C8
Banningham....81 E8
Banniskirk
  House....158 E3
Bannister Green....42 B2
Bannockburn....127 E7
Banstead....28 D3
Bantham....6 E4
Banton....119 B7
Banwell....23 D5
Banyard's Green....57 B6
Bapchild....30 C3
Barabhas....155 B8
Barabhas
  Iarach....155 C8
Barabhas
  Uarach....155 B8
Barachandroman....124 C2
Barassie....118 F3
Baravullin....124 E4
Barbaraville....151 D10
Barber Booth....88 F2
Barbieston....112 C4
Barbon....99 F8
Barbridge....74 D3
Barbrook....21 E6
Barby....52 B3
Barcaldine....130 E3
Barcheston....51 F7
Barcombe....17 C8
Barcombe Cross....17 C8
Barden....101 E6
Bardennoch....113 E5
Barden Scale....94 D3
Bardfield Saling..42 B2
Bardister....160 F5
Bardney....78 C4
Bardon....63 C8
Bardon Mill....109 C7
Bardowie....119 B5
Bardrainney....118 B3
Bardsea....92 B3
Bardsey....95 E6
Bardwell....56 B3
Bare....92 C4
Barfad....145 G7
Barford
  Norf....68 D4
  Warks....51 C7
Barford St John....52 F2
Barford
  St Martin....25 F5
Barford
  St Michael....52 F2
Barfrestone....31 D6
Bargod
  =Bargoed....35 E5
Bargoed
  =Bargod....35 E5
Bargrennan....105 B7
Barham
  Cambs....54 B2
  Kent....31 D6
  Suff....56 D5
Barharrow....106 D3
Barholm....65 C7
Barkby....64 D3
Barkestone-
  le-Vale....77 F7
Barkham....27 C5
Barking
  London....41 F7
  Suff....56 D4
Barkingside....41 F7
Barking Tye....56 D4
Barkisland....87 C8
Barkston
  Lincs....78 E2
  N Yorks....95 F7
Barkway....54 F4
Barlaston....75 F5
Barlavington....16 C3
Barlborough....76 B4
Barlby....96 F2
Barley
  Herts....54 F4
  Lancs....93 E8
Barley Mow....111 D5
Barleythorpe....64 D5
Barling....43 F5
Barlow
  Derbys....76 B3
  N Yorks....89 B7
  T&W....110 C4
Barmby Moor....96 E3
Barmby on the
  Marsh....89 B7
Barmer....80 D4
Barmoor Castle 123 F5
Barmoor Lane
  End....123 F6
Barmouth
  =Abermaw....58 C3
Barmpton....101 C8
Barmston....97 C7
Barnack....65 D7
Barnacle....63 F7
Barnard Castle....101 C5

Barnard Gate 38 C4
Barnardiston 55 E8
Barnbarroch 106 D5
Barnburgh 89 D5
Barnby 69 F7
Barnby Dun 89 D7
Barnby in the Willows 77 D8
Barnby Moor 89 F7
Barnes Street 29 E7
Barnet 41 E5
Barnetby le Wold 90 D4
Barney 81 D5
Barnham
Suff 56 B2
W Sus 16 D3
Barnham Broom 68 D3
Barnhead 135 D6
Barnhill
Ches W 73 D8
Dundee 134 F4
Moray 152 C1
Barnhills 104 B3
Barningham
Durham 101 C5
Suff 56 B3
Barnoldby le Beck 91 D6
Barnoldswick 93 E8
Barns Green 16 B5
Barnsley
Glos 37 D7
S Yorks 88 D4
Barnstaple 20 F4
Barnston
Essex 42 C2
Mers 85 F3
Barnstone 77 F7
Barnt Green 50 B5
Barnton
Ches W 74 B3
Edin 120 B4
Barnwell All Saints 65 F7
Barnwell St Andrew 65 F7
Barnwood 37 C5
Barochreal 124 C4
Barons Cross 49 D6
Barr 112 E2
Barra Castle 141 B6
Barrachan 105 E7
Barrack 153 D8
Barraglom 154 D6
Barrahormid 144 E6
Barran 124 C4
Barrapol 146 G2
Barras
Aberds 141 F7
Cumb 100 C3
Barrasford 110 B2
Barravullin 124 E4
Barregarrow 84 D3
Barrhead 118 D4
Barrhill 112 F2
Barrington
Cambs 54 E4
Som 11 C8
Barripper 2 C5
Barrmill 118 D3
Barrock 158 C4
Barrock House 158 D4
Barrow
Lancs 93 F7
Rutland 65 C5
Suff 55 C8
Barroway Drove 67 D5
Barrowburn 116 C4
Barrowby 77 F8
Barrowcliff 103 F8
Barrowden 65 D6
Barrowford 93 F8
Barrow Green 30 C3
Barrow Gurney 23 C7
Barrow Haven 90 B4
Barrow-in-Furness 92 C2
Barrow Island 92 C1
Barrow Nook 86 D2
Barrows Green
Ches E 74 D3
Cumb 99 F7
Barrow's Green 86 F3
Barrow Street 24 F3
Barrow upon Humber 90 B4
Barrow upon Soar 64 C2
Barrow upon Trent 63 B7
Barry 135 F5
Barry = Y Barri 22 C3
Barry Island 22 C3
Barsby 64 C3
Barsham 69 F6
Barston 51 B7
Bartestree 49 E7
Barthol Chapel 153 E8
Barthomley 74 D4
Bartley 14 C4
Bartley Green 62 F4
Bartlow 55 E6
Barton
Cambs 54 D5
Ches W 73 D8
Glos 37 B8
Lancs 85 D4
Lancs 92 F5
N Yorks 101 D7
Oxon 39 D5
Torbay 7 C7
Warks 51 D6
Barton Bendish 67 D7
Barton Hartshorn 52 F4
Barton in Fabis 76 F5
Barton in the Beans 63 D7
Barton-le-Clay 53 F8
Barton-le-Street 96 B3
Barton-le-Willows 96 C3
Barton Mills 55 B8
Barton on Sea 14 E3
Barton on the Heath 51 F7
Barton St David 23 F7
Barton Seagrave 53 B6
Barton Stacey 26 E2
Barton Turf 69 B6
Barton-under-Needwood 63 C5
Barton-upon-Humber 90 B4
Barton Waterside 90 B4
Barugh 88 D4
Barway 55 B6
Barwell 63 E8
Barwick
Herts 41 C6
Som 12 C3
Barwick in Elmet 95 F6
Baschurch 60 B4
Bascote 52 C2
Basford Green 75 D6
Bashall Eaves 93 E6
Bashley 14 E3
Basildon 42 F3
Basingstoke 26 D4
Baslow 76 B2
Bason Bridge 22 E5
Bassaleg 35 F6
Bassenthwaite 108 F2
Bassett 14 C5
Bassingbourn 54 E4
Bassingfield 77 F6
Bassingham 78 C2
Bassingthorpe 65 B6
Basta 160 D7
Baston 65 C8
Bastwick 69 C7
Baswick Steer 97 E6
Batchworth Heath 40 E3
Batcombe
Dorset 12 D4
Som 23 F8
Bate Heath 74 B3
Batford 40 C4
Bath 24 C2
Bathampton 24 C2
Bathealton 11 B5
Batheaston 24 C2
Bathford 24 C2
Bathgate 120 C2
Bathley 77 D7
Bathpool
Corn 5 B7
Som 11 B7
Bathville 120 C2
Batley 88 B3
Batsford 51 F6
Battersby 102 D3
Battersea 28 B3
Battisborough Cross 6 E3
Battisford 56 D4
Battisford Tye 56 D4
Battle
E Sus 18 D4
Powys 48 F2
Battledown 37 B6
Battlefield 60 C5
Battlesbridge 42 E3
Battlesden 40 B2
Battlesea Green 57 B6
Battleton 10 B4
Battram 63 D8
Battramsley 14 E4
Baughton 50 E3
Baughurst 26 D3
Baulking 38 E3
Baumber 78 B5
Baunton 37 D7
Baverstock 24 F5
Bawburgh 68 D4
Bawdeswell 81 E6
Bawdrip 22 F5
Bawdsey 57 E7
Bawtry 89 E7
Baxenden 87 B5
Baxterley 63 E6
Baybridge 15 B6
Baycliff 92 B2
Baydon 25 B7
Bayford
Herts 41 D6
Som 12 B5
Bayles 109 E7
Baylham 56 D5
Baynard's Green 39 B5
Bayston Hill 60 D4
Baythorn End 55 E8
Bayton 49 B8
Beach 130 D1
Beachampton 53 F5
Beachamwell 67 D7
Beachans 151 G13
Beacharr 143 D7
Beachborough 19 B8
Beachley 36 E2
Beacon 11 D6
Beacon End 43 B5
Beacon Hill 27 F6
Beacon's Bottom 39 E7
Beaconsfield 40 F2
Beacrabhaic 154 H6
Beadlam 102 F4
Beadlow 54 F2
Beadnell 117 B8
Beaford 9 C7
Beal
Northumb 123 E6
N Yorks 89 B6
Beamhurst 75 F7
Beaminster 12 D2
Beamish 110 D5
Beamsley 94 D3
Bean 29 B6
Beanacre 24 C4
Beanley 117 C6
Beaquoy 159 F4
Bear Cross 13 E8
Beardwood 86 B4
Beare Green 28 E2
Bearley 51 C6
Bearnus 146 G6
Bearpark 110 E5
Bearsbridge 109 D7
Bearsden 118 B5
Bearsted 29 D8
Bearstone 74 F4
Bearwood
BCP 13 E8
Hereford 49 D5
W Mid 62 F4
Beattock 114 D3
Beauchamp Roding 42 C1
Beauchief 88 F4
Beaufort 35 C5
Beaufort Castle 151 G8
Beaulieu 14 D4
Beauly 151 G8
Beaumaris 83 D6
Beaumont
Cumb 108 D3
Essex 43 B7
Beaumont Hill 101 C7
Beausale 51 B7
Beauworth 15 B6
Beaworthy 9 E6
Beazley End 42 B3
Bebington 85 F4
Bebside 117 F8
Beccles 69 E7
Becconsall 86 B2
Beckbury 61 D7
Beckenham 28 C4
Beckermet 98 D2
Beckfoot
Cumb 98 D3
Cumb 107 E7
Beck Foot 99 E8
Beckford 50 F4
Beckhampton 25 C5
Beck Hole 103 D6
Beckingham
Lincs 77 D8
Notts 89 F8
Beckington 24 D3
Beckley
E Sus 19 C5
Hants 14 E3
Oxon 39 C5
Beck Row 55 B7
Beck Side 98 F4
Beckton 41 F7
Beckwithshaw 95 D5
Becontree 41 F7
Bedale 101 F7
Bedburn 110 F4
Bedchester 13 C6
Beddau 34 F4
Beddgelert 71 C6
Beddingham 17 D8
Beddington 28 C4
Bedfield 57 C6
Bedford 53 D8
Bedham 16 B4
Bedhampton 15 D8
Bedingfield 57 C5
Bedlam 95 C5
Bedlington 117 F8
Bedlington Station 117 F8
Bedlinog 34 D4
Bedminster 23 B7
Bedmond 40 D3
Bednall 62 C3
Bedrule 116 C2
Bedstone 49 B5
Bedwas 35 F5
Bedworth 63 F7
Bedworth Heath 63 F7
Bed-y-coedwr 71 E8
Beeby 64 D3
Beech
Hants 26 F4
Staffs 75 F5
Beech Hill
Gtr Man 86 D3
W Berks 26 C4
Beechingstoke 25 D5
Beedon 26 B2
Beeford 97 D7
Beeley 76 C2
Beelsby 91 D6
Beenham 26 C3
Beeny 8 E3
Beer 11 F7
Beercrocombe 11 B8
Beer Hackett 12 C3
Beesands 7 E6
Beesby 91 F8
Beeson 7 E6
Beeston
C Beds 54 E2
Ches W 74 D2
Norf 68 C2
Notts 76 F5
W Yorks 95 F5
Beeston Regis 81 C7
Beeswing 107 C5
Beetham 92 B4
Beetley 68 C2
Begbroke 38 C4
Begelly 32 D2
Beggar's Bush 48 C4
Beguildy 48 B3
Beighton
Norf 69 D6
S Yorks 88 F5
Beighton Hill 76 D2
Beith 118 D3
Bekesbourne 31 D5
Belaugh 69 C5
Belbroughton 50 B4
Belchamp Otten 56 E2
Belchamp St Paul 55 E8
Belchamp Walter 56 E2
Belchford 79 B5
Belford 123 F7
Belhaven 122 B2
Belhelvie 141 C8
Belhinnie 140 B3
Bellabeg 140 C2
Bellamore 112 F2
Bellanoch 144 D6
Bellaty 134 D2
Bell Bar 41 D5
Bell Busk 94 D2
Belleau 79 B7
Bellehiglash 152 E1
Bell End 50 B4
Bellerby 101 E6
Bellever 6 B4
Belliehill 135 C5
Bellingdon 40 D2
Bellingham 116 F4
Belloch 143 E7
Bellochantuy 143 E7
Bell o'th'Hill 74 E2
Bellsbank 112 D4
Bellshill
N Lanark 119 C7
Northumb 123 F7
Bellspool 120 F4
Bellsquarry 120 C3
Bells Yew Green 18 B3
Belmaduthy 151 F9
Belmesthorpe 65 C7
Belmont
Blackburn 86 C4
London 28 C3
S Ayrs 112 B3
Shetland 160 C7
Belnacraig 140 C2
Belowda 4 C4
Belper 76 E3
Belper Lane End 76 E3
Belsay 110 B4
Belses 115 B8
Belsford 7 D5
Belstead 56 E5
Belston 112 B3
Belstone 9 E8
Belthorn 86 B5
Beltinge 31 C5
Beltoft 90 D2
Belton
Leics 63 B8
Lincs 78 F2
N Lincs 89 D8
Norf 69 D7
Belton in Rutland 64 D5
Beltring 29 E7
Belts of Collonach 141 E5
Belvedere 29 B5
Belvoir 77 F8
Bembridge 15 F7
Bemersyde 121 F8
Bemerton 25 F6
Bempton 97 B7
Benacre 69 F8
Ben Alder Lodge 132 B2
Ben Armine Lodge 157 H10
Benbuie 113 E7
Ben Casgro 155 E9
Benderloch 124 B5
Bendronaig Lodge 150 H3
Benenden 18 B5
Benfield 105 C7
Bengate 69 B6
Bengeworth 50 E5
Benhall Green 57 C7
Benhall Street 57 C7
Benholm 135 C8
Beningbrough 95 D8
Benington
Herts 41 B5
Lincs 79 E6
Benllech 82 C5
Benmore
Argyll 145 E10
Stirling 126 B3
Benmore Lodge 156 H6
Bennacott 8 E4
Bennan 143 F10
Benniworth 91 F6
Benover 29 E8
Bensham 110 C5
Benslie 118 E3
Benson 39 E6
Bent 135 B6
Bent Gate 87 B5
Benthall
Northumb 117 B8
Shrops 61 D6
Bentham 37 C6
Benthoul 141 D7
Bentlawnt 60 D3
Bentley
E Yorks 97 F6
Hants 27 E5
Suff 56 F5
S Yorks 89 D6
Warks 63 E6
Worcs 50 C4
Bentley Heath 51 B6
Benton 21 F5
Bentpath 115 E6
Bents 120 C2
Bentworth 26 E4
Benvie 134 F3
Benwick 66 E3
Beoley 51 C5
Beoraidbeg 147 B9
Bepton 16 C2
Berden 41 B7
Bere Alston 6 C2
Bere Ferrers 6 C2
Berepper 3 D5
Bere Regis 13 E6
Bergh Apton 69 D6
Berinsfield 39 E5
Berkeley 36 E3
Berkhamsted 40 D2
Berkley 24 E3
Berkswell 51 B7
Bermondsey 28 B4
Bernera 149 F13
Bernice 145 D10
Bernisdale 149 C9
Berrick Salome 39 E6
Berriedale 158 H3
Berrier 99 B5
Berriew 59 D8
Berrington
Northumb 123 E6
Shrops 60 D5
Berrow 22 D5
Berrow Green 50 D2
Berry Down Cross 20 E4
Berryfield 39 C7
Berry Hill
Glos 36 C2
Pembs 45 E2
Berryhillock 152 B5
Berrynarbor 20 E4
Berry Pomeroy 7 C6
Bersham 73 E7
Berstane 159 G5
Berwick 18 E2
Berwick Bassett 25 B5
Berwick Hill 110 B4
Berwick St James 25 F5
Berwick St John 13 B7
Berwick St Leonard 24 F4
Berwick-upon-Tweed 123 D5
Bescar 85 C4
Besford 50 E4
Bessacarr 89 D7
Bessels Leigh 38 D4
Bessingby 97 C7
Bessingham 81 D7
Bestbeech Hill 18 B3
Besthorpe
Norf 68 E3
Notts 77 C8
Bestwood 77 E5
Bestwood Village 77 E5
Beswick 97 E6
Betchworth 28 E3
Bethania
Ceredig 46 C4
Gwyn 71 C8
Gwyn 83 F6
Bethel
Anglesey 82 D3
Gwyn 72 F3
Gwyn 82 E5
Bethersden 30 E3
Bethesda
Gwyn 83 E6
Pembs 32 C1
Bethlehem 33 B7
Bethnal Green 41 F6
Betley 74 E4
Betsham 29 B7
Betteshanger 31 D7
Bettiscombe 11 E8
Bettisfield 73 F8
Betton
Shrops 60 D3
Shrops 74 F3
Bettws
Bridgend 34 F3
Mon 35 C6
Newport 35 E6
Bettws Cedewain 59 E8
Bettws Gwerfil Goch 72 E4
Bettws Ifan 46 E2
Bettws Newydd 35 D7
Bettws-y-crwyn 60 F2
Bettyhill 157 C10
Betws 33 C7
Betws Bledrws 46 D4
Betws-Garmon 82 F5
Betws-y-Coed 83 F7
Betws-yn-Rhos 72 B3
Beulah
Ceredig 45 E4
Powys 47 D8
Bevendean 17 D7
Bevercotes 77 B6
Beverley 97 F6
Beverston 37 E5
Bevington 36 E3
Bewaldeth 108 F2
Bewcastle 109 B5
Bewdley 50 B2
Bewerley 94 C4
Bewholme 97 D7
Bexhill 18 E4
Bexley 29 B5
Bexleyheath 29 B5
Bexwell 67 D6
Beyton 56 C3
Bhaltos 154 D5
Bhatarsaigh 148 J1
Bibury 37 D8
Bicester 39 B5
Bickenhall 11 C7
Bickenhill 63 F5
Bicker 78 F5
Bickershaw 86 D4
Bickerstaffe 86 D2
Bickerton
Ches E 74 D2
N Yorks 95 D7
Bickington
Devon 7 B5
Devon 20 F4
Bickleigh
Devon 6 C3
Devon 10 D4
Bickleton 20 F4
Bickley 28 C5
Bickley Moss 74 E2
Bicknacre 42 D3
Bicknoller 22 F3
Bicknor 30 D2
Bickton 14 C2
Bicton
Shrops 60 C4
Shrops 60 F2
Bidborough 29 E6
Biddenden 19 B5
Biddenham 53 E8
Biddestone 24 B3
Biddisham 23 D5
Biddlesden 52 E4
Biddlestone 117 D5
Biddulph 75 D5
Biddulph Moor 75 D6
Bideford 9 B6
Bidford-on-Avon 51 D6
Bidston 85 E3
Bielby 96 E3
Bieldside 141 D7
Bierley
IoW 15 G6
W Yorks 94 F4
Bierton 39 C8
Bigbury 6 E4
Bigbury on Sea 6 E4
Bigby 90 D4
Biggar
Cumb 92 C1
S Lanark 120 F3
Biggin
Derbys 75 D8
Derbys 76 E2
N Yorks 95 F8
Biggings 160 G3
Biggin Hill 28 D5
Biggleswade 54 E2
Bighouse 157 C11
Bighton 26 F4
Bignor 16 C3
Big Sand 149 A12
Bigton 160 L5
Bilberry 4 C5
Bilborough 76 E5
Bilbrook 22 E2
Bilbrough 95 E8
Bilbster 158 E4
Bildershaw 101 B7
Bildeston 56 E3
Billericay 42 E2
Billesdon 64 D4
Billesley 51 D6
Billingborough 78 F4
Billinge 86 D3
Billingford 81 E6
Billingham 102 B2
Billinghay 78 D4
Billingley 88 D5
Billingshurst 16 B4
Billingsley 61 F7
Billington
C Beds 40 B2
Lancs 93 F7
Billockby 69 C7
Billy Row 110 F4
Bilsborrow 92 F5
Bilsby 79 B7
Bilsham 16 D3
Bilsington 19 B7
Bilson Green 36 C3
Bilsthorpe 77 C6
Bilsthorpe Moor 77 D6
Bilston
Midloth 121 C5
W Mid 62 E3
Bilstone 63 D7
Bilting 30 E4
Bilton
E Yorks 97 F7
Northumb 117 C8
Warks 52 B2
Bilton in Ainsty 95 E7
Bimbister 159 G4
Binbrook 91 E6
Binchester Blocks 110 F5
Bincombe 12 F4
Bindal 151 C12
Binegar 23 E8
Binfield 27 B6
Binfield Heath 26 B5
Bingfield 110 B2
Bingham 77 F7
Bingley 94 F4
Bings Heath 60 C5
Binham 81 D5
Binley
Hants 26 D2
W Mid 51 B8
Binley Woods 51 B8
Binniehill 119 B8
Binsoe 94 B5
Binstead 15 E6
Binsted 27 E5
Binton 51 D6
Bintree 81 E6
Binweston 60 D3
Birch
Essex 43 C5
Gtr Man 87 D6
Bircham Newton 80 D3
Bircham Tofts 80 D3
Birchanger 41 B8
Birchencliffe 88 C2
Bircher 49 C6
Birch Green 43 C5
Birchgrove
Cardiff 22 B3
Swansea 33 E8
Birch Heath 74 C2
Birch Hill 74 B2
Birchington 31 C6
Birchmoor 63 D6
Birchover 76 C2
Birch Vale 87 F8
Birchwood
Lincs 78 C2
Warr 86 E4
Bircotes 89 E7
Birdbrook 55 E8
Birdforth 95 B7
Birdham 16 E2
Birdholme 76 C3
Birdingbury 52 C2
Birdlip 37 C6
Birdsall 96 C4
Birds Edge 88 D3
Birdsgreen 61 F7
Birdsmoor Gate 11 D8
Birdston 119 B6
Birdwell 88 D4
Birdwood 36 C4
Birgham 122 F3
Birkby 101 D8
Birkdale 85 C4
Birkenhead 85 F4
Birkenhills 153 D7
Birkenshaw
N Lanark 119 C6
W Yorks 88 B3
Birkhall 140 E2
Birkhill
Angus 134 F3
Borders 114 C5
Birkholme 65 B6
Birkin 89 B6
Birley 49 D6
Birling
Kent 29 C7
Northumb 117 D8
Birling Gap 18 F2
Birlingham 50 E4
Birmingham 62 F4
Birnam 133 E7
Birse 140 E4
Birsemore 140 E4
Birstall
Leics 64 D2
W Yorks 88 B3
Birstwith 94 D5
Birthorpe 78 F4
Birtley
Hereford 49 C5
Northumb 109 B8
T&W 111 D5
Birts Street 50 F2
Bisbrooke 65 E5
Biscathorpe 91 F6
Biscot 40 B3
Bisham 39 F8
Bishampton 50 D4
Bish Mill 10 B2
Bishop Auckland 101 B7
Bishopbridge 90 E4
Bishopbriggs 119 C6
Bishop Burton 97 F5
Bishop Middleham 111 F6
Bishopmill 152 B2
Bishop Monkton 95 C6
Bishop Norton 90 E3
Bishopsbourne 31 D5
Bishops Cannings 24 C5
Bishop's Castle 60 F3
Bishop's Caundle 12 C4
Bishop's Cleeve 37 B6
Bishops Frome 49 E8
Bishop's Green 42 C2
Bishop's Hull 11 B7
Bishop's Itchington 51 D8
Bishops Lydeard 11 B6
Bishops Nympton 10 B2
Bishop's Offley 61 B7
Bishop's Stortford 41 B7
Bishop's Sutton 26 F4
Bishop's Tachbrook 51 C8
Bishops Tawton 20 F4
Bishopsteignton 7 B7
Bishopstoke 15 C5
Bishopston 33 F6
Bishopstone
Bucks 39 C8
E Sus 17 D8
Hereford 49 E6
Swindon 38 F2
Wilts 13 B8
Bishopstrow 24 E3
Bishop Sutton 23 D7
Bishop's Waltham 15 C6
Bishopswood 11 C7
Bishop's Wood 62 D2
Bishopsworth 23 C7
Bishop Thornton 95 C5
Bishopthorpe 95 E8
Bishopton
Darl 102 B1
Dumfries 105 E8
N Yorks 95 B6
Renfs 118 B4
Warks 51 D6
Bishop Wilton 96 D3
Bishton 35 F7
Bisley
Glos 37 D6
Sur 27 D7
Bispham 92 E3
Bispham Green 86 C2
Bissoe 3 B6
Bisterne Close 14 D3
Bitchfield 65 B6
Bittadon 20 E4
Bittaford 6 D4
Bittering 68 C2
Bitterley 49 B7
Bitterne 15 C5
Bitteswell 64 F2
Bitton 23 C8
Bix 39 F7
Bixter 160 H5
Blaby 64 E2
Blackacre 114 E3
Blackadder West 122 D4
Blackawton 7 D6
Blackborough 11 D5
Blackborough End 67 C6
Black Bourton 38 D2
Blackboys 18 C2
Blackbrook
Derbys 76 E3
Mers 86 E3
Staffs 74 F4
Blackburn
Aberds 141 C7
Aberds 152 E5
Blackburn 86 B4
W Loth 120 C2
Black Callerton 110 C4
Black Clauchrie 112 F2
Black Corries Lodge 131 D6
Blackcraig 113 F7
Black Crofts 124 B5
Blackden Heath 74 B4
Blackdog 141 C8
Black Dog 10 D3
Blackfell 111 D5
Blackfield 14 D5
Blackford
Cumb 108 C3
Perth 127 D7
Som 12 B4
Som 23 E6
Blackfordby 63 C7
Blackgang 15 G5
Blackhall Colliery 111 F7
Blackhall Mill 110 D4
Blackhall Rocks 111 F7
Blackham 29 F5
Blackhaugh 121 F7
Blackheath
Essex 43 B6
Suff 57 B8
Sur 27 E8
W Mid 62 F3
Black Heddon 110 B3
Blackhill
Aberds 153 C10
Aberds 153 D10
Highld 149 C8
Blackhills
Highld 151 F12
Moray 152 C2
Blackhorse 23 B8
Blackland 24 C5
Black Lane 87 D5
Blacklaw 153 C6
Blackley 87 D6
Blacklunans 134 C1
Black Marsh 60 E3
Blackmill 34 F3
Blackmoor 27 F5
Blackmoor Gate 21 E5
Blackmore 42 D2
Blackmore End
Essex 55 F8
Herts 40 C4
Black Mount 131 E6
Blackness 120 B3
Blacknest 27 E5
Black Notley 42 B3
Blacko 93 E8
Black Pill 33 E7
Blackpool
Blackpool 92 F3
Devon 7 E6
Pembs 32 C1
Blackpool Gate 108 B5
Blackridge 119 C8
Blackrock
Argyll 142 B4
Mon 35 C6
Blackrod 86 C4
Blackshaw 107 C7
Blackshaw Head 87 B7
Blacksmith's Green 56 C5
Blackstone 17 C6
Black Tar 44 E4
Blackthorn 39 C6
Blackthorpe 56 C3
Blacktoft 90 B2
Blacktop 141 D7
Black Torrington 9 D6
Blacktown 35 F6
Blackwall Tunnel 41 F6
Blackwater
Corn 3 B6
Hants 27 D6
IoW 15 F6
Blackwaterfoot 143 F9
Blackwell
Darl 101 C7
Derbys 75 B8
Derbys 76 D4
Warks 51 E7
Worcs 50 B4
W Sus 28 F4
Blackwood 119 E7
Blackwood = Coed Duon 35 E5
Blackwood Hill 75 D6
Blacon 73 C7
Bladnoch 105 D8
Bladon 38 C4
Blaenannerch 45 E4
Blaenau Ffestiniog 71 C8
Blaenavon 35 D6
Blaencelyn 46 D2
Blaendyryn 47 F8
Blaenffos 45 F3
Blaengarw 34 E3
Blaengwrach 34 D2
Blaen-gwynfi 34 E2
Blaenpennal 46 C5
Blaenplwyf 46 B4
Blaenporth 45 E4
Blaenrhondda 34 D3
Blaen-waun 32 B3
Blaen-y-coed 32 B4
Blaenycwm 47 B7
Blaen-y-Cwm
Denb 72 F4
Gwyn 71 E8
Powys 59 B7
Blagdon
N Som 23 D7
Torbay 7 C6
Blagdon Hill 11 C7
Blagill 109 E7
Blaguegate 86 D2
Blaich 130 B4
Blain 147 E9
Blaina 35 D6
Blair Atholl 133 C5
Blairbeg 143 E11
Blairdaff 141 C5
Blair Drummond 127 E6
Blairglas 126 F2
Blairgowrie 134 E1
Blairhall 128 F2
Blairingone 127 E8
Blairland 118 E3
Blairlogie 127 E7
Blairlomond 125 F7
Blairmore 145 E10
Blairnamarrow 139 C8
Blairquhosh 126 F4
Blair's Ferry 145 G8
Blairskaith 119 B5
Blaisdon 36 C4
Blakebrook 50 B3
Blakedown 50 B3
Blakelaw 122 F3
Blakeley 62 E2
Blakeley Lane 75 E6
Blakemere 49 E5
Blakeney
Glos 36 D3
Norf 81 C6
Blakenhall
Ches E 74 E4
W Mid 62 E3
Blakeshall 62 F2
Blakesley 52 D4
Blanchland 110 D2
Blandford Forum 13 D6
Blandford St Mary 13 D6
Bland Hill 94 D5
Blanefield 119 B5
Blankney 78 C3
Blantyre 119 D6
Blar a'Chaorainn 131 C5
Blaran 124 D4
Blarghour 125 D5
Blarmachfoldach 130 C4
Blarnalearoch 150 B4
Blashford 14 D2
Blaston 64 E5
Blatherwycke 65 E6
Blawith 98 F4
Blaxhall 57 D7
Blaxton 89 D7
Blaydon 110 C4
Bleadon 22 D5
Bleak Hey Nook 87 D8
Blean 30 C5
Bleasby
Lincs 90 F5
Notts 77 E7
Bleasdale 93 E5
Bleatarn 100 C2
Blebocraigs 129 C6
Bleddfa 48 C4
Bledington 38 B2
Bledlow 39 D7
Bledlow Ridge 39 E7
Blegbie 121 C7
Blencarn 109 F6
Blencogo 107 E8
Blendworth 15 C8
Blenheim Park 80 D4
Blennerhasset 107 E8
Blervie Castle 151 F13
Bletchingdon 39 C5
Bletchingley 28 D4
Bletchley
M Keynes 53 F6
Shrops 74 F3
Bletherston 32 B1
Bletsoe 53 D8
Blewbury 39 F5
Blickling 81 E7
Blidworth 77 D5
Blindburn 116 C4
Blindcrake 107 F8
Blindley Heath 28 E4
Blisland 5 B6
Blissford 14 C2
Bliss Gate 50 B2
Blisworth 52 D5
Blithbury 62 B4
Blitterlees 107 D8
Blockley 51 F6
Blofield 69 D6
Blofield Heath 69 C6
Blo' Norton 56 B4
Bloomfield 115 B8
Blore 75 E8
Blount's Green 75 F7
Blowick 85 C4
Bloxham 52 F2
Bloxholm 78 D3
Bloxwich 62 D3
Bloxworth 13 E6
Blubberhouses 94 D4
Blue Anchor
Som 22 E2
Swansea 33 E6
Blue Row 43 C6
Blundeston 69 E8
Blunham 54 D2
Blunsdon St Andrew 37 F8
Bluntington 50 B3
Bluntisham 54 B4
Blunts 5 C8
Blyborough 90 E3
Blyford 57 B8
Blymhill 62 C2
Blyth
Northumb 117 F9
Notts 89 F7
Blyth Bridge 120 E4
Blythburgh 57 B8
Blythe 121 E8
Blythe Bridge 75 E6
Blyton 90 E2
Boarhills 129 C7
Boarhunt 15 D7
Boarshead 18 B2
Boars Head 86 D3
Boars Hill 38 D4
Boarstall 39 C6
Boasley Cross 9 E6
Boath 151 D8
Boat of Garten 138 C5
Bobbing 30 C2
Bobbington 62 E2
Bobbingworth 41 D8
Bocaddon 5 D6
Bochastle 126 D5
Bocking 42 B3
Bocking Churchstreet 42 B3
Boddam
Aberds 153 D11
Shetland 160 M5
Boddington 37 B5
Bodedern 82 C3
Bodelwyddan 72 B4
Bodenham
Hereford 49 D7
Wilts 14 B2
Bodenham Moor 49 D7
Bodermid 70 E2
Bodewryd 82 B3
Bodfari 72 B4
Bodffordd 82 D4
Bodham 81 C7
Bodiam 18 C4
Bodicote 52 F2
Bodieve 4 B4
Bodinnick 5 D6
Bodle Street Green 18 D3
Bodmin 5 C5
Bodney 67 E8
Bodorgan 82 E3
Bodsham 30 E5
Boduan 70 D4
Bodymoor Heath 63 E5
Bogallan 151 F9
Bogbrae 153 E10
Bogend
Borders 122 E3
S Ayrs 118 F3
Boghall 120 C2
Boghead 119 E7
Bogmoor 152 B3
Bogniebrae 152 D5
Bognor Regis 16 E3
Bograxie 141 C6
Bogside 119 D8
Bogton 153 C6
Bogue 113 F6
Bohenie 137 F5
Bohortha 3 C7
Bohuntine 137 F5

Boirseam 154 J5
Bojewyan 2 C2
Bolam
Durham 101 B6
Northumb 117 F6
Bolberry 6 F4
Bold Heath 86 F3
Boldon 111 C6
Boldon Colliery 111 C6
Boldre 14 E4
Boldron 101 C5
Bole 89 F8
Bolehill 76 D2
Boleside 121 F7
Bolham 10 C4
Bolham Water 11 C6
Bolingey 4 D2
Bollington 75 B6
Bollington Cross 75 B6
Bolney 17 B6
Bolnhurst 53 D8
Bolshan 135 D6
Bolsover 76 B4
Bolsterstone 88 E3
Bolstone 49 F7
Boltby 102 F2
Bolter End 39 E7
Bolton
Cumb 99 B8
E Loth 121 B8
E Yorks 96 D3
Gtr Man 86 D5
Northumb 117 C7
Bolton Abbey 94 D3
Bolton Bridge 94 D3
Bolton-by-Bowland 93 E7
Boltonfellend 108 C4
Boltongate 108 E2
Bolton-le-Sands 92 C4
Bolton Low Houses 108 E2
Bolton-on-Swale 101 E7
Bolton Percy 95 E8
Bolton Town End 92 C4
Bolton upon Dearne 89 D5
Bolventor 5 B6
Bomere Heath 60 C4
Bonar Bridge 151 B9
Bonawe 125 B6
Bonby 90 C4
Boncath 45 F4
Bonchester Bridge 115 C8
Bonchurch 15 G6
Bondleigh 9 D8
Bonehill
Devon 6 B5
Staffs 63 D5
Bo'ness 127 F8
Bonhill 118 B3
Boningale 62 D2
Bonjedward 116 B2
Bonkle 119 D8
Bonnavoulin 147 F8
Bonnington
Edin 120 C4
Kent 19 B7
Bonnybank 129 D5
Bonnybridge 127 F7
Bonnykelly 153 C8
Bonnyrigg and Lasswade 121 C6
Bonnyton
Aberds 153 E6
Angus 134 F3
Angus 135 D6
Bonsall 76 D2
Bonskeid House 133 C5
Bont 35 C7
Bontddu 58 C3
Bont-Dolgadfan 59 D5
Bont-goch 58 F3
Bonthorpe 79 B7
Bontnewydd
Ceredig 46 C5
Gwyn 82 F4
Bont-newydd 72 B4
Bont Newydd
Gwyn 71 C8
Gwyn 71 E8
Bontuchel 72 D4
Bonvilston 22 B2
Bon-y-maen 33 E7
Booker 39 E8
Boon 121 E8
Boosbeck 102 C4
Boot 98 D3
Booth 87 B8
Boothby Graffoe 78 D2
Boothby Pagnell 78 F2
Boothen 75 E5
Boothferry 89 B8
Boothville 53 C5
Booth Wood 87 C8
Bootle
Cumb 98 F3
Mers 85 E4
Booton 81 E7
Boot Street 57 E6
Boquhan 126 F4
Boraston 49 B8
Borden
Kent 30 C2
W Sus 16 B2
Bordley 94 C2
Bordon 27 F6
Bordon Camp 27 F5
Boreham
Essex 42 D3
Wilts 24 E3
Boreham Street 18 D3
Borehamwood 40 E4
Boreland
Dumfries 114 E4
Stirling 132 F2
Borgh
W Isles 148 H1
W Isles 154 J4
Borghastan 154 C7
Borgie 157 D9
Borgue
Dumfries 106 E3
Borgue *continued*
Highld 158 H3
Borley 56 E2
Bornais 148 F2
Bornesketaig 149 A8
Borness 106 E3
Boroughbridge 95 C6
Borough Green 29 D7
Borras Head 73 D7
Borreraig 148 C6
Borrobol Lodge 157 G11
Borrowash 76 F4
Borrowby 102 F2
Borrowdale 98 C4
Borrowfield 141 E7
Borth 58 E3
Borthwickbrae 115 C7
Borthwickshiels 115 C7
Borth-y-Gest 71 D6
Borve 149 D9
Borve Lodge 154 H5
Borwick 92 B5
Bosavern 2 C2
Bosbury 49 E8
Boscastle 8 E3
Boscombe
BCP 14 E2
Wilts 25 F7
Boscoppa 4 D5
Bosham 16 D2
Bosherston 44 F4
Boskenna 2 D3
Bosley 75 C6
Bossall 96 C3
Bossiney 8 F2
Bossingham 31 E5
Bossington 21 E7
Bostock Green 74 C3
Boston 79 E6
Boston Long Hedges 79 E6
Boston Spa 95 E7
Boston West 79 E5
Boswinger 3 B8
Botallack 2 C2
Botany Bay 41 E5
Botcherby 108 D4
Botcheston 63 D8
Botesdale 56 B4
Bothal 117 F8
Bothamsall 77 B6
Bothel 107 F8
Bothenhampton 12 E2
Bothwell 119 D7
Botley
Bucks 40 D2
Hants 15 C6
Oxon 38 D4
Botolph Claydon 39 B7
Botolphs 17 D5
Bottacks 150 E7
Bottesford
Leics 77 F8
N Lincs 90 D2
Bottisham 55 C6
Bottlesford 25 D6
Bottom Boat 88 B4
Bottomcraig 129 B5
Bottom House 75 D7
Bottom of Hutton 86 B2
Bottom o'th'Moor 86 C4
Botusfleming 6 C2
Botwnnog 70 D3
Bough Beech 29 E5
Boughrood 48 F3
Boughspring 36 E2
Boughton
Norf 67 D6
Notts 77 C6
W Nhants 53 C5
Boughton Aluph 30 E4
Boughton Lees 30 E4
Boughton Malherbe 30 E2
Boughton Monchelsea 29 D8
Boughton Street 30 D4
Boulby 103 C5
Boulden 60 F5
Boulmer 117 C8
Boulston 44 D4
Boultenstone 140 C3
Boultham 78 C2
Bourn 54 D4
Bourne 65 B7
Bourne End
Bucks 40 F1
C Beds 53 E7
Herts 40 D3
Bournemouth 13 E8
Bournes Green
Glos 37 D6
Southend 43 F5
Bournheath 50 B4
Bournmoor 111 D6
Bournville 62 F4
Bourton
Dorset 24 F2
N Som 23 C5
Oxon 38 F2
Shrops 61 E5
Bourton on Dunsmore 52 B2
Bourton on the Hill 51 F6
Bourton-on-the-Water 38 B1
Bousd 146 E5
Boustead Hill 108 D2
Bouth 99 F5
Bouthwaite 94 B4
Boveney 27 B7
Boverton 21 C8
Bovey Tracey 7 B6
Bovingdon 40 D3
Bovingdon Green
Bucks 39 F8
Herts 40 D3
Bovinger 41 D8
Bovington Camp 13 F6
Bow
Borders 121 E7
Devon 10 D2
Orkney 159 J4
Bowbank 100 B4
Bow Brickhill 53 F7
Bowburn 111 F6
Bowcombe 15 F5
Bowd 11 E6
Bowden
Borders 121 F8
Devon 7 E6
Bowden Hill 24 C4
Bowderdale 100 D1
Bowdon 87 F5
Bower 116 F3
Bowerchalke 13 B8
Bowerhill 24 C4
Bower Hinton 12 C2
Bowermadden 158 D4
Bowers Gifford 42 F3
Bowershall 128 E2
Bowertower 158 D4
Bowes 100 C4
Bowgreave 92 E4
Bowgreen 87 F5
Bowhill 115 B7
Bowhouse 107 C7
Bowland Bridge 99 F6
Bowley 49 D7
Bowlhead Green 27 F7
Bowling
W Dunb 118 B4
W Yorks 94 F4
Bowling Bank 73 E7
Bowling Green 50 D3
Bowmanstead 99 E5
Bowmore 142 C4
Bowness-on-Solway 108 C2
Bowness-on-Windermere 99 E6
Bow of Fife 128 C5
Bowsden 123 E5
Bowside Lodge 157 C11
Bowston 99 E6
Bow Street 58 F3
Bowthorpe 68 D4
Box
Glos 37 D5
Wilts 24 C3
Boxbush 36 C4
Box End 53 E8
Boxford
Suff 56 E3
W Berks 26 B2
Boxgrove 16 D3
Boxley 29 D8
Boxmoor 40 D3
Boxted
Essex 56 F4
Suff 56 D2
Boxted Cross 56 F4
Boxted Heath 56 F4
Boxworth 54 C4
Boxworth End 54 C4
Boyden Gate 31 C6
Boylestone 75 F8
Boyndie 153 B6
Boynton 97 C7
Boysack 135 E6
Boyton
Corn 8 E5
Suff 57 E7
Wilts 24 F4
Boyton Cross 42 D2
Boyton End 55 E8
Bozeat 53 D7
Braaid 84 E3
Braal Castle 158 D3
Brabling Green 57 C6
Brabourne 30 E4
Brabourne Lees 30 E4
Brabster 158 D5
Bracadale 149 E8
Bracara 147 B10
Braceborough 65 C7
Bracebridge 78 C2
Bracebridge Heath 78 C2
Bracebridge Low Fields 78 C2
Braceby 78 F3
Bracewell 93 E8
Brackenfield 76 D3
Brackenthwaite
Cumb 108 E2
N Yorks 95 D5
Bracklesham 16 E2
Brackletter 136 F4
Brackley
Argyll 143 D8
W Nhants 52 F3
Brackloch 156 G4
Bracknell 27 C6
Braco 127 D7
Bracobrae 152 C5
Bracon Ash 68 E4
Bracorina 147 B10
Bradbourne 76 D2
Bradbury 101 B8
Bradda 84 F1
Bradden 52 E4
Braddock 5 C6
Bradeley 75 D5
Bradenham
Bucks 39 E8
Norf 68 D2
Bradenstoke 24 B5
Bradfield
Essex 56 F5
Norf 81 D8
W Berks 26 B4
Bradfield Combust 56 D2
Bradfield Green 74 D3
Bradfield Heath 43 B7
Bradfield St Clare 56 D3
Bradfield St George 56 C3
Bradford
Corn 5 B6
Derbys 76 C2
Devon 9 D6
Northumb 123 F7
W Yorks 94 F4
Bradford Abbas 12 C3
Bradford Leigh 24 C3
Bradford-on-Avon 24 C3
Bradford-on-Tone 11 B6
Bradford Peverell 12 E4
Brading 15 F7
Bradley
Derbys 76 E2
Hants 26 E4
NE Lincs 91 D6
Staffs 62 C2
W Mid 62 E3
W Yorks 88 B2
Bradley Green 50 C4
Bradley in the Moors 75 E7
Bradley Stoke 36 F3
Bradlow 50 F2
Bradmore
Notts 77 F5
W Mid 62 E2
Bradninch 10 D5
Bradnop 75 D7
Bradpole 12 E2
Bradshaw
Gtr Man 86 C5
W Yorks 87 C8
Bradstone 9 F5
Bradwall Green 74 C4
Bradway 88 F4
Bradwell
Derbys 88 F2
Essex 42 B4
M Keynes 53 F6
Norf 69 D8
Staffs 74 E5
Bradwell Grove 38 D2
Bradwell on Sea 43 D6
Bradwell Waterside 43 D5
Bradworthy 8 C5
Bradworthy Cross 8 C5
Brae
Dumfries 107 B5
Highld 155 J13
Highld 156 J7
Shetland 160 G5
Braeantra 151 D8
Braedownie 134 B2
Braefield 150 H7
Braegrum 128 B2
Braehead
Dumfries 105 D8
Orkney 159 D5
Orkney 159 H6
S Lanark 119 F8
S Lanark 120 D2
Braehead of Lunan 135 D6
Braehoulland 160 F4
Braehungie 158 G3
Braelangwell Lodge 151 B8
Braemar 139 E7
Braemore
Highld 150 D4
Highld 158 G2
Brae of Achnahaird 156 H3
Brae Roy Lodge 137 E6
Braeside 118 B2
Braes of Enzie 152 C3
Braeswick 159 E7
Braewick 160 H5
Brafferton
Darl 101 B7
N Yorks 95 B7
Brafield-on-the-Green 53 D6
Bragar 155 C7
Bragbury End 41 B5
Bragleenmore 124 C5
Braichmelyn 83 E6
Braid 120 C5
Braides 92 D4
Braidley 101 F5
Braidwood 119 E8
Braigo 142 B3
Brailsford 76 E2
Brainshaugh 117 D8
Braintree 42 B3
Braiseworth 56 B5
Braishfield 14 B4
Braithwaite
Cumb 98 B4
S Yorks 89 C7
W Yorks 94 E3
Braithwell 89 E6
Bramber 17 C5
Bramcote
Notts 76 F5
Warks 63 F8
Bramdean 15 B7
Bramerton 69 D5
Bramfield
Herts 41 C5
Suff 57 B7
Bramford 56 E5
Bramhall 87 F6
Bramham 95 E7
Bramhope 95 E5
Bramley
Hants 26 D4
Sur 27 E8
S Yorks 89 E5
W Yorks 94 F5
Bramling 31 D6
Brampford Speke 10 E4
Brampton
Cambs 54 B3
Cumb 100 B1
Cumb 108 C5
Derbys 76 B3
Hereford 49 F6
Lincs 77 B8
Norf 81 E8
Suff 69 F7
S Yorks 88 D5
Brampton Abbotts 36 B3
Brampton Ash 64 F4
Brampton Bryan 49 B5
Brampton en le Morthen 89 F5
Bramshall 75 F7
Bramshaw 14 C3
Bramshill 26 C5
Bramshott 27 F6
Branault 147 E8
Brancaster 80 C3
Brancaster Staithe 80 C3
Brancepeth 110 F5
Branch End 110 C3
Branchill 151 F13
Branderburgh 152 A2
Brandesburton 97 E7
Brandeston 57 C6
Brand Green 36 B4
Brandhill 49 B6
Brandis Corner 9 D6
Brandiston 81 E7
Brandon
Durham 110 F5
Lincs 78 E2
Northumb 117 C6
Suff 67 F7
Warks 52 B2
Brandon Bank 67 F6
Brandon Creek 67 E6
Brandon Parva 68 D3
Brandsby 95 B8
Brandy Wharf 90 E4
Brane 2 D3
Bran End 42 B2
Branksome 13 E8
Branksome Park 13 E8
Bransby 77 B8
Branscombe 11 F6
Bransford 50 D2
Bransgore 14 E2
Branshill 127 E7
Bransholme 97 F7
Branson's Cross 51 B5
Branston
Leics 64 B5
Lincs 78 C3
Staffs 63 B6
Branston Booths 78 C3
Branstone 15 F6
Bransty 98 C1
Brant Broughton 78 D2
Brantham 56 F5
Branthwaite
Cumb 98 B2
Cumb 108 F2
Brantingham 90 B3
Branton
Northumb 117 C6
S Yorks 89 D7
Branxholme 115 C7
Branxholm Park 115 C7
Branxton 122 F4
Brassey Green 74 C2
Brassington 76 D2
Brasted 29 D5
Brasted Chart 29 D5
Brathens 141 E5
Bratoft 79 C7
Brattleby 90 F3
Bratton
Telford 61 C6
Wilts 24 D4
Bratton Clovelly 9 E6
Bratton Fleming 20 F5
Bratton Seymour 12 B4
Braughing 41 B6
Braunston 52 C3
Braunstone Town 64 D2
Braunston-in-Rutland 64 D5
Braunton 20 F3
Brawby 96 B3
Brawl 157 C11
Brawlbin 158 E2
Bray 27 B7
Braybrooke 64 F4
Braye 16 I1
Brayford 21 F5
Bray Shop 5 B8
Braystones 98 D2
Braythorn 94 E5
Brayton 95 F9
Bray Wick 27 B6
Brazacott 8 E4
Breach 30 C2
Breachacha Castle 146 F4
Breachwood Green 40 B4
Breacleit 154 D6
Breaden Heath 73 F8
Breadsall 76 F3
Breadstone 36 D4
Breage 2 D5
Breakachy 150 G7
Bream 36 D3
Breamore 14 C2
Brean 22 D4
Breanais 154 E4
Brearton 95 C6
Breascleit 154 D7
Breaston 76 F4
Brechfa 46 F4
Brechin 135 C5
Breckan 159 H3
Breck of Cruan 159 G4
Breckrey 149 B10
Brecon
= *Aberhonddu* 34 B4
Bredbury 87 E7
Brede 18 D5
Bredenbury 49 D8
Bredfield 57 D6
Bredgar 30 C2
Bredhurst 29 C8
Bredicot 50 D4
Bredon 50 F4
Bredon's Norton 50 F4
Bredwardine 48 E5
Breedon on the Hill 63 B8
Breibhig
W Isles 148 J1
W Isles 155 D9
Breich 120 C2
Breightmet 86 D5
Breighton 96 F3
Breinton 49 F6
Breinton Common 49 E6
Breiwick 160 J6
Bremhill 24 B4
Bremirehoull 160 L6
Brenchley 29 E7
Brendon 21 E6
Brenkley 110 B5
Brent Eleigh 56 E3
Brentford 28 B2
Brentingby 64 C4
Brent Knoll 22 D5
Brent Pelham 54 F5
Brentwood 42 E1
Brenzett 19 C7
Brereton 62 C4
Brereton Green 74 C4
Brereton Heath 74 C5
Bressingham 68 F3
Bretby 63 B6
Bretford 52 B2
Bretforton 51 E5
Bretherdale Head 99 D7
Bretherton 86 B2
Brettabister 160 H6
Brettenham
Norf 68 F2
Suff 56 D3
Bretton
Derbys 76 B2
Flint 73 C7
Brewer Street 28 D4
Brewlands Bridge 134 C1
Brewood 62 D2
Briach 151 F13
Briants Puddle 13 E6
Brick End 42 B1
Brickendon 41 D6
Bricket Wood 40 D4
Bricklehampton 50 E4
Bride 84 B4
Bridekirk 107 F8
Bridell 45 E3
Bridestowe 9 F7
Brideswell 152 E5
Bridford 10 F3
Bridfordmills 10 F3
Bridge 31 D5
Bridge End 78 F4
Bridgefoot
Angus 134 F3
Cumb 98 B2
Bridge Green 55 F5
Bridgehampton 12 B3
Bridge Hewick 95 B6
Bridgehill 110 D3
Bridgemary 15 D6
Bridgemont 87 F8
Bridgend
Aberds 140 C4
Aberds 152 E5
Angus 135 C5
Argyll 142 B4
Argyll 143 E8
Argyll 145 D7
Cumb 99 C5
Fife 129 C5
Moray 152 E3
N Lanark 119 B6
Pembs 45 E3
W Loth 120 B3
Bridgend = *Pen-y-Bont Ar Ogwr* 21 B8
Bridgend of Lintrathen 134 D2
Bridge of Alford 140 C4
Bridge of Allan 127 E6
Bridge of Avon 152 E1
Bridge of Awe 125 C6
Bridge of Balgie 132 E2
Bridge of Cally 133 D8
Bridge of Canny 141 E5
Bridge of Craigisla 134 D2
Bridge of Dee 106 D4
Bridge of Don 141 C8
Bridge of Dun 135 D6
Bridge of Dye 141 F5
Bridge of Earn 128 C3
Bridge of Ericht 132 D2
Bridge of Feugh 141 E6
Bridge of Forss 157 C13
Bridge of Gairn 140 E2
Bridge of Gaur 132 D2
Bridge of Muchalls 141 E7
Bridge of Oich 137 D6
Bridge of Orchy 125 B8
Bridge of Waith 159 G3
Bridge of Walls 160 H4
Bridge of Weir 118 C3
Bridgerule 8 D4
Bridges 60 E3
Bridge Sollers 49 E6
Bridge Street 56 E2
Bridgeton 119 C6
Bridgetown
Corn 8 F5
Som 21 F8
Bridge Trafford 73 B8
Bridge Yate 23 B8
Bridgham 68 F2
Bridgnorth 61 E7
Bridgtown 62 D3
Bridgwater 22 F5
Bridlington 97 C7
Bridport 12 E2
Bridstow 36 B2
Brierfield 93 F8
Brierley
Glos 36 C3
Hereford 49 D6
S Yorks 88 C5
Brierley Hill 62 F3
Briery Hill 35 D5
Brigg 90 D4
Briggswath 103 D6
Brigham
Cumb 107 F7
E Yorks 97 D6
Brighouse 88 B2
Brighstone 14 F5
Brightgate 76 D2
Brighthampton 38 D3
Brightling 18 C3
Brightlingsea 43 C6
Brighton
Brighton 17 D7
Corn 4 D4
Brighton Hill 26 E4
Brightons 120 B2
Brightwalton 26 B2
Brightwell 57 E6
Brightwell Baldwin 39 E6
Brightwell cum Sotwell 39 E5
Brignall 101 C5
Brig o'Turk 126 D4
Brigsley 91 D6
Brigsteer 99 F6
Brigstock 65 F6
Brill 39 C6
Brilley 48 E4
Brimaston 44 C4
Brimfield 49 C7
Brimington 76 B4
Brimley 7 B5
Brimpsfield 37 C6
Brimpton 26 C3
Brims 159 K3
Brimscombe 37 D5
Brimstage 85 F4
Brinacory 147 B10
Brind 96 F3
Brindister
Shetland 160 H4
Shetland 160 K6
Brindle 86 B4
Brindley Ford 75 D5
Brineton 62 C2
Bringhurst 64 E5
Brington 53 B8
Brinian 159 F5
Briningham 81 D6
Brinkhill 79 B6
Brinkley 55 D7
Brinklow 52 B2
Brinkworth 37 F7
Brinmore 138 B2
Brinscall 86 B4
Brinsea 23 C6
Brinsley 76 E4
Brinsop 49 E6
Brinsworth 88 F5
Brinton 81 D6
Brisco 108 D4
Brisley 81 E5
Brislington 23 B8
Bristol 23 B7
Briston 81 D6
Britannia 87 B6
Britford 14 B2
Brithdir 58 C4
British Legion Village 29 D8
Briton Ferry 33 E8
Britwell Salome 39 E6
Brixham 7 D7
Brixton
Devon 6 D3
London 28 B4
Brixton Deverill 24 F3
Brixworth 52 B5
Brize Norton 38 D3
Broad Blunsdon 38 E1
Broadbottom 87 E7
Broadbridge 16 D2
Broadbridge Heath 28 F2
Broad Campden 51 F6
Broad Chalke 13 B8
Broadclyst 10 E4
Broadfield
Gtr Man 87 C6
Lancs 86 B3
Pembs 32 D2
W Sus 28 F3
Broadford 149 F11
Broadford Bridge 16 B4
Broad Green
C Beds 53 E7
Essex 42 B4
Worcs 50 D2
Broadhaugh 115 D7
Broadhaven 158 E5
Broad Haven 44 D3
Broadheath 87 F5
Broad Heath 49 C8
Broadhembury 11 D6
Broadhempston 7 C6
Broad Hill 55 B6
Broad Hinton 25 B6
Broadholme
Derbys 76 E3
Lincs 77 B8
Broadland Row 18 D5
Broadlay 32 D4
Broad Laying 26 C2
Broadley
Lancs 87 C6
Moray 152 B3
Broadley Common 41 D7
Broad Marston 51 E6
Broadmayne 12 F5
Broadmeadows 121 F7
Broadmere 26 E4
Broadmoor 32 D1
Broadoak 31 C5
Broad Oak
Carms 33 B6
Cumb 98 E3
Dorset 12 E2
Dorset 13 C5
E Sus 18 C3
E Sus 18 D5
Hereford 36 B1
Mers 86 E3
Broadrashes 152 C4
Broadsea 153 B9
Broadstairs 31 C7
Broadstone
BCP 13 E8
Shrops 60 F5
Broad Street 30 D2
Broad Street Green 42 D4
Broad Town 25 B5
Broadtown Lane 25 B5
Broadwas 50 D2
Broadwater
Herts 41 B5
W Sus 17 D5
Broadway
Carms 32 D3
Pembs 44 D3
Som 11 C8
Suff 57 B7
Worcs 51 F5
Broadwell
Glos 36 C2
Glos 38 B2
Oxon 38 D2
Warks 52 C2
Broadwell House 110 D2
Broadwey 12 F4
Broadwindsor 12 D2
Broadwood Kelly 9 D8
Broadwoodwidger 9 F6
Brobury 48 E5
Brochel 149 D10
Brochloch 113 E5
Brochroy 125 B6
Brockamin 50 D2
Brockbridge 15 C7
Brockdam 117 B7
Brockdish 57 B6
Brockenhurst 14 D4
Brocketsbrae 119 F8
Brockford Street 56 C5
Brockhall 52 C4
Brockham 28 E2
Brockhampton
Glos 37 B7
Hereford 49 F7
Brockholes 88 C2
Brockhurst
Derbys 76 C3
Hants 15 D7
Brocklebank 108 E3
Brocklesby 90 C5
Brockley 23 C6
Brockley Green 56 D2
Brockleymoor 108 F4
Brockton
Shrops 60 D3
Shrops 60 F3
Shrops 61 D7
Shrops 61 E5
Telford 61 C7
Brockweir 36 D2
Brockwood 15 B7
Brockworth 37 C5
Brocton 62 C3
Brodick 143 E11
Brodsworth 89 D6
Brogaig 149 B9
Brogborough 53 F7
Brokenborough 37 F6
Broken Cross
Ches E 75 B5
Ches W 74 B3
Bromborough 85 F4
Brome 56 B5
Brome Street 57 B5
Bromeswell 57 D7
Bromfield
Cumb 107 E8
Shrops 49 B6
Bromham
Bedford 53 D8
Wilts 24 C4
Bromley
London 28 C5
W Mid 62 F3
Bromley Common 28 C5
Bromley Green 19 B6
Brompton
Medway 29 C8
N Yorks 102 E1
N Yorks 103 F7
Brompton-on-Swale 101 E7
Brompton Ralph 22 F2
Brompton Regis 21 F8
Bromsash 36 B3
Bromsberrow Heath 50 F2
Bromsgrove 50 B4
Bromyard 49 D8
Bromyard Downs 49 D8
Bronaber 71 D8
Brongest 46 E2
Bronington 73 F8
Bronllys 48 F3
Bronnant 46 C5
Bronwydd Arms 33 B5
Bronydd 48 E4
Bronygarth 73 F6
Brook
Carms 32 D3
Hants 14 B4
Hants 14 C3
IoW 14 F4
Kent 30 E4
Sur 27 E8
Sur 27 F7
Brooke
Norf 69 E5
Rutland 64 D5
Brookenby 91 E6
Brookend 36 E2
Brook End 53 C8
Brookfield 118 C4
Brook Hill 14 C3
Brookhouse 92 C5
Brookhouse Green 74 C5
Brookland 19 C6
Brooklands
Dumfries 106 B5
Gtr Man 87 E5
Shrops 74 E2
Brookmans Park 41 D5
Brooks 59 E8
Brooks Green 16 B5
Brook Street
Kent 19 B6
Kent 29 E6
W Sus 17 B7
Brookthorpe 37 C5
Brookville 67 E7
Brookwood 27 D7
Broom
C Beds 54 E2
S Yorks 88 E5
Warks 51 D5
Worcs 50 B4
Broome
Norf 69 E6
Shrops 60 F4
Broomedge 86 F5
Broome Park 117 C7
Broomer's Corner 16 B5
Broomfield
Aberds 153 E9
Essex 42 C3
Kent 30 D2
Kent 31 C5
Som 22 F4
Broomfleet 90 B2
Broom Green 81 E5
Broomhall
Ches E 74 E3
Windsor 27 C7
Broomhaugh 110 C3
Broomhill
Norf 67 D6
Northumb 117 D8
S Yorks 88 D5
Broom Hill 13 D8
Broomholm 81 D9
Broomley 110 C3
Broompark 110 E5
Broom's Green 50 F2
Broomy Lodge 14 C3
Brora 157 J12
Broseley 61 D6
Brotherhouse Bar 66 C2
Brotherstone 122 F2
Brothertoft 79 E5
Brotherton 89 B5
Brotton 102 C4
Broubster 157 C13
Brough
Cumb 100 C2
Derbys 88 F2
E Yorks 90 B3
Highld 158 C4
Notts 77 D8
Orkney 159 G4
Shetland 160 F6
Shetland 160 F7
Shetland 160 G7
Shetland 160 H6
Shetland 160 J7
Broughall 74 E2
Brough Lodge 160 D7
Brough Sowerby 100 C2
Broughton
Borders 120 F4
Cambs 54 B3
Flint 73 C7
Hants 25 F8
Lancs 92 F5
M Keynes 53 E6
N Lincs 90 D3
N Nhants 53 B6
N Yorks 94 D2
N Yorks 96 B3
Orkney 159 D5
Oxon 52 F2
V Glam 21 B8
Broughton Astley 64 E2
Broughton Beck 98 F4
Broughton Common 24 C3
Broughton Gifford 24 C3
Broughton Hackett 50 D4
Broughton in Furness 98 F4
Broughton Mills 98 E4
Broughton Moor 107 F7
Broughton Park 87 D6
Broughton Poggs 38 D2
Broughtown 159 D7
Broughty Ferry 134 F4
Browhouses 108 C2
Browland 160 H4
Brown Candover 26 F3
Brown Edge
Lancs 85 C4
Staffs 75 D6
Brown Heath 73 C8
Brownhill
Aberds 153 D6
Aberds 153 D8
Blackburn 93 F6
Shrops 60 B4
Brownhills
Fife 129 C7
W Mid 62 D4
Brownlow 74 C5
Brownlow Heath 74 C5
Brownmuir 135 B7
Brown's End 50 F2
Brownshill 37 D5
Brownston 6 D4
Brownyside 117 B7
Broxa 103 E7
Broxbourne 41 D6
Broxburn
E Loth 122 B2
W Loth 120 B3
Broxholme 78 B2
Broxted 42 B1
Broxton 73 D8
Broxwood 49 D5
Broyle Side 17 C8
Brù 155 C8
Bruairnis 148 H2
Bruan 158 G5
Bruar Lodge 133 B5
Brucehill 118 B3
Bruera 73 C8
Bruern Abbey 38 B2
Bruichladdich 142 B3
Bruisyard 57 C7
Brumby 90 D2
Brund 75 C8
Brundall 69 D6
Brundish 57 C6
Brundish Street 57 B6
Brunery 147 D10
Brunshaw 93 F8
Brunswick Village 110 B5
Bruntcliffe 88 B3
Bruntingthorpe 64 E3
Brunton
Fife 128 B5
Northumb 117 B8
Wilts 25 D7
Brushford
Devon 9 D8
Som 10 B4
Bruton 23 F8
Bryanston 13 D6
Brydekirk 107 B8
Bryher 2 E3
Brymbo 73 D6
Brympton 12 C3
Bryn
Carms 33 D6
Gtr Man 86 D3
Neath 34 E2

**Bryn** continued
Shrops . . . . . . . . . . .60 F2
Brynamman . . . . . .33 C8
Brynberian . . . . . . .45 F3
Brynbryddan . . . . .34 E1
Bryncae . . . . . . . . . .34 F3
Bryncethin . . . . . . .34 F3
Bryn-coch
Neath . . . . . . . . . . .33 E8
Bryncroes . . . . . . . .70 D3
Bryncrug . . . . . . . . .58 D3
Bryn Du . . . . . . . . . .82 D3
Bryneglwys . . . . . . .72 E5
Brynford . . . . . . . . .73 B5
Bryn Gates . . . . . . .86 D3
Bryn-glas . . . . . . . . .83 E8
Bryn Golau . . . . . . .34 F3
Bryngwran . . . . . . .82 D3
Bryngwyn
Ceredig . . . . . . . . . .45 E4
Mon . . . . . . . . . . . . .35 D7
Powys . . . . . . . . . . .48 E3
Brynhenllan . . . . . .45 F2
Brynhoffnant . . . . .46 D2
Brynithel . . . . . . . . .35 D6
Bryn-Iwan . . . . . . . .46 F2
Brynmawr . . . . . . . .35 C5
Bryn-mawr . . . . . . .70 D3
Brynmenyn . . . . . . .34 F3
Brynmill . . . . . . . . . .33 E7
Brynna . . . . . . . . . . .34 F3
Bryn-nantllech . . . .72 C3
Bryn-penarth . . . . .59 D8
Brynrefail
Anglesey . . . . . . . . .82 C4
Gwyn . . . . . . . . . . . .83 E5
Bryn Rhyd-yr-
Arian . . . . . . . . . . . .72 C3
Brynsadler . . . . . . .34 F4
Bryn Saith
Marchog . . . . . . . . .72 D4
Brynsiencyn . . . . . .82 E4
Bryn Sion . . . . . . . .59 C5
Brynteg
Anglesey . . . . . . . . .82 C4
Ceredig . . . . . . . . . .46 E3
Bryn-y-gwenin . . . .35 C7
Bryn-y-maen . . . . . .83 D8
Bryn-yr-eryr . . . . . .70 C4
Buaile nam
Bodach . . . . . . . . .148 H2
Bualintur . . . . . . .149 F9
Buarthmeini . . . . . .72 F2
Bubbenhall . . . . . . .51 B8
Bubwith . . . . . . . . . .96 F3
Buccleuch . . . . . . .115 C6
Buchanty . . . . . . . .127 B8
Buchlyvie . . . . . . . .126 E4
Buckabank . . . . . .108 E3
Buckden
Cambs . . . . . . . . . . .54 C2
N Yorks . . . . . . . . . .94 B2
Buckenham . . . . . . .69 D6
Buckerell . . . . . . . . .11 D6
Buckfast . . . . . . . . . . .6 C5
Buckfastleigh . . . . . .6 C5
Buckhaven . . . . . .129 E5
Buckholm . . . . . . .121 F7
Buckholt . . . . . . . . .36 C2
Buckhorn Weston 13 B5
Buckhurst Hill . . . .41 E7
Buckie . . . . . . . . . .152 B4
Buckies . . . . . . . . .158 D3
Buckingham . . . . . .52 F4
Buckland
Bucks . . . . . . . . . . . .40 C1
Devon . . . . . . . . . . . .6 E4
Glos . . . . . . . . . . . . .51 F5
Hants . . . . . . . . . . . .14 E4
Herts . . . . . . . . . . . .54 F4
Kent . . . . . . . . . . . . .31 E7
Oxon . . . . . . . . . . . .38 E3
Sur . . . . . . . . . . . . . .28 D3
Buckland Brewer . . .9 B6
Buckland
Common . . . . . . . . .40 D2
Buckland
Dinham . . . . . . . . . .24 D2
Buckland Filleigh . . .9 D6
Buckland in the
Moor . . . . . . . . . . . . .6 B5
Buckland
Monachorum . . . . .6 C2
Buckland Newton 12 D4
Buckland St Mary .11 C7
Bucklebury . . . . . . .26 B3
Bucklegate . . . . . . .79 F6
Bucklerheads . . . .134 F4
Bucklers Hard . . . .14 E5
Bucklesham . . . . . .57 E6
Buckley = Bwcle . . .73 C6
Bucklow Hill . . . . . .86 F5
Buckminster . . . . . .65 B5
Bucknall
Lincs . . . . . . . . . . . .78 C4
Stoke . . . . . . . . . . . .75 E6
Bucknell
Oxon . . . . . . . . . . . .39 B5
Shrops . . . . . . . . . . .49 B5
Buckpool . . . . . . . .152 B4
Bucksburn . . . . . .141 D7
Buck's Cross . . . . . . .8 B5
Bucks Green . . . . . .27 F8
Buckshaw Village 86 B3
Bucks Horn Oak . .27 E6
Buckton
E Yorks . . . . . . . . . .97 B7
Hereford . . . . . . . . .49 B5
Northumb . . . . . . .123 F6
Buckworth . . . . . . .54 B2
Budbrooke . . . . . . .51 C7
Budby . . . . . . . . . . . .77 C6
Budd's Titson . . . . . .8 D4
Bude . . . . . . . . . . . . . .8 D4
Budlake . . . . . . . . . .10 E4
Budle . . . . . . . . . .123 F7
Budleigh
Salterton . . . . . . . .11 F5
Budock Water . . . . . .3 C6
Buerton . . . . . . . . . .74 E3
Buffler's Holt . . . . .52 F4
Bugbrooke . . . . . . .52 D4
Buglawton . . . . . . . .75 C5
Bugle . . . . . . . . . . . . .4 D5

Bugley . . . . . . . . . . .24 E3
Bugthorpe . . . . . . . .96 D3
Buildwas . . . . . . . . .61 D6
Buildwas Road . . . .48 D2
Builth Wells = Llanfair-
ym-Muallt . . . . . . . .48 D2
Buirgh . . . . . . . . . .154 H5
Bulby . . . . . . . . . . . .65 B7
Bulcote . . . . . . . . . .77 E6
Buldoo . . . . . . . . . .157 C12
Bulford . . . . . . . . . .25 E6
Bulford Camp . . . . .25 E6
Bulkeley . . . . . . . . .74 D2
Bulkington
Warks . . . . . . . . . . .63 F7
Wilts . . . . . . . . . . . .24 D4
Bulkworthy . . . . . . . .9 C5
Bullamoor . . . . . . .102 E1
Bullbridge . . . . . . . .76 D3
Bullbrook . . . . . . . .27 C6
Bulley . . . . . . . . . . . .36 C4
Bullgill . . . . . . . . . .107 F7
Bull Hill . . . . . . . . . .14 E4
Bullington
Hants . . . . . . . . . . . .26 E2
Lincs . . . . . . . . . . . .78 B3
Bull's Green . . . . . . .41 C5
Bullwood . . . . . . . .145 F10
Bulmer
Essex . . . . . . . . . . . .56 E2
N Yorks . . . . . . . . . .96 C2
Bulmer Tye . . . . . . .56 F2
Bulphan . . . . . . . . . .42 F2
Bulverhythe . . . . . .18 E4
Bulwark . . . . . . . . .153 D9
Bulwell . . . . . . . . . .76 E5
Bulwick . . . . . . . . . .65 E6
Bumble's Green . . .41 D7
Bun Abhainn
Eadarra . . . . . . . .154 G6
Bunacaimb . . . . . .147 C9
Bunarkaig . . . . . . .136 F4
Bunbury . . . . . . . . .74 D2
Bunbury Heath . . . .74 D2
Bundalloch . . . . . .149 F13
Buness . . . . . . . . . .160 C8
Bunessan . . . . . . .146 J6
Bungay . . . . . . . . . . .69 F6
Bunker's Hill . . . . . .38 C4
Bunkers Hill
Lincs . . . . . . . . . . . .78 B2
Lincs . . . . . . . . . . . .79 D5
Bunloit . . . . . . . . . .137 B8
Bun Loyne . . . . . . .136 D5
Bunnahabhain . . .142 A5
Bunny . . . . . . . . . . . .64 B2
Buntait . . . . . . . . . .150 H6
Buntingford . . . . . .41 B6
Bunwell . . . . . . . . . .68 E4
Burbage
Derbys . . . . . . . . . . .75 B7
Leics . . . . . . . . . . . .63 E8
Wilts . . . . . . . . . . . .25 C7
Burchett's Green .39 F8
Burcombe . . . . . . . .25 F5
Burcot . . . . . . . . . . .39 E5
Burcott . . . . . . . . . .40 B1
Burdon . . . . . . . . . .111 D6
Bures . . . . . . . . . . . .56 F3
Bures Green . . . . . .56 F3
Burford
Ches E . . . . . . . . . . .74 D3
Oxon . . . . . . . . . . . .38 C2
Shrops . . . . . . . . . . .49 C7
Burg . . . . . . . . . . . .146 G6
Burgar . . . . . . . . . .159 F4
Burgate
Hants . . . . . . . . . . . .14 C2
Suff . . . . . . . . . . . . .56 B4
Burgess Hill . . . . . .17 C7
Burgh . . . . . . . . . . . .57 D6
Burgh by Sands . .108 D3
Burgh Castle . . . . . .69 D7
Burghclere . . . . . . .26 C2
Burghead . . . . . . . .151 E14
Burghfield . . . . . . . .26 C4
Burghfield
Common . . . . . . . . .26 C4
Burghfield Hill . . . .26 C4
Burgh Heath . . . . . .28 D3
Burghill . . . . . . . . . .49 E6
Burgh le Marsh . . .79 C7
Burgh Muir . . . . . .141 B6
Burgh next
Aylsham . . . . . . . . .81 E8
Burgh on Bain . . . .91 F6
Burgh
St Margaret . . . . .69 C7
Burgh St Peter . . . .69 E7
Burghwallis . . . . . .89 C6
Burham . . . . . . . . . .29 C8
Buriton . . . . . . . . . .15 B8
Burland . . . . . . . . . .74 D3
Burlawn . . . . . . . . . . .4 B4
Burleigh . . . . . . . . . .27 C6
Burlescombe . . . . . .11 C5
Burleston . . . . . . . . .13 E5
Burley
Hants . . . . . . . . . . . .14 D3
Rutland . . . . . . . . . .65 C5
W Yorks . . . . . . . . . .95 F5
Burleydam . . . . . . .74 E3
Burley Gate . . . . . . .49 E7
Burley in
Wharfedale . . . . . .94 E4
Burley Lodge . . . . .14 D3
Burley Street . . . . .14 D3
Burlingjobb . . . . . .48 D4
Burlow . . . . . . . . . . .18 D2
Burlton . . . . . . . . . . .60 B4
Burmarsh . . . . . . . .19 B7
Burmington . . . . . . .51 F7
Burn . . . . . . . . . . . . .89 B6
Burnaston . . . . . . . .76 F2
Burnbank . . . . . . . .119 D7
Burnby . . . . . . . . . . .96 E4
Burncross . . . . . . . .88 E4
Burnded . . . . . . . . . .99 E7
Burness . . . . . . . . .159 D7
Burneside . . . . . . .101 E8
Burness . . . . . . . . . .99 E7
Burnett . . . . . . . . . .23 C8
Burnfoot
Borders . . . . . . . . .115 C7
Borders . . . . . . . . .115 C8
E Ayrs . . . . . . . . . .112 D4
Perth . . . . . . . . . . .127 D8

**Burnham**
Bucks . . . . . . . . . . . .40 F2
N Lincs . . . . . . . . . .90 C4
**Burnham**
Deepdale . . . . . . . .80 C4
Burnham Green . . .41 C5
Burnham Market 80 C4
Burnham Norton . .80 C4
**Burnham-**
on-Crouch . . . . . . .43 E5
Burnham-on-Sea 22 E5
**Burnham Overy**
Staithe . . . . . . . . . .80 C4
**Burnham Overy**
Town . . . . . . . . . . . .80 C4
Burnham Thorpe 80 C4
Burnhead
Dumfries . . . . . . . .113 E8
S Ayrs . . . . . . . . . .112 D2
Burnhervie . . . . . .141 C6
Burnhope . . . . . . . .110 E4
Burnhouse . . . . . . .118 D3
Burniston . . . . . . . .103 E8
Burnlee . . . . . . . . . .88 D2
Burnley . . . . . . . . . .93 F8
Burnley Lane . . . . .93 F8
Burnmouth . . . . . .123 C5
Burnopfield . . . . . .110 D4
Burnsall . . . . . . . . . .94 C3
**Burnside**
Angus . . . . . . . . . .135 D5
E Ayrs . . . . . . . . . .113 C5
Fife . . . . . . . . . . . .128 D3
Shetland . . . . . . . .160 F4
S Lanark . . . . . . . .119 C6
W Loth . . . . . . . . . .120 B3
**Burnside of**
Duntrune . . . . . . .134 F4
Burnswark . . . . . .107 B8
Burntcommon . . . . .27 D8
Burnt Heath . . . . . .76 B2
Burnthouse . . . . . . . .3 C6
Burnt Houses . . . .101 B6
Burntisland . . . . . .128 F4
Burnton . . . . . . . . .112 D4
Burnwood . . . . . . . .62 D4
Burnt Yates . . . . . . .95 C5
Burnwynd . . . . . . .120 C4
**Burpham**
Sur . . . . . . . . . . . . . .27 D8
W Sus . . . . . . . . . . . .16 D4
**Burradon**
Northumb . . . . . . .117 D5
T&W . . . . . . . . . . .111 B5
Burrafirth . . . . . . .160 B8
**Burraland**
Shetland . . . . . . . .160 F5
Shetland . . . . . . . .160 J4
Burras . . . . . . . . . . . .3 C5
Burravoe
Shetland . . . . . . . .160 F7
Shetland . . . . . . . .160 G5
Burray Village . . .159 J5
Burrells . . . . . . . . .100 C1
Burrelton . . . . . . .134 F2
**Burridge**
Devon . . . . . . . . . . .20 F4
Hants . . . . . . . . . . . .15 C6
Burrill . . . . . . . . . . .101 F7
Burringham . . . . . . .90 D2
**Burrington**
Devon . . . . . . . . . . . .9 C8
Hereford . . . . . . . . .49 B6
N Som . . . . . . . . . . .23 D6
**Burrough Green . .55 D7**
Burrough on the
Hill . . . . . . . . . . . . .64 C4
Burrow-bridge . . . .11 B8
Burrowhill . . . . . . .27 C7
Burry . . . . . . . . . . . .33 E5
Burry Green . . . . . .33 E5
**Burry Port**
= Porth Tywyn . . .33 D5
Burscough . . . . . . .86 C2
**Burscough**
Bridge . . . . . . . . . .86 C2
Bursea . . . . . . . . . . .96 F4
Burshill . . . . . . . . . .97 E6
Bursledon . . . . . . . .15 D5
Burslem . . . . . . . . . .75 E5
Burstall . . . . . . . . . .56 E4
Burstock . . . . . . . . .12 D2
**Burston**
Norf . . . . . . . . . . . . .68 F4
Staffs . . . . . . . . . . . .75 F6
Burstow . . . . . . . . . .28 E4
Burstwick . . . . . . . .91 B6
Burtersett . . . . . . .100 F3
Burthorpe . . . . . . . .55 C8
Burthwaite . . . . . . .108 E4
Burtle . . . . . . . . . . . .23 E5
**Burton**
BCP . . . . . . . . . . . . .14 E2
Ches W . . . . . . . . . .73 B7
Ches W . . . . . . . . . .74 C2
Lincs . . . . . . . . . . . .78 B2
Northumb . . . . . . .123 F7
Pembs . . . . . . . . . . .44 E4
Som . . . . . . . . . . . . .22 E3
Wilts . . . . . . . . . . . .24 B3
Burton Agnes . . . . .97 C7
Burton Bradstock 12 F2
Burton Dassett . . .51 D8
Burton Fleming . .97 B6
**Burton Green**
W Mid . . . . . . . . . . .51 B7
Wrex . . . . . . . . . . . .73 D7
Burton Hastings .63 E8
**Burton-in-**
Kendal . . . . . . . . . .92 B5
**Burton in**
Lonsdale . . . . . . . .93 B6
Burton Joyce . . . . .77 E6
Burton Latimer . . .53 B7
Burton Lazars . . . .64 C4
Burton Leonard . .95 C6
**Burton on the**
Wolds . . . . . . . . . . .64 B2
Burton Overy . . . . .64 E3
**Burton**
Pedwardine . . . . .78 E4
Burton Pidsea . . . .97 F8
Burton Salmon . . .89 B5
Burton Stather . . .90 C2
**Burton upon**
Stather . . . . . . . . . .90 C2

**Burton**
upon Trent . . . . . .63 B6
Burtonwood . . . . . .86 E3
Burwardsley . . . . . .74 D2
Burwarton . . . . . . . .61 F6
Burwash . . . . . . . . .18 C3
**Burwash**
Common . . . . . . . . .18 C3
Burwash Weald . . .18 C3
**Burwell**
Cambs . . . . . . . . . . .55 C6
Lincs . . . . . . . . . . . .79 B6
Burwen . . . . . . . . . .82 B4
Burwick . . . . . . . . .159 K5
**Bury**
Cambs . . . . . . . . . . .66 F2
Gtr Man . . . . . . . . . .87 C6
Som . . . . . . . . . . . . .10 B4
W Sus . . . . . . . . . . . .16 C4
Bury Green . . . . . . .41 B7
Bury St Edmunds 56 C2
Burythorpe . . . . . . .96 C3
Busby . . . . . . . . . . .119 D5
Buscot . . . . . . . . . . .38 E2
Bush Bank . . . . . . . .49 D6
Bushbury . . . . . . . . .62 D3
Bushby . . . . . . . . . . .64 D3
Bush Crathie . . . .139 E8
**Bush Green** . . . . . .68 F5
Bushey . . . . . . . . . . .40 E4
Bushey Heath . . . . .40 E4
Bushley . . . . . . . . . .50 F3
Bushton . . . . . . . . . .25 B5
Buslingthorpe . . . .90 F4
Busta . . . . . . . . . . .160 G5
Butcher's Cross .18 C2
Butcombe . . . . . . . .23 C7
Butetown . . . . . . . . .22 B3
Butleigh . . . . . . . . . .23 F7
**Butleigh**
Wootton . . . . . . . .23 F7
Butler's Cross . . . .39 D8
Butler's End . . . . . .63 F6
Butlers Marston . .51 E8
Butley . . . . . . . . . . . .57 D7
**Butley High**
Corner . . . . . . . . . .57 E7
Butterburn . . . . . .109 B6
Buttercrambe . . . . .96 D3
Butterknowle . . . .101 B6
Butterleigh . . . . . . .10 D4
**Buttermere**
Cumb . . . . . . . . . . . .98 C3
Wilts . . . . . . . . . . . .25 C8
Buttershaw . . . . . . .88 B2
Butterstone . . . . . .133 E7
Butterton . . . . . . . . .75 D7
**Butterwick**
Durham . . . . . . . . .102 B1
Lincs . . . . . . . . . . . .79 E6
N Yorks . . . . . . . . . .96 B3
N Yorks . . . . . . . . . .97 B5
Butt Green . . . . . . . .74 D3
Buttington . . . . . . . .60 D2
Buttonoak . . . . . . . .50 B2
Buttsash . . . . . . . . .14 D5
Butt's Green . . . . . .14 B4
Buxhall . . . . . . . . . .56 D4
**Buxhall Fen**
Street . . . . . . . . . . .56 D4
Buxley . . . . . . . . . .122 D4
Buxted . . . . . . . . . . .17 B8
**Buxton**
Derbys . . . . . . . . . . .75 B7
Norf . . . . . . . . . . . . .81 E8
Buxworth . . . . . . . . .87 F8
Bwcle = Buckley . .73 C6
Bwlch . . . . . . . . . . . .35 B5
Bwlchgwyn . . . . . . .73 D6
Bwlch-Llan . . . . . . .46 D4
Bwlchnewydd . . . . .32 B4
Bwlchtocyn . . . . . . .70 E4
Bwlch-y-cibau . . . .59 C8
Bwlchyddar . . . . . . .59 B8
Bwlch-y-fadfa . . . . .46 E3
Bwlch-y-ffridd . . . .59 E7
Bwlchgroes . . . . . . .45 F4
Bwlch-y-sarnau . . .48 B2
Byermoor . . . . . . . .110 D4
Byers Green . . . . .110 F5
Byfield . . . . . . . . . . .52 D3
Byfleet . . . . . . . . . . .27 C8
Byford . . . . . . . . . . .49 E5
Bygrave . . . . . . . . . .54 F3
Byker . . . . . . . . . . .111 C5
Bylchau . . . . . . . . . .72 C3
Byley . . . . . . . . . . . .74 C4
Bynea . . . . . . . . . . . .33 E6
Byness . . . . . . . . . .116 D3
Bythorn . . . . . . . . . .53 B8
Byton . . . . . . . . . . . .49 C5
Byworth . . . . . . . . . .16 B3

**C**

Cabharstadh . . . .155 E8
Cablea . . . . . . . . . .133 F6
Cabourne . . . . . . . .90 D5
**Cabrach**
Argyll . . . . . . . . . . .144 G3
Moray . . . . . . . . . .140 B2
Cabrich . . . . . . . . .151 G8
Cabus . . . . . . . . . . . .92 E4
Cackle Street . . . . .17 B8
Cadbury . . . . . . . . . .10 D4
Cadbury Barton . . .9 C8
Cadder . . . . . . . . . .119 B6
Caddington . . . . . . .40 C3
Caddonfoot . . . . . .121 F7
**Cadeby**
Leics . . . . . . . . . . . .63 D8
S Yorks . . . . . . . . . .89 D6
Cadeleigh . . . . . . . .10 D4
Cade Street . . . . . .18 C3
Cadgwith . . . . . . . . . .3 E6
Cadham . . . . . . . . .128 D4
Cadishead . . . . . . . .86 E5
Cadle . . . . . . . . . . . .33 E7
**Cadley**
Lancs . . . . . . . . . . . .92 F5
Wilts . . . . . . . . . . . .25 C7
Wilts . . . . . . . . . . . .25 D7
Cadmore End . . . . .39 E7
Cadnam . . . . . . . . . .14 C3
Cadney . . . . . . . . . . .90 D4
Cadole . . . . . . . . . . .73 C6
Cadoxton . . . . . . . . .22 C3

**Cadoxton-**
Juxta-Neath . . . .34 E1
Cadshaw . . . . . . . . .86 C5
Cadzow . . . . . . . . .119 D7
**Caeathro** . . . . . . . .82 E4
Caehopkin . . . . . . . .34 C2
Caenby . . . . . . . . . . .90 F4
Caenby Corner . . . .90 F3
**Caerau**
Bridgend . . . . . . . . .34 E2
Cardiff . . . . . . . . . . .22 B3
Caér-bryn . . . . . . . .33 C6
Caerdeon . . . . . . . . .58 C3
**Caerdydd**
= Cardiff . . . . . . . . .22 B3
Caerfarchell . . . . . .44 C2
Caerffili
= Caerphilly . . . . . .35 F5
Caerfyrddin
= Carmarthen . . . .33 B5
Caergeiliog . . . . . . .82 D3
Caergwrle . . . . . . . .73 D7
Caergybi
= Holyhead . . . . . . .82 C2
Caerleon
= Caerllion . . . . . . .35 E7
Caer Llan . . . . . . . . .36 D1
Caerllion
= Caerleon . . . . . . .35 E7
Caerphilly
= Caerffili . . . . . . . .35 F5
Caersws . . . . . . . . . .59 E7
Caerwedros . . . . . . .46 D2
Caerwent . . . . . . . . .36 E1
Caerwych . . . . . . . . .71 D7
Caerwys . . . . . . . . . .72 B5
Caethle . . . . . . . . . . .58 E3
Caim . . . . . . . . . . . . .83 C6
Caio . . . . . . . . . . . . .47 F5
Cairinis . . . . . . . . .148 B3
Cairisiadar . . . . . .154 D5
Cairminis . . . . . . .154 J5
Cairnbaan . . . . . . .145 D7
Cairnbanno
House . . . . . . . . . . .153 D8
Cairnborrow . . . . .152 D4
Cairnbrogie . . . . .141 B7
**Cairnbulg**
Castle . . . . . . . . . .153 B10
**Cairncross**
Angus . . . . . . . . . .134 B4
Borders . . . . . . . . .122 C4
Cairndow . . . . . . . .125 D7
Cairness . . . . . . . .153 B10
Cairneyhill . . . . . .128 F2
**Cairnfield**
House . . . . . . . . . . .152 B4
Cairngaan . . . . . . .104 F5
Cairngarroch . . . .104 E4
Cairnhill . . . . . . . .153 E6
**Cairnie**
Aberds . . . . . . . . . .141 D7
Aberds . . . . . . . . . .152 D4
Cairnorrie . . . . . . .153 D8
Cairnpark . . . . . . .141 C7
Cairnryan . . . . . . .104 C4
Cairnton . . . . . . . .159 H4
Caister-on-Sea . . .69 C8
**Caistor**
Lincs . . . . . . . . . . . .90 D5
**Caistor**
St Edmund . . . . . .68 D5
Caistron . . . . . . . .117 D5
Caitha Bowland 121 E7
Calais Street . . . . .56 F3
Calanais . . . . . . . .154 D7
Calbost . . . . . . . . .155 F9
Calbourne . . . . . . . .14 F5
Calceby . . . . . . . . . .79 B6
Calcot Row . . . . . . .26 B4
Calcott . . . . . . . . . . .31 C5
Caldback . . . . . . . .160 C8
Caldbeck . . . . . . . .108 F3
Caldbergh . . . . . . .101 F5
**Caldecote**
Cambs . . . . . . . . . . .54 D4
Cambs . . . . . . . . . . .65 F8
Herts . . . . . . . . . . . .54 F3
W Nhants . . . . . . . .52 D4
**Caldecott**
N Nhants . . . . . . . .53 C7
Oxon . . . . . . . . . . . .38 E4
Rutland . . . . . . . . . .65 E5
Calderbank . . . . . .119 C7
Calderbrook . . . . . .87 C7
Caldercruix . . . . . .119 C8
Calder Hall . . . . . . .98 D2
Calder Mains . . . .158 E2
Caldermill . . . . . . .119 E6
Calder Vale . . . . . . .92 E5
Calderwood . . . . . .119 D6
Caldhame . . . . . . .134 E4
Caldicot . . . . . . . . .36 F1
**Caldwell**
Derbys . . . . . . . . . . .63 C6
N Yorks . . . . . . . . .101 C6
Caldy . . . . . . . . . . . .85 F3
Caledrhydiau . . . . .46 D3
Calfsound . . . . . . .159 E6
Calgary . . . . . . . . .146 F6
Califer . . . . . . . . . .151 F13
**California**
Falk . . . . . . . . . . . .120 B2
Norf . . . . . . . . . . . . .69 C8
Calke . . . . . . . . . . . .63 B7
Callakille . . . . . . .149 C11
Callaly . . . . . . . . . .117 D6
Callander . . . . . . .126 D5
Callaughton . . . . . .61 E6
Callestick . . . . . . . . .4 D2
Calligarry . . . . . . .149 H11
Callington . . . . . . . . .5 C8
Callow . . . . . . . . . . .49 F6
Callow End . . . . . . .50 E3
Callow Hill
Wilts . . . . . . . . . . . .37 F7
Worcs . . . . . . . . . . .50 B2
**Callows Grave** . . . .49 C7
Calmore . . . . . . . . . .14 C4
Calmsden . . . . . . . .37 D7
Calne . . . . . . . . . . . .24 B5
Calow . . . . . . . . . . . .76 B4
Calshot . . . . . . . . . .15 D5
**Calstock** . . . . . . . . . .6 C2
Calstone
Wellington . . . . . . .24 C5
Calthorpe . . . . . . . .81 D7

Calthwaite . . . . . .108 E4
**Calton**
N Yorks . . . . . . . . . .94 D2
Staffs . . . . . . . . . . . .75 D8
Calveley . . . . . . . . . .74 D2
Calver . . . . . . . . . . . .76 B2
Calverhall . . . . . . . .74 F3
Calver Hill . . . . . . . .49 E5
Calverleigh . . . . . . .10 C4
Calverley . . . . . . . . .94 F5
Calvert . . . . . . . . . . .39 B6
Calverton
M Keynes . . . . . . . .53 F5
Notts . . . . . . . . . . . .77 E6
Calvine . . . . . . . . . .133 C5
Calvo . . . . . . . . . . .107 D8
Cam . . . . . . . . . . . . .36 E4
Camas-luinie . . . .136 B2
Camasnacroise . .130 D2
Camastianavaig
. . . . . . . . . . . . . . . .149 E10
Camasunary . . . . .149 G10
Camault Muir . . . .151 G8
Camb . . . . . . . . . . .160 D7
Camber . . . . . . . . . .19 D6
Camberley . . . . . . . .27 C6
Camberwell . . . . . .28 B4
Camblesforth . . . . .89 B7
Cambo . . . . . . . . . .117 F6
Cambois . . . . . . . .117 F9
Camborne . . . . . . . . .3 C5
Cambourne . . . . . . .54 D4
**Cambridge**
Cambs . . . . . . . . . . .55 D5
Glos . . . . . . . . . . . . .36 D4
Cambridge Town .43 F5
Cambus . . . . . . . . .127 E7
Cambusavie
Farm . . . . . . . . . . .151 B10
Cambusbarron . . .127 E6
Cambuskenneth 127 E7
Cambuslang . . . . .119 C6
Cambusmore
Lodge . . . . . . . . . .151 B10
Camden . . . . . . . . . .41 F5
Camelford . . . . . . . . .8 F3
Camelsdale . . . . . . .27 F6
Camerory . . . . . . .151 H13
Camer's Green . . . .50 F2
Camerton
Bath . . . . . . . . . . . .23 D8
Cumb . . . . . . . . . .107 F7
E Yorks . . . . . . . . . .91 B6
Camghouran . . . .132 D2
Cammachmore . . .141 E8
Cammeringham . .90 F3
Camore . . . . . . . . .151 B10
Campbeltown . . . .143 F8
Camperdown . . . .111 B5
Camp Hill . . . . . . . .63 E7
Campmuir . . . . . . .134 F2
Campsall . . . . . . . . .89 C6
Campsey Ash . . . . .57 D7
**Campton** . . . . . . . . .54 F2
Camptown . . . . . .116 C2
Camrose . . . . . . . . .44 C4
Camserney . . . . . .133 E5
Camster . . . . . . . .158 F4
Camuschoirk . . . .130 C1
Camuscross . . . . .149 G11
**Camusnagaul**
Highld . . . . . . . . . .130 B4
Highld . . . . . . . . . .150 C3
Camusrory . . . . . .147 B11
Camusterrach . . .149 D12
Camusvrachan . .132 E3
Canada . . . . . . . . . .14 C3
Canadia . . . . . . . . .18 D4
Canal Side . . . . . . .89 C7
**Candacraig**
House . . . . . . . . . . .140 C2
Candlesby . . . . . . . .79 C7
Candy Mill . . . . . . .120 E3
Cane End . . . . . . . . .26 B4
Canewdon . . . . . . . .42 E4
Canford Bottom . .13 D8
Canford Magna . . .13 E8
Canham's Green . .56 C4
**Cann** . . . . . . . . . . . .13 B6
Cann Common . . .13 B6
Cannich . . . . . . . . .150 H6
Cannington . . . . . . .22 F4
Cannock . . . . . . . . .62 D3
Cannock Wood . . .62 D4
Canon Bridge . . . .49 E6
Canon Frome . . . . .49 E8
Canon Pyon . . . . . .49 E6
Canons Ashby . . . .52 D3
Canonstown . . . . . . .2 C4
Canterbury . . . . . . .30 D5
**Cantley**
Norf . . . . . . . . . . . . .69 D6
S Yorks . . . . . . . . . .89 D7
Cantlop . . . . . . . . . .60 D5
Canton . . . . . . . . . . .22 B3
Cantraybruich . . .151 G10
Cantraydoune . . .151 G10
Cantraywood . . . .151 G10
Canwick . . . . . . . . .78 C2
Canworthy Water . .8 E4
Caol . . . . . . . . . . . .131 B5
Caolas . . . . . . . . . .146 G3
**Caolas**
Scalpaigh . . . . . .154 H7
Caolas Stocinis 154 H6
Caol Ila . . . . . . . . .142 A5
Caol Loch . . . . . . . . . . .
Capel . . . . . . . . . . . .28 E2
Capel Bangor . . . . .58 F3
Capel Betws
Lleucu . . . . . . . . . .46 D5
Capel Carmel . . . . .70 E2
Capel Coch . . . . . . .82 C4
Capel Curig . . . . . . .83 F7
Capel Cynon . . . . . .46 E2
**Capel Dewi**
Carms . . . . . . . . . . .33 B5
Ceredig . . . . . . . . . .46 E3
Ceredig . . . . . . . . . .58 F3
Capel Garmon . . . .83 F8
Capel-gwyn . . . . . .82 D3

Capel Gwyn . . . . . .33 B5
Capel Gwynfe . . . . .33 B8
Capel Hendre . . . . .33 C6
Capel Hermon . . . .71 E8
Capel Isaac . . . . . . .33 B6
Capel Iwan . . . . . . .45 F3
Capel le Ferne . . . .31 F6
Capel Llanilltern . .34 F4
Capel Mawr . . . . . . .82 D4
Capel St Andrew . .57 E7
Capel St Mary . . . . .56 F4
Capel Seion . . . . . . .46 B5
Capel Tygwydd . . . .45 E4
Capel Uchaf . . . . . .70 C5
Capelulo . . . . . . . . .83 D7
Capel-y-graig . . . . .82 E5
Capenhurst . . . . . . .73 B7
Capernwray . . . . . . .92 B5
Capheaton . . . . . . .117 F6
Cappercleuch . . . .115 B5
Capplegill . . . . . . .114 D4
Capton . . . . . . . . . . . .7 D6
Caputh . . . . . . . . . .133 F7
Carbis Bay . . . . . . . . .2 C4
**Carbost**
Highld . . . . . . . . . .149 D9
Highld . . . . . . . . . .149 E8
Carbrook . . . . . . . . .88 F4
Carbrooke . . . . . . . .68 D2
Carburton . . . . . . . .77 B6
Carcant . . . . . . . . .121 D6
Carcary . . . . . . . . .135 D6
Carclaze . . . . . . . . . .4 D5
Car Colston . . . . . . .77 E7
Carcroft . . . . . . . . . .89 C6
Cardenden . . . . . . .128 E4
Cardeston . . . . . . . .60 C3
**Cardiff**
= Caerdydd . . . . . . .22 B3
**Cardigan**
= Aberteifi . . . . . . .45 E3
Cardington
Bedford . . . . . . . . . .53 E8
Shrops . . . . . . . . . . .60 E5
Cardinham . . . . . . . .5 C6
Cardonald . . . . . . .118 C5
Cardow . . . . . . . . .152 D1
Cardrona . . . . . . . .121 F6
Cardross . . . . . . . .118 B3
Cardurnock . . . . . .107 D8
Careby . . . . . . . . . . .65 C7
Careston Castle 135 D5
Carew . . . . . . . . . . . .32 D1
Carew Cheriton . . .32 D1
Carew Newton . . . .32 D1
Carey . . . . . . . . . . . .49 F7
Carfrae . . . . . . . . . .121 C8
Cargenbridge . . . .107 B6
Cargill . . . . . . . . . .134 F1
Cargo . . . . . . . . . . .108 D4
Cargreen . . . . . . . . . .6 C2
Carham . . . . . . . . .122 F4
Carhampton . . . . . .22 E2
Carharrack . . . . . . . .3 B6
**Carie**
Perth . . . . . . . . . . .132 D3
Perth . . . . . . . . . . .132 F3
Carines . . . . . . . . . . .4 D2
Carisbrooke . . . . . .15 F5
Cark . . . . . . . . . . . . .92 B3
Carlabhagh . . . . . .154 C7
Carland Cross . . . . .4 D3
Carlby . . . . . . . . . . .65 C7
Carlecotes . . . . . . . .88 D2
Carleton
Cumb . . . . . . . . . . . .99 B7
Cumb . . . . . . . . . . .108 D4
Lancs . . . . . . . . . . . .92 F3
N Yorks . . . . . . . . . .94 E2
Carleton Forehoe 68 C3
Carleton Rode . . . .68 E4
Carlin How . . . . . . .103 C5
**Carlingcott** . . . . . .23 D8
Carlin How . . . . . . .103 C5
Carlisle . . . . . . . . .108 D4
Carlops . . . . . . . . . .120 D4
**Carlton**
Bedford . . . . . . . . . .53 D7
Cambs . . . . . . . . . . .55 D7
Leics . . . . . . . . . . . .63 D7
N Yorks . . . . . . . . . .77 B6
N Yorks . . . . . . . . .101 C6
N Yorks . . . . . . . . .102 A4
Stockton . . . . . . . .102 B1
Suff . . . . . . . . . . . . .57 C7
S Yorks . . . . . . . . . .88 C4
W Yorks . . . . . . . . . .88 B4
Carlton Colville . . .69 E8
Carlton Curlieu . . .64 E3
**Carlton**
Husthwaite . . . . . .95 B7
**Carlton in**
Cleveland . . . . . . .102 D3
**Carlton in**
Lindrick . . . . . . . . .89 F6
**Carlton le**
Moorland . . . . . . .78 D2
Carlton Miniott . .102 F1
Carlton on Trent . .77 C7
Carlton Scroop . . .78 E2
Carluke . . . . . . . . .119 D8
**Carmarthen**
= Caerfyrddin . . . .33 B5
Carmel
Anglesey . . . . . . . . .82 C3
Carms . . . . . . . . . . .33 C6
Flint . . . . . . . . . . . .73 B5
Guern . . . . . . . . . . .16 I2
Gwyn . . . . . . . . . . . .82 F4
Carmont . . . . . . . .141 F7
Carmunnock . . . . .119 D6
Carmyle . . . . . . . . .119 C6
Carmyllie . . . . . . . .135 E5
Carnaby . . . . . . . . . .97 C7
Carnach
Highld . . . . . . . . . .136 B3
Highld . . . . . . . . . .150 B3
W Isles . . . . . . . . . .154 H7
Carnachy . . . . . . . .157 D10
Cárnais . . . . . . . . .154 D5
Carnbee . . . . . . . . .129 D7
Carnbo . . . . . . . . . .128 D2
Carnbrea . . . . . . . . . .3 B5
Carnduff . . . . . . . .119 E6
Carnduncan . . . . .142 B3

Carnforth . . . . . . . .92 B4
Carn-gorm . . . . . .136 B2
Carnhedryn . . . . . .44 C3
Carnhell Green . . . .2 C5
Carnkie
Corn . . . . . . . . . . . . .3 C5
Corn . . . . . . . . . . . . .3 C6
Carnoch
Highld . . . . . . . . . .150 H5
Highld . . . . . . . . . .150 H6
Carnock . . . . . . . . .128 F2
Carnon Downs . . . .3 B6
Carnousie . . . . . . .153 C6
Carnoustie . . . . . .135 F5
Carnwath . . . . . . .120 E2
Carnyorth . . . . . . . . .2 C2
Carperby . . . . . . . .101 F5
Carpley Green . . . .100 F4
Carr . . . . . . . . . . . . .89 E6
Carradale . . . . . . . .143 E9
Carragraich . . . . .154 H6
Carrbridge . . . . . .138 B5
Carrefour Selous .17 I3
Carreglefn . . . . . . .82 C3
Carreg-wen . . . . . . .45 E4
Carr Hill . . . . . . . . .111 C5
Carrick
Argyll . . . . . . . . . .145 E8
Fife . . . . . . . . . . . .129 B6
Carrick Castle . . .145 D10
Carrick House . . .159 E6
Carriden . . . . . . . .128 F2
Carrington
Gtr Man . . . . . . . . .86 E5
Lincs . . . . . . . . . . . .79 D6
Midloth . . . . . . . . .121 C6
Carrog
Conwy . . . . . . . . . . .71 C8
Denb . . . . . . . . . . . .72 E5
Carron
Falk . . . . . . . . . . . .127 F7
Moray . . . . . . . . . .152 D2
Carron Bridge . . .127 F6
Carronbridge . . . .113 E8
Carronshore . . . . .127 F7
Carrshield . . . . . . .109 E8
Carrutherstown . .107 B8
Carrville . . . . . . . .111 E6
Carsaig
Argyll . . . . . . . . . .144 E6
Argyll . . . . . . . . . .147 J8
Carscreugh . . . . . .105 D6
Carse Gray . . . . . .134 D4
Carsegowan . . . . .105 D8
Carse House . . . . .144 G6
Carseriggan . . . . .105 C7
Carsethorn . . . . . .107 D6
Carshalton . . . . . . .28 C3
Carsington . . . . . . .76 D2
Carskiey . . . . . . . .143 H7
Carsluith . . . . . . . .105 D8
Carsphairn . . . . . .113 E5
Carstairs . . . . . . . .120 E2
Carstairs
Junction . . . . . . . .120 E2
Carswell Marsh . .38 E3
Carter's Clay . . . . .14 B4
Carterton . . . . . . . .38 D2
Carterway
Heads . . . . . . . . . . .110 D3
Carthew . . . . . . . . . .4 D5
Carthorpe . . . . . . .101 F8
Cartington . . . . . . .117 D6
Cartland . . . . . . . .119 E8
Cartmel . . . . . . . . . .92 B3
Cartmel Fell . . . . . .99 F6
Carway . . . . . . . . . .33 D5
Cary Fitzpaine . . . .12 B3
Cas-gwent
= Chepstow . . . . . .36 E2
Cashlie . . . . . . . . .132 E1
Cashmoor . . . . . . . .13 C7
Casnewydd
= Newport . . . . . . .35 F7
Cassey Compton . .37 C7
Cassington . . . . . . .38 C4
Cassop . . . . . . . . . .111 F6
Castell . . . . . . . . . . .72 C5
Castellau . . . . . . . . .34 F4
Castell-Howell . . . .46 E3
Castell-Nedd
= Neath . . . . . . . . . .33 E8
Castell Newydd
Emlyn =
Newcastle Emlyn .46 E2
Castell-y-bwch . . . .35 E6
Casterton . . . . . . . .93 B6
Castle Acre . . . . . . .67 C8
Castle Ashby . . . . .53 D6
Castle Bolton . . . .101 E5
Castle Bromwich .62 F5
Castle Bytham . . . .65 C6
Castlebythe . . . . . .32 B1
Castle
Caereinion . . . . . .59 D8
Castle Camps . . . . .55 E7
Castle Carrock . . .108 D5
Castlecary . . . . . . .119 B7
Castle Cary . . . . . . .23 F8
Castle Combe . . . . .24 B3
Castlecraig . . . . . .151 E11
Castle
Donington . . . . . . .63 B8
Castle
Douglas . . . . . . . .106 C4
Castle Eaton . . . . . .37 E8
Castle Eden . . . . . .111 F7
Castlefairn . . . . . .113 F7
Castleford . . . . . . . .88 B5
Castle Frome . . . . .49 E8
Castle Green . . . . . .27 C7
Castle Gresley . . . .63 C6
Castle Heaton . . .122 E5
Castle
Hedingham . . . . . .55 F8
Castlehill
Borders . . . . . . . . .120 F5
Highld . . . . . . . . . .158 D3
W Dunb . . . . . . . . .118 B3
Castle Hill . . . . . . . .29 E7
Castle Huntly . . . .128 B5
Castle Kennedy . .104 D5
Castlemaddy . . . .113 E5
Castlemartin . . . . .44 F4

Castlemilk
Dumfries . . . . . . .107 B8
Glasgow . . . . . . . .119 D6
Castlemorris . . . . .44 B4
Castlemorton . . . . .50 F2
Castle O'er . . . . . .115 E5
Castle
Pulverbatch . . . . .60 D4
Castle Rising . . . . .67 B6
Castleside . . . . . . .110 E3
Castle Stuart . . . .151 G10
Castlethorpe . . . . .53 E6
Castleton
Angus . . . . . . . . . .134 E3
Argyll . . . . . . . . . .145 E1
Derbys . . . . . . . . . . .88 F2
Gtr Man . . . . . . . . . .87 C6
Newport . . . . . . . . .35 F6
N Yorks . . . . . . . . .102 D4
Castletown
Ches W . . . . . . . . . .73 D8
Highld . . . . . . . . . .151 G10
Highld . . . . . . . . . .158 D3
IoM . . . . . . . . . . . . .84 F2
T&W . . . . . . . . . . .111 D6
Castleweary . . . . .115 D7
Castley . . . . . . . . . . .95 E5
Caston . . . . . . . . . . .68 E2
Castor . . . . . . . . . . .65 E8
Catacol . . . . . . . . .143 D10
Catbrain . . . . . . . . .36 F2
Catbrook . . . . . . . . .36 D2
Catchall . . . . . . . . . . .2 D3
Catchems Corner .51 B7
Catchgate . . . . . . .110 D4
Catcleugh . . . . . . .116 D3
Catcliffe . . . . . . . . .88 F5
Catcott . . . . . . . . . .23 F5
Caterham . . . . . . . .28 D4
Catfield . . . . . . . . . .69 B6
Catfirth . . . . . . . . .160 H6
Catford . . . . . . . . . .28 B4
Catforth . . . . . . . . .92 F4
Cathays . . . . . . . . . .22 B3
Cathcart . . . . . . . .119 C5
Cathedine . . . . . . . .35 B5
Catherington . . . . .15 C7
Catherton . . . . . . . .49 B8
Catlodge . . . . . . . .138 E2
Catlowdy . . . . . . . .108 B4
Catmore . . . . . . . . .38 F4
Caton . . . . . . . . . . . .92 C5
Caton Green . . . . . .92 C5
Catrine . . . . . . . . . .113 B5
Cat's Ash . . . . . . . .35 E7
Catsfield . . . . . . . . .18 D4
Catshill . . . . . . . . . .50 B4
Cattal . . . . . . . . . . . .95 D7
Cattawade . . . . . . .56 F5
Catterall . . . . . . . . .92 E4
Catterick . . . . . . . .101 E7
Catterick Bridge 101 E7
Catterick
Garrison . . . . . . . .101 E6
Catterlen . . . . . . . .108 F4
Catterline . . . . . . .135 B8
Catterton . . . . . . . .95 E8
Catthorpe . . . . . . . .52 B3
Cattistock . . . . . . . .12 E4
Catton
Northumb . . . . . . .109 D8
N Yorks . . . . . . . . . .95 B6
Catwick . . . . . . . . . .97 E7
Catworth . . . . . . . .53 B8
Caudlespring . . . . .68 D2
Caulcott . . . . . . . . .39 B5
Cauldcots . . . . . . .135 E6
Cauldhame . . . . . .126 E5
Cauldon . . . . . . . . . .75 E7
Cauldmill . . . . . . . .115 C8
Caulkerbush . . . . .107 D6
Caulside . . . . . . . . .115 F7
Caunsall . . . . . . . . .62 F2
Caunton . . . . . . . . .77 D7
Causewayend . . . .120 E3
Causeway End . . .105 C8
Causeway Foot . . .94 F3
Causewayhead
Cumb . . . . . . . . . . .107 D8
Stirling . . . . . . . . .127 E6
Causeyend . . . . . .141 C8
**Causey Park**
Bridge . . . . . . . . . .117 E7
Cautley . . . . . . . . .100 E1
Cavendish . . . . . . . .56 E2
Cavendish Bridge 63 B8
Cavenham . . . . . . . .55 C8
Caversfield . . . . . . .39 B5
Caversham . . . . . . .26 B5
Caverswall . . . . . . .75 E6
Cavil . . . . . . . . . . . .96 F3
Cawdor . . . . . . . . .151 F11
Cawkwell . . . . . . . .79 B5
Cawood . . . . . . . . . .95 F8
Cawsand . . . . . . . . . .6 D2
Cawston . . . . . . . . .81 E7
Cawthorne . . . . . . .88 D3
Cawthorpe . . . . . . .65 B7
Cawton . . . . . . . . . .96 B2
Caxton . . . . . . . . . . .54 D4
Caynham . . . . . . . . .49 B7
**Caythorpe**
Lincs . . . . . . . . . . . .78 E2
Notts . . . . . . . . . . . .77 E6
Cayton . . . . . . . . . .103 F8
Ceannacroc
Lodge . . . . . . . . . .136 C5
Ceann a Deas Loch
Baghasdail . . . . . .148 G2
Ceann Shiphoirt 155 F7
Ceann
Tarabhaigh . . . . .154 F7
Cearsiadair . . . . . .155 E8
Cefn Berain . . . . . .72 C3
Cefn-brith . . . . . . . .72 D3
Cefn Canol . . . . . . .73 F6
Cefn-coch
Conwy . . . . . . . . . . .83 E8
Cefn Coch . . . . . . . .59 B8
Cefn-coed-y-
cymmer . . . . . . . . .34 D4
Cefn Cribwr . . . . . .34 F2
Cefn Cross . . . . . . .34 F2
Cefn-ddwysarn . . .72 F3
Cefn Einion . . . . . .60 F2

Cefneithin ... 33 C6
Cefn-gorwydd ... 47 E8
Cefn-mawr ... 73 E6
Cefn-y-bedd ... 73 D7
Cefn-y-pant ... 32 B2
Cei-bach ... 46 D3
Ceinewydd
  =New Quay ... 46 D2
Ceint ... 82 D4
Cellan ... 46 E5
Cellarhead ... 75 E6
Cemaes ... 82 B3
Cemmaes ... 58 D5
Cemmaes Road ... 58 D5
Cenarth ... 45 E4
Cenin ... 71 C5
Central ... 118 B2
Ceos ... 155 F6
Ceres ... 129 C6
Cerne Abbas ... 12 D4
Cerney Wick ... 37 E7
Cerrigceinwen ... 82 D4
Cerrigydrudion ... 72 E3
Cessford ... 116 B3
Ceunant ... 82 E5
Chaceley ... 50 F3
Chacewater ... 3 B6
Chackmore ... 52 F4
Chacombe ... 52 E2
Chadderton ... 87 D7
Chadderton Fold 87 D6
Chaddesden ... 76 F3
Chaddesley
  Corbett ... 50 B3
Chaddleworth ... 26 B2
Chadlington ... 38 B3
Chadshunt ... 51 D8
Chadwell ... 64 B4
Chadwell St Mary.29 B7
Chadwick End ... 51 B7
Chadwick Green.86 E3
Chaffcombe ... 11 C8
Chagford ... 10 F2
Chailey ... 17 C7
Chainbridge ... 66 D4
Chain Bridge ... 79 E6
Chainhurst ... 29 E8
Chalbury ... 13 D8
Chalbury
  Common ... 13 D8
Chaldon ... 28 D4
Chaldon Herring.13 F5
Chale ... 15 G5
Chale Green ... 15 G5
Chalfont
  Common ... 40 E3
Chalfont St Giles..40 E2
Chalfont St Peter.40 E3
Chalford ... 37 D5
Chalgrove ... 39 E6
Chalk ... 29 B7
Challacombe ... 21 E5
Challoch ... 105 C7
Challock ... 30 D4
Chalton
  C Beds ... 40 B3
  Hants ... 15 C8
Chalvington ... 18 E2
Chancery ... 46 B4
Chandler's Ford..14 B5
Channel Tunnel..19 B8
Channerwick ... 160 L6
Chantry
  Som ... 24 E2
  Suff ... 56 E5
Chapel ... 128 E4
Chapel Allerton
  Som ... 23 D6
  W Yorks ... 95 F6
Chapel Amble ... 4 B4
Chapel Brampton.52 F5
Chapel Chorlton..74 F5
Chapel End ... 63 E7
Chapel-en-
  le-Frith ... 87 F8
Chapelgate ... 66 B4
Chapel Green
  Warks ... 52 C2
  Warks ... 63 F6
Chapel Haddlesey 89 B6
Chapelhall ... 119 C7
Chapel Head ... 66 F3
Chapelhill
  Dumfries ... 114 E3
  Highld ... 151 D11
  N Ayrs ... 118 E3
  Perth ... 128 B4
  Perth ... 133 F7
Chapel Hill
  Aberds ... 153 E10
  Lincs ... 78 D5
  Mon ... 36 E2
  N Yorks ... 95 E6
Chapelknowe ... 108 B3
Chapel Lawn ... 48 B5
Chapel-le-Dale..93 B7
Chapel Milton ... 87 F8
Chapel of
  Garioch ... 141 B6
Chapel Row ... 26 C3
Chapel
  St Leonards ... 79 B8
Chapel Stile ... 99 D5
Chapelton
  Angus ... 135 E6
  Devon ... 9 B7
  Highld ... 138 C5
  S Lanark ... 119 E6
Chapeltown
  Blackburn ... 86 C5
  Moray ... 139 B8
  S Yorks ... 88 E4
Chapmanslade ... 24 E3
Chapmans Well ... 9 E5
Chapmore End ... 41 C6
Chappel ... 42 B4
Chard ... 11 D8
Chardstock ... 11 D8
Charfield ... 36 E4
Charford ... 50 C4
Charing ... 30 E3
Charing Cross ... 14 C2
Charing Heath ... 30 E3
Charingworth ... 51 F7

Charlbury ... 38 C3
Charlcombe ... 24 C2
Charlecote ... 51 D7
Charles ... 21 F5
Charlesfield ... 107 C8
Charleston
  Angus ... 134 E3
  Renfs ... 118 C4
Charlestown
  Aberdeen ... 141 D8
  Corn ... 4 D5
  Derbys ... 87 E8
  Dorset ... 12 G4
  Fife ... 128 F2
  Gtr Man ... 87 D6
  Highld ... 149 A13
  Highld ... 151 G9
  W Yorks ... 87 B7
Charlestown
  of Aberlour ... 152 D2
Charles Tye ... 56 D4
Charlesworth ... 87 E8
Charleton ... 7 E5
Charlton
  Hants ... 25 E8
  Herts ... 40 B4
  London ... 28 B5
  Northumb ... 116 F4
  Som ... 23 D8
  Telford ... 61 C5
  Wilts ... 13 B7
  Wilts ... 25 D6
  Wilts ... 37 F6
  W Nhants ... 52 F3
  Worcs ... 50 E5
  W Sus ... 16 C2
Charlton Abbots..37 B7
Charlton Adam ... 12 B3
Charlton-
  All-Saints ... 14 B2
Charlton Down ... 12 E4
Charlton
  Horethorne ... 12 B4
Charlton Kings ... 37 B6
Charlton
  Mackerell ... 12 B3
Charlton
  Marshall ... 13 D6
Charlton
  Musgrove ... 12 B5
Charlton on
  Otmoor ... 39 C5
Charltons ... 102 C4
Charlwood ... 28 E3
Charlynch ... 22 F4
Charminster ... 12 E4
Charmouth ... 11 E8
Charndon ... 39 B6
Charney Bassett.38 E3
Charnock
  Richard ... 86 C3
Charsfield ... 57 D6
Chart Corner ... 29 D8
Charter Alley ... 26 D3
Charterhouse ... 23 D6
Charterville
  Allotments ... 38 C3
Chartham ... 30 D5
Chartham Hatch..30 D5
Chartridge ... 40 D2
Charvil ... 27 B5
Charwelton ... 52 D3
Chasetown ... 62 D4
Chastleton ... 38 B2
Chasty ... 8 D5
Chatburn ... 93 E7
Chatcull ... 74 F4
Chatham ... 29 C8
Chathill ... 117 B7
Chattenden ... 29 B8
Chatteris ... 66 F3
Chattisham ... 56 E4
Chatto ... 116 C3
Chatton ... 117 B6
Chawleigh ... 10 C2
Chawley ... 38 D4
Chawston ... 54 D2
Chawton ... 26 F5
Cheadle
  Gtr Man ... 87 F6
  Staffs ... 75 E7
Cheadle Heath ... 87 F6
Cheadle Hulme ... 87 F6
Cheam ... 28 C3
Cheapside ... 27 D8
Chearsley ... 39 C7
Chebsey ... 62 B2
Checkendon ... 39 F6
Checkley
  Ches E ... 74 E4
  Hereford ... 49 F7
  Staffs ... 75 F7
Chedburgh ... 55 D8
Cheddar ... 23 D6
Cheddington ... 40 C2
Cheddleton ... 75 D6
Cheddon
  Fitzpaine ... 11 B7
Chedglow ... 37 E6
Chedgrave ... 69 E6
Chedington ... 12 D2
Chediston ... 57 B7
Chedworth ... 37 C7
Chedzoy ... 22 F5
Cheeklaw ... 122 D3
Cheeseman's
  Green ... 19 B7
Cheglinch ... 20 E4
Cheldon ... 10 C2
Chelford ... 74 B5
Chellaston ... 76 F3
Chell Heath ... 75 D5
Chellington ... 53 D7
Chelmarsh ... 61 F7
Chelmer Village..42 D3
Chelmondiston ... 57 F6
Chelmorton ... 75 C8
Chelmsford ... 42 D3
Chelsea ... 28 B3
Chelsfield ... 29 C5
Chelsworth ... 56 E3
Cheltenham ... 37 B6
Chelveston ... 53 C7
Chelvey ... 23 C6
Chelwood ... 23 C8
Chelwood
  Common ... 17 B8

Chelwood Gate ... 17 B8
Chelworth ... 37 E7
Chelworth Green.37 E7
Chemistry ... 74 E2
Chenies ... 40 E3
Chepstow
  =Cas-gwent ... 36 E2
Chequerfield ... 89 B5
Cherhill ... 24 B5
Cherington
  Glos ... 37 E6
  Warks ... 51 F7
Cheriton
  Devon ... 21 E6
  Hants ... 15 B6
  Kent ... 19 B8
  Swansea ... 33 E5
Cheriton Bishop..10 E2
Cheriton
  Fitzpaine ... 10 D3
Cheriton or
  Stackpole Elidor.44 F4
Cherrington ... 61 B6
Cherrybank ... 128 B3
Cherry Burton ... 97 E5
Cherry Hinton ... 55 D5
Cherry Orchard..50 D3
Cherry
  Willingham ... 78 B3
Chertsey ... 27 C8
Cheselbourne ... 13 E5
Chesham ... 40 D2
Chesham Bois ... 40 E2
Cheshunt ... 41 D6
Cheslyn Hay ... 62 D3
Chessington ... 28 C2
Chester ... 73 C8
Chesterblade ... 23 E8
Chesterfield ... 76 B3
Chester-
  le-Street ... 111 D5
Chester Moor ... 111 E5
Chesters
  Borders ... 116 B2
  Borders ... 116 C2
Chesterton
  Cambs ... 55 C5
  Cambs ... 65 E8
  Glos ... 37 D7
  Oxon ... 39 B5
  Shrops ... 61 E7
  Staffs ... 74 E5
  Warks ... 51 D8
Chesterwood ... 109 C8
Chestfield ... 30 C5
Cheston ... 6 D4
Cheswardine ... 61 B7
Cheswick ... 123 E6
Chetnole ... 12 D4
Chettiscombe ... 10 C4
Chettisham ... 66 F5
Chettle ... 13 C7
Chetton ... 61 E6
Chetwode ... 39 B6
Chetwynd Aston..61 C7
Cheveley ... 55 C7
Chevening ... 29 D5
Chevington ... 55 D8
Chevithorne ... 10 C4
Chew Magna ... 23 C7
Chew Stoke ... 23 C7
Chewton
  Keynsham ... 23 C8
Chewton Mendip 23 D7
Chicheley ... 53 E7
Chichester ... 16 D2
Chickerell ... 12 F4
Chicklade ... 24 F4
Chicksgrove ... 24 F4
Chidden ... 15 C7
Chiddingfold ... 27 F7
Chiddingly ... 18 D2
Chiddingstone ... 29 E5
Chiddingstone
  Causeway ... 29 E6
Chiddingstone
  Hoath ... 29 E5
Chideock ... 12 E2
Chidham ... 15 D8
Chidswell ... 88 B3
Chieveley ... 26 B2
Chignall
  St James ... 42 D2
Chignall Smealy..42 C2
Chigwell ... 41 E7
Chigwell Row ... 41 E7
Chilbolton ... 25 F8
Chilcomb ... 15 B6
Chilcombe ... 12 E3
Chilcompton ... 23 D8
Chilcote ... 63 C6
Childer Thornton.73 B7
Child Okeford ... 13 C6
Childrey ... 38 F3
Child's Ercall ... 61 B6
Childswickham ... 51 F5
Childwall ... 86 F2
Childwick Green. 40 C4
Chilfrome ... 12 E3
Chilgrove ... 16 C2
Chilham ... 30 D4
Chilhampton ... 25 F5
Chilla ... 9 D6
Chillaton ... 9 F6
Chillenden ... 31 D6
Chillerton ... 15 F5
Chillesford ... 57 D7
Chillingham ... 117 B6
Chillington
  Devon ... 7 E5
  Som ... 11 C8
Chilmark ... 24 F4
Chilson ... 38 C3
Chilsworthy
  Corn ... 6 B2
  Devon ... 8 D5
Chilthorne
  Domer ... 12 C3
Chiltington ... 17 C7
Chilton
  Bucks ... 39 C6
  Durham ... 101 B7
  Oxon ... 38 F4
Chilton Cantelo..12 B3
Chilton Foliat ... 25 B8
Chilton Lane ... 111 F6
Chilton Polden ... 23 F5

Chilton Street ... 55 E8
Chilton Trinity ... 22 F4
Chilvers Coton ... 63 F7
Chilwell ... 76 F5
Chilworth
  Hants ... 14 C5
  Sur ... 27 E8
Chimney ... 38 D3
Chineham ... 26 D4
Chingford ... 41 E6
Chinley ... 87 F8
Chinley Head ... 87 F8
Chinnor ... 39 D7
Chipnall ... 74 F4
Chippenhall
  Green ... 57 B6
Chippenham
  Cambs ... 55 C7
  Wilts ... 24 B4
Chipperfield ... 40 D3
Chipping
  Herts ... 54 F4
  Lancs ... 93 E6
Chipping
  Campden ... 51 F6
Chipping Hill ... 42 C4
Chipping Norton.38 B3
Chipping Ongar..42 D1
Chipping Sodbury 36 F4
Chipping Warden.52 E2
Chipstable ... 10 B5
Chipstead
  Kent ... 29 D5
  Sur ... 28 D3
Chirbury ... 60 E2
Chirk =Y Waun ... 73 F6
Chirk Bank ... 73 F6
Chirmorrie ... 105 B6
Chirnside ... 122 D4
Chirnsidebridge 122 D4
Chirton ... 25 D5
Chisbury ... 25 C7
Chiselborough ... 12 C2
Chiseldon ... 25 B6
Chiserley ... 87 B8
Chislehampton ... 39 E5
Chislehurst ... 28 B5
Chislet ... 31 C6
Chiswell Green..40 D4
Chiswick ... 28 B3
Chiswick End ... 54 E4
Chisworth ... 87 E7
Chithurst ... 16 B2
Chittering ... 55 B5
Chitterne ... 24 E4
Chittlehamholt ... 9 B8
Chittlehampton ... 9 B8
Chittoe ... 24 C4
Chivenor ... 20 F4
Chobham ... 27 C7
Choicelee ... 122 D3
Cholderton ... 25 E7
Cholesbury ... 40 D2
Chollerford ... 110 B2
Chollerton ... 110 B2
Cholmondeston ... 74 C3
Cholsey ... 39 F5
Cholstrey ... 49 D6
Chop Gate ... 102 E3
Choppington ... 117 F8
Chopwell ... 110 D4
Chorley
  Ches E ... 74 D2
  Lancs ... 86 C3
  Shrops ... 61 F6
  Staffs ... 62 C4
Chorleywood ... 40 E3
Chorlton cum
  Hardy ... 87 E6
Chorlton Lane ... 73 E8
Choulton ... 60 F3
Chowdene ... 111 D5
Chowley ... 73 D8
Chrishall ... 54 F5
Christchurch
  BCP ... 14 E2
  Cambs ... 66 E4
  Glos ... 36 C2
  Newport ... 35 F7
Christian Malford.24 B4
Christleton ... 73 C8
Christmas
  Common ... 39 E7
Christon ... 23 D5
Christon Bank ... 117 B8
Christow ... 10 F3
Chryston ... 119 B6
Chudleigh ... 7 B6
Chudleigh
  Knighton ... 7 B6
Chulmleigh ... 9 C8
Chunal ... 87 E8
Church ... 86 B5
Churcham ... 36 C4
Church Aston ... 61 C7
Churchbank ... 48 B4
Church
  Brampton ... 52 C5
Churchbridge ... 62 D3
Church
  Broughton ... 76 F2
Church
  Crookham ... 27 D6
Churchdown ... 37 C5
Church Eaton ... 62 C2
Churchend
  Essex ... 42 B2
  Essex ... 43 E6
  S Glos ... 36 E4
Church End
  Cambs ... 66 D3
  Cambs ... 66 F2
  C Beds ... 40 B2
  C Beds ... 53 F7
  C Beds ... 54 F2
  Essex ... 42 B3
  Essex ... 55 E6
  E Yorks ... 97 D6
  Hants ... 26 D4
  Herts ... 41 B7
  Lincs ... 78 B5
  London ... 28 B3
  N Yorks ... 93 D7
  Warks ... 63 E6
  Warks ... 63 E6
  Wilts ... 24 B5
Church Enstone..38 B3
Church Fenton ... 95 F8

Church Green
  Devon ... 11 E6
  Norf ... 68 E3
Church Gresley ... 63 C6
Church
  Hanborough ... 38 C4
Church Hill ... 74 C3
Church Houses ... 102 E4
Churchill
  Devon ... 11 D8
  Devon ... 20 E4
  N Som ... 23 D6
  Oxon ... 38 B2
  Worcs ... 50 B3
  Worcs ... 50 D4
Churchinford ... 11 C7
Church Knowle ... 13 F7
Church Laneham..77 B8
Church Langton..64 E4
Church Lawford..52 B2
Church Lawton ... 74 D5
Church Leigh ... 75 F7
Church Lench ... 50 D5
Church Mayfield..75 E8
Church Minshull..74 C3
Church Norton ... 16 E2
Churchover ... 64 F2
Church Preen ... 60 E5
Church
  Pulverbatch ... 60 D4
Churchstanton ... 11 C6
Church Stoke ... 60 E2
Churchstow ... 6 E5
Church Stowe ... 52 D4
Church Street ... 29 B8
Church Stretton..60 E4
Churchtown
  Derbys ... 76 C2
  IoM ... 84 C4
  Lancs ... 92 E4
  Mers ... 85 C4
Church Town
  N Lincs ... 89 D8
  Sur ... 28 D4
Church Village ... 34 F4
Church Warsop ... 77 C5
Churnsike
  Lodge ... 109 B6
Churston Ferrers..7 D7
Churt ... 27 F6
Churton ... 73 D8
Churwell ... 88 B3
Chute Standen ... 25 D8
Chwilog ... 70 D4
Chyandour ... 2 C3
Cilan Uchaf ... 70 E3
Cilcain ... 73 C5
Cilcennin ... 46 C4
Cilfor ... 71 D7
Cilfrew ... 34 D1
Cilfynydd ... 34 E4
Cilgerran ... 45 E3
Cilgwyn
  Carms ... 33 B8
  Gwyn ... 82 F4
  Pembs ... 45 F2
Ciliau Aeron ... 46 D3
Cill Donnain ... 148 F2
Cille Bhrighde ... 148 G2
Cille Pheadair ... 148 G2
Cilmery ... 48 D2
Cilsan ... 33 B6
Ciltalgarth ... 72 E2
Cilwendeg ... 45 F4
Cilybebyll ... 33 D8
Cilycwm ... 47 F6
Cimla ... 34 E1
Cinderford ... 36 C3
Cippyn ... 45 E3
Circebost ... 154 D6
Cirencester ... 37 D7
Ciribhig ... 154 C6
City
  London ... 41 F6
  Powys ... 60 F2
City Dulas ... 82 C4
Clachaig ... 145 E10
Clachan
  Argyll ... 124 D3
  Argyll ... 125 D7
  Argyll ... 130 E2
  Argyll ... 144 H6
  Highld ... 149 E10
  W Isles ... 148 D2
Clachan of
  Campsie ... 119 B6
Clachan of
  Glendaruel ... 145 E8
Clachan-Seil ... 124 D3
Clachan
  Strachur ... 125 D6
Clachbreck ... 144 F6
Clachnabrain ... 134 C3
Clachtoll ... 156 G3
Clackmannan ... 127 E8
Clacton-on-Sea..43 C7
Cladach
  Chireboist ... 148 B2
Cladach-
  knockline ... 148 B2
Cladich ... 125 C6
Claggan
  Highld ... 131 B5
  Highld ... 147 G9
Claigan ... 148 C7
Claines ... 50 D3
Clandown ... 23 D8
Clanfield
  Hants ... 15 C7
  Oxon ... 38 D2
Clanville ... 25 D8
Claonaig ... 145 H7
Claonel ... 157 J8
Clapgate
  Dorset ... 13 D8
  Herts ... 41 B7
Clapham
  Bedford ... 53 D8
  London ... 28 B3
  N Yorks ... 93 C7
  W Sus ... 16 D4
Clap Hill ... 19 B7
Clappers ... 122 D5
Clappersgate ... 99 D5
Clapton
  Som ... 12 D2

Clapton-in-
  Gordano ... 23 B6
Clapton-on-
  the-Hill ... 38 C1
Clapworthy ... 9 B8
Clarach ... 58 F3
Clara Vale ... 110 C4
Clarbeston ... 32 B1
Clarbeston Road..32 B1
Clarborough ... 89 F8
Clardon ... 158 D3
Clare ... 55 E8
Clarebrand ... 106 C4
Clarencefield ... 107 C7
Clarilaw ... 115 C8
Clark's Green ... 28 F2
Clarkston ... 119 D5
Clashandorran ... 151 G8
Clashcoig ... 151 B9
Clashindarroch ... 152 E4
Clashmore
  Highld ... 151 C10
  Highld ... 156 F3
Clashnessie ... 156 F3
Clashnoir ... 139 B8
Clate ... 160 G7
Clathy ... 127 C8
Clatt ... 140 B4
Clatter ... 59 E6
Clatterford ... 15 F5
Clatterin Bridge 135 B6
Clatworthy ... 22 F2
Claughton
  Lancs ... 92 E5
  Lancs ... 93 C5
  Mers ... 85 F4
Claverdon ... 51 C6
Claverham ... 23 C6
Clavering ... 55 F5
Claverley ... 61 E7
Claverton ... 24 C2
Clawdd-newydd ... 72 D4
Clawthorpe ... 92 B5
Clawton ... 9 E5
Claxby
  Lincs ... 79 B7
  Lincs ... 90 E5
Claxton
  Norf ... 69 D6
  N Yorks ... 96 C2
Claybokie ... 139 E6
Claybrooke
  Magna ... 63 F8
Claybrooke Parva 63 F8
Clay Common ... 69 F7
Clay Coton ... 52 B3
Clay Cross ... 76 C3
Claydon
  Oxon ... 52 D2
  Suff ... 56 D5
Claygate
  Dumfries ... 108 B3
  Kent ... 29 E8
  Sur ... 28 C2
Claygate Cross ... 29 D7
Clayhanger
  Devon ... 10 B5
  W Mid ... 62 D4
Clayhidon ... 11 C6
Clayhill
  E Sus ... 18 C5
  Hants ... 14 D4
Clay Hill ... 26 B3
Clay Lake ... 66 B2
Clayock ... 158 E3
Claypole ... 77 E8
Clayton
  Staffs ... 75 E5
  S Yorks ... 89 D5
  W Sus ... 17 C6
  W Yorks ... 94 F4
Clayton Green ... 86 B3
Clayton-le-Moors 93 F7
Clayton-le-
  Woods ... 86 B3
Clayton West ... 88 C3
Clayworth ... 89 F8
Cleadale ... 146 C7
Cleadon ... 111 C6
Clearbrook ... 6 C3
Clearwell ... 36 D2
Cleasby ... 101 C7
Cleat ... 159 K5
Cleatlam ... 101 C6
Cleator ... 98 C2
Cleator Moor ... 98 C2
Clebrig ... 157 F8
Cleckheaton ... 88 B2
Cleedownton ... 61 F5
Cleehill ... 49 B7
Clee St Margaret .61 F5
Cleethorpes ... 91 D7
Cleeton St Mary .49 B8
Cleeve ... 23 C6
Cleeve Hill ... 37 B6
Cleeve Prior ... 51 E5
Clehonger ... 49 F6
Cleish ... 128 E2
Cleland ... 119 D8
Clench Common. 25 C6
Clenchwarton ... 67 B5
Clent ... 50 B4
Cleobury
  Mortimer ... 49 B8
Cleobury North ... 61 F6
Clephanton ... 151 F11
Clerklands ... 115 B8
Clestrain ... 159 H4
Cleuch Head ... 115 C8
Clevancy ... 25 B5
Clevedon ... 23 B6
Cleveley ... 38 B3
Cleveleys ... 92 E3
Cleverton ... 37 F6
Clevis ... 21 B7
Clewer ... 23 D6
Cley next the Sea 81 C6
Cliaid ... 148 H1
Cliasmol ... 154 G5
Cliburn ... 99 B8
Click Mill ... 159 F4
Cliddesden ... 26 E4
Cliff ... 87 B7
Cliffburn ... 135 E6
Cliffe
  Medway ... 29 B8

Cliffe continued
  N Yorks ... 96 F2
Cliff End ... 19 D5
Cliffe Woods ... 29 B8
Clifford
  Hereford ... 48 E4
  W Yorks ... 95 E7
Clifford
  Chambers ... 51 D6
Clifford's Mesne.36 B4
Cliffsend ... 31 C7
Clifton
  Bristol ... 23 B7
  C Beds ... 54 F2
  Cumb ... 99 B7
  Derbys ... 75 E8
  Lancs ... 92 F4
  Northum ... 117 F8
  Nottingham ... 77 F5
  N Yorks ... 94 E4
  Oxon ... 52 F2
  Stirling ... 131 F7
  S Yorks ... 89 E6
  Worcs ... 50 E3
  York ... 95 D8
Clifton Campville 63 C6
Cliftoncote ... 116 B4
Clifton Green ... 87 D5
Clifton Hampden.39 E5
Clifton Reynes ... 53 D7
Clifton upon
  Dunsmore ... 52 B3
Clifton upon
  Teme ... 50 C2
Cliftonville ... 31 B7
Climaen gwyn ... 33 D8
Climping ... 16 D4
Climpy ... 120 D2
Clink ... 24 E2
Clint ... 95 D5
Clint Green ... 68 C3
Clintmains ... 122 F2
Cliobh ... 154 D5
Clippesby ... 69 C7
Clipsham ... 65 C6
Clipston ... 64 F4
Clipstone ... 77 C5
Clitheroe ... 93 E7
Cliuthar ... 154 H6
Clive ... 60 B5
Clivocast ... 160 C8
Clixby ... 90 D5
Clocaenog ... 72 D4
Clochan ... 152 B4
Clock Face ... 86 E3
Clockmill ... 122 D3
Cloddiau ... 60 D2
Clodock ... 35 B7
Clola ... 153 D10
Clophill ... 53 F8
Clopton
  N Nhants ... 65 F7
  Suff ... 57 D6
Clopton Corner ... 57 D6
Clopton Green ... 55 D8
Closeburn ... 113 E8
Close Clark ... 84 E2
Closworth ... 12 C3
Clothall ... 54 F3
Clotton ... 74 C2
Clough Foot ... 87 B7
Cloughton ... 103 E8
Cloughton
  Newlands ... 103 E8
Clousta ... 160 H5
Clouston ... 159 G3
Clova
  Aberds ... 140 B3
  Angus ... 134 B3
Clovelly ... 8 B5
Clove Lodge ... 100 C4
Clovenfords ... 121 F7
Clovenstone ... 141 C6
Clovullin ... 130 C4
Clow Bridge ... 87 B6
Clowne ... 76 B4
Clows Top ... 50 B2
Cloy ... 73 E7
Cluanie Inn ... 136 C3
Cluanie Lodge ... 136 C3
Clun ... 60 F3
Clunbury ... 60 F3
Clunderwen ... 32 C2
Clune ... 138 B3
Clunes ... 136 F5
Clungunford ... 49 B5
Clunie
  Aberds ... 153 C6
  Perth ... 133 E8
Clunton ... 60 F3
Cluny ... 128 E4
Cluny Castle ... 138 E2
Clutton
  Bath ... 23 D8
  Ches W ... 73 D8
Clwt-grugoer ... 72 C3
Clwt-y-bont ... 83 E5
Clydach
  Mon ... 35 C6
  Swansea ... 33 D7
Clydach Vale ... 34 E3
Clydebank ... 118 B4
Clydey ... 45 F4
Clyffe Pypard ... 25 B5
Clynder ... 145 E11
Clyne ... 34 D2
Clynelish ... 157 J11
Clynnog-fawr ... 82 F4
Clyro ... 48 E4
Clyst Honiton ... 10 E4
Clyst Hydon ... 10 D5
Clyst St George...10 F4
Clyst
  St Lawrence ... 10 D5
Clyst St Mary ... 10 E4
Cnoc Amhlaigh 155 D10
Cnwch-coch ... 47 B5
Coachford ... 152 D4
Coad's Green ... 5 B7
Coal Aston ... 76 B3
Coalbrookdale ... 61 D6
Coalbrookvale ... 35 D5
Coalburn ... 119 F8
Coalburns ... 110 C4
Coalcleugh ... 109 E8
Coaley ... 36 D4
Coalfair Green ... 57 C8
Coalhall ... 112 C4
Coalhill ... 42 E3

Coalpit Heath ... 36 F3
Coalport ... 61 D6
Coalsnaughton ... 127 E8
Coaltown of
  Balgonie ... 128 E4
Coaltown of
  Wemyss ... 128 E5
Coalville ... 63 C8
Coalway ... 36 C2
Coat ... 12 B2
Coatbridge ... 119 C7
Coatdyke ... 119 C7
Coate
  Swindon ... 38 F1
  Wilts ... 24 C5
Coates
  Cambs ... 66 E3
  Glos ... 37 D6
  Lancs ... 93 E8
  Notts ... 90 F2
  W Sus ... 16 C3
Coatham ... 102 B3
Coatham
  Mundeville ... 101 B7
Coatsgate ... 114 D3
Cobbaton ... 9 B8
Cobbler's Green..69 E5
Coberley ... 37 C6
Cobham
  Kent ... 29 C7
  Sur ... 28 C2
Cobholm Island...69 D8
Cobleland ... 126 E4
Cobnash ... 49 C6
Coburty ... 153 B9
Cockayne ... 102 E4
Cockayne Hatley .54 E3
Cock Bank ... 73 E7
Cock Bridge ... 139 D8
Cockburnspath ... 122 B3
Cock Clarks ... 42 D4
Cockenzie and
  Port Seton ... 121 B7
Cockerham ... 92 D4
Cockermouth ... 107 F8
Cockernhoe
  Green ... 40 B4
Cockfield
  Durham ... 101 B6
  Suff ... 56 D3
Cockfosters ... 41 E5
Cocking ... 16 C2
Cockington ... 7 C6
Cocklake ... 23 E6
Cockley Beck ... 98 D4
Cockley Cley ... 67 D7
Cockshutt ... 60 B4
Cockthorpe ... 81 C5
Cockwood ... 10 F4
Cockyard ... 49 F6
Codda ... 5 B6
Coddenham ... 56 D5
Coddington
  Ches W ... 73 D8
  Hereford ... 50 E2
  Notts ... 77 D8
Codford St Mary .24 F4
Codford St Peter .24 F4
Codicote ... 41 C5
Codmore Hill ... 16 B4
Codnor ... 76 E4
Codrington ... 24 B2
Codsall ... 62 D2
Codsall Wood ... 62 D2
Coed Duon
  =Blackwood ... 35 E5
Coedely ... 34 F4
Coedkernew ... 35 F6
Coed Mawr ... 83 D5
Coed Morgan ... 35 C7
Coedpoeth ... 73 D6
Coed-Talon ... 73 D6
Coedway ... 60 C3
Coed-y-bryn ... 46 E2
Coed-y-paen ... 35 E7
Coed-yr-ynys ... 35 B5
Coed
  Ystumgwern ... 71 E6
Coelbren ... 34 C2
Coffinswell ... 7 C6
Cofton Hackett ... 50 B5
Cogan ... 22 B3
Cogenhoe ... 53 C6
Cogges ... 38 D3
Coggeshall ... 42 B4
Coggeshall
  Hamlet ... 42 B4
Coggins Mill ... 18 C2
Coignafearn
  Lodge ... 138 C2
Coig
  Peighinnean 155 A10
Coig Peighinnean
  Bhuirgh ... 155 B9
Coilacriech ... 140 E2
Coilantogle ... 126 D4
Coilleag ... 148 G2
Coillore ... 149 E8
Coity ... 34 F3
Col ... 155 C9
Colaboll ... 157 H8
Colan ... 4 C3
Colaton Raleigh...11 F5
Colbost ... 148 D7
Colburn ... 101 E6
Colby
  Cumb ... 100 B1
  IoM ... 84 E2
  Norf ... 81 D8
Colchester ... 43 B6
Colcot ... 22 C3
Cold Ash ... 26 C3
Cold Ashby ... 52 B4
Cold Ashton ... 24 B2
Cold Aston ... 37 C8
Coldbackie ... 157 D9
Coldbeck ... 100 D2
Cold Blow ... 32 C2
Cold Brayfield ... 53 D7
Coldean ... 17 D7
Coldeast ... 7 B6
Colden ... 87 B7
Colden
  Common ... 15 B5
Coldfair Green ... 57 C8
Coldham ... 66 D4

Coldharbour
  Glos ... 36 D2
  Kent ... 29 D6
  Sur ... 28 E2
Cold Harbour ... 78 F2
Cold Hatton ... 61 B6
Cold Hesledon ... 111 E7
Cold Higham ... 52 D4
Cold Kirby ... 102 F3
Cold Newton ... 64 D4
Cold Northcott ... 8 F4
Cold Norton ... 42 D4
Cold Overton ... 64 C5
Coldrain ... 128 D2
Coldred ... 31 E6
Coldridge ... 9 D8
Coldstream
  Angus ... 134 F3
  Borders ... 122 F4
Coldwaltham ... 16 C4
Coldwells ... 153 D11
Coldwells Croft. 140 B4
Coldyeld ... 60 E3
Cole ... 23 F8
Colebatch ... 60 F3
Colebrook ... 10 D5
Colebrooke ... 10 D2
Coleby
  Lincs ... 78 C2
  Lincs ... 90 B2
Coleford
  Devon ... 10 D2
  Glos ... 36 C2
  Som ... 23 E8
Cole Green ... 41 C5
Cole Henley ... 26 D2
Colehill ... 13 D8
Coleman's Hatch .29 F5
Colemere ... 73 F8
Colemore ... 26 F5
Coleorton ... 63 C8
Colerne ... 24 B3
Colesbourne ... 37 C6
Colesden ... 54 D2
Coles Green ... 56 E4
Cole's Green ... 57 C6
Coleshill
  Bucks ... 40 E2
  Oxon ... 38 E2
  Warks ... 63 F6
Colestocks ... 11 D5
Colgate ... 28 F3
Colgrain ... 126 F2
Colinsburgh ... 129 D6
Colinton ... 120 C5
Colintraive ... 145 F9
Colkirk ... 80 E5
Collace ... 134 F2
Collafirth ... 160 G6
Collaton St Mary .7 D6
College Milton ... 119 D6
Collessie ... 128 C4
Collier Row ... 41 E8
Collier's End ... 41 B6
Collier's Green ... 18 B4
Collier Street ... 29 E8
Colliery Row ... 111 E6
Collieston ... 141 B9
Collin ... 107 B7
Collingbourne
  Ducis ... 25 D7
Collingbourne
  Kingston ... 25 D7
Collingham
  Notts ... 77 C8
  W Yorks ... 95 E6
Collington ... 49 C8
Collingtree ... 53 D5
Collins Green ... 86 E3
Colliston ... 135 E6
Collycroft ... 63 F7
Collynie ... 153 E8
Collyweston ... 65 D6
Colmonell ... 104 A5
Colmworth ... 54 D2
Colnabaichin ... 139 D8
Colnbrook ... 27 B8
Colne
  Cambs ... 54 B4
  Lancs ... 93 E8
Colne Edge ... 93 E8
Colne Engaine ... 56 F2
Colney ... 68 D4
Colney Heath ... 41 D5
Colney Street ... 40 D4
Coln Rogers ... 37 D7
Coln St Aldwyn's .37 D8
Coln St Dennis ... 37 C7
Colpy ... 153 E6
Colquhar ... 121 E6
Colsterdale ... 101 F6
Colsterworth ... 65 B6
Colston Bassett..77 F6
Coltfield ... 151 E13
Colthouse ... 99 E5
Coltishall ... 69 C5
Coltness ... 119 D8
Colton
  Cumb ... 99 F5
  Norf ... 68 D4
  N Yorks ... 95 E8
  Staffs ... 62 B4
  W Yorks ... 95 F6
Colva ... 48 D4
Colvend ... 107 D5
Colvister ... 160 D7
Colwall Green ... 50 E2
Colwall Stone ... 50 E2
Colwell ... 110 B2
Colwich ... 62 B4
Colwick ... 77 E6
Colwinston ... 21 B8
Colworth ... 16 D3
Colwyn Bay
  =Bae Colwyn ... 83 D8
Colyford ... 11 E7
Colyton ... 11 E7
Combe
  Hereford ... 48 C5
  Oxon ... 38 C4
  W Berks ... 25 C8
Combe Common..25 B5
Combe Down ... 24 C2
Combe Florey ... 22 F3
Combe Hay ... 24 D2
Combeinteignhead 7 B7

Combe Martin....20 E4
Combe Moor....49 C5
Combe Raleigh..11 D6
Comberbach....74 B3
Comberton
 Cambs....54 D4
 Hereford....49 C6
Combe
St Nicholas..11 C8
Combpyne....11 E7
Combridge....75 F7
Combrook....51 E8
Combs
 Derbys....75 B8
 Suff....56 D4
Combs Ford....56 D4
Combwich....22 E4
Comers....141 D7
Comins Coch....58 F3
Commercial End..55 C6
Commins Capel
 Betws....46 D3
Commins Coch..58 D5
Commondale....102 C4
Common Edge..92 F3
Commonmoor....5 C7
Commonside....74 B2
Common Side..76 B3
Compstall....87 E7
Compton
 Devon....7 C6
 Hants....15 B5
 Sur....27 E6
 Sur....27 E7
 W Berks....26 B3
 Wilts....25 D6
 W Sus....15 C8
Compton Abbas..13 C6
Compton Abdale..37 C7
Compton Bassett..24 C5
Compton
Beauchamp....38 F2
Compton Bishop..23 D5
Compton
Chamberlayne..13 B8
Compton Dando..23 C8
Compton Dundon..23 F7
Compton Martin..23 D7
Compton
Pauncefoot....12 B4
Compton Valence 12 E3
Comrie
 Fife....128 F2
 Perth....127 B6
Conaglen House 130 C4
Concraigie....133 E8
Conder Green..92 D4
Conderton....50 F4
Condicote....38 B1
Condorrat....119 B7
Condover....60 D4
Coneyhurst....16 B5
Coneythorpe..96 B3
Coneythorpe....95 D6
Coney Weston..56 B3
Conford....27 F6
Congash....139 B6
Congdon's Shop..5 B7
Congerstone....63 D7
Congham....80 E3
Congleton....75 C5
Congl-y-wal....71 C8
Congresbury....23 C6
Congreve....62 C3
Conicavel....151 F12
Coningsby....78 D5
Conington
 Cambs....54 C4
 Cambs....65 F8
Conisbrough....89 E6
Conisby....142 B3
Conisholme....91 E8
Coniston
 Cumb....99 E5
 E Yorks....97 F7
Coniston Cold..94 D2
Conistone....94 C2
Connah's Quay..73 C6
Connel....124 B5
Connel Park....113 C6
Connor Downs....2 C4
Conon Bridge..151 F8
Conon House..151 F8
Cononley....94 E2
Conordan....149 E10
Consall....75 E6
Consett....110 D4
Constable
Burton....101 E6
Constantine....3 D6
Constantine Bay..4 B3
Contin....150 F7
Contlaw....141 D7
Conwy....83 D7
Conyer....30 C3
Conyers Green..56 C2
Cooden....18 E4
Cooil....84 E3
Cookbury....9 D6
Cookham....40 F1
Cookham Dean..40 F1
Cookham Rise..40 F1
Cookhill....51 D5
Cookley
 Suff....57 B7
 Worcs....62 F2
Cookley Green..39 E6
Cookney....141 E7
Cookridge....95 E5
Cooksbridge....17 C8
Cooksmill Green 42 D2
Coolham....16 B5
Cooling....29 B8
Coombe
 Corn....4 D4
 Corn....8 C4
 Hants....15 B7
 Wilts....25 D6
Coombe Bissett..14 B2
Coombe Hill..37 B5
Coombe Keynes..13 F6
Coombes....17 D5
Coopersale
Common....41 D7
Cootham....16 C4
Copdock....56 E5
Copford Green..43 B5

Copgrove....95 C6
Copister....160 F6
Cople....54 E2
Copley....101 B5
Coplow Dale....75 B8
Copmanthorpe..95 E8
Coppathorne....8 D4
Coppenhall....62 C3
Coppenhall Moss 74 D4
Copperhouse....2 C4
Coppingford....65 F8
Copplestone....10 D2
Coppull....86 C3
Coppull Moor..86 C3
Copsale....17 B5
Copster Green..93 F6
Copston Magna..63 F8
Copt Heath....51 B6
Copt Hewick....95 B6
Copthorne
 Shrops....60 C4
 Sur....28 F4
Copt Oak....63 C8
Copy's Green..80 D5
Copythorne....14 C4
Corbets Tey....42 F1
Corbridge....110 C2
Corby....65 F5
Corby Glen....65 B6
Cordon....143 E11
Coreley....49 B8
Cores End....40 F2
Corfe....11 C7
Corfe Castle....13 F7
Corfe Mullen..13 E7
Corfton....60 F4
Corgarff....139 D8
Corhampton....15 B7
Corlae....113 E6
Corley....63 F7
Corley Ash....63 F6
Corley Moor....63 F6
Cornaa....84 D4
Cornabus....142 D4
Cornel....83 E7
Corner Row....92 F4
Corney....98 E3
Cornforth....111 F6
Cornhill....152 C5
Cornhill-
on-Tweed....122 F4
Cornholme....87 B7
Cornish Hall End..55 F6
Cornquoy....159 J6
Cornsay....110 E4
Cornsay Colliery 110 E4
Corntown
 Highld....151 F8
 V Glam....21 B8
Cornwell....38 B2
Cornwood....6 D4
Cornworthy....7 D6
Corpach....130 B4
Corpusty....81 D7
Corran
 Highld....130 C4
 Highld....149 H13
Corranbuie....145 G7
Corrany....84 D4
Corrie....143 D11
Corrie Common..114 F5
Corriecravie....143 F10
Corriemoillie....150 E6
Corriemulzie
Lodge....150 B6
Corrievarkie
Lodge....132 B2
Corrievorrie....138 B3
Corrimony....150 H6
Corringham
 Lincs....90 E2
 Thurrock....42 F3
Corris....58 D4
Corris Uchaf....58 D4
Corrour Shooting
Lodge....131 C9
Corrow....125 E7
Corry....149 F11
Corrykinloch....156 G6
Corrymuckloch..133 F5
Corrynachenchy 147 G9
Corry of
Ardnagrask..151 B8
Corsback....158 C4
Corscombe....12 D3
Corse
 Aberds....152 D6
 Glos....36 B4
Corse Lawn....50 F3
Corse of Kinnoir 152 D5
Corsewall....104 C4
Corsham....24 B3
Corsindae....141 D5
Corsley....24 E3
Corsley Heath..24 E3
Corsock....106 B4
Corston
 Bath....23 C8
 Wilts....37 F6
Corstorphine..120 B4
Cors-y-Gedol..71 E6
Cortachy....134 D3
Corton
 Suff....69 E8
 Wilts....24 E4
Corton Denham..12 B4
Coruanan Lodge 130 C4
Corunna....148 B3
Corwen....72 E4
Coryton
 Devon....9 F6
 Thurrock....42 F3
Cosby....64 E2
Coseley....62 E3
Cosgrove....53 E5
Cosham....15 D7
Cosheston....32 D1
Cossall....76 E4
Cossington
 Leics....64 C3
 Som....23 E5
Costa....159 F4
Costessey....68 C4
Costock....64 B2
Coston....64 C5
Cote....38 D3
Cotebrook....74 C2
Cotehill....108 D4

Cotes
 Leics....99 F6
 Leics....64 B2
 Staffs....74 F5
Cotesbach....64 F2
Cotgrave....77 F6
Cothall....141 C7
Cotham....77 E7
Cothelstone....22 F3
Cotherstone....101 C5
Cothill....38 E4
Cotleigh....11 D7
Cotmanhay....76 E4
Cotmaton....11 F6
Coton
 Cambs....54 D5
 Staffs....62 B2
 Staffs....74 F5
 W Nhants....52 B4
Coton Clanford..62 B2
Coton Hill
 Shrops....60 C4
 Staffs....75 F6
Coton in the
Elms....63 C6
Cott....7 C5
Cottam
 E Yorks....97 C5
 Lancs....92 F5
 Notts....77 B8
Cottartown....151 H13
Cottenham....54 C5
Cotterdale....100 E3
Cottered....41 B6
Cotteridge....50 B5
Cotterstock....65 E7
Cottesbrooke..52 B5
Cottesmore....65 C6
Cotteylands....10 C4
Cottingham
 E Yorks....97 F6
 N Nhants....64 E5
Cottingley....94 F4
Cottisford....52 F3
Cotton
 Staffs....75 E7
 Suff....56 C4
Cotton End....53 E8
Cottown
 Aberds....140 B4
 Aberds....141 C6
 Aberds....153 D8
Cotwalton....75 F6
Couch's Mill....5 D6
Coughton
 Hereford....36 B2
 Warks....51 C5
Coulaghailtro..144 G6
Coulags....150 G2
Coulby
 Newham....102 C3
Coulderton....98 D1
Coulin....150 F3
Coull
 Aberds....140 D4
 Argyll....142 B3
Coulport....145 E11
Coulsdon....28 D3
Coulston....24 D4
Coulter....120 F3
Coulton....96 B2
Cound....61 D5
Coundon
 Durham....101 B7
 W Mid....63 F7
Coundon
Grange....101 B7
Countersett....100 F4
Countess....25 E6
Countess Wear..10 F4
Countesthorpe..64 E2
Countisbury....21 E6
County Oak....28 F3
Coupar Angus..134 E2
Coup Green....86 B3
Coupland....122 F5
Cour....143 D9
Courance....114 E3
Court-at-Street..19 B7
Courteenhall....53 D5
Court Henry....33 B6
Courtsend....43 E6
Courtway....22 F4
Cousland....121 C6
Cousley Wood..18 B3
Cove
 Argyll....145 E11
 Borders....122 B3
 Devon....10 C4
 Hants....27 D6
 Highld....155 H13
Cove Bay....141 D8
Cove Bottom....57 B8
Covehithe....69 F8
Coven....62 D3
Coveney....66 F4
Covenham
St Bartholomew.91 E7
Covenham
St Mary....91 E7
Coventry....51 B8
Coverack....3 E6
Coverham....101 F6
Covesea....152 A1
Covington
 Cambs....53 B8
 S Lanark....120 F2
Cowan Bridge..93 B6
Cow Ark....93 E6
Cowbeech....18 D3
Cowbit....66 C2
Cowbridge
 Lincs....79 E6
 Som....21 E8
Cowbridge
=Y Bont-Faen..21 B8
Cowdale....75 B7
Cowden....29 E5
Cowdenbeath..128 E3
Cowdenburn....120 D5
Cowers Lane....76 E3
Cowes....15 E5
Cowesby....102 F2
Cowfold....17 B6
Cowgill....100 F2
Cowie
 Aberds....141 F7
 Stirling....127 F7

Cowley
 Devon....10 E4
 Glos....37 C6
 London....40 F3
 Oxon....39 D5
Cowleymoor....10 C4
Cowling
 Lancs....86 C3
 N Yorks....94 E2
 N Yorks....101 F7
Cowlinge....55 D8
Cowpe....87 B6
Cowpen....117 F8
Cowpen Bewley 102 B2
Cowplain....15 C7
Cowshill....109 E8
Cowslip Green..23 C6
Cowstrandburn 128 E2
Cowthorpe....95 D7
Coxbank....74 E3
Coxbench....76 E3
Cox Common..69 F6
Coxford
 Norf....80 E4
 Soton....14 C4
Cox Green....27 B6
Coxheath....31 E6
Coxhoe....111 F6
Coxley....23 E7
Cox Moor....76 D5
Coxwold....95 B8
Coychurch....21 B8
Coylton....112 B4
Coylumbridge..138 C5
Coynach....140 D3
Coynachie....152 E4
Coytrahen....34 F2
Crabadon....7 D5
Crabbs Cross....50 C5
Crabtree....17 B6
Crackenthorpe 100 B1
Crackington Haven 8 E3
Crackley....51 B7
Crackleybank....61 C7
Crackpot....100 E4
Cracoe....94 C2
Craddock....11 C5
Cradhlastadh....154 D5
Cradley....50 E2
Cradley Heath..62 F3
Crafthole....5 D8
Craggan....139 B6
Craggie
 Highld....151 H10
 Highld....157 H11
Crai....34 B2
Craibstone....152 C4
Craichie....135 E5
Craig
 Dumfries....106 B3
 Dumfries....106 C3
 Highld....150 G3
Craiganor
Lodge....132 D3
Craig Castle....140 B3
Craig-cefn-parc..33 D7
Craigdam....153 E8
Craigdarroch
 Dumfries....113 E7
 Highld....150 F7
Craigdhu....150 G7
Craigearn....141 C6
Craigellachie....152 D2
Craigencross....104 C4
Craigend
 Perth....128 B3
 Stirling....127 F6
Craigendive....145 E9
Craigendoran..126 F2
Craigends....118 C4
Craigens
 Argyll....142 B3
 E Ayrs....113 C5
Craighat....126 F3
Craighead....129 D8
Craighlaw
Mains....105 C7
Craighouse....144 G4
Craigie
 Aberds....141 C8
 Dundee....134 F4
 Perth....128 B3
 Perth....133 E8
 S Ayrs....118 F4
Craigiefield....159 G5
Craigielaw....121 B7
Craiglockhart..120 B5
Craigmalloch..112 F4
Craigmaud....153 C8
Craigmillar....121 B5
Craigmore....145 G10
Craignant....73 F6
Craigneuk
 N Lanark....119 C7
 N Lanark....119 D7
Craignure....124 B3
Craigo....135 C6
Craigow....128 D2
Craig Penllyn...21 B8
Craigrothie....129 C5
Craigroy....151 F14
Craigruie....126 B3
Craigston Castle 153 C7
Craigton
 Aberdeen....141 D7
 Angus....134 D3
 Angus....135 F5
Cranage....74 C4
Cranberry....74 F5
Cranborne....13 C8

Cranbourne....27 B7
Cranbrook
 Devon....10 E5
 Kent....18 B4
Cranbrook
Common....18 B4
Crane Moor....88 D4
Crane's Corner..68 C2
Cranfield....53 E7
Cranford....28 B2
Cranford
St Andrew....53 B7
Cranford St John 53 B7
Cranham
 Glos....37 C5
 London....42 F1
Crank....86 E3
Crank Wood....86 D4
Cranleigh....27 F8
Cranmer Green..56 B4
Cranmore....14 F4
Cranna....153 C6
Crannich....147 G8
Crannoch....152 C4
Cranoe....64 E4
Cransford....57 C7
Cranshaws....122 C2
Cranstal....84 B4
Crantock....4 C2
Cranwell....78 E3
Cranwich....67 E7
Cranworth....68 D2
Craobh Haven..124 E3
Crapstone....6 C3
Crarae....125 F5
Crask Inn....157 G8
Craskins....140 D3
Crask of Aigas..150 G7
Craster....117 C8
Craswall....48 F4
Cratfield....57 B7
Crathes....141 E6
Crathie
 Aberds....139 E8
 Highld....137 E8
Crathorne....102 D2
Craven Arms....60 F4
Crawcrook....110 C4
Crawford
 Lancs....86 D3
 S Lanark....114 B2
Crawfordjohn..113 B8
Crawick....113 C7
Crawley
 Hants....26 F2
 Oxon....38 C3
 W Sus....28 F3
Crawley Down..28 F4
Crawleyside....110 E2
Crawshawbooth..87 B6
Crawton....135 B8
Cray
 N Yorks....94 B2
 Perth....133 C8
Crayford....29 B6
Crayke....95 B8
Crays Hill....42 E3
Cray's Pond....39 F6
Creacombe....10 C3
Creagan....130 E3
Creag Ghoraidh 148 D2
Creaguaineach
Lodge....131 C7
Creaksea....43 E5
Creaton....52 B5
Creca....108 B2
Credenhill....49 E6
Crediton....10 D3
Creebridge....105 C8
Creech
Heathfield....11 B7
Creech
St Michael....11 B7
Creed....3 B8
Creekmouth....41 F7
Creeting Bottoms 56 D5
Creeting St Mary 56 D4
Creeton....65 B7
Creetown....105 D8
Creggans....125 E6
Cregneash....84 F1
Creg-ny-Baa....84 D3
Cregrina....48 D3
Creich....128 B5
Creigiau....34 F4
Cremyll....6 D2
Creslow....39 B8
Cressage....61 D5
Cressbrook....75 B8
Cresselly....32 D1
Cressing....42 B3
Cresswell
 Northumb....117 E8
 Staffs....75 F6
Cresswell Quay..32 D1
Creswell....76 B5
Cretingham....57 C6
Cretshengan..144 G6
Crewe
 Ches E....74 D4
 Ches W....73 D8
Crewgreen....60 C3
Crewkerne....12 D2
Crianlarich....126 B2
Cribyn....46 D4
Criccieth....71 D5
Crich....76 D3
Crichie....153 D9
Crichton....121 C6
Crick
 Mon....36 E1
 W Nhants....52 B3
Crickadarn....48 E2
Cricket
Malherbie....11 C8
Cricket
St Thomas....11 D8
Crickheath....60 B2
Crickhowell....35 C6
Cricklade....37 E8
Cricklewood....41 F5
Cridling Stubbs..89 B6
Crieff....127 B7
Criggion....60 C2
Crigglestone....88 C4
Crimond....153 C10
Crimonmogate 153 C10

Crimplesham....67 D6
Cringleford....68 D4
Crinan....144 D6
Cringles....94 E3
Crinow....32 C2
Cripplesease....2 C4
Cripplestyle....13 C8
Cripp's Corner..18 C4
Croasdale....98 C2
Crockenhill....29 C6
Crockernwell....10 E2
Crockerton....24 E3
Crockey Hill....96 E2
Crockham Hill..28 D5
Crockleford....43 B6
Crock Street....11 C8
Crockness....159 J4
Croes-goch....44 B3
Croeserw....34 E2
Croes-lan....46 E2
Croesor....71 C7
Croesyceiliog
 Carms....33 C5
 Torf....35 E7
Croes-y-
mwyalch....35 E7
Croesywaun....82 F5
Croft
 Leics....64 E2
 Lincs....79 C8
 Pembs....45 E3
 Warr....86 E4
Croftamie....126 F3
Croftmalloch..120 C2
Crofton
 Wilts....25 C7
 W Yorks....88 C4
Croft-on-Tees..101 D7
Crofts of
Benachielt....158 G3
Crofts of Haddo 153 E8
Crofts of
Inverthernie...153 D7
Crofts of Meikle
Ardo....153 D8
Croggan....124 C3
Croglin....109 E5
Croich....150 B7
Crois Dughaill..148 F2
Cromarty....151 E10
Cromblet....153 E7
Cromdale....139 B6
Cromer
 Herts....41 B5
 Norf....81 C8
Cromford....76 D2
Cromhall....36 E3
Cromhall Common 36 F3
Cromor....155 E9
Cromra....137 E8
Cromwell....77 C7
Cronberry....113 B6
Crondall....27 E5
Cronk-y-Voddy..84 D3
Cronton....86 F2
Crook
 Cumb....99 E6
 Durham....110 F4
Crookedholm..118 F4
Crookes....88 F4
Crookham
 Northumb....122 F5
 W Berks....26 C3
Crookham
Village....27 D5
Crookhaugh....114 B4
Crookhouse....116 B3
Crooklands....99 F7
Crook of Devon 128 D2
Cropredy....52 E2
Cropston....64 C2
Cropthorne....50 E4
Cropton....103 F5
Cropwell Bishop..77 F6
Cropwell Butler..77 F6
Cros....155 A10
Crosbost....155 E8
Crosby
 Cumb....107 F7
 IoM....84 E3
 N Lincs....90 C2
Crosby Garrett 100 D2
Crosby
Ravensworth..99 C8
Crosby Villa....107 F7
Croscombe....23 E7
Cross....23 D6
Crossaig....143 C9
Crossal....149 E9
Crossapol....146 G2
Cross Ash....35 C8
Cross-at-Hand..29 E8
Crossburn....119 B8
Crossbush....16 D4
Crosscanonby..107 F7
Crossdale Street 81 D8
Crossens....85 C4
Crossflatts....94 E4
Crossford
 Fife....128 F2
 S Lanark....119 E8
Crossgate....66 B2
Crossgatehall..121 C6
Crossgates
 Fife....128 F3
 Powys....48 C2
Crossgill....93 C5
Cross Green
 Devon....9 F5
 Suff....56 D2
 Suff....56 D3
 Warks....51 D8
Cross-hands....32 C2
Cross Hands
 Carms....33 C6
 Pembs....32 C1
Crosshill
 E Ayrs....112 B4
 Fife....128 E3
 S Ayrs....112 D3
Crosshouse....118 F3
Cross Houses....60 D5

Crossings....108 B5
Cross in Hand
 E Sus....18 C2
 Leics....64 F2
Cross Inn
 Ceredig....46 C4
 Ceredig....46 D2
 Rhondda....34 F4
Crosskeys....35 E6
Crosskirk....157 B13
Cross Lane Head..61 E7
Cross Lanes
 Corn....3 D5
 N Yorks....95 C8
 Wrex....73 E7
Crosslanes....60 C3
Crosslee....115 C6
Crossmichael..106 C4
Crossmoor....92 F4
Cross Oak....35 B5
Cross of
Jackston....153 E7
Cross o'th'hands 76 E2
Crossroads
 Aberds....141 E6
 E Ayrs....118 F4
Cross Street....57 B5
Crossway
 Hereford....49 F8
 Mon....35 C8
 Powys....48 D2
Crossway Green..50 C3
Crossways....13 F5
Crosswell....45 F3
Crosswood....47 B5
Crosthwaite....99 E6
Croston....86 C2
Crostwick....69 C5
Crostwight....69 B6
Crothair....154 D6
Crouch....29 D7
Croucheston....13 B8
Crouch Hill....12 C5
Crouch House
Green....28 E5
Croughton....52 F3
Crovie....153 B8
Crow....14 D2
Crowan....2 C5
Crowborough..18 B2
Crowcombe....22 F3
Crowdecote....75 C8
Crowden....87 E8
Crow Edge....88 D2
Crowell....39 E7
Crowfield
 Suff....56 D5
 W Nhants....52 E4
Crow Hill....36 B3
Crowhurst
 E Sus....18 D4
 Sur....28 E4
Crowhurst Lane
End....28 E4
Crowland....66 C2
Crowlas....2 C4
Crowle
 N Lincs....89 C8
 Worcs....50 D4
Crowmarsh
Gifford....39 F6
Crown Corner..57 B6
Crownhill....6 D2
Crownland....56 C4
Crownthorpe....68 D3
Crowntown....2 C5
Crows-an-wra....2 D2
Crowshill....68 D2
Crowsnest....60 D3
Crowthorne....27 C6
Crowton....74 B2
Croxall....63 C5
Croxby....91 E5
Croxdale....111 F5
Croxden....75 F7
Croxley Green..40 E3
Croxton
 Cambs....54 C3
 N Lincs....90 C4
 Norf....67 F8
 Staffs....74 F4
Croxtonbank....74 F4
Croxton Kerrial..64 B5
Croy
 Highld....151 G10
 N Lanark....119 B7
Croyde....20 F3
Croydon
 Cambs....54 E4
 London....28 C4
Crubenmore
Lodge....138 E2
Cruckmeole....60 D4
Cruckton....60 C4
Cruden Bay....153 E10
Crudgington....61 C6
Crudwell....37 E6
Crug....48 B3
Crugmeer....4 B4
Crugybar....47 F5
Crulabhig....154 D6
Crumlin
 =Crymlyn....35 E6
Crumpsall....87 D6
Crundale
 Kent....30 E4
 Pembs....44 D4
Cruwys Morchard 10 C3
Crux Easton....26 D2
Crwbin....33 C5
Crya....159 H4
Cryers Hill....40 E1
Crymlyn....83 D6
Crymych....45 F3
Crynant....34 D1
Crynfryn....46 C4
Cuaig....149 C12
Cuan....124 D3
Cubbington....51 C8
Cubeck....100 F4
Cubert....4 D2
Cubley....88 D3
Cubley Common..75 F8
Cublington
 Bucks....39 B8

Cublington continued
 Hereford....49 F6
Cuckfield....17 B7
Cucklington....13 B5
Cuckney....77 B5
Cuckoo Hill....89 E8
Cuddesdon....39 D6
Cuddington
 Bucks....39 C7
 Ches W....74 B3
Cuddington
Heath....73 E8
Cuddy Hill....92 F4
Cudham....28 D5
Cudliptown....6 B3
Cudworth
 Som....11 C8
 S Yorks....88 D4
Cuffley....41 D6
Cuiashader....155 B10
Cuidhir....148 H1
Cuidhtinis....154 J5
Culbo....151 E9
Culbokie....151 F9
Culburnie....150 G7
Culcabock....151 G9
Culcairn....151 F11
Culcharry....151 F11
Culcheth....86 E4
Culdrain....152 E5
Culduie....149 E12
Culford....56 B2
Culgaith....99 B8
Culham....39 E5
Culkein....156 F3
Culkein
 Drumbeg....156 F4
Culkerton....37 E6
Cullachie....139 B5
Cullen....152 B5
Cullercoats....111 B6
Cullicudden....151 E9
Cullingworth....94 F3
Cullipool....124 D3
Cullivoe....160 C7
Culloch....127 C6
Culloden....151 G10
Cullompton....10 D5
Culmaily....151 B11
Culmazie....105 D7
Culmington....60 F4
Culmstock....11 C6
Culnacraig....156 H3
Culnaknock....149 B10
Culpho....57 E6
Culrain....151 B8
Culross....127 F8
Culroy....112 C3
Culsh
 Aberds....140 E2
 Aberds....153 D8
Culshabbin....105 D7
Culswick....160 J4
Cultercullen....141 B8
Cults
 Aberdeen....141 D7
 Aberds....152 E5
 Dumfries....105 E8
Culverstone
Green....29 C7
Culverthorpe....78 E3
Culworth....52 E3
Culzie Lodge....151 D8
Cumbernauld..119 B7
Cumbernauld
Village....119 B7
Cumberworth..79 B8
Cuminestown..153 C8
Cumlewick....160 L6
Cummersdale..108 D3
Cummertrees..107 C8
Cummingston..152 B1
Cumnock....113 B5
Cumnor....38 D4
Cumrew....108 D5
Cumwhinton..108 D4
Cumwhitton....108 D5
Cundall....95 B7
Cunninghamhead
....118 E3
Cunister....160 D7
Cupar....129 C5
Cupar Muir....129 C5
Cupernham....14 B4
Curbar....76 B2
Curbridge
 Hants....15 C6
 Oxon....38 D3
Curdridge....15 C6
Curdworth....63 E5
Curland....11 C7
Curlew Green....57 C7
Currarie....112 E1
Curridge....26 B2
Currie....120 C4
Curry Mallet....11 B8
Curry Rivel....11 B8
Curtisden Green..29 E8
Curtisknowle....6 D5
Cury....3 D5
Cushnie....153 B7
Cushuish....22 F3
Cusop....48 E4
Cutcloy....105 F8
Cutcombe....21 F8
Cutgate....87 C6
Cutiau....58 C3
Cutlers Green....55 F6
Cutnall Green....50 C3
Cutsdean....51 F5
Cutthorpe....76 B3
Cutts....160 K6
Cuxham....39 E6
Cuxton....29 C8
Cuxwold....91 D5
Cwm
 Bl Gwent....35 D5
 Denb....72 B4
Cwmafan....34 E1
Cwmaman....34 D4
Cwmann....46 E4
Cwmavon....35 D6
Cwmbach
 Carms....32 B3
 Carms....33 D5

Cwmbâch....34 D4
Cwmbelan....59 F6
Cwmbrân
 =Cwmbran....35 E6
Cwmbran
 =Cwmbrân....35 E6
Cwmbrwyno....58 F4
Cwm-byr....46 F5
Cwmcarn....35 E6
Cwmcarvan....36 D1
Cwm-Cewydd....59 C5
Cwm-cou....45 E4
Cwmcych....45 F4
Cwmdare....34 D3
Cwmdu
 Carms....46 F5
 Powys....35 B5
Cwmduad....46 F2
Cwm-Dulais....33 D7
Cwmdwr....47 F6
Cwmfelin
 Bridgend....34 F2
 M Tydf....34 D4
Cwmfelin Boeth..32 C2
Cwm-felin-fach..35 E5
Cwmfelin Mynach 32 B3
Cwmffrwd....33 C5
Cwm Ffrwd-oer..35 D6
Cwmgiedd....34 C1
Cwmgors....33 C8
Cwmgwili....33 C6
Cwmgwrach....34 D2
Cwm-hesgen....71 E8
Cwmhiraeth....46 F2
Cwm-hwnt....34 D3
Cwmifor....33 B7
Cwm Irfon....47 E7
Cwmisfael....33 C5
Cwm-Llinau....58 D5
Cwmllynfell....33 C8
Cwm-mawr....33 C6
Cwmorgan....45 F4
Cwm-parc....34 E3
Cwmpengraig....46 F2
Cwm Penmachno 71 C8
Cwmrhos....35 B5
Cwmsychpant....46 E3
Cwmtillery....35 D6
Cwm-twrch Isaf 34 C1
Cwm-twrch
Uchaf....34 C1
Cwmwysg....34 B2
Cwm-y-glo
 Carms....33 C6
 Gwyn....82 E5
Cwmyoy....35 B6
Cwmystwyth....47 B6
Cwrt....58 D3
Cwrt-newydd....46 E3
Cwrt-y-cadno..47 E5
Cwrt-y-gollen..35 C6
Cydweli
 =Kidwelly....33 D5
Cyffordd Llandudno
Junction....83 D7
Cyffylliog....72 D4
Cyfronydd....59 D8
Cymer....34 E2
Cyncoed....35 F5
Cynghordy....47 E7
Cynheidre....33 D5
Cynwyd....72 E4
Cynwyl Elfed....32 B4
Cywarch....59 C5

**D**

Dacre
 Cumb....99 B6
 N Yorks....94 C4
Dacre Banks....94 C4
Daddry Shield..109 F8
Dadford....52 F4
Dadlington....63 E8
Dafarn Faig....71 C5
Dafen....33 D6
Daffy Green....68 D2
Dagenham....41 F7
Daglingworth..37 D6
Dagnall....40 C2
Dail Beag....154 C7
Dail bho Dheas 155 A9
Dail bho Thuath 155 A9
Daill....142 B4
Dailly....112 D2
Dail Mor....154 C7
Dairsie or
Osnaburgh....129 C6
Daisy Hill....86 D4
Dalabrog....148 F2
Dalavich....125 D5
Dalbeattie....106 C5
Dalblair....113 C6
Dalbog....135 B5
Dalby
 IoM....84 E2
 N Yorks....96 B2
Dalchalloch....132 C4
Dalchalm....157 J12
Dalchenna....125 E6
Dalchirach....152 E1
Dalchork....157 H8
Dalchreichart..137 C5
Dalchruin....127 C6
Dalderby....78 C5
Dale
 Pembs....44 E3
Dale Abbey....76 F4
Dale Head....99 C6
Dalelia....147 E10
Dale of Walls..160 H3
Daless....151 H11
Dalfaber....138 C5
Dalgarven....118 E2
Dalgety Bay....128 F3
Dalginross....127 B6
Dalguise....133 E6
Dalhalvaig....157 D11
Dalham....55 C8
Dalinlongart..145 E10
Dalkeith....121 C6

Dallam 86 E3
Dallas 151 F14
Dalleagles 113 C5
Dallinghoo 57 D6
Dallington
E Sus 18 D3
W Nhants 52 C5
Dallow 94 B4
Dalmadilly 141 C6
Dalmally 125 C7
Dalmarnock 119 C6
Dalmary 126 E4
Dalmellington 112 D4
Dalmeny 120 B4
Dalmigavie 138 C3
Dalmigavie Lodge 138 B3
Dalmore 151 E9
Dalmuir 118 B4
Dalnabreck 147 E9
Dalnacardoch Lodge 132 B4
Dalnacroich 150 F6
Dalnaglar Castle 133 C8
Dalnahaitnach 138 B4
Dalnaspidal Lodge 132 B3
Dalnavaid 133 C7
Dalnavie 151 D9
Dalnawillan Lodge 157 E13
Dalness 131 D5
Dalnessie 157 H9
Dalqueich 128 D2
Dalreavoch 157 J10
Dalry 118 E2
Dalrymple 112 C3
Dalserf 119 D8
Dalston 108 D3
Dalswinton 114 F2
Dalton
Dumfries 107 B8
Lancs 86 D2
Northumb 110 B4
Northumb 110 D2
N Yorks 95 B7
N Yorks 101 D6
S Yorks 89 E5
Dalton-in-Furness 92 B2
Dalton-le-Dale 111 E7
Dalton-on-Tees 101 D7
Dalton Piercy 111 F7
Dalveich 126 B5
Dalvina Lodge 157 E9
Dalwhinnie 138 F2
Dalwood 11 D7
Dalwyne 112 E3
Damerham 14 C2
Damgate 69 D7
Dam Green 68 F3
Damnaglaur 104 F5
Damside 120 E4
Dam Side 92 E4
Danbury 42 D3
Danby 103 D5
Danby Wiske 101 E8
Dandaleith 152 D2
Danderhall 121 C6
Danebridge 75 C6
Dane End 41 B6
Danehill 17 B8
Danemoor Green 68 D3
Danesford 61 E7
Daneshill 26 D4
Dangerous Corner 86 C3
Danskine 121 C8
Darcy Lever 86 D5
Darenth 29 B6
Daresbury 86 F3
Darfield 88 D5
Darfoulds 77 B5
Dargate 30 C4
Darite 5 C7
Darlaston 62 E3
Darley 94 D5
Darley Bridge 76 C2
Darley Head 94 D4
Darlingscott 51 E7
Darlington 101 C7
Darliston 74 F2
Darlton 77 B7
Darnall 88 F4
Darnick 121 F8
Darowen 58 D5
Darra 153 D7
Darracott 20 F3
Darras Hall 110 B4
Darrington 89 B5
Darsham 57 C8
Dartford 29 B6
Dartford Crossing 29 B6
Dartington 7 C5
Dartmeet 6 B4
Dartmouth 7 D6
Darton 88 D4
Darvel 119 F5
Darwell Hole 18 D3
Darwen 86 B4
Datchet 27 B7
Datchworth 41 C5
Datchworth Green 41 C5
Daubhill 86 D5
Daugh of Kinermony 152 D2
Dauntsey 37 F6
Dava 151 H13
Davenham 74 B3
Davenport Green 74 B5
Daventry 52 C3
Davidson's Mains 120 B5
Davidstow 8 F3
David's Well 48 B2
Davington 115 D5
Daviot
Aberds 141 B6
Highld 151 H10
Davoch of Grange 152 C4
Davyhulme 87 E5
Dawley 61 D6
Dawlish 7 B7
Dawlish Warren 7 B7
Dawn 83 D8
Daws Heath 42 F4
Daw's House
Corn 8 F5
Corn 8 F5
Dawsmere 79 F7
Dayhills 75 F6
Daylesford 38 B2
Ddôl-Cownwy 59 C7
Ddrydwy 82 D3
Deadwater 116 E2
Deaf Hill 111 F6
Deal 31 D7
Deal Hall 43 E6
Dean
Cumb 98 B2
Devon 6 C5
Devon 20 E4
Dorset 13 C7
Hants 15 C6
Som 23 E8
Deanburnhaugh 115 C6
Deane
Gtr Man 86 D4
Hants 26 D3
Deanich Lodge 150 C6
Deanland 13 C7
Dean Prior 6 C5
Dean Row 87 F6
Deans 120 C3
Deanscales 98 B2
Deanshanger 53 F5
Deanston 127 D6
Dearham 107 F7
Debach 57 D6
Debden
Essex 41 E7
Essex 55 F6
Debden Cross 55 F6
Debenham 57 C5
Dechmont 120 B3
Deddington 52 F2
Dedham 56 F4
Dedham Heath 56 F4
Deebank 141 E5
Deene 65 E6
Deenethorpe 65 E6
Deepcar 88 E3
Deepcut 27 D7
Deepdale 100 F2
Deeping Gate 65 D8
Deeping St James 65 D8
Deeping St Nicholas 66 C2
Deerhill 152 C4
Deerhurst 37 B5
Deerness 159 H6
Defford 50 E4
Defynnog 34 B3
Deganwy 83 D7
Deighton
N Yorks 102 D1
W Yorks 88 C2
York 96 E2
Deiniolen 83 E5
Delabole 8 F2
Delamere 74 C2
Delfrigs 141 B8
Delliefure 151 H13
Dell Lodge 139 C6
Delnabo 139 C7
Delnadamph 139 D8
Delph 87 D7
Delves 110 E4
Delvine 133 E8
Dembleby 78 F3
Denaby Main 89 E5
Denbigh = Dinbych 72 C4
Denbury 7 C6
Denby 76 E3
Denby Dale 88 D3
Denchworth 38 E3
Dendron 92 B2
Denel End 53 F8
Denend 152 E6
Denford 53 B7
Dengie 43 D5
Denham
Bucks 40 F3
Suff 55 C8
Suff 57 B5
Denham Street 57 B5
Denhead
Aberds 153 C9
Fife 129 C6
Denhead of Arbilot 135 E5
Denhead of Gray 134 F3
Denholm 115 C8
Denholme 94 F3
Denholme Clough 94 F3
Denio 70 D4
Denmead 15 C7
Denmore 141 C8
Denmoss 153 D6
Dennington 57 C6
Denny 127 F7
Dennyloanhead 127 F7
Denny Lodge 14 D4
Denshaw 87 C7
Denside 141 E7
Densole 31 E6
Denston 55 D8
Denstone 75 E8
Dent 100 F2
Denton
Cambs 65 F8
Darl 101 C7
E Sus 17 D8
Gtr Man 87 E7
Kent 31 E6
Lincs 77 F8
Norf 69 F5
N Yorks 94 E4
Oxon 39 D5
W Nhants 53 D6
Denton's Green 86 E2
Denver 67 D6
Denwick 117 C8
Deopham 68 D3
Deopham Green 68 E3
Depden 55 D8
Depden Green 55 D8
Deptford
London 28 B4
Wilts 24 F5
Derby 76 F3
Derbyhaven 84 F2
Dereham 68 C2
Deri 35 D5
Derril 8 D5
Derringstone 31 E6
Derrington 62 B2
Derriton 8 D5
Derryguaig 146 H7
Derry Hill 24 B4
Derrythorpe 90 D2
Dersingham 80 D2
Dervaig 146 F7
Derwen 72 D4
Derwenlas 58 E4
Desborough 64 F5
Desford 63 D8
Detchant 123 F6
Detling 29 D8
Deuddwr 60 C2
Devauden 36 E1
Devil's Bridge 47 B6
Devizes 24 C5
Devol 118 B3
Devonport 6 D2
Devonside 127 E8
Devoran 3 C6
Dewar 121 E6
Dewlish 13 E5
Dewsbury 88 B3
Dewsbury Moor 88 B3
Dewshall Court 49 F6
Dhoon 84 D4
Dhoor 84 C4
Dhowin 84 B4
Dial Post 17 C5
Dibden 14 D5
Dibden Purlieu 14 D5
Dickleburgh 68 F4
Didbrook 51 F5
Didcot 39 F5
Diddington 54 C2
Diddlebury 60 F5
Didley 49 F6
Didling 16 C2
Didmarton 37 F5
Didsbury 87 E6
Didworthy 6 C4
Digby 78 D3
Digg 149 B9
Diggle 87 D8
Digmoor 86 D2
Digswell Park 41 C5
Dihewyd 46 D3
Dilham 69 B6
Dilhorne 75 E6
Dillarburn 119 E8
Dillington 54 C2
Dilston 110 C2
Dilton Marsh 24 E3
Dilwyn 49 D6
Dinas
Carms 45 F4
Gwyn 70 D3
Dinas Cross 45 F2
Dinas Dinlle 82 F4
Dinas-Mawddwy 59 C5
Dinas Powys 22 B3
Dinbych = Denbigh 72 C4
Dinbych-y-Pysgod = Tenby 32 D2
Dinder 23 E7
Dinedor 49 F7
Dingestow 36 C1
Dingle 85 F4
Dingleden 18 B5
Dingley 64 F4
Dingwall 151 F8
Dinlabyre 115 E8
Dinmael 72 E4
Dinnet 140 E3
Dinnington
Som 12 C2
S Yorks 89 F6
T&W 110 B5
Dinorwic 83 E5
Dinton
Bucks 39 C7
Wilts 24 F5
Dinwoodie Mains 114 E4
Dinworthy 8 C5
Dippen 143 F11
Dippenhall 27 E6
Dipple
Moray 152 C3
S Ayrs 112 D2
Diptford 6 D5
Dipton 110 D4
Dirdhu 139 B6
Dirleton 129 F7
Dirt Pot 109 E8
Discoed 48 C4
Diseworth 63 B8
Dishes 159 F7
Dishforth 95 B6
Disley 87 F7
Diss 56 B5
Disserth 48 D2
Distington 98 B2
Ditchampton 25 F5
Ditcheat 23 F8
Ditchingham 69 E6
Ditchling 17 C7
Ditherington 60 C5
Dittisham 7 D6
Ditton
Halton 86 F2
Kent 29 D8
Ditton Green 55 D7
Ditton Priors 61 F6
Divach 137 B7
Divlyn 47 F6
Dixton
Glos 50 F4
Mon 36 C2
Dobcross 87 D7
Dobwalls 5 C7
Doccombe 10 F2
Dochfour House 151 H9
Dochgarroch 151 G9
Docking 80 D3
Docklow 49 D7
Dockray 99 B5
Dockroyd 94 F3
Doc Penfro = Pembroke Dock 44 E4
Dodburn 115 D7
Doddinghurst 42 E1
Doddington
Cambs 66 E3
Kent 30 D3
Lincs 78 B2
Northumb 123 F5
Shrops 49 B8
Doddiscombsleigh 10 F3
Dodford
W Nhants 52 C4
Worcs 50 B4
Dodington 24 A2
Dodleston 73 C7
Dods Leigh 75 F7
Dodworth 88 D4
Doe Green 86 F3
Doe Lea 76 C4
Dogdyke 78 D5
Dogmersfield 27 D5
Dogridge 37 F7
Dogsthorpe 65 D8
Dog Village 10 E4
Dolanog 59 C7
Dolau
Powys 48 C3
Rhondda 34 F3
Dolbenmaen 71 C6
Dolfach 59 D6
Dolfor 59 F8
Dol-fôr 58 D5
Dolgarrog 83 E7
Dolgellau 58 C4
Dolgran 46 F3
Dolhendre 72 F2
Doll 157 J11
Dollar 127 E8
Dolley Green 48 C4
Dollwen 58 F3
Dolphin 73 B5
Dolphinholme 92 D5
Dolphinton 120 E4
Dolton 9 C7
Dolwen
Conwy 83 D8
Powys 59 D6
Dolwyd 83 D8
Dolwyddelan 83 F7
Dôl-y-Bont 58 F3
Dol-y-cannau 48 E4
Dolyhir 48 D4
Doncaster 89 D6
Dones Green 74 B3
Donhead St Andrew 13 B7
Donhead St Mary 13 B7
Donibristle 128 F3
Donington 78 F5
Donington on Bain 91 F6
Donington South Ing 78 F5
Donisthorpe 63 C7
Donkey Town 27 C7
Donnington
Glos 38 B1
Hereford 50 F2
Shrops 61 D5
Telford 61 C7
W Berks 26 C2
W Sus 16 D2
Donnington Wood 61 C7
Donyatt 11 C8
Doonfoot 112 C3
Dorback Lodge 139 C6
Dorchester
Dorset 12 E4
Oxon 39 E5
Dordon 63 D6
Dore 88 F4
Dores 151 H8
Dorking 28 E2
Dormansland 28 E5
Dormanstown 102 B3
Dormington 49 E7
Dormston 50 D4
Dornal 105 B6
Dorney 27 B7
Dornie 149 F13
Dornoch 151 C10
Dornock 108 C2
Dorrery 158 E2
Dorridge 51 B6
Dorrington
Lincs 78 D3
Shrops 60 D4
Dorsington 51 E6
Dorstone 48 E5
Dorton 39 C6
Dorusduain 136 B2
Dosthill 63 E6
Dottery 12 E2
Doublebois 5 C6
Dougarie 143 E9
Doughton 37 E5
Douglas
IoM 84 E3
S Lanark 119 F8
Douglas & Angus 134 F4
Douglastown 134 E4
Douglas Water 119 F8
Douglas West 119 F8
Doulting 23 E8
Dounby 159 F3
Doune
Highld 156 J7
Stirling 127 D6
Doune Park 153 B7
Douneside 140 D3
Dounie 151 B8
Dounreay 157 C12
Dousland 6 C3
Dovaston 60 B3
Dove Holes 75 B7
Dovenby 107 F7
Dover 31 E7
Dovercourt 57 F6
Doverdale 50 C3
Doveridge 75 F8
Doversgreen 28 E3
Dowally 133 E7
Dowbridge 92 F4
Dowdeswell 37 C6
Dowlais 34 D4
Dowland 9 C7
Dowlish Wake 11 C8
Down Ampney 37 E8
Downcraig Ferry 145 H10
Downderry 5 D8
Downe 28 C5
Downend
IoW 15 F6
S Glos 23 B8
W Berks 26 B2
Downfield 134 F3
Downgate 5 B8
Downham
Essex 42 E3
Lancs 93 E7
Northumb 122 F4
Downham Market 67 D6
Down Hatherley 37 B5
Downhead 23 E8
Downhill
Perth 133 F7
T&W 111 D6
Downholland Cross 85 D4
Downholme 101 E6
Downies 141 E8
Downley 39 E8
Down St Mary 10 D2
Downside
Som 23 E8
Sur 28 D2
Down Thomas 6 D3
Downton
Hants 14 E3
Wilts 14 B2
Downton on the Rock 49 B6
Dowsby 65 B8
Dowsdale 66 C2
Dowthwaitehead 99 B5
Doxey 62 B3
Doxford 117 B7
Doxford Park 111 D6
Doynton 24 B2
Draffan 119 E7
Dragonby 90 C3
Drakeland Corner 6 D3
Drakemyre 118 D2
Drake's Broughton 50 E4
Drakes Cross 51 B5
Drakewalls 6 B2
Draughton
N Yorks 94 D3
W Nhants 53 B5
Drax 89 B7
Draycote 52 B2
Draycott
Derbys 76 F4
Glos 51 F6
Som 23 D6
Draycott in the Clay 63 B5
Draycott in the Moors 75 E6
Drayford 10 C2
Drayton
Leics 64 E5
Lincs 78 F5
Norf 68 C4
Oxon 38 E4
Oxon 52 E2
Ptsmth 15 D7
Som 12 B2
Worcs 50 B4
Drayton Bassett 63 D5
Drayton Beauchamp 40 C2
Drayton Parslow 39 B8
Drayton St Leonard 39 E5
Drebley 94 D3
Dreemskerry 84 C4
Dreenhill 44 D4
Drefach
Carms 33 C6
Carms 46 F2
Dre-fach
Carms 33 C7
Ceredig 46 E4
Drefelin 46 F2
Dreghorn 118 F3
Drellingore 31 E6
Drem 121 B8
Dresden 75 E6
Dreumasdal 148 E2
Drewsteignton 10 E2
Driby 79 B6
Driffield
E Yorks 97 D6
Glos 37 E7
Drigg 98 E2
Drighlington 88 B3
Drimnin 147 F8
Drimpton 12 D2
Drimsynie 125 E7
Drinisiadar 154 H6
Drinkstone 56 C3
Drinkstone Green 56 C3
Drishaig 125 D7
Drissaig 124 D5
Drochil 120 E4
Drointon 62 B4
Droitwich Spa 50 C3
Droman 156 D4
Dron 128 C3
Dronfield 76 B3
Dronfield Woodhouse 76 B3
Drongan 112 C4
Dronley 134 F3
Droxford 15 C7
Droylsden 87 E7
Druid 72 E4
Druidston 44 D3
Druimarbin 130 B4
Druimavuic 130 E4
Druimdrishaig 144 F6
Druimindarroch 147 C9
Druimyeon More 143 C7
Drum
Argyll 145 F8
Perth 128 D2
Drumbeg 156 F4
Drumblade 152 D5
Drumblair 153 D6
Drumbuie
Dumfries 113 F5
Highld 149 E12
Drumburgh 108 D2
Drumburn 107 C6
Drumchapel 118 B5
Drumchardine 151 G8
Drumchork 155 J13
Drumclog 119 F6
Drumderfit 151 F9
Drumeldrie 129 D6
Drumelzier 120 F4
Drumfearn 149 G11
Drumgask 138 E2
Drumgley 134 D4
Drumguish 138 E3
Drumin 152 E1
Drumlasie 140 D5
Drumlemble 143 G7
Drumligair 141 C8
Drumlithie 141 F6
Drummoddie 105 E7
Drummond 151 E9
Drummore 104 F5
Drummuir 152 D3
Drummuir Castle 152 D3
Drumnadrochit 137 B8
Drumnagorrach 152 C5
Drumoak 141 E6
Drumpark 107 A5
Drumphail 105 C6
Drumrash 106 B3
Drumrunie 156 J4
Drums 141 B8
Drumsallie 130 B3
Drumstinchall 107 D5
Drumsturdy 134 F4
Drumtochty Castle 135 B6
Drumtroddan 105 E7
Drumuie 149 D9
Drumuillie 138 B5
Drumvaich 127 D5
Drumwhindle 153 E9
Drunkendub 135 E6
Drury 73 C6
Drury Square 68 C2
Drybeck 100 C1
Drybridge
Moray 152 B4
N Ayrs 118 F3
Drybrook 36 C3
Dryburgh 121 F8
Dry Doddington 77 E8
Dry Drayton 54 C4
Dryhope 115 B5
Drylaw 120 B5
Drym 2 C5
Drymen 126 F3
Drymuir 153 D9
Drynoch 149 E9
Dryslwyn 33 B6
Dryton 61 D5
Dubford 153 B8
Dubton 135 D5
Duchally 156 H6
Duchlage 126 F2
Duck Corner 57 E7
Duckington 73 D8
Ducklington 38 D3
Duckmanton 76 B4
Duck's Cross 54 D2
Duddenhoe End 55 F5
Duddingston 121 B5
Duddington 65 D6
Duddleswell 17 B8
Duddo 122 E5
Duddon 74 C2
Duddon Bridge 98 F4
Dudleston 73 F7
Dudleston Heath 73 F7
Dudley
T&W 111 B5
W Mid 62 E3
Dudley Port 62 E3
Duffield 76 E3
Duffryn
Neath 34 E2
Newport 35 F6
Dufftown 152 E3
Duffus 152 B1
Dufton 100 B1
Duggleby 96 C4
Duirinish 149 E12
Duisdalemore 149 G12
Duisky 130 B4
Dukestown 35 C5
Dukinfield 87 E7
Dulas 82 C4
Dulcote 23 E7
Dulford 11 D5
Dull 133 E5
Dullatur 119 B7
Dullingham 55 D7
Dulnain Bridge 139 B5
Duloe
Bedford 54 C2
Corn 5 D7
Dulsie 151 G12
Dulverton 10 B4
Dulwich 28 B4
Dumbarton 118 B3
Dumbleton 50 F5
Dumcrieff 114 D4
Dumfries 107 B6
Dumgoyne 126 F4
Dummer 26 E3
Dumpford 16 B2
Dumpton 31 C7
Dun 135 D6
Dunain House 151 G9
Dunalastair 132 D4
Dunan 149 F10
Dunans 145 D9
Dunball 22 E5
Dunbar 122 B2
Dunbeath 158 H3
Dunbeg 124 B4
Dunblane 127 D6
Dunbog 128 C4
Duncanston 151 F8
Duncanstone 140 B4
Dun Charlabhaigh 154 C6
Dunchurch 52 B2
Duncote 52 D4
Duncow 114 F2
Duncraggan 126 D4
Duncrievie 128 D3
Duncton 16 C3
Dundas House 159 K5
Dundee 134 F4
Dundeugh 113 F5
Dundon 23 F6
Dundonald 118 F3
Dundonnell 150 C3
Dundonnell Hotel 150 C3
Dundonnell House 150 C4
Dundraw 108 E2
Dundreggan 137 C6
Dundreggan Lodge 137 C6
Dundrennan 106 E4
Dundry 23 C7
Dunecht 141 D6
Dunfermline 128 F2
Dunfield 37 E8
Dunford Bridge 88 D2
Dungworth 88 F3
Dunham 77 B8
Dunham-on-the-Hill 73 B8
Dunhampton 50 C3
Dunham Town 86 F5
Dunholme 78 B3
Dunino 129 C7
Dunipace 127 F7
Dunira 127 B6
Dunkeld 133 E7
Dunkerton 24 D2
Dunkeswell 11 D6
Dunkeswick 95 E6
Dunkirk
Kent 30 D4
Norf 81 E8
Dunk's Green 29 D7
Dunlappie 135 C5
Dunley
Hants 26 D2
Worcs 50 C2
Dunlichity Lodge 151 H9
Dunlop 118 E4
Dunmaglass Lodge 137 B8
Dunmore
Argyll 144 G6
Falk 127 F7
Dunnet 158 C4
Dunnichen 135 E5
Dunninald 135 D7
Dunning 128 C2
Dunnington
E Yorks 97 D7
Warks 51 D5
York 96 D2
Dunnockshaw 87 B6
Dunollie 124 B4
Dunoon 145 F10
Dunragit 105 D5
Dunrostan 144 E6
Duns 122 D3
Dunsby 65 B8
Dunscore 113 F8
Dunscroft 89 D7
Dunsdale 102 C4
Dunsden Green 26 B5
Dunsfold 27 F8
Dunsford 10 F3
Dunshalt 128 C4
Dunshillock 153 D9
Dunskey House 104 D4
Dunsley 103 C6
Dunsmore 40 D1
Dunsop Bridge 93 D6
Dunstable 40 B3
Dunstall 63 B5
Dunstall Common 50 E3
Dunstall Green 55 C8
Dunstan 117 C8
Dunstan Steads 117 B8
Dunster 21 E8
Duns Tew 38 B4
Dunston
Lincs 78 C3
Norf 68 D5
Staffs 62 C3
T&W 110 C5
Dunsville 89 D7
Dunswell 97 F6
Dunsyre 120 E3
Dunterton 5 B8
Duntisbourne Abbots 37 D6
Duntisbourne Leer 37 D6
Duntisbourne Rouse 37 D6
Duntish 12 D4
Duntocher 118 B4
Dunton
Bucks 39 B8
C Beds 54 E3
Norf 80 D4
Dunton Bassett 64 E2
Dunton Green 29 D6
Dunton Wayletts 42 E2
Duntulm 149 A9
Dunure 112 C2
Dunvant 33 E6
Dunvegan 148 D7
Dunwich 57 B8
Dunwood 75 D6
Dupplin Castle 128 C2
Durdar 108 D4
Durgates 18 B3
Durham 111 E5
Durisdeer 113 D8
Durisdeermill 113 D8
Durkar 88 C4
Durleigh 22 F4
Durley
Hants 15 C6
Wilts 25 C7
Durnamuck 150 B3
Durness 156 C7
Durno 141 B6
Duror 130 D3
Durran
Argyll 125 E5
Highld 158 D3
Durrington
Wilts 25 E6
W Sus 16 D5
Dursley 36 E4
Durston 11 B7
Durweston 13 D6
Dury 160 G6
Duston 52 C5
Duthil 138 B5
Dutlas 48 B4
Duton Hill 42 B2
Dutson 8 F5
Dutton 74 B2
Duxford
Cambs 55 E5
Oxon 38 E3
Dwygyfylchi 83 D7
Dwyran 82 E4
Dyce 141 C7
Dye House 110 D2
Dyffryn
Bridgend 34 E2
Carms 32 B4
Pembs 44 B4
Dyffryn Ardudwy 71 E6
Dyffryn Castell 58 F4
Dyffryn Ceidrych 33 B8
Dyffryn Cellwen 34 D2
Dyke
Lincs 65 B8
Moray 151 F12
Dykehead
Angus 134 C3
N Lanark 119 D8
Stirling 126 E4
Dykelands 135 C7
Dykends 134 D2
Dykeside 153 D7
Dykesmains 118 E2
Dylife 59 E5
Dymchurch 19 C7
Dymock 50 F2
Dyrham 24 B2
Dysart 128 E5
Dyserth 72 B4


## E


Eadar Dha Fhadhail 154 D5
Eagland Hill 92 E4
Eagle 77 C8
Eagle Barnsdale 77 C8
Eagle Moor 77 C8
Eaglescliffe 102 C2
Eaglesfield
Cumb 98 B2
Dumfries 108 B2
Eaglesham 119 D5
Eaglethorpe 65 E7
Eairy 84 E2
Eakley Lanes 53 D6
Eakring 77 C6
Ealand 89 C8
Ealing 40 F4
Eals 109 D6
Eamont Bridge 99 B7
Earby 94 E2
Earcroft 86 B4
Eardington 61 E7
Eardisland 49 D6
Eardisley 48 E5
Eardiston
Shrops 60 B3
Worcs 49 C8
Earith 54 B4
Earle 117 B5
Earley 27 B5
Earlham 68 D5
Earlish 149 B8
Earls Barton 53 C6
Earls Colne 42 B4
Earl's Croome 50 E3
Earlsdon 51 B8
Earlsferry 129 E6
Earlsfield 78 F2
Earlsford 153 E8
Earl's Green 56 C4
Earlsheaton 88 B3
Earl Shilton 63 E8
Earlsmill 151 F12
Earl Soham 57 C6
Earl Sterndale 75 C7
Earlston
Borders 121 F8
E Ayrs 118 F4
Earl Stonham 56 D5
Earlswood
Mon 36 E1
Sur 28 E3
Warks 51 B6
Earnley 16 E2
Earsairidh 148 J2
Earsdon 111 B6
Earsham 69 F6
Earswick 96 D2
Eartham 16 D3
Easby
N Yorks 101 D6
N Yorks 102 D3
Easdale 124 D3
Easebourne 16 B2
Easenhall 52 B2
Eashing 27 E7
Easington
Bucks 39 C6
Durham 111 E7
E Yorks 91 C7
Northumb 123 F7
Oxon 39 E6
Oxon 52 F2
Redcar 103 C5
Easington Colliery 111 E7
Easington Lane 111 E6
Easingwold 95 C8
Easole Street 31 D6
Eassie 134 E3
East Aberthaw 22 C2
East Adderbury 52 F2
East Allington 7 E5
East Anstey 10 B3
East Appleton 101 E7
East Ardsley 88 B4
East Ashling 16 D2
East Auchronie 141 D7
East Ayton 103 F7
East Bank 35 D6
East Barkwith 91 F5
East Barming 29 D8
East Barnby 103 C6
East Barnet 41 E5
East Barns 122 B3
East Barsham 80 D5
East Beckham 81 D7
East Bedfont 27 B8
East Bergholt 56 F4
East Bilney 68 C2
East Blatchington 17 D8
East Boldre 14 D4
Eastbourne 18 F3
East Brent 22 D5
Eastbridge 57 C8
East Bridgford 77 E6
East Buckland 21 F5
East Budleigh 11 F5
Eastburn 94 E3
East Burrafirth 160 H5
East Burton 13 F6
Eastbury
London 40 E3
W Berks 25 B8
East Butsfield 110 E4
East Butterwick 90 D2
Eastby 94 D3
East Cairnbeg 135 B7
East Calder 120 C3
East Carleton 68 D4
East Carlton
N Nhants 64 F5
W Yorks 94 E5
East Chaldon 13 F5
East Challow 38 F3
East Chiltington 17 C7
East Chinnock 12 C2
East Chisenbury 25 D6
Eastchurch 30 B3
East Clandon 27 D8
East Claydon 39 B7
East Clyne 157 J12
East Coker 12 C3
Eastcombe 37 D5
East Combe 22 F3
East Common 96 F2
East Compton 23 E8
Eastcote
London 40 F4
W Mid 51 B6
W Nhants 52 D4
Eastcott
Corn 8 C4
Wilts 24 D5
East Cottingwith 96 E3
Eastcourt
Wilts 25 C7
Wilts 37 E6
East Cowes 15 E6
East Cowick 89 B7
East Cowton 101 D8
East Cramlington 111 B5
East Cranmore 23 E8
East Creech 13 F7
East Croachy 138 B2
East Croftmore 139 C5
East Curthwaite 108 E3
East Dean
E Sus 18 F2
Hants 14 B3
W Sus 16 C3
East Down 20 E5
East Drayton 77 B7
East Ella 90 B4
East End
Dorset 13 E7
E Yorks 91 B6
Hants 14 E4
Hants 15 B7
Hants 26 C2
Herts 41 B7
Kent 18 B5
N Som 23 B6
Oxon 38 C3
Easter Ardross 151 D9
Easter Balmoral 139 E8
Easter Boleskine 137 B8
Easter Compton 36 F2
Easter Cringate 127 F6
Easter Davoch 140 D3
Easter Earshaig 114 D3
Easter Fearn 151 C9
Easter Galcantray 151 G11
Eastergate 16 D3
Easterhouse 119 C6
Easter Howgate 120 C5
Easter Howlaws 122 E3
Easter Kinkell 151 F8
Easter Lednathie 134 C3
Easter Milton 151 F12
Easter Moniack 151 G8
Eastern Green 63 F6
Easter Ord 141 D7
Easter Quarff 160 K6
Easter Rhynd 128 C3
Easter Row 127 E6
Easter Silverford 153 B7
Easter Skeld 160 J5
Easterton 24 D5
Eastertown 22 D5
Eastertown of Auchleuchries 153 E10
Easter Whyntie 152 B6
East Farleigh 29 D8
East Farndon 64 F4
East Ferry 90 E2
Eastfield
N Lanark 119 C8
N Yorks 103 F8
Eastfield Hall 117 D8
East Fortune 121 B8
East Garston 25 B8
Eastgate
Durham 110 F2
Norf 81 E7
East Ginge 38 F4
East Goscote 64 C3

East Grafton . . . . 25 C7
East Grimstead . . 14 B3
East Grinstead . . 28 F4
East Guldeford . . 19 C6
East Haddon . . . . 52 C4
East Hagbourne . 39 F5
East Halton . . . . 90 C5
Eastham . . . . . . 85 F4
Eastham Ferry . . 85 F4
Easthampstead . 27 C6
East Hanney . . . . 38 E4
East Hanningfield . . 42 D3
East Hardwick . . 89 C5
East Harling . . . . 68 F2
East Harlsey . . . . 102 E2
East Harnham . . 14 B2
East Harptree . . . 23 D7
East Hartford . . . 111 B5
East Harting . . . . 15 C8
East Hatley . . . . 54 D3
East Hauxwell . . 101 E6
East Haven . . . . 135 F5
Eastheath . . . . . 27 C6
East Heckington . 78 E4
East Hedleyhope . 110 E4
East Hendred . . . 38 F4
East Herrington 111 E6
East Hesleyside . 96 B5
East Hoathly . . . 18 D2
Easthope . . . . . . 61 E5
Easthorpe
 Essex . . . . . . . 43 B5
 Leics . . . . . . . 77 F8
 Notts . . . . . . . 77 D7
East Horrington . 23 E7
East Horsley . . . . 27 D8
East Horton . . . . 123 F6
Easthouses . . . . 121 C6
East Huntspill . . 22 E5
East Hyde . . . . . 40 C4
East Ilkerton . . . 21 E6
East Ilsley . . . . . 38 F4
Eastington
 Devon . . . . . . . 10 D2
 Glos . . . . . . . . 36 C4
 Glos . . . . . . . . 37 C8
East Keal . . . . . . 79 C6
East Kennett . . . 25 C6
East Keswick . . . 95 E6
East Kilbride . . . 119 D6
East Kirkby . . . . 79 C6
East Knapton . . . 96 B4
East Knighton . . 13 F6
East Knoyle . . . . 24 F3
East Kyloe . . . . . 123 F6
East Lambrook . . 12 C2
East Lamington . 151 D10
East Langdon . . . 31 E7
East Langton . . . 64 E4
East Langwell . 157 J10
East Lavant . . . . 16 D2
East Lavington . . 16 C3
Eastleach Martin 38 D2
Eastleach
 Turville . . . . . . 38 D1
East Leake . . . . . 64 B2
East Learmouth 122 F4
Eastleigh
 Devon . . . . . . . 9 B6
 Hants . . . . . . . 14 C5
East Leigh . . . . . 9 D8
East Lexham . . . 67 C8
East Lilburn . . . . 117 B6
Eastling . . . . . . . 30 D3
East Linton . . . . 121 B8
East Liss . . . . . . 15 B8
East Looe . . . . . . 5 D7
East Lound . . . . . 89 E8
East Lulworth . . 13 F6
East Lutton . . . . 96 C5
East Lydford . . . 23 F7
East Mains . . . . 141 E5
East Malling . . . 29 D8
East March . . . . 134 F4
East Marden . . . 16 C2
East Markham . . 77 B7
East Marton . . . . 94 D2
East Meon . . . . . 15 B7
East Mere . . . . . 10 C4
East Mersea . . . . 43 C6
East Mey . . . . . . 158 C5
East Molesey . . . 28 C2
Eastmoor
 Derbys . . . . . . 76 B3
 Norf . . . . . . . . 67 D7
East Morden . . . 13 E7
East Morton . . . . 94 E3
East Ness . . . . . 96 B2
East Newton . . . . 97 F8
Eastney . . . . . . . 15 E7
Eastnor . . . . . . . 50 F2
East Norton . . . . 64 D4
East Nynehead . . 11 B6
East Oakley . . . . 26 D3
Eastoft . . . . . . . 90 C2
East Ogwell . . . . 7 B6
Eastoke . . . . . . . 15 E8
Easton
 Cambs . . . . . . 54 B2
 Cumb . . . . . . . 108 B4
 Cumb . . . . . . . 108 D2
 Devon . . . . . . . 10 C4
 Dorset . . . . . . 12 G4
 Hants . . . . . . . 26 F3
 Lincs . . . . . . . 65 B6
 Norf . . . . . . . . 68 C4
 Som . . . . . . . . 23 E7
 Suff . . . . . . . . 57 D6
 Wilts . . . . . . . 24 B3
Easton Grey . . . . 37 F5
Easton-in-
 Gordano . . . . . 23 B8
Easton Maudit . . 53 D6
Easton on the
 Hill . . . . . . . . 65 D7
Easton Royal . . . 25 C7
East Orchard . . . 13 C6
East Ord . . . . . . 123 D6
East Panson . . . . 9 E5
Eastpark . . . . . . 107 C7
East Peckham . . 29 E7
East Pennard . . . 23 F7
East Perry . . . . . 54 C2

East Portlemouth . . 6 F5
East Prawle . . . . . 7 F5
East Preston . . . . 16 D4
East Putford . . . . . 9 C5
East
 Quantoxhead . . 22 E3
East Rainton . . . 111 E6
East Ravendale . . 91 E6
East Raynham . . 80 E4
East Rhidorroch
 Lodge . . . . . . 150 B5
Eastriggs . . . . . 108 C2
East Rigton . . . . 95 E6
Eastrington . . . . 89 B8
East Rounton . . . 102 D2
East Row . . . . . . 103 C6
East Rudham . . . 80 E4
East Runton . . . . 81 C7
East Ruston . . . . 69 B6
Eastry . . . . . . . . 31 D7
East Saltoun . . . 121 C7
East Sleekburn . 117 F8
East Somerton . . 69 C7
East Stockwith . . 89 E8
East Stoke
 Dorset . . . . . . 13 F6
 Notts . . . . . . . 77 E7
East Stour . . . . . 13 B6
East Stourmouth . 31 C6
East Stowford . . . 9 B8
East Stratton . . . 26 F3
East Studdal . . . 31 E7
East Suisnish . . 149 E10
East Taphouse . . 5 C6
East-the-Water . . 9 B6
East Thirston . . 117 E7
East Tilbury . . . . 29 B7
East Tisted . . . . . 26 F5
East Torrington . . 90 F5
East Tuddenham 68 C3
East Tytherley . . 14 B3
East Tytherton . . 24 B4
East Village . . . . 10 D3
Eastville
 Bristol . . . . . . . 23 B8
 Lincs . . . . . . . 79 D7
East Wall . . . . . . 60 E5
East Walton . . . . 67 C7
Eastwell . . . . . . 64 B4
East Wellow . . . . 14 B4
East Wemyss . . . 128 E5
East Whitburn . . 120 C2
Eastwick
 Herts . . . . . . . 41 C7
 Shetland . . . . 160 H5
East Williamston 32 D1
East Winch . . . . 67 C6
East Winterslow . 25 F7
East Wittering . . 15 E8
East Witton . . . . 101 F6
Eastwood
 Notts . . . . . . . 76 E4
 Southend . . . . 42 F4
 W Yorks . . . . . 87 B7
East Woodburn 116 F5
East Woodhay . . 26 C2
East Worldham . . 26 F5
East Worlington . 10 C2
East Worthing . . 17 D5
Eathorpe . . . . . . 51 C8
Eaton
 Ches E . . . . . . . 75 C5
 Ches W . . . . . . 74 C2
 Leics . . . . . . . 64 B4
 Norf . . . . . . . . 68 D5
 Notts . . . . . . . 77 B7
 Oxon . . . . . . . 38 D4
 Shrops . . . . . . 60 F3
 Shrops . . . . . . 60 E5
Eaton Bishop . . . 49 F6
Eaton Bray . . . . 40 B2
Eaton
 Constantine . . 61 D5
Eaton Green . . . 40 B2
Eaton Hastings . 38 E2
Eaton on Tern . . 61 B6
Eaton Socon . . . 54 D2
Eavestone . . . . . 94 C5
Ebberston . . . . 103 F6
Ebbesbourne
 Wake . . . . . . . 13 B7
Ebbw Vale
 = Glyn Ebwy . . 35 D5
Ebchester . . . . 110 D4
Ebford . . . . . . . . 10 F4
Ebley . . . . . . . . 37 D5
Ebnal . . . . . . . . 73 E8
Ebrington . . . . . 51 E6
Ecchinswell . . . . 26 D2
Ecclaw . . . . . . 122 C3
Ecclefechan . . . 107 B8
Eccles
 Borders . . . . . 122 E3
 Gtr Man . . . . . . 87 E5
 Kent . . . . . . . . 29 C8
Ecclesall . . . . . . 88 F4
Ecclesfield . . . . 88 E4
Ecclesgreig . . . 135 C7
Eccleshall . . . . . 62 B2
Eccleshill . . . . . 94 F4
Ecclesmachan . 120 B3
Eccles on Sea . . 69 B7
Eccles Road . . . 68 E3
Eccleston
 Ches W . . . . . . 73 C8
 Lancs . . . . . . . 86 C3
 Mers . . . . . . . . 86 E2
Eccleston Park . 86 E2
Eccup . . . . . . . . 95 E5
Echt . . . . . . . . 141 D6
Eckford . . . . . . 116 B3
Eckington
 Derbys . . . . . . 76 B4
 Worcs . . . . . . . 50 E4
Ecton . . . . . . . . 53 C6
Edale . . . . . . . . 88 F2
Edburton . . . . . . 17 C6
Edderside . . . . 107 E7
Edderton . . . . . 151 C10
Eddistone . . . . . 8 B4
Eddleston . . . . 120 E5
Edenbridge . . . . 28 E5
Edenfield . . . . . 87 C5
Edenham . . . . . . 65 B7
Eden Park . . . . . 28 C4
Edensor . . . . . . 76 C2

Edentaggart . . 126 E2
Edenthorpe . . . . 89 D7
Edentown . . . . 108 D3
Ederline . . . . . 124 E4
Edern . . . . . . . . 70 D3
Edgarley . . . . . . 23 F7
Edgbaston . . . . . 62 F4
Edgcott
 Bucks . . . . . . . 39 B6
 Som . . . . . . . . 21 F7
Edge . . . . . . . . . 60 D3
Edgebolton . . . . 61 B5
Edge End . . . . . . 36 C2
Edgefield . . . . . . 81 D6
Edgefield Street . 81 D6
Edge Green . . . . 73 D8
Edge Hill . . . . . . 85 F4
Edgeside . . . . . . 87 B6
Edgeworth . . . . . 37 D6
Edgmond . . . . . . 61 C7
Edgmond Marsh . 61 B7
Edgton . . . . . . . . 60 F3
Edgware . . . . . . 40 E4
Edgworth . . . . . 86 C5
Edinample . . . . 126 B4
Edinbane . . . . . 149 C8
Edinburgh . . . . 121 B5
Edingale . . . . . . 63 C6
Edingight
 House . . . . . . 152 C5
Edingley . . . . . . 77 D6
Edingthorpe . . . 69 A6
Edingthorpe
 Green . . . . . . 69 A6
Edington
 Som . . . . . . . . 23 F5
 Wilts . . . . . . . 24 D4
Edintore . . . . . 152 D4
Edithmead . . . . 22 E5
Edith Weston . . 65 D6
Edlaston . . . . . . 76 E2
Edlesborough . . 40 C2
Edlingham . . . . 117 D7
Edlington . . . . . 78 B5
Edmondsham . . 13 C8
Edmondsley . . . 110 E5
Edmondthorpe . 65 C5
Edmonstone . . 159 F6
Edmonton . . . . . 41 E6
Edmundbyers . . 110 D3
Ednam . . . . . . 122 F3
Ednaston . . . . . 76 E2
Edradynate . . . 133 D5
Edrom . . . . . . . 122 D4
Edstaston . . . . . 74 F2
Edstone . . . . . . 51 C6
Edvin Loach . . . . 49 D8
Edwalton . . . . . . 77 F5
Edwardstone . . . 56 E3
Edwinsford . . . . 46 F5
Edwinstowe . . . . 77 C6
Edworth . . . . . . 54 E3
Edwyn Ralph . . . 49 D8
Edzell . . . . . . . 135 C5
E Eachwick . . . 110 B4
Efail Isaf . . . . . . 34 F4
Efailnewydd . . . 70 D4
Efailwen . . . . . . 32 B2
Efenechtyd . . . . 72 D5
Effingham . . . . . 28 D2
Effirth . . . . . . . 160 H5
Efford . . . . . . . . 10 D3
Egdon . . . . . . . . 50 D4
Egerton
 Gtr Man . . . . . . 86 C5
 Kent . . . . . . . . 30 E3
Egerton Forstal . 30 E3
Eggborough . . . . 89 B6
Eggbuckland . . . . 6 D3
Eggington . . . . . 40 B2
Egginton . . . . . . 63 B6
Egglescliffe . . . 102 C2
Eggleston . . . . 100 B4
Egham . . . . . . . . 27 B8
Egleton . . . . . . . 65 D5
Eglingham . . . . 117 C7
Egloshayle . . . . . 4 B5
Egloskerry . . . . . 8 F4
Eglwysbach . . . . 83 D8
Eglwys-Brewis . . 22 C2
Eglwys Cross . . . 73 E8
Eglwys Fach . . . 58 E3
Eglwyswen . . . . 45 F3
Eglwyswrw . . . . 45 F3
Egmanton . . . . . 77 C7
Egremont
 Cumb . . . . . . . 98 C2
 Mers . . . . . . . . 85 E4
Egton . . . . . . . 103 D6
Egton Bridge . . 103 D6
Eight Ash Green . 43 B5
Eignaig . . . . . . 130 E1
Eil . . . . . . . . . 138 C4
Eilanreach . . . . 149 G13
Eileanach Lodge 151 E8
Eilean Darach . . 150 C4
Einacleite . . . . 154 E6
Eisgean . . . . . . 155 F8
Eisingrug . . . . . 71 D7
Elan Village . . . 47 C8
Elberton . . . . . . 36 F3
Elburton . . . . . . . 6 D3
Elcho . . . . . . . 128 B3
Elcombe . . . . . . 37 F8
Eldernell . . . . . . 66 E3
Eldersfield . . . . 50 F3
Eldersli . . . . . . 118 C4
Eldon . . . . . . . 101 B7
Eldrick . . . . . . . 112 F2
Eldroth . . . . . . . 93 C7
Eldwick . . . . . . . 94 E4
Elfhowe . . . . . . 99 E6
Elford
 Northumb . . . 123 F7
 Staffs . . . . . . . 63 C5
Elgin . . . . . . . 152 B2
Elgol . . . . . . . 149 G10
Elham . . . . . . . . 31 E5
Elie . . . . . . . . 129 D6
Eling
 Hants . . . . . . . 14 C4
 W Yorks . . . . . 96 E2
Elishader . . . . 149 B10
Elishaw . . . . . . 116 E4
Elkesley . . . . . . 77 B6
Elkstone . . . . . . 37 C6
Ellan . . . . . . . 138 B4
Elland . . . . . . . . 88 B2
Ellary . . . . . . . 144 F6
Ellastone . . . . . 75 E8

Ellemford . . . . 122 C3
Ellenbrook . . . . . 84 E3
Ellenhall . . . . . . 62 B2
Ellen's Green . . . 27 F8
Ellerbeck . . . . . 102 E2
Ellerburn . . . . . 103 F6
Ellerby . . . . . . . 103 C5
Ellerdine Heath . 61 B6
Ellerhayes . . . . . 10 D4
Elleric . . . . . . . 130 E4
Ellerker . . . . . . . 90 B3
Ellerton
 E Yorks . . . . . . 96 F3
 Shrops . . . . . . 61 B7
Ellesborough . . . 39 D8
Ellesmere . . . . . 73 F8
Ellesmere Port . 73 B8
Ellingham
 Norf . . . . . . . . 69 E6
 Northumb . . . 117 B7
Ellingstring . . . 101 F6
Ellington
 Cambs . . . . . . 54 B2
 Northumb . . . 117 E8
Elliot . . . . . . . 135 F6
Ellisfield . . . . . . 26 E4
Ellistown . . . . . . 63 C8
Ellon . . . . . . . 153 E9
Ellonby . . . . . . 108 F4
Ellough . . . . . . . 69 F7
Elloughton . . . . 90 B3
Ellwood . . . . . . 36 D2
Elm . . . . . . . . 66 D4
Elmbridge . . . . . 50 C4
Elmdon
 Essex . . . . . . . 55 F5
 W Mid . . . . . . 63 F5
Elmdon Heath . . 63 F5
Elmers End . . . . 28 C4
Elmesthorpe . . . 63 E8
Elmfield . . . . . . 15 E7
Elm Hill . . . . . . 13 B6
Elmhurst . . . . . . 62 C5
Elmley Castle . . 50 E4
Elmley Lovett . . 50 C3
Elmore . . . . . . . 36 C4
Elmore Back . . . 36 C4
Elm Park . . . . . . 41 F8
Elmscott . . . . . . 8 B4
Elmsett . . . . . . . 56 E4
Elmstead Market . 43 B6
Elmsted . . . . . . 30 E5
Elmstone . . . . . . 31 C6
Elmstone
 Hardwicke . . . 37 B6
Elmswell
 E Yorks . . . . . . 97 D5
 Suff . . . . . . . . 56 C3
Elmton . . . . . . . 76 B5
Elphin . . . . . . . 156 H5
Elphinstone . . . 121 B6
Elrick . . . . . . . 141 D7
Elrig . . . . . . . . 105 E7
Elsdon . . . . . . . 117 E5
Elsecar . . . . . . . 88 E4
Elsenham . . . . . 41 B8
Elsfield . . . . . . . 39 C5
Elsham . . . . . . . 90 C4
Elsing . . . . . . . 68 C3
Elslack . . . . . . . 94 E2
Elson . . . . . . . 73 F7
Elsrickle . . . . . 120 E3
Elstead . . . . . . . 27 E7
Elsted . . . . . . . 16 C2
Elsthorpe . . . . . 65 B7
Elstob . . . . . . . 101 B8
Elston
 Notts . . . . . . . 77 E7
 Wilts . . . . . . . 25 E5
Elstone . . . . . . . 9 C8
Elstow . . . . . . . 53 E8
Elstree . . . . . . . 40 E4
Elstronwick . . . . 97 F8
Elswick . . . . . . . 92 F4
Elsworth . . . . . . 54 C4
Elterwater . . . . . 99 D5
Eltham . . . . . . . 28 B5
Eltisley . . . . . . . 54 D3
Elton
 Cambs . . . . . . 65 E7
 Ches W . . . . . . 73 B8
 Derbys . . . . . . 76 C2
 Glos . . . . . . . . 36 C4
 Hereford . . . . . 49 B6
 Notts . . . . . . . 77 F7
 Stockton . . . . 102 C2
Elton Green . . . 73 B8
Elvanfoot . . . . . 114 C2
Elvaston . . . . . . 76 F4
Elveden . . . . . . 56 B2
Elvingston . . . . 121 B7
Elvington
 Kent . . . . . . . . 31 D6
 York . . . . . . . . 96 E2
Elwick
 Hrtlpl . . . . . . . 111 F7
 Northumb . . . 123 F7
Elworth . . . . . . 74 C4
Elworthy . . . . . . 22 F2
Ely
 Cambs . . . . . . 66 F5
 Cardiff . . . . . . 22 B3
Emberton . . . . . 53 E6
Embleton
 Cumb . . . . . . 107 F8
 Northumb . . . 117 B8
Embo . . . . . . . 151 B11
Emborough . . . . 23 D8
Embo Street . . . 151 B11
Embsay . . . . . . 94 D3
Emersons Green . 23 B8
Emery Down . . . 14 D3
Emley . . . . . . . . 88 C3
Emmbrook . . . . 27 C5
Emmer Green . . 26 B5
Emmington . . . . 39 D7
Emneth . . . . . . 66 D4
Emneth Hungate 66 D5
Empingham . . . 65 D6
Empshott . . . . . 27 F5
Emstrey . . . . . . 60 C5
Emsworth . . . . . 15 D8
Enborne . . . . . . 26 C2
Enchmarsh . . . . 60 E5
Enderby . . . . . . 64 E2
Endmoor . . . . . . 99 F7
Endon . . . . . . . 75 D6
Endon Bank . . . 75 D6

Enfield . . . . . . . 41 E6
Enfield Wash . . . 41 E6
Enford . . . . . . . 25 D6
Engamoor . . . . 160 H4
Engine Common . 36 F3
Englefield . . . . . 26 B4
Englefield Green . 27 B7
Englesea-brook . 74 D4
English Bicknor . 36 C2
Englishcombe . . 24 C2
English Frankton . 60 B4
Enham Alamein . 25 E8
Enmore . . . . . . . 22 F4
Ennerdale Bridge 98 C2
Enoch . . . . . . . 113 D8
Enochdhu . . . . 133 C7
Ensay . . . . . . . 146 G6
Ensbury . . . . . . . 13 E8
Ensdon . . . . . . . 60 C4
Ensis . . . . . . . . . 9 B7
Enstone . . . . . . . 38 B3
Enterkinfoot . . . 113 D8
Enterpen . . . . . 102 D2
Enville . . . . . . . . 62 F2
Eolaigearraidh . 148 H2
Eorabus . . . . . 146 J6
Eòropaidh . . . . 155 A10
Epperstone . . . . 77 E6
Epping . . . . . . . 41 D7
Epping Green
 Essex . . . . . . . 41 D7
 Herts . . . . . . . 41 D5
Epping Upland . . 41 D7
Eppleby . . . . . . 101 C6
Eppleworth . . . . 97 F6
Epsom . . . . . . . . 28 C3
Epwell . . . . . . . 51 E8
Epworth . . . . . . . 89 D8
Epworth Turbary 89 D8
Erbistock . . . . . 73 E7
Erbusaig . . . . . 149 F12
Erchless Castle . 150 G7
Erdington . . . . . 62 E5
Eredine . . . . . . 125 E5
Eriboll . . . . . . . 156 D7
Ericstane . . . . . 114 C3
Eridge Green . . . 18 B2
Erines . . . . . . . 145 F7
Eriswell . . . . . . . 55 B8
Erith . . . . . . . . . 29 B6
Erlestoke . . . . . . 24 D4
Ermine . . . . . . . . 78 B2
Ermington . . . . . . 6 D4
Erpingham . . . . . 81 D7
Errogie . . . . . . 137 B8
Errol . . . . . . . . 128 B4
Erskine . . . . . . 118 B4
Erskine Bridg. . 118 B4
Ervie . . . . . . . . 104 C4
Erwarton . . . . . . 57 F6
Erwood . . . . . . . 48 E2
Eryholme . . . . . 101 D8
Eryrys . . . . . . . . 73 D6
Escomb . . . . . . 101 B6
Escrick . . . . . . . 96 E2
Esgairdawe . . . . 46 E5
Esgairgeiliog . . . 58 D4
Esh . . . . . . . . 110 E4
Esher . . . . . . . . 28 C2
Esholt . . . . . . . . 94 E4
Eshott . . . . . . . 117 E8
Eshton . . . . . . . 94 D2
Esh Winning . . . 110 E4
Eskadale . . . . . 150 H7
Eskbank . . . . . . 121 C6
Eskdale Green . . 98 D3
Eskdalemuir . . . 115 E5
Eske . . . . . . . . . 97 E6
Eskham . . . . . . . 91 E7
Esk Valley . . . . 103 D6
Esprick . . . . . . . 92 F4
Essendine . . . . . 65 C7
Essendon . . . . . . 41 D5
Essich . . . . . . . 151 H9
Essington . . . . . 62 D3
Esslemont . . . . 141 B8
Eston . . . . . . . 102 C3
Eswick . . . . . . . 160 H6
Etal . . . . . . . . 122 F5
Etchilhampton . . 24 C5
Etchingham . . . . 18 C4
Etchinghill
 Kent . . . . . . . . 19 B8
 Staffs . . . . . . . 62 C4
Ethie Castle . . . 135 E6
Ethie Mains . . . 135 E6
Etling Green . . . 68 C3
Eton . . . . . . . . . 27 B7
Eton Wick . . . . . 27 B7
Etteridge . . . . . 138 E2
Ettersgill . . . . . 100 B3
Ettingshall . . . . . 62 E3
Ettington . . . . . . 51 E7
Etton
 E Yorks . . . . . . 97 E5
 Pboro . . . . . . . 65 D8
Ettrick . . . . . . . 115 C5
Ettrickbridge . . 115 B6
Ettrickhill . . . . . 115 C5
Etwall . . . . . . . . 76 F2
Euston . . . . . . . 56 B2
Euximoor Drove . 66 E4
Euxton . . . . . . . 86 C3
Evanstown . . . . . 34 F3
Evanton . . . . . . 151 E9
Evedon . . . . . . . 78 E3
Evelix . . . . . . . 151 B10
Evenjobb . . . . . . 48 C4
Evenley . . . . . . . 52 F3
Evenlode . . . . . . 38 B2
Evenwood . . . . 101 B6
Evenwood Gate . 101 B6
Everbay . . . . . . 159 F7
Evercreech . . . . . 23 F8
Everdon . . . . . . . 52 D3
Everingham . . . . 96 E4
Everleigh . . . . . . 25 D7
Everley . . . . . . 103 F7
Eversholt . . . . . . 53 F7
Evershot . . . . . . 12 D3
Eversley . . . . . . 27 C5
Eversley Cross . . 27 C5
Everthorpe . . . . . 96 F5
Everton
 C Beds . . . . . . 54 D3
 Hants . . . . . . . 14 E3
 Mers . . . . . . . . 85 E4
 Notts . . . . . . . 89 E7

Evertown . . . . 108 B3
Evesbatch . . . . . 49 E8
Evesham . . . . . . 50 E5
Evington . . . . . . 64 D3
Ewden Village . . 88 E3
Ewell . . . . . . . . 28 C3
Ewell Minnis . . . 31 E6
Ewelme . . . . . . . 39 E6
Ewen . . . . . . . . 37 E7
Ewenny . . . . . . . 21 B8
Ewerby . . . . . . . 78 E4
Ewerby Thorpe . 78 E4
Ewes . . . . . . . 115 E6
Ewesley . . . . . . 117 E6
Ewhurst . . . . . . . 27 E8
Ewhurst Green
 E Sus . . . . . . . 18 C4
 Sur . . . . . . . . . 27 E8
Ewloe . . . . . . . . 73 C7
Ewloe Green . . . 73 C6
Ewood . . . . . . . . 86 B4
Eworthy . . . . . . . 9 E6
Ewshot . . . . . . . 27 E6
Ewyas Harold . . 35 B7
Exbourne . . . . . . 9 D8
Exbury . . . . . . . 14 E5
Exebridge . . . . . 10 B4
Exelby . . . . . . . 101 F7
Exeter . . . . . . . 10 E4
Exford . . . . . . . 21 F7
Exhall . . . . . . . . 51 D6
Exley Head . . . . 94 F3
Exminster . . . . . 10 F4
Exmouth . . . . . . 10 F5
Exnaboe . . . . . 160 M5
Exning . . . . . . . 55 C7
Exton
 Devon . . . . . . . 10 F4
 Hants . . . . . . . 15 B7
 Rutland . . . . . 65 C6
 Som . . . . . . . . 21 F8
Exwick . . . . . . . 10 E4
Eyam . . . . . . . . 76 B2
Eydon . . . . . . . . 52 D3
Eye
 Hereford . . . . . 49 C6
 Pboro . . . . . . . 66 D2
 Suff . . . . . . . . 56 B5
Eye Green . . . . . 66 D2
Eyemouth . . . . 122 C5
Eyeworth . . . . . . 54 E3
Eyhorne Street . . 30 D2
Eyke . . . . . . . . 57 D7
Eynesbury . . . . . 54 D2
Eynort . . . . . . . 149 F8
Eynsford . . . . . . 29 C6
Eynsham . . . . . . 38 D4
Eype . . . . . . . . 12 E2
Eyre
 Highld . . . . . . 149 C9
 Highld . . . . . 149 E10
Eythorne . . . . . . 31 E6
Eyton
 Hereford . . . . . 49 C6
 Shrops . . . . . . 60 F3
 Wrex . . . . . . . . 73 E7
Eyton upon the
 Weald Moors . 61 C6

**F**

Faceby . . . . . . 102 D2
Facit . . . . . . . . . 87 C6
Faddiley . . . . . . 74 D2
Fadmoor . . . . . 102 F4
Faerdre . . . . . . . 33 D7
Failand . . . . . . . 23 B7
Failford . . . . . . 112 B4
Failsworth . . . . . 87 D6
Fain . . . . . . . . 150 D4
Fairbourne . . . . . 58 C3
Fairburn . . . . . . . 89 B5
Fairfield
 Derbys . . . . . . 75 B7
 Stockton . . . . 102 C2
 Worcs . . . . . . . 50 B4
 Worcs . . . . . . . 50 E5
Fair Green . . . . . 67 C6
Fairhaven . . . . . 85 B4
Fair Hill . . . . . . 108 F5
Fairlie . . . . . . . 118 D2
Fairlight . . . . . . 19 D5
Fairlight Cove . . 19 D5
Fairmile . . . . . . 11 E5
Fairmilehead . . 120 C5
Fairoak . . . . . . . 74 F4
Fair Oak . . . . . . 15 C5
Fair Oak Green . 26 C4
Fairseat . . . . . . 29 C7
Fairstead
 Essex . . . . . . . 42 C3
 Norf . . . . . . . . 67 C6
Fairwarp . . . . . . 17 B8
Fairy Cottage . . 84 D4
Fairy Cross . . . . . 9 B6
Fakenham . . . . . 80 E5
Fakenham Magna 56 B3
Fala . . . . . . . . 121 C7
Fala Dam . . . . . 121 C7
Falahill . . . . . . . 121 D6
Falcon . . . . . . . . 49 F8
Faldingworth . . . 90 F4
Falfield . . . . . . . 36 E3
Falkenham . . . . . 57 F6
Falkirk . . . . . . . 119 B8
Falkland . . . . . . 128 D4
Falla . . . . . . . . 116 C3
Fallgate . . . . . . . 76 C3
Fallin . . . . . . . . 127 E7
Fallowfield . . . . . 87 E6
Fallsidehill . . . . 122 E2
Falmer . . . . . . . 17 D7
Falmouth . . . . . . 3 C7
Falsgrave . . . . . 103 F8
Falstone . . . . . 116 F3
Fanagmore . . . . 156 E4
Fangdale Beck . 102 E3
Fangfoss . . . . . . 96 D3
Fankerton . . . . 127 F6
Fanmore . . . . . 146 G7
Fannich Lodge . 150 E5
Fans . . . . . . . . 122 E2
Far Bank . . . . . . 89 C7
Far Bletchley . . . 53 F6
Farcet . . . . . . . . 66 E2
Far Cotton . . . . . 52 D5

Farden . . . . . . . 49 B7
Fareham . . . . . . 15 D6
Farewell . . . . . . 62 C4
Far Forest . . . . . 50 B2
Farforth . . . . . . . 79 B6
Faringdon . . . . . 38 E2
Farington . . . . . . 86 B3
Farlam . . . . . . . 109 D5
Farlary . . . . . . 157 J10
Far Laund . . . . . 76 E3
Farleigh
 N Som . . . . . . 23 C6
 Sur . . . . . . . . . 28 C4
Farleigh
 Hungerford . . 24 D3
Farleigh Wallop . 26 E4
Farlesthorpe . . . 79 B7
Farleton
 Cumb . . . . . . . 99 F7
 Lancs . . . . . . . 93 C5
Farley
 Shrops . . . . . . 60 D3
 Staffs . . . . . . . 75 E7
 Wilts . . . . . . . 14 B3
Farley Green . . . 27 E8
Farley Hill
 Luton . . . . . . . 40 B3
 Wokingham . . 26 C5
Farleys End . . . . 36 C4
Farlington . . . . . 96 C2
Farlow . . . . . . . . 61 F6
Farmborough . . 23 C8
Farmcote
 Glos . . . . . . . . 37 B7
 Shrops . . . . . . 61 E7
Farmington . . . . 37 C8
Farmoor . . . . . . 38 D4
Farmtown . . . . 152 C5
Farnborough
 Hants . . . . . . . 27 D6
 London . . . . . . 28 C5
 Warks . . . . . . . 52 E2
 W Berks . . . . . 38 F4
Farnborough
 Green . . . . . . 27 D6
Farncombe . . . . 27 E7
Farndish . . . . . . 53 C7
Farndon
 Ches W . . . . . . 73 D8
 Notts . . . . . . . 77 D7
Farnell . . . . . . 135 D6
Farnham
 Dorset . . . . . . 13 C7
 Essex . . . . . . . 41 B7
 N Yorks . . . . . 95 C6
 Suff . . . . . . . . 57 C7
 Sur . . . . . . . . . 27 E6
Farnham
 Common . . . . 40 F2
Farnham Green . 41 B7
Farnham Royal . 40 F2
Farnhill . . . . . . 94 E3
Farningham . . . 29 C6
Farnley
 N Yorks . . . . . 94 E5
 W Yorks . . . . . 95 F5
Farnley Tyas . . . 88 C2
Farnsfield . . . . . 77 D6
Farnworth
 Gtr Man . . . . . 86 D5
 Halton . . . . . . 86 F3
Farr
 Highld . . . . . . 138 D4
 Highld . . . . . . 151 H9
 Highld . . . . . 157 C10
Farr House . . . . 151 H9
Farringdon . . . . 10 E5
Farrington
 Gurney . . . . . 23 D8
Far Sawrey . . . . 99 E5
Farsley . . . . . . . 94 F5
Farthinghoe . . . 52 F3
Farthingloe . . . . 31 E6
Farthingstone . . 52 D4
Fartown . . . . . . 88 C2
Farway . . . . . . . 11 E6
Fasag . . . . . . . 149 C13
Fascadale . . . . 147 D8
Faslane Port . . . 145 E11
Fasnacloich . . . 130 E4
Fasnakyle Ho . . 137 B6
Fassfern . . . . . 130 B4
Fatfield . . . . . . 111 D6
Fattahead . . . . 153 C6
Faugh . . . . . . . 108 D5
Fauldhouse . . . 120 C2
Faulkbourne . . . 42 C3
Faulkland . . . . . 24 D2
Fauls . . . . . . . . 74 F2
Faversham . . . . 30 C4
Favillar . . . . . . 152 E2
Fawdington . . . . 95 B7
Fawfieldhead . . 75 C7
Fawkham Green . 29 C6
Fawler . . . . . . . 38 C3
Fawley
 Bucks . . . . . . . 39 F7
 Hants . . . . . . . 15 D5
 W Berks . . . . . 38 F3
Fawley Chapel . . 36 B2
Faxfleet . . . . . . 90 B2
Faygate . . . . . . 28 F3
Fazakerley . . . . 85 E4
Fazeley . . . . . . . 63 D6
Fearby . . . . . . 101 F6
Fearn . . . . . . . 151 D11
Fearnan . . . . . . 132 E4
Fearnbeg . . . . . 149 C12
Fearnhead . . . . . 86 E4
Fearn Lodge . . . 151 C9
Fearnmore . . . . 149 B12
Fearn Station . . 151 D11
Featherstone
 Staffs . . . . . . . 62 D3
 W Yorks . . . . . 88 B5
Featherwood . . 116 D4
Feckenham . . . . 50 C5
Feering . . . . . . . 42 B4
Feetham . . . . . 100 E4
Feizor . . . . . . . . 93 C7
Felbridge . . . . . 28 F4
Felbrigg . . . . . . 81 D8
Felcourt . . . . . . 28 E4
Felden . . . . . . . 40 D3
Felin-Crai . . . . . 34 B2
Felindre
 Carms . . . . . . 33 B6
 Carms . . . . . . 33 B8

Felindre continued
 Carms . . . . . . 46 F2
 Carms . . . . . . 47 F5
 Ceredig . . . . . 46 D4
 Powys . . . . . . 59 F8
 Swansea . . . . 33 D7
Felindre Farchog 45 F3
Felinfach
 Ceredig . . . . . 46 D4
 Powys . . . . . . 48 F2
Felinfoel . . . . . . 33 D6
Felingwmisaf . . 33 B6
Felingwmuchaf . 33 B6
Felinwynt . . . . . 45 D4
Felixkirk . . . . . 102 F2
Felixstowe . . . . . 57 F6
Felixstowe Ferry .57 F7
Felkington . . . . 122 E5
Felkirk . . . . . . . . 88 C4
Felling . . . . . . . 111 C5
Fell Side . . . . . 108 F3
Felmersham . . . 53 D7
Felmingham . . . 81 E8
Felpham . . . . . . 16 E3
Felsham . . . . . . 56 D3
Felsted . . . . . . . 42 B2
Feltham . . . . . . 28 B2
Felthorpe . . . . . 68 C4
Felton
 Hereford . . . . . 49 E7
 Northumb . . . 117 D7
 N Som . . . . . . 23 C7
Felton Butler . . . 60 C3
Feltwell . . . . . . . 67 E7
Fenay Bridge . . . 88 C2
Fence . . . . . . . . 93 F8
Fence Houses . . 111 D6
Fen Ditton . . . . . 55 C5
Fen Drayton . . . 54 C4
Fen End . . . . . . 51 B7
Fengate
 Norf . . . . . . . . 81 E7
 Pboro . . . . . . . 66 E2
Fenham . . . . . . 123 E6
Fenhouses . . . . . 79 E5
Feniscliffe . . . . . 86 B4
Feniscowles . . . 86 B4
Feniton . . . . . . . 11 E6
Fenlake . . . . . . . 53 E8
Fenny Bentley . . 75 D8
Fenny Bridges . . 11 E6
Fenny Compton . 52 D2
Fenny Drayton . . 63 E7
Fenny Stratford . 53 F6
Fenrother . . . . 117 E7
Fen Side . . . . . . 79 D6
Fenstanton . . . . 54 C4
Fenton
 Cambs . . . . . . 54 B4
 Lincs . . . . . . . 77 B8
 Lincs . . . . . . . 77 D8
 Stoke . . . . . . . 75 E5
Fenton Barns . . 129 F7
Fenton Town . . 123 F5
Fenwick
 E Ayrs . . . . . . 118 E4
 Northumb . . . 110 B3
 Northumb . . . 123 E6
 S Yorks . . . . . 89 C6
Feochaig . . . . . 143 G8
Feock . . . . . . . . . 3 C7
Feolin Ferry . . . 144 G3
Ferindonald . . . 149 H11
Feriniquarrie . . 148 C6
Ferlochan . . . . 130 E3
Fern . . . . . . . . 134 C4
Ferndale . . . . . . 34 E4
Ferndown . . . . . 13 D8
Ferness . . . . . . 151 G12
Ferney Green . . . 99 E6
Fernham . . . . . . 38 E2
Fernhill Heath . . 50 D3
Fernhurst . . . . . 16 B2
Fernie . . . . . . . 128 C5
Ferniegair . . . . 119 D7
Fernilea . . . . . . 149 E8
Fernilee . . . . . . . 75 B7
Ferrensby . . . . . 95 C6
Ferring . . . . . . . 16 D4
Ferrybridge . . . . 89 B5
Ferryden . . . . . 135 D7
Ferryhill
 Aberdeen . . . 141 D8
 Durham . . . . . 111 F5
Ferry Hill . . . . . 66 F3
Ferryhill Station . 111 F6
Ferry Point . . . 151 C10
Ferryside . . . . . 32 C4
Fersfield . . . . . . 68 F3
Fersit . . . . . . . 131 B7
Ferwig . . . . . . . 45 E3
Feshiebridge . . 138 D4
Fetcham . . . . . . 28 D2
Fetterangus . . . 153 C9
Fettercairn . . . . 135 B6
Fettes . . . . . . . 151 F8
Fewcott . . . . . . . 39 B5
Fewston . . . . . . 94 D4
F Faccombe . . . . 25 D8
Ffairfach . . . . . . 33 B7
Ffair-Rhos . . . . . 47 C6
Ffaldybrenin . . . 46 E5
Ffarmers . . . . . . 47 E5
Ffawyddog . . . . 35 C6
Fforest . . . . . . . 33 D6
Fforest-fach . . . 33 E7
Ffostrasol . . . . . 46 E2
Ffos-y-ffin . . . . 46 C3
Ffridd-Uchaf . . . 83 F5
Ffrith . . . . . . . . 73 D6
Ffrwd . . . . . . . . 82 F4
Ffynnon ddrain . 33 B5
Ffynnongroyw . . 85 F2
Ffynnon-oer . . . 46 D4
Fidden . . . . . . 146 J6
Fiddes . . . . . . . 141 F7
Fiddington
 Glos . . . . . . . . 50 F4
 Som . . . . . . . . 22 E4
Fiddleford . . . . . 13 C6
Fiddlers Hamlet . 41 D7
Field . . . . . . . . 75 F7
Field Broughton . 99 F5
Field Dalling . . . 81 D6
Field Head . . . . 63 D8
Fifehead
 Magdalen . . . 13 B5
Fifehead Neville . 13 C5

Fifield
 Oxon . . . . . . . 38 C2
 Wilts . . . . . . . 25 D6
 Windsor . . . . . 27 B7
Fifield Bavant . . 13 B8
Fifieldean . . . . . 25 E6
Filands . . . . . . . 37 F6
Filby . . . . . . . . 69 C7
Filey . . . . . . . . 97 A7
Filgrave . . . . . . 53 E6
Filkins . . . . . . . 38 D2
Filleigh
 Devon . . . . . . . 9 B8
 Devon . . . . . . . 10 C2
Fillingham . . . . 90 F3
Fillongley . . . . . 63 F6
Filton . . . . . . . . 23 B8
Fimber . . . . . . . 96 C4
Finavon . . . . . . 134 D4
Finchairn . . . . . 124 E5
Fincham . . . . . . 67 D6
Finchampstead . 27 C5
Finchdean . . . . . 15 C8
Finchingfield . . 55 F7
Finchley . . . . . . 41 E5
Findern . . . . . . . 76 F3
Findhorn . . . . . 151 E13
Findhorn Bridge 138 B4
Findochty . . . . . 152 B4
Findo Gask . . . . 128 B2
Findon
 Aberds . . . . . 141 E8
 W Sus . . . . . . 16 D5
Findon Mains . . 151 E9
Findrack House 140 D5
Finedon . . . . . . 53 B7
Fingal Street . . . 57 C6
Fingask . . . . . . 141 B6
Fingerpost . . . . . 50 B2
Fingest . . . . . . . 39 E7
Finghall . . . . . 101 F6
Fingland
 Cumb . . . . . . 108 D2
 Dumfries . . . . 113 C7
Finglesham . . . . 31 D7
Fingringhoe . . . . 43 B6
Finlarig . . . . . . 132 F2
Finmere . . . . . . 52 F4
Finnart . . . . . . 132 D2
Finningham . . . . 56 C4
Finningley . . . . . 89 E7
Finnygaud . . . . 152 C5
Finsbury . . . . . . 41 F6
Finstall . . . . . . . 50 C4
Finsthwaite . . . . 99 F5
Finstock . . . . . . 38 C3
Finstown . . . . . 159 G4
Fintry
 Aberds . . . . . 153 C7
 Dundee . . . . . 134 F4
 Stirling . . . . . 126 F5
Finzean . . . . . . 140 E5
Fionnphort . . . . 146 J6
Fionnsbhagh . . 154 J5
Firbeck . . . . . . . 89 F6
Firby
 N Yorks . . . . . 96 C3
 N Yorks . . . . . 101 F7
Firgrove . . . . . . 87 C7
Firsby . . . . . . . 79 C7
Firsdown . . . . . . 25 F7
First Coast . . . . 150 B2
Fir Tree . . . . . . 110 F4
Fishbourne
 IoW . . . . . . . . 15 E6
 W Sus . . . . . . 16 D2
Fishburn . . . . . 111 F6
Fishcross . . . . . 127 E7
Fisherford . . . . 153 E6
Fisher Place . . . 99 C5
Fisher's Pond . . 15 B5
Fisherstreet . . . 27 F7
Fisherton
 Highld . . . . . . 151 F10
 S Ayrs . . . . . . 112 C2
Fishguard
 = Abergwaun . 44 B4
Fishlake . . . . . . 89 C7
Fishleigh Barton . 9 B7
Fishponds . . . . . 23 B8
Fishpool . . . . . . 36 B3
Fishtoft . . . . . . . 79 E6
Fishtoft Drove . . 79 E6
Fishtown of
 Usan . . . . . . 135 D7
Fishwick . . . . . 122 D5
Fiskavaig . . . . . 149 E8
Fiskerton
 Lincs . . . . . . . 78 B3
 Notts . . . . . . . 77 D7
Fitling . . . . . . . . 97 F8
Fittleton . . . . . . 25 E6
Fittleworth . . . . 16 C4
Fitton End . . . . . 66 C4
Fitz . . . . . . . . . 60 C4
Fitzhead . . . . . . 11 B6
Fitzwilliam . . . . 88 C5
Fiunary . . . . . . 147 G9
Five Acres . . . . 36 C2
Five Ashes . . . . 18 C2
Fivecrosses . . . . 74 B2
Fivehead . . . . . . 11 B8
Five Oak Green . 29 E7
Five Oaks
 Jersey . . . . . . 17 I3
 W Sus . . . . . . 16 B4
Five Roads . . . . 33 D5
Flack's Green . . 42 C3
Flackwell Heath . 40 F1
Fladbury . . . . . . 50 E4
Fladdabister . . . 160 K6
Flagg . . . . . . . . 75 C8
Flamborough . . 97 B8
Flamstead . . . . . 40 C3
Flamstead End . 41 D6
Flansham . . . . . 16 D3
Flanshaw . . . . . 88 B4
Flasby . . . . . . . 94 D2
Flash . . . . . . . . 75 C7
Flashader . . . . 149 C7
Flask Inn . . . . . 103 D7
Flaunden . . . . . 40 D3
Flawborough . . . 77 E7
Flawith . . . . . . . 95 C7
Flax Bourton . . . 23 C7

Flaxby 95 D6
Flaxholme 76 E3
Flaxley 36 C3
Flaxpool 22 F3
Flaxton 96 C2
Fleckney 64 E3
Flecknoe 52 C3
Fledborough 77 B8
Fleet
  Hants 15 D8
  Hants 27 D6
  Lincs 66 B3
Fleetham 117 B7
Fleet Hargate 66 B3
Fleetlands 15 D6
Fleetville 40 D4
Fleetwood 92 E3
Flemingston 22 B2
Flemington 119 D6
Flempton 56 C2
Fleoideabhagh 154 J5
Fletchertown 108 E2
Fletching 17 B8
Flexbury 8 D4
Flexford 27 E7
Flimby 107 F7
Flimwell 18 B4
Flint = Y Fflint 73 B6
Flintham 77 E7
Flint Mountain 73 B6
Flinton 97 F8
Flintsham 48 D5
Flitcham 80 E3
Flitton 53 F8
Flitwick 53 F8
Flixborough 90 C2
Flixborough
  Stather 90 C2
Flixton
  Gtr Man 86 E5
  N Yorks 97 B6
  Suff 69 F6
Flockton 88 C3
Flodaigh 148 C3
Flodden 122 F5
Flodigarry 149 A9
Flood's Ferry 66 E3
Flookburgh 92 B3
Florden 68 E4
Flore 52 C4
Flotterton 117 D5
Flowton 56 E4
Flush House 88 D2
Flushing
  Aberds 153 D10
  Corn 3 C7
Flyford Flavell 50 D4
Foals Green 57 B6
Fobbing 42 F3
Fochabers 152 C3
Fochriw 35 D5
Fockerby 90 C2
Fodderletter 139 B7
Fodderty 151 F8
Foel 59 C6
Foel-gastell 33 C6
Foffarty 134 E4
Foggathorpe 96 F3
Fogo 122 E3
Fogorig 122 E3
Foindle 156 E4
Folda 134 C1
Fole 75 F7
Foleshill 63 F7
Folke 12 C4
Folkestone 31 F6
Folkingham 78 F3
Folkington 18 E2
Folksworth 65 F8
Folkton 97 B6
Folla Rule 153 E7
Follifoot 95 D6
Folly Gate 9 E7
Fonthill Bishop 24 F4
Fonthill Gifford 24 F4
Fontmell Magna 13 C6
Fontwell 16 D3
Foolow 75 B8
Foots Cray 29 B5
Forbestown 140 C2
Force Mills 99 E5
Forcett 101 C6
Ford
  Argyll 124 E4
  Bucks 39 D7
  Devon 9 B6
  Glos 37 B7
  Northumb 122 F5
  Shrops 60 C4
  Staffs 75 D7
  Wilts 24 B3
  W Sus 16 D3
Fordcombe 29 E6
Fordell 128 F3
Forden 60 D2
Ford End 42 C2
Forder Green 7 C5
Fordham
  Cambs 55 B7
  Essex 43 B5
  Norf 67 E6
Fordhouses 62 D3
Fordingbridge 14 C2
Fordon 97 B6
Fordoun 135 B7
Ford's Green 56 C4
Fordstreet 43 B5
Ford Street 11 C6
Fordwells 38 C3
Fordwich 31 D5
Fordyce 152 B5
Forebridge 62 B3
Forest 109 F8
Forest Becks 93 D7
Forestburn Gate 117 E6
Foresterseat 152 C1
Forest Gate 41 F7
Forest Green 28 E2
Forest Hall 99 D7
Forest Head 109 D5
Forest Hill 39 D5
Forest Lane Head 95 D6
Forest Lodge
  Argyll 131 E6
  Highld 139 C6

Forest Lodge continued
  Perth 133 B6
Forest Mill 127 E8
Forest Row 28 F5
Forestside 15 C8
Forest Town 77 C5
Forfar 134 D4
Forgandenny 128 C2
Forge 58 E4
Forge Side 35 D6
Forgewood 119 D7
Forgie 152 C3
Forglen House 153 C6
Formby 85 D4
Forncett End 68 E4
Forncett St Mary 68 E4
Forncett St Peter 68 E4
Forneth 133 E7
Fornham All
  Saints 56 C2
Fornham
  St Martin 56 C2
Forres 151 F13
Forrestfield 119 C8
Forrest Lodge 113 F5
Forsbrook 75 E6
Forse 158 G4
Forse House 158 G4
Forsinain 157 E12
Forsinard 157 E11
Forsinard
  Station 157 E11
Forston 12 E4
Forteviot 128 C2
Fort George
  Guern 16 I2
  Highld 151 F10
Forth 120 D2
Forthampton 50 F3
Forth Road
  Bridge 120 B4
Fortingall 132 E4
Forton
  Hants 26 E2
  Lancs 92 D4
  Shrops 60 C4
  Som 11 D8
  Staffs 61 B7
Forton Heath 60 C4
Fortrie 153 D6
Fortrose 151 F10
Fortuneswell 12 G4
Fort William 131 B5
Forty Green 40 E2
Forty Hill 41 E6
Forward Green 56 D4
Fosbury 25 D8
Fosdyke 79 F6
Foss 132 D4
Foss Cross 37 D7
Fossebridge 37 C7
Fosterhouses 89 C7
Foster Street 41 D7
Foston
  Derbys 75 F8
  Lincs 77 E8
  N Yorks 96 C2
Foston on the
  Wolds 97 D7
Fotherby 91 E7
Fotheringhay 65 E7
Foubister 159 H6
Foulby 88 C4
Foulden
  Borders 122 D5
  Norf 67 E7
Foulis Castle 151 E8
Foul Mile 18 D3
Foulridge 93 E8
Foulsham 81 E6
Fountainhall 121 E7
Four Ashes
  Staffs 62 F2
  Suff 56 B4
Four Crosses
  Powys 59 D7
  Powys 60 C2
  Wrex 73 D6
Four Elms 29 E5
Four Forks 22 F4
Four Gotes 66 C4
Fourlane Ends 76 D3
Four Lane Ends 74 C2
Four Lanes 3 C5
Fourlanes End 74 D5
Four Marks 26 F4
Four Mile Bridge 82 D2
Four Oaks
  E Sus 19 C5
  W Mid 62 E5
  W Mid 63 F6
Fourpenny 151 B11
Four Roads
  Carms 33 D5
  IoM 84 F2
Fourstones 109 C8
Four Throws 18 C4
Fovant 13 B8
Foveran 141 B8
Fowey 5 D6
Fowley Common 86 E4
Fowlis 134 F3
Fowlis Wester 127 B8
Fowlmere 54 E5
Fownhope 49 F7
Foxbar 118 C4
Foxcombe Hill 38 D4
Fox Corner 27 D7
Foxdale 84 E2
Foxearth 56 E2
Foxfield 98 F4
Foxham 24 B4
Foxhole
  Corn 4 D4
  Swansea 33 E7
Foxholes 97 B6
Foxhunt Green 18 D2
Fox Lane 27 D6
Foxley
  Norf 81 E6
  Wilts 37 F5
Fox Street 43 B6
Foxt 75 E7
Foxton
  Cambs 54 E5
  Durham 102 B1
  Leics 64 E4

Foxup 93 B8
Foxwist Green 74 C3
Foxwood 49 B8
Foy 36 B2
Foyers 137 B7
Fraddam 2 C4
Fraddon 4 D4
Fradley 63 C5
Fradswell 75 F6
Fraisthorpe 97 C7
Framfield 17 B8
Framingham Earl 69 E5
Framingham
  Pigot 69 D5
Framlingham 57 C6
Frampton
  Dorset 12 E4
  Lincs 79 F6
Frampton
  Cotterell 36 F3
Frampton
  Mansell 37 D6
Frampton on
  Severn 36 D4
Frampton West
  End 79 E5
Framsden 57 D5
Framwellgate
  Moor 111 E5
Franche 50 B3
Frankby 85 F3
Frankley 62 F3
Frank's Bridge 48 D3
Frankton 52 B2
Frant 18 B2
Fraserburgh 153 B9
Frating Green 43 B6
Fratton 15 E7
Freathy 5 D8
Freckenham 55 B7
Freckleton 86 B2
Freeby 64 B5
Freehay 75 E7
Freeland 38 C4
Freester 160 H6
Freethorpe 69 D7
Freiston 79 E6
Fremington
  Devon 20 F4
  N Yorks 101 E5
Frenchay 23 B8
Frenchbeer 9 F8
Frenich 126 D3
Frensham 27 E6
Fresgoe 157 C12
Freshfield 85 D3
Freshford 24 C2
Freshwater 14 F4
Freshwater Bay 14 F4
Freshwater East 32 E1
Fressingfield 57 B6
Freston 57 F5
Freswick 158 D5
Fretherne 36 D4
Frettenham 68 C5
Freuchie 128 D4
Freuchies 134 C2
Freystrop 44 D4
Friar's Gate 29 F5
Friarton 128 B3
Friday Bridge 66 D4
Friday Street 18 E3
Fridaythorpe 96 D4
Friern Barnet 41 E5
Friesland 146 F4
Friesthorpe 90 F4
Frieston 78 E2
Frieth 39 E7
Frilford 38 E4
Frilsham 26 B3
Frimley 27 D6
Frimley Green 27 D6
Frindsbury 29 B8
Fring 80 D3
Fringford 39 B6
Frinsted 30 D2
Frinton-on-Sea 43 B8
Friockheim 135 E5
Friog 58 C3
Frisby on the
  Wreake 64 C3
Friskney 79 D7
Friskney Eaudike 79 D7
Friskney Tofts 79 D7
Friston
  E Sus 18 F2
  Suff 57 C8
Fritchley 76 D3
Fritham 14 C3
Frith Bank 79 E6
Frith Common 49 C8
Frithelstock 9 C6
Frithelstock Stone 9 C6
Frithville 79 D6
Frittenden 30 E2
Frittiscombe 7 E6
Fritton
  Norf 68 E5
  Norf 69 D7
Fritwell 39 B5
Frizinghall 94 F4
Frizington 98 C2
Frocester 36 D4
Frodesley 60 D5
Frodingham 90 C2
Frodsham 74 B2
Frogden 116 B3
Froggatt 76 B2
Froghall 75 E7
Frogmore
  Devon 7 E5
  Hants 27 D6
Frognall 65 C8
Frogshail 81 D8
Frolesworth 64 E2
Frome 24 E2
Frome St Quentin 12 D3
Fromes Hill 49 E8
Fron
  Denb 72 C4
  Gwyn 70 D4
  Gwyn 82 F5
  Powys 48 C2
  Powys 59 E8
  Powys 60 D2
Froncysyllte 73 E6
Frongoch 72 F3
Frostenden 69 F7

Frosterley 110 F3
Frotoft 159 F5
Froxfield 25 C7
Froxfield Green 15 B8
Froyle 27 E5
Fryerning 42 D2
Fryton 96 B2
Fulbeck 78 D2
Fulbourn 55 D6
Fulbrook 38 C2
Fulford
  Som 11 B7
  Staffs 75 F6
  York 96 E2
Fulham 28 B3
Fulking 17 C6
Fullarton
  Glasgow 119 C6
  N Ayrs 118 F3
Fuller's Moor 73 D8
Fuller Street 42 C3
Fullerton 25 F8
Fulletby 79 B5
Full Sutton 96 D3
Fullwood 118 D4
Fulmer 40 F2
Fulmodestone 81 D5
Fulnetby 78 B3
Fulstow 91 E7
Fulwell 111 D6
Fulwood
  Lancs 92 F5
  S Yorks 88 F4
Fundenhall 68 E4
Fundenhall
  Street 68 E4
Funtington 15 D8
Funtley 15 D6
Funtullich 127 B6
Funzie 160 D8
Furley 11 D7
Furnace
  Argyll 125 E6
  Carms 33 D6
Furnace End 63 E6
Furneaux Pelham 41 B7
Furness Vale 87 F8
Furzehill 21 E6
Furze Platt 40 F1
Fyfett 11 C7
Fyfield
  Essex 42 D1
  Glos 38 D2
  Hants 25 E7
  Oxon 38 E4
  Wilts 25 C6
Fylingthorpe 103 D7
Fyvie 153 E7

**G**
Gabhsann bho
  Dheas 155 B9
Gabhsann bho
  Thuath 155 B9
Gablon 151 B10
Gabroc Hill 118 D4
Gaddesby 64 C3
Gadebridge 40 D3
Gaer 35 B5
Gaerllwyd 35 E8
Gaerwen 82 D4
Gagingwell 38 B4
Gaick Lodge 138 F3
Gailey 62 C3
Gainford 101 C6
Gainsborough
  Lincs 90 E2
  Suff 57 E5
Gainsford End 55 F8
Gairloch 149 A13
Gairlochy 136 F4
Gairney Bank 128 E3
Gairnshiel
  Lodge 139 D8
Gaisgill 99 D8
Gaitsgill 108 E3
Galashiels 121 F7
Galgate 92 D4
Galhampton 12 B4
Gallaberry 114 F2
Gallachoille 144 E6
Gallanach
  Argyll 124 C4
  Argyll 146 E5
Gallantry Bank 74 D2
Gallatown 128 E4
Galley Common 63 E7
Galleyend 42 D3
Galley Hill 54 C4
Galleywood 42 D3
Gallin 132 E2
Gallowfauld 134 E4
Gallows Green 75 E7
Galltair 149 F13
Galmisdale 146 C7
Galmpton
  Devon 6 E4
  Torbay 7 D6
Galphay 95 B5
Galston 118 F5
Galtrigill 148 C6
Gamblesby 109 F6
Gamesley 87 E8
Gamlingay 54 D3
Gammersgill 101 F5
Gamston 77 B7
Ganarew 36 C2
Ganavan 124 B4
Gang 5 C8
Ganllwyd 71 E8
Gannochy
  Angus 135 B5
  Perth 128 B3
Gansclet 158 F5
Ganstead 97 F7
Ganthorpe 96 B2
Ganton 97 B5
Garbat 150 E7
Garbhallt 125 F6
Garboldisham 68 F3
Garden City 73 C7
Gardenstown 153 B7
Garden Village
  Wrex 73 D7
  W Yorks 95 F7
Garderhouse 160 J5

Gardham 97 E5
Gardin 160 G6
Gare Hill 24 E2
Garelochhead 145 D11
Garford 38 E4
Garforth 95 F7
Gargrave 94 D2
Gargunnock 127 E6
Garlic Street 68 F5
Garlieston 105 E8
Garlinge Green 30 D5
Garlogie 141 D6
Garmond 153 C8
Garmony 147 G9
Garmouth 152 B3
Garn-dolbenmaen 71 C5
Garndiffaith 35 D6
Garnant 33 C7
Garnfadryn 70 D3
Garnkirk 119 C6
Garnlydan 35 C5
Garnswllt 33 D7
Garn-yr-erw 35 C6
Garrabost 155 D10
Garraron 124 E4
Garras 3 D6
Garreg 71 C7
Garrick 127 C7
Garrigill 109 E7
Garriston 101 E6
Garroch 113 F5
Garrogie Lodge 137 C8
Garros 149 B9
Garrow 133 E5
Garryhorn 113 E5
Garsdale 100 F2
Garsdale Head 100 E2
Garsdon 37 F6
Garshall Green 75 F6
Garsington 39 D5
Garstang 92 E4
Garston 86 F2
Garswood 86 E3
Gartcosh 119 C6
Garth
  Bridgend 34 E2
  Gwyn 83 D5
  Powys 47 E8
  Shetland 160 H4
  Wrex 73 E6
Garthamlock 119 C6
Garthbrengy 48 F2
Garthdee 141 D8
Gartheli 46 D4
Garthmyl 59 E8
Garthorpe
  Leics 64 B5
  N Lincs 90 C2
Garth Row 99 E7
Gartly 152 E5
Gartmore 126 E4
Gartnagrenach 144 H6
Gartness
  N Lanark 119 C7
  Stirling 126 F4
Gartocharn 126 F3
Garton 97 F8
Garton-on-
  the-Wolds 97 D5
Gartsherrie 119 C7
Gartymore 157 H13
Garvald 121 B8
Garvamore 137 E8
Garvard 144 D2
Garvault Hotel 157 F10
Garve 150 E6
Garvestone 68 D3
Garvock
  Aberds 135 B7
  Invclyd 118 B2
Garway 36 B1
Garway Hill 35 B8
Gaskan 130 B1
Gastard 24 C3
Gasthorpe 68 F2
Gatcombe 15 F5
Gate Burton 90 F2
Gateford 89 F6
Gateforth 89 B6
Gatehead 118 F3
Gate Helmsley 96 D2
Gatehouse 116 F3
Gatehouse of
  Fleet 106 D3
Gatelawbridge 114 E2
Gateley 81 E5
Gatenby 101 F8
Gateshead 111 C5
Gatesheath 73 C8
Gateside
  Aberds 140 C5
  Angus 134 E4
  E Renf 118 D4
  Fife 128 C3
  N Ayrs 118 D3
Gathurst 86 D3
Gatley 87 F6
Gattonside 121 F8
Gatwick Airport 28 E3
Gaufron 47 C8
Gaulby 64 D3
Gauldry 129 B5
Gaunt's Common 13 D8
Gautby 78 B4
Gavinton 122 D3
Gawber 88 D4
Gawcott 52 F4
Gawsworth 75 C5
Gawthorpe 88 B3
Gawthrop 100 F1
Gawthwaite 98 F4
Gaydon 51 D8
Gayfield 159 C5
Gayhurst 53 E6
Gayle 100 F3
Gayles 101 D6
Gay Street 16 B4
Gayton
  Mers 85 F3
  Norf 67 C7
  Northants 52 D5
  Staffs 62 B3
Gayton le Marsh 91 F8
Gayton le Wold 91 F6

Gayton Thorpe 67 C7
Gaywood 67 B6
Gazeley 55 C8
Geanies House 151 D11
Gearraidh
  Bhaileas 148 F2
Gearraidh
  Bhaird 155 E8
Gearraidh na
  h-Aibhne 154 D7
Gearraidh na
  Monadh 148 G2
Geary 148 B7
Geddes House 151 F11
Gedding 56 D3
Geddington 65 F5
Gedintailor 149 E10
Gedling 77 E6
Gedney 66 B4
Gedney
  Broadgate 66 B4
Gedney Drove
  End 66 B4
Gedney Dyke 66 B4
Gedney Hill 66 C3
Gee Cross 87 E7
Geilston 118 B3
Geirinis 148 D2
Geise 158 D3
Geisiadar 154 D6
Geldeston 69 E6
Gell 83 E8
Gelli
  Pembs 32 C1
  Rhondda 34 E3
Gellideg 34 D4
Gellifor 72 C5
Gelligaer 35 E5
Gellilydan 71 D7
Gellinudd 33 D8
Gellyburn 133 F7
Gellywen 32 B3
Gelston
  Dumfries 106 D4
  Lincs 78 E2
Gembling 97 D7
Gentleshaw 62 C4
Geocrab 154 H6
Georgefield 115 E5
Georgeham 20 F3
George Green 40 F3
George Nympton 10 B2
Georgetown 35 D5
Gerlan 83 E6
Germansweek 9 E6
Germoe 2 D4
Gerrans 3 C7
Gerrards Cross 40 F3
Gestingthorpe 56 F2
Geuffordd 60 C2
Gibbet Hill 64 F2
Gibbshill 106 B4
Gib Hill 74 B3
Gidea Park 41 F8
Gidleigh 9 F8
Giffnock 119 D5
Gifford 121 C8
Giffordland 118 E2
Giffordtown 128 C4
Giggleswick 93 C8
Gilberdyke 90 B2
Gilchriston 121 C7
Gilcrux 107 F8
Gildersome 88 B3
Gildingwells 89 F6
Gileston 22 C2
Gilfach 35 E5
Gilfach Goch 34 F3
Gilfachrheda 46 D3
Gillamoor 102 F4
Gillar's Green 86 E2
Gillen 148 C7
Gilling East 96 B2
Gillingham
  Dorset 13 B6
  Medway 29 C8
  Norf 69 E7
Gilling West 101 D6
Gillock 158 E4
Gillow Heath 75 D5
Gills 158 C5
Gill's Green 18 B4
Gilmanscleuch 115 B6
Gilmerton
  Edin 121 C5
  Perth 127 B7
Gilmonby 100 C4
Gilmorton 64 F2
Gilmourton 119 E6
Gilsland 109 C6
Gilsland Spa 109 C6
Gilston
  Borders 121 D7
  Herts 41 C7
Gilwern 35 C6
Gimingham 81 D8
Giosla 154 E6
Gipping 56 C4
Gipsey Bridge 79 E5
Girdle Toll 118 E3
Girlsta 160 H6
Girsby 102 D1
Girtford 54 D2
Girthon 106 D3
Girton
  Cambs 54 C5
  Notts 77 C8
Girvan 112 E1
Gisburn 93 E8
Gisleham 69 F8
Gislingham 56 B4
Gissing 68 F4
Gittisham 11 E6
Gladestry 48 D4
Gladsmuir 121 B7
Glais 33 D8
Glaisdale 103 D5
Glame 149 D10
Glamis 134 E3
Glan Adda 83 D5
Glanaman 33 C7
Glan Conwy
  Conwy 83 D8
  Conwy 83 B8
Glandford 81 C6
Glan-Duar 46 E4
Glandwr 32 B2
Glan-Dwyfach 71 C5

Glandy Cross 32 B2
Glandyfi 58 E3
Glan Gors 82 D4
Glangrwyney 35 C6
Glanmule 59 E8
Glanrafon 58 F3
Glanrhyd
  Gwyn 70 D3
  Pembs 45 E3
Glan-rhyd 82 F4
Glanton 117 C6
Glanton Pike 117 C6
Glan-traeth 82 D2
Glanvilles
  Wootton 12 D4
Glan-y-don 73 B5
Glan-y-nant 59 F6
Glan-yr-afon
  Anglesey 83 C6
  Gwyn 72 E3
  Gwyn 72 E4
Glan-y-wern 71 D7
Glapthorn 65 E7
Glapwell 76 C4
Glas-allt Shiel 139 F8
Glasbury 48 F3
Glaschoil 151 H13
Glascoed
  Denb 72 B3
  Mon 35 D7
  Powys 59 C8
Glascorrie 140 E2
Glascote 63 D6
Glascwm 48 D3
Glasdrum 130 E4
Glasfryn 72 D3
Glasgow 119 C5
Glashvin 149 B9
Glasinfryn 83 E5
Glasnacardoch 147 B9
Glasnakille 149 G10
Glasphein 148 D6
Glaspwll 58 E4
Glassburn 150 H6
Glasserton 105 F8
Glassford 119 E7
Glasshouse Hill 36 B4
Glasshouses 94 C4
Glasslie 128 D4
Glasson
  Cumb 108 C2
  Lancs 92 D4
Glassonby 109 F5
Glasterlaw 135 D5
Glaston 65 D5
Glastonbury 23 F7
Glatton 65 F8
Glazebrook 86 E4
Glazebury 86 E4
Glazeley 61 F7
Gleadless 88 F4
Gleadsmoss 74 C5
Gleann
  Tholàstaidh 155 C10
Gleaston 92 B2
Gleiniant 59 E6
Glemsford 56 E2
Glen
  Dumfries 106 B5
  Dumfries 106 D2
Glenamachrie 124 C5
Glen Auldyn 84 C4
Glenbarr 143 E7
Glenbeg
  Highld 139 B6
  Highld 147 E8
Glen Bernisdale 149 D9
Glenbervie 141 F6
Glenboig 119 C7
Glenborrodale 147 E9
Glenbranter 125 F7
Glenbreck 114 B3
Glenbrein
  Lodge 137 C7
Glenbrittle
  House 149 F9
Glenbuchat
  Lodge 140 C2
Glenbuck 113 B7
Glenburn 118 C4
Glencalvie
  Lodge 150 C7
Glencanisp
  Lodge 156 G4
Glencaple 107 C6
Glencarron
  Lodge 150 F3
Glencarse 128 B3
Glencassley
  Castle 156 J7
Glenceitlein 131 E5
Glencoe 130 D4
Glencraig 128 E3
Glencripesdale 147 E9
Glencrosh 113 F7
Glendavan
  House 140 D3
Glendevon 127 D8
Glendoebeg 137 D7
Glendoe Lodge 137 D7
Glendoick 128 B4
Glendoll Lodge 134 B2
Glendoune 112 E1
Glenduckie 128 C4
Glendye Lodge 140 F5
Gleneagles
  Hotel 127 C8
Gleneagles
  House 127 D8
Glenegedale 142 C4
Glenelg 149 G13
Glenernie 151 G13
Glenfarg 128 C3
Glenfarquhar
  Lodge 141 F6
Glenferness
  House 151 G12
Glenfeshie
  Lodge 138 E4
Glenfield 64 D2
Glenfinnan 147 C11
Glenfoot 128 C3
Glenfyne Lodge 125 D8
Glengap 106 D3
Glengarnock 118 D3
Glengorm Castle 146 F7
Glengrasco 149 D9
Glenhead Farm 134 C1

Glen Ho 121 F5
Glenhoul 113 F6
Glenhurich 130 C2
Glenkerry 115 C5
Glenkiln 106 B5
Glenkindie 140 C3
Glenlatterach 152 C1
Glenlee 113 F6
Glenlichorn 127 C6
Glenlivet 139 B7
Glenlochsie 133 B7
Glenloig 143 E10
Glenluce 105 D6
Glenmallan 125 E8
Glenmarksie 150 F6
Glenmassan 145 E10
Glenmavis 119 C7
Glenmaye 84 E2
Glenmidge 113 F8
Glen Mona 84 D4
Glenmore
  Argyll 124 D4
  Highld 149 D9
Glenmore
  Lodge 139 D5
Glenmoy 134 C4
Glen Nevis
  House 131 B5
Glenogil 134 C4
Glen Parva 64 E2
Glenprosen
  Lodge 134 C2
Glenprosen
  Village 134 C3
Glenquiech 134 C3
Glenreasdell
  Mains 145 H7
Glenree 143 F10
Glenridding 99 C5
Glenrossal 156 J7
Glenrothes 128 D4
Glensanda 130 E2
Glensaugh 135 B6
Glenshero
  Lodge 137 E8
Glen Sluain 125 F6
Glenstockadale 104 C4
Glenstriven 145 F9
Glentaggart 113 B8
Glen Tanar
  House 140 E3
Glentham 90 E4
Glentirranmuir 127 E5
Glenton 140 B5
Glentress 121 F5
Glentromie
  Lodge 138 E3
Glen Trool
  Lodge 112 F4
Glentrool
  Village 105 B8
Glentruan 84 B4
Glentruim
  House 138 E2
Glentworth 90 F3
Glenuig 147 D9
Glen Village 119 B8
Glenurquhart 151 E10
Glespin 113 B8
Gletness 160 H6
Glewstone 36 B2
Glinton 65 D8
Glooston 64 E4
Glororum 123 F7
Glossop 87 E8
Gloster Hill 117 D8
Gloucester 37 C5
Gloup 160 C7
Glusburn 94 E3
Glutt Lodge 157 F12
Glutton Bridge 75 C7
Glympton 38 B4
Glynarthen 46 E2
Glynbrochan 59 F6
Glyn-Ceiriog 73 F6
Glyncoch 34 E4
Glyncorrwg 34 E2
Glyn-cywarch 71 D7
Glynde 17 D8
Glyndebourne 17 C8
Glyndyfrdwy 72 E5
Glyn Ebwy
  =Ebbw Vale 35 D5
Glynedd
  =Glynneath 34 D2
Glyn-neath
  =Glynedd 34 D2
Glynogwr 34 F3
Glyntaff 34 F4
Glyntawe 34 C2
Gnosall 62 B2
Gnosall Heath 62 B2
Goadby 64 E4
Goadby Marwood 64 B4
Goatacre 25 B5
Goathill 12 C4
Goathland 103 D6
Goathurst 22 F4
Goat Lees 30 E4
Gobernuisgach
  Lodge 156 E7
Gobhaig 154 G5
Gobowen 73 F7
Godalming 27 E7
Godley 87 E7
Godmanchester 54 B3
Godmanstone 12 E4
Godmersham 30 D4
Godney 23 E6
Godolphin Cross 2 C5
Godre'r-graig 34 D1
Godshill
  Hants 14 C2
  IoW 15 F6
Godstone 28 D4
Godwinscroft 14 E2
Goetre 35 D7
Goferydd 82 C2
Goff's Oak 41 D6
Gogar 120 B4
Goginan 58 F3
Golan 71 C6
Golant 5 D6
Golberdon 5 B8
Golborne 86 E4
Golcar 88 C2
Goldcliff 35 F7

Golden Cross 18 D2
Golden Green 29 E7
Golden Grove 33 C6
Goldenhill 75 D5
Golden Pot 26 E5
Golden Valley 37 B6
Golders Green 41 F5
Goldhanger 43 D5
Gold Hill 66 E5
Golding 60 D5
Goldington 53 D8
Goldsborough
  N Yorks 95 D6
  N Yorks 103 C5
Goldsithney 2 C4
Goldsworthy 9 B5
Goldthorpe 89 D5
Gollanfield 151 F11
Gollinglith Foot 101 F6
Golspie 157 J11
Golval 157 C11
Gomeldon 25 F6
Gomersal 88 B3
Gomshall 27 E8
Gonalston 77 E6
Gonfirth 160 G5
Good Easter 42 C2
Gooderstone 67 D7
Goodleigh 20 F5
Goodmanham 96 E4
Goodnestone
  Kent 30 C4
  Kent 31 D6
Goodrich 36 C2
Goodrington 7 D6
Goodshaw 87 B6
Goodwick =Wdig 44 B4
Goodworth
  Clatford 25 E8
Goole 89 B8
Goonbell 3 B6
Goonhavern 4 D2
Goose Eye 94 E3
Goose Green
  Gtr Man 86 D3
  Norf 68 F4
  W Sus 16 C5
Gooseham 8 C4
Goosey 38 E3
Goosnargh 93 F5
Goostrey 74 B4
Gorcott Hill 51 C5
Gord 160 L6
Gordon 122 E2
Gordonbush 157 J11
Gordonsburgh 152 B4
Gordonstoun 152 B1
Gordonstown
  Aberds 152 C5
  Aberds 153 E7
Gore 31 D7
Gorebridge 121 C6
Gore Cross 24 D5
Gorefield 66 C4
Gore Pit 42 C4
Gorey 17 I3
Gorgie 120 B5
Goring 39 F6
Goring-by-Sea 16 D5
Goring Heath 26 B4
Gorleston-
  on-Sea 69 D8
Gornalwood 62 E3
Gorrachie 153 C7
Gorran
  Churchtown 3 B8
Gorran Haven 3 B9
Gorrenberry 115 E7
Gors 46 B5
Gorsedd 73 B5
Gorse Hill 38 F1
Gorseinon 33 E6
Gorseness 159 G5
Gorsgoch 46 D3
Gorslas 33 C6
Gorsley 36 B3
Gorstan 150 E6
Gorstanvorran 130 B2
Gorsteyhill 74 D4
Gorsty Hill 62 B5
Gortantaoid 142 A4
Gorton 87 E6
Gosbeck 57 D5
Gosberton 78 F5
Gosberton
  Clough 65 B8
Gosfield 42 B3
Gosford 49 C7
Gosforth
  Cumb 98 D2
  T&W 110 C5
Gosmore 40 B4
Gosport 15 E7
Gossabrough 160 E7
Gossington 36 D4
Goswick 123 E6
Gotham 76 F5
Gotherington 37 B6
Gott 160 J6
Goudhurst 18 B4
Goulceby 79 B5
Gourdas 153 D7
Gourdon 135 B8
Gourock 118 B2
Govan 119 C5
Govanhill 119 C5
Goveton 7 E5
Govilon 35 C6
Gowanhill 153 B10
Gowdall 89 B7
Gowerton 33 E6
Gowkhall 128 F2
Gowthorpe 96 D3
Goxhill
  E Yorks 97 E7
  N Lincs 90 B5
Goxhill Haven 90 B5
Goytre 34 F1
Grabhair 155 F8
Graby 65 B7
Grade 3 E6
Graffham 16 C3
Grafham
  Cambs 54 C2
  Sur 27 E8
Grafton
  Hereford 49 F6
  N Yorks 95 C7

Grafton *continued*
Oxon 38 D2
Shrops 60 C4
Worcs 49 C7
Grafton Flyford 50 D4
Grafton Regis 53 E5
Grafton Underwood 65 F6
Grafty Green 30 E2
Graianrhyd 73 D6
Graig
Conwy 83 D8
Denb 72 B4
Graig-fechan 72 D5
Grain 30 B2
Grainsby 91 E6
Grainthorpe 91 E7
Grampound 3 B8
Grampound Road 4 D4
Gramsdal 148 C3
Granborough 39 B7
Granby 77 F7
Grandborough 52 C2
Grandtully 133 D6
Grange
Cumb 98 C4
E Ayrs 118 F4
Medway 29 C8
Mers 85 F3
Perth 128 B4
Grange Crossroads 152 C4
Grange Hall 151 E13
Grange Hill 41 E7
Grangemill 76 D2
Grange Moor 88 C3
Grangemouth 127 F8
Grange of Lindores 128 C4
Grange-over-Sands 92 B4
Grangepans 128 F2
Grangetown
Cardiff 22 B3
Redcar 102 B3
Grange Villa 110 D5
Granish 138 C5
Gransmoor 97 D7
Granston 44 B3
Grantchester 54 D5
Grantham 78 F2
Grantley 94 C5
Grantlodge 141 C6
Granton
Dumfries 114 D3
Edin 120 B5
Grantown-on-Spey 139 B6
Grantshouse 122 C4
Grappenhall 86 F4
Grasby 90 D4
Grasmere 99 D5
Grasscroft 87 D7
Grassendale 85 F4
Grassholme 100 B4
Grassington 94 C3
Grassmoor 76 C4
Grassthorpe 77 C7
Grateley 25 E7
Gratwich 75 F7
Graveley
Cambs 54 C3
Herts 41 B5
Gravelly Hill 62 E5
Gravels 60 D3
Graven 160 F6
Graveney 30 C4
Gravesend
Herts 41 B7
Kent 29 B7
Grayingham 90 E3
Grayrigg 99 E7
Grays 29 B7
Grayshott 27 F6
Grayswood 27 F7
Graythorp 102 B3
Grazeley 26 C4
Greasbrough 88 E5
Greasby 85 F3
Great Abington 55 E6
Great Addington 53 B7
Great Alne 51 D6
Great Altcar 85 D4
Great Amwell 41 C6
Great Asby 100 C1
Great Ashfield 56 C3
Great Ayton 102 C3
Great Baddow 42 D3
Great Bardfield 55 F7
Great Barford 54 D2
Great Barr 62 E4
Great Barrington 38 C2
Great Barrow 73 C8
Great Barton 56 C2
Great Barugh 96 B3
Great Bavington 117 F5
Great Bealings 57 E6
Great Bedwyn 25 C7
Great Bentley 43 B7
Great Billing 53 C6
Great Bircham 80 D3
Great Blakenham 56 D5
Great Blencow 108 F4
Great Bolas 61 B6
Great Bookham 28 D2
Great Bourton 52 E2
Great Bowden 64 F4
Great Bradley 55 D7
Great Braxted 42 C4
Great Bricett 56 D4
Great Brickhill 53 F7
Great Bridge 62 E3
Great Bridgeford 62 B2
Great Brington 52 C4
Great Bromley 43 B6
Great Broughton
Cumb 107 F7
N Yorks 102 D3
Great Budworth 74 B3
Great Burdon 101 C8
Great Burgh 28 D3
Great Burstead 42 E2
Great Busby 102 D3
Great Canfield 42 C1
Great Carlton 91 F8
Great Casterton 65 D7
Great Chart 30 E3
Great Chatwell 61 C7
Great Chesterford 55 E6
Great Cheverell 24 D4
Great Chishill 54 F5
Great Clacton 43 C7
Great Cliff 88 C4
Great Clifton 98 B2
Great Coates 91 D6
Great Comberton 50 E4
Great Corby 108 D4
Great Cornard 56 E2
Great Cowden 97 E8
Great Coxwell 38 E2
Great Crakehall 101 E7
Great Cransley 53 B6
Great Cressingham 67 D8
Great Crosby 85 E4
Great Cubley 75 F8
Great Dalby 64 C4
Great Denham 53 E8
Great Doddington 53 C6
Great Dunham 67 C8
Great Dunmow 42 B2
Great Durnford 25 F6
Great Easton
Essex 42 B2
Leics 64 E5
Great Eccleston 92 E4
Great Edstone 103 F5
Great Ellingham 68 E3
Great Elm 24 E2
Greater Doward 36 C2
Great Eversden 54 D4
Great Fencote 101 E7
Great Finborough 56 D4
Greatford 65 C7
Great Fransham 67 C8
Great Gaddesden 40 C3
Greatgate 75 E7
Great Gidding 65 F8
Great Givendale 96 D4
Great Glemham 57 C7
Great Glen 64 E3
Great Gonerby 77 F8
Great Gransden 54 D3
Great Green
Norf 69 F5
Suff 56 D3
Great Habton 96 B3
Great Hale 78 E4
Great Hallingbury 41 C8
Greatham
Hants 27 F5
Hrtlpl 102 B2
W Sus 16 C4
Great Hampden 39 D8
Great Harrowden 53 B6
Great Harwood 93 F7
Great Haseley 39 D6
Great Hatfield 97 E7
Great Haywood 62 B4
Great Heath 63 F7
Great Heck 89 B6
Great Henny 56 F2
Great Hinton 24 D4
Great Hockham 68 E2
Great Holland 43 C8
Great Horkesley 56 F3
Great Hormead 41 B6
Great Horton 94 F4
Great Horwood 53 F5
Great Houghton
S Yorks 88 D5
W Nhants 53 D5
Great Hucklow 75 B8
Great Kelk 97 D7
Great Kimble 39 D8
Great Kingshill 40 E1
Great Langton 101 E7
Great Leighs 42 C3
Great Lever 86 D5
Great Limber 90 D5
Great Linford 53 E6
Great Livermere 56 B2
Great Longstone 76 B2
Great Lumley 111 E5
Great Lyth 60 D4
Great Malvern 50 E2
Great Maplestead 56 F2
Great Marton 92 F3
Great Massingham 80 E3
Great Melton 68 D4
Great Milton 39 D6
Great Missenden 40 D1
Great Mitton 93 F7
Great Mongeham 31 D7
Great Moulton 68 E4
Great Munden 41 B6
Great Musgrave 100 C2
Great Ness 60 C3
Great Notley 42 B3
Great Oakley
Essex 43 B7
N Nhants 65 F5
Great Offley 40 B4
Great Ormside 100 C2
Great Orton 108 D3
Great Ouseburn 95 C7
Great Oxendon 64 F4
Great Oxney Green 42 D2
Great Palgrave 67 C8
Great Parndon 41 D7
Great Paxton 54 C3
Great Plumpton 92 F3
Great Plumstead 69 C6
Great Ponton 78 F2
Great Preston 88 B5
Great Raveley 66 F2
Great Rissington 38 C1
Great Rollright 51 F8
Great Ryburgh 81 E5
Great Ryle 117 C6
Great Ryton 60 D4
Great Saling 42 B3
Great Salkeld 109 F5
Great Sampford 55 F7
Great Sankey 86 F3
Great Saxham 55 C8
Great Shefford 25 B8
Great Shelford 55 D5
Great Smeaton 101 D8
Great Snoring 80 D5
Great Somerford 37 F6
Great Stainton 101 B8
Great Stambridge 42 E4
Great Staughton 54 C2
Great Steeping 79 C7
Great Stonar 31 D7
Greatstone on Sea 19 C7
Great Strickland 99 B7
Great Stukeley 54 B3
Great Sturton 78 B5
Great Sutton
Ches W 73 B7
Shrops 60 F5
Great Swinburne 110 B2
Great Tew 38 B3
Great Tey 42 B4
Great Thurkleby 95 B7
Great Thurlow 55 D7
Great Torrington 9 C6
Great Tosson 117 D6
Great Totham
Essex 42 C4
Essex 42 C4
Great Tows 91 E6
Great Urswick 92 B2
Great Wakering 43 F5
Great Waldingfield 56 E3
Great Walsingham 80 D5
Great Waltham 42 C2
Great Warley 42 E1
Great Washbourne 50 F4
Great Weldon 65 F6
Great Welnetham 56 D2
Great Wenham 56 F4
Great Whittington 110 B3
Great Wigborough 43 C5
Great Wilbraham 55 D6
Great Wishford 25 F5
Great Witcombe 37 C6
Great Witley 50 C2
Great Wolford 51 F7
Greatworth 52 E3
Great Wratting 55 E7
Great Wymondley 41 B5
Great Wyrley 62 D3
Great Wytheford 61 C5
Great Yarmouth 69 D8
Great Yeldham 55 F8
Greave 87 B6
Greeba 84 D3
Green 72 C4
Greenbank 160 C7
Greenburn 120 C2
Greendikes 117 B6
Green End 54 D2
Greenfield
C Beds 53 F8
Flint 73 B5
Gtr Man 87 D7
Highld 136 D5
Oxon 39 E7
Greenford 40 F4
Greengairs 119 B7
Greenham 26 C2
Green Hammerton 95 D7
Greenhaugh 116 F3
Greenhead 109 C6
Greenhill
Falk 119 B8
Kent 31 C5
Leics 63 C8
London 40 F4
Greenhills 118 D3
Greenhithe 29 B6
Greenholm 118 F5
Greenholme 99 D7
Greenhouse 115 B8
Greenhow Hill 94 C4
Greenigoe 159 H5
Greenland 158 D4
Greenlands 39 F7
Green Lane 59 E8
Greenlaw
Aberds 153 C6
Borders 122 E3
Greenlea 107 B7
Greenloaning 127 D7
Greenmount 87 C5
Greenmow 160 L6
Greenock 118 B2
Greenock West 118 B2
Greenodd 99 F5
Green Ore 23 D7
Greenrow 107 D8
Green St Green 29 C5
Greenside 110 C4
Greensidehill 117 C5
Greens Norton 52 E4
Greenstead Green 42 B4
Greensted 41 D8
Green Street 40 E4
Greenwich 28 B4
Greet 50 F5
Greete 49 B7
Greetham
Lincs 79 B6
Rutland 65 C6
Greetland 87 B8
Gregg Hall 99 E6
Gregson Lane 86 B3
Greinetobht 148 A3
Greinton 23 F6
Gremista 160 J6
Grenaby 84 E2
Grendon
N Nhants 53 C6
Warks 63 D6
Grendon Common 63 E6
Grendon Green 49 D7
Grendon Underwood 39 B6
Grenofen 6 B2
Grenoside 88 E4
Greosabhagh 154 H6
Gresford 73 D7
Gresham 81 D7
Greshornish 149 C8
Gressenhall 68 C2
Gressingham 93 C5
Gresty Green 74 D4
Greta Bridge 101 C5
Gretna 108 C3
Gretna Green 108 C3
Gretton
Glos 50 F5
N Nhants 65 E5
Shrops 60 E5
Grewelthorpe 94 B5
Greygarth 94 B4
Grey Green 89 D8
Greynor 33 D6
Greysouthen 98 B2
Greystoke 108 F4
Greystone
Angus 135 E5
Dumfries 107 B6
Greywell 26 D5
Griais 155 C9
Grianan 155 D9
Gribthorpe 96 F3
Gridley Corner 9 E5
Griff 63 F7
Griffithstown 35 E6
Grimbister 159 G4
Grimblethorpe 91 F6
Grimeford Village 86 C4
Grimethorpe 88 D5
Griminis 148 C2
Grimister 160 D6
Grimley 50 C3
Grimness 159 J5
Grimoldby 91 F7
Grimpo 60 B3
Grimsargh 93 F5
Grimsbury 52 E2
Grimsby 91 C6
Grimscote 52 D4
Grimscott 8 D4
Grimsthorpe 65 B7
Grimston
E Yorks 97 F8
Leics 64 B3
Norf 80 E3
York 96 D2
Grimstone 12 E4
Grinacombe Moor 9 E6
Grindale 97 B7
Grindigar 159 H6
Grindiscol 160 K6
Grindle 61 D7
Grindleford 76 B2
Grindleton 93 E7
Grindley 62 B4
Grindley Brook 74 E2
Grindlow 75 B8
Grindon
Northumb 122 E5
Staffs 75 D7
Grindonmoor Gate 75 D7
Gringley on the Hill 89 E8
Grinsdale 108 D3
Grinshill 60 B5
Grinton 101 E5
Griomsidar 155 E8
Grishipoll 146 F4
Grisling Common 17 B8
Gristhorpe 103 F8
Griston 68 E2
Gritley 159 H6
Grittenham 37 F7
Grittleton 37 F5
Grizebeck 98 F4
Grizedale 99 E5
Grobister 159 F7
Groby 64 D2
Groes
Conwy 72 C4
Neath 34 F1
Groes-faen 34 F4
Groesffordd Marli 72 B4
Groeslon
Gwyn 82 E5
Gwyn 82 F4
Groes-lwyd 60 C2
Grogport 143 D9
Gromford 57 D7
Gronant 72 A4
Groombridge 18 B2
Grosmont
Mon 35 B8
N Yorks 103 D6
Groton 56 E3
Grougfoot 120 B3
Grouville 17 I3
Grove
Dorset 12 G5
Kent 31 C6
Notts 77 B7
Oxon 38 E4
Grove Park 28 B5
Grovesend 33 D6
Grove Vale 62 E4
Grudie 150 E6
Gruids 157 J8
Gruinard House 150 B2
Grula 149 F8
Gruline 147 G8
Grunasound 160 K5
Grundisburgh 57 D6
Grunsagill 93 D7
Gruting 160 J4
Grutness 160 N6
Gualachulain 131 E5
Gualin House 156 D6
Guardbridge 129 C6
Guarlford 50 E3
Guay 133 E7
Guestling Green 19 D5
Guestling Thorn 18 D5
Guestwick 81 E6
Guestwick Green 81 E6
Guide 86 B5
Guide Post 117 F8
Guilden Morden 54 E3
Guilden Sutton 73 C8
Guildford 27 E7
Guildtown 133 F8
Guilsborough 52 B4
Guilsfield 60 C2
Guilton 31 D6
Guineaford 20 F4
Guisborough 102 C4
Guiseley 94 E4
Guist 81 E5
Guith 159 E6
Guiting Power 37 B7
Gulberwick 160 K6
Gullane 129 F6
Gulval 2 C3
Gulworthy 6 B2
Gumfreston 32 D2
Gumley 64 E3
Gummow's Shop 4 D3
Gunby
E Yorks 96 F3
Lincs 65 B6
Gundleton 26 F4
Gun Hill 18 D2
Gunn 20 F5
Gunnerside 100 E4
Gunnerton 110 B2
Gunness 90 C2
Gunnislake 6 B2
Gunnista 160 J7
Gunthorpe
Norf 81 D6
Notts 77 E6
Pboro 65 D8
Gunville 15 F5
Gunwalloe 3 D5
Gurnard 15 E5
Gurnett 75 B6
Gurney Slade 23 E8
Gurnos 34 D1
Gussage All Saints 13 C8
Gussage St Michael 13 C7
Guston 31 E7
Gutcher 160 D7
Guthrie 135 D5
Guyhirn 66 D3
Guyhirn Gull 66 D3
Guy's Head 66 B4
Guy's Marsh 13 B6
Guyzance 117 D8
Gwaenysgor 72 A4
Gwalchmai 82 D3
Gwaun-Cae-Gurwen 33 C8
Gwaun-Leision 33 C8
Gwbert 45 E3
Gweek 3 D6
Gwehelog 35 D7
Gwenddwr 48 E2
Gwennap 3 C6
Gwenter 3 E6
Gwernaffield 73 C6
Gwernesney 35 D8
Gwernogle 46 F4
Gwernymynydd 73 C6
Gwersyllt 73 D7
Gwespyr 85 F2
Gwithian 2 B4
Gwredog 82 C4
Gwyddelwern 72 E4
Gwyddgrug 46 F3
Gwydyr Uchaf 83 E7
Gwynfryn 73 D6
Gwystre 48 C2
Gwytherin 83 E8
Gyfelia 73 E7
Gyffi 83 D7
Gyre 159 H4
Gyrn-goch 70 C5

## H

Habberley 60 D3
Habergham 93 F8
Habrough 90 C5
Haceby 78 F3
Hacheston 57 D7
Hackbridge 28 C3
Hackenthorpe 88 F5
Hackford 68 D3
Hackforth 101 E7
Hackland 159 F4
Hackleton 53 D6
Hackness
N Yorks 103 E7
Orkney 159 J4
Hackney 41 F6
Hackthorn 90 F3
Hackthorpe 99 B7
Haconby 65 B8
Hacton 41 F8
Hadden 122 F3
Haddenham
Bucks 39 D7
Cambs 55 B5
Haddington
E Loth 121 B8
Lincs 78 C2
Haddiscoe 69 E7
Haddon
Cambs 65 E8
Ches E 75 C6
Hade Edge 88 D2
Hademore 63 D5
Hadfield 87 E8
Hadham Cross 41 C7
Hadham Ford 41 B7
Hadleigh
Essex 42 F4
Suff 56 E4
Hadley 61 C6
Hadley End 62 B5
Hadlow 29 E7
Hadlow Down 18 C2
Hadnall 60 C5
Hadstock 55 E6
Hady 76 B3
Hadzor 50 C4
Haffenden Quarter 30 E2
Hafod-Dinbych 83 F8
Hafod-Iom 83 D8
Haggate 93 F8
Haggbeck 108 B4
Haggerston 123 E6
Haggrister 160 F5
Hagley
Hereford 49 E7
Worcs 62 F3
Hagworthingham 79 C6
Haigh
Gtr Man 86 D4
S Yorks 88 C3
Haigh Moor 88 B3
Haighton Green 93 F5
Haile 98 D2
Hailes 50 F5
Hailey
Herts 41 C6
Oxon 38 C3
Hailsham 18 E2
Hail Weston 54 C2
Haimer 158 D3
Hainault 41 E7
Hainford 68 C5
Hainton 91 F5
Hairmyres 119 D6
Haisthorpe 97 C7
Hakin 44 E3
Halam 77 D6
Halbeath 128 F3
Halberton 10 C5
Halcro 158 D4
Hale
Gtr Man 87 F5
Halton 86 F2
Hants 14 C2
Hale Bank 86 F2
Halebarns 87 F5
Hales
Norf 69 E6
Staffs 74 F4
Halesfield 61 D7
Halesgate 66 B3
Halesowen 62 F3
Hales Place 30 D5
Hale Street 29 E7
Halesworth 57 B7
Halewood 86 F2
Halford
Shrops 60 F4
Warks 51 E7
Halfpenny Furze 32 C3
Halfpenny Green 62 E2
Halfway
Carms 46 F5
Carms 47 F7
W Berks 26 C2
Halfway Bridge 16 B3
Halfway House 60 C3
Halfway Houses 30 B3
Halifax 87 B8
Halket 118 D4
Halkirk 158 E3
Halkyn 73 B6
Halland 18 D2
Hallaton 64 E4
Hallatrow 23 D8
Hallbankgate 109 D5
Hall Dunnerdale 98 E4
Hallen 36 F2
Hall Green
W Mid 62 F5
W Yorks 88 C4
Hall Grove 41 C5
Halliburton 122 E2
Hallin 148 C7
Halling 29 C8
Hallington
Lincs 91 F7
Northumb 110 B2
Halliwell 86 C5
Hall of Tankerness 159 H6
Hall of the Forest 60 F2
Halloughton 77 D6
Hallow 50 D3
Hallrule 115 C8
Halls 122 B2
Hallsands 7 F6
Hall's Green 41 B5
Hallthwaites 98 F3
Hallworthy 8 F3
Hallyburton House 134 F2
Hallyne 120 E4
Halmer End 74 E4
Halmore 36 D3
Halmyre Mains 120 E4
Halnaker 16 D3
Halsall 85 C4
Halse
Som 11 B6
W Nhants 52 E3
Halsetown 2 C4
Halsham 91 B6
Halsinger 20 F4
Halstead
Essex 56 F2
Kent 29 C5
Leics 64 D4
Halstock 12 D3
Haltham 78 C5
Haltoft End 79 E6
Halton
Bucks 40 C1
Halton 86 F3
Lancs 92 C5
Northumb 110 C2
Wrex 73 F7
W Yorks 95 F6
Halton East 94 D3
Halton Gill 93 B8
Halton Holegate 79 C7
Halton Lea Gate 109 D6
Halton West 93 D8
Haltwhistle 109 C7
Halvergate 69 D7
Halwell 7 D5
Halwill 9 E6
Halwill Junction 9 D6
Ham
Devon 11 D7
Glos 36 E3
Highld 158 C4
Kent 31 D7
London 28 B2
Shetland 160 K1
Wilts 25 C8
Hambleden 39 F7
Hambledon
Hants 15 C7
Sur 27 F7
Hamble-le-Rice 15 D5
Hambleton
Lancs 92 E3
N Yorks 95 F8
Hambridge 11 B8
Hambrook
S Glos 23 B8
W Sus 15 D8
Ham Common 13 B6
Hameringham 79 C6
Hamerton 54 B2
Hametoun 160 K1
Ham Green
Hereford 50 E2
Kent 19 C5
Kent 30 C2
N Som 23 B7
Worcs 50 C5
Hamilton 119 D7
Hammer 27 F6
Hammerpot 16 D4
Hammersmith 28 B3
Hammerwich 62 D4
Hammerwood 28 F5
Hammond Street 41 D6
Hammoon 13 C6
Hamnavoe
Shetland 160 E4
Shetland 160 E6
Shetland 160 F6
Shetland 160 K5
Hampden Park 18 E3
Hamperden End 55 F6
Hampnett 37 C7
Hampole 89 C6
Hampreston 13 E8
Hampstead 41 F5
Hampstead Norreys 26 B3
Hampsthwaite 95 D5
Hampton
London 28 C2
Shrops 61 F7
Worcs 50 E5
Hampton Bishop 49 F7
Hampton Heath 73 E8
Hampton in Arden 63 F6
Hampton Loade 61 F7
Hampton Lovett 50 C3
Hampton Lucy 51 D7
Hampton on the Hill 51 C7
Hampton Poyle 39 C5
Hamrow 80 E5
Hamsey 17 C8
Hamsey Green 28 D4
Hamstall Ridware 62 C5
Hamstead
IoW 14 E5
W Mid 62 E4
Hamstead Marshall 26 C2
Hamsterley
Durham 110 D4
Durham 110 F4
Hamstreet 19 B7
Ham Street 23 F7
Hamworthy 13 E7
Hanbury
Staffs 63 B5
Worcs 50 C4
Hanbury Woodend 63 B5
Hanby 78 F3
Hanchurch 74 E5
Handbridge 73 C8
Handcross 17 B6
Handforth 87 F6
Handley 73 D8
Handsacre 62 C4
Handsworth
S Yorks 88 F5
W Mid 62 E4
Handy Cross 9 B6
Hanford 75 E5
Hanging Langford 24 F5
Hangleton 16 D4
Hanham 23 B8
Hankelow 74 E3
Hankerton 37 E6
Hankham 18 E3
Hanley 75 E5
Hanley Castle 50 E3
Hanley Child 49 C8
Hanley Swan 50 E3
Hanley William 49 C8
Hanlith 94 C2
Hanmer 73 F8
Hannah 79 B8
Hannington
Hants 26 D3
Swindon 38 E1
W Nhants 53 B6
Hannington Wick 38 E1
Hansel Village 118 F3
Hanslope 53 E6
Hanthorpe 65 B7
Hanwell
London 40 F4
Oxon 52 E2
Hanwood 60 D4
Hanworth
London 28 B2
Norf 81 D7
Happendon 119 F8
Happisburgh 69 A6
Happisburgh Common 69 B6
Hapsford 73 B8
Hapton
Lancs 93 F7
Norf 68 E4
Harberton 7 D5
Harbertonford 7 D5
Harbledown 30 D5
Harborne 62 F4
Harborough Magna 52 B2
Harbottle 117 D5
Harbury 51 D8
Harby
Leics 77 F7
Notts 77 B8
Harcombe 11 E6
Harden
W Mid 62 D4
W Yorks 94 F3
Hardenhuish 24 B4
Hardgate 141 D6
Hardham 16 C4
Hardingham 68 D3
Hardingstone 53 D5
Hardington 24 D2
Hardington Mandeville 12 C3
Hardington Marsh 12 D3
Hardley 14 D5
Hardley Street 69 D6
Hardmead 53 E7
Hardrow 100 E3
Hardstoft 76 C4
Hardway
Hants 15 D7
Som 24 F2
Hardwick
Bucks 39 C8
Cambs 54 D4
N Nhants 53 C6
Norf 67 C6
Norf 68 F5
Notts 77 B6
Oxon 38 D3
Oxon 39 B5
W Mid 62 E4
Hardwicke
Glos 36 C4
Glos 37 B6
Hereford 48 E4
Hardy's Green 43 B5
Hareby 79 C6
Hareden 93 D6
Harefield 40 E3
Hare Green 43 B6
Hare Hatch 27 B6
Harehills 95 F6
Harehope 117 B6
Hareseugh 109 E6
Harescombe 37 C5
Haresfield 37 C5
Hareshaw 119 C8
Hareshaw Head 116 F4
Hare Street 41 B6
Harewood 95 E6
Harewood End 36 B2
Harford
Carms 46 E5
Devon 6 D4
Hargate 68 E4
Hargatewall 75 B8
Hargrave
Ches W 73 C8
N Nhants 53 B8
Suff 55 D8
Harker 108 C3
Harkland 160 E6
Harkstead 57 F5
Harlaston 63 C6
Harlaw House 141 B6
Harlaxton 77 F8
Harlech 71 D6
Harlequin 77 F6
Harlescott 60 C5
Harlesden 41 F5
Harleston
Devon 7 E5
Norf 68 F5
Suff 56 D4
Harlestone 52 C5
Harle Syke 93 F8
Harley
Shrops 61 D5
S Yorks 88 E4
Harleyholm 120 F2
Harlington
C Beds 53 F8
London 27 B8
S Yorks 89 D5
Harlosh 149 D7
Harlow 41 C7
Harlow Hill
Northumb 110 C3
N Yorks 95 D5
Harlthorpe 96 F3
Harlton 54 D4
Harman's Cross 13 F7
Harmby 101 F6
Harmer Green 41 C5
Harmer Hill 60 B4
Harmondsworth 27 B8
Harmston 78 C2
Harnham 110 B3
Harnhill 37 D7
Harold Hill 41 E8
Haroldston West 44 D3
Haroldswick 160 B8
Harold Wood 41 E8
Harome 102 F4
Harpenden 40 C4
Harpford 11 E5
Harpham 97 C6
Harpley
Norf 80 E3
Worcs 49 C8
Harpole 52 C4
Harpsdale 158 E3
Harpsden 39 F7
Harpswell 90 F3
Harpurhey 87 D6
Harpur Hill 75 B7
Harraby 108 D4
Harrapool 149 F11
Harrier 160 J1
Harrietfield 127 B8
Harrietsham 30 D2
Harrington
Cumb 98 B1
Lincs 79 B6
N Nhants 64 F4
Harringworth 65 E6
Harris 146 B6
Harrogate 95 D6
Harrold 53 D7
Harrow 40 F4
Harrowbarrow 5 C8
Harrowden 53 E8
Harrowgate Hill 101 C7
Harrow on the Hill 40 F4
Harrow Street 56 F3
Harrow Weald 40 E4
Harston
Cambs 54 D5
Leics 77 F8
Harswell 96 E4
Hart 111 F7
Hartburn
Northumb 117 F6
Stockton 102 C2
Hart Common 86 D4
Hartest 56 D2
Hartfield 29 F5
Hartford
Cambs 54 B3
Ches W 74 B3
Hartfordbridge 27 D5
Hartford End 42 C2
Hartforth 101 D6
Harthill
Ches W 74 D2
N Lanark 120 C2
S Yorks 89 F5
Hart Hill 40 B4
Hartington 75 C8
Hartland 8 B4
Hartlebury 50 B3
Hartlepool 111 F8
Hartley
Cumb 100 D2
Kent 18 B4
Kent 29 C7
Northumb 111 B6
Hartley Westpall 26 D4
Hartley Wintney 27 D5
Hartlip 30 C2
Hartoft End 103 E5
Harton
N Yorks 96 C3
Shrops 60 F4
T&W 111 C6
Hartpury 36 B4
Hartshead 88 B2
Hartshill 63 E7
Hartshorne 63 B7
Hartsop 99 C6
Hart Station 111 F7
Hartwell 53 D5
Hartwood 119 D8
Harvieston 126 F4
Harvington 51 E5
Harvington Cross 51 E5
Harwell 38 F4
Harwich 57 F6
Harwood
Durham 109 F8
Gtr Man 86 C5
Harwood Dale 103 E7
Harworth 89 E7
Hasbury 62 F3
Hascombe 27 E7
Haselbech 52 B5
Haselbury Plucknett 12 C2
Haseley 51 C7
Haselor 51 D6
Hasfield 37 B5
Hasguard 44 E3
Haskayne 85 D4
Hasketon 57 D6
Hasland 76 C3
Haslemere 27 F7
Haslingden 87 B5
Haslingfield 54 D5
Haslington 74 D4
Hassall 74 D4
Hassall Green 74 D4
Hassell Street 30 E4
Hassendean 115 B8
Hassingham 69 D6
Hassocks 17 C6
Hassop 76 B2
Hastigrow 158 D4
Hastingleigh 30 E4
Hastings 18 E5
Hastingwood 41 D7
Hastoe 40 D2
Haswell 111 E6
Haswell Plough 111 E6
Hatch
C Beds 54 E2
Hants 26 D4
Wilts 13 B7
Hatch Beauchamp 11 B8
Hatch End 40 E4
Hatchet Gate 14 D4
Hatch Green 11 C8
Hatching Green 40 C4
Hatchmere 74 B2
Hatcliffe 91 D6
Hatfield
Hereford 49 D7
Herts 41 D5
S Yorks 89 D7
Worcs 50 D3
Hatfield Broad Oak 41 C8
Hatfield Garden Village 41 D5
Hatfield Heath 41 C8
Hatfield Hyde 41 C5
Hatfield Peverel 42 C3
Hatfield Woodhouse 89 D7
Hatford 38 E3
Hatherden 25 D8
Hatherleigh 9 D7
Hathern 63 B8
Hatherop 38 D1
Hathersage 88 F3
Hathershaw 87 D7
Hatherton
Ches E 74 E3
Staffs 62 C3
Hatley St George 54 D3
Hatt 5 C8
Hattingley 26 F4
Hatton
Aberds 153 E10
Derbys 63 B6
Lincs 78 B4
Shrops 60 E4
Warks 51 C7
Warr 86 F3
Hatton Castle 153 D7
Hattoncrook 141 B7
Hatton Heath 73 C8
Hatton of Fintray 141 C7
Haugh
E Ayrs 112 B4
Gtr Man 87 C7
Lincs 79 B7
Haugham 91 F7
Haugh Head 117 B6
Haughley 56 C4
Haughley Green 56 C4

Haugh of Glass . 152 E4
Haugh of Urr . . . 106 C5
Haughs of
  Clinterty . . . . 141 C7
Haughton
  Notts . . . . . . . .77 B6
  Shrops . . . . . . .60 B3
  Shrops . . . . . . .61 C5
  Shrops . . . . . . .61 D7
  Shrops . . . . . . .61 E6
  Staffs . . . . . . . .62 B2
Haughton Castle 110 B2
Haughton Green. .87 E7
Haughton Moss. .74 D2
Haultwick . . . . . .41 B6
Haunn
  Argyll . . . . . . .146 G6
  W Isles . . . . . . .148 G2
Haunton . . . . . . .63 C6
Hauxley . . . . . . .117 D8
Hauxton . . . . . . .54 D5
Havant . . . . . . . .15 D8
Haven. . . . . . . . .49 D6
Haven Bank . . . .78 D5
Haven Side . . . . .91 B5
Havenstreet. . . . .15 E6
Havercroft . . . . . .88 C4
Haverfordwest
  =Hwlffordd . . . .44 D4
Haverhill . . . . . . .55 E7
Haverigg. . . . . . .92 B1
Havering-
  atte-Bower . . . .41 E8
Haveringland. . . .81 E7
Haversham. . . . . .53 E6
Haverthwaite . . . .99 F5
Haverton Hill . . .102 B2
Hawarden
  =Penarlâg . . . .73 C7
Hawcoat . . . . . . .92 B2
Hawen . . . . . . . .46 E2
Hawes . . . . . . . .100 F3
Hawes' Green . . .68 E5
Hawes Side . . . . .92 F3
Hawford . . . . . . .50 C3
Hawick . . . . . . .115 C8
Hawkchurch . . . .11 D8
Hawkedon . . . . . .55 D8
Hawkenbury
  Kent . . . . . . . .18 B2
  Kent . . . . . . . .30 E2
Hawkeridge . . . . .24 D3
Hawkerland . . . . .11 F5
Hawkesbury
  S Glos . . . . . . .36 F4
  Warks . . . . . . .63 F7
Hawkesbury
  Upton. . . . . . .36 F4
Hawkes End . . . . .63 F7
Hawk Green . . . . .87 F7
Hawkhill . . . . . . .117 C8
Hawkhurst . . . . . .18 B4
Hawkinge . . . . . . .31 F6
Hawkley . . . . . . .15 B8
Hawkridge . . . . . .21 F7
Hawkshead . . . . .99 E5
Hawkshead Hill. .99 E5
Hawksland . . . . .119 F8
Hawkswick. . . . . .94 B2
Hawksworth
  Notts . . . . . . . .77 E7
  W Yorks . . . . . .94 E4
  W Yorks . . . . . .95 F5
Hawkwell . . . . . . .42 E4
Hawley
  Hants . . . . . . .27 D6
  Kent . . . . . . . .29 B6
Hawling. . . . . . . .37 B7
Hawnby . . . . . . .102 F3
Haworth . . . . . . .94 F3
Hawstead . . . . . .56 D2
Hawthorn
  Durham . . . . . .111 E7
  Rhondda . . . . .35 F5
  Wilts . . . . . . . .24 C3
Hawthorn Hill
  Brack . . . . . . . .27 B6
  Lincs . . . . . . . .78 D5
Hawthorpe . . . . .65 B7
Hawton . . . . . . . .77 D7
Haxby . . . . . . . . .96 D2
Haxey . . . . . . . . .89 D8
Haydock . . . . . . .86 E3
Haydon . . . . . . . .12 C4
Haydon Bridge . 109 C8
Haydon Wick . . . .37 F8
Haye . . . . . . . . . . .5 C8
Hayes
  London . . . . . .28 C5
  London . . . . . .40 E4
Hayfield
  Derbys . . . . . . .87 F8
  Fife . . . . . . . .128 E4
Hay Green. . . . . .66 C5
Hayhill . . . . . . . .112 C4
Hayhillock . . . . .135 E5
Hayle . . . . . . . . . .2 C4
Haynes . . . . . . . .53 E8
Haynes Church
  End . . . . . . . .53 E8
Hay-on-Wye
  =Y Gelli Gandryll. .48 E4
Hayscastle . . . . .44 C4
Hayscastle Cross 44 C4
Hayshead . . . . . .135 E6
Hay Street . . . . . .41 B6
Hayton
  Aberdeen . . . . .141 D8
  Cumb . . . . . . .107 D8
  Cumb . . . . . . .108 D5
  E Yorks . . . . . .96 E4
  Notts . . . . . . .89 F8
Hayton's Bent . . .60 F5
Haytor Vale . . . . . .7 B5
Haywards Heath. .17 B7
Haywood. . . . . . .89 C6
Haywood Oaks . .77 D6
Hazelbank . . . . .119 E8
Hazelbury Bryan. 12 D5
Hazeley . . . . . . . .26 D5
Hazel Grove . . . . .87 F7
Hazelhurst . . . . . .87 D6
Hazelslade . . . . . .62 C4
Hazel Street. . . . .18 B3
Hazelton . . . . . . . .37 C7

Hazelton Walls . 128 B5
Hazelwood. . . . . .76 E3
Hazlemere. . . . . .40 E1
Hazlerigg . . . . . .110 B5
Hazlewood . . . . . .94 D3
Hazon . . . . . . . .117 D7
Heacham . . . . . . .80 D2
Headbourne
  Worthy. . . . . . .26 F2
Headbrook . . . . . .48 D5
Headcorn . . . . . . .30 E2
Headingley. . . . . .95 F5
Headington . . . . .39 D5
Headlam . . . . . . .101 C6
Headless Cross. . .50 C5
Headley
  Hants . . . . . . .26 C3
  Hants . . . . . . .27 F6
  Sur . . . . . . . . .28 D3
Head of Muir . . .127 F7
Headon . . . . . . . .77 B7
Heads Nook . . . .108 D4
Heage . . . . . . . . .76 D3
Healaugh
  N Yorks . . . . . .95 E7
  N Yorks . . . . . .101 E5
Heale
  Devon . . . . . . .20 E5
  Som. . . . . . . . .23 E8
Healey
  Gtr Man. . . . . .87 C6
  Northumb . . . . .110 D3
  N Yorks . . . . . .101 F6
Healing . . . . . . . .91 C6
Heamoor. . . . . . . .2 C3
Heanish . . . . . . .146 G3
Heanor . . . . . . . .76 E4
Heanton
  Punchardon. . . .20 F4
Heapham . . . . . . .90 F2
Hearthstane . . . .114 B4
Heasley Mill . . . . .21 F6
Heast . . . . . . . . .149 G11
Heath
  Cardiff. . . . . . .22 B3
  Derbys . . . . . . .76 C4
Heath and Reach .40 B2
Heathcote . . . . . .75 C8
Heath End
  Hants . . . . . . .26 C3
  Sur . . . . . . . . .27 E6
  Warks . . . . . . .51 C7
Heather . . . . . . . .63 C7
Heatherfield . . . .149 D9
Heathfield
  Devon . . . . . . . .7 B6
  E Sus. . . . . . . .18 C2
  Som. . . . . . . . .11 B6
Heath Hayes . . . . .62 C4
Heath Hill . . . . . . .61 C7
Heath House . . . .23 E6
Heathrow Airport.27 B8
Heathstock . . . . .11 D7
Heathton . . . . . . .62 E2
Heath Town . . . . .62 E3
Heatley . . . . . . . .86 F5
Heaton
  Lancs . . . . . . .92 C4
  Staffs . . . . . . .75 C6
  T&W . . . . . . .111 C5
  W Yorks . . . . . .94 F4
Heaton Moor . . . .87 E6
Heaverham . . . . .29 D6
Heaviley . . . . . . . .87 F7
Heavitree . . . . . . .10 E4
Hebburn . . . . . . .111 C6
Hebden . . . . . . . .94 C3
Hebden Bridge . . .87 B7
Hebron
  Anglesey . . . . .82 C4
  Carms. . . . . . .32 B2
  Northumb . . . . .117 F7
Heck. . . . . . . . . .114 F3
Heckfield . . . . . . .26 C5
Heckfield Green. .57 B5
Heckfordbridge . . .43 B5
Heckington . . . . . .78 E4
Heckmondwike. . .88 B3
Heddington . . . . .24 C4
Heddle . . . . . . . .159 G4
Heddon-on-
  the-Wall . . . . .110 C4
Hedenham . . . . . .69 E6
Hedge End . . . . . .15 C5
Hedgerley. . . . . . .40 F2
Hedging . . . . . . . .11 B8
Hedley on
  the Hill . . . . . .110 D3
Hednesford . . . . .62 C4
Hedon . . . . . . . . .91 B5
Hedsor. . . . . . . . .40 F2
Hedworth . . . . . .111 C6
Hegdon Hill . . . . .49 D7
Heggerscales . . .100 C3
Heglibister . . . . .160 H5
Heighington
  Darl. . . . . . . . .101 B7
  Lincs . . . . . . . .78 C3
Heights of Brae. 151 E8
Heights of
  Kinlochewe . . .150 E3
Heilam . . . . . . . .156 C7
Heiton . . . . . . . .122 F3
Hele
  Devon . . . . . . .10 C4
  Devon . . . . . . .20 E4
Helensburgh . . . .145 E11
Helford . . . . . . . . .3 D6
Helford Passage. . .3 D6
Helhoughton. . . . .80 E4
Helions
  Bumpstead . . . .55 E7
Hellaby . . . . . . . .89 E6
Helland . . . . . . . . .5 C5
Hellesdon . . . . . .68 C5
Hellidon . . . . . . . .52 D3
Hellifield . . . . . . .93 D8
Hellingly . . . . . . .18 D2
Hellington . . . . . .69 D6
Hellister . . . . . . .160 J5
Helm . . . . . . . . . .117 F7
Helmdon . . . . . . .52 E3
Helmingham . . . . .57 D5
Helmington Row 110 F4

Helmshore . . . . . .87 B5
Helmsley. . . . . . .102 F4
Helperby . . . . . . .95 C7
Helperthorpe . . . .97 B5
Helpringham . . . . .78 E4
Helpston . . . . . . .65 D8
Helsby . . . . . . . . .73 B8
Helsey . . . . . . . . .79 B8
Helston . . . . . . . . .3 D5
Helstone . . . . . . . .8 F2
Helton . . . . . . . . .99 B7
Helwith Bridge . .93 C8
Hemblington . . . .69 C6
Hemel
  Hempstead. . . .40 D3
Hemingbrough. . .96 F2
Hemingby . . . . . .78 B5
Hemingford
  Abbots . . . . . .54 B3
  Hemingford Grey.54 B3
Hemingstone. . . .57 D5
Hemington
  Leics . . . . . . . .63 B8
  N Nhants . . . . .65 F7
  Som. . . . . . . . .24 D2
Hemley. . . . . . . . .57 E6
Hemlington . . . . .102 C3
Hemp Green . . . . .57 C7
Hempholme. . . . . .97 D6
Hempnall . . . . . . .68 E5
Hempnall Green. .68 E5
Hempriggs
  House. . . . . . .158 F5
Hempstead
  Essex . . . . . . . .55 F7
  Medway . . . . . .29 C8
  Norf . . . . . . . .69 B7
  Norf . . . . . . . .81 D7
Hempsted. . . . . . .37 C5
Hempton
  Norf . . . . . . . .80 E5
  Oxon . . . . . . .52 F2
Hemsby . . . . . . . .69 C7
Hemswell . . . . . . .90 F3
Hemswell Cliff. . .90 F3
Hemsworth . . . . .88 C5
Hemyock . . . . . . .11 C6
Henbury
  Bristol. . . . . . .23 B7
  Ches E. . . . . . .75 B5
Hendon
  London . . . . . .41 F5
  T&W . . . . . . .111 D7
Hendre . . . . . . . .73 C5
Hendre-ddu . . . . .83 E8
Hendreforgan . . . .34 F3
Hendy . . . . . . . . .33 D6
Heneglwys . . . . . .82 D4
Hen-feddau fawr.45 F4
Henfield . . . . . . . .17 C6
Henford . . . . . . . . .9 E5
Henghurst . . . . . .19 B6
Hengoed
  Caerph . . . . . .35 E5
  Powys . . . . . . .48 D4
  Shrops . . . . . . .73 F6
Hengrave . . . . . . .56 C2
Henham . . . . . . . .41 B8
Heniarth . . . . . . .59 D8
Henlade . . . . . . . .11 B7
Henley
  Shrops . . . . . . .49 B7
  Som. . . . . . . . .23 F6
  Suff. . . . . . . . .57 D5
  W Sus . . . . . . .16 B2
Henley-in-Arden .51 C6
Henley-on-
  Thames . . . . .39 F7
Henley's Down . .18 D4
Henllan
  Ceredig . . . . . .46 E2
  Denb . . . . . . . .72 C4
Henllan Amgoed .32 B2
Henllys . . . . . . . .35 E6
Henlow . . . . . . . .54 F2
Hennock . . . . . . .10 F3
Henny Street . . . .56 F2
Henryd . . . . . . . . .83 D7
Henry's Moat. . . .32 B1
Hensall . . . . . . . .89 B6
Henshaw . . . . . . .109 C7
Hensingham . . . . .98 C1
Henstead . . . . . . .69 F7
Henstridge. . . . . .12 C5
Henstridge Ash. . .12 B5
Henstridge Marsh 12 B5
Henton
  Oxon . . . . . . .39 D7
  Som. . . . . . . . .23 E6
Henwood . . . . . . . .5 B7
Heogan . . . . . . . .160 J6
Heol-las . . . . . . . .33 E7
Heol Senni . . . . . .34 B3
Heol-y-Cyw . . . . .34 F3
Hepburn . . . . . . .117 B6
Hepple . . . . . . . .117 D5
Hepscott . . . . . . .117 F8
Heptonstall . . . . .87 B7
Hepworth
  Suff. . . . . . . . .56 B3
  W Yorks . . . . . .88 D2
Herbrandston. . . .44 E3
Hereford. . . . . . . .49 E7
Heriot . . . . . . . . .121 D6
Hermiston . . . . . .120 B4
Hermitage
  Borders. . . . . .115 E8
  Dorset. . . . . . .12 E4
  W Berks . . . . . .26 B3
  W Sus . . . . . . .15 D8
Hermon
  Anglesey . . . . .82 E3
  Carms. . . . . . .33 B7
  Carms. . . . . . .45 F4
  Pembs . . . . . . .45 F3
Herne . . . . . . . . .31 C5
Herne Bay. . . . . . .31 C5
Herner . . . . . . . . . .9 B7
Hernhill . . . . . . . .30 C4
Herodsfoot . . . . . .5 C7
Herongate . . . . . .42 E2
Heronsford . . . . .104 A5
Herriard . . . . . . . .26 E4
Herringfleet. . . . .69 E7
Herringswell . . . .55 B8
Herrington . . . . . .111 D6
Hersham
  Corn . . . . . . . . .8 D4

Hersham *continued*
  Sur . . . . . . . . .28 C2
Herstmonceux . . .18 D3
Herston. . . . . . . .159 J5
Hertford . . . . . . . .41 C6
Hertford Heath. . .41 C6
Hertingfordbury. .41 C6
Hesket
  Newmarket . . . .108 F3
Heskin Green . . . .86 C3
Hesleden . . . . . . .111 F7
Hesleyside . . . . . .116 F4
Heslington . . . . . .96 D2
Hessay . . . . . . . . .95 D8
Hessenford . . . . . .5 D8
Hessett . . . . . . . .56 C3
Hessle . . . . . . . . .90 B4
Hest Bank . . . . . .92 C4
Heston. . . . . . . . .28 B2
Hestwall . . . . . . .159 G3
Heswall . . . . . . . .85 F3
Hethe . . . . . . . . .39 B5
Hethersett . . . . . .68 D4
Hethersgill . . . . .108 C4
Hethpool . . . . . . .116 B4
Hett . . . . . . . . . .111 F5
Hetton . . . . . . . . .94 D2
Hetton-le-Hole . .111 E6
Hetton Steads . . .123 F6
Heugh . . . . . . . . .110 B3
Heugh-head . . . .140 C2
Heveningham. . . .57 B7
Hever . . . . . . . . . .29 E5
Heversham. . . . . .99 F6
Hevingham. . . . . .81 E7
Hewas Water. . . . . .3 B8
Hewelsfield . . . . .36 D2
Hewish
  N Som . . . . . . .23 C6
  Som. . . . . . . . .12 D2
Heworth . . . . . . .96 D2
Hexham . . . . . . .110 C2
Hextable . . . . . . .29 B6
Hexton . . . . . . . . .54 F2
Hexworthy . . . . . . .6 B4
Hey . . . . . . . . . . .93 E8
Heybridge
  Essex . . . . . . . .42 D4
  Essex . . . . . . . .42 E2
Heybridge Basin. 42 D4
Heybrook Bay. . . . .6 E3
Heydon
  Cambs . . . . . . .54 E5
  Norf . . . . . . . .81 E7
Heydour . . . . . . . .78 F3
Heylipol . . . . . . .146 G2
Heylor . . . . . . . .160 E4
Heysham . . . . . . .92 C4
Heyshott. . . . . . . .16 C2
Heyside . . . . . . . .87 D7
Heytesbury . . . . . .24 E4
Heythrop . . . . . . .38 B3
Heywood
  Gtr Man. . . . . .87 C6
  Wilts . . . . . . . .24 D3
Hibaldstow. . . . . .90 D3
Hickleton . . . . . . .89 D5
Hickling
  Norf . . . . . . . .69 B7
  Notts . . . . . . . .64 B3
Hickling Green . . .69 B7
Hickling Heath . . .69 B7
Hickstead . . . . . . .17 B6
Hidcote Boyce. . . .51 E6
High Ackworth . . .88 C5
Higham
  Derbys . . . . . . .76 D3
  Kent . . . . . . . .29 B8
  Lancs . . . . . . . .93 F8
  Suff. . . . . . . . .55 C8
  Suff. . . . . . . . .56 F4
Higham Dykes . . 110 B4
Higham Ferrers . .53 C7
Higham Gobion . .54 F2
Higham on
  the Hill . . . . . .63 E7
Highampton . . . . . .9 D6
Higham Wood . . .29 E6
High Angerton . . .117 F6
High Bankhill. . . .109 E5
High Barnes . . . .111 D6
High Beach . . . . .41 E7
High Bentham . . .93 C6
High Bickington . .9 B8
High Birkwith . . . .93 B7
High Blantyre . . .119 D6
High
  Bonnybridge . .119 B8
High Bradfield . . .88 E3
High Bray . . . . . . .21 F5
Highbridge
  Highld . . . . . . .136 F4
  Som. . . . . . . . .22 E5
Highbrook . . . . . .28 F4
High Brooms . . . .29 E6
High Bullen . . . . . .9 B7
Highburton . . . . . .88 C2
Highbury. . . . . . . .23 E8
High Buston . . . .117 D8
High Callerton . . .110 B4
High Catton . . . . .96 D3
Highclere . . . . . . .26 C2
Highcliffe . . . . . . .14 E3
High Coggs . . . . . .38 D3
High Coniscliffe 101 C7
High Cross
  Hants . . . . . . .15 B8
  Herts . . . . . . . .41 C6
High Easter . . . . .42 C2
High Eggborough.89 B6
High Ellington . .101 F6
Higher Ansty . . . .13 D5
Higher Ashton . . .10 F3
Higher Ballam . . .92 F3
Higher Bartle . . . .92 F5
Higher Boscaswell. 2 C1
Higher
  Burwardsley . . .74 D2
High Ercall . . . . . .61 C5
Higher Clovelly . . .8 B5
Higher End. . . . . .86 D3
Higher
  Kinnerton 73 C7
Higher
  Penwortham. . .86 B3
Higher Town . . . . .2 E4
Higher Walreddon 6 B2

Higher Walton
  Lancs . . . . . . .86 B3
  Warr . . . . . . . .86 F3
Higher Wheelon .86 B4
Higher Whitley . .86 F4
Higher Wincham .74 B3
Higher Wych . . . .73 E8
Hill Head
  Hants . . . . . . .15 D6
  Northumb . . . . .110 C2
Highfield
  E Yorks . . . . . .96 F3
  Gtr Man. . . . . .86 D5
  N Ayrs . . . . . . .118 D3
  Oxon . . . . . . .39 B5
  S Yorks . . . . . .88 F4
  T&W . . . . . . .110 D4
Highfields
  Cambs. . . . . . .54 D4
  Northumb . . . . .123 D5
Hillgarth . . . . . . . .42 B3
Highgate . . . . . . .41 F5
High Grange . . . .110 F4
High Green
  Norf . . . . . . . .68 D4
  S Yorks . . . . . .88 E4
  Worcs . . . . . . .50 E3
High Halden. . . . .19 B5
High Halstow. . . .29 B8
High Ham . . . . . . .23 F6
High Harrington. .98 B2
High Hatton . . . . .61 B6
High Hawsker . . .103 D7
High Hesket. . . . .108 E4
High Hesleden . .111 F7
High Hoyland . . . .88 C3
High Hunsley . . . .97 F5
High Hurstwood. .17 B8
High Hutton . . . . .96 C3
High Ireby . . . . . .108 F2
High Kelling. . . . .81 C7
High Kilburn . . . .95 B8
High Lands . . . . .101 B6
Highlane
  Ches E. . . . . . .75 C5
  Derbys . . . . . . .88 F5
High Lane
  Gtr Man. . . . . .87 F7
  Worcs . . . . . . .49 C8
High Laver . . . . . .41 D8
Highlaws . . . . . . .107 E8
Highleadon . . . . .36 B4
High Legh. . . . . . .86 F5
Highleigh . . . . . . .16 E2
High Leven . . . . .102 C2
Highley . . . . . . . . .61 F7
High Littleton . . . .23 D8
High Lorton . . . . .98 B3
High Marishes . . .96 B4
High Marnham . . .77 B8
High Melton . . . . .89 D6
High Mickley . . . .110 C3
High Mindork . . .106 D4
Highmoor Cross . .39 F7
Highmoor Hill . . . .36 F1
Highnam . . . . . . .36 C4
Highnam Green . .36 B4
High Newton. . . . .99 F6
High Newton-
  by-the-Sea. . .117 B8
High Nibthwaite. .98 F4
High Offley . . . . . .61 B7
High Ongar . . . . . .42 D1
High Onn. . . . . . .62 C2
High Roding . . . . .42 C2
High Row . . . . . .108 F3
High Salvington .16 D5
High Sellafield . . .98 D2
High Shaw . . . . .100 E3
High Spen . . . . . .110 D4
Highsted . . . . . . .30 C3
High Stoop . . . . .110 E3
High Street
  Corn . . . . . . . . .4 D4
  Kent . . . . . . . .18 B4
  Suff. . . . . . . . .56 E2
  Suff. . . . . . . . .57 B8
  Suff. . . . . . . . .57 D8
Highstreet Green 55 F8
High Street
  Green . . . . . . .56 D4
Hightae . . . . . . . .107 B7
High Throston . . .111 F7
Hightown
  Ches E. . . . . . .75 C5
  Mers . . . . . . . .85 D4
Hightown Green. .56 D3
High Toynton . . . .79 C5
High Trewhitt . . .117 D6
High Valleyfield 128 F2
Highway . . . . . . . .24 B5
Highweek . . . . . . . .7 B6
High Westwood 110 D4
Highworth . . . . . .38 E2
High Wray . . . . . . .99 E5
High Wych . . . . . .41 C7
High Wycombe . . .40 E1
Hilborough . . . . . .67 D8
Hilcote . . . . . . . . .76 D4
Hilcott . . . . . . . . .25 D6
Hildenborough . . .29 E6
Hilden Park . . . . .29 E6
Hilderstone . . . . .75 F6
Hilderthorpe . . . .97 C7
Hilfield . . . . . . . . .12 D4
Hilgay . . . . . . . . .67 E6
Hill
  Pembs . . . . . . .32 D2
  S Glos . . . . . . .36 E3
  W Mid . . . . . . .62 E5
Hillam . . . . . . . . .89 B6
Hillbeck . . . . . . .100 C2
Hillborough . . . . .31 C6
Hillbrae
  Aberds . . . . . . .141 B6
  Aberds . . . . . . .152 D6
Hill Brow . . . . . . .15 B8
Hillbutts . . . . . . . .13 D7
Hillclifflane . . . . .76 E2
Hillcommon. . . . . .11 B6
Hill Dale . . . . . . .86 C3
Hill Dyke . . . . . . .79 E6
Hillend . . . . . . . .128 F3
Hill End
  Durham . . . . . .110 F3
  Fife . . . . . . . . .128 E2
  N Yorks . . . . . .94 D3
Hillerton . . . . . . . .10 E2
Hillesden . . . . . . .39 B6

Hillesley . . . . . . . .36 F4
Hillfarance . . . . . .11 B6
Hillhead
  Aberds . . . . . . .152 E6
  Devon . . . . . . . .7 D7
  S Ayrs . . . . . . .112 C4
Hillhead of
  Auchentumb . .153 C9
Hillhead of
  Cocklaw . . . . .153 D10
Hillhouse . . . . . . .121 D8
Hilliclay. . . . . . . .158 D3
Hillingdon . . . . . .40 F3
Hillington
  Glasgow . . . . . .118 C5
  Norf . . . . . . . .80 E3
Hillmorton. . . . . . .52 B3
Hill Mountain. . . .44 E4
Hillockhead
  Aberds . . . . . . .140 C3
  Aberds . . . . . . .140 D2
Hill of Beath. . . . .128 E3
Hill of Fearn. . . .151 D11
Hill of
  Mountblairy . .153 C6
Hill Ridware . . . . .62 C4
Hillside
  Aberds . . . . . . .141 E8
  Angus . . . . . . .135 C6
  Mers . . . . . . . .85 C4
  Orkney . . . . . .159 J5
  Shetland . . . . .160 G6
Hillswick . . . . . . .160 F4
Hill Top
  Durham . . . . . .100 B4
  Hants . . . . . . .14 D5
  W Mid . . . . . . .62 E3
  W Yorks . . . . . .88 C4
Hill View . . . . . . .13 E7
Hillway . . . . . . . . .15 F7
Hillwell . . . . . . . .160 M5
Hilmarton . . . . . . .24 B5
Hilperton . . . . . . .24 D3
Hilsea . . . . . . . . . .15 D7
Hilston . . . . . . . . .97 F8
Hilton
  Aberds . . . . . . .153 E9
  Cambs. . . . . . .54 C3
  Cumb . . . . . . .100 B2
  Derbys . . . . . . .76 F2
  Dorset. . . . . . .13 D5
  Durham . . . . . .101 B6
  Highld . . . . . . .151 D10
  Shrops . . . . . . .61 E7
  Stockton . . . . .102 C2
Hilton of
  Cadboll . . . . .151 D11
Himbleton . . . . . .50 D4
Himley . . . . . . . . .62 E2
Hincaster . . . . . . .99 F7
Hinckley . . . . . . . .63 E8
Hinderclay . . . . . .56 B4
Hinderton . . . . . . .73 B7
Hinderwell . . . . .103 C5
Hindford . . . . . . . .73 F7
Hindhead . . . . . . .27 F6
Hindley . . . . . . . . .86 D4
Hindley Green . . .86 D4
Hindlip. . . . . . . . .50 D3
Hindolveston. . . .81 E6
Hindon. . . . . . . . .24 F4
Hindringham . . . .81 D5
Hingham . . . . . . .68 D3
Hinstock . . . . . . .61 B6
Hintlesham . . . . . .56 E4
Hinton
  Hants . . . . . . .14 E3
  Hereford . . . . . .48 F5
  S Glos . . . . . . .24 B2
  Shrops . . . . . . .60 D4
  W Nhants . . . . .52 D3
Hinton Ampner . . .15 B6
Hinton Blewett . . .23 D7
Hinton
  Charterhouse . .24 D2
Hinton-in-
  the-Hedges . . .52 F3
Hinton Martell . . .13 D8
Hinton on
  the Green . . . .50 E5
Hinton Parva . . . .38 F2
Hinton St George.12 C2
Hinton St Mary . .13 C5
Hinton Waldrist . .38 E3
Hints
  Shrops . . . . . . .49 B8
  Staffs . . . . . . .63 D5
Hinwick . . . . . . . .53 C7
Hinxhill . . . . . . . .30 E4
Hinxton . . . . . . . .55 E5
Hinxworth . . . . . .54 E3
Hipperholme. . . . .88 B2
Hipswell . . . . . . .101 E6
Hirael . . . . . . . . . .83 D5
Hiraeth . . . . . . . .32 B2
Hirn . . . . . . . . . .141 D6
Hirnant . . . . . . . . .59 B7
Hirst
  N Lanark . . . . .119 C8
  Northumb . . . .117 F8
Hirst Courtney . . .89 B7
Hirwaen . . . . . . . .72 C5
Hirwaun . . . . . . . .34 D3
Hiscott . . . . . . . . . .9 B7
Histon . . . . . . . . .54 C5
Hitcham . . . . . . . .56 D3
Hither Green. . . . .28 B4
Hittisleigh . . . . . .10 E2
Hive. . . . . . . . . . .96 F4
Hixon . . . . . . . . . .62 B4
Hoaden . . . . . . . .31 D6
Hoaldalbert. . . . . .35 B7
Hoar Cross . . . . . .62 B5
Hoarwithy . . . . . .36 B2
Hoath . . . . . . . . . .31 C6
Hobarris. . . . . . . .48 B5
Hobbister . . . . . .159 H4
Hobkirk . . . . . . . .115 C8
Hobson . . . . . . . .110 D4
Hoby . . . . . . . . . .64 C3
Hockering . . . . . . .68 C3
Hockerton . . . . . .77 D7
Hockley . . . . . . . .42 E4
Hockley Heath . . .51 B6

Hockliffe. . . . . . . .40 B2
Hockwold cum
  Wilton . . . . . . .67 F7
Hockworthy. . . . . .10 C5
Hoddesdon . . . . . .41 D6
Hoddlesden. . . . . .86 B5
Hoddomcross . . .107 B8
Hoddom Mains . .107 B8
Hodgeston. . . . . . .32 E1
Hodley . . . . . . . . .59 E8
Hodnet . . . . . . . . .61 B6
Hodthorpe . . . . . .76 B5
Hoe
  Hants . . . . . . .15 C6
  Norf . . . . . . . .68 C2
Hoe Gate . . . . . . .15 C7
Hoff . . . . . . . . . . .100 C1
Hoggard's Green 56 D2
Hoggeston. . . . . . .39 B8
Hogha
  Gearraidh . . . .148 A2
Hoghton . . . . . . . .86 B4
Hognaston . . . . . .76 D2
Hog Patch. . . . . . .27 E6
Hogsthorpe . . . . .79 B8
Holbeach . . . . . . .66 B3
Holbeach Bank . . .66 B3
Holbeach Clough .66 B3
Holbeach Drove . .66 C3
Holbeach Hurn . . .66 B3
Holbeach
  St Johns . . . . .66 C3
Holbeach
  St Marks . . . . .79 F6
Holbeach
  St Matthew. . . .79 F7
Holbeck
  Notts . . . . . . . .76 B5
  W Yorks . . . . . .95 F5
Holbeck
  Woodhouse . . .76 B5
Holberrow Green 50 D5
Holbeton. . . . . . . .6 D4
Holborn . . . . . . . .41 F6
Holbrook
  Derbys . . . . . . .76 E3
  Suff. . . . . . . . .57 F5
  S Yorks . . . . . .88 F5
Holburn . . . . . . .123 F6
Holbury. . . . . . . . .14 D5
Holcombe
  Devon . . . . . . . .7 B7
  Som. . . . . . . . .23 E8
Holcombe Rogus .11 C5
Holcot . . . . . . . . .53 C5
Holden . . . . . . . . .93 E7
Holdenby . . . . . . .52 C4
Holdenhurst . . . . .14 E2
Holdgate . . . . . . .61 F5
Holdingham . . . . .78 E3
Holditch . . . . . . . .11 D8
Holefield . . . . . . .122 F4
Holehouses . . . . .74 B4
Hole-in-the-Wall.36 B3
Holemoor . . . . . . . .9 D6
Holestane . . . . . .113 E8
Holford . . . . . . . . .22 E3
Holgate . . . . . . . .95 D8
Holker . . . . . . . . .92 B3
Holkham . . . . . . . .80 C4
Hollacombe . . . . . .9 D5
Holland
  Orkney . . . . . .159 C5
  Orkney . . . . . .159 F7
Holland Fen . . . . .78 E5
Holland-on-Sea . .43 C8
Hollandstoun . . .159 C8
Hollee . . . . . . . . .108 C2
Hollesley . . . . . . .57 E7
Hollicombe . . . . . .7 C6
Hollingbourne . . .30 D2
Hollington
  Derbys . . . . . . .76 F2
  E Sus. . . . . . . .18 D4
  Staffs . . . . . . .75 F7
Hollington Grove.76 F2
Hollingworth. . . . .87 E8
Hollins . . . . . . . . .87 D6
Hollinsclough. . . .75 C7
Hollins Green . . . .86 E4
Hollins Lane . . . . .92 D4
Hollinwood
  Gtr Man. . . . . .87 D7
  Shrops . . . . . . .74 F2
Hollocombe . . . . . .9 C8
Holloway . . . . . . . .76 D3
Hollowell . . . . . . .52 B4
Hollow Meadows .88 F3
Hollybush
  Caerph . . . . . .35 D5
  E Ayrs . . . . . . .112 C3
  Worcs . . . . . . .50 F2
Holly End . . . . . . .66 D4
Holly Green . . . . .50 E3
Hollym. . . . . . . . .91 B7
Hollywood . . . . . .51 B5
Holmbridge . . . . .88 D2
Holmbury
  St Mary . . . . . .28 E2
Holmbush. . . . . . . .4 D5
Holmcroft . . . . . . .62 B3
Holme
  Cambs . . . . . . .65 F8
  Cumb . . . . . . .92 B5
  Notts . . . . . . . .77 D8
  N Yorks . . . . . .102 F1
  W Yorks . . . . . .88 D2
Holme Chapel. . . .87 B6
Holme Green. . . . .95 E8
Holme Hale . . . . .67 D8
Holme Lacy. . . . . .49 F7
Holme Marsh . . . .48 D5
Holme next the
  Sea . . . . . . . .80 C3
Holme-on-
  Spalding-Moor.96 F4
Holme on the
  Wolds . . . . . . .97 E5
Holme Pierrepont 77 F6
Holmer . . . . . . . . .49 E7
Holmer Green. . . .40 E2
Holme
  St Cuthbert . . .107 E8
Holmes Chapel . .74 C4
Holmesfield . . . . .76 B3
Holmeswood . . . .86 C2
Holmewood . . . . .76 C4
Holme Wood . . . .94 F4

Holmfirth . . . . . . .88 D2
Holmhead
  Dumfries . . . . .113 F7
  E Ayrs . . . . . . .113 B5
Holmisdale . . . . .148 D6
Holmpton . . . . . . .91 B7
Holmrook . . . . . . .98 E2
Holmsgarth . . . . .160 J6
Holmwrangle . . .108 E5
Holne . . . . . . . . . .6 C5
Holnest . . . . . . . .12 D4
Holsworthy . . . . . .8 D5
Holsworthy
  Beacon . . . . . . .9 D5
Holt
  Dorset. . . . . . .13 D8
  Norf . . . . . . . .81 D6
  Wilts . . . . . . . .24 C3
  Worcs . . . . . . .50 C3
  Wrex . . . . . . . .73 D8
Holtby . . . . . . . . .96 D2
Holt End
  Hants . . . . . . .26 F4
  Worcs . . . . . . .51 C5
Holt Fleet . . . . . . .50 C3
Holt Heath . . . . . .50 C3
Holton
  Oxon . . . . . . .39 D6
  Som. . . . . . . . .12 B4
  Suff. . . . . . . . .57 B7
Holton cum
  Beckering . . . .90 F5
Holton Heath . . . .13 E7
Holton le Clay . . .91 D6
Holton le Moor . . .90 E4
Holton St Mary . .56 F4
Holt Park . . . . . . .95 E5
Holwell
  Dorset. . . . . . .12 C5
  Herts . . . . . . . .54 F2
  Leics . . . . . . . .64 B4
  Oxon . . . . . . .38 D2
Holwick . . . . . . . .100 B4
Holworth . . . . . . .13 F5
Holybourne . . . . .26 E5
Holy Cross . . . . . .50 B4
Holyhead
  =Caergybi. . . . .82 C2
Holy Island . . . . .123 E7
Holymoorside . . . .76 C3
Holyport . . . . . . . .27 B6
Holystone . . . . . .117 D5
Holytown . . . . . . .119 C7
Holywell
  Cambs . . . . . . .54 B4
  Corn . . . . . . . . .4 D2
  Dorset. . . . . . .12 D3
  E Sus. . . . . . . .18 F2
  Northumb . . . .111 B6
Holywell
  =Treffynnon . . .73 B5
Holywell Green . . .87 C8
Holywell Lake . . . .11 B6
Holywell Row . . . .55 B8
Holywood . . . . . .114 F2
Homer . . . . . . . . .61 D6
Homersfield . . . . .69 F5
Hom Green . . . . . .36 B2
Homington . . . . . .14 B2
Honey Hill . . . . . . .30 C5
Honeybourne . . . .51 E6
Honeychurch. . . . . .9 D8
Honey Street . . . .25 C6
Honey Tye . . . . . .56 F3
Honiley . . . . . . . .51 B7
Honing . . . . . . . . .69 B6
Honingham . . . . . .68 C4
Honington
  Lincs . . . . . . . .78 E2
  Suff. . . . . . . . .56 B3
  Warks . . . . . . .51 E7
Honiton . . . . . . . .11 D6
Honley . . . . . . . . .88 C2
Hood Green . . . . .88 D4
Hooe
  E Sus. . . . . . . .18 E3
  Plym . . . . . . . . .6 D3
Hooe Common . . .18 D3
Hoo Green . . . . . .86 F5
Hook
  E Yorks . . . . . .89 B8
  Hants . . . . . . .26 D5
  London . . . . . .28 C2
  Pembs . . . . . . .44 D4
  Wilts . . . . . . . .37 F7
Hooke . . . . . . . . .12 E3
Hookgate . . . . . . .74 F4
Hook Green
  Kent . . . . . . . .18 B3
  Kent . . . . . . . .29 C7
Hook Norton . . . .51 F8
Hookway. . . . . . . .10 E3
Hookwood . . . . . .28 E3
Hoole . . . . . . . . . .73 C8
Hooley . . . . . . . . .28 D3
Hoop. . . . . . . . . . .36 D2
Hoo St Werburgh 29 B8
Hooton . . . . . . . . .73 B7
Hooton Levitt . . . .89 E6
Hooton Pagnell. . .89 D5
Hooton Roberts . .89 E5
Hope
  Derbys . . . . . . .88 F2
  Devon . . . . . . . .6 F4
  Highld . . . . . . .156 D7
  Powys . . . . . . .60 D2
  Shrops . . . . . . .60 D3
  Staffs . . . . . . .75 D8
Hope =Yr Hôb. . . .73 D7
Hope Bagot . . . . .49 B7
Hope End Green . .42 B1
Hopeman . . . . . .152 B1
Hope Mansell . . . .36 C3
Hopesay. . . . . . . .60 F3
Hope's Green . . . .42 F3
Hope under
  Dinmore . . . . .49 D7
Hopley's Green . . .48 D5
Hopperton . . . . . .95 D7
Hopstone . . . . . . .61 E7
Hopton
  Shrops . . . . . . .60 B3
  Shrops . . . . . . .61 B5
  Staffs . . . . . . .62 B3

Hopton *continued*
  Suff. . . . . . . . .56 B3
Hopton
  Cangeford . . . .60 F5
Hopton Castle . . .49 B5
Hoptonheath . . . .49 B5
Hopton on Sea . . .69 D8
Hopton Wafers . . .49 B8
Hopwas . . . . . . . .63 D5
Hopwood . . . . . . .87 D6
Horam . . . . . . . . .18 D2
Horbling . . . . . . . .78 F4
Horbury . . . . . . . .88 C3
Horcott . . . . . . . .38 D1
Horden . . . . . . . .111 E7
Horderley . . . . . . .60 F4
Hordle . . . . . . . . .14 E3
Hordley . . . . . . . .73 F7
Horeb
  Carms . . . . . . .33 B6
  Carms . . . . . . .33 D8
  Ceredig . . . . . .46 E2
Horfield . . . . . . . .23 B8
Horham . . . . . . . .57 B6
Horkesley Heath. .43 B5
Horkstow . . . . . . .90 C3
Horley
  Oxon . . . . . . .52 E2
  Sur . . . . . . . . .28 E3
Hornblotton
  Green . . . . . . .23 F7
Hornby
  Lancs . . . . . . .93 C5
  N Yorks . . . . . .101 E7
  N Yorks . . . . . .102 D1
Horncastle . . . . . .79 C5
Hornchurch . . . . .41 F8
Horncliffe. . . . . . .122 E4
Horndean
  Borders. . . . . .122 E4
  Hants . . . . . . .15 C8
Horndon . . . . . . . .6 B3
Horndon on the
  Hill . . . . . . . .42 F2
Horne. . . . . . . . . .28 E4
Horniehaugh . . . .134 C4
Horning . . . . . . . .69 C6
Horninghold . . . . .64 E5
Horninglow . . . . .63 B6
Horningsea . . . . .55 C5
Horningsham . . . .24 E3
Horningtoft. . . . . .80 E5
Hornsby . . . . . . .108 D5
Horns Corner. . . .18 C4
Horns Cross
  Devon . . . . . . . .9 B5
  E Sus. . . . . . . .18 C5
Hornsea . . . . . . . .97 E8
Hornsea Bridge . .97 E8
Hornsey. . . . . . . .41 F6
Hornton . . . . . . . .51 E8
Horrabridge. . . . . .6 C3
Horringer . . . . . . .56 C2
Horringford. . . . . .15 F6
Horsebridge
  Devon . . . . . . . .6 B2
  Hants . . . . . . .25 F8
Horse Bridge . . . .75 D6
Horsebrook . . . . .62 C2
Horsehay . . . . . . .61 D6
Horseheath . . . . .55 E7
Horsehouse . . . .101 F5
Horsell. . . . . . . . .27 D7
Horseman's
  Green . . . . . . .73 E8
Horseway . . . . . . .66 F4
Horsey. . . . . . . . .69 B7
Horsford . . . . . . .68 C4
Horsforth . . . . . . .94 F5
Horsham
  Worcs . . . . . . .50 D2
  W Sus . . . . . . .28 F2
Horsham St Faith 68 C5
Horsington
  Lincs . . . . . . . .78 C4
  Som. . . . . . . . .12 B5
Horsley
  Derbys . . . . . . .76 E3
  Glos . . . . . . . . .37 E5
  Northumb . . . . .110 C3
  Northumb . . . .116 F4
Horsley Cross . . .43 B7
Horsleycross
  Street. . . . . . .43 B7
Horsleyhill . . . . .115 C8
Horsleyhope . . . .110 E3
Horsley
  Woodhouse . . .76 E3
Horsmonden . . . .29 E7
Horspath . . . . . . .39 D5
Horstead . . . . . . .69 C5
Horsted Keynes . .17 B7
Horton
  Bucks . . . . . . .40 C2
  Dorset. . . . . . .13 D8
  Lancs . . . . . . . .93 D8
  S Glos . . . . . . .36 F4
  Shrops . . . . . . .60 B4
  Som. . . . . . . . .11 C8
  Staffs . . . . . . .75 D6
  Swansea . . . . .33 F5
  Wilts . . . . . . . .25 C5
  Windsor . . . . . .27 B8
  W Nhants . . . . .53 D6
Horton-cum-
  Studley . . . . . .39 C5
Horton Green . . . .73 E8
Horton Heath . . . .15 C5
Horton in
  Ribblesdale . . .93 B8
Horton Kirby . . . .29 C6
Hortonlane . . . . . .60 C4
Horwich . . . . . . . .86 C4
Horwich End . . . . .87 F8
Horwood . . . . . . . .9 B7
Hose. . . . . . . . . . .64 B4
Hoselaw . . . . . . .122 F4
Hoses. . . . . . . . . .98 E4
Hosh . . . . . . . . . .127 B7
Hosta . . . . . . . . .148 A2
Hoswick . . . . . . .160 L6
Hotham . . . . . . . .96 F4
Hothfield . . . . . . .30 E3
Houbie . . . . . . . .160 D8
Houdston . . . . . .112 E1

Hough
Ches E.......74 D4
Ches E.......75 B5
Hougham.......77 E8
Hough Green.......86 F2
Hough-on-the-Hill.......78 E2
Houghton
Cambs.......54 B3
Cumb.......108 D4
Hants.......25 F8
Pembs.......44 E4
W Sus.......16 C4
Houghton Conquest.......53 E8
Houghton Green
E Sus.......19 C6
Warr.......86 E4
Houghton-le-Side.......101 B7
Houghton-le-Spring.......111 E6
Houghton on the Hill.......64 D3
Houghton Regis..40 B3
Houghton St Giles.......80 D5
Houlland
Shetland.......160 F7
Shetland.......160 H5
Houlsyke.......103 D5
Hound.......15 D5
Hound Green.......26 D5
Houndslow.......122 E2
Houndwood.......122 C4
Hounslow.......28 B2
Hounslow Green..42 C2
Housay.......160 F8
House of Daviot.......151 G10
House of Glenmuick..140 E2
Housetter.......160 E5
Houss.......160 K5
Houston.......118 C4
Houstry.......158 G3
Houton.......159 H4
Hove.......17 D6
Hoveringham..77 E6
Hoveton.......69 C6
Hovingham..96 B2
How.......108 D5
Howbrook.......88 E4
How Caple.......49 F8
Howden
Borders.......116 B2
E Yorks.......89 B8
Howden-le-Wear.......110 F4
Howe
Highld.......158 D5
Norf.......69 D5
N Yorks.......101 F8
Howe Bridge..86 D4
Howe Green..42 D3
Howell.......78 E4
How End.......53 E8
Howe of Teuchar.......153 D7
Howe Street
Essex.......42 C2
Essex.......55 F7
Howey.......48 D2
Howgate.......120 D5
How Green.......29 E5
Howick.......117 C8
Howle
Durham.......101 B5
Telford.......61 B6
Howlett End...55 F6
Howley.......11 D7
Hownam.......116 C3
Hownam Mains.116 B3
Howpasley.......115 D6
Howsham
N Lincs.......90 D4
N Yorks.......96 C3
Howslack.......114 D3
Howtel.......122 F4
Howton.......35 B8
Howtown.......99 C6
Howwood.......118 C3
Hoxne.......57 B5
Hoy.......159 H3
Hoylake.......85 F3
Hoyland.......88 D4
Hoylandswaine..88 D3
Hubberston..94 B2
Hubbert's Bridge.79 E5
Huby
N Yorks.......95 C8
N Yorks.......95 B5
Hucclecote.......37 C5
Hucking.......30 D2
Hucknall.......76 E5
Huddersfield.......88 C2
Huddington.......50 D4
Hudswell.......101 D6
Huggate.......96 D4
Hugglescote..63 C8
Hughenden Valley.......40 E1
Hughley.......61 E5
Hugh Town......2 E4
Huish
Devon.......9 C7
Wilts.......25 C6
Huish Champflower...11 B5
Huish Episcopi..12 B2
Huisinis.......154 F4
Hulcott.......40 C1
Hulland.......76 E2
Hulland Ward..76 E2
Hullavington..37 F5
Hullbridge.......42 E4
Hulme.......87 E6
Hulme End.......75 D8
Hulme Walfield..74 C5
Hulverstone..14 F4
Hulver Street...69 F7
Humber.......49 D7
Humber Bridge..90 B4
Humberston..91 D7
Humbie.......121 C7
Humbleton
E Yorks.......97 F8
Northumb.......117 B5

Humby.......78 F3
Hume.......122 E3
Humshaugh.......110 B2
Huna.......158 C5
Huncoat.......93 F7
Huncote.......64 E2
Hundalee.......116 C2
Hunderthwaite.100 B4
Hundle Houses.79 D5
Hundleby.......79 C6
Hundleton.......44 E4
Hundon.......55 E8
Hundred Acres.15 C6
Hundred End.......86 B2
Hundred House.48 D3
Hungarton.......64 D3
Hungerford
Hants.......14 C2
W Berks.......25 C8
Hungerford Newtown.......25 B8
Hungerton.......65 B5
Hungladder..149 A8
Hunmanby.......97 B6
Hunmanby Moor.97 B7
Hunningham..51 C8
Hunny Hill.......15 F5
Hunsdon.......41 C7
Hunsingore..95 D7
Hunslet.......95 F6
Hunsonby.......109 F5
Hunspow.......158 C4
Hunstanton.......80 C2
Hunstanworth.110 E2
Hunsterson..74 E3
Hunston
Suff.......56 C3
W Sus.......16 D2
Hunstrete.......23 C8
Hunt End.......50 C5
Hunter's Quay.145 F10
Hunthill Lodge.134 B4
Huntingdon.......54 B3
Huntingfield..57 B7
Huntingford..24 F3
Huntington
E Loth.......121 B7
Hereford.......48 D4
Staffs.......62 C3
York.......96 D2
Huntingtower.128 B2
Huntley.......36 C4
Huntly.......152 E5
Huntlywood..122 E2
Hunton
Kent.......29 E8
N Yorks.......101 E6
Hunt's Corner..68 F3
Hunt's Cross..86 F2
Huntsham.......10 B5
Huntspill.......22 E5
Huntworth..22 F5
Hunwick.......110 F4
Hunworth.......81 D6
Hurdsfield.......75 B6
Hurley
Warks.......63 E6
Windsor.......39 F8
Hurlford.......118 F4
Hurliness.......159 K3
Hurn.......14 E2
Hurn's End.......79 E7
Hursley.......14 B5
Hurst
N Yorks.......101 D5
Som.......12 C2
Wokingham..27 B5
Hurstbourne Priors.......26 E2
Hurstbourne Tarrant.......25 D8
Hurst Green
E Sus.......18 C4
Lancs.......93 F6
Hurstpierpoint..17 C6
Hurst Wickham..17 C6
Hurstwood..93 F8
Hurtmore.......27 E7
Hurworth Place.......101 D7
Hury.......100 C4
Husabost.......148 C7
Husbands Bosworth..64 F3
Husborne Crawley.......53 F7
Husthwaite..95 B8
Hutchwns.......21 B7
Huthwaite.......76 D4
Huttoft.......79 B8
Hutton
Borders.......122 D5
Cumb.......99 B6
Essex.......42 E2
E Yorks.......97 D6
Lancs.......86 B3
N Som.......22 D5
Hutton Buscel..103 F7
Hutton Conyers..95 B6
Hutton Cranswick..97 D6
Hutton End.......108 F4
Hutton Gate.......102 C3
Hutton Henry..111 F7
Hutton-le-Hole 103 E5
Hutton Magna.101 D6
Hutton Roof
Cumb.......93 B6
Cumb.......108 F3
Hutton Rudby.102 D2
Hutton Sessay..95 B7
Hutton Village.102 C3
Hutton Wandesley.....95 D8
Huxley.......74 C2
Huxter
Shetland.......160 G4
Shetland.......160 H5
Huxton.......122 C4
Huyton.......86 E2
Hycemoor.......98 F2
Hyde
Glos.......37 D5
Gtr Man.......87 E7
Hants.......14 C2
Hyde Heath..40 D2

Hyde Park.......89 D6
Hydestile.......27 E7
Hylton Castle..111 D6
Hyndford Bridge 120 E2
Hynish.......146 H2
Hyssington..60 E3
Hythe
Hants.......14 D5
Kent.......19 B8
Hythe End.......27 B8
Hythie.......153 C10

I
Ibberton.......13 D5
Ible.......76 D2
Ibsley.......14 D2
Ibstock.......63 C8
Ibstone.......39 E7
Ibthorpe.......25 D8
Ibworth.......26 D3
Ichrachan.125 B6
Ickburgh.......67 E8
Ickenham.......40 F3
Ickford.......39 D6
Ickham.......31 D6
Ickleford.......54 F2
Icklesham.......19 D5
Ickleton.......55 E5
Icklingham..55 B8
Ickwell Green..54 E2
Icomb.......38 B2
Idbury.......38 C2
Iddesleigh......9 D7
Ide.......10 E3
Ideford......7 B6
Iden.......19 C6
Iden Green
Kent.......18 B4
Kent.......18 B5
Idle......94 F4
Idlicote.......51 E7
Idmiston.......25 F6
Idole.......33 C5
Idridgehay..76 E2
Idrigill.......149 B8
Idstone.......38 F2
Idvies.......135 E5
Iffley.......39 D5
Ifield.......28 F3
Ifold.......27 F8
Iford.......17 D8
Ifton Heath..73 F7
Ightfield.......74 F2
Ightham.......29 D6
Iken.......57 D8
Ilam.......75 D8
Ilchester.......12 B3
Ilderton.......117 B6
Ilford.......41 F7
Ilfracombe..20 E4
Ilkeston.......76 E4
Ilketshall St Andrew.....69 F6
Ilketshall St Lawrence...69 F6
Ilketshall St Margaret...69 F6
Ilkley.......94 E4
Illey.......62 F3
Illingworth..87 B8
Illogan.......3 B5
Illston on the Hill.64 E4
Ilmer.......39 D7
Ilmington.......51 E7
Ilminster.......11 C8
Ilsington......7 B5
Ilston.......33 E6
Ilton
N Yorks.......94 B4
Som.......11 C8
Imachar.......143 D9
Imeraval.......142 D4
Immingham..91 C5
Impington.......54 C5
Ince.......73 B8
Ince Blundell..85 D4
Ince in Makerfield..86 D3
Inchbare.......135 C6
Inchberry.......152 C3
Inchbraoch..135 D7
Incheril.......150 E3
Inchgrundle..134 B4
Inchina.......150 B2
Inchinnan.......118 C4
Inchkinloch..157 E8
Inchlaggan..136 D4
Inchlumpie..151 D8
Inchmore.......150 G6
Inchnacardoch Hotel.......137 C6
Inchnadamph.156 H5
Inch of Arnhall.135 B6
Inchree.......130 C4
Inchture.......128 B4
Inchyra.......128 B3
Indian Queens.....4 D4
Inerval.......142 D4
Ingatestone.......42 E2
Ingbirchworth.88 D3
Ingestre.......62 B3
Ingham
Lincs.......90 F3
Norf.......69 B6
Suff.......56 B2
Ingham Corner..69 B6
Ingleborough..66 C4
Ingleby
Derbys.......63 B7
Lincs.......77 B8
Ingleby Arncliffe.102 D2
Ingleby Barwick 102 C2
Ingleby Greenhow.102 D3
Inglemire.......97 F6
Inglesbatch..24 C2
Inglesham.......38 E2
Ingleton
Durham.......101 B6
N Yorks.......93 B6
Inglewhite..92 E5
Ingoe.......110 B3
Ingol.......92 F5

Ingoldisthorpe..80 D2
Ingoldmells..79 C8
Ingoldsby.......78 F3
Ingon.......51 D7
Ingram.......117 C6
Ingrow.......94 F3
Ings.......99 E6
Ingst.......36 F2
Ingworth.......81 E7
Inham's End..66 E2
Inkberrow.......50 D5
Inkpen.......25 C8
Inkstack.......158 C4
Inn.......99 D6
Innellan.......145 F10
Innerleithen..121 F6
Innerleven..129 D5
Innermessan..104 C4
Innerwick
E Loth.......122 B3
Perth.......132 E2
Innis Chonain.125 C7
Insch.......140 B5
Insh.......138 D4
Inshore.......156 C6
Inskip.......92 F4
Instoneville..89 C6
Instow.......20 F3
Intake.......89 D6
Inver
Aberds.......139 E8
Highld.......151 C11
Perth.......133 E7
Inverailort.147 C10
Inveraldie.......134 F4
Inverallochy.153 B10
Inveran.......151 B8
Inveraray.......125 E6
Inverarish.......149 E10
Inverarity.......134 E4
Inverarnan..126 C2
Inverasdale.155 J13
Inverbeg.......126 E2
Inverbervie.135 B8
Inverboyndie.153 B6
Inverbroom..150 C4
Invercassley..156 J7
Invercauld House.......139 E7
Inverchaolain..145 F9
Invercharnan.131 E5
Inverchoran.150 F5
Invercreran..130 E4
Inverdruie.......138 C5
Inverebrie.......153 E9
Invereck.......145 E10
Inverernan House.......140 C2
Invereshie House.......138 D4
Inveresk.......121 B6
Inverey.......139 F6
Inverfarigaig..137 B8
Invergarry.......137 D6
Invergelder.......139 E8
Invergeldie..127 B6
Invergordon..151 E10
Invergowrie..134 F3
Inverguseran.149 H12
Inverhadden..132 D3
Inverharroch..152 E3
Inverherive..126 B2
Inverie.......147 B10
Inverinan.......125 D5
Inverinate.......136 B2
Inverkeilor..135 E6
Inverkeithing.128 F3
Inverkeithny.153 D6
Inverkip.......118 B2
Inverkirkaig..156 H3
Inverlael.......150 C4
Inverlochlarig.126 C3
Inverlochy
Argyll.......125 C7
Highld.......131 B5
Inverlussa.......144 E5
Inver Mallie..136 F4
Invermark Lodge.......140 F3
Invermoidart..147 D9
Invermoriston.137 C7
Invernaver.157 C10
Inverneill.......145 E7
Inverness.......151 G9
Invernettie..153 D11
Invernoaden..125 F7
Inveroran Hotel 131 E6
Inverpolly Lodge.......156 H3
Inverquharity.134 D4
Inverquhomery 153 D10
Inverroy.......137 F5
Inversanda..130 D3
Invershiel.......136 C2
Invershin.......151 B8
Inversnaid Hotel 132 D3
Inveruglas.......126 C2
Inveruglass.......138 D4
Inverurie.......141 B6
Invervar.......132 E3
Inverythan..153 D7
Inwardleigh......9 E7
Inworth.......42 C4
Iochdar.......148 D2
Iping.......16 B2
Ipplepen......7 C6
Ipsden.......39 F6
Ipsley.......51 C5
Ipstones.......75 D7
Ipswich.......57 E5
Irby.......85 F3
Irby in the Marsh 79 C7
Irby upon Humber..91 D5
Irchester.......53 C7
Ireby
Cumb.......108 F2
Lancs.......93 B6
Ireland
Orkney.......159 H4
Shetland.......160 L5
Ireland's Cross..74 E4
Ireleth......92 B2
Ireshopeburn 109 F8
Irlam.......86 E5
Irnham.......65 B7

Iron Acton.......36 F3
Ironbridge.......61 D6
Iron Cross.......51 D5
Irongray.......107 B6
Ironmacannie..106 B3
Ironside.......153 C8
Ironville.......76 D4
Irstead.......69 B6
Irthington.......108 C4
Irthlingborough..53 B7
Irton.......103 F8
Irvine.......118 F3
Isauld.......157 C12
Isbister
Orkney.......159 F3
Orkney.......159 G4
Shetland.......160 D5
Shetland.......160 G7
Isfield.......17 C8
Isham.......53 B6
Isle Abbotts..11 B8
Isle Brewers..11 B8
Isleham.......55 B7
Isle of Whithorn.105 F8
Isleornsay.......149 G12
Islesburgh..160 G5
Islesteps.......107 B6
Isleworth.......28 B2
Isley Walton..63 B8
Islibhig.......154 E4
Islington.......41 F6
Islip
N Nhants.......53 B7
Oxon.......39 C5
Istead Rise.......29 C7
Isycoed.......73 D8
Itchen.......14 C5
Itchen Abbas..26 F3
Itchen Stoke..26 F3
Itchingfield..16 B5
Itchington.......36 F3
Itteringham..81 D7
Itton......9 E8
Itton Common..36 E1
Ivegill.......108 E4
Iver.......40 F3
Iver Heath..40 F3
Iveston.......110 D4
Ivinghoe.......40 C2
Ivinghoe Aston..40 C2
Ivington.......49 D6
Ivington Green..49 D6
Ivybridge......6 D4
Ivy Chimneys..41 D7
Ivychurch.......19 C7
Ivy Cross.......13 B6
Ivy Hatch.......29 D6
Iwade.......30 C3
Iwerne Courtney or Shroton..13 C6
Iwerne Minster..13 C6
Ixworth.......56 B3
Ixworth Thorpe..56 B3

J
Jack Hill.......94 D5
Jack in the Green.10 E5
Jacksdale.......76 D4
Jackstown.......153 E7
Jacobstow......8 E3
Jacobstowe......9 D7
Jameston.......32 E1
Jamestown
Dumfries.......115 E6
Highld.......150 F7
W Dunb.......126 F2
Jarrow.......111 C6
Jarvis Brook..18 C2
Jasper's Green..42 B3
Java.......124 B3
Jawcraig.......119 B8
Jaywick.......43 C7
Jealott's Hill..27 B6
Jedburgh.......116 B2
Jeffreyston..32 D1
Jellyhill.......119 B6
Jemimaville..151 E10
Jersey Farm..40 D4
Jesmond.......111 C5
Jevington.......18 E2
Jockey End.......40 C3
Johnby.......108 F4
John o'Groats.158 C5
John's Cross..18 C4
Johnshaven..135 C7
Johnston
E Renfs.......118 C4
Pembs.......44 D4
Johnstonebridge..114 E3
Johnstown
Carms.......33 C5
Wrex.......73 E7
Joppa
Edin.......121 B6
S Ayrs.......112 C4
Jordans.......40 E2
Jordanthorpe..88 F4
Jump.......88 D4
Jumpers Green..14 E2
Juniper Green.120 C4
Jurby East..84 C3
Jurby West..84 C3

K
Kaber.......100 C2
Kaimend.......120 E2
Kaimes.......121 C5
Kalemouth..116 B3
Kames
Argyll.......124 D4
Argyll.......145 F8
E Ayrs.......113 B6
Kea......3 B7
Keadby.......90 C2
Keal Cotes..79 C6
Kearsley.......87 D5
Kearstwick..99 F8
Kearton.......100 E4
Kearvaig.......156 B5
Keasden......93 C7
Keckwick.......86 F3
Keddington..91 F7
Kedington..55 E8

Kedleston.......76 E3
Keelby.......91 C5
Keele.......74 E5
Keeley Green..53 E8
Keeston.......44 D4
Keevil.......24 D4
Kegworth.......63 B8
Kehelland......2 B5
Keig.......140 C5
Keighley.......94 E3
Keil.......130 D3
Keilarsbrae..127 E7
Keillmore.......144 E5
Keillor.......134 E2
Keillour.......127 B8
Keills.......142 B5
Keils.......144 G5
Keinton Mandeville..23 F7
Keir Mill.......113 E8
Keisby.......65 B7
Keiss.......158 D5
Keith.......152 C4
Keith Inch..153 D11
Keithock.......135 C6
Kelbrook.......94 E2
Kelby.......78 E3
Keld
Cumb.......99 C7
N Yorks.......100 D3
Keldholme.......103 F5
Kelfield
N Lincs.......90 D2
N Yorks.......95 F8
Kelham.......77 D7
Kellan.......147 G8
Kellas
Angus.......134 F4
Moray.......152 C1
Kellaton......7 F6
Kelleth.......100 D1
Kelleythorpe..97 D5
Kelling.......81 C6
Kellingley..89 B6
Kellington..89 B6
Kelloe.......111 F6
Kelloholm.......113 C7
Kelly......9 F5
Kelly Bray......5 B8
Kelmarsh.......52 B5
Kelmscot.......38 E2
Kelsale.......57 C7
Kelsall.......74 C2
Kelsall Hill..74 C2
Kelshall.......54 F4
Kelsick.......107 D8
Kelso.......122 F3
Kelstedge.......76 C3
Kelsterton..91 E6
Kelston.......24 C2
Keltneyburn..132 E4
Kelton.......107 B6
Kelty.......128 E3
Kelvedon.......42 C4
Kelvedon Hatch..42 E1
Kelvin.......119 D6
Kelvinside.......119 C5
Kelynack......2 C2
Kemback.......129 C6
Kemberton..61 D7
Kemble.......37 E6
Kemerton.......50 F4
Kemeys Commander..35 D7
Kemnay.......141 C6
Kempley.......36 B3
Kempsey.......50 E3
Kempsford..38 E1
Kemps Green..51 B6
Kempshott.......26 D4
Kempston.......53 E8
Kempston Hardwick..53 E8
Kempton.......60 F3
Kemp Town..17 D7
Kemsing.......29 D6
Kemsley.......30 C3
Kenardington..19 B6
Kenchester..49 E6
Kencot.......38 D2
Kendal.......99 E7
Kendoon.......113 F6
Kendray.......88 D4
Kenfig.......34 F2
Kenfig Hill..34 F2
Kenilworth..51 B7
Kenknock.......132 F1
Kenley
London.......28 D4
Shrops.......61 D5
Kenmore
Highld.......149 C12
Perth.......132 E4
Kenn
Devon.......10 F4
N Som.......23 C6
Kennacley.......154 H6
Kennacraig.145 G7
Kennerleigh..10 D3
Kennet.......127 E8
Kennethmont.140 B4
Kennett.......55 C7
Kennford.......10 F4
Kenninghall..68 F3
Kenninghall Heath..68 F3
Kennington
Kent.......30 E4
Oxon.......39 D5
Kennoway.......129 D5
Kenny Hill..55 B7
Kennythorpe..96 C3
Kenovay.......146 G2
Kensaleyre..149 C9
Kensington..28 B3
Kensworth..40 C3
Kensworth Common..40 C3
Kentallen.......130 D4
Kentchurch..35 B8
Kentford.......55 C8
Kentisbeare..11 D5
Kentisbury..20 E5
Kentisbury Ford..20 E5
Kentmere.......99 D6
Kenton
Devon.......10 F4

Kenton continued
Suff.......57 C5
T&W.......110 C5
Kenton Bankfoot..110 C5
Kentra.......147 E9
Kents Bank..92 B3
Kent's Green..36 B4
Kent's Oak..14 B4
Kent Street
E Sus.......18 D4
Kent.......29 D7
W Sus.......17 B6
Kenwick.......73 F8
Kenwyn......3 B7
Keoldale.......156 C6
Keppanach..130 C4
Keppoch.......136 B2
Keprigan.......143 G7
Kepwick.......102 E2
Kerchesters.122 F3
Keresley.......63 F7
Kernborough......7 E5
Kerne Bridge..36 C2
Kerris......2 D3
Kerry.......59 F8
Kerrycroy.......145 G10
Kerrysdale.......149 A13
Kerry's Gate..49 F5
Kersall.......77 C7
Kersey.......56 E4
Kershopefoot..115 F7
Kersoe.......50 F4
Kerswell.......11 D5
Kerswell Green..50 E3
Kesgrave.......57 E6
Kessingland..69 F8
Kessingland Beach.......69 F8
Kessington..119 B5
Kestle......3 B8
Kestle Mill......4 D3
Keston.......28 C5
Keswick
Cumb.......98 B4
Norf.......68 D5
Norf.......81 D9
Ketley.......61 C6
Ketley Bank..61 C6
Ketsby.......79 B6
Kettering.......53 B6
Ketteringham..68 D4
Kettins.......134 F2
Kettlebaston..56 D3
Kettlebridge..128 D5
Kettleburgh..57 C6
Kettlehill.......128 D5
Kettleholm..107 B8
Kettleness..103 C6
Kettleshume..75 B6
Kettlesing Bottom..94 D5
Kettlesing Head..94 D5
Kettlestone..81 D5
Kettlethorpe..77 B8
Kettletoft.......159 E7
Kettlewell..94 B2
Ketton.......65 D6
Kew.......28 B2
Kew Bridge..28 B2
Kewstoke.......22 C5
Kexbrough..88 D4
Kexby
Lincs.......90 F2
York.......96 D3
Key Green.......75 C5
Keyham.......64 D3
Keyhaven.......14 E4
Keyingham..91 B6
Keymer.......17 C7
Keynsham..23 C8
Keysoe.......53 C8
Keysoe Row..53 C8
Keyston.......53 B8
Keyworth.......77 F6
Kibblesworth..110 D5
Kibworth Beauchamp..64 E3
Kibworth Harcourt..64 E3
Kidbrooke..28 B5
Kiddemore Green.......62 D2
Kidderminster..50 B3
Kiddington..38 B4
Kidlington..38 C4
Kidmore End..26 B4
Kidsgrove..74 D5
Kidstones.......100 F4
Kidwelly =Cydweli..33 D5
Kiel Crofts..124 B5
Kielder.......116 E2
Kierfield Ho..159 G3
Kilbagie.......127 F8
Kilbarchan..118 C4
Kilbeg.......149 H11
Kilberry.......144 G6
Kilbirnie.......118 D3
Kilbride
Argyll.......124 C4
Argyll.......124 C5
Highld.......149 F10
Kilburn
Angus.......134 C3
Derbys.......76 E3
London.......41 F5
N Yorks.......95 B8
Kilby.......64 E3
Kilchamaig..145 G7
Kilchattan..144 D2
Kilchattan Bay..145 H10
Kilchenzie..143 F7
Kilcheran..124 B4
Kilchiaran..142 B3
Kilchoan
Argyll.......124 D3
Highld.......146 E7
Kilchoman..142 B3
Kilchrenan..125 C6
Kilconquhar.129 D6
Kilcot.......36 B3
Kilcoy.......151 F8
Kilcreggan..145 E11
Kildale.......102 D4
Kildalloig.......143 G8
Kildary.......151 D10

Kildermorie Lodge.......151 D8
Kildonan.......143 F11
Kildonan Lodge.......157 G12
Kildonnan.......146 C7
Kildrummy.......140 C3
Kildwick.......94 E3
Kilfinan.......145 F8
Kilfinnan.......137 E5
Kilgetty.......32 D2
Kilgwrrwg Common.......36 E1
Kilham
E Yorks.......97 C6
Northumb.......122 F4
Kilkenneth..146 G2
Kilkerran.......143 G8
Kilkhampton......9 E6
Killamarsh..89 F5
Killay.......33 E7
Killbeg.......147 G9
Killean.......143 D7
Killen.......151 F9
Killerby.......101 C6
Killichonan.132 D2
Killiechonate..136 F5
Killiechronan.147 G8
Killiecrankie.133 C6
Killiemor.......146 H7
Killiemore House.......146 J7
Killilan.......150 H2
Killimster.......158 E5
Killin.......132 F2
Killinallan..142 A4
Killinghall..95 D5
Killington..99 F8
Killingworth..111 B5
Killin Lodge.137 D8
Killmahumaig.144 D6
Killochyett..121 E7
Killocraw.......143 E7
Killundine.......147 G8
Kilmacolm..118 C3
Kilmaha.......124 E5
Kilmahog.......126 D5
Kilmalieu.......130 D2
Kilmaluag.......149 A9
Kilmany.......129 B5
Kilmarie.......149 G10
Kilmarnock..118 F4
Kilmaron Castle 129 C5
Kilmartin.......124 E4
Kilmaurs.......118 E4
Kilmelford..124 D4
Kilmeny.......142 B4
Kilmersdon..23 D8
Kilmeston..15 B6
Kilmichael..143 F7
Kilmichael Glassary..145 D7
Kilmichael of Inverlussa..144 E6
Kilmington
Devon.......11 E7
Wilts.......24 F2
Kilmonivaig..136 F4
Kilmorack..150 G7
Kilmore
Argyll.......124 C4
Highld.......149 H11
Kilmory
Argyll.......144 F6
Highld.......147 D8
Highld.......149 H8
N Ayrs.......143 F10
Kilmuir
Highld.......148 D7
Highld.......149 A8
Highld.......151 D10
Highld.......151 G9
Kilmun
Argyll.......124 D5
Argyll.......145 E10
Kilncadzow.119 E8
Kilndown.......18 B4
Kilnhurst.......89 E5
Kilninian.......146 G6
Kilninver.......124 C4
Kiln Pit Hill..110 D3
Kilnsea.......91 C8
Kilnsey.......94 C2
Kilnwick.......97 E5
Kilnwick Percy..96 D4
Kiloran.......144 D2
Kilpatrick..143 F10
Kilpeck.......49 F6
Kilphedir.......157 H12
Kilpin.......89 B8
Kilpin Pike..89 B8
Kilrenny.......129 D7
Kilsby.......52 B3
Kilspindie.......128 B4
Kilsyth.......119 B7
Kiltarlity.......151 G8
Kilton
Notts.......77 B5
Som.......22 E3
Kilton Thorpe..102 C4
Kilvaxter.......149 B8
Kilve.......22 E3
Kilvington..77 E7
Kilwinning..118 E3
Kimberworth..88 E5
Kimberley
Norf.......68 D3
Notts.......76 E5
Kimble Wick..39 D8
Kimbolton
Cambs.......53 C8
Hereford.......49 C7
Kimcote.......64 F2
Kimmeridge..13 G7
Kimmerston..123 F5
Kimpton
Hants.......25 E7
Herts.......40 C4
Kinbrace.......157 F11
Kinbuck.......127 D6
Kincaple.......129 C6
Kincardine
Fife.......127 F8
Highld.......151 C9
Kincardine Bridge.......127 F8

Kincardine O'Neil.......140 E4
Kinclaven.......134 F1
Kincorth.......141 D8
Kincorth House.......151 E13
Kincraig.......138 D4
Kincraigie.......133 E6
Kindallachan.133 E6
Kineton
Glos.......37 B7
Warks.......51 D8
Kinfauns.......128 B3
Kingairloch..130 D2
Kingarth.......145 H9
Kingcoed.......35 D8
King Edward..153 C7
Kingerby.......90 E4
Kingham.......38 B2
Kingholm Quay.107 B6
Kinghorn.......128 F4
Kingie.......136 D4
Kinglassie..128 E4
Kingoodie..128 B5
King's Acre..49 E6
Kingsand......6 D2
Kingsbarns..129 C7
Kingsbridge
Devon......6 E5
Som.......21 F8
King's Bromley..62 C5
Kingsburgh..149 C8
Kingsbury
London.......41 F5
Warks.......63 E6
Kingsbury Episcopi..12 B2
King's Caple..36 B2
Kingsclere..26 D3
King's Cliffe..65 E7
Kingscote.......37 E5
Kingscott......9 C7
King's Coughton..51 D5
Kingscross..143 F11
Kingsdon.......12 B3
Kingsdown..31 E7
Kingseat.......128 E3
Kingsey.......39 D7
Kingsfold.......28 F2
Kingsford
E Ayrs.......118 E4
Worcs.......62 F2
Kingsforth..90 C4
Kingsgate..31 B7
Kingsheanton..20 F4
King's Heath..62 F4
Kings Hedges..55 C5
King's Hill..29 D7
Kingshouse Hotel.......131 D6
Kingside Hill..107 D8
Kingskerswell..7 C6
Kingskettle..128 D5
Kingsland
Anglesey.......82 C2
Hereford.......49 C6
Kings Langley..40 D3
Kingsley
Ches W.......74 B2
Hants.......27 F5
Staffs.......75 E7
Kingsley Green..27 F6
Kingsley Holt..75 E7
Kingsley Park..53 C5
King's Lynn..67 B6
King's Meaburn..99 B8
King's Mills..73 E7
Kingsmuir
Angus.......134 E4
Fife.......129 D7
Kings Muir..121 F5
King's Newnham..52 B2
King's Newton..63 B7
Kingsnorth..19 B7
King's Norton
Leics.......64 D3
W Mid.......51 B5
King's Nympton......9 C8
King's Pyon..49 D6
King's Ripton..54 B3
King's Somborne..25 F8
King's Stag.......12 C5
King's Stanley..37 D5
King's Sutton..52 F2
Kingstanding..62 E4
Kingsteignton......7 B6
King's Sterndale..75 B7
King's Thorn..49 F7
Kingsthorpe..53 C5
Kingston
Cambs.......54 D4
Devon......6 E4
Dorset.......13 D5
Dorset.......13 G7
E Loth.......129 F7
Hants.......14 D2
IoW.......15 F5
Kent.......31 D5
Moray.......152 B3
Kingston Bagpuize..38 E4
Kingston Blount..39 E7
Kingston by Sea..17 D6
Kingston Deverill.24 F3
Kingstone
Hereford.......49 F6
Som.......11 C8
Staffs.......62 B4
Kingston Gorse..16 D4
Kingston Lisle..38 F3
Kingston Maurward..12 E5
Kingston near Lewes.......17 D7
Kingston on Soar.64 B2
Kingston Russell..12 E3
Kingston St Mary..11 B7
Kingston Seymour..23 C6
Kingston upon Hull..90 B4
Kingston upon Thames..28 C2
Kingston Vale..28 B3
Kingstown.......108 D3

King's Walden . . . .40 B4
Kingswear . . . . . . . .7 D6
Kingswells . . . . . .141 D7
Kingswinford . . . . .62 F2
Kingswood
 Bucks . . . . . . . . . .39 C6
 Glos . . . . . . . . . . .36 E4
 Hereford . . . . . . .48 D4
 Kent . . . . . . . . . . .30 D2
 Powys . . . . . . . . .60 D2
 S Glos . . . . . . . . .23 B8
 Sur . . . . . . . . . . . .28 D3
 Warks . . . . . . . . .51 B6
Kings Worthy . . . .26 F2
Kingthorpe . . . . . .78 B4
Kington
 Hereford . . . . . . .48 D4
 Worcs . . . . . . . . .50 D4
Kington Langley . .24 B4
Kington Magna . . .13 B5
Kington
 St Michael . . . . .24 B4
Kingussie . . . . . . .138 D3
Kingweston . . . . . .23 F7
Kininvie House . . .152 D3
Kinkell Bridge . . .127 C8
Kinknockie . . . . . .153 D10
Kinlet . . . . . . . . . . .61 F7
Kinloch
 Fife . . . . . . . . . . .128 C4
 Highld . . . . . . . .146 B6
 Highld . . . . . . . .149 G11
 Highld . . . . . . . .156 F6
 Perth . . . . . . . . . .133 B8
 Perth . . . . . . . . . .134 E2
Kinlochan . . . . . . .130 C2
Kinlochard . . . . . .126 D3
Kinlochbeoraid 147 C11
Kinlochbervie . . . .156 D5
Kinlocheil . . . . . . .130 B3
Kinlochetive . . . . .150 E3
Kinloch Hourn . . .136 D2
Kinloch Laggan . .137 F8
Kinlochleven . . . . .131 C5
Kinloch Lodge . . .157 D8
Kinlochmoidart
 . . . . . . . . . . . . . . .147 D10
Kinlochmorar . . . .147 B11
Kinlochmore . . . . .131 C5
Kinloch
 Rannoch . . . . . .132 D3
Kinlochspelve . . . .124 C2
Kinloid . . . . . . . . .147 C9
Kinloss . . . . . . . . .151 E13
Kinmel Bay . . . . . .72 A3
Kinmuck . . . . . . . .141 C7
Kinmundy . . . . . . .141 C7
Kinnadie . . . . . . . .153 D9
Kinnaird . . . . . . . .128 B4
Kinnaird Castle . .135 D6
Kinneff . . . . . . . . .135 B8
Kinnelhead . . . . . .114 D3
Kinnell . . . . . . . . .135 D6
Kinnerley . . . . . . . .60 B3
Kinnersley
 Hereford . . . . . . .48 E5
 Worcs . . . . . . . . .50 E3
Kinnerton . . . . . . .48 C4
Kinnesswood . . . .128 D3
Kinninvie . . . . . . .101 B5
Kinnordy . . . . . . .134 D3
Kinoulton . . . . . . . .77 F6
Kinross . . . . . . . . .128 D3
Kinrossie . . . . . . .134 F1
Kinsbourne
 Green . . . . . . . . .40 C4
Kinsey Heath . . . . .74 E3
Kinsham
 Hereford . . . . . . .49 C5
 Worcs . . . . . . . . .50 F4
Kinsley . . . . . . . . . .88 C5
Kinson . . . . . . . . . .13 E8
Kintbury . . . . . . . .25 C8
Kintessack . . . . . .151 E12
Kintillo . . . . . . . . .128 C3
Kintocher . . . . . . .140 D4
Kinton
 Hereford . . . . . . .49 B6
 Shrops . . . . . . . . .60 C3
Kintore . . . . . . . . .141 C6
Kintour . . . . . . . . .142 C5
Kintra
 Argyll . . . . . . . . .142 D4
 Argyll . . . . . . . . .146 J6
Kintraw . . . . . . . . .124 E4
Kinuachdrachd . .124 F3
Kinveachy . . . . . . .138 C5
Kinver . . . . . . . . . .62 F2
Kippax . . . . . . . . . .95 F7
Kippen . . . . . . . . .127 E6
Kippford or
 Scaur . . . . . . . .106 D5
Kirbister
 Orkney . . . . . . . .159 F3
 Orkney . . . . . . . .159 H4
Kirbuster . . . . . . . .159 F3
Kirby Bedon . . . . .69 D5
Kirby Bellars . . . . .64 C4
Kirby Cane . . . . . .69 E6
Kirby Cross . . . . . .43 B8
Kirby Grindalythe 96 C5
Kirby Hill
 N Yorks . . . . . . . .95 C6
 N Yorks . . . . . . .101 E6
Kirby Knowle . . . .102 F2
Kirby-le-Soken . . .43 B8
Kirby Misperton . .96 B3
Kirby Muxloe . . . .64 D2
Kirby Row . . . . . . .69 E6
Kirby Sigston . . . .102 E2
Kirby Underdale . .96 D4
Kirby Wiske . . . . .102 F1
Kirdford . . . . . . . . .16 B4
Kirk . . . . . . . . . . . .158 E4
Kirkabister . . . . . .160 K6
Kirkandrews . . . . .106 E3
Kirkandrews upon
 Eden . . . . . . . . .108 D3
Kirkbampton . . . .108 D3
Kirkbean . . . . . . . .107 D6
Kirk Bramwith . . .89 C7
Kirkbride . . . . . . .108 D2
Kirkbuddo . . . . . .135 E5
Kirkburn
 Borders . . . . . . .121 F5

Kirkburn continued
 E Yorks . . . . . . . .97 D5
Kirkburton . . . . . . .88 C2
Kirkby
 Lincs . . . . . . . . . .90 E4
 Mers . . . . . . . . . .86 E2
 N Yorks . . . . . . .102 D3
Kirkby Fleetham 101 E7
Kirkby Green . . . . .78 D3
Kirkby-in-
 Ashfield . . . . . . .76 D5
Kirkby-in-
 Furness . . . . . . .98 F4
Kirkby la Thorpe . .78 E3
Kirkby Lonsdale . .93 B6
Kirkby Malham . . .93 C8
Kirkby Mallory . . .63 D8
Kirkby Malzeard . .94 B5
Kirkby Mills . . . . .103 F5
Kirkby
 Overflow . . . . . .95 D5
Kirkby Stephen . .100 D2
Kirkby Thore . . . . .99 B8
Kirkby
 Underwood . . . .65 B7
Kirkby Wharfe . . . .95 E6
Kirkcaldy . . . . . . .128 E4
Kirkcambeck . . . .108 C5
Kirkcarswell . . . . .106 E4
Kirkcolm . . . . . . . .104 C4
Kirkconnel . . . . . .113 C7
Kirkconnell . . . . .107 C6
Kirkcowan . . . . . .105 C7
Kirkcudbright . . . .106 D3
Kirkdale . . . . . . . . .85 E4
Kirk Deighton . . . .95 D6
Kirk Ella . . . . . . . . .90 B4
Kirkfieldbank . . . .119 E8
Kirkgunzeon . . . .107 C5
Kirk Hallam . . . . . .76 E4
Kirkham
 Lancs . . . . . . . . . .92 F4
 N Yorks . . . . . . . .96 C3
Kirkhamgate . . . . .88 B3
Kirk Hammerton . .95 D7
Kirkharle . . . . . . . .117 F6
Kirkheaton
 Northumb . . . . .110 B3
 W Yorks . . . . . . .88 C2
Kirkhill
 Angus . . . . . . . .135 C6
 Highld . . . . . . . .151 G8
 Midloth . . . . . . .120 C5
 Moray . . . . . . . .152 E2
Kirkhope . . . . . . . .115 B6
Kirkhouse . . . . . . .121 F6
Kirkibost . . . . . . .149 G10
Kirkinch . . . . . . . .134 E3
Kirkinner . . . . . . .105 D8
Kirkintilloch . . . . .119 B6
Kirk Ireton . . . . . . .76 D2
Kirkland
 Cumb . . . . . . . . .98 C2
 Cumb . . . . . . . .109 F6
 Dumfries . . . . . .113 C7
 Dumfries . . . . . .113 E8
Kirk Langley . . . . .76 F2
Kirkleatham . . . . .102 B3
Kirklevington . . . .102 D2
Kirkley . . . . . . . . . .69 E8
Kirklington
 Notts . . . . . . . . . .77 D6
 N Yorks . . . . . . .101 F8
Kirklinton . . . . . . .108 C4
Kirkliston . . . . . . .120 B4
Kirkmaiden . . . . .104 F5
Kirkmichael
 Perth . . . . . . . . .133 D7
 S Ayrs . . . . . . . .112 C3
Kirk Michael . . . . .84 C3
Kirkmuirhill . . . . .119 E7
Kirknewton
 Northumb . . . . .122 F4
 W Loth . . . . . . . .120 C4
Kirkney . . . . . . . . .152 E5
Kirk of Shotts . . .119 C8
Kirkoswald
 Cumb . . . . . . . .109 E5
 S Ayrs . . . . . . . .112 D2
Kirkpatrick
 Durham . . . . . . .106 B4
Kirkpatrick-
 Fleming . . . . . .108 B2
Kirk Sandall . . . . .89 D7
Kirksanton . . . . . .98 F3
Kirk Smeaton . . . .89 C6
Kirkstall . . . . . . . . .95 F5
Kirkstead . . . . . . . .78 C4
Kirkstile . . . . . . . .152 E5
Kirkstyle . . . . . . . .158 C5
Kirkton
 Aberds . . . . . . . .140 B6
 Aberds . . . . . . . .153 D6
 Angus . . . . . . . .134 E4
 Angus . . . . . . . .134 E3
 Borders . . . . . . .115 C8
 Dumfries . . . . . .114 F2
 Fife . . . . . . . . . .129 B5
 Highld . . . . . . . .149 F13
 Highld . . . . . . . .150 G2
 Highld . . . . . . . .151 B10
 Highld . . . . . . . .151 F10
 Perth . . . . . . . . .127 C8
 S Lanark . . . . . .114 B2
 Stirling . . . . . . .126 D4
Kirktonhill . . . . . .121 D7
Kirkton Manor . . .120 F5
Kirkton of Airlie 134 D3
Kirkton of
 Auchterhouse . .134 F3
Kirkton of
 Auchterless . . .153 D7
Kirkton of
 Barevan . . . . . .151 G11
Kirkton of
 Bourtie . . . . . . .141 B7
Kirkton of
 Collace . . . . . . .134 F1
Kirkton of Craig 135 D7
Kirkton of
 Culsalmond . . .153 E6
Kirkton of
 Durris . . . . . . . .141 E6
Kirkton of
 Glenbuchat . . .140 C2

Kirkton of
 Glenisla . . . . . .134 C2
Kirkton of
 Kingoldrum . . .134 D3
Kirkton of Largo 129 D6
Kirkton of
 Lethendy . . . . .133 E8
Kirkton of Logie
 Buchan . . . . . .141 B8
Kirkton of
 Maryculter . . . .141 E7
Kirkton of
 Menmuir . . . . .135 C5
Kirkton of
 Monikie . . . . . .135 F5
Kirkton of Oyne .141 B5
Kirkton of
 Rayne . . . . . . . .153 F6
Kirkton of
 Skene . . . . . . . .141 D7
Kirkton of
 Tough . . . . . . . .140 C5
Kirktown . . . . . . . .153 C10
Kirktown of
 Alvah . . . . . . . .153 B6
Kirktown of
 Deskford . . . . .152 B5
Kirktown of
 Fetteresso . . . .141 F7
Kirktown of
 Mortlach . . . . .152 E3
Kirktown of
 Slains . . . . . . . .141 B9
Kirkurd . . . . . . . . .120 E4
Kirkwall . . . . . . . .159 G5
Kirkwhelpington 117 F5
Kirk Yetholm . . . .116 B4
Kirmington . . . . . .90 C5
Kirmond le Mire . .90 E5
Kirn . . . . . . . . . . . .145 F10
Kirriemuir . . . . . . .134 D3
Kirstead Green . . .69 E5
Kirtlebridge . . . . .108 B2
Kirtleton . . . . . . . .115 F5
Kirtling . . . . . . . . .55 D7
Kirtling Green . . . .55 D7
Kirtlington . . . . . . .38 C4
Kirtomy . . . . . . . .157 C10
Kirton
 Lincs . . . . . . . . . .79 F6
 Notts . . . . . . . . . .77 C6
 Suff . . . . . . . . . . .57 F6
Kirton End . . . . . . .79 E5
Kirton Holme . . . . .79 E5
Kirton in Lindsey . .90 E3
Kislingbury . . . . . .52 D4
Kites Hardwick . . .52 C2
Kittisford . . . . . . . .11 B5
Kittle . . . . . . . . . . .33 F6
Kitt's Green . . . . . .63 F5
Kitt's Moss . . . . . . .87 F6
Kittybrewster . . . .141 D8
Kitwood . . . . . . . . .26 F4
Kivernoll . . . . . . . .49 F6
Kiveton Park . . . . .89 F5
Knaith . . . . . . . . . .90 F2
Knaith Park . . . . . .90 F2
Knap Corner . . . . .13 B6
Knaphill . . . . . . . . .27 D7
Knapp
 Perth . . . . . . . . .134 F2
 Som . . . . . . . . . .11 B8
Knapthorpe . . . . . .77 D7
Knapton
 Norf . . . . . . . . . .81 D9
 York . . . . . . . . . . .95 D8
Knapton Green . . .49 D6
Knapwell . . . . . . . .54 C4
Knaresborough . . .95 D6
Knarsdale . . . . . . .109 D6
Knauchland . . . . .152 C5
Knaven . . . . . . . . .153 D8
Knayton . . . . . . . .102 F2
Knebworth . . . . . . .41 B5
Knedlington . . . . . .89 B8
Kneesall . . . . . . . . .77 C7
Kneesworth . . . . . .54 E4
Kneeton . . . . . . . . .77 E7
Knelston . . . . . . . .33 F5
Knenhall . . . . . . . .75 F6
Knettishall . . . . . . .68 F2
Knightacott . . . . . .21 E5
Knightcote . . . . . . .51 D8
Knightley Dale . . .62 B2
Knighton
 Devon . . . . . . . . .6 E3
 Leicester . . . . . .64 D2
 Staffs . . . . . . . . .61 B7
 Staffs . . . . . . . . .74 E4
Knighton
 = Tref-y-Clawdd . .48 B4
Knightswood . . . .118 C5
Knightwick . . . . . .50 D2
Knill . . . . . . . . . . .48 C4
Knipton . . . . . . . . .77 F8
Knitsley . . . . . . . .110 E4
Kniveton . . . . . . . .76 D2
Knock
 Argyll . . . . . . . .147 H8
 Cumb . . . . . . . .100 B1
 Moray . . . . . . . .152 C5
Knockally . . . . . . .158 H3
Knockan . . . . . . . .156 H5
Knockandhu . . . . .139 B8
Knockando . . . . . .152 D1
Knockando
 House . . . . . . . .152 D2
Knockbain . . . . . .151 F9
Knockbreck . . . . .148 B7
Knockdee . . . . . . .158 D3
Knockdolian . . . . .104 A5
Knockenkelly . . . .143 F11
Knockentiber . . . .118 F3
Knockespock
 House . . . . . . . .140 B4
Knockfarrel . . . . . .151 F8
Knockglass . . . . . .104 D4
Knockholt . . . . . . .29 D5
Knockholt Pound 29 D5
Knockie Lodge . . .137 C7
Knockin . . . . . . . . .60 B3
Knockinlaw . . . . . .118 F4
Knocklearn . . . . . .106 B4
Knocknaha . . . . . .143 G7
Knocknain . . . . . .104 C3
Knockrome . . . . . .144 F4
Knocksharry . . . . .84 D2

Knodishall . . . . . . .57 C8
Knolls Green . . . . .74 B5
Knolton . . . . . . . . .73 F7
Knolton Bryn . . . . .73 F7
Knook . . . . . . . . . . .24 E4
Knossington . . . . .64 D5
Knott End-
 on-Sea . . . . . . .92 E3
Knotting . . . . . . . . .53 C8
Knotting Green . . .53 C8
Knottingley . . . . . .89 B6
Knotts
 Cumb . . . . . . . . .99 B6
 Lancs . . . . . . . . .93 D7
Knotty Ash . . . . . . .86 E2
Knotty Green . . . . .40 E2
Knowbury . . . . . . .49 B7
Knowe . . . . . . . . .105 B7
Knowehead . . . . .113 E6
Knowesgate . . . . .117 F5
Knowes of
 Elrick . . . . . . . .152 C6
Knoweton . . . . . . .119 D7
Knowhead . . . . . .153 C9
Knowle
 Bristol . . . . . . . . .23 B8
 Devon . . . . . . . . .10 D2
 Devon . . . . . . . . .11 F5
 Devon . . . . . . . . .20 F3
 Shrops . . . . . . . .49 B7
 W Mid . . . . . . . .51 B6
Knowle Green . . . .93 F6
Knowle Park . . . . .94 E3
Knowl Hill . . . . . . .27 B6
Knowlton
 Dorset . . . . . . . .13 C8
 Kent . . . . . . . . . .31 D6
Knowsley . . . . . . . .86 E2
Knowstone . . . . . .10 B3
Knox Bridge . . . . .29 E8
Knucklas . . . . . . . .48 B4
Knuston . . . . . . . . .53 C7
Knutsford . . . . . . .74 B4
Knutton . . . . . . . . .74 E5
Knypersley . . . . . .75 D5
Kuggar . . . . . . . . . .3 E6
Kyleakin . . . . . . . .149 F12
Kyle of
 Lochalsh . . . . .149 F12
Kylerhea . . . . . . .149 F12
Kylesknoydart . . .147 B11
Kylesku . . . . . . . .156 F5
Kylesmorar . . . . .147 B11
Kylestrome . . . . . .156 F5
Kyllachy House . .138 B3
Kynaston . . . . . . . .60 B3
Kynnersley . . . . . .61 C6
Kyre Magna . . . . . .49 C8

## L

Labost . . . . . . . . .155 C7
Lacasaidh . . . . . .155 E8
Lacasdal . . . . . . .155 D9
Laceby . . . . . . . . . .91 D6
Lacey Green . . . . .39 E8
Lach Dennis . . . . .74 B4
Lackford . . . . . . . .55 B8
Lacock . . . . . . . . . .24 C4
Ladbroke . . . . . . . .52 D2
Laddingford . . . . .29 E7
Lade Bank . . . . . . .79 D6
Ladock . . . . . . . . . .4 D3
Lady . . . . . . . . . . .159 D7
Ladybank . . . . . . .128 C5
Ladykirk . . . . . . . .122 E4
Ladysford . . . . . . .153 B9
La Fontenelle . . . .16 I2
Laga . . . . . . . . . . .147 E9
Lagalochan . . . . .124 D4
Lagavulin . . . . . . .142 D5
Lagg
 Argyll . . . . . . . .144 F4
 N Ayrs . . . . . . . .143 F10
Laggan
 Argyll . . . . . . . .142 C3
 Highld . . . . . . . .137 E5
 Highld . . . . . . . .138 E2
 Highld . . . . . . . .147 D10
 S Ayrs . . . . . . . .112 F2
Lagganulva . . . . .146 G7
Laide . . . . . . . . . .155 H13
Laigh Fenwick . . .118 E4
Laigh Glengall . . .112 C3
Laighmuir . . . . . . .118 E4
Laindon . . . . . . . . .42 F2
Lair . . . . . . . . . . . .150 G3
Lairg . . . . . . . . . . .157 J8
Lairg Lodge . . . . .157 J8
Lairgmore . . . . . .151 H8
Lairg Muir . . . . . .157 J8
Laisterdyke . . . . . .94 F4
Laithes . . . . . . . . .108 F4
Lake
 IoW . . . . . . . . . . .15 F6
 Wilts . . . . . . . . . .25 F6
Lakenham . . . . . . .68 D5
Lakenheath . . . . . .67 F7
Lakesend . . . . . . . .66 E5
Lakeside . . . . . . . .99 F5
Laleham . . . . . . . .27 C8
Laleston . . . . . . . .21 B7
Lamarsh . . . . . . . .56 F2
Lamas . . . . . . . . . .81 E8
Lambden . . . . . . .122 E3
Lamberhurst . . . . .18 B3
Lamberhurst
 Quarter . . . . . . .18 B3
Lamberton . . . . . .123 D5
Lambeth . . . . . . . .28 B4
Lambhill . . . . . . . .119 C5
Lambley
 Northumb . . . . .109 D6
 Notts . . . . . . . . . .77 E6
Lamborough Hill 38 D4
Lambourn . . . . . . .25 B8
Lambourne End . .41 E7
Lambs Green . . . . .28 F3
Lambston . . . . . . .44 D4
Lambton . . . . . . . .111 D5
Lamerton . . . . . . . .6 B2
Lamesley . . . . . . .111 D5
Laminess . . . . . . .159 E7
Lamington
 Highld . . . . . . . .151 D10
 S Lanark . . . . . .120 F2
Lamlash . . . . . . . .143 E11

Lamloch . . . . . . . .112 E5
Lamonby . . . . . . .108 F4
Lamorna . . . . . . . . .2 D3
Lamorran . . . . . . . .3 B7
Lampardbrook . . .57 C6
Lampeter = Llanbedr
 Pont Steffan . . .46 E4
Lampeter Velfrey .32 C2
Lamphey . . . . . . . .32 D1
Lamplugh . . . . . . .98 B2
Lamport . . . . . . . .53 B5
Lamyatt . . . . . . . . .23 F8
Lana
 Devon . . . . . . . . .8 E5
 Devon . . . . . . . . .8 D5
Lanark . . . . . . . . .119 E8
Lancaster . . . . . . .92 C4
Lanchester . . . . . .110 E4
Lancing . . . . . . . . .17 D5
Landbeach . . . . . .55 C5
Landcross . . . . . . .9 B6
Landerberry . . . . .141 D6
Landford . . . . . . . .14 C3
Landford Manor . .14 C3
Landimore . . . . . .33 E5
Landkey . . . . . . . . .20 F4
Landore . . . . . . . . .33 E7
Landrake . . . . . . . .5 C8
Landscove . . . . . . .7 C5
Landshipping . . . .32 C1
Landshipping
 Quay . . . . . . . . .32 C1
Landulph . . . . . . . .6 C2
Landwade . . . . . . .55 C7
Lane . . . . . . . . . . . .4 C3
Laneast . . . . . . . . .8 F4
Lane End
 Bucks . . . . . . . . .39 E8
 Cumb . . . . . . . . .98 E3
 Dorset . . . . . . . .13 E6
 Hants . . . . . . . . .15 F7
 IoW . . . . . . . . . . .15 F7
 Lancs . . . . . . . . .93 E8
Lane Ends
 Lancs . . . . . . . . .93 D7
 Lancs . . . . . . . . .93 F6
 N Yorks . . . . . . .94 E2
Laneham . . . . . . . .77 B7
Lanehead
 Durham . . . . . . .109 E8
 Northumb . . . . .116 F3
Lane Head
 Derbys . . . . . . . .75 B8
 Durham . . . . . . .101 C6
 Gtr Man . . . . . . .86 E4
 W Yorks . . . . . . .88 D2
Lanercost . . . . . . .109 C5
Laneshaw Bridge .94 E2
Lane Side . . . . . . .87 B5
Lanfach . . . . . . . . .35 E6
Langar . . . . . . . . . .77 F7
Langbank . . . . . . .118 B3
Langbar . . . . . . . . .94 D3
Langburnshiels . .115 D8
Langcliffe . . . . . . .93 C8
Langdale . . . . . . . .157 E9
Langdale End . . . .103 E7
Langdon . . . . . . . .8 F5
Langdon Beck . . .109 F8
Langdon Hills . . . .42 F2
Langdyke . . . . . . .128 D5
Langenhoe . . . . . .43 C6
Langford
 C Beds . . . . . . . .54 E2
 Devon . . . . . . . . .10 D5
 Essex . . . . . . . . .42 D4
 Notts . . . . . . . . . .77 D8
 Oxon . . . . . . . . .38 D2
Langford Budville 11 B6
Langham
 Essex . . . . . . . . .56 F4
 Norf . . . . . . . . . .81 C6
 Rutland . . . . . . .64 C5
 Suff . . . . . . . . . .56 C3
Langhaugh . . . . . .120 F5
Langho . . . . . . . . .93 F7
Langholm . . . . . . .115 F6
Langleeford . . . . .117 B5
Langley
 Ches E . . . . . . . .75 B6
 Hants . . . . . . . . .14 D4
 Herts . . . . . . . . .41 B5
 Kent . . . . . . . . . .30 D2
 Northumb . . . . .109 C8
 Slough . . . . . . . .27 B8
 Warks . . . . . . . .51 C6
 W Sus . . . . . . . .16 B2
Langley Burrell . . .24 B4
Langley Common 76 F2
Langley Heath . . .30 D2
Langley Lower
 Green . . . . . . . .54 F5
Langley Marsh . . .11 B5
Langley Park . . . .110 E5
Langley Street . . .69 D6
Langley Upper
 Green . . . . . . . .54 F5
Langney . . . . . . . .18 E3
Langold . . . . . . . . .89 F6
Langore . . . . . . . . .8 F5
Langport . . . . . . . .12 B2
Langrick . . . . . . . .79 E5
Langridge . . . . . . .24 C2
Langridge Ford . .9 B7
Langrigg . . . . . . .107 E8
Langrish . . . . . . . .15 B8
Langsett . . . . . . . .88 D3
Langshaw . . . . . . .121 F8
Langside . . . . . . . .127 C6
Langskaill . . . . . .159 D5
Langstone
 Hants . . . . . . . . .15 D8
 Newport . . . . . . .35 E7
Langthorne . . . . .101 E7
Langthorpe . . . . . .95 C6
Langthwaite . . . .101 D5
Langtoft
 E Yorks . . . . . . . .97 C6
 Lincs . . . . . . . . . .65 C8
Langton
 Durham . . . . . . .101 C6
 Lincs . . . . . . . . . .78 C5
 Lincs . . . . . . . . . .79 B6
 N Yorks . . . . . . . .96 C3
Langton by
 Wragby . . . . . .78 B4
Langton Green
 Kent . . . . . . . . . .18 B2
 Suff . . . . . . . . . .56 B5
Langton Herring . .12 F4

Langton
 Matravers . . . . .13 G8
Langtree . . . . . . . .9 C6
Langwathby . . . . .109 F5
Langwell House 158 H3
Langwell Lodge .156 J4
Langwith . . . . . . . .76 C5
Langwith
 Junction . . . . . .76 C5
Langworth . . . . . . .78 B3
Lanivet . . . . . . . . . .4 C5
Lanlivery . . . . . . . .5 D5
Lanner . . . . . . . . . .3 C6
Lanreath . . . . . . . .5 D6
Lansallos . . . . . . . .5 D6
Lansdown . . . . . . .37 B6
Lanteglos Highway 5 D7
Lanton
 Borders . . . . . . .116 B2
 Northumb . . . . .122 F5
Lapford . . . . . . . . .10 D2
Laphroaig . . . . . .142 D4
La Planque . . . . . .16 I2
Lapley . . . . . . . . . .62 C2
Lapworth . . . . . . . .51 B6
Larachbeg . . . . . .147 G9
Larbert . . . . . . . . .127 F7
Larden Green . . . .74 D2
Largie . . . . . . . . . .152 E6
Largiemore . . . . .145 E8
Largoward . . . . . .129 D6
Largs . . . . . . . . . .118 D2
Largybeg . . . . . . .143 F11
Largymore . . . . . .143 F11
Larkfield . . . . . . . .118 B2
Larkhall . . . . . . . .119 D7
Larkhill . . . . . . . . .25 E6
Larling . . . . . . . . . .68 F2
Larriston . . . . . . . .115 E8
Lartington . . . . . .101 C5
Lary . . . . . . . . . . . .140 D2
Lasham . . . . . . . . .26 E4
Lashenden . . . . . .30 E2
Lassington . . . . . .36 B4
Lassodie . . . . . . . .128 E3
Lastingham . . . . .103 E5
Latcham . . . . . . . .23 E6
Latchford
 Herts . . . . . . . . .41 B6
 Warr . . . . . . . . . .86 F4
Latchingdon . . . . .42 D4
Latchley . . . . . . . . .6 B2
Lately Common . .86 E4
Lathbury . . . . . . . .53 E6
Latheron . . . . . . .158 G3
Latheronwheel . .158 G3
Latheronwheel
 House . . . . . . . .158 G3
Lathones . . . . . . .129 D6
Latimer . . . . . . . . .40 E3
Latteridge . . . . . . .36 F3
Lattiford . . . . . . . .12 B4
Latton . . . . . . . . . .37 E7
Latton Bush . . . . .41 D7
Lauchintilly . . . . .141 C6
Lauder . . . . . . . . .121 E8
Laugharne . . . . . .32 C4
Laughterton . . . . .77 B8
Laughton
 E Sus . . . . . . . . .18 D2
 Leics . . . . . . . . .64 F3
 Lincs . . . . . . . . . .78 F3
 Lincs . . . . . . . . . .90 E2
Laughton
 Common . . . . . .89 F6
Laughton en
 le Morthen . . . .89 F6
Launcells . . . . . . . .8 D4
Launceston . . . . . .8 F5
Launton . . . . . . . . .39 B6
Laurencekirk . . . .135 B7
Laurieston
 Dumfries . . . . .106 C3
 Falk . . . . . . . . . .120 B2
Lavendon . . . . . . .53 D7
Lavenham . . . . . . .56 E3
Laverhay . . . . . . .114 E4
Laversdale . . . . . .108 C4
Laverstock . . . . . .25 F6
Laverstoke . . . . . .26 E2
Laverton
 Glos . . . . . . . . . .51 F5
 N Yorks . . . . . . .94 B5
 Som . . . . . . . . . .24 D2
Lavister . . . . . . . . .73 D7
Law . . . . . . . . . . .119 D8
Lawers
 Perth . . . . . . . . .127 B6
 Perth . . . . . . . . .132 F3
Lawford . . . . . . . . .56 F4
Lawhitton . . . . . . . .9 F5
Lawkland . . . . . . .93 C7
Lawley . . . . . . . . . .61 D6
Lawnhead . . . . . . .62 B2
Lawrenny . . . . . . .32 D1
Lawshall . . . . . . . .56 D2
Lawton . . . . . . . . .49 D6
Laxay . . . . . . . . . .84 D4
Laxfield . . . . . . . . .57 B6
Laxfirth
 Shetland . . . . . .160 H6
 Shetland . . . . . .160 J6
Laxo . . . . . . . . . . .160 G6
Laxobigging . . . . .160 F6
Laxton
 E Yorks . . . . . . . .89 B8
 N Nhants . . . . . .65 E6
 Notts . . . . . . . . . .77 C7
Laycock . . . . . . . . .94 E3
Layer Breton . . . . .43 C5
Layer de la Haye . .43 C5
Layer Marney . . . .43 C5
Layham . . . . . . . . .56 E4
Laylands Green . .25 C8
Laytham . . . . . . . . .96 F3
Layton . . . . . . . . . .92 F3
Lazenby . . . . . . . .102 B3
Lazonby . . . . . . . .108 F5
Lea
 Derbys . . . . . . . .76 D3
 Hereford . . . . . . .36 B3
 Lincs . . . . . . . . . .90 F2
 Shrops . . . . . . . .60 D4
 Shrops . . . . . . . .60 F4
 Wilts . . . . . . . . . .37 F6
Leabrooks . . . . . . .76 D4
Leac a Li . . . . . . .154 H6

Leachkin . . . . . . .151 G9
Leadburn . . . . . . .120 D5
Leadenham . . . . . .78 D2
Leaden Roding . . .42 C1
Leadgate
 Cumb . . . . . . . .109 E7
 Durham . . . . . . .110 D4
 T&W . . . . . . . . .110 D4
Leadhills . . . . . . .113 C8
Leafield . . . . . . . . .38 C3
Leagrave . . . . . . . .40 B3
Leake . . . . . . . . . .102 E2
Leake
 Commonside . . .79 D6
Lealholm . . . . . . .103 D5
Lealt
 Argyll . . . . . . . .144 D5
 Highld . . . . . . . .149 B10
Leamington
 Hastings . . . . . .52 C2
Leamonsley . . . . . .62 D5
Leamside . . . . . . .111 E6
Leanaig . . . . . . . .151 F8
Leargybreck . . . .144 F4
Leasgill . . . . . . . . .99 F6
Leasingham . . . . .78 E3
Leasingthorne . .101 B7
Leasowe . . . . . . . .85 E3
Leatherhead . . . . .28 D2
Leatherhead
 Common . . . . . .28 D2
Leathley . . . . . . . .94 E5
Leaton . . . . . . . . . .60 C4
Lea Town . . . . . . . .92 F4
Leaveland . . . . . . .30 D4
Leavening . . . . . . .96 C3
Leaves Green . . . .28 C5
Leazes . . . . . . . . .110 D4
Lebberston . . . . .103 F8
Lechlade-
 on-Thames . . . .38 E2
Leck . . . . . . . . . . .93 B6
Leckford . . . . . . . .25 F8
Leckfurin . . . . . . .157 D10
Leckgruinart . . . .142 B3
Leckhampstead
 Bucks . . . . . . . . .52 F5
 W Berks . . . . . . .26 B2
Leckhampstead
 Thicket . . . . . . .26 B2
Leckhampton . . . .37 C6
Leckie . . . . . . . . . .150 E3
Leckmelm . . . . . .150 B4
Leckwith . . . . . . . .22 B3
Leconfield . . . . . . .97 E6
Ledaig . . . . . . . . .124 B5
Ledburn . . . . . . . . .40 B2
Ledbury . . . . . . . . .50 F2
Ledcharrie . . . . . .126 B4
Ledgemoor . . . . . .49 D6
Ledicot . . . . . . . . .49 C6
Ledmore . . . . . . .156 H5
Lednagullin . . . . .157 C10
Ledsham
 Ches W . . . . . . . .73 B7
 W Yorks . . . . . . .89 B5
Ledston . . . . . . . . .88 B5
Ledston Luck . . . .95 F7
Ledwell . . . . . . . . .38 B4
Lee
 Argyll . . . . . . . .146 J7
 Devon . . . . . . . . .20 E3
 Hants . . . . . . . . .14 C4
 Lancs . . . . . . . . .93 D5
 Shrops . . . . . . . .73 F8
Leeans . . . . . . . . .160 J5
Leebotten . . . . . .160 L6
Leebotwood . . . . .60 E4
Lee Brockhurst . .60 B5
Leece . . . . . . . . . . .92 C2
Leechpool . . . . . . .44 D4
Lee Clump . . . . . .40 D2
Leeds
 Kent . . . . . . . . . .30 D2
 W Yorks . . . . . . .95 F5
Leedstown . . . . . .2 C5
Leek . . . . . . . . . . .75 D6
Leekbrook . . . . . .75 D6
Lee Moor . . . . . . . .6 C3
Lees
 Derbys . . . . . . . .76 F2
 Gtr Man . . . . . . .87 D7
 W Yorks . . . . . . .94 F3
Leeswood . . . . . . .73 C6
Legbourne . . . . . .91 F7
Legerwood . . . . . .121 E8
Legsby . . . . . . . . . .90 F5
Leicester . . . . . . . .64 D2
Leicester Forest
 East . . . . . . . . . .64 D2
Leigh
 Dorset . . . . . . . .12 D4
 Glos . . . . . . . . . .37 B5
 Gtr Man . . . . . . .86 D4
 Kent . . . . . . . . . .29 E6
 Shrops . . . . . . . .60 D3
 Sur . . . . . . . . . . .28 E3
 Wilts . . . . . . . . . .37 E7
 Worcs . . . . . . . . .50 D2
Leigh Beck . . . . . .42 F4
Leigh Common . . .12 B5
Leigh Delamere . .24 B3
Leigh Green . . . . .19 B6
Leigh on Sea . . . .42 F4
Leigh Park . . . . . . .15 D8
Leigh Sinton . . . . .50 D2
Leighswood . . . . .62 D4
Leighterton . . . . . .37 E5
Leighton
 N Yorks . . . . . . .94 B5
 Powys . . . . . . . .60 D2
 Shrops . . . . . . . .61 D6
 Som . . . . . . . . . .24 E2
Leighton
 Bromswold . . . .54 B2
Leighton Buzzard 40 B2
Leigh upon
 Mendip . . . . . . .23 E8
Leigh Woods . . . . .23 B7
Leinthall Earls . . .49 C6
Leinthall Starkes 49 C6

Leintwardine . . . . .49 B6
Leire . . . . . . . . . . .64 E2
Leirinmore . . . . . .156 C7
Leiston . . . . . . . . . .57 C8
Leitfie . . . . . . . . . .134 E2
Leith . . . . . . . . . . .121 B5
Leitholm . . . . . . . .122 E3
Lelant . . . . . . . . . . .2 C4
Lelley . . . . . . . . . . .97 F8
Lem Hill . . . . . . . . .50 B2
Lemington
 Hall . . . . . . . . .117 C7
Lempitlaw . . . . . .122 F3
Lenchwick . . . . . . .50 E5
Lendalfoot . . . . . .112 F1
Lendrick Lodge . .126 D4
Lenham . . . . . . . . .30 D2
Lenham Heath . . .30 E2
Lennel . . . . . . . . .122 E4
Lennoxtown . . . . .119 B6
Lenton
 Lincs . . . . . . . . . .78 F3
 Nottingham . . . .77 F5
Lentran . . . . . . . .151 G8
Lenwade . . . . . . . .68 C3
Leny House . . . . .126 D5
Lenzie . . . . . . . . .119 B6
Leoch . . . . . . . . . .134 F3
Leochel-
 Cushnie . . . . . .140 C4
Leominster . . . . . .49 D6
Leonard Stanley . 37 D5
Leorin . . . . . . . . .142 D4
Lepe . . . . . . . . . . .15 E5
Lephin . . . . . . . . .148 D6
Lephinchapel . . .145 D8
Lephinmore . . . . .145 D8
Le Planel . . . . . . .16 I2
Leppington . . . . . .96 C3
Lepton . . . . . . . . . .88 C3
Lerryn . . . . . . . . . .5 D6
Lerwick . . . . . . . .160 J6
Lesbury . . . . . . . .117 C8
Le Skerne
 Haughton . . . . .101 C8
Leslie
 Aberds . . . . . . .140 B4
 Fife . . . . . . . . . .128 D4
Lesmahagow . . .119 E8
Lesnewth . . . . . . . .8 E3
Lessendrum . . . .152 D5
Lessingham . . . . .69 B6
Lessonhall . . . . . .108 D2
Leswalt . . . . . . . .104 C4
Letchmore Heath 40 E4
Letchworth . . . . . .54 F3
Letcombe Bassett 38 F3
Letcombe Regis . .38 F3
Letham
 Angus . . . . . . . .135 E5
 Falk . . . . . . . . . .127 F7
 Fife . . . . . . . . . .128 C5
Letham Grange . .135 E6
Lethenty . . . . . . .153 D8
Letheringham . . . .57 D6
Letheringsett . . . .81 D6
Lettaford . . . . . . . .10 F2
Lettan . . . . . . . . .159 D8
Letterewe . . . . . .150 D2
Letterfearn . . . . .149 F13
Letterfinlay . . . . .137 E5
Lettermorar . . . . .147 C10
Lettermore . . . . . .146 G7
Letters . . . . . . . . .150 C4
Letterston . . . . . . .44 C4
Lettoch
 Highld . . . . . . . .139 C6
 Highld . . . . . . . .151 H13
Letton
 Hereford . . . . . . .48 E5
 Hereford . . . . . . .49 B5
Letton Green . . . .68 D2
Letty Green . . . . . .41 C5
Letwell . . . . . . . . .89 F6
Leuchars . . . . . . .129 B6
Leuchars House 152 B2
Leumrabhagh . . .155 F8
Levan . . . . . . . . . .118 B2
Levaneap . . . . . . .160 G6
Levedale . . . . . . . .62 C2
Leven
 E Yorks . . . . . . . .97 E7
 Fife . . . . . . . . . .129 D5
Levencorroch . . .143 F11
Levens . . . . . . . . . .99 F6
Levens Green . . . .41 B6
Levenshulme . . . .87 E6
Levenwick . . . . . .160 L6
Leverburgh
 = An t-Ob . . . . .154 J5
Leverington . . . . .66 C4
Leverton . . . . . . . .79 E7
Leverton
 Highgate . . . . . .79 E7
Leverton Outgate 79 E7
Levington . . . . . . .57 F6
Levisham . . . . . .103 E6
Levishie . . . . . . . .137 C7
Lew . . . . . . . . . . . .38 D3
Lewannick . . . . . . .8 F4
Lewdown . . . . . . . .9 F6
Lewes . . . . . . . . . .17 C8
Leweston . . . . . . .44 C4
Lewisham . . . . . . .28 B4
Lewiston . . . . . . .137 B8
Lewistown . . . . . . .34 F3
Lewknor . . . . . . . .39 E7
Leworthy
 Devon . . . . . . . . .8 D5
 Devon . . . . . . . . .21 F5
Lewtrenchard . . . .9 F6
Lexden . . . . . . . . . .43 B5
Ley
 Aberds . . . . . . .140 C4
 Corn . . . . . . . . . .5 C6
Leybourne . . . . . . .29 D7
Leyburn . . . . . . . .101 E6
Leyfields . . . . . . . .63 D6
Leyhill . . . . . . . . . .40 D2
Leyland . . . . . . . . .86 B3
Leylodge . . . . . . .141 C6
Leymoor . . . . . . . .88 C2
Leys
 Aberds . . . . . . . .153 C10

Leys continued
 Perth . . . . . . . . .134 F2
Leys Castle . . . . .151 G9
Leysdown-
 on-Sea . . . . . . .30 B4
Leysmill . . . . . . . .135 E6
Leys of Cossans 134 E3
Leysters Pole . . . .49 C7
Leyton . . . . . . . . . .41 F6
Leytonstone . . . . .41 F6
Lezant . . . . . . . . . .5 B8
Leziate . . . . . . . . . .67 C6
Lhanbryde . . . . . .152 B2
Liatrie . . . . . . . . .150 H5
Libanus . . . . . . . . .34 B3
Libberton . . . . . . .120 E2
Liberton . . . . . . . .121 C5
Liceasto . . . . . . . .154 H6
Lichfield . . . . . . . .62 D5
Lickey . . . . . . . . . .50 B4
Lickey End . . . . . . .50 B4
Lickfold . . . . . . . . .16 B3
Liddel . . . . . . . . . .159 K5
Liddesdale . . . . . .130 D1
Liddington . . . . . . .38 F2
Lidgate . . . . . . . . .55 D8
Lidget . . . . . . . . . .89 D7
Lidget Green . . . . .94 F4
Lidgett . . . . . . . . . .77 C6
Lidlington . . . . . . .53 F7
Lidstone . . . . . . . .38 B3
Lieurary . . . . . . . .158 C2
Liff . . . . . . . . . . . .134 F3
Lifton . . . . . . . . . . .9 F5
Liftondown . . . . . . .9 F5
Lighthorne . . . . . .51 D8
Lightwater . . . . . . .27 C7
Lightwood . . . . . . .75 E6
Lightwood Green
 Ches E . . . . . . . .74 E3
 Wrex . . . . . . . . . .73 E7
Lilbourne . . . . . . . .52 B3
Lilburn Tower . . .117 B6
Lilleshall . . . . . . . .61 C7
Lilley
 Herts . . . . . . . . .40 B4
 W Berks . . . . . . .26 B2
Lilliesleaf . . . . . .115 B8
Lillingstone
 Dayrell . . . . . . .52 F5
Lillingstone
 Lovell . . . . . . . .52 E5
Lillington
 Dorset . . . . . . . .12 C4
 Warks . . . . . . . .51 C8
Lilliput . . . . . . . . . .13 E8
Lilstock . . . . . . . . .22 E3
Lilyhurst . . . . . . . .61 C7
Limbury . . . . . . . . .40 B3
Limebrook . . . . . . .49 C5
Limefield . . . . . . . .87 C6
Limekilnburn . . . .119 D7
Limekilns . . . . . . .128 F2
Limerigg . . . . . . .119 B8
Limerstone . . . . . .14 F5
Limington . . . . . . .12 B3
Limpenhoe . . . . . .69 D6
Limpley Stoke . . . .24 C2
Limpsfield . . . . . . .28 D5
Limpsfield Chart .28 D5
Linby . . . . . . . . . . .76 D5
Linchmere . . . . . . .27 F6
Lincluden . . . . . . .107 B6
Lincoln . . . . . . . . . .78 B2
Lincomb . . . . . . . . .50 C3
Lindale . . . . . . . . . .99 F6
Lindal in Furness .92 B2
Lindean . . . . . . . .121 F7
Lindfield . . . . . . . .17 B7
Lindford . . . . . . . . .27 F6
Lindifferon . . . . . .128 C5
Lindley . . . . . . . . . .88 C2
Lindley Green . . . .94 E5
Lindores . . . . . . .128 C4
Lindridge . . . . . . . .49 C8
Lindsell . . . . . . . . .42 B2
Lindsey . . . . . . . . .56 E3
Linford
 Hants . . . . . . . . .14 D2
 Thurrock . . . . . .29 B7
Lingague . . . . . . . .84 E2
Lingards Wood . . .87 C8
Lingbob . . . . . . . . .94 F3
Lingdale . . . . . . .102 C4
Lingen . . . . . . . . . .49 C5
Lingfield . . . . . . . .28 E4
Lingreabhagh . . .154 J5
Lingwood . . . . . . .69 D6
Linicro . . . . . . . . .149 B8
Linkenholt . . . . . . .25 D8
Linkhill . . . . . . . . . .18 C5
Linkinhorne . . . . . .5 B8
Linklater . . . . . . .159 K5
Linksness . . . . . . .159 H3
Linktown . . . . . . .128 E4
Linley . . . . . . . . . . .60 E3
Linley Green . . . . .49 D8
Linlithgow . . . . . .120 B3
Linlithgow
 Bridge . . . . . . .120 B2
Linshiels . . . . . . .116 D4
Linsiadar . . . . . . .154 D7
Linsidemore . . . .151 B8
Linslade . . . . . . . . .40 B2
Linstead Parva . . .57 B7
Linstock . . . . . . . .108 D4
Linthwaite . . . . . . .88 C2
Lintlaw . . . . . . . . .122 D4
Lintmill . . . . . . . . .152 B5
Linton
 Borders . . . . . . .116 B3
 Cambs . . . . . . . .55 E6
 Derbys . . . . . . . .63 C6
 Hereford . . . . . . .36 B3
 Kent . . . . . . . . . .29 E8
 Northumb . . . . .117 E8
 N Yorks . . . . . . .94 C2
Linton-on-Ouse . .95 C7
Linwood
 Hants . . . . . . . . .14 D2
 Lincs . . . . . . . . . .90 F5
 Renfs . . . . . . . . .118 C4
Lionacleit . . . . . .148 D2
Lional . . . . . . . . .155 A10
Liphook . . . . . . . . .27 F6
Liscard . . . . . . . . .85 E4

Liscombe . . . 21 F7
Liskeard . . . 5 C7
L'Islet . . . 16 I2
Liss . . . 15 B8
Lissett . . . 97 D7
Liss Forest . . . 90 F5
Lisvane . . . 35 F5
Liswerry . . . 35 F7
Litcham . . . 67 C8
Litchborough . . . 52 D4
Litchfield . . . 26 D2
Litherland . . . 85 E4
Litlington
  Cambs. . . . 54 E4
  E Sus. . . . 18 E2
Little Abington . . . 55 E6
Little Addington . . . 53 B7
Little Alne . . . 51 C6
Little Altcar . . . 85 D4
Little Assynt . . . 156 G4
Little Aston . . . 62 D4
Little Atherfield . . . 15 G5
Little Ayre . . . 159 J4
Little-ayre . . . 160 G5
Little Ayton . . . 102 C3
Little Baddow . . . 42 D3
Little Badminton . . . 37 F5
Little Ballinluig . . . 133 D6
Little Bampton . . . 108 D2
Little Bardfield . . . 55 F7
Little Barford . . . 54 D2
Little
  Barningham . . . 81 D7
Little Barrington . . . 38 C2
Little Barrow . . . 73 B8
Little Barugh . . . 96 B3
Little Bavington . . . 110 B2
Little Bealings . . . 57 E6
Littlebeck . . . 103 D6
Little Bedwyn . . . 25 C7
Little Bentley . . . 43 B7
Little
  Berkhamsted . . . 41 D5
Little Billing . . . 53 C6
Little Birch . . . 49 F7
Little Blakenham . . . 56 E5
Little Blencow . . . 108 F4
Little Bollington . . . 86 F5
Little Bookham . . . 28 D2
Littleborough
  Gtr Man. . . . 87 C7
  Notts. . . . 90 F2
Littlebourne . . . 31 D6
Little Bowden . . . 64 F4
Little Bradley . . . 55 D7
Little Brampton . . . 60 F3
Little Brechin . . . 135 C5
Littlebredy . . . 12 F3
Little Brickhill . . . 53 F7
Little Brington . . . 52 C4
Little Bromley . . . 43 B6
Little Broughton . . . 107 F7
Little Budworth . . . 74 C2
Little Burstead . . . 42 E2
Littlebury . . . 55 F6
Littlebury Green . . . 55 F6
Little Bytham . . . 65 C7
Little Carlton
  Lincs. . . . 91 F7
  Notts. . . . 77 D7
Little Casterton . . . 65 D7
Little Cawthorpe . . . 91 F7
Little Chalfont . . . 40 E2
Little Chart . . . 30 E3
Little Chesterford . . . 55 E6
Little Cheverell . . . 24 D4
Little Chishill . . . 54 F5
Little Clacton . . . 43 C7
Little Clifton . . . 98 B2
Little Colp . . . 153 D7
Little Comberton . . . 50 E4
Little Common . . . 51 F7
Little Compton . . . 51 F7
Little Cornard . . . 56 F2
Little Cowarne . . . 49 D8
Little Coxwell . . . 38 E2
Little Crakehall . . . 101 E7
Little
  Cressingham . . . 67 D8
Little Crosby . . . 85 D4
Little Dalby . . . 64 C4
Little Dawley . . . 61 D6
Littledean . . . 36 C3
Little Dens . . . 153 D10
Little Dewchurch . . . 49 F7
Little Downham . . . 66 F5
Little Driffield . . . 97 D6
Little Dunham . . . 67 C8
Little Dunkeld . . . 133 E7
Little Dunmow . . . 42 B2
Little Easton . . . 42 B2
Little Eaton . . . 76 E3
Little Eccleston . . . 92 E4
Little Ellingham . . . 68 E2
Little End . . . 41 D8
Little Eversden . . . 54 D4
Little Faringdon . . . 38 D2
Little Fencote . . . 101 E7
Little Fenton . . . 95 F8
Littleferry . . . 151 E14
Little Finborough 56 D4
Little Fransham . . . 68 C2
Little Gaddesden 40 C2
Little Gidding . . . 65 F8
Little Glemham . . . 57 D7
Little Glenshee . . . 133 F6
Little Gransden . . . 54 D3
Little Green . . . 24 E2
Little Grimsby . . . 91 E7
Little Gruinard . . . 150 C2
Little Habton . . . 96 B3
Little Hale . . . 78 E4
Little Hallingbury . . . 41 C7
Littleham
  Devon . . . . 9 B6
  Devon . . . . 10 F5
Little Hampden . . . 40 D1
Littlehampton . . . 16 D4
Little Harrowden . . . 53 B6
Little Haseley . . . 39 D6
Little Hatfield . . . 97 E7
Little Hautbois . . . 81 E8
Little Haven . . . 44 D3
Little Hay . . . 62 D5
Little Hayfield . . . 87 F8

Little Haywood . . . 62 B4
Little Heath . . . 63 F7
Littlehempston . . . 7 C6
Little Hereford . . . 49 C7
Little Horkesley . . . 56 F3
Little Horsted . . . 17 C8
Little Horton . . . 94 F4
Little Horwood . . . 53 F5
Littlehoughton . . . 117 C8
Little Houghton
  S Yorks. . . . 88 D5
  W Nhants. . . . 53 D6
Little Hucklow . . . 75 B8
Little Hulton . . . 86 D5
Little Humber . . . 91 B5
Little Hungerford . . . 26 B3
Little Irchester . . . 53 C7
Little Kimble . . . 39 D8
Little Kineton . . . 51 D8
Little Kingshill . . . 40 E1
Little Langdale . . . 99 D5
Little Langford . . . 25 F5
Little Laver . . . 41 D8
Little Leigh . . . 74 B3
Little Leighs . . . 42 C3
Little Lever . . . 87 D5
Little London
  Bucks. . . . 39 C6
  E Sus. . . . 18 D2
  Hants. . . . 25 E8
  Hants. . . . 26 D4
  Lincs. . . . 66 B2
  Lincs. . . . 66 B4
  Norf . . . . 81 E7
  Powys . . . 59 F7
Little Longstone . . . 75 B8
Little Lynturk . . . 140 C4
Little Malvern . . . 50 E2
Little Maplestead . . . 56 F2
Little Marcle . . . 49 F8
Little Marlow . . . 40 F1
Little Marsden . . . 93 F8
Little
  Massingham . . . 80 E3
Little Melton . . . 68 D4
Littlemill
  Aberds. . . . 140 E2
  E Ayrs. . . . 112 C4
  Highld. . . . 151 F12
  Northumb . . . 117 C8
Little Mill . . . 35 D7
Little Milton . . . 39 D6
Little Missenden . . . 40 E2
Littlemoor . . . 12 F4
Littlemore . . . 39 D5
Little Musgrave . . . 100 C2
Little Ness . . . 60 C4
Little Neston . . . 73 B6
Little Newcastle . . . 44 C4
Little Newsham . . . 101 C6
Little Oakley
  Essex . . . . 43 B8
  N Nhants. . . . 65 F5
Little Orton . . . 108 D3
Little Ouseburn . . . 95 C7
Littleover . . . 76 F3
Little Paxton . . . 54 C2
Little Petherick . . . 4 B4
Little Pitlurg . . . 152 D4
Little Plumpton . . . 92 F3
Little Plumstead . . . 69 C6
Little Ponton . . . 78 F2
Littleport . . . 67 F5
Little Raveley . . . 54 B3
Little Reedness . . . 90 B2
Little Ribston . . . 95 D6
Little Rissington . . . 38 C1
Little Ryburgh . . . 81 E5
Little Ryle . . . 117 C6
Little Salkeld . . . 109 F5
Little Sampford . . . 55 F7
Little Sandhurst . . . 27 C6
Little Saxham . . . 55 C8
Little Scatwell . . . 150 F6
Little Sessay . . . 95 B7
Little Shelford . . . 54 D5
Little Singleton . . . 92 F3
Little
  Skillymarno . . . 153 C9
Little Smeaton . . . 89 C6
Little Snoring . . . 81 D5
Little Sodbury . . . 36 F4
Little Somborne . . . 25 F8
Little Somerford . . . 37 F6
Little Stainforth . . . 93 C8
Little Stainton . . . 101 B8
Little Stanney . . . 73 B8
Little Staughton . . . 54 C2
Little Steeping . . . 79 C7
Little Stoke . . . 75 F6
Little Stonham . . . 56 C5
Little Stretton
  Leics. . . . 64 D3
  Shrops. . . . 60 E4
Little Strickland . . . 99 C7
Little Stukeley . . . 54 B3
Little Sutton . . . 73 B7
Little Tew . . . 38 B3
Little Thetford . . . 55 B6
Little Thirkleby . . . 95 B7
Little Thurlow . . . 55 D7
Little Thurrock . . . 29 B7
Littlethorpe
  Leics. . . . 64 E2
  N Yorks. . . . 95 C6
Littleton
  Ches W . . . 73 C8
  Hants. . . . 26 F2
  Perth. . . . 134 F2
  Som. . . . 23 F6
  Sur . . . . 27 C8
  Sur . . . . 27 E7
Littleton Drew . . . 37 F5
Littleton-
  on-Severn . . . 36 F2
Littleton Pannell 24 D5
Little Torboll . . . 151 B10
Little Torrington . . . 9 C6
Little Totham . . . 42 C4
Little Toux . . . 152 C5
Littletown . . . 111 E6
Little Town
  Cumb . . . . 98 C4
  Lancs . . . . 93 F6
Little Urswick . . . 92 B2
Little Wakering . . . 43 F5

Little Walden . . . 55 E6
Little
  Waldingfield . . . 56 E3
Little
  Walsingham . . . 80 D5
Little Waltham . . . 42 C3
Little Warley . . . 42 E2
Little Weighton . . . 97 F5
Little Welnetham 56 C2
Little Wenham . . . 56 F4
Little Wenlock . . . 61 D6
Little Whittingham
  Green . . . . 57 B6
Littlewick Green . . . 27 B6
Little Wilbraham 55 D6
Little Wishford . . . 25 F5
Little Witley . . . 50 C2
Little Wittenham . . . 39 E5
Little Wolford . . . 51 F7
Littleworth
  Bedford. . . . 53 E8
  Glos . . . . 37 D5
  Oxon . . . . 38 E3
  Staffs . . . . 62 C4
  Worcs . . . 50 D3
Little Wratting . . . 55 E7
Little Wymington 53 C7
Little Wymondley . . . 41 B5
Little Wyrley . . . 62 D4
Little Yeldham . . . 55 F8
Litton
  Derbys . . . 75 B8
  N Yorks . . . 94 B2
  Som. . . . 23 D7
Litton Cheney . . . 12 E3
Liurbost . . . 155 E9
Liverpool . . . 85 E4
Liverpool Airport . . . 86 F2
Liversedge . . . 88 B3
Liverton
  Devon . . . . 7 B6
  Redcar . . . 103 C5
Livingston . . . 120 C3
Livingston
  Village . . . 120 C3
Lixwm . . . 73 B5
Lizard . . . 3 E6
Llaingoch . . . 82 C2
Llaithddu . . . 59 F7
Llan . . . 59 D5
Llanaber . . . 58 C3
Llanaelhaearn . . . 70 C4
Llanafan . . . 47 B5
Llanafan-fawr . . . 47 D8
Llanallgo . . . 82 C4
Llanandras
  = Presteigne . . . 48 C5
Llanarmon . . . 70 D5
Llanarmon Dyffryn
  Ceiriog . . . 73 F5
Llanarmon-
  yn-Ial . . . 73 D5
Llanarth
  Ceredig . . . 46 D3
  Mon. . . . 35 C7
Llanarthne . . . 33 B6
Llanasa . . . 85 F2
Llanbabo . . . 82 C3
Llanbadarn Fawr . . . 58 F3
Llanbadarn
  Fynydd . . . 48 B3
Llanbadarn-
  y-Garreg . . . 48 E3
Llanbadoc . . . 35 E7
Llanbadrig . . . 82 B3
Llanbeder . . . 35 E7
Llanbedr
  Gwyn. . . . 71 E6
  Powys . . . 35 B6
  Powys . . . 48 E3
Llanbedr-
  Dyffryn-Clwyd . . . 72 D5
Llanbedrgoch . . . 82 C5
Llanbedrog . . . 70 D4
Llanbedr Pont Steffan
  = Lampeter . . . 46 E4
Llanbedr-
  y-cennin . . . 83 E7
Llanberis . . . 83 E5
Llanbethery . . . 22 C2
Llanbister . . . 48 B3
Llanblethian . . . 21 B8
Llanboidy . . . 32 B3
Llanbradach . . . 35 E5
Llanbrynmair . . . 59 D5
Llancarfan . . . 22 B2
Llancayo . . . 35 D7
Llancloudy . . . 36 B1
Llancynfelyn . . . 58 E3
Llandaff . . . 22 B3
Llandanwg . . . 71 E6
Llandarcy . . . 33 E8
Llandawke . . . 32 C3
Llanddaniel Fab . . . 82 D4
Llanddarog . . . 33 C6
Llanddeiniol . . . 46 B4
Llanddeiniolen . . . 82 E5
Llandderfel . . . 72 F3
Llanddeusant
  Anglesey . . . 82 C3
  Carms. . . . 34 B1
Llanddew . . . 48 F2
Llanddewi . . . 33 F5
Llanddewi-Brefi . . . 47 D5
Llanddewi'r Cwm . . . 48 E2
Llanddewi
  Rhydderch . . . 35 C7
Llanddewi
  Velfrey . . . 32 C2
Llanddoged . . . 83 E8
Llanddona . . . 83 D5
Llanddowror . . . 32 C3
Llanddulas . . . 72 B3
Llanddwywe . . . 71 E6
Llanddyfnan . . . 82 D5
Llandefaelog
  Fach . . . 48 F2
Llandefaelog-
  tre'rgraig . . . 35 B5
Llandefalle . . . 48 F2
Llandegai . . . 83 D5
Llandegfan . . . 83 D5
Llandegla . . . 73 D5
Llandegley . . . 48 C3
Llandegveth . . . 35 E7
Llandegwning . . . 70 D3
Llandeilo . . . 33 B7
Llandeilo Graban . . . 48 E2

Llandeilo'r Fan . . . 47 F7
Llandeloy . . . 44 C3
Llandenny . . . 35 D8
Llandevenny . . . 35 F8
Llandewednock . . . 3 E6
Llandewi
  Ystradenny . . . 48 C3
Llandinabo . . . 36 B2
Llandinam . . . 59 F7
Llandissilio . . . 32 B2
Llandogo . . . 36 D2
Llandough
  V Glam. . . . 21 B8
  V Glam. . . . 22 B3
Llandovery
  = Llanymddyfri . . . 47 F6
Llandow . . . 21 B8
Llandre
  Carms. . . . 47 E5
  Ceredig . . . 58 F3
Llandrillo . . . 72 F4
Llandrillo-yn-
  Rhos . . . 83 C8
Llandrindod
  = Llandrindod
  Wells . . . 48 C2
Llandrindod Wells
  = Llandrindod . . . 48 C2
Llandrinio . . . 60 C2
Llandudno . . . 83 C7
Llandudno Junction
  = Cyffordd
  Llandudno . . . 83 D7
Llandwrog . . . 82 F4
Llandybie . . . 33 C7
Llandyfaelog . . . 33 C5
Llandyfan . . . 33 C7
Llandyfriog . . . 46 E2
Llandyfrydog . . . 82 C4
Llandygwydd . . . 45 E4
Llandynan . . . 73 E5
Llandyrnog . . . 72 C5
Llandysilio . . . 60 C2
Llandyssil . . . 59 E8
Llandysul . . . 46 E3
Llanedeyrn . . . 35 F6
Llanedi . . . 33 D6
Llaneglwys . . . 48 F2
Llanegryn . . . 58 D2
Llanegwad . . . 33 B6
Llaneilian . . . 82 B4
Llanelian-yn-
  Rhos . . . 83 D8
Llanelidan . . . 72 D5
Llanelieu . . . 48 F3
Llanellen . . . 35 C7
Llanelli . . . 33 E6
Llanelltyd . . . 58 C4
Llanelly . . . 35 C6
Llanelly Hill . . . 35 C6
Llanelwedd . . . 48 D2
Llanelwy
  = St Asaph . . . 72 B4
Llanenddwyn . . . 71 E6
Llanengan . . . 70 E3
Llanerchymedd . . . 82 C4
Llanerfyl . . . 59 D7
Llanfachraeth . . . 82 C3
Llanfachreth . . . 71 E8
Llanfaelog . . . 82 D3
Llanfaelrhys . . . 70 E3
Llanfaenor . . . 35 C8
Llanfaes
  Anglesey . . . 83 D6
  Powys . . . 34 B4
Llanfaethlu . . . 82 C3
Llanfaglan . . . 82 E4
Llanfair . . . 71 E6
Llanfair-ar-
  y-bryn . . . 47 F7
Llanfair
  Caereinion . . . 59 D8
Llanfair Clydogau 46 D5
Llanfair-
  Dyffryn-Clwyd . . . 72 D5
Llanfairfechan . . . 83 D6
Llanfair
  Kilgheddin . . . 35 D7
Llanfair-
  Nant-Gwyn . . . 45 F3
Llanfairpwllgwyngyll
Llanfair Talhaiarn 72 B3
Llanfair
  Waterdine . . . 48 B4
Llanfair-ym-Muallt
  = Builth Wells. . . 48 E2
Llanfairyneubwll 82 D3
Llanfairynghornwy
  . . . 82 B3
Llanfallteg . . . 32 C2
Llanfaredd . . . 48 D2
Llanfarian . . . 46 B4
Llanfechain . . . 59 B8
Llanfechan . . . 47 E8
Llanfechell . . . 82 B3
Llanfendigaid . . . 58 D2
Llanferres . . . 73 C5
Llan Ffestiniog . . . 71 C8
Llanfihangel-
  ararth . . . 46 F3
Llanfihangel-
  Crucorney . . . 35 B7
Llanfihangel Glyn
  Myfyr . . . 72 D3
Llanfihangel Nant
  Bran . . . 47 F8
Llanfihangel-
  nant-Melan . . . 48 D3
Llanfihangel
  Rhydithon . . . 48 C3
Llanfihangel
  Rogiet . . . 35 F8
Llanfihangel
  Tal-y-llyn . . . 35 B5
Llanfihangel-
  uwch-Gwili . . . 33 B5
Llanfihangel-
  y-Creuddyn . . . 47 B5
Llanfihangel-
  yn-Ngwynfa . . . 59 C7
Llanfihangel yn
  Nhowyn . . . 82 D3
Llanfihangel-
  ypennant
  Gwyn. . . . 58 D3
  Gwyn. . . . 71 C6

Llanfihangel-
  ytraethau . . . 71 D6
Llanfilo . . . 48 F3
Llanfoist . . . 35 C6
Llanfor . . . 72 F3
Llanfrechfa . . . 35 E7
Llanfrothen . . . 71 C7
Llanfrynach . . . 34 B4
Llanfwrog
  Anglesey . . . 82 C3
  Denb . . . . 72 D5
Llanfyllin . . . 59 C8
Llanfynydd
  Carms. . . . 33 B6
  Flint . . . . 73 D6
Llanfyrnach . . . 45 F4
Llangadfan . . . 59 C7
Llangadog . . . 33 B8
Llangadwaladr
  Anglesey . . . 82 E3
  Powys . . . 73 F5
Llangaffo . . . 82 E4
Llangain . . . 32 C4
Llangammarch
  Wells . . . 47 E8
Llangan . . . 21 B8
Llangarron . . . 36 B2
Llangasty Talyllyn 35 B5
Llangathen . . . 33 B6
Llangattock . . . 35 C6
Llangattock
  Lingoed . . . 35 B7
Llangattock nigh
  Usk . . . 35 D7
Llangattock-
  Vibon-Avel . . . 36 C1
Llangedwyn . . . 59 B8
Llangefni . . . 82 D4
Llangeinor . . . 34 F3
Llangeitho . . . 46 D5
Llangeler . . . 46 F2
Llangelynin . . . 58 D2
Llangendeirne . . . 33 C5
Llangennech . . . 33 D6
Llangennith . . . 33 E5
Llangenny . . . 35 C6
Llangernyw . . . 83 E8
Llangian . . . 70 E3
Llanglydwen . . . 32 B2
Llangoed . . . 83 D6
Llangoedmor . . . 45 E3
Llangollen . . . 73 E6
Llangolman . . . 32 B2
Llangorse . . . 35 B5
Llangovan . . . 36 D1
Llangower . . . 72 F3
Llangrannog . . . 46 D2
Llangristiolus . . . 82 D4
Llangrove . . . 36 C2
Llangua . . . 35 B7
Llangunllo . . . 48 B4
Llangunnor . . . 33 C5
Llangurig . . . 47 B8
Llangwm
  Conwy . . . 72 E3
  Mon. . . . 35 D8
  Pembs. . . . 44 E4
Llangwnnadl . . . 70 D3
Llangwyfan . . . 72 C5
Llangwyfan-isaf . . . 82 D3
Llangwyllog . . . 82 D4
Llangwyryfon . . . 46 B4
Llangybi
  Ceredig . . . 46 D5
  Gwyn. . . . 70 C5
  Mon. . . . 35 E7
Llangyfelach . . . 33 E7
Llangynhafal . . . 72 C5
Llangynidr . . . 35 C5
Llangynin . . . 32 C3
Llangynog
  Carms. . . . 32 C4
  Powys . . . 59 B7
Llangynwyd . . . 34 F2
Llanhamlach . . . 34 B4
Llanharan . . . 34 F4
Llanharry . . . 34 F4
Llanhennock . . . 35 E7
Llanhilleth
  = Llanhiledd . . . 35 D6
Llanhiledd
  = Llanhilleth . . . 35 D6
Llanidloes . . . 59 F6
Llaniestyn . . . 70 D3
Llanifyny . . . 59 F5
Llanigon . . . 48 F4
Llanilar . . . 46 B5
Llanilid . . . 34 F3
Llanilltud Fawr
  = Llantwit Major . . . 21 C8
Llanishen
  Cardiff. . . . 35 F5
  Mon. . . . 36 D1
Llanllawddog . . . 33 B5
Llanllechid . . . 83 E6
Llanllowell . . . 35 E7
Llanllugan . . . 59 D7
Llanllwch . . . 32 C4
Llanllwchaiarn . . . 59 E8
Llanllwni . . . 46 F3
Llanllyfni . . . 82 F4
Llanmadoc . . . 33 E5
Llanmaes . . . 21 C8
Llanmartin . . . 35 F7
Llanmihangel . . . 21 B8
Llanmorlais . . . 33 E6
Llannefydd . . . 72 B3
Llannon . . . 33 D6
Llannor . . . 70 D4
Llanon . . . 46 C4
Llanover . . . 35 D7
Llanpumsaint . . . 33 B5
Llanreithan . . . 44 C3
Llanrhaeadr . . . 72 C4
Llanrhaeadr-
  ym-Mochnant . . . 59 B8
Llanrhian . . . 44 B3
Llanrhidian . . . 33 E5
Llanrhos . . . 83 C7
Llanrhyddlad . . . 82 C3
Llanrhystud . . . 46 C4
Llanrosser . . . 48 F4
Llanrothal . . . 36 C1
Llanrug . . . 82 E5
Llanrumney . . . 35 F6
Llanrwst . . . 83 E8
Llansadurnen . . . 32 C3

Llansadwrn
  Anglesey . . . 83 D5
  Carms. . . . 47 F5
Llansaint . . . 32 D4
Llansamlet . . . 33 E7
Llansannan . . . 72 C3
Llansannor . . . 21 B8
Llansantffraed
  Ceredig . . . 46 C4
  Powys . . . 35 B5
Llansantffraed
  Cwmdeuddwr . . . 47 C8
Llansantffraed-
  in-Elvel . . . 48 D2
Llansawel . . . 46 F5
Llansilin . . . 60 B2
Llansoy . . . 35 D8
Llanspyddid . . . 34 B4
Llanstadwell . . . 44 E4
Llansteffan . . . 32 C4
Llanstephan . . . 48 E3
Llantarnam . . . 35 E7
Llanteg . . . 32 C2
Llanthony . . . 35 B6
Llantilio
  Crossenny . . . 35 C7
Llantilio
  Pertholey . . . 35 C7
Llantood . . . 45 E3
Llantrisant
  Anglesey . . . 82 C3
  Mon. . . . 35 E7
  Rhondda . . . 34 F4
Llantrithyd . . . 22 B2
Llantwit Fardre . . . 34 F4
Llantwit Major
  = Llanilltud Fawr . . . 21 C8
Llanuwchllyn . . . 72 F2
Llanvaches . . . 35 E8
Llanvair
  Discoed . . . 35 E8
Llanvapley . . . 35 C7
Llanvetherine . . . 35 C7
Llanveynoe . . . 48 F5
Llanvihangel
  Gobion . . . 35 D7
Llanvihangel-
  Ystern-Llewern . . . 35 C8
Llanwarne . . . 36 B2
Llanwddyn . . . 59 C7
Llanwenog . . . 46 E3
Llanwern . . . 35 F7
Llanwinio . . . 32 B3
Llanwnda
  Gwyn. . . . 82 F4
  Pembs. . . . 44 B4
Llanwnnen . . . 46 E4
Llanwnog . . . 59 E7
Llanwrda . . . 47 F6
Llanwrin . . . 58 D4
Llanwrthwl . . . 47 C8
Llanwrtud
  = Llanwrtyd Wells . . . 47 E7
Llanwrtyd . . . 47 E7
Llanwrtyd Wells
  = Llanwrtud . . . 47 E7
Llanwyddelan . . . 59 D7
Llanyblodwel . . . 60 B2
Llanybri . . . 32 C4
Llanybydder . . . 46 E4
Llanycefn . . . 32 B1
Llanychaer . . . 44 B4
Llanycil . . . 72 F3
Llanycrwys . . . 46 E5
Llanymawddwy . . . 59 C6
Llanymddyfri
  = Llandovery . . . 47 F6
Llanymynech . . . 60 B2
Llanynghenedl . . . 82 C3
Llanynys . . . 72 C5
Llan-y-pwll . . . 73 D7
Llanyre . . . 48 C2
Llanystumdwy . . . 71 D5
Llanywern . . . 35 B5
Llawhaden . . . 32 C1
Llawnt . . . 73 F6
Llawr Dref . . . 70 E3
Llawryglyn . . . 59 E6
Llay . . . 73 D7
Llechcynfarwy . . . 82 C3
Llecheiddior . . . 71 C5
Llechfaen . . . 34 B4
Llechryd
  Caerph. . . . 35 D5
  Ceredig . . . 45 E4
Llechrydau . . . 73 F6
Lledrod . . . 46 B5
Llenmerewig . . . 59 E8
Llethrid . . . 33 E6
Llidiad Nenog . . . 46 F4
Llidiardau . . . 72 F2
Llidiart-y-parc . . . 72 E5
Llithfaen . . . 70 C4
Llong . . . 73 C6
Llowes . . . 48 E3
Llundain-fach . . . 46 D4
Llwydcoed . . . 34 D3
Llwyn . . . 60 F2
Llwyncelyn . . . 46 D3
Llwyndafydd . . . 46 D2
Llwynderw . . . 60 D2
Llwyn-du . . . 35 C6
Llwyndyrys . . . 70 C4
Llwyngwril . . . 58 D2
Llwyn-hendy . . . 33 E6
Llwynmawr . . . 73 F6
Llwyn-têg . . . 33 D6
Llwyn-y-brain . . . 32 C2
Llwyn-y-groes . . . 46 D4
Llwynypia . . . 34 E3
Llynclys . . . 60 B2
Llynfaes . . . 82 D4
Llysfaen . . . 83 D8
Llyswen . . . 48 F3
Llysworney . . . 21 B8
Llys-y-frân . . . 32 B1
Llywel . . . 47 F7
Loan . . . 120 B2
Loanend . . . 122 E5
Loanhead . . . 121 C5
Loans . . . 118 F3
Loans of
  Tullich . . . 151 D11
Lobb . . . 20 F3
Loch a
  Charnain . . . 148 D3

Loch a'
  Ghainmhich . . . 155 E7
Lochailort . . . 147 C10
Lochaline . . . 147 G9
Lochans . . . 104 D4
Lochanhully . . . 138 B5
Lochassynt
  House . . . 156 G4
Lochavich
  House . . . 124 D5
Lochawe . . . 125 C7
Loch Baghasdail
  = Lochboisdale . . . 148 G2
Lochboisdale
  = Loch Baghasdail . . . 148 G2
Lochbuie . . . 124 C2
Lochcarron . . . 149 E13
Loch Choire
  Lodge . . . 157 F9
Lochdhu . . . 157 E13
Lochdochart
  House . . . 126 B3
Lochdon . . . 124 B3
Lochdrum . . . 150 D5
Lochead . . . 144 F6
Lochearnhead . . . 126 B4
Lochee . . . 134 F3
Lochend
  Highld . . . 151 H8
  Highld . . . 158 D4
Locherben . . . 114 E2
Lochfoot . . . 107 B5
Lochgair . . . 145 D8
Lochgarthside . . . 137 C8
Lochgelly . . . 128 E3
Lochgilphead . . . 145 E7
Lochgoilhead . . . 125 E8
Loch Head . . . 105 F7
Lochhill . . . 152 B2
Lochindorb
  Lodge . . . 151 H12
Lochinver . . . 156 G3
Lochlane . . . 127 B7
Loch Loyal
  Lodge . . . 157 E9
Lochluichart . . . 150 E6
Lochmaben . . . 114 F3
Lochmaddy = Loch
  nam Madadh . . . 148 B4
Lochmore
  Cottage . . . 158 F2
Lochmore
  Lodge . . . 156 F5
Loch nam Madadh
  = Lochmaddy . . . 148 B4
Lochore . . . 128 E3
Lochportain . . . 148 A4
Lochranza . . . 143 C10
Lochs Crofts . . . 152 B3
Loch Sgioport . . . 148 E3
Lochside
  Aberds . . . 135 C7
  Highld . . . 151 F11
  Highld . . . 156 D7
  Highld . . . 157 F11
Lochslin . . . 151 C11
Lochstack
  Lodge . . . 156 F5
Lochton . . . 141 E6
Lochty
  Angus . . . 135 C5
  Fife . . . . 129 D7
  Perth. . . . 128 B2
Lochuisge . . . 130 D1
Lochurr . . . 113 F7
Lochwinnoch . . . 118 D3
Lochwood
  Borders . . . 115 B8
  Stockton . . . 102 C1
Lochyside . . . 131 B5
Lockengate . . . 4 C5
Lockerbie . . . 114 F4
Lockeridge . . . 25 C6
Lockerley . . . 14 B3
Locking . . . 23 D5
Lockington
  E Yorks . . . 97 E5
  Leics. . . . 63 B8
Lockleywood . . . 61 B6
Locks Heath . . . 15 D6
Lockton . . . 103 E6
Lockwood . . . 88 C2
Loddington
  Leics. . . . 64 D4
  N Nhants. . . . 53 B6
Loddiswell . . . 6 E5
Loddon . . . 69 E6
Lode . . . 55 C6
Loders . . . 12 E2
Lodsworth . . . 16 B3
Lofthouse
  N Yorks . . . 94 B4
  W Yorks . . . 88 B4
Loftus . . . 103 C5
Logan . . . 113 B5
Loganlea . . . 120 C2
Logan Mains . . . 104 E4
Loggerheads . . . 74 F4
Logie
  Angus . . . 135 C6
  Fife . . . . 129 B6
  Moray . . . 151 F13
Logiealmond
  Lodge . . . 133 F6
Logie
  Coldstone . . . 140 D3
Logie Hill . . . 151 D10
Logie Newton . . . 153 D6
Logie Pert . . . 135 C6
Logierait . . . 133 D6
Login . . . 32 B2
Lolworth . . . 54 C4
Lonbain . . . 149 C11
Londesborough . . . 96 E4
London Colney . . . 40 D4
Londonderry . . . 101 F8
Londonthorpe . . . 78 F2
Londubh . . . 155 J13
Lonemore . . . 151 C10
Long Ashton . . . 23 B7
Longbar . . . 118 D3
Long Bennington . . . 77 E8
Longborough . . . 38 B1
Long Bredy . . . 12 E3
Longbridge
  Warks . . . 51 C7

Longbridge continued
  W Mid . . . 50 B5
Longbridge
  Deverill . . . 24 E3
Long Buckby . . . 52 C4
Longburton . . . 12 C4
Long Clawson . . . 64 B4
Longcliffe . . . 76 D2
Long Common . . . 15 C6
Long Compton
  Staffs . . . 62 B2
  Warks . . . 51 F7
Longcot . . . 38 E2
Long Crendon . . . 39 D6
Long Crichel . . . 13 C7
Longcroft . . . 119 B7
Longden . . . 60 D4
Long Ditton . . . 28 C2
Longdon
  Staffs . . . 62 C4
  Worcs . . . 50 F3
Longdon Green . . . 62 C4
Longdon on Tern . . . 61 C6
Longdown . . . 10 E3
Longdowns . . . 3 C6
Long Drax . . . 89 B7
Long
  Duckmanton . . . 76 B4
Long Eaton . . . 76 F4
Longfield
  Kent . . . 29 C7
  Shetland . . . 160 M5
Longford
  Derbys . . . 76 F2
  Glos . . . . 37 B5
  London . . . 27 B8
  Shrops . . . 74 F3
  Telford . . . 61 C7
  W Mid . . . 63 F7
Longfordlane . . . 76 F2
Longforgan . . . 128 B5
Longformacus . . . 122 D2
Longframlington
  . . . 117 D7
Long Green . . . 50 F3
Longham
  Dorset. . . . 13 E8
  Norf . . . . 68 C2
Long
  Hanborough . . . 38 C4
Longhaven . . . 153 E11
Longhill . . . 153 C9
Longhirst . . . 117 F8
Longhope
  Glos . . . . 36 C3
  Orkney . . . 159 J4
Longhorsley . . . 117 E7
Longhoughton . . . 117 C8
Long Itchington . . . 52 C2
Longlane
  Derbys . . . 76 F2
  W Berks . . . 26 B2
Long Lawford . . . 52 B2
Longlevens . . . 37 B5
Longley . . . 88 D2
Longley Green . . . 50 D2
Long Load . . . 12 B2
Longmanhill . . . 153 B7
Long Marston
  Herts. . . . 40 C1
  N Yorks . . . 95 D8
  Warks . . . 51 E6
Long Marton . . . 100 B1
Long Melford . . . 56 E2
Longmoor Camp . . . 27 F5
Longmorn . . . 152 C2
Long Newnton . . . 37 E6
Longnewton
  Borders . . . 115 B8
  Stockton . . . 102 C1
Longney . . . 36 C4
Longniddry . . . 121 B7
Longnor
  Shrops . . . 60 D4
  Staffs . . . 75 C7
Longparish . . . 26 E2
Longport . . . 75 E5
Long Preston . . . 93 D8
Longridge
  Lancs . . . . 93 F6
  Staffs . . . 62 C3
  W Loth. . . . 120 C2
Longriggend . . . 119 B8
Long Riston . . . 97 E7
Longsdon . . . 75 D6
Longshaw . . . 86 D3
Longside . . . 153 D10
Long Sight . . . 87 D7
Longstanton . . . 54 C4
Longstock . . . 25 F8
Longstone . . . 32 D2
Longstowe . . . 54 D4
Long Stratton . . . 68 E4
Long Street . . . 53 E5
Long Sutton
  Hants . . . 26 E5
  Lincs. . . . 66 B4
  Som. . . . 12 B2
Longthorpe . . . 65 E8
Long Thurlow . . . 56 C4
Longthwaite . . . 99 B6
Longton
  Lancs . . . . 86 B2
  Stoke . . . 75 E6
Longtown
  Cumb . . . 108 C3
  Hereford . . . 35 B7
Longview . . . 86 E2
Longville in the
  Dale . . . 60 E5
Long Whatton . . . 63 B8
Longwick . . . 39 D7
Long Wittenham . . . 39 E5
Longwitton . . . 117 F6
Longwood . . . 61 D6
Longworth . . . 38 E3
Longyester . . . 121 C8
Lonmay . . . 153 C10
Lonmore . . . 148 D7
Looe . . . 5 D7
Loose . . . 29 D8
Loosley Row . . . 39 D8
Lopcombe Corner 25 F7
Lopen . . . 12 C2
Loppington . . . 60 B4
Lopwell . . . 6 C2
Lorbottle . . . 117 D6

Lorbottle Hall . . . 117 D6
Lornty . . . 134 E1
Loscoe . . . 76 E4
Losgaintir . . . 154 H5
Lossiemouth . . . 152 A2
Lossit . . . 142 C2
Lostford . . . 74 F3
Lostock Gralam . . . 74 B3
Lostock Green . . . 74 B3
Lostock Hall . . . 86 B3
Lostock Junction 86 D4
Lostwithiel . . . 5 D6
Loth . . . 159 E7
Lothbeg . . . 157 H12
Lothersdale . . . 94 E2
Lothmore . . . 157 H12
Loudwater . . . 40 E2
Loughborough . . . 64 C2
Loughor . . . 33 E6
Loughton
  Essex . . . . 41 E7
  M Keynes . . . 53 F6
  Shrops . . . 61 F6
Lound
  Lincs. . . . 65 C7
  Notts. . . . 89 F7
  Suff. . . . 69 E8
Lount . . . 63 C7
Louth . . . 91 F7
Love Clough . . . 87 B6
Lovedean . . . 15 C7
Lover . . . 14 B3
Loversall . . . 89 E6
Loves Green . . . 42 D2
Lovesome Hill . . . 102 E1
Loveston . . . 32 D1
Lovington . . . 23 F7
Low Ackworth . . . 89 C5
Low Barlings . . . 78 B3
Low Bentham . . . 93 C6
Low Bradfield . . . 88 E3
Low Bradley . . . 94 E3
Low Braithwaite 108 E4
Low Brunton . . . 110 B2
Low Burnham . . . 89 D8
Low Burton . . . 101 F7
Low Buston . . . 117 D8
Lowca . . . 98 B1
Low Catton . . . 96 D3
Low Clanfield . . . 104 F5
Low Coniscliffe . . . 101 C7
Low Crosby . . . 108 D4
Low Dalby . . . 103 F6
Lowdham . . . 77 E6
Low Dinsdale . . . 101 C8
Lowe . . . 74 F2
Lowe Hill . . . 75 D6
Low Ellington . . . 101 F7
Lower Aisholt . . . 22 F4
Lower Arncott . . . 39 C6
Lower Ashton . . . 10 F3
Lower Assendon . . . 39 F7
Lower Badcall . . . 156 E4
Lower Bartle . . . 92 F4
Lower Basildon . . . 26 B4
Lower Beeding . . . 17 B6
Lower Benefield . . . 65 F7
Lower
  Boddington . . . 52 D2
Lower Brailes . . . 51 F8
Lower Breakish 149 F11
Lower
  Broadheath . . . 50 D3
Lower
  Bullingham . . . 49 F7
Lower Cam . . . 36 D4
Lower Chapel . . . 48 F2
Lower Chute . . . 25 D8
Lower Crossings . . . 87 F8
Lower
  Cumberworth . . . 88 D3
Lower Darwen . . . 86 B4
Lower Dean . . . 53 C8
Lower Diabaig . . . 149 B12
Lower Dicker . . . 18 D2
Lower Dinchope . . . 60 F4
Lower Down . . . 60 F3
Lower Drift . . . 2 D3
Lower Dunsforth . . . 95 C7
Lower Egleton . . . 49 E8
Lower Elkstone . . . 75 D7
Lower End . . . 40 B2
Lower Everleigh 25 D6
Lower Farringdon 26 F5
Lower Foxdale . . . 84 E2
Lower Frankton . . . 73 F7
Lower Froyle . . . 27 E5
Lower Gledfield 151 B8
Lower Green . . . 81 D5
Lower Hacheston 57 D7
Lower Halistra . . . 148 C7
Lower Halstow . . . 30 C2
Lower Hardres . . . 31 D5
Lower
  Hawthwaite . . . 98 F4
Lower Heath . . . 75 C5
Lower
  Hempriggs . . . 151 E14
Lower Hergest . . . 48 D4
Lower Heyford . . . 38 B4
Lower Higham . . . 29 B8
Lower Holbrook . . . 57 F5
Lower Hordley . . . 60 B3
Lower
  Horsebridge . . . 18 D2
Lower Killeyan . . . 142 D3
Lower
  Kingswood . . . 28 D3
Lower Kinnerton 73 C7
Lower Langford . . . 23 C6
Lower Largo . . . 129 D6
Lower Leigh . . . 75 F7
Lower Lemington 51 F7
Lower Lenie . . . 137 B8
Lower Lydbrook . . . 36 C2
Lower Lye . . . 49 C6
Lower Machen . . . 35 F6
Lower
  Maes-coed . . . 48 F5
Lower Mayland . . . 43 D5
Lower Midway . . . 63 B7
Lower Milovaig . . . 148 C6
Lower Moor . . . 50 E4

Lower Nazeing . . 41 D6
Lower
 Netchwood. . . . .61 E6
Lower Ollach . . 149 E10
Lower Penarth . . 22 B4
Lower Penn . . . . .62 E2
Lower
 Pennington . . . .14 E4
Lower Peover . . .74 B4
Lower Pexhill . . .75 B5
Lower Place. . . . .87 C7
Lower Quinton . .51 E6
Lower Rochford .49 C8
Lower Seagry . . .37 F6
Lower Shelton. . .53 E7
Lower Shiplake . .27 B5
Lower
 Shuckburgh. . . .52 C2
Lower Slaughter .38 B1
Lower Stanton
 St Quintin . . . . .37 F6
Lower Stoke. . . .30 B2
Lower Stondon . .54 F2
Lower Stow
 Bedon . . . . . . . .68 E2
Lower Street
 Norf . . . . . . . . . .69 C6
 Norf . . . . . . . . . .81 D8
Lower Strensham.50 E4
Lower Stretton . .86 F4
Lower Sundon . .40 B3
Lower Swanwick 15 D5
Lower Swell . . . .38 B1
Lower Tean . . . . .75 F7
Lower Thurlton . .69 E7
Lower Tote . . 149 B10
Lower Town . . . .44 B4
Lower Tysoe . . . .51 E8
Lower Upham . . .15 C6
Lower Vexford . .22 F3
Lower Weare . . . .23 D6
Lower Welson . . .48 D4
Lower Whitley . . .74 B3
Lower Wield . . . .26 E4
Lower
 Winchendon . . .39 C7
Lower
 Withington. . . .74 C5
Lower Woodend . .39 F7
Lower Woodford .25 F6
Lower Wyche. . . .50 E2
Lowesby . . . . . . .64 D4
Lowestoft . . . . . .69 E8
Loweswater . . . .98 B3
Low Etherley . . 101 B6
Low Fell. . . . . . 111 D5
Lowford . . . . . . .15 C5
Low Fulney . . . . .66 B2
Low Garth . . . . 103 D5
Low Gate. . . . . 110 C2
Lowgill
 Cumb . . . . . . . . .99 E8
 Lancs . . . . . . . . .93 C6
Low Grantley . . .94 B5
Low Habberley . .50 B3
Low Ham . . . . . .12 B2
Low Hesket . . . 108 E4
Low Hesleyhurst 117 E6
Low Hutton . . . . 96 C3
Lowick
 N Nhants. . . . . . .65 F6
 Northumb. . . . . 123 F6
Lowick Bridge . .98 F4
Lowick Green . .98 F4
Low Laithe . . . .94 C4
Lowlands . . . . . .35 E6
Low Leighton. . . .87 F8
Low Lorton. . . . .98 B3
Low Marishes . .96 B4
Low Marnham . .77 C8
Low Mill. . . . . . 102 E4
Low Moor
 Lancs . . . . . . . . .93 E4
 W Yorks. . . . . . .88 B2
Lowmoor Row . .99 B8
Low Moorsley . 111 E6
Low Newton . . . .99 F6
Low Newton-
 by-the-Sea. . . 117 B8
Lownie Moor . . 134 E4
Low Row
 Cumb . . . . . . . 108 F3
 Cumb . . . . . . . 109 C5
 N Yorks . . . . . 100 E4
Low Salchrie . . 104 C4
Low Smerby . . . 143 F6
Lowsonford . . . .51 C6
Lowther . . . . . . .99 B7
Lowthorpe . . . . .97 C6
Lowton . . . . . . . .86 E4
Lowton Common .86 E4
Low Torry . . . . 128 F2
Low Worsall . . . 102 D1
Low Wray . . . . . .99 D5
Loxbeare. . . . . . .10 C4
Loxhill . . . . . . . .27 E8
Loxhore. . . . . . . .20 F5
Loxley . . . . . . . . .51 D7
Loxton . . . . . . . .23 D5
Loxwood. . . . . . .27 F8
Lubcroy. . . . . . 156 J6
Lubenham . . . . .64 F4
Luccombe . . . . . .21 E8
Luccombe
 Village . . . . . . .15 G6
Lucker . . . . . . . 123 F7
Luckett . . . . . . . . .5 B8
Luckington . . . . .37 F5
Lucklawhill . . . 129 B6
Lucton . . . . . . . .49 C6
Ludag . . . . . . . 148 G2
Ludborough . . . .91 E6
Ludchurch . . . . .32 C2
Luddenden . . . . .87 B8
Luddenden Foot .87 B8
Luddesdown . . . .29 C7
Luddington
 N Lincs . . . . . . . .90 C2
 Warks . . . . . . . . .51 D6
Luddington in the
 Brook. . . . . . . .65 F8
Lude House . . . 133 C5
Ludford
 Lincs . . . . . . . . .91 F6

Ludford continued
 Shrops . . . . . . . .49 B7
Ludgershall
 Bucks . . . . . . . . .39 C6
 Wilts . . . . . . . . .25 D7
Ludgvan . . . . . . . .2 C4
Ludham . . . . . . .69 C6
Ludlow . . . . . . . .49 B7
Ludwell . . . . . . . .13 B7
Ludworth . . . . . 111 E6
Luffincott . . . . . . .8 E5
Lugar . . . . . . . . 113 B5
Luggate Burn . . 122 B2
Lugg Green . . . .49 C6
Lugton . . . . . . . 118 D4
Lugwardine . . . .49 E7
Luib . . . . . . . . 149 F10
Lulham . . . . . . . .49 E6
Lullenden . . . . . .28 E5
Lullington
 Derbys . . . . . . . .63 C6
 Som. . . . . . . . . . .24 D2
Lulsgate Bottom. 23 C7
Lulsley . . . . . . . .50 D2
Lumb . . . . . . . . . .87 B8
Lumby . . . . . . . . .95 F7
Lumloch . . . . . . 119 C6
Lumphanan . . . 140 D4
Lumphinnans . . 128 E3
Lumsdaine . . . . 122 C4
Lumsden . . . . . 140 B3
Lunan . . . . . . . . 135 D6
Lunanhead . . . . 134 D4
Luncarty . . . . . 128 B2
Lund
 E Yorks . . . . . . .97 E5
 N Yorks . . . . . . .96 F3
 Shetland . . . . . 160 C7
Lunderton . . . 153 D11
Lundie
 Angus . . . . . . . 134 F2
 Highld . . . . . . . 136 C4
Lundin Links . . 129 D6
Lunga . . . . . . . . 124 E3
Lunna . . . . . . . . 160 G6
Lunning . . . . . . 160 G7
Lunnon . . . . . . . .33 F6
Lunsford's Cross 18 D4
Lunt . . . . . . . . . .85 D4
Luntley . . . . . . . .49 D5
Luppitt . . . . . . . .11 D6
Lupset . . . . . . . .88 C4
Lupton . . . . . . . .99 F7
Lurgashall . . . . .16 B3
Lusby . . . . . . . . .79 C6
Luson . . . . . . . . . .6 E4
Lussagiven. . . . 144 E5
Lusta . . . . . . . . 149 C7
Lustleigh . . . . . . .10 F2
Luston . . . . . . . .49 C6
Luthermuir . . . 135 C6
Luthrie . . . . . . . 128 C5
Luton
 Devon . . . . . . . . . .7 B7
 Luton . . . . . . . . .40 B3
 Medway . . . . . . .29 C8
Lutterworth . . . .64 F2
Lutton
 Devon . . . . . . . . . .6 D3
 Lincs . . . . . . . . .66 B4
 N Nhants . . . . . .65 F8
Lutworthy . . . . . .10 C2
Luxborough . . . .21 F8
Luxulyan . . . . . . .5 D5
Lybster . . . . . . 158 G4
Lydbury North . .60 F3
Lydcott . . . . . . . .21 F5
Lydd . . . . . . . . . .19 C7
Lydden . . . . . . . .31 E6
Lyddington . . . .65 E5
Lydd on Sea . . . .19 C7
Lydeard
 St Lawrence. . . .22 F3
Lyde Green . . . .26 D5
Lydford . . . . . . . . .9 F7
Lydford-on-
 Fosse. . . . . . . .23 F7
Lydgate . . . . . . . .87 B7
Lydham . . . . . . .60 E3
Lydiard Green . .37 F7
Lydiard Millicent .37 F7
Lydiate . . . . . . . .85 D4
Lydlinch . . . . . . .12 C5
Lydney . . . . . . . .36 D3
Lydstep . . . . . . . .32 E1
Lye . . . . . . . . . . .62 F3
Lye Green
 Bucks . . . . . . . . .40 D2
 E Sus . . . . . . . . .18 B2
Lyford . . . . . . . .38 E3
Lymbridge Green.30 E5
Lyme Regis . . . . .11 E8
Lyminge . . . . . . .31 E5
Lymington . . . . .14 E4
Lyminster . . . . . .16 D4
Lymm . . . . . . . . .86 F4
Lymore . . . . . . . .14 E3
Lympne . . . . . . . .19 B8
Lympsham . . . . .22 D5
Lympstone . . . . .10 F4
Lynchat . . . . . . 138 D3
Lyndale House . 149 C8
Lyndhurst . . . . . .14 D4
Lyndon . . . . . . . .65 D6
Lyne . . . . . . . . . .27 C8
Lyneal . . . . . . . . .73 F8
Lyne Down . . . . .49 F8
Lyneham
 Oxon . . . . . . . . .38 B2
 Wilts . . . . . . . . .24 B5
Lynemore . . . . 139 B6
Lynemouth . . . . 117 E8
Lyne of
 Gorthleck . . . . 137 B8
Lyne of Skene . 141 C6
Lyness . . . . . . . 159 J4
Lyng
 Norf . . . . . . . . . .68 C3
 Som. . . . . . . . . . .11 B8
Lynmouth . . . . . .21 E6
Lynsted . . . . . . . .30 C3
Lynton . . . . . . . .21 E6
Lyon's Gate . . . .12 D4
Lyonshall . . . . . .48 D5
Lytchett
 Matravers . . . .13 E7

Lytchett Minster. .13 E7
Lyth . . . . . . . . . 158 D4
Lytham . . . . . . . .85 B4
Lytham St Anne's.85 B4
Lythe . . . . . . . . 103 C6
Lythes . . . . . . . 159 K5

# M

Mabe Burnthouse .3 C6
Mabie . . . . . . . . 107 B6
Mablethorpe . . .91 F9
Macclesfield . . .75 B6
Macclesfield
 Forest . . . . . . . .75 B6
Macduff . . . . . . 153 B7
Mace Green . . . .56 E5
Macharioch . . . 143 H8
Machen . . . . . . . .35 F6
Machrihanish . . 143 F7
Machynlleth . . . .58 D4
Machynys . . . . . .33 E6
Mackerel's
 Common . . . . . .16 B4
Mackworth . . . . .76 F3
Macmerry . . . . 121 B7
Madderty . . . . . 127 B8
Maddiston . . . . 120 B2
Madehurst . . . . .16 C3
Madeley
 Staffs . . . . . . . . .74 E4
 Telford . . . . . . . .61 D6
Madeley Heath . .74 E4
Madeley Park . . .74 E4
Madingley . . . . .54 C4
Madley. . . . . . . . .49 F6
Madresfield . . . .50 E3
Madron . . . . . . . . .2 C3
Maenaddwyn . . .82 C4
Maenclochog . . .32 B1
Maendy . . . . . . . .22 B2
Maentwrog . . . . .71 C7
Maen-y-groes . . .46 D2
Maer . . . . . . . . . .74 F4
Maerdy
 Conwy . . . . . . . .72 E4
 Rhondda . . . . . . .34 E3
Maesbrook . . . . .60 B2
Maesbury . . . . . .60 B3
Maesbury Marsh .60 B3
Maesgwyn-Isaf . .59 C8
Maesgwynne . . . .32 B3
Maeshafn . . . . . .73 C6
Maesllyn . . . . . . .46 E2
Maesteg . . . . . . .34 E2
Maes-Treylow . . .48 C4
Maesybont . . . . .33 C6
Maesycrugiau . . .46 E3
Maesy cwmmer . .35 E5
Maesymeillion . .46 E3
Magdalen Laver. 41 D8
Maggieknockater
 . . . . . . . . . . . . 152 D3
Magham Down . .18 D3
Maghull . . . . . . .85 D4
Magor . . . . . . . . .35 F8
Magpie Green . . .68 F4
Maiden Bradley . 24 F3
Maidencombe . . . .7 C7
Maidenhall . . . . .57 E5
Maidenhead . . . .40 F1
Maiden Law . . . 110 E4
Maiden Newton . 12 E3
Maidens . . . . . . 112 D2
Maidensgrave . . .57 E6
Maiden's Green . .27 B6
Maidenwell
 Corn . . . . . . . . . .5 B6
 Lincs . . . . . . . . .79 B6
Maiden Wells . . .44 F4
Maidford . . . . . . .52 D4
Maids Moreton . .52 F5
Maidstone . . . . .29 D8
Maidwell . . . . . .52 B5
Mail . . . . . . . . . 160 L6
Main . . . . . . . . . .59 C8
Maindee . . . . . . .35 F7
Mainsforth . . . . 111 F6
Mains of Airies . 104 C3
Mains of
 Allardice . . . . 135 B8
Mains of
 Annochie . . . . 153 D9
Mains of
 Ardestie . . . . . 135 F5
Mains of Balhall 135 C5
Mains of
 Ballindarg . . . 134 D4
Mains of
 Balnakettle . . 135 B6
Mains of
 Birness . . . . . 153 E9
Mains of
 Burgie . . . . . . 151 F13
Mains of
 Clunas . . . . . . 151 G11
Mains of
 Crichie . . . . . . 153 D9
Mains of
 Dalvey . . . . . . 151 H14
Mains of
 Dellavaird . . . 141 F6
Mains of Drum . 141 E7
Mains of
 Edingight . . . . 152 C5
Mains of
 Fedderate . . . 153 D8
Mains of
 Inkhorn . . . . . 153 E9
Mains of Mayen 152 D5
Mains of
 Melgund . . . . 135 D5
Mains of
 Thornton . . . . 135 B6
Mains of Watten 158 E4
Mainsriddle . . . 107 D6
Mainstone . . . . .60 F2
Maisemore . . . . .37 B5
Malacleit . . . . . 148 A2
Malborough . . . . .6 F5
Malcoff . . . . . . . .87 F8
Maldon . . . . . . . .42 D4
Maligar . . . . . . 149 B9
Mallaig . . . . . . 147 B9

Malleny Mills . . 120 C4
Malling . . . . . . . 126 D4
Malltraeth . . . . . .82 E4
Mallwyd . . . . . . .59 C5
Malmesbury . . . .37 F6
Malmsmead. . . . .21 E6
Malpas
 Ches W . . . . . . . .73 E8
 Corn . . . . . . . . . . .3 B7
 Newport . . . . . . .35 E7
Malswick . . . . . . .36 B4
Maltby
 Stockton . . . . . 102 C2
 S Yorks . . . . . . . .89 E6
Maltby le Marsh . .91 F8
Malting Green . . .43 B5
Maltman's Hill . . .30 E3
Malton . . . . . . . .96 B3
Malvern Link . . .50 E2
Malvern Wells . . .50 E2
Mamble . . . . . . . .49 B8
Mamhilad . . . . . .35 D7
Manaccan. . . . . . .3 D6
Manafon . . . . . . .59 D8
Manais . . . . . . . 154 J6
Manar House . . 141 B6
Manaton . . . . . . .10 F2
Manby . . . . . . . . .91 F7
Mancetter . . . . . .63 E7
Manchester . . . . .87 E6
Manchester
 Airport . . . . . . .87 F6
Mancot . . . . . . . .73 C7
Mandally . . . . . 137 D5
Manea. . . . . . . . .66 F4
Manfield . . . . . . 101 C7
Mangaster . . . . 160 F5
Mangotsfield . . . .23 B8
Mangurstadh . . 154 D5
Mankinholes . . . .87 B7
Manley . . . . . . . .74 B2
Manmoel . . . . . .35 D5
Mannal . . . . . . . 146 G2
Mannerston . . . 120 B3
Manningford
 Bohune . . . . . . .25 D6
Manningford
 Bruce . . . . . . . .25 D6
Manningham . . .94 F4
Mannings Heath. 17 B6
Mannington . . . .13 D8
Manningtree . . . .56 F4
Mannofield . . . 141 D8
Manor . . . . . . . . .41 F7
Manorbier . . . . .32 E1
Manordeilo . . . . .33 B7
Manor Estate. . . .88 F4
Manorhill . . . . . 122 F2
Manorowen . . . .44 B4
Mansel field . . . .33 F6
Mansell Lacy . . . .49 E6
Mansell Gamage .49 E5
Mansergh . . . . . .99 F8
Mansfield
 E Ayrs . . . . . . . 113 C6
 Notts . . . . . . . . .76 C5
Mansfield
 Woodhouse . . .76 C5
Mansriggs . . . . . .98 F4
Manston
 Dorset . . . . . . . .13 C6
 Kent . . . . . . . . . .31 C7
 W Yorks . . . . . . .95 F6
Manswood . . . . .13 D7
Manthorpe
 Lincs . . . . . . . . .65 C7
 Lincs . . . . . . . . .78 F2
Manton
 N Lincs . . . . . . . .90 D3
 Notts . . . . . . . . .77 B5
 Rutland . . . . . . .65 D5
 Wilts . . . . . . . . .25 C6
Manuden . . . . . .41 B7
Maperton . . . . . .12 B4
Maplebeck . . . . .77 C7
Maple Cross . . . .40 E3
Mapledurham . . .26 B4
Mapledurwell . . .26 D4
Maplehurst . . . . .17 B5
Maplescombe . . .29 C6
Mapleton . . . . . .75 E8
Mapperley . . . . .76 E4
Mapperley Park . .77 E5
Mapperton . . . . .12 E3
Mappleborough
 Green . . . . . . . .51 C5
Mappleton . . . . .97 E8
Mappowder . . . .12 D5
Maraig . . . . . . . 154 G6
Marazanvose . . . .4 D3
Marazion . . . . . . .2 C4
Marbhig . . . . . . 155 F9
Marbury . . . . . . .74 E2
March
 Cambs . . . . . . . .66 E4
 S Lanark . . . . . 114 C2
Marcham . . . . . .38 E4
Marchamley . . . .61 B5
Marchington . . . .75 F7
Marchington
 Woodlands . . . .62 B5
Marchroes . . . . .70 E4
Marchwiel . . . . . .73 E7
Marchwood . . . .14 C4
Marcross . . . . . .21 C8
Marden
 Hereford . . . . . .49 E7
 Kent . . . . . . . . . .29 E8
 T&W . . . . . . . . 111 B6
 Wilts . . . . . . . . .25 D5
Marden Beech . .29 E8
Marden Thorn . .29 E8
Mardy . . . . . . . . .35 C7
Marefield . . . . . .64 D4
Mareham le Fen .79 C5
Mareham on the
 Hill . . . . . . . . . .79 C5
Marehay . . . . . . .76 E3
Marehill . . . . . . .16 C4
Maresfield . . . . .17 B8
Marfleet . . . . . . .90 B5
Marford . . . . . . .73 D7
Margam . . . . . . .34 F1
Margaret Marsh .13 C6
Margaret Roding .42 C1
Margaretting . . .42 D2
Margate . . . . . . .31 B7
Margnaheglish 143 E11
Margrove Park . 102 C4

Marham . . . . . . .67 C7
Marhamchurch. . .8 D4
Marholm . . . . . . .65 D8
Marian-glas . . . .82 C4
Mariandyrus . . . .83 C6
Marianglas . . . . .82 C5
Marianleigh . . . . .10 B2
Marishader . . . . 149 B9
Marjoriebanks . 114 F3
Mark
 Dumfries . . . . 104 D5
 S Ayrs . . . . . . . 104 B4
 Som. . . . . . . . . . .23 E5
Markbeech . . . . .29 E5
Markby . . . . . . . .79 B7
Mark Causeway . .23 E5
Mark Cross
 E Sus . . . . . . . . .17 C8
 E Sus . . . . . . . . .18 B2
Market Bosworth 63 D8
Market Deeping . 65 D8
Market Drayton . .74 F3
Market
 Harborough. . . .64 F4
Markethill . . . . 134 F2
Market Lavington 24 D5
Market Overton . 65 C5
Market Rasen . . .90 F5
Market Stainton . 78 B5
Market Warsop . .77 C5
Market Weighton .96 E4
Market Weston . .56 B3
Markfield . . . . . .63 C8
Markham . . . . . .35 D5
Markham Moor . .77 B7
Markinch . . . . . 128 D4
Markington . . . . .95 C5
Marksbury . . . . .23 C8
Marks Tey . . . . . .43 B5
Markyate . . . . . .40 C3
Marland . . . . . . .87 C6
Marlborough . . .25 C6
Marlbrook
 Hereford . . . . . .49 D7
 Worcs . . . . . . . . .50 B4
Marlcliff . . . . . . .51 D5
Marldon . . . . . . . .7 C6
Marlesford . . . . .57 D7
Marley Green . . .74 E2
Marley Hill . . . . 110 D5
Marley Mount . . .14 E3
Marlingford . . . .68 D4
Marloes . . . . . . .44 E2
Marlow
 Bucks . . . . . . . . .39 F8
 Hereford . . . . . .49 B6
Marlow Bottom . .40 F1
Marlpit Hill . . . . .28 E5
Marlpool . . . . . . .76 E4
Marnhull . . . . . . .13 C5
Marnoch . . . . . 152 C5
Marnock . . . . . 119 C7
Marple . . . . . . . .87 F7
Marple Bridge. . .87 F7
Marr . . . . . . . . . .89 D6
Marrel . . . . . . . 157 H13
Marrick . . . . . . . 101 E5
Marrister . . . . . 160 G7
Marros . . . . . . . .32 D3
Marsden
 T&W . . . . . . . . 111 C6
 W Yorks . . . . . . .87 C8
Marsett . . . . . . . 100 F4
Marsh
 Devon . . . . . . . . .11 C7
 W Yorks . . . . . . .94 F3
Marshall's Heath 40 C4
Marshalsea . . . . .11 D8
Marshalswick . . .40 D4
Marsham . . . . . .81 E7
Marshaw . . . . . . .93 D5
Marsh Baldon . . .39 E5
Marshborough . .31 D7
Marshbrook . . . .60 F4
Marshchapel . . . .91 E7
Marshfield
 Newport . . . . . .35 F6
 S Glos . . . . . . . .24 B2
Marshgate . . . . . .8 E3
Marsh Gibbon . . .39 B6
Marsh Green
 Devon . . . . . . . . .10 E5
 Kent . . . . . . . . . .28 E5
 Staffs . . . . . . . . .75 D5
Marshland
 St James . . . . . .66 D5
Marsh Lane . . . . .76 B4
Marshside . . . . . .85 C4
Marsh Street . . . .21 E8
Marshwood . . . . .11 E8
Marske . . . . . . . 101 D6
Marske-by-
 the-Sea . . . . . 102 B4
Marston
 Ches W . . . . . . . .74 B3
 Hereford . . . . . .49 D5
 Lincs . . . . . . . . .77 E8
 Oxon . . . . . . . . .39 D5
 Staffs . . . . . . . . .62 B3
 Staffs . . . . . . . . .62 C2
 Warks . . . . . . . . .63 E6
 Wilts . . . . . . . . .24 D4
Marston Doles . . .52 D2
Marston Green. . .63 F5
Marston Magna . .12 B3
Marston Meysey . .37 E8
Marston
 Montgomery . . .75 F8
Marston
 Moretaine . . . . .53 E7
Marston on Dove .63 B6
Marston
 St Lawrence. . . .52 E3
Marston Stannett .49 D7
Marston Trussell .64 F3
Marstow . . . . . . .36 C2
Marsworth . . . . .40 C2
Marten . . . . . . . .25 D7
Marthall . . . . . . .74 B5
Martham . . . . . . .69 C7
Martin
 Hants . . . . . . . . .13 C8
 Kent . . . . . . . . . .31 E7
 Lincs . . . . . . . . .78 C5
 Lincs . . . . . . . . .78 D4
Martin Dales . . . .78 C4
Martin Drove End .13 B8

Martinhoe . . . . . .21 E5
Martinhoe Cross .21 E5
Martin
 Hussingtree . . .50 C3
Martin Mill . . . . .31 E7
Martinscroft . . . .86 F4
Martinstown . . . .12 F4
Martlesham . . . . .57 E6
Martlesham
 Heath . . . . . . . .57 E6
Martletwy . . . . . .32 C1
Martley . . . . . . . .50 D2
Martock . . . . . . .12 C2
Marton
 Ches E . . . . . . . .75 C5
 E Yorks . . . . . . .97 F7
 Lincs . . . . . . . . .90 F2
 Mbro . . . . . . . . 102 C3
 N Yorks . . . . . . .95 C7
 N Yorks . . . . . . 103 F5
 Shrops . . . . . . . .60 D2
 Shrops . . . . . . . .60 B3
 Warks . . . . . . . . .52 C2
Marton-le-Moor .95 B6
Martyr's Green . .27 D8
Martyr Worthy . .26 F3
Marwick . . . . . . 159 F3
Marwood . . . . . .20 F4
Marybank . . . . . 150 F7
Maryburgh . . . . 151 F8
Maryhill . . . . . . 119 C5
Marykirk . . . . . 135 C6
Marylebone . . . .86 D3
Marypark . . . . . 152 E1
Maryport
 Cumb . . . . . . . 107 F7
 Dumfries . . . . 104 F5
Mary Tavy . . . . . . .6 B4
Maryton . . . . . . 135 D6
Marywell
 Aberds . . . . . . 140 E4
 Aberds . . . . . . 141 E8
 Angus . . . . . . . 135 E6
Masham . . . . . . 101 F7
Mashbury . . . . . .42 C2
Masongill . . . . . .93 B6
Masonhill . . . . . 112 B3
Mastin Moor . . . .76 B4
Mastrick . . . . . . 141 D7
Matching . . . . . .41 C8
Matching Green . .41 C8
Matching Tye . . . .41 C8
Matfen . . . . . . . 110 B3
Matfield . . . . . . .29 E7
Mathern . . . . . . .36 E2
Mathon . . . . . . . .50 E2
Mathry . . . . . . . .44 B3
Matlaske . . . . . . .81 D7
Matlock . . . . . . . .76 C2
Matlock Bath . . . .76 D2
Matson . . . . . . . .37 C5
Matterdale End . .99 B5
Mattersey . . . . . .89 F7
Mattersey Thorpe 89 F7
Mattingley . . . . .26 D5
Mattishall . . . . . .68 C3
Mattishall Burgh .68 C3
Mauchline . . . . 112 B4
Maud . . . . . . . . 153 D9
Maugersbury. . . .38 B2
Maughold . . . . . .84 C4
Mauld . . . . . . . . 150 H7
Maulden . . . . . . .53 E8
Maulds Meaburn .99 C8
Maunby . . . . . . 102 F2
Maund Bryan . . .49 D7
Maundown . . . . . .11 B5
Mautby . . . . . . . .69 C7
Mavis Enderby . . 79 C6
Mawbray. . . . . . 107 E7
Mawdesley . . . . .86 C2
Mawdlam . . . . . .34 F2
Mawgan . . . . . . . .3 D6
Maw Green . . . . .74 D4
Mawla . . . . . . . . . .3 B6
Mawnan . . . . . . . .3 D6
Mawnan Smith . . .3 D6
Mawsley . . . . . . .53 B6
Maxey . . . . . . . . .65 D8
Maxstoke . . . . . .63 F6
Maxton
 Borders . . . . . 122 F2
 Kent . . . . . . . . . .31 E7
Maxwellheugh . 122 F3
Maxwelltown . . 107 B6
Maxworthy. . . . . .8 E4
Mayals . . . . . . . .33 E7
May Bank . . . . . .75 E5
Maybole . . . . . . 112 D3
Mayfield
 E Sus . . . . . . . . .18 C2
 Midloth . . . . . . 121 C6
 Staffs . . . . . . . . .75 E8
 W Loth. . . . . . . 120 C2
Mayford . . . . . . .27 D7
Mayland . . . . . . .43 D5
Maynard's Green 18 D2
Maypole
 Mon. . . . . . . . . .36 C1
 Scilly . . . . . . . . . .2 E4
Maypole Green
 Essex . . . . . . . . .43 B5
 Norf . . . . . . . . . .69 E7
 Suff . . . . . . . . . .57 C6
Maywick . . . . . . 160 L5
Meadle . . . . . . . .39 D8
Meadowtown . . .60 D3
Meadway . . . . . .35 F7
Meaford . . . . . . .75 F5
Meal Bank . . . . .99 E7
Mealabost
 Bhuirgh . . . . . 155 B9
Mealabost
 Bhuirgh . . . . . 155 D9
Meal Bank . . . . .99 E7
Mealsgate . . . . 108 E2
Meanwood . . . . .95 F5
Mearbeck . . . . . .93 C8
Meare . . . . . . . . .23 E6
Mears Ashby . . . .53 C6
Measham . . . . . .63 C7
Meath Green . . . .28 E3
Meathop . . . . . . .99 F6
Meaux . . . . . . . . .97 F6
Meavy . . . . . . . . . .6 C3
Medbourne . . . . .64 E4
Medburn . . . . . 110 B4
Meddon . . . . . . . .8 C5
Meden Vale . . . . .77 C5
Medlam . . . . . . . .79 D6

Medmenham . . .39 F8
Medomsley . . . 110 D4
Medstead . . . . . .26 F4
Meerbrook . . . . .75 C6
Meer End . . . . . .51 B7
Meers Bridge. . . .91 F8
Meesden . . . . . . .54 F5
Meeth . . . . . . . . . .9 D7
Meggethead . . . 114 C4
Meidrim . . . . . . .32 B3
Meifod
 Denb . . . . . . . . .72 D4
 Powys . . . . . . . .59 C8
Meigle . . . . . . . 134 E2
Meikle Earnock . .119 D7
Meikle Ferry . . 151 C10
Meikle Forter . . 134 C1
Meikle Gluich . . 151 C9
Meikleour . . . . 134 F1
Meikle
 Pinkerton . . . 122 B3
Meikle Strath . . 135 B6
Meikle Tarty . . . 141 B8
Meikle Wartle . . 153 E7
Meinciau . . . . . .33 C5
Meir . . . . . . . . . .75 E6
Meir Heath . . . . .75 E6
Melbourn . . . . . .54 E4
Melbourne
 Derbys . . . . . . . .63 B7
 E Yorks . . . . . . .96 E3
 S Lanark . . . . . 120 E3
Melbury Abbas . .13 B6
Melbury Bubb . . .12 D3
Melbury Osmond 12 D3
Melbury
 Sampford . . . . .12 D3
Melby . . . . . . . . 160 H3
Melchbourne . . .53 C8
Melcombe
 Bingham . . . . . .13 D5
Melcombe Regis. .12 F4
Meldon
 Devon . . . . . . . . .9 E7
 Northumb . . . . 117 F7
Meldreth . . . . . . .54 E4
Meldrum House .141 F7
Melfort . . . . . . . 124 D4
Melgarve . . . . . 137 E7
Meliden . . . . . . .72 A4
Melinbyrhedyn . .58 E5
Melincourt . . . . .34 D2
Melin-y-coed . . .83 E8
Melin-y-ddôl . . . .59 D7
Melin-y-grug . . . .59 D7
Melin-y-Wig . . . .72 E4
Melkinthorpe . . .99 B7
Melkridge . . . . . 109 C7
Melksham . . . . . .24 C4
Melldalloch . . . 145 F8
Melling
 Lancs . . . . . . . . .93 B5
 Mers . . . . . . . . .85 D4
Melling Mount . .86 D2
Mellis . . . . . . . . .56 B5
Mellon Charles 155 H13
Mellon Udrigle 155 H13
Mellor
 Gtr Man. . . . . . .87 F7
 Lancs . . . . . . . . .93 F6
Mellor Brook . . .93 F6
Mells . . . . . . . . . .24 E2
Melmerby
 Cumb . . . . . . . 109 F6
 N Yorks . . . . . . .95 B6
 N Yorks . . . . . . 101 F6
Melplash . . . . . . .12 E2
Melrose . . . . . . 121 F8
Melsetter . . . . . 159 K3
Melsonby . . . . . 101 D6
Meltham . . . . . . .88 C2
Melton . . . . . . . .57 D6
Meltonby . . . . . . .96 D3
Melton Constable 81 D6
Melton Mowbray 64 C4
Melton Ross . . . .90 C4
Melvaig . . . . . . 155 J12
Melverley . . . . . .60 C3
Melverley Green . 60 C3
Melvich . . . . . . 157 C11
Membury . . . . . . .11 D7
Memsie . . . . . . 153 B9
Memus . . . . . . . 134 D4
Menabilly . . . . . . .5 D5
Menai Bridge
 =Porthaethwy . 83 D5
Mendham . . . . . .69 F5
Mendlesham . . . .56 C5
Mendlesham
 Green . . . . . . . .56 C4
Menheniot . . . . . .5 C3
Mennock . . . . . 113 D8
Menston . . . . . . .94 E4
Menstrie . . . . . 127 E7
Menthorpe . . . . .96 F2
Mentmore . . . . . .40 C2
Meoble . . . . . . . 147 C10
Meole Brace . . . .60 C4
Meols . . . . . . . . .85 E3
Meonstoke . . . . .15 C7
Meopham . . . . . .29 C7
Meopham Station 29 C7
Mepal . . . . . . . . .66 F4
Meppershall . . . .54 F2
Merbach . . . . . . .48 E5
Mere
 Ches E . . . . . . . .86 F5
 Wilts . . . . . . . . .24 F3
Mere Brow . . . . .86 C2
Mereclough . . . . .93 F8
Mere Green . . . .62 E5
Mereside . . . . . . .92 F3
Merevale . . . . . . .63 E7
Mergie . . . . . . . 141 F6
Meriden . . . . . . .63 F6
Merkadale . . . . 149 E8
Merkland
 Dumfries . . . . 106 A4
 S Ayrs . . . . . . . 112 E2
Merkland Lodge 156 G7
Merley . . . . . . . .13 E8
Merlin's Bridge . .44 D4
Merrington . . . . .60 B4
Merrion . . . . . . .44 F4
Merriott . . . . . . .12 C2
Merrivale . . . . . . .6 B3

Merrow . . . . . . . .27 D8
Merrymeet . . . . . .5 C7
Mersham . . . . . . .19 B7
Merstham . . . . . .28 D3
Merston . . . . . . .16 D2
Merstone . . . . . .15 F6
Merther . . . . . . . . .3 B7
Merthyr . . . . . . . .32 B4
Merthyr Cynog . .47 F8
Merthyr-Dyfan . .22 B3
Merthyr Mawr . .21 B7
Merthyr Tudful
 =Merthyr Tydfil . 34 D4
Merthyr Tydfil . . .34 D4
Merthyr Vale . . . .34 D4
Merton
 Devon . . . . . . . . .9 C7
 London . . . . . . .28 B3
 Norf . . . . . . . . . .68 E2
 Oxon . . . . . . . . .39 C5
Mervinslaw . . . 116 C2
Meshaw . . . . . . . .10 C2
Messing . . . . . . .42 C4
Messingham . . . .90 D2
Metfield . . . . . . .69 F5
Metheringham . . 78 C3
Methil . . . . . . . 129 E5
Methlem . . . . . . .70 D2
Methley . . . . . . . .88 B4
Methlick . . . . . . 153 E8
Methven . . . . . . 128 B2
Methwold . . . . . .67 E7
Methwold Hythe . 67 E7
Mettingham . . . .69 F6
Mevagissey . . . . . .3 B9
Mewith Head . . .93 C7
Mexborough . . . .89 D5
Mey . . . . . . . . . 158 C4
Meysey
 Hampton . . . . . .37 E8
Miabhag
 W Isles . . . . . . 154 G5
 W Isles . . . . . . 154 H6
Miabhig. . . . . . . 154 D5
Miabhig
 W Yorks . . . . . . .87 B8
 W Yorks . . . . . . .88 C3
Michaelchurch . .36 B2
Michaelchurch
 Escley . . . . . . .48 F5
Michaelchurch
 on Arrow . . . . .48 D4
Michaelston-
 le-Pit . . . . . . . .22 B3
Michaelston-
 y-Fedw . . . . . .35 F6
Michaelston-
 super-Ely . . . . .22 B3
Micheldever . . . .26 F3
Michelmersh . . . .14 B4
Mickfield . . . . . .56 C5
Mickle Trafford . .73 C8
Mickleby . . . . . 103 C6
Mickleham . . . . .28 D2
Mickleover . . . . .76 F3
Micklethwaite . . .94 E4
Mickleton
 Durham . . . . . 100 B4
 Glos . . . . . . . . . .51 E6
Mickletown . . . . .88 B4
Mickle Trafford . .73 C8
Mickley . . . . . . . .95 B5
Mickley Square. 110 C3
Mid Ardlaw . . . 153 B9
Mid Auchinleck 118 B3
Midbea . . . . . . 159 D5
Mid Beltie . . . . 140 D5
Mid Calder . . . . 120 C3
Mid Cloch
 Forbie . . . . . . 153 C7
Mid Clyth . . . . . 158 G4
Middle Assendon .39 F7
Middle Aston . . . .38 B4
Middle Barton . . .38 B4
Middlebie . . . . . 108 B2
Middle
 Cairncake . . . 153 D8
Middle Claydon . .39 B7
Middle Drums . . 135 D5
Middleforth
 Green . . . . . . . .86 B3
Middleham . . . . 101 F6
Middle Handley . .76 B4
Middlehope . . . . .60 F4
Middle Littleton . 51 E5
Middle
 Maes-coed. . . .48 F5
Middle Mill . . . . .44 C3
Middlemuir . . . . 141 B8
Middle Rasen . . .90 F4
Middle Rigg . . . 128 D2
Middleshaw
 Cumb . . . . . . . . .99 F7
 Dumfries . . . . 107 B8
Middlesmoor . . . .94 B3
Middlestone . . . 111 F5
Middlestone
 Moor . . . . . . . 110 F5
Middlestown . . . .88 C3
Middlethird . . . 122 E2
Middleton
 Aberds . . . . . . 141 C7
 Argyll . . . . . . . 146 G2
 Cumb . . . . . . . . .99 F8
 Derbys . . . . . . . .75 C8
 Derbys . . . . . . . .76 C2
 Essex . . . . . . . . .56 F2
 Gtr Man. . . . . . .87 D6
 Hants . . . . . . . . .26 E2
 Hereford . . . . . .49 C7
 Midloth . . . . . . 121 D6
 N Nhants . . . . . .64 F5
 Norf . . . . . . . . . .67 C6
 Northumb . . . . 117 F6
 Northumb . . . . 123 F7
 N Yorks . . . . . . .94 E4
 N Yorks . . . . . . 103 F5
 Perth . . . . . . . . 128 D3
 Shrops . . . . . . . .49 B7
 Shrops . . . . . . . .60 B3
 Suff . . . . . . . . . .57 C8
 Swansea . . . . . .33 F5
 Warks . . . . . . . . .63 E5
 W Yorks . . . . . . .88 B3

Middleton
 Cheney . . . . . . .52 E2
Middleton Green .75 F6
Middleton Hall . 117 B5
Middleton-
 in-Teesdale . . 100 B4
Middleton Moor . 57 C8
Middleton One
 Row . . . . . . . . 102 C1
Middleton-
 on-Leven . . . . 102 D2
Middleton-
 on-Sea. . . . . . .16 D3
Middleton on
 the Hill . . . . . . .49 C7
Middleton-on-
 the-Wolds . . . .96 E5
Middleton Priors .61 E6
Middleton
 Quernham. . . . .95 B6
Middleton
 St George . . . 101 C7
Middleton
 Scriven . . . . . . .61 F6
Middleton Stoney 39 B5
Middleton Tyas . 101 D7
Middletown
 Cumb . . . . . . . . .98 D1
 Powys . . . . . . . .60 C3
Middle Tysoe . . .51 E8
Middle Wallop . .25 F7
Middlewich . . . . .74 C3
Middle
 Winterslow . . .25 F7
Middle Woodford 25 F6
Middlewood
 Green . . . . . . . .56 C4
Middlezoy . . . . . .23 F5
Midfield . . . . . . 157 C8
Midge Hall . . . . .86 B3
Midgeholme . . . 109 D6
Midgham . . . . . .26 C3
Midgley
 W Yorks . . . . . . .87 B8
 W Yorks . . . . . . .88 C3
Midhopestones . .88 E3
Midhurst . . . . . .16 B2
Mid Lavant . . . . .16 D2
Midlem . . . . . . 115 B8
Mid Main . . . . . 150 H7
Midsomer
 Norton . . . . . . .23 D8
Midton . . . . . . . 118 B2
Midtown
 Highld . . . . . . 155 J13
 Highld . . . . . . 157 C8
Midtown of
 Buchromb . . . 152 D3
Mid Urchany . . 151 G11
Midville . . . . . . .79 D6
Mid Walls . . . . . 160 H4
Mid Yell . . . . . . 160 D7
Migdale . . . . . . 151 C9
Migvie . . . . . . . 140 D3
Milarrochy . . . . 126 E3
Milborne Port . . .12 C4
Milborne
 St Andrew . . . .13 E6
Milborne Wick . .12 B4
Milbourne
 Northumb . . . . 110 B4
 Wilts . . . . . . . . 100 B1
Milburn . . . . . . . .99 B8
Milbury Heath . . .36 E3
Milcombe . . . . . .52 F2
Milden . . . . . . . .56 E3
Mildenhall
 Suff . . . . . . . . . .55 B8
 Wilts . . . . . . . . .25 C7
Milebrook . . . . . .48 B5
Milebush . . . . . . .29 E8
Mile Cross . . . . .68 C5
Mile Elm . . . . . . .24 C4
Mile End
 Essex . . . . . . . . .43 B5
 Glos . . . . . . . . . .36 C2
Mileham . . . . . . .68 C2
Mile Oak . . . . . . .17 D6
Milesmark . . . . 128 F2
Milfield . . . . . . 122 F5
Milford
 Derbys . . . . . . . .76 E3
 Devon . . . . . . . . .8 B4
 Powys . . . . . . . .59 E7
 Staffs . . . . . . . . .62 B3
 Sur . . . . . . . . . .27 E7
 Wilts . . . . . . . . .14 B2
Milford Haven =
 Aberdaugleddau .44 E4
Milford on Sea . .14 E3
Milkwall . . . . . . .36 D2
Milkwell . . . . . . .13 B7
Milland . . . . . . .16 B2
Millarston . . . . 118 C4
Millbank
 Aberds . . . . . . 153 D11
 Highld . . . . . . 158 D3
Mill Bank. . . . . . .87 B8
Millbeck . . . . . . .98 B4
Millbounds . . . 159 E6
Millbreck . . . . . 153 D10
Millbridge . . . . . .27 E6
Millbrook
 C Beds. . . . . . . .53 E7
 Corn . . . . . . . . . .6 D2
 Soton . . . . . . . . .14 C4
Millcombe . . . . . .7 E6
Mill Common . . .69 F7
Millcorner . . . . .18 C5
Milldale . . . . . . .75 D8
Millden Lodge . 135 B5
Milldens . . . . . 135 D5
Mill End
 Bucks . . . . . . . . .39 F7
 Herts . . . . . . . . .54 F4
Millerhill . . . . . 121 C6
Miller's Dale . . . .75 B8
Miller's Green . .76 D2
Millgreen . . . . . .61 B6
Mill Green
 Essex . . . . . . . . .42 D2
 Norf . . . . . . . . . .68 F4
 Suff . . . . . . . . . .56 E3
Millhalf . . . . . . .48 E4
Millhayes . . . . . .11 D7
Millhead . . . . . . .92 B4

Mil–New 217


Millheugh 119 D7
Mill Hill 41 E5
Millholme 99 E7
Millhouse
Argyll 145 F8
Cumb 108 F3
Millhousebridge 114 F4
Millhouse Green 88 D3
Millhouses 88 F4
Millikenpark 118 C4
Millin Cross 44 D4
Millington 96 D4
Mill Lane 27 D5
Millmeece 74 F5
Mill of Kingoodie 141 B7
Mill of Muiresk 153 D6
Mill of Sterin 140 E2
Mill of Uras 141 F7
Millom 98 F3
Millook 8 E3
Mill Place 90 D3
Millpool 5 B6
Millport 145 H10
Millquarter 113 F6
Mill Side 99 F6
Mill Street 68 C3
Millthorpe 78 F4
Millthrop 100 E1
Milltimber 141 D7
Milltown
Corn 5 D6
Derbys 76 C3
Devon 20 F4
Dumfries 108 B3
Milltown of Aberdalgie 128 B2
Milltown of Auchindoun 152 D3
Milltown of Craigston 153 C7
Milltown of Edinvillie 152 D2
Milltown of Kildrummy 140 C3
Milltown of Rothiemay 152 D5
Milltown of Towie 140 C3
Milnathort 128 D3
Milner's Heath 73 C8
Milngavie 119 B5
Milnrow 87 C7
Milnshaw 87 B5
Milnthorpe 99 F6
Milo 33 C6
Milson 49 B8
Milstead 30 D3
Milston 25 E6
Milton
Angus 134 E3
Cambs 55 C5
Cumb 109 C5
Derbys 63 B7
Dumfries 105 D6
Dumfries 106 B5
Dumfries 113 F8
Highld 150 F6
Highld 150 H7
Highld 151 D10
Highld 151 G8
Highld 158 E5
Moray 152 B5
Notts 77 B7
N Som 22 C5
Oxon 38 E4
Oxon 52 F2
Pembs 32 D1
Perth 127 C8
Ptsmth 15 E7
Stirling 126 D4
Stoke 75 D6
W Dunb 118 B4
Milton Abbas 13 D6
Milton Abbot 6 B2
Milton Bridge 120 C5
Milton Bryan 53 F7
Milton Clevedon 23 F8
Milton Coldwells 153 E9
Milton Combe 6 C2
Milton Damerel 9 C5
Miltonduff 152 B1
Milton End 37 D8
Milton Ernest 53 D8
Milton Green 73 D8
Miltonhill 151 E13
Milton Hill 38 E4
Miltonise 105 B5
Milton Keynes 53 F6
Milton Keynes Village 53 F6
Milton Lilbourne 25 C6
Milton Malsor 52 D5
Milton Morenish 132 F3
Milton of Auchinhove 140 D4
Milton of Balgonie 128 D5
Milton of Buchanan 126 E3
Milton of Campfield 140 D5
Milton of Campsie 119 B6
Milton of Corsindae 141 D5
Milton of Cushnie 140 C4
Milton of Dalcapon 133 D6
Milton of Edradour 133 D6
Milton of Gollanfield 151 F10
Milton of Lesmore 140 B3
Milton of Logie 140 D3
Milton of Murtle 141 D7
Milton of Noth 140 B4
Milton of Tullich 140 E2
Milton on Stour 13 B5
Milton Regis 30 C3
Milton under Wychwood 38 C2
Milverton
Som 11 B6
Warks 51 C8
Milwich 75 F6
Minard 125 F5
Minchinhampton 37 D5
Mindrum 122 F4
Minehead 21 E8
Minera 73 D6
Minety 37 E7
Minffordd
Gwyn 58 C4
Gwyn 71 D6
Gwyn 83 D5
Miningsby 79 C6
Minions 5 B7
Minishant 112 C3
Minllyn 59 C5
Minnes 141 B8
Minngearraidh 148 F2
Minnigaff 105 C8
Minnonie 153 B7
Minskip 95 C6
Minstead 14 C3
Minsted 16 B2
Minster
Kent 30 B3
Kent 31 C7
Minsterley 60 D3
Minster Lovell 38 C3
Minsterworth 36 C4
Minterne Magna 12 D4
Minting 78 B4
Mintlaw 153 D9
Minto 115 B8
Minton 60 E4
Minwear 32 C1
Minworth 63 E5
Mirbister 159 F4
Mirehouse 98 C1
Mireland 158 D5
Mirfield 88 C3
Miserden 37 D6
Miskin 34 F4
Misson 89 E7
Misterton
Leics 64 F2
Notts 89 E8
Som 12 D2
Mistley 56 F5
Mitcham 28 C3
Mitcheldean 36 C3
Mitchell 4 D3
Mitchel Troy 36 C1
Mitcheltroy Common 36 D1
Mitford 117 F7
Mithian 4 D2
Mitton 62 C2
Mixbury 52 F4
Moat 108 B4
Moats Tye 56 D4
Mobberley
Ches E 74 B4
Staffs 75 E7
Moccas 49 E5
Mochdre
Conwy 83 D8
Powys 59 F7
Mochrum 105 E7
Mockbeggar 14 D2
Mockerkin 98 B2
Modbury 6 D4
Moddershall 75 F6
Moelfre
Anglesey 82 C5
Powys 59 B8
Moffat 114 D3
Moggerhanger 54 E2
Moira 63 C7
Molash 30 D4
Mol-chlach 149 G9
Mold
= Yr Wyddgrug 73 C6
Moldgreen 88 C2
Molehill Green 42 B1
Molescroft 97 E6
Molesden 117 F7
Molesworth 53 B8
Moll 149 E10
Molland 10 B3
Mollington
Ches W 73 B7
Oxon 52 E2
Mollinsburn 119 B7
Monachty 46 C4
Monachylemore 126 C3
Monar Lodge 150 G5
Monaughty 48 C4
Monboddo House 135 B7
Mondynes 135 B7
Monevechadan 125 E7
Monewden 57 D6
Moneydie 128 B2
Moniaive 113 E7
Monifieth 134 F4
Monikie 135 F4
Monimail 128 C4
Monington 45 E3
Monk Bretton 88 D4
Monken Hadley 41 E5
Monk Fryston 89 B6
Monkhopton 61 E6
Monkland 49 D6
Monkleigh 9 B6
Monknash 21 B8
Monkokehampton 9 D7
Monkseaton 111 B6
Monks Eleigh 56 E3
Monk's Gate 17 B6
Monks Heath 74 B5
Monk Sherborne 26 D4
Monkshill 153 D7
Monksilver 22 F2
Monks Kirby 63 F8
Monk Soham 57 C6
Monkspath 51 B6
Monks Risborough 39 D8
Monk Street 42 B2
Monkswood 35 D7
Monkton
Devon 11 D6
Kent 31 C6
Pembs 44 E4
S Ayrs 112 B3
Monkton Combe 24 C2
Monkton Deverill 24 F3
Monkton Farleigh 24 C3
Monkton Heathfield 11 B7
Monkton Up Wimborne 13 C8
Monkwearmouth 111 D6
Monkwood 26 F4
Monmouth
= Trefynwy 36 C2
Monmouth Cap 35 B7
Monnington on Wye 49 E5
Monreith 105 E7
Monreith Mains 105 E7
Montacute 12 C2
Montcoffer House 153 B6
Montford
Argyll 145 G10
Shrops 60 C4
Montford Bridge 60 C4
Montgarrie 140 C4
Montgomery
= Trefaldwyn 60 E2
Montrave 129 D5
Montrose 135 D7
Mont Saint 16 I2
Montsale 43 E6
Monxton 25 E8
Monyash 75 C8
Monymusk 141 C5
Monzie 127 B7
Monzie Castle 127 B7
Moodiesburn 119 B6
Moonzie 128 C5
Moor Allerton 95 F5
Moorby 79 C5
Moor Crichel 13 D7
Moordown 13 E8
Moore 86 F3
Moorend 36 D4
Moor End
E Yorks 96 F4
York 96 D2
Moorends 89 C7
Moorgate 88 E5
Moorgreen 76 E4
Moorhall 76 B3
Moorhampton 49 E5
Moorhead 94 F4
Moorhouse
Cumb 108 D3
Notts 77 C7
Moorlinch 23 F5
Moor Monkton 95 D8
Moor of Granary 151 F13
Moor of Ravenstone 105 E7
Moor Row 98 C2
Moorsholm 102 C4
Moorside 87 D7
Moor Street 30 C2
Moorthorpe 89 C5
Moortown
Hants 14 D2
IoW 14 F5
Lincs 90 E4
Morangie 151 C10
Morar 147 B9
Morborne 65 E8
Morchard Bishop 10 D2
Morcombelake 12 E2
Morcott 65 D6
Morda 60 B2
Morden
Dorset 13 E7
London 28 C3
Mordiford 49 F7
Mordon 101 B8
More 60 E3
Morebath 10 B4
Morebattle 116 B3
Morecambe 92 C4
Morefield 150 B4
Moreleigh 7 D5
Morenish 132 F2
Moresby 98 B1
Moresby Parks 98 C1
Morestead 15 B6
Moreton
Dorset 13 F6
Essex 41 D8
Mers 85 E3
Oxon 39 D6
Staffs 61 C7
Moreton Corbet 61 B5
Moretonhampstead 10 F2
Moreton-in-Marsh 51 F7
Moreton Jeffries 49 E8
Moreton Morrell 51 D8
Moreton on Lugg 49 E7
Moreton Pinkney 52 E3
Moreton Say 74 F3
Moreton Valence 36 D4
Morfa
Carms 33 C6
Carms 33 E6
Morfa Bach 32 C4
Morfa Bychan 71 D6
Morfa Dinlle 82 F4
Morfa Glas 34 D2
Morfa Nefyn 70 C3
Morfydd 72 E5
Morgan's Vale 14 B2
Moriah 46 B5
Morland 99 B7
Morley
Derbys 76 E3
Durham 101 B6
W Yorks 88 B3
Morley Green 87 F6
Morley St Botolph 68 E3
Morningside
Edin 120 B5
N Lanark 119 D8
Morningthorpe 68 E5
Morpeth 117 F8
Morphie 135 C7
Morrey 62 C5
Morris Green 55 F8
Morriston 33 E7
Morston 81 C6
Mortehoe 20 E3
Mortimer 26 C4
Mortimer's Cross 49 C6
Mortimer West End 26 C4
Mortlake 28 B3
Morton
Cumb 108 D3
Derbys 76 C4
Lincs 65 B7
Lincs 77 C8
Lincs 90 E2
Norf 68 C4
Notts 77 D7
S Glos 36 E3
Shrops 60 B2
Morton Bagot 51 C6
Morton-on-Swale 101 E8
Morvah 2 C3
Morval 5 D7
Morvich
Highld 136 B2
Highld 157 J10
Morville 61 E6
Morville Heath 61 E6
Morwenstow 8 C4
Mosborough 88 F5
Moscow 118 E4
Mosedale 108 F3
Moseley
W Mid 62 E3
W Mid 62 F4
Worcs 50 D3
Moss
Argyll 146 G2
Highld 147 E9
S Yorks 89 C6
Wrex 73 D7
Mossat 140 C3
Mossbank 160 F6
Moss Bank 86 E3
Mossbay 98 B1
Mossblown 112 B4
Mossbrow 86 F5
Mossburnford 116 C2
Mossdale 106 B3
Moss Edge 92 E4
Mossend 119 C7
Moss End 27 B6
Mosser 98 B3
Mossfield 151 D9
Mossgiel 112 B4
Mosside 134 D4
Mossley
Ches E 75 C5
Gtr Man 87 D7
Mossley Hill 85 F4
Moss of Barmuckity 152 B2
Moss Pit 62 B3
Moss-side 151 F11
Moss Side 92 F3
Mosstodloch 152 B3
Mosston 135 E5
Mossy Lea 86 C3
Mosterton 12 D2
Moston
Gtr Man 87 D6
Shrops 61 B5
Moston Green 74 C4
Mostyn 85 F2
Mostyn Quay 85 F2
Motcombe 13 B6
Mothecombe 6 E4
Motherby 99 B6
Motherwell 119 D7
Mottingham 28 B5
Mottisfont 14 B4
Mottistone 14 F5
Mottram in Longdendale 87 E7
Mottram St Andrew 75 B5
Mouilpied 16 I2
Mouldsworth 74 B2
Moulin 133 D6
Moulsecoomb 17 D7
Moulsford 39 F5
Moulsoe 53 E7
Moulton
Ches W 74 C3
Lincs 66 B3
N Yorks 101 D7
Suff 55 C7
V Glam 22 B2
W Nhants 53 C5
Moulton Chapel 66 C2
Moulton Eaugate 66 C3
Moulton St Mary 69 D6
Moulton Seas End 66 B3
Mounie Castle 141 B6
Mount
Corn 4 D2
Corn 5 C6
Highld 151 G12
Mountain 94 F3
Mountain Ash
= Aberpennar 34 E4
Mountain Cross 120 E4
Mountain Water 44 C4
Mountbenger 115 B6
Mount Bures 56 F3
Mount Canisp 151 D10
Mountfield 18 C4
Mountgerald 151 E8
Mount Hawke 3 B6
Mountjoy 4 C3
Mountnessing 42 E2
Mounton 36 E2
Mount Pleasant
Ches E 74 D5
Derbys 63 C6
Derbys 76 E3
Flint 73 B6
Hants 14 E3
W Yorks 88 B3
Mountsorrel 64 C2
Mount Sorrel 13 B8
Mount Tabor 87 B8
Mousehole 2 D3
Mousen 123 F7
Mouswald 107 B7
Mow Cop 75 D5
Mowhaugh 116 B4
Mowsley 64 F3
Moxley 62 E3
Moy
Highld 137 F7
Moy *continued*
Highld 151 H10
Moy Hall 151 H10
Moy House 151 E13
Moyles Court 14 D2
Moylgrove 45 E3
Moy Lodge 137 F7
Muasdale 143 D7
Muchalls 141 E8
Much Birch 49 F7
Much Cowarne 49 E8
Much Dewchurch 49 F6
Muchelney 12 B2
Much Hadham 41 C7
Much Hoole 86 B2
Muchlarnick 5 D7
Much Marcle 49 F8
Muchrachd 150 H5
Much Wenlock 61 D6
Muckernich 151 F8
Mucking 42 F2
Muckleford 12 E4
Mucklestone 74 F4
Muckleton 61 B5
Muckletown 140 B4
Muckley Corner 62 D4
Muckton 91 F7
Mudale 157 F8
Muddiford 20 F4
Mudeford 14 E2
Mudford 12 C3
Mudgley 23 E6
Mugdock 119 B5
Mugeary 149 E9
Mugginton 76 E2
Muggleswick 110 E3
Muie 157 J9
Muir 139 F6
Muirden 153 C7
Muirdrum 135 F5
Muirhead
Angus 134 F3
Fife 128 D4
N Lanark 119 C6
S Ayrs 118 F3
Muirhouselaw 116 B2
Muirhouses 128 F2
Muirkirk 113 B6
Muirmill 127 F6
Muir of Fairburn 150 F7
Muir of Fowlis 140 C4
Muir of Ord 151 F8
Muir of Pert 134 F4
Muirshearlich 136 F4
Muirskie 141 E7
Muirtack 153 E9
Muirton
Highld 151 E10
Perth 127 C8
Perth 128 B3
Muirton Mains 150 F7
Muirton of Ardblair 134 E1
Muirton of Ballochy 135 C6
Muiryfold 153 C7
Muker 100 E4
Mulbarton 68 D4
Mulben 152 C3
Mulindry 142 C4
Mullardoch House 150 H5
Mullion 3 E5
Mullion Cove 3 E5
Mumby 79 B8
Munderfield Row 49 D8
Munderfield Stocks 49 D8
Mundesley 81 D9
Mundford 67 E8
Mundham 69 E6
Mundon 42 D4
Mundurno 141 C8
Munerigie 137 D5
Muness 160 C8
Mungasdale 150 B2
Mungrisdale 108 F3
Munlochy 151 F9
Munsley 49 E8
Munslow 60 F5
Murchington 9 F8
Murcott 39 C5
Murkle 158 D3
Murlaggan
Highld 136 E3
Highld 137 F6
Murra 159 H3
Murrayfield 120 B5
Murrow 66 D3
Mursley 39 B8
Murthill 134 D4
Murthly 133 F7
Murton
Cumb 100 B2
Durham 111 E6
Northumb 123 E5
York 96 D2
Musbury 11 E7
Muscoates 102 F4
Musdale 124 C5
Musselburgh 121 B6
Muston
Leics 77 F8
N Yorks 97 B6
Mustow Green 50 B3
Mutehill 106 E3
Mutford 69 F7
Muthill 127 C7
Mutterton 10 D5
Muxton 61 C7
Mybster 158 E3
Myddfai 34 B1
Myddle 60 B4
Mydroilyn 46 D3
Myerscough 92 F4
Mylor Bridge 3 C7
Mynachlog-ddu 45 F3
Myndtown 60 F3
Mynydd Bach 47 B6
Mynydd-bach 36 E1
Mynydd Bodafon 82 C4
Mynydd Isa 73 C6
Mynyddygarreg 33 D5
Mynytho 70 D4
Myrebird 141 E6
Myrelandhorn 158 E4
Myreside 128 B4
Myrtle Hill 47 F6
Mytchett 27 D6
Mytholm 87 B7
Mytholmroyd 87 B8
Myton-on-Swale 95 C7
Mytton 60 C4


## N


Naast 155 J13
Naburn 95 E8
Nackington 31 D5
Nacton 57 E6
Nafferton 97 D6
Na Gearrannan 154 C6
Nailbridge 36 C3
Nailsbourne 11 B7
Nailsea 23 B6
Nailstone 63 D8
Nailsworth 37 E5
Nairn 151 F11
Nalderswood 28 E3
Nancegollan 2 C5
Nancledra 2 C3
Nanhoron 70 D3
Nannau 71 E8
Nannerch 73 C5
Nanpantan 64 C2
Nanpean 4 D4
Nanstallon 4 C5
Nant-ddu 34 C4
Nanternis 46 D2
Nantgaredig 33 B5
Nantgarw 35 F5
Nant-glas 47 C8
Nantglyn 72 C4
Nantgwyn 47 B8
Nantlle 82 F5
Nantmawr 60 B2
Nantmel 48 C2
Nantmor 71 C7
Nant Peris 83 F6
Nant Uchaf 72 D4
Nantwich 74 D3
Nant-y-Bai 47 E6
Nant-y-cafn 34 D2
Nantycaws 33 C5
Nant-y-derry 35 D7
Nant-y-ffi 46 F4
Nantyffyllon 34 E2
Nantyglo 35 C5
Nant-y-moel 34 E3
Nant-y-pandy 83 D6
Naphill 39 E8
Nappa 93 D8
Napton on the Hill 52 C2
Narberth
= Arberth 32 C2
Narborough
Leics 64 E2
Norf 67 C7
Nasareth 82 F4
Naseby 52 B4
Nash
Bucks 53 F5
Hereford 48 C5
Newport 35 F7
Shrops 49 B8
Nash Lee 39 D8
Nassington 65 E7
Nasty 41 B6
Nateby
Cumb 100 D2
Lancs 92 E4
Natland 99 F7
Naughton 56 E4
Naunton
Glos 37 B8
Worcs 50 F3
Naunton Beauchamp 50 D4
Navenby 78 D2
Navestock Heath 41 E8
Navestock Side 42 E1
Navidale 157 H13
Nawton 102 F4
Nayland 56 F3
Nazeing 41 D7
Neacroft 14 E2
Neal's Green 63 F7
Neap 160 H7
Near Sawrey 99 E5
Neasham 101 C8
Neath
= Castell-Nedd 33 E8
Neath Abbey 33 E8
Neatishead 69 B6
Nebo
Anglesey 82 B4
Ceredig 46 C4
Conwy 83 F8
Gwyn 82 F4
Necton 67 D8
Nedd 156 F4
Nedderton 117 F8
Nedging Tye 56 E4
Needham 68 F5
Needham Market 56 D4
Needingworth 54 B4
Needwood 63 B5
Neen Savage 49 B8
Neen Sollars 49 B8
Neenton 61 F6
Nefyn 70 C4
Neilston 118 D4
Neinthirion 59 D6
Neithrop 52 E2
Nelly Andrews Green 60 D2
Nelson
Caerph 35 E5
Lancs 93 F8
Nelson Village 111 B5
Nemphlar 119 E8
Nempnett Thrubwell 23 C7
Nene Terrace 66 D2
Nenthall 109 E7
Nenthead 109 E7
Nenthorn 122 F2
Nerabus 142 C3
Nercwys 73 C6
Nerston 119 D6
Nesbit 123 F5
Ness 73 B7
Nesscliffe 60 C3
Neston
Ches W 73 B6
Wilts 24 C3
Nether Alderley 74 B5
Netheravon 25 E6
Nether Blainslie 121 E8
Nether Booth 88 F2
Netherbrae 153 C7
Netherbrough 159 G4
Nether Broughton 64 B3
Netherburn 119 E8
Nether Burrow 93 B6
Netherbury 12 E2
Netherby
Cumb 108 B3
N Yorks 95 E6
Nether Cerne 12 E4
Nether Compton 12 C3
Nethercote 52 C3
Nethercott 20 F3
Nether Crimond 141 B7
Nether Dalgliesh 115 D5
Nether Dallachy 152 B3
Netherend 36 D2
Nether Exe 10 D4
Netherfield 18 D4
Nether Glasslaw 153 C8
Netherhampton 14 B2
Nether Handwick 134 E3
Nether Haugh 88 E5
Nether Heage 76 D3
Nether Heyford 52 D4
Nether Hindhope 116 C3
Nether Howecleuch 114 C3
Nether Kellet 92 C5
Nether Kinmundy 153 D10
Nether Langwith 76 B5
Netherlaw 106 E4
Nether Leask 153 E10
Nether Lenshie 153 D6
Netherley
Aberds 141 E7
Mers 86 F2
Nethermill 114 F3
Nether Monynut 122 C3
Nethermuir 153 D9
Nether Padley 76 B2
Nether Park 153 C10
Netherplace 118 D5
Nether Poppleton 95 D8
Netherseal 63 C6
Nether Silton 102 E2
Nether Stowey 22 F3
Netherthird 113 C5
Netherthong 88 D2
Netherthorpe 89 F6
Netherton
Angus 135 D5
Devon 7 B6
Hants 25 D8
Mers 85 D4
Northumb 117 D5
Oxon 38 E4
Perth 133 D8
Stirling 119 B5
W Mid 62 F3
Worcs 50 E4
W Yorks 88 C2
W Yorks 88 C3
Nethertown
Cumb 98 D1
Highld 158 C5
Nether Urquhart 128 D3
Nether Wallop 25 F8
Nether Wasdale 98 D3
Nether Whitacre 63 E6
Netherwitton 117 E7
Netherwood 113 B6
Nether Worton 52 F2
Nethy Bridge 139 B6
Netley 15 D5
Netley Marsh 14 C4
Netteswell 41 C7
Nettlebed 39 F7
Nettlebridge 23 E8
Nettlecombe 12 E3
Nettleden 40 C3
Nettleham 78 B3
Nettlestead 29 D7
Nettlestead Green 29 D7
Nettlestone 15 E7
Nettlesworth 111 E5
Nettleton
Lincs 90 D5
Wilts 24 B3
Neuadd 33 B7
Nevendon 42 E3
Nevern 45 E2
New Abbey 107 C6
New Aberdour 153 B8
New Addington 28 C4
Newall 94 E4
New Alresford 26 F3
New Alyth 134 E2
Newark
Orkney 159 D8
Pboro 66 D2
Newark-on-Trent 77 D7
New Arley 63 F6
Newarthill 119 D7
New Ash Green 29 C7
New Barn 29 C7
New Barnetby 90 C4
Newbarns 92 B2
New Barton 53 C6
Newbattle 121 C6
New Bewick 117 B6
Newbiggin
Cumb 92 C2
Cumb 98 E2
Cumb 99 B6
Cumb 99 B8
Cumb 109 E5
Durham 100 B4
N Yorks 100 E4
N Yorks 100 F4
Newbiggin-by-the-Sea 117 F9
Newbigging
Angus 134 E2
Angus 134 F4
Angus 134 F4
S Lanark 120 E3
Newbiggin-on-Lune 100 D2
New Bilton 52 B2
Newbold
Derbys 76 B3
Leics 63 C8
Newbold on Avon 52 B2
Newbold on Stour 51 E7
Newbold Pacey 51 D7
Newbold Verdon 63 D8
New Bolingbroke 79 D6
Newborough
Anglesey 82 E4
Pboro 66 D2
Staffs 62 B5
Newbottle
T&W 111 D6
W Nhants 52 F3
New Boultham 78 B2
Newbourne 57 E6
New Bradwell 53 E6
New Brancepeth 110 E5
Newbridge
Caerph 35 E6
Ceredig 46 D4
Corn 2 C3
Corn 5 C8
Dumfries 107 B6
Edin 120 B4
Hants 14 C3
IoW 14 F5
Pembs 44 B4
New Bridge 73 E6
Newbridge Green 50 F3
Newbridge-on-Usk 35 E7
Newbridge on Wye 48 D2
New Brighton
Flint 73 C6
Mers 85 E4
New Brinsley 76 D4
Newbrough 109 C8
New Broughton 73 D7
New Buckenham 68 E3
Newbuildings 10 D2
Newburgh
Aberds 141 B8
Aberds 153 C9
Borders 115 C6
Fife 128 C4
Lancs 86 C2
Newburn 110 C4
Newbury 26 C2
Newbury Park 41 F7
Newby
Cumb 99 B7
Lancs 93 E8
N Yorks 93 B7
N Yorks 102 C3
N Yorks 103 E8
Newby Bridge 99 F5
Newby East 108 D4
New Byth 153 C8
Newby West 108 D3
Newby Wiske 102 F1
Newcastle
Mon 35 C8
Shrops 60 F2
Newcastle Emlyn
= Castell Newydd
Emlyn 46 E2
Newcastleton or Copshaw Holm 115 F7
Newcastle-under-Lyme 74 E5
Newcastle upon Tyne 110 C5
New Catton 68 C5
Newchapel
Pembs 45 F4
Powys 59 F6
Staffs 75 D5
Sur 28 E4
New Cheriton 15 B6
Newchurch
Carms 32 B4
IoW 15 F6
Kent 19 B7
Lancs 93 F8
Mon 36 E1
Powys 48 D4
Staffs 62 B5
New Costessey 68 C4
Newcott 11 D7
New Cowper 107 E8
Newcraighall 121 B6
New Cross
Ceredig 46 B5
London 28 B4
New Cumnock 113 C6
New Deer 153 D8
New Delaval 111 B5
New Duston 52 C5
New Earswick 96 D2
New Edlington 89 E6
New Elgin 152 B2
New Ellerby 97 F7
Newell Green 27 B6
New Eltham 28 B5
New End 51 D5
Newenden 18 C5
Newent 36 B4
Newerne 36 D3
New Farnley 94 F5
New Ferry 85 F4
Newfield
Durham 110 F5
Highld 151 D10
Newford 2 E4
Newfound 26 D3
New Fryston 89 B5
Newgale 44 C3
New Galloway 106 B3
Newgate 81 C6
Newgate Street 41 D6
New Gilston 129 D6
New Grimsby 2 E3
New Hainford 68 C5
Newhall
Ches E 74 E3
Newhall *continued*
Derbys 63 B6
Newhall House 151 E9
Newhall Point 151 E10
Newham 117 B7
Newham Hall 117 B7
New Hartley 111 B6
Newhaven
Derbys 75 D8
Edin 121 B5
E Sus 17 D8
New Haw 27 C8
New Hedges 32 D2
New Herrington 111 D6
Newhey 87 C7
New Hinksey 39 D5
New Holkham 80 D4
New Holland 90 B4
Newholm 103 C6
New Houghton
Derbys 76 C4
Norf 80 E3
Newhouse 119 C7
New Houses 93 B8
New Humberstone 64 D3
New Hutton 99 E7
New Hythe 29 D8
Newick 17 B8
Newingreen 19 B8
Newington
Kent 19 B8
Kent 30 C2
Kent 31 C7
Notts 89 E7
Oxon 39 E6
Shrops 60 F4
New Inn
Carms 46 F3
Mon 36 D1
Pembs 45 F2
Torf 35 E7
New Invention
Shrops 48 B4
W Mid 62 D3
New Kelso 150 G2
New Kingston 64 B2
New Lanark 119 E8
Newland
Glos 36 D2
Hull 97 F6
N Yorks 89 B7
Worcs 50 E2
Newlandrig 121 C6
Newlands
Borders 115 E8
Highld 151 G10
Moray 152 C3
Northumb 110 D3
Newland's Corner 27 E8
Newlandsmuir 119 D6
Newlands of Geise 158 D2
Newlands of Tynet 152 B3
Newlands Park 82 C2
New Lane 86 C2
New Lane End 86 E4
New Leake 79 D7
New Leeds 153 C9
New Longton 86 B3
Newlot 159 G6
New Luce 105 C5
Newlyn 2 D3
Newmachar 141 C7
Newmains 119 D8
New Malden 28 C3
Newmarket
Suff 55 C7
W Isles 155 D9
New Marske 102 B4
New Marton 73 F7
New Micklefield 95 F7
Newmill
Borders 115 C7
Corn 2 C3
Moray 152 C4
New Mill
Aberds 141 F6
Herts 40 C2
Wilts 25 C6
W Yorks 88 D2
Newmill of Inshewan 134 C4
New Mills
Ches E 87 F5
Corn 4 D3
Derbys 87 F7
Powys 59 D7
Newmills of Boyne 152 C5
Newmiln 133 F8
Newmilns 118 F5
New Milton 14 E3
New Moat 32 B1
Newnham
Cambs 54 D5
Glos 36 C3
Hants 26 D5
Herts 54 F3
Kent 30 D3
W Nhants 52 D3
Newnham Bridge 49 C8
New Ollerton 77 C6
New Oscott 62 E4
Newpark 129 C6
New Park 95 D5
New Pitsligo 153 C8
New Polzeath 4 B4
Newport
Devon 20 F4
Essex 55 F6
E Yorks 96 F4
Highld 158 H3
IoW 15 F6
Norf 69 C8
Telford 61 C7
Newport
= Casnewydd 35 F7
Newport
= Trefdraeth 45 F2
Newport-on-Tay 129 B6
Newport Pagnell 53 E6

**Newpound**
Common . . . . . . 16 B4
Newquay . . . . . . 4 C3
**New Quay**
=Ceinewydd . . . 46 D2
New Rackheath . 69 C5
New Radnor . . . . 48 C4
New Rent . . . . . 108 F4
New Ridley . . . . . 110 D3
New Road Side . . 94 E2
New Romney . . . 19 C7
New Rossington . 89 E7
**New Row**
Ceredig . . . . . . . 47 B6
Lancs . . . . . . . . 93 F6
N Yorks . . . . . . 102 C4
New Sarum . . . . 25 F6
Newsbank . . . . . 74 C5
**Newseat**
Aberds . . . . . . 153 D10
Aberds . . . . . . 153 E7
**Newsham**
Northumb . . . . 111 B6
N Yorks . . . . . . 101 C6
N Yorks . . . . . . 102 F1
**Newsholme**
E Yorks . . . . . . 89 B8
Lancs . . . . . . . . 93 D8
New Silksworth 111 D6
Newsome . . . . . 88 C2
**Newstead**
Borders . . . . . . 121 F8
Northumb . . . . 117 B7
Notts . . . . . . . . 76 D5
New Stevenston 119 D7
New Street . . . . . 75 D7
New Street Lane . 74 F3
New Swanage . . 13 F8
Newthorpe . . . . 95 F7
**Newton**
Argyll . . . . . . . 125 F6
Borders . . . . . . 116 B2
Bridgend . . . . . . 21 B7
Cambs . . . . . . . 54 E5
Cambs . . . . . . . 66 C4
Cardiff . . . . . . . 22 B4
Ches W . . . . . . . 73 C8
Ches W . . . . . . . 74 B2
Ches W . . . . . . . 74 D2
Cumb . . . . . . . . 92 B2
Derbys . . . . . . . 76 D4
Dorset . . . . . . . 13 C5
Dumfries . . . . . 108 B2
Dumfries . . . . . 114 E4
Gtr Man . . . . . . 87 E7
Hereford . . . . . . 48 F5
Hereford . . . . . . 49 D7
Highld . . . . . . 151 E10
Highld . . . . . . 151 G10
Highld . . . . . . 156 F5
Highld . . . . . . 158 F3
Lancs . . . . . . . . 92 F4
Lancs . . . . . . . . 93 B5
Lancs . . . . . . . . 93 D6
Lincs . . . . . . . . 78 F3
Moray . . . . . . . 152 B1
N Nhants . . . . . 65 F5
Norf . . . . . . . . . 67 C8
Northumb . . . . 110 C3
Notts . . . . . . . . 77 D7
Perth . . . . . . . . 133 F5
S Lanark . . . . . 119 C6
S Lanark . . . . . 120 F2
Staffs . . . . . . . . 62 B4
Suff . . . . . . . . . 56 E3
Swansea . . . . . . 33 F7
S Yorks . . . . . . . 89 D6
Warks . . . . . . . . 52 B3
Wilts . . . . . . . . 14 B3
W Loth . . . . . . 120 B3
Newton Abbot . . . 7 B6
Newtonairds . . . 113 F8
Newton Arlosh . 107 D8
Newton Aycliffe . 101 B7
Newton Bewley . 102 B2
**Newton**
Blossomville . . 53 D7
**Newton**
Bromswold . . . . 53 C7
**Newton**
Burgoland . . . . . 63 D7
Newton by Toft . 90 F4
Newton Ferrers . . 6 E3
Newton Flotman . 68 E5
Newtongrange . 121 C6
Newton Hall . . . . 110 C3
Newton Harcourt 64 E3
Newton Heath . . 87 D6
**Newtonhill**
Aberds . . . . . . 141 E8
Highld . . . . . . 151 E8
Newton House . . 141 B5
Newton Kyme . . . 95 E7
**Newton-le-Willows**
Mers . . . . . . . . 86 E3
N Yorks . . . . . . 101 F7
Newton Longville 53 F6
Newton Mearns 118 D6
Newtonmill . . . . 135 C6
Newtonmore . . . 138 E3
Newton Morrell 101 D7
**Newton**
Mulgrave . . . . . 103 C5
**Newton of**
Ardtoe . . . . . . 147 D9
**Newton of**
Balcanquhal . . 128 C3
**Newton of**
Falkland . . . . . 128 D4
Newton on Ayr . 112 B3
Newton on Ouse . 95 D8
**Newton-on-**
Rawcliffe . . . . . 103 E6
**Newton-on-**
the-Moor . . . . . 117 D7
Newton on Trent . 77 B8
Newton Park . . . 145 G10
**Newton**
Poppleford . . . . 11 F5
Newton Purcell . 52 F4
Newton Regis . . . 63 D6
Newton Reigny 108 F4
Newton St Cyres . 10 E3
Newton St Faith . 68 C5
Newton St Loe . . 24 C2

Newton St Petrock 9 C6
Newton Solney . . 63 B6
Newton Stacey . . 26 E2
Newton Stewart 105 C8
Newton Tony . . . 25 E7
Newton Tracey . . . 9 B7
**Newton under**
Roseberry . . . . 102 C3
**Newton upon**
Derwent . . . . . . 96 E3
Newton Valence . 26 F5
New Totley . . . . . 76 B3
**Newtown**
Argyll . . . . . . . 125 E6
BCP . . . . . . . . 13 E8
Ches W . . . . . . . 74 B2
Corn . . . . . . . . . 3 D6
Cumb . . . . . . . 107 E7
Cumb . . . . . . . 108 C5
Derbys . . . . . . . 87 F7
Devon . . . . . . . 10 B2
Glos . . . . . . . . . 36 D3
Glos . . . . . . . . . 50 F4
Hants . . . . . . . . 14 B4
Hants . . . . . . . . 14 C3
Hants . . . . . . . . 15 C6
Hants . . . . . . . . 15 C7
Hants . . . . . . . . 15 D5
Hants . . . . . . . . 26 C2
Hereford . . . . . . 49 E8
Highld . . . . . . 137 D6
IoM . . . . . . . . . 84 E3
IoW . . . . . . . . . 14 E5
Northumb . . . . 117 B6
Northumb . . . . 117 D6
Northumb . . . . 123 F5
Shrops . . . . . . . 73 F8
Staffs . . . . . . . . 75 C6
Staffs . . . . . . . . 75 C7
Wilts . . . . . . . . 13 B7
**Newtown**
=Y Dreneuydd . . 59 E8
**Newtown**
Linford . . . . . . 64 D2
**Newtown**
St Boswells . . . 121 F8
**Newtown**
Unthank . . . . . . 63 D8
**New Tredegar =**
Tredegar Newydd 35 D5
New Trows . . . . 119 F8
Newtyle . . . . . . 134 E2
New Ulva . . . . . 144 E6
New Walsoken . . 66 D4
New Waltham . . 91 D6
New Whittington 76 B3
New Wimpole . . 54 E4
New Winton . . . 121 B7
New Yatt . . . . . . 38 C3
**New York**
Lincs . . . . . . . . 78 D5
N Yorks . . . . . . 94 C4
Neyland . . . . . . 44 E4
Niarbyl . . . . . . . 84 E2
Nibley . . . . . . . 36 F3
Nibley Green . . . 36 E4
Nibon . . . . . . . 160 F5
Nicholashayne . 11 C6
Nicholaston . . . 33 F6
Nidd . . . . . . . . 95 C6
**Nigg**
Aberdeen . . . . . 141 D8
Highld . . . . . . 151 D11
Nigg Ferry . . . . 151 E10
Nightcott . . . . . 10 B3
Nilig . . . . . . . . 72 D4
Nine Ashes . . . . 42 D1
Ninebanks . . . . 109 D7
Nine Mile Burn 120 D4
Nine Wells . . . . 44 C2
Ninfield . . . . . . 18 D4
Ningwood . . . . 14 F4
Nisbet . . . . . . . 116 B2
**Nisthouse**
Orkney . . . . . . 159 G4
Shetland . . . . . 160 G7
Niton . . . . . . . . 15 G6
Nitshill . . . . . . 118 C5
Noak Hill . . . . . 41 E8
Noblethorpe . . . 88 D3
Nobottle . . . . . . 52 C4
Nocton . . . . . . 78 C3
Noke . . . . . . . . 39 C5
Nolton . . . . . . . 44 D3
Nolton Haven . . 44 D3
**No Man's Heath**
Ches W . . . . . . . 74 E2
Warks . . . . . . . . 63 D6
**Nomansland**
Devon . . . . . . . 10 C3
Wilts . . . . . . . . 14 C3
Noneley . . . . . . 60 B4
Nonikiln . . . . . 151 D9
Nonington . . . . 31 D6
Noonsborough 160 H4
Norbreck . . . . . 92 E3
Norbridge . . . . . 50 E2
**Norbury**
Ches E . . . . . . . 74 E2
Derbys . . . . . . . 75 E8
Shrops . . . . . . . 60 E3
Staffs . . . . . . . . 61 B7
Nordelph . . . . . 67 D5
Norden . . . . . . 87 C6
Norden Heath . . 13 F7
Nordley . . . . . . 61 E6
Norham . . . . . 122 E5
Norley . . . . . . . 74 B2
Norleywood . . . 14 E4
**Normanby**
N Lincs . . . . . . 90 C2
N Yorks . . . . . . 103 F5
Redcar . . . . . . 102 C3
**Normanby-**
by-Spital . . . . . 90 F4
**Normanby**
by Stow . . . . . . 90 F2
**Normanby**
le Wold . . . . . . 90 E5
Norman Cross . . 65 E8
Normandy . . . . 27 D7
Norman's Bay . . 18 E3
Norman's Green 11 D5
Normanstone . . 69 E8
**Normanton**
Derby . . . . . . . 76 F3
Leics . . . . . . . . 77 D8

**Normanton** continued
Lincs . . . . . . . . 78 E2
Notts . . . . . . . . 77 D7
Rutland . . . . . . 65 D6
W Yorks . . . . . . 88 B4
**Normanton**
le Heath . . . . . . 63 C7
**Normanton**
on Soar . . . . . . 64 B2
**Normanton**
on Trent . . . . . . 77 D7
**Normanton-on-**
the-Wolds . . . . 77 F6
Normoss . . . . . 92 F3
Norney . . . . . . 27 E7
**Norrington**
Common . . . . . 24 C3
Norris Green . . . 85 E4
Norris Hill . . . . 63 C7
Northacre . . . . . 68 E2
Northallerton . . 102 E1
**Northam**
Devon . . . . . . . . 9 B6
Soton . . . . . . . . 14 C5
Northampton . . 53 C5
North Anston . . 89 F6
North Aston . . . 38 B4
Northaw . . . . . . 41 D5
North Baddesley 14 C4
**North**
Ballachulish . . 130 C4
North Barrow . . 23 F8
North Barsham . 80 D5
Northbeck . . . . 78 E3
North Benfleet . 42 F3
North Bersted . . 16 D3
North Berwick . 129 F7
North Boarhunt . 15 C7
Northborough . . 65 D8
North Bourne . . 31 D7
North Bovey . . . . 7 B6
North Bradley . . 24 D3
North Brentor . . . 9 F6
North Brewham . 24 F2
**Northbridge**
Street . . . . . . . 18 C4
North Buckland . 20 E3
**North**
Burlingham . . . 69 C6
North Cadbury . 12 B4
North Cairn . . . 104 B3
North Carlton . . 78 B2
North Carrine . 143 H7
North Cave . . . . 96 F4
North Cerney . . 37 D7
Northchapel . . . 16 B3
North Charford . 14 C2
North Charlton 117 B7
North Cheriton . 12 B4
Northchurch . . . 40 D2
North Cliff . . . . 97 E8
North Cliffe . . . 96 F4
North Clifton . . 77 B8
**North**
Cockerington . 91 E7
North Coker . . . 12 C3
North Collafirth 160 E5
North Common . 17 B7
North Connel . . 124 B5
North Cornelly . 34 F2
North Cotes . . . 91 D7
Northcott . . . . . . 8 E5
North Cove . . . . 69 F7
North Cowton . 101 D7
North Crawley . 53 E7
North Cray . . . . 29 B5
North Creake . . 80 D4
North Curry . . . 11 B8
North Dalton . . 96 D5
North Dawn . . . 159 H5
North Deighton . 95 D6
Northdown . . . . 31 B7
North Duffield . 96 F2
Northdyke . . . . 159 F3
North Elkington . 91 E6
North Elmham . 81 E6
North Elmsall . . 89 C5
**Northend**
Bath . . . . . . . . 24 C2
Bucks . . . . . . . 39 E7
Warks . . . . . . . 51 D8
**North End**
Bucks . . . . . . . 39 B8
Essex . . . . . . . 42 C2
E Yorks . . . . . . 97 F8
Hants . . . . . . . 26 C2
Lincs . . . . . . . . 78 E5
N Som . . . . . . . 23 C6
Ptsmth . . . . . . 15 D7
Som . . . . . . . . 11 B7
W Sus . . . . . . . 16 D5
North Erradale 155 F11
North Fambridge 42 E4
North Fearns . . 149 E10
**North**
Featherstone . . 88 B5
North Ferriby . . 90 B3
**Northfield**
Aberdeen . . . . . 141 D8
Borders . . . . . . 122 C5
E Yorks . . . . . . 90 B4
W Mid . . . . . . . 50 B5
Northfields . . . . 65 D7
Northfleet . . . . 29 B7
**North**
Frodingham . . 97 D7
Northgate . . . . 65 B6
North Gluss . . . 160 F5
North Gorley . . 14 C2
**North Green**
Norf . . . . . . . . 68 F5
Suff . . . . . . . . . 57 C7
North Greetwell 78 B3
North Grimston . 96 C4
North Halley . . . 159 J5
North Halling . . 29 C8
North Hayling . . 15 D8
North Hazelrigg 123 F6
North Heasley . . 21 F6
North Heath . . . 16 B4
**North Hill**
Cambs . . . . . . . 55 B5
Corn . . . . . . . . . 5 B7
North Hinksey . 38 D4
North Holmwood 28 E2
Northhouse . . . 115 D7
North Howden . 96 F3

North Huish . . . . 6 D5
North Hykeham . 78 C2
Northiam . . . . . 18 C5
Northill . . . . . . 54 E2
Northington . . . 26 F3
North Johnston . 44 D4
North Kelsey . . . 90 D4
**North Kelsey**
Moor . . . . . . . . 90 D4
North Kessock . 151 G9
**North**
Killingholme . . 90 C5
North Kilvington 102 F1
North Kilworth . 64 F3
North Kirkton . 153 C11
**North**
Kiscadale . . . 143 F11
North Kyme . . . 78 D4
North Lancing . . 17 D5
Northlands . . . . 79 D6
Northlea . . . . . 111 D7
Northleach . . . . 37 C8
North Lee . . . . . 39 D8
Northleigh . . . . 11 E6
North Leigh . . . 38 C3
**North Leverton with**
Habblesthorpe 89 F8
Northlew . . . . . . 9 E7
North Littleton . 51 E5
North Lopham . 68 F3
North Luffenham 65 D6
North Marden . 16 C2
North Marston . 39 B7
**North Middleton**
Midloth . . . . . 121 D6
Northumb . . . . 117 B6
North Molton . . 10 B2
Northmoor . . . . 38 D4
**Northmoor Green**
or Moorland . . 22 F5
North Moreton . 39 F5
Northmuir . . . . 134 D3
North Mundham 16 D2
North Muskham 77 D7
North Newbald . 96 F5
North Newington 52 F2
North Newnton . 25 D6
North Newton . . 22 F4
Northney . . . . . 15 D8
North Nibley . . 36 E4
North Oakley . . 26 D3
North Ockendon 42 F1
Northolt . . . . . . 40 F4
Northop . . . . . . 73 C6
Northop Hall . . 73 C6
North Ormesby . 91 E6
North Ormsby . . 91 E6
**Northorpe**
Lincs . . . . . . . . 65 C7
Lincs . . . . . . . . 78 F5
Lincs . . . . . . . . 90 E2
**North**
Otterington . . 102 F1
**Northover**
Som . . . . . . . . 12 B3
Som . . . . . . . . 23 F6
North Owersby . 90 E4
Northowram . . . 88 B2
North Perrott . . 12 D2
North Petherton 22 F4
North Petherwin . 8 F4
North Pickenham 67 D8
North Piddle . . . 50 D4
North Poorton . 12 E3
Northport . . . . . 13 F7
North Port . . . . 125 C6
Northpunds . . . 160 L6
**North**
Queensferry . . 128 F3
North Radworthy 21 F6
North Rauceby . 78 E3
Northrepps . . . . 81 D8
North Reston . . 91 F7
North Rigton . . 95 E5
North Roe . . . . 160 E5
North Runcton . 67 C6
North Sandwick 160 D7
North Scale . . . . 92 C1
North Scarle . . . 77 C8
North Seaton . . 117 F8
North Shian . . . 130 E3
North Shields . . 111 C6
North Shoebury . 43 F5
North Shore . . . 92 F3
**North Side**
Cumb . . . . . . . 98 B2
Pboro . . . . . . . 66 E2
North Skelton . 102 C4
**North**
Somercotes . . . 91 E8
North Stainley . 95 B5
**North**
Stainmore . . . 100 C3
North Stifford . . 42 F2
**North Stoke**
Bath . . . . . . . . 24 C2
Oxon . . . . . . . 39 F6
W Sus . . . . . . . 16 C4
Northstowe . . . 54 C5
**North Street**
Hants . . . . . . . 26 F4
Kent . . . . . . . . 30 D4
Medway . . . . . 30 B2
W Berks . . . . . . 26 B4
**North**
Sunderland . . 123 F8
North Tamerton . 8 E5
North Tawton . . . 9 D8
North Thoresby . 91 E6
North Tidworth . 25 E7
North Togston . 117 D8
**North**
Tuddenham . . 68 C3
North Walbottle 110 C4
North Walsham . 81 D8
North Waltham . 26 E3
**North**
Warnborough . 26 D5
**North Water**
Bridge . . . . . . 135 C6
North Watten . . 158 E4
Northway . . . . . 50 F4
**North Weald**
Bassett . . . . . . 41 D7
**North**
Wheatley . . . . 89 F8

**North**
Whilborough . . 7 C6
Northwich . . . . 74 B3
Northwick . . . . 36 F2
North Wick . . . . 23 C7
North Willingham 91 F5
North Wingfield 76 C4
North Witham . 65 B6
Northwold . . . . 67 E7
**Northwood**
Derbys . . . . . . . 76 C2
IoW . . . . . . . . 15 E5
Kent . . . . . . . . 31 C7
London . . . . . . 40 E3
Shrops . . . . . . . 73 F8
**Northwood**
Green . . . . . . . 36 C4
North Woolwich 28 B5
**North Wootton**
Dorset . . . . . . . 12 C4
Norf . . . . . . . . 67 B6
Som . . . . . . . . 23 E7
North Wraxall . 24 B3
North Wroughton 38 F1
**Norton**
E Sus . . . . . . . 17 D8
Glos . . . . . . . . 37 B5
Halton . . . . . . 86 F3
Herts . . . . . . . 54 F4
IoW . . . . . . . . 14 F4
Mon . . . . . . . . 35 C8
Notts . . . . . . . 77 B5
Powys . . . . . . . 48 C5
Shrops . . . . . . . 60 F4
Shrops . . . . . . . 61 D5
Shrops . . . . . . . 61 D7
Stockton . . . . . 102 B2
Suff . . . . . . . . . 56 C3
S Yorks . . . . . . 89 C6
Wilts . . . . . . . . 37 F5
Worcs . . . . . . . 50 D3
Worcs . . . . . . . 50 E5
W Sus . . . . . . . 16 D3
W Sus . . . . . . . 16 E2
Norton Bavant . 24 E4
Norton Bridge . 75 F5
Norton Canes . . 62 D4
Norton Canon . 49 E5
Norton Corner . 81 E6
Norton Disney . 77 D8
Norton East . . . 62 D4
Norton Ferris . . 24 F2
**Norton**
Fitzwarren . . . . 11 B6
Norton Green . . 14 F4
Norton Hawkfield 23 C7
Norton Heath . . 42 D2
Norton in Hales 74 F4
**Norton-in-**
the-Moors . . . . 75 D6
**Norton-Juxta-**
Twycross . . . . 63 D7
Norton-le-Clay . 95 B7
Norton Lindsey . 51 C7
**Norton**
Malreward . . . 23 C8
**Norton**
Mandeville . . . 42 D1
**Norton-on-**
Derwent . . . . . 96 B3
Norton St Philip . 24 D2
**Norton sub**
Hamdon . . . . 12 C2
**Norton**
Woodseats . . . 88 F4
Norwell . . . . . . 77 C7
**Norwell**
Woodhouse . . . 77 C7
Norwich . . . . . 160 E4
Norwood . . . . . 89 F5
Norwood Hill . . 28 E3
Norwoodside . . 66 E4
Noseley . . . . . . 64 E4
Noss . . . . . . . 160 M5
Noss Mayo . . . . . 6 E3
Nosterfield . . . 101 F7
Nostie . . . . . . 149 F13
Notgrove . . . . . 37 B8
Nottage . . . . . . 21 B7
Nottingham . . . 77 F5
**Notton**
Wilts . . . . . . . . 24 C4
W Yorks . . . . . . 88 C4
Nounsley . . . . . 42 C3
Noutard's Green 50 C2
Novar House . . 151 E9
Nox . . . . . . . . 60 C4
Nuffield . . . . . . 39 F6
Nunburnholme . 96 E4
Nuncargate . . . 76 D5
Nuneaton . . . . . 63 E7
**Nuneham**
Courtenay . . . . 39 E5
Nun Hills . . . . . 87 B6
Nun Monkton . 95 D8
Nunney . . . . . . 24 E2
Nunnington . . . 96 B2
Nunnykirk . . . . 117 E6
Nunsthorpe . . . 91 D6
**Nunthorpe**
Mbro . . . . . . . 102 C3
York . . . . . . . . 96 D2
Nunton . . . . . . 14 B2
Nunwick . . . . . 95 B6
Nupend . . . . . . 36 D4
Nursling . . . . . 14 C4
Nursted . . . . . . 15 B8
**Nutbourne**
W Sus . . . . . . . 15 D8
W Sus . . . . . . . 16 C4
Nutfield . . . . . . 28 D4
Nuthall . . . . . . 76 E5
Nuthampstead . 54 F5
Nuthurst . . . . . 17 B5
Nutley E Sus . . . 17 B8
Hants . . . . . . . 26 E4
Nutwell . . . . . . 89 D7
Nybster . . . . . . 158 D5
Nyetimber . . . . 16 E2
Nyewood . . . . . 16 B2
Nymet Rowland 10 D2
Nymet Tracey . . 10 D2
Nympsfield . . . . 37 D5
Nynehead . . . . 11 B6
Nyton . . . . . . . 16 D3

**O**

Oadby . . . . . . . 64 D3
Oad Street . . . . 30 C2
Oakamoor . . . . 75 D7
Oakbank . . . . . 120 C3
Oak Cross . . . . . 9 E7
Oakdale . . . . . . 35 E5
Oake . . . . . . . . 11 B6
Oaken . . . . . . . 62 D2
Oakenclough . . 92 E5
Oakengates . . . 61 C7
Oakenholt . . . . 73 B6
**Oakenshaw**
Durham . . . . . 110 F5
W Yorks . . . . . . 88 B3
Oakerthorpe . . . 76 D3
Oakes . . . . . . . 88 C2
Oakfield . . . . . . 35 E7
**Oakford**
Ceredig . . . . . . 46 D3
Devon . . . . . . . 10 B4
Oakfordbridge . 10 B4
Oakgrove . . . . . 75 C6
Oakham . . . . . . 65 D5
Oakhanger . . . . 27 F5
Oakhill . . . . . . 23 E8
Oakhurst . . . . . 29 D6
Oakington . . . . 54 C5
**Oaklands**
Herts . . . . . . . . 41 C5
Powys . . . . . . . 48 D2
Oakle Street . . . 36 C4
**Oakley**
BCP . . . . . . . . 13 E8
Bedford . . . . . . 53 D8
Bucks . . . . . . . 39 C6
Fife . . . . . . . . 128 F2
Hants . . . . . . . 26 D3
Oxon . . . . . . . 39 D7
Suff . . . . . . . . . 57 B5
Oakley Green . . 27 B7
Oakley Park . . . 59 F6
Oakmere . . . . . 74 C2
**Oakridge**
Glos . . . . . . . . 37 D6
Hants . . . . . . . 26 D4
Oaks . . . . . . . . 60 D4
Oaksey . . . . . . 37 E6
Oaks Green . . . 75 F8
Oakthorpe . . . . 63 C7
Oakwoodhill . . 28 F2
Oakworth . . . . . 94 F3
Oape . . . . . . . 156 J7
**Oare**
Kent . . . . . . . . 30 C4
Som . . . . . . . . 21 E7
W Berks . . . . . . 26 B3
Wilts . . . . . . . . 25 C6
Oasby . . . . . . . 78 F3
Oathlaw . . . . . 134 D4
Oatlands . . . . . 95 D6
**Oban**
Argyll . . . . . . . 124 C4
Highld . . . . . . 147 C11
Oborne . . . . . . 12 C4
Obthorpe . . . . . 65 C7
**Occlestone**
Green . . . . . . . 74 C3
Occold . . . . . . 57 B5
Ochiltree . . . . . 112 B5
Ochtermuthill 127 C7
Ochtertyre . . . . 127 B7
Ockbrook . . . . . 76 F4
Ockham . . . . . . 27 D8
Ockle . . . . . . . 147 D8
Ockley . . . . . . . 28 F2
Ocle Pychard . . 49 E7
Octon . . . . . . . 97 C6
**Octon Cross**
Roads . . . . . . . 97 C6
Odcombe . . . . . 12 C3
Odd Down . . . . 24 C2
Oddendale . . . . 99 C7
Odder . . . . . . . 78 B2
Oddingley . . . . 50 D4
Oddington . . . . 39 C5
Odell . . . . . . . 53 D7
Odie . . . . . . . 159 F7
Odiham . . . . . . 26 D5
Odstock . . . . . . 14 B2
Odstone . . . . . . 63 D7
Offchurch . . . . 51 C8
Offenham . . . . 51 E5
**Offham**
E Sus . . . . . . . 17 C7
Kent . . . . . . . . 29 D7
W Sus . . . . . . . 16 D4
Offord Cluny . . 54 C3
Offord Darcy . . 54 C3
Offton . . . . . . . 56 E4
Offwell . . . . . . 11 E6
**Ogbourne**
Maizey . . . . . . 25 B6
**Ogbourne**
St Andrew . . . . 25 B6
**Ogbourne**
St George . . . . 25 B7
Ogil . . . . . . . . 134 C4
Ogle . . . . . . . . 110 B4
Ogmore . . . . . . 21 B7
Ogmore-by-Sea 34 E3
Ogmore Vale . . 34 E3
**Okeford**
Fitzpaine . . . . 13 C6
Okehampton . . . 9 E7
**Okehampton**
Camp . . . . . . . . 9 E7
Okraquoy . . . . 160 K6
Old . . . . . . . . . 53 B6
Old Aberdeen . 141 D8
Old Alresford . . 26 F3
Oldany . . . . . . 156 F4
Old Arley . . . . . 63 E6
Old Basford . . . 76 E5
Old Basing . . . . 26 D4
Oldberrow . . . . 51 C6
Old Bewick . . . 117 B6
**Old**
Bolingbroke . . 79 C6
Oldborough . . . 10 D2
Old Brampton . 76 B3
Old Bramhope . 94 E5
**Old Bridge of**
Tilt . . . . . . . . 133 C5

**Old Bridge of**
Urr . . . . . . . . 106 C4
Old Buckenham 68 E3
Old Burghclere . 26 D2
**Oldbury**
Shrops . . . . . . . 61 E7
Warks . . . . . . . 63 E7
W Mid . . . . . . . 62 F3
**Oldbury-**
on-Severn . . . . 36 E3
**Oldbury on**
the Hill . . . . . . 37 F5
Old Byland . . . 102 F3
Old Cassop . . . 111 F6
**Oldcastle**
Bridgend . . . . . 21 B8
Mon . . . . . . . . 35 B7
Old Castleton . 115 E8
Old Catton . . . . 68 C5
Old Clee . . . . . 91 D6
Old Cleeve . . . . 22 E2
Old Clipstone . . 77 C6
Old Colwyn . . . 83 D8
Old Coulsdon . . 28 D4
Old Crombie . . 152 C5
Old Dailly . . . . 112 E2
Old Dalby . . . . 64 B3
Old Deer . . . . . 153 D9
Old Denaby . . . 89 E5
Old Edlington . . 89 E6
Old Eldon . . . . 101 B7
Old Ellerby . . . 97 F7
Oldfallow . . . . 62 C3
Old Felixstowe . 57 F7
Oldfield . . . . . . 50 C3
Old Fletton . . . 65 E8
Oldford . . . . . . 24 D2
Old Glossop . . . 87 E8
Old Goole . . . . 89 B8
Old Hall . . . . . 59 F6
Oldham . . . . . . 87 D7
Oldhamstocks . 122 B3
Old Heath . . . . 43 B6
Old Heathfield . 18 C2
Old Hill . . . . . . 62 F3
Old Hunstanton 80 C2
Old Hurst . . . . 54 B3
Old Hutton . . . 99 F7
Old Kea . . . . . . . 3 B7
Old Kilpatrick . 118 B4
Old Kinnernie . 141 D6
Old Knebworth . 41 B5
Oldland . . . . . . 23 B8
Old Langho . . . 93 F7
Old Laxey . . . . 84 D4
Old Leake . . . . 79 D7
Old Malton . . . 96 B3
Oldmeldrum . . 141 B7
Old Micklefield . 95 F7
Old Milton . . . . 14 E3
Old Milverton . 51 C7
Old Monkland . 119 C7
Old Netley . . . . 15 D5
Old Philpstoun 120 B3
Old Quarrington 111 F6
Old Radnor . . . 48 D4
Old Rattray . . . 153 C10
Old Rayne . . . . 141 B5
Old Romney . . . 19 C7
Oldshore Beg . . 156 D4
Oldshoremore . 156 D5
Old Sodbury . . . 36 F4
Old Somerby . . 78 F2
Oldstead . . . . . 102 F3
Old Stratford . . 53 E5
Old Thirsk . . . . 102 F2
Oldtown . . . . . 140 B4
**Old Town**
Cumb . . . . . . . 99 F7
Cumb . . . . . . . 108 E4
Northumb . . . . 116 E4
Scilly . . . . . . . . 2 E4
Oldtown of Ord 152 C6
Old Trafford . . . 87 E6
Old Tupton . . . . 76 C3
Old Warden . . . 54 E2
Oldway . . . . . . 33 F6
Oldways End . . 10 B3
Old Weston . . . 53 B8
Oldwhat . . . . . 153 C8
Old Whittington 76 B3
Old Wick . . . . . 158 E5
Old Windsor . . . 27 B7
Old Wives Lees . 30 D4
Old Woking . . . 27 D8
Old Woodhall . . 78 C5
Olgrinmore . . . 158 E2
Oliver's Battery . 15 B5
Ollaberry . . . . . 160 E5
**Ollerton**
Ches E . . . . . . . 74 B4
Notts . . . . . . . 77 C6
Shrops . . . . . . . 61 B6
Olmarch . . . . . 46 D5
Olney . . . . . . . 53 D6
Olrig House . . . 158 D3
Olton . . . . . . . 62 F5
Olveston . . . . . 36 F3
Olwen . . . . . . . 46 E4
Ombersley . . . . 50 C3
Ompton . . . . . . 77 C6
Onchan . . . . . . 84 E3
Onecote . . . . . . 75 D7
Onen . . . . . . . . 35 C8
Ongar Hill . . . . 67 B5
Ongar Street . . 49 C5
Onibury . . . . . . 49 B6
Onich . . . . . . . 130 C4
Onllwyn . . . . . 34 C2
Onneley . . . . . . 74 E4
Onslow Village . 27 E7
Onthank . . . . . 118 E4
Openwoodgate . 76 E3
**Opinan**
Highld . . . . . . 149 A12
Highld . . . . . . 155 H13
Orange Lane . . 122 E3
Orange Row . . . 66 B5
Orasaigh . . . . . 155 F8
Orbliston . . . . . 152 C3
Orbost . . . . . . 148 D7
Orby . . . . . . . . 79 C7
Orchard Hill . . . . 9 B6
Orchard Portman 11 B7
Orcheston . . . . 25 E5
Orcop . . . . . . . 36 B1
Orcop Hill . . . . 36 B1

Ord . . . . . . . . 149 G11
Ordhead . . . . . 141 C5
Ordie . . . . . . . 140 D3
Ordiequish . . . 152 C3
Ordsall . . . . . . 89 F7
Ore . . . . . . . . . 18 D5
Oreton . . . . . . 61 F6
**Orford**
Suff . . . . . . . . . 57 E8
Warr . . . . . . . . 86 E4
Orgreave . . . . . 63 C5
Orlestone . . . . . 19 B6
**Orleton**
Hereford . . . . . 49 C6
Worcs . . . . . . . 49 C8
Orlingbury . . . . 53 B6
Ormesby . . . . . 102 C3
**Ormesby**
St Margaret . . 69 C7
**Ormesby**
St Michael . . . 69 C7
**Ormiclate**
Castle . . . . . . 148 E2
Ormiscaig . . . . 155 H13
Ormiston . . . . . 121 C7
Ormsaigbeg . . 146 E7
Ormsaigmore . 146 E7
Ormsary . . . . . 144 F6
Ormsgill . . . . . 92 B1
Ormskirk . . . . . 86 D2
Orpington . . . . 29 C5
**Orrell**
Gtr Man . . . . . . 86 D3
Mers . . . . . . . . 85 E4
Orrisdale . . . . . 84 C3
Orroland . . . . . 106 E4
Orsett . . . . . . . 42 F2
Orslow . . . . . . 62 C2
Orston . . . . . . . 77 E7
Orthwaite . . . . 108 F2
Ortner . . . . . . . 92 D5
**Orton**
Cumb . . . . . . . 99 D8
N Nhants . . . . . 53 B6
**Orton**
Longueville . . 65 E8
**Orton-on-**
the-Hill . . . . . . 63 D7
Orton Waterville 65 E8
Orwell . . . . . . . 54 D4
Osbaldeston . . . 93 F6
Osbaldwick . . . 96 D2
Osbaston . . . . . 60 B3
Osbournby . . . . 78 F3
Oscroft . . . . . . 74 C2
Ose . . . . . . . . 149 D8
Osgathorpe . . . 63 C8
**Osgodby**
Lincs . . . . . . . . 90 E4
N Yorks . . . . . . 96 F2
N Yorks . . . . . . 103 F8
Oskaig . . . . . . 149 E10
Oskamull . . . . 146 G7
**Osmaston**
Derby . . . . . . . 76 F3
Derbys . . . . . . . 76 E2
Osmington . . . . 12 F5
Osmington Mills 12 F5
Osmotherley . . 102 E2
Ospisdale . . . . 151 C10
Ospringe . . . . . 30 C4
Ossett . . . . . . . 88 B3
Ossington . . . . 77 C7
Ostend . . . . . . 43 E5
Oswaldkirk . . . 96 B2
Oswaldtwistle . 86 B5
Oswestry . . . . . 60 B2
Otford . . . . . . . 29 D6
Otham . . . . . . . 29 D8
Othery . . . . . . . 23 F5
**Otley**
Suff . . . . . . . . . 57 D6
W Yorks . . . . . . 94 E5
Otterbourne . . . 15 B5
**Otterburn**
Northumb . . . . 116 E4
N Yorks . . . . . . 93 D8
Otterburn Camp 116 E4
Otter Ferry . . . 145 E8
Otterham . . . . . . 8 E3
Otterhampton . 22 E4
Ottershaw . . . . 27 C8
Otterswick . . . 160 E7
Otterton . . . . . 11 F5
Ottery St Mary . 11 E6
Ottinge . . . . . . 31 E5
Ottringham . . . 91 B6
Oughterby . . . 108 D2
Oughtershaw . . 100 F3
Oughterside . . 107 E8
Oughtibridge . . 88 E4
Oughtrington . . 86 F4
Oulston . . . . . . 95 B8
**Oulton**
Cumb . . . . . . . 108 D2
Norf . . . . . . . . 81 E7
Staffs . . . . . . . . 75 F6
Suff . . . . . . . . . 69 E8
W Yorks . . . . . . 88 B4
Oulton Broad . . 69 E8
Oulton Street . . 81 E7
Oundle . . . . . . 65 F7
Ousby . . . . . . . 109 F6
Ousdale . . . . . 158 H2
Ousden . . . . . . 55 D8
Ousefleet . . . . . 90 B2
**Ouston**
Durham . . . . . 111 D5
Northumb . . . . 110 B3
Outgate . . . . . . 99 E5
Outhgill . . . . . 100 D2
Outlane . . . . . . 87 C8
Out Newton . . . 91 B7
Out Rawcliffe . . 92 E4
Outwell . . . . . . 66 D5
Outwick . . . . . . 14 C2
**Outwood**
Sur . . . . . . . . . 28 E4
W Yorks . . . . . . 88 B4
Outwoods . . . . 61 C7
Ovenden . . . . . 87 B8
Ovenscloss . . . 121 F7
**Over**
Cambs . . . . . . . 54 B4
Ches W . . . . . . . 74 C3
S Glos . . . . . . . 36 F2
Overbister . . . . 159 D7

Overbury . . . . . 50 F4
Overcombe . . . . 12 F4
Over Compton . 12 C3
Overgreen . . . . 76 B3
Over Green . . . . 63 E5
Over Haddon . . 76 C2
Over Hulton . . . 86 D4
Over Kellet . . . . 92 B5
Over Kiddington 38 B4
Over Knutsford . 74 B4
Overleigh . . . . . 23 F6
Overley Green . . 51 D5
Over Monnow . . 36 C2
Over Norton . . . 38 B3
Over Peover . . . 74 B4
Overpool . . . . . 73 B7
Overscaig Hotel 156 G7
Overseal . . . . . 63 C6
Over Silton . . . 102 E2
Oversland . . . . 30 D4
Overstone . . . . 53 C6
Over Stowey . . . 22 F3
Overstrand . . . . 81 C8
Over Stratton . . 12 C2
Over Tabley . . . 86 F5
Overthorpe . . . . 52 E2
**Overton**
Aberdeen . . . . . 141 C7
Ches W . . . . . . . 74 B2
Dumfries . . . . . 107 C6
Hants . . . . . . . 26 E3
Lancs . . . . . . . . 92 D4
N Yorks . . . . . . 95 D8
Shrops . . . . . . . 49 B7
Swansea . . . . . . 33 F5
W Yorks . . . . . . 88 C3
Overton = Owrtyn 73 E7
Overton Bridge . 73 E7
Overtown . . . . 119 D8
Over Wallop . . . 25 F7
Over Whitacre . 63 E6
Over Worton . . 38 B4
**Oving**
Bucks . . . . . . . 39 B7
W Sus . . . . . . . 16 D3
Ovingdean . . . . 17 D7
Ovingham . . . . 110 C3
**Ovington**
Durham . . . . . 101 C6
Essex . . . . . . . 55 E8
Hants . . . . . . . 26 F3
Norf . . . . . . . . 68 D2
Northumb . . . . 110 C3
Ower . . . . . . . . 14 C4
Owermoigne . . 13 F5
Owlbury . . . . . 60 E3
Owler Bar . . . . 76 B2
Owlerton . . . . . 88 F4
Owl's Green . . . 57 C6
Owlswick . . . . . 39 D7
Owmby . . . . . . 90 D4
Owmby-by-Spital 90 F4
Owrtyn = Overton 73 E7
Owslebury . . . . 15 B6
**Owston**
Leics . . . . . . . . 64 D4
S Yorks . . . . . . 89 C6
Owston Ferry . . 90 D2
Owstwick . . . . . 97 F8
Owthorne . . . . 91 B7
Owthorpe . . . . 77 F6
Oxborough . . . . 67 D7
Oxcombe . . . . . 79 B6
Oxen End . . . . . 42 B2
Oxenholme . . . 99 F7
Oxenhope . . . . 94 F3
Oxen Park . . . . 99 F5
Oxenton . . . . . 50 F4
Oxenwood . . . . 25 D8
Oxford . . . . . . . 39 D5
Oxhey . . . . . . . 40 E4
Oxhill . . . . . . . 51 E8
Oxley . . . . . . . 62 D3
Oxley Green . . . 43 C5
Oxley's Green . . 18 C3
Oxnam . . . . . . 116 C2
Oxshott . . . . . . 28 C2
Oxspring . . . . . 88 D3
Oxted . . . . . . . 28 D4
**Oxton**
Borders . . . . . . 121 D7
Notts . . . . . . . 77 D6
Oxwich . . . . . . 33 F5
Oxwich Green . . 33 F5
Oykel Bridge . . 156 J6
Oyne . . . . . . . 141 B5

**P**

Pabail Iarach . . 155 D10
Pabail Uarach . . 155 D10
Pace Gate . . . . . 94 D4
Packington . . . . 63 C7
Padanaram . . . 134 D4
Padbury . . . . . . 52 F5
Paddington . . . . 41 F5
Paddlesworth . . 19 B8
Paddockhaugh 152 C2
Paddockhole . . 115 F5
Paddock Wood . 29 E7
Padfield . . . . . . 87 E8
Padiham . . . . . . 93 F7
Padog . . . . . . . 83 F8
Padside . . . . . . 94 D4
Padstow . . . . . . . 4 B4
Padworth . . . . . 26 C4
Page Bank . . . . 110 F5
**Pagelsham**
Eastend . . . . . 43 E5
**Pagelsham**
Churchend . . . 43 E5
Paibeil . . . . . . 148 B2
Paible . . . . . . . 154 H5
Paignton . . . . . . 7 C6
Pailton . . . . . . 63 F8
Painscastle . . . . 48 E3
Painshawfield 110 C3
Painsthorpe . . . 96 D4
Painswick . . . . 37 D5
Pairc Shiaboist 154 C7
Paisley . . . . . . 118 C4
Pakefield . . . . . 69 E8
Pakenham . . . . 56 C3
Pale . . . . . . . . 72 F3
Palestine . . . . . 25 E7
Paley Street . . . 27 B6
Palfrey . . . . . . 62 E4

Palgowan 112 F3
Palgrave 56 B5
Pallion 111 D6
Palmarsh 19 B8
Palnackie 106 D5
Palnure 105 C8
Palterton 76 C4
Pamber End 26 D4
Pamber Green 26 D4
Pamber Heath 26 C4
Pamphill 13 D7
Pampisford 55 E5
Pan 159 J4
Panbride 135 F5
Pancrasweek 8 D4
Pandy
  Gwyn. 58 D3
  Mon. 35 B7
  Powys 59 D6
  Wrex. 73 F5
Pandy Tudur 83 E8
Panfield 42 B3
Pangbourne 26 B4
Pannal 95 D6
Panshanger 41 C5
Pant 60 B2
Pant-glas
  Carms. 33 B6
  Gwyn. 71 C5
Pant-glâs 58 E4
Pant-glas 73 F6
Pantgwyn
  Carms. 33 B6
  Ceredig. 45 E4
Pant Mawr 59 F5
Panton 78 B4
Pantperthog 58 D4
Pant-teg 33 B5
Pant-y-Caws 32 B2
Pant-y-dwr 47 B8
Pant-y-ffridd 59 D8
Pantyffynnon 33 C7
Pantymwyn 73 C5
Pant-yr-awel 34 F3
Pant-y-Wacco 72 B5
Panxworth 69 C6
Papcastle 107 F8
Papigoe 158 E5
Papil 160 K5
Papley 159 J5
Papple 121 B8
Papplewick 76 D5
Papworth Everard 54 C3
Papworth St Agnes 54 C3
Par 5 D5
Parbold 86 C2
Parbrook
  Som. 23 F7
  W Sus 16 B4
Parc 72 F2
Parcllyn 45 D4
Parc-Seymour 35 E8
Parc-y-rhôs 46 E4
Pardshaw 98 B2
Parham 57 C7
Park 114 E2
Park Corner
  Oxon 39 F6
  Windsor 40 F1
Parkend 36 D3
Park End
  Mbro. 102 C3
  Northumb 109 B8
Parkeston 57 F6
Parkgate
  Ches W 73 B6
  Dumfries 114 F3
  Kent 19 B5
  Sur 28 E3
Park Gate 15 D6
Parkham 9 B5
Parkham Ash 9 B5
Park Hill
  Notts 77 D6
  N Yorks 95 C6
Parkhill House 141 C7
Parkhouse 36 D1
Parkhouse Green 76 C4
Parkhurst 15 E5
Parkmill 33 F6
Parkneuk 135 B7
Parkstone 13 E8
Park Street 28 E2
Parley Cross 13 E8
Parracombe 21 E5
Parrog 45 F2
Parsley Hay 75 C8
Parsonage Green 42 D3
Parsonby 107 F8
Parson Cross 88 E4
Parson Drove 66 D3
Parson's Heath 43 B6
Partick 119 C5
Partington 86 E5
Partney 79 C7
Parton
  Cumb 98 B1
  Dumfries 106 B3
  Glos 37 B5
Partridge Green 17 C5
Parwich 75 D8
Passenham 53 F5
Paston 81 D9
Patchacott 9 E6
Patcham 17 D7
Patching 16 D4
Patchole 20 E5
Pateley Bridge 94 C4
Paternoster Heath 43 C5
Pathe 23 F5
Pathhead
  Aberds 135 C7
  E Ayrs 113 C6
  Fife 128 E4
  Midloth 121 C7
Path of Condie 128 C2
Pathstruie 128 C2
Patna 112 C4
Patney 25 D5
Patrick Brompton 101 E7
Patrington 91 B7
Patrixbourne 31 D5

Patterdale 99 C5
Pattingham 62 E2
Pattishall 52 D4
Pattiswick Green 42 B4
Patton Bridge 99 E7
Paul 2 D3
Paulerspury 52 E5
Paull 91 B5
Paulton 23 D8
Pavenham 53 D7
Pawlett 22 E5
Pawston 122 F4
Paxford 51 F6
Paxton 122 D5
Payhembury 11 D5
Paythorne 93 D8
Peacehaven 17 D8
Peak Dale 75 B7
Peak Forest 75 B8
Peakirk 65 E8
Pearsie 134 D3
Peasedown St John 24 D2
Peasemore 26 B2
Peasenhall 57 C7
Pease Pottage 28 F3
Peaslake 27 E8
Peasley Cross 86 E3
Peasmarsh 19 C5
Peaston 121 C7
Peastonbank 121 C7
Peathill 153 B9
Peat Inn 129 D6
Peatling Magna 64 E2
Peatling Parva 64 F2
Peaton 60 F5
Peats Corner 57 C5
Pebmarsh 56 F2
Pebworth 51 E6
Pecket Well 87 B7
Peckforton 74 D2
Peckham 28 B4
Peckleton 63 D8
Pedlinge 19 B8
Pedmore 62 F3
Pedwell 23 F6
Peebles 121 E5
Peel 84 D2
Peel Common 15 D6
Peel Park 119 D6
Pegsdon 54 F2
Pegswood 117 F8
Pegwell 31 C7
Peinchorran 149 E10
Peinlich 149 C9
Pelaw 111 C5
Pelcomb Bridge 44 D4
Pelcomb Cross 44 D4
Peldon 43 C5
Pellon 87 B8
Pelsall 62 D4
Pelton 111 D5
Pelutho 107 E8
Pelynt 5 D7
Pemberton 86 D3
Pembrey 33 D5
Pembridge 49 D5
Pembroke = Penfro 44 E4
Pembroke Dock = Doc Penfro 44 E4
Pembury 29 E7
Penallt 36 C2
Penally 32 E2
Penalt 36 B2
Penare 3 B8
Penarlâg = Hawarden 73 C7
Penarth 22 B3
Pen-bont Rhydybeddau 58 F3
Penbryn 45 D4
Pencader 46 F3
Pencaenewydd 70 C5
Pencaitland 121 C7
Pencarnisiog 82 D3
Pencarreg 46 E4
Pencelli 34 B4
Pen-clawdd 33 E6
Pencoed 34 F3
Pencombe 49 D7
Pencoyd 36 B2
Pencraig
  Hereford 36 B2
  Powys 59 B7
Pendeen 2 C2
Penderyn 34 D3
Pendine 32 D3
Pendlebury 87 D5
Pendleton 93 F7
Pendock 50 F2
Pendoggett 4 B5
Pendomer 12 C3
Pendoylan 22 B2
Pendre 34 F3
Penegoes 58 D4
Pen-ffordd 32 B1
Penfro = Pembroke 44 E4
Pengam 35 E5
Penge 28 B4
Pengenffordd 48 F3
Pengorffwysfa 82 B4
Pengover Green 5 C7
Penhale
  Corn 3 E5
  Corn 4 D4
Penhalvaen 3 C6
Penhill 38 F1
Penhow 35 E8
Penhurst 18 D3
Peniarth 58 D3
Penicuik 120 C5
Peniel
  Carms 33 B5
  Denb 72 C4
Penifiler 149 D9
Peninver 143 F9
Penisarwaun 83 E5
Penistone 88 D3
Penjerrick 3 C6
Penketh 86 F3
Penkill 112 E2
Penkridge 62 C3
Penley 73 F8
Penllergaer 33 E7

Penllyn 21 B8
Pen-llyn 82 C3
Pen-lon 82 E4
Penmachno 83 F7
Penmaen 33 F6
Penmaenan 83 D7
Penmaenmawr 83 D7
Penmaenpool 58 C3
Penmark 22 C2
Penmarth 3 C6
Penmon 83 C6
Penmore Mill 146 F7
Penmorfa
  Ceredig 46 D2
  Gwyn 71 C6
Penmynydd 82 D5
Penn
  Bucks 40 E2
  W Mid 62 E2
Pennal 58 D4
Pennan 153 B8
Pennant
  Ceredig 46 C4
  Denb 72 D4
  Denb 72 F4
  Powys 59 E5
Pennant Melangell 59 B7
Pennar 44 E4
Pennard 33 F6
Pennerley 60 E3
Pennington
  Cumb 92 B2
  Gtr Man 86 E4
  Hants 14 E4
Penny Bridge 99 F5
Pennycross 147 J8
Pennygate 69 B6
Pennygown 147 G8
Pennymoor 10 C3
Pennywell 111 D6
Penparc
  Ceredig 45 E4
  Pembs 44 B3
Penparcau 58 F2
Penperlleni 35 D7
Penpillick 5 D6
Penpol 3 C7
Penpont
  Dumfries 113 E8
  Powys 34 B3
Penprysg 34 F3
Penquit 6 D4
Penrherber 45 F4
Penrhiw-goch 33 C6
Penrhiwceiber 34 E4
Penrhiw-llan 46 E2
Penrhiw-pâl 46 E2
Penrhos 70 D4
Penrhôs 35 C8
Penrhos 34 C1
Penrhosfeilw 82 C2
Penrhyn Bay 83 C8
Penrhyn-coch 58 F3
Penrhyndeudraeth 71 D7
Penrhynside 83 C8
Penrice 33 F5
Penrose 4 B3
Penruddock 99 B6
Penryn 3 C6
Pensarn
  Gwyn 70 C5
  Gwyn 71 E6
Pen-sarn 71 E6
Pensax 50 C2
Pensby 85 F3
Penselwood 24 F2
Pensford 23 C8
Penshaw 111 D6
Penshurst 29 E6
Pensilva 5 C7
Penston 121 B7
Pentewan 3 B9
Pentir 83 E5
Pentire 4 C2
Pentlow 56 E2
Pentney 67 C7
Penton Mewsey 25 E8
Pentraeth 82 D5
Pentre
  Carms 33 C6
  Powys 59 F7
  Powys 60 E2
  Rhondda 34 E3
  Shrops 60 C3
  Wrex. 72 F5
  Wrex. 73 E6
Pentrebach
  M Tydf 34 D4
  Swansea 33 D7
Pentre-bâch 46 E4
Pentre-bach 47 F8
Pentrebeirdd 59 C8
Pentre Berw 82 D4
Pentre-bont 83 F7
Pentrecagal 46 E2
Pentre-celyn
  Denb 72 D5
  Powys 59 D5
Pentre-chwyth 33 E7
Pentre-cwrt 46 F2
Pentre Dolau-Honddu 47 E8
Pentredwr 73 E5
Pentre-dwr 33 E7
Pentrefelin
  Carms 33 B6
  Ceredig 46 E5
  Conwy 83 D8
  Gwyn 71 D6
Pentrefoelas 83 F8
Pentre-galar 45 F3
Pentregat 46 D2
Pentre-Gwenlais 33 C7
Pentre Gwynfryn 71 E6
Pentre Halkyn 73 B6
Pentreheyling 60 E2
Pentre-Isaf 83 E8
Pentre Llanrhaeadr 72 C4
Pentre-llwyn-llŵyd 47 D8
Pentre-llyn 46 B5

Pentre-llyn cymmer 72 D3
Pentre Meyrick 21 B8
Pentre-poeth 35 F6
Pentre'r Felin 83 E8
Pentre'r-felin 47 F8
Pentre-rhew 47 D5
Pentre-tafarn-y-fedw 83 E8
Pentre-ty-gwyn 47 F7
Pentrich 76 D3
Pentridge 13 C8
Pen-twyn 36 D2
Pentyrch 35 F5
Penuchadre 21 B7
Penuwch 46 C4
Penwithick 4 D5
Penwyllt 34 C2
Penybanc 33 B7
Pen-y-banc 33 B7
Penybont
  Carms 32 B4
  Gwyn 58 D4
  Gwyn 71 E7
  Powys 59 E5
Pen-y-Bont Ar Ogwr = Bridgend 21 B8
Penybontfawr 59 B7
Pen-y-bryn
  Gwyn 58 C3
  Pembs 45 E3
Penycae 73 E6
Pen-y-cae 34 C2
Pen-y-cae-mawr 35 E8
Pen-y-cefn 72 B5
Pen-y-clawdd 36 D1
Pen-y-coedcae 34 F4
Penycwm 44 C3
Pen-y-fai 34 F2
Penyffordd 73 C7
Penyffridd 82 F5
Pen-y-garn
  Carms 46 F4
  Ceredig 58 F3
Pen-y-garnedd
  Anglesey 82 D5
  Powys 59 B8
Pen-y-gop 72 E3
Pen-y-graig 34 E3
Penygraig 70 D2
Penygroes
  Gwyn 70 C4
  Pembs 45 F3
Pen-y-groes 33 C6
Pen-y-groeslon 70 D3
Pen-y-Gwryd Hotel 83 F6
Penyrheol 35 F5
Pen-yr-heol 35 C8
Pen-yr-Heolgerrig 34 D4
Penysarn 82 B4
Pen-y-stryt 73 D5
Penywaun 34 D3
Penzance 2 C3
Peopleton 50 D4
Peover Heath 74 B4
Peper Harow 27 E7
Perceton 118 E3
Percie 140 E4
Percyhorner 153 B9
Periton 21 E8
Perivale 40 F4
Perkinsville 111 D5
Perlethorpe 77 B6
Perranarworthal 3 C6
Perranporth 4 D2
Perranuthnoe 2 D4
Perranzabuloe 4 D2
Perry Barr 62 E4
Perry Green
  Herts 41 C7
  Wilts 37 F6
Perry Street 29 B7
Pershall 74 F5
Pershore 50 E4
Pert 135 C6
Pertenhall 53 C8
Perth 128 B3
Perthy 73 F7
Perton 62 E2
Pertwood 24 F3
Peterborough 65 E8
Peterburn 155 J12
Peterchurch 48 F5
Peterculter 141 D7
Peterhead 153 D11
Peterlee 111 E7
Petersfield 15 B8
Peter's Green 40 C4
Peters Marland 9 C6
Peterstone Wentlooge 35 F6
Peterston-super-Ely 22 B2
Peterstow 36 B2
Peter Tavy 6 B3
Petertown 159 H4
Petham 30 D5
Petrockstow 9 D7
Pett 19 D5
Pettaugh 57 D5
Petteridge 29 E7
Pettinain 120 E2
Pettistree 57 D6
Petton
  Devon 10 B5
  Shrops 60 B4
Petts Wood 28 C5
Petty 153 E7
Pettycur 128 F4
Pettymuick 141 B8
Petworth 16 B3
Pevensey 18 E3
Pevensey Bay 18 E3
Pewsey 25 C6
Philham 8 B4
Philiphaugh 115 B7
Phillack 2 C4
Philleigh 3 C7
Philpstoun 120 B3
Phocle Green 36 B3
Phoenix Green 27 D5
Pica 98 B2
Piccotts End 41 D4
Pickering 103 F5

Picket Post 14 D2
Pickhill 101 F8
Picklescott 60 E4
Pickletillem 129 B6
Pickmere 74 B3
Pickney 11 B6
Pickstock 61 B7
Pickwell
  Devon 20 E3
  Leics 64 C4
Pickworth
  Lincs 78 F3
  Rutland 65 C6
Picton
  Ches W 73 B8
  Flint 85 F7
  N Yorks 102 D2
Piddinghoe 17 D8
Piddington
  Oxon 39 C6
  W Nhants 53 D6
Piddlehinton 12 E5
Piddletrenthide 12 E5
Pidley 54 B4
Piercebridge 101 C7
Pierowall 159 D5
Pigdon 117 F7
Pikehall 75 D8
Pilgrims Hatch 42 E1
Pilham 90 E2
Pill 23 B7
Pillaton 5 C8
Pillerton Hersey 51 E8
Pillerton Priors 51 E8
Pilleth 48 C4
Pilley
  Hants 14 E4
  S Yorks 88 D4
Pilling 92 E4
Pilling Lane 92 E3
Pillowell 36 D3
Pillwell 13 C5
Pilning 36 F2
Pilsbury 75 C8
Pilsdon 12 E2
Pilsgate 65 D7
Pilsley
  Derbys 76 B2
  Derbys 76 C4
Pilton
  Devon 20 F4
  N Nhants 65 F7
  Rutland 65 D6
  Som 23 E7
Pilton Green 33 F5
Pimperne 13 D7
Pinchbeck 66 B2
Pinchbeck Bars 65 B8
Pinchbeck West 66 B2
Pincheon Green 89 C7
Pinehurst 38 F1
Pinfold 85 C4
Pinged 33 D5
Pinhoe 10 E4
Pinkneys Green 40 F1
Pinley 51 B8
Pin Mill 57 F6
Pinminnoch 112 E1
Pinmore 112 E2
Pinmore Mains 112 E2
Pinner 40 F4
Pinvin 50 E4
Pinwherry 112 F1
Pinxton 76 D4
Pipe and Lyde 49 E7
Pipe Gate 74 E4
Piperhill 151 F11
Piper's Pool 8 F4
Pippacott 20 F4
Pipton 48 F3
Pirbright 27 D7
Pirnmill 143 D9
Pirton
  Herts 54 F2
  Worcs 50 E3
Pisgah
  Ceredig 47 B5
  Stirling 127 D6
Pishill 39 F7
Pistyll 70 C4
Pitagowan 133 C5
Pitblae 153 B9
Pitcairngreen 128 B2
Pitcalnie 151 D11
Pitcaple 141 B6
Pitchcombe 37 D5
Pitchcott 39 B7
Pitchford 60 D5
Pitch Green 39 D7
Pitch Place 27 D7
Pitcombe 23 F8
Pitcorthie 129 D7
Pitcox 122 B2
Pitcur 128 B3
Pitfichie 141 C5
Pitforthie 135 B8
Pitgrudy 151 B10
Pitkennedy 135 D5
Pitkevy 128 D4
Pitkierie 129 D7
Pitlessie 128 D5
Pitlochry 133 D6
Pitmachie 141 B5
Pitmain 138 D3
Pitmedden 141 B7
Pitminster 11 C7
Pitmuies 135 E5
Pitmunie 141 C5
Pitney 12 B2
Pitscottie 129 C6
Pitsea 42 F3
Pitsford 53 C5
Pitsmoor 88 F4
Pitstone 40 C2
Pitstone Green 40 C2
Pittendreich 152 B1
Pittentrail 157 J10
Pittenweem 129 D7
Pittington 111 E6
Pittodrie 141 B5
Pitton 25 F7
Pittswood 29 E7
Pittulie 153 B9
Pityme 4 B4
Pity Me 111 E5
Pityoulish 138 C5
Pixey Green 57 B6

Pixham 28 D2
Pixley 49 F8
Place Newton 96 B4
Plaidy 153 C7
Plains 119 C7
Plaish 60 E5
Plaistow 27 F8
Plaitford 14 C3
Plank Lane 86 E4
Plas-canol 58 C2
Plas Gogerddan 58 F3
Plas Llwyngwern 58 D4
Plas Nantyr 73 F5
Plastow Green 26 C3
Plas-yn-Cefn 72 B4
Platt 29 D7
Platt Bridge 86 D4
Platts Common 88 D4
Plawsworth 111 E5
Plaxtol 29 D7
Playden 19 C6
Playford 57 E6
Play Hatch 26 B5
Playing Place 3 C7
Playley Green 50 F2
Plealey 60 D4
Pleasington 86 B4
Pleasley 76 C5
Pleckgate 93 F6
Plenmeller 109 C7
Pleshey 42 C2
Plockton 149 E13
Plocrapol 154 H6
Ploughfield 49 E5
Plowden 60 F3
Ploxgreen 60 D3
Pluckley 30 E3
Pluckley Thorne 30 E3
Plumbland 107 F8
Plumley 74 B4
Plumpton
  Cumb 108 F4
  E Sus 17 C7
Plumpton Green 17 C7
Plumpton Head 108 F5
Plumstead
  London 29 B5
  Norf 81 D7
Plumtree 77 F6
Plungar 77 F7
Plush 12 D5
Plwmp 46 D2
Plymouth 6 D2
Plympton 6 D3
Plymstock 6 D3
Plymtree 10 D5
Pockley 102 F4
Pocklington 96 E4
Pode Hole 66 B2
Podimore 12 B3
Podington 53 C7
Podmore 74 F4
Point Clear 43 C6
Pointon 78 F4
Pokesdown 14 E2
Pol a Charra 148 G2
Polbae 105 B6
Polbain 156 H2
Polbathic 5 D8
Polbeth 120 C3
Polchar 138 D4
Polebrook 65 F7
Pole Elm 50 E3
Polegate 18 E2
Poles 151 B10
Polesworth 63 D6
Polgigga 2 D2
Polglass 156 J3
Polgooth 4 D4
Poling 16 D4
Polkerris 5 D5
Polla 156 D6
Pollington 89 C7
Polloch 130 C1
Pollok 118 C5
Pollokshields 119 C5
Polmassick 3 B8
Polmont 120 B2
Polnessan 112 C4
Polnish 147 C10
Polperro 5 D7
Polruan 5 D6
Polsham 23 E7
Polstead 56 F3
Poltalloch 124 F4
Poltimore 10 E4
Polton 121 C5
Polwarth 122 D3
Polyphant 8 F4
Polzeath 4 B4
Ponders End 41 E6
Pondersbridge 66 E2
Ponsanooth 3 C6
Ponsonby 98 D2
Ponsworthy 6 B5
Pont Aber 33 B8
Pont Aber-Geirw 71 E8
Pontamman 33 C7
Pontantwn 33 C5
Pontardawe 33 D8
Pontarddulais 33 D6
Pont-ar-gothi 33 B6
Pont-ar-Hydfer 34 B2
Pont-ar-llechau 33 B8
Pontarsais 33 B5
Pontblyddyn 73 C6
Pontbren Araeth 33 B7
Pontbren Llwyd 34 D3
Pont Cwm Pydew 72 F4
Pont Cyfyng 83 F7
Pont Cysyllte 73 E6
Pont Dolydd Prysor 71 D8
Pontefract 89 B5
Ponteland 110 B4
Ponterwyd 58 F4
Pontesbury 60 D3
Pontfadog 73 F6
Pontfaen 45 F2
Pont-faen 34 B3
Pont Fronwydd 58 B5
Pont-gareg 45 E2
Pontgarreg 46 D2
Pont-Henri 33 D5
Ponthir 35 E7
Ponthirwaun 45 E3
Pontllanfraith 35 E6

Pontlliw 33 D7
Pont-Llogel 59 C7
Pontllyfni 82 F4
Pontlottyn 35 D5
Pontneddfechan 34 D3
Pontnewydd 35 E6
Pont Pen-y-benglog 83 E6
Pontrhydfendigaid 47 C6
Pont Rhyd-goch 83 E6
Pont-Rhyd-sarn 59 B5
Pont Rhyd-y-cyff 34 E2
Pont-rhyd-y-fen 34 E1
Pont-rhyd-y-groes 47 B6
Pontrilas 35 B7
Pontrobert 59 C8
Pont-rug 82 E5
Ponts Green 18 D3
Pontshill 36 B3
Pont-siân 46 E3
Pontsticill 34 C4
Pontwgan 83 D7
Pontyates 33 D5
Pontyberem 33 C6
Pontyclun 34 E3
Pontycymer 34 E3
Pontyglasier 45 F3
Pont-y-gwaith 34 E4
Pont-y-pant 83 F7
Pont y Pennant 59 B6
Pontypool = Pont-y-pŵl 35 D6
Pontypridd 34 E4
Pont-y-pŵl = Pontypool 35 D6
Pont yr Afon-Gam 71 C8
Pont-yr-hafod 44 C4
Pontywaun 35 E6
Pool
  Corn 3 B5
  W Yorks 94 E5
Poole 13 E8
Poole Keynes 37 E6
Poolend 75 D6
Poolewe 155 J13
Pooley Bridge 99 B6
Poolfold 75 D5
Poolhill 36 B4
Pool o'Muckhart 128 D2
Poolsbrook 76 B4
Pootings 29 E5
Pope Hill 44 D4
Popeswood 27 C6
Popham 26 E3
Poplar 41 F6
Popley 26 D4
Porchester 77 E5
Porchfield 14 E5
Porin 150 F6
Poringland 69 D5
Porkellis 3 C5
Porlock 21 E7
Porlock Weir 21 E7
Port Ann 145 E8
Port Appin 130 E3
Port Arthur 160 K5
Port Askaig 142 B4
Portavadie 145 G8
Port Bannatyne 145 G9
Port Carlisle 108 C2
Port Charlotte 142 C3
Port Clarence 102 B2
Port Driseach 145 F8
Port Ellen 142 D4
Port Elphinstone 141 C6
Portencalzie 104 B4
Portencross 118 E1
Port Erin 84 F1
Port Erroll 153 E10
Portesham 12 F4
Port e Vullen 84 C4
Port-Eynon 33 F5
Portfield Gate 44 D4
Port Gaverne 8 F2
Port Glasgow 118 B3
Portgordon 152 B3
Portgower 157 H13
Porth
  Corn 4 C3
  Rhondda 34 E4
Porthaethwy = Menai Bridge 83 D5
Porthallow
  Corn 3 D6
  Corn 5 D7
Porthcawl 21 B7
Porthcothan 4 C3
Porthcurno 2 D2
Port Henderson 149 A12
Porthgain 44 B3
Porthill 60 C4
Porthkerry 22 C2
Porthleven 2 D5
Porthllechog 82 B4
Porthmadog 71 D6
Porthmeor 2 C3
Porth Navas 3 D6
Portholland 3 B8
Porthoustock 3 D7
Porthpean 4 D5
Porth Tywyn = Burry Port 33 D5
Porthyrhyd
  Carms 33 C6
Porth-y-waen 60 B2
Portincaple 145 D11
Portington 96 F3
Portinnisherrich 125 D5
Portinscale 98 B4
Port Isaac 4 A4

Portishead 23 B6
Portkil 145 E11
Portknockie 152 B5
Port Lamont 145 F9
Portlethen 141 E8
Portling 107 D5
Port Lion 44 E4
Port Logan 104 E4
Portmahomack 151 C12
Portmeirion 71 D6
Portmellon 3 B9
Port Mholair 155 D10
Port Mor 146 F7
Portmore 14 E4
Port Mulgrave 103 C5
Portnacroish 130 E3
Portnahaven 142 C2
Portnalong 149 E8
Portnaluchaig 147 C9
Portnancon 156 C7
Port Nan Giùran 155 D10
Port nan Long 148 A3
Portnellan 126 B3
Port Nis 155 A10
Portobello 121 B6
Port of Menteith 126 D4
Porton 25 F6
Portpatrick 104 D4
Port Quin 4 A4
Port Ramsay 130 E2
Portreath 3 B5
Portree 149 D9
Port St Mary 84 F2
Portscatho 3 C7
Portsea 15 D7
Portskerra 157 C11
Portskewett 36 F2
Portslade 17 D6
Portslade-by-Sea 17 D6
Portsmouth 15 D7
Portsonachan 125 C6
Portsoy 152 B5
Port Sunlight 85 F4
Portswood 14 C5
Port Talbot 34 E1
Port Tennant 33 E7
Portuairk 146 E7
Portway
  Hereford 49 F6
  Worcs 51 B5
Port Wemyss 142 C2
Port William 105 E7
Portwrinkle 5 D8
Poslingford 55 E8
Postbridge 6 B4
Postcombe 39 E7
Postling 19 B8
Postwick 69 D5
Potholm 115 F6
Potsgrove 40 B2
Potten End 40 D3
Potter Brompton 97 B5
Potterhanworth 78 C3
Potterhanworth Booths 78 C3
Potter Heigham 69 C7
Potterne 24 D4
Potterne Wick 24 D5
Potternewton 95 F6
Potters Bar 41 D5
Potter's Cross 62 F2
Potterspury 53 E5
Potter Street 41 D7
Potterton
  Aberds 141 C8
  W Yorks 95 F7
Potto 102 D2
Potton 54 E3
Pott Row 80 E3
Pott Shrigley 75 B6
Poughill
  Corn 8 D4
  Devon 10 D3
Poulshot 24 D4
Poulton
  Glos 37 D8
  Mers 85 E4
Poulton-le-Fylde 92 F3
Pound Bank 50 B2
Poundbury 12 E4
Poundfield 18 B2
Pound Green
  E Sus 18 C2
  IoW 14 F4
  Worcs 50 B2
Pound Hill 28 F3
Poundland 112 F1
Poundon 39 B6
Poundsgate 6 B5
Poundstock 8 E4
Powburn 117 C6
Powderham 10 F4
Powerstock 12 E3
Powfoot 107 C8
Powick 50 D3
Powmill 128 E2
Poxwell 12 F5
Poyle 27 B8
Poynings 17 C6
Poyntington 12 C4
Poynton 87 F7
Poynton Green 61 C5
Poystreet Green 56 D3
Praa Sands 2 D4
Pratt's Bottom 29 C5
Praze 2 C5
Praze-an-Beeble 2 C5
Predannack Wollas 3 E5
Prees 74 F2
Preesall 92 E3
Prees Green 74 F2
Preesgweene 73 F6
Prees Heath 74 F2
Prees Higher Heath 74 F2
Prees Lower Heath 74 F2

Prenteg 71 C6
Prenton 85 F4
Prescot 86 E2
Prescott 60 B4
Pressen 122 F4
Prestatyn 72 A4
Prestbury
  Ches E 75 B6
  Glos 37 B6
Presteigne = Llanandras 48 C5
Presthope 61 E5
Prestleigh 23 E8
Preston
  Borders 122 D3
  Brighton 17 D7
  Devon 7 B6
  Dorset 12 F5
  E Loth 121 B8
  E Yorks 97 F7
  Glos 37 D7
  Glos 49 F8
  Herts 40 B4
  Kent 30 C4
  Kent 31 C6
  Lancs 86 B3
  Northumb 117 B7
  Rutland 65 D5
  Shrops 60 C5
  Wilts 24 B5
  Wilts 25 B7
Preston Bagot 51 C6
Preston Bissett 39 B6
Preston Bowyer 11 B6
Preston Brockhurst 60 B5
Preston Brook 86 F3
Preston Candover 26 E4
Preston Capes 52 D3
Preston Crowmarsh 39 E6
Preston Gubbals 60 C4
Prestonmill 107 D6
Preston on Stour 51 E7
Preston on the Hill 86 F3
Preston on Wye 49 E5
Prestonpans 121 B7
Preston Plucknett 12 C3
Preston St Mary 56 D3
Prestwich 87 D6
Prestwick
  Northumb 110 B4
  S Ayrs 112 B3
Prestwood 40 D1
Price Town 34 E3
Prickwillow 67 F5
Priddy 23 D7
Priesthaugh 115 D7
Priest Hutton 92 B5
Priest Weston 60 E2
Primethorpe 64 E2
Primrose Green 68 C3
Primrosehill 40 D3
Primrose Valley 97 B7
Princes Risborough 39 D8
Princethorpe 52 B2
Princetown
  Caerph 35 C5
  Devon 6 B3
Prion 72 C4
Prior Muir 129 C7
Prior Park 123 D5
Priors Frome 49 F7
Priors Hardwick 52 D2
Priorslee 61 C7
Priors Marston 52 D2
Priory Wood 48 E4
Priston 23 C8
Pristow Green 68 F4
Prittlewell 42 F4
Privett 15 B7
Prixford 20 F4
Probus 3 B7
Proncy 151 B10
Prospect 107 E8
Prudhoe 110 C3
Ptarmigan Lodge 126 D2
Pubil 132 E1
Puckeridge 41 B6
Puckington 11 C8
Pucklechurch 23 B8
Pucknall 14 B4
Puckrup 50 F3
Puddinglake 74 C4
Puddington
  Ches W 73 B7
  Devon 10 C3
Puddledock 68 E3
Puddletown 12 E5
Pudleston 49 D7
Pudsey 94 F5
Pulborough 16 C4
Puleston 61 B7
Pulford 73 D7
Pulham 12 D5
Pulham Market 68 F4
Pulham St Mary 68 F5
Pulloxhill 53 F8
Pumpherston 120 C3
Pumsaint 47 E5
Puncheston 32 B1
Puncknowle 12 F3
Punnett's Town 18 C3
Purbrook 15 D7
Purewell 14 E2
Purfleet 29 B6
Puriton 22 E5
Purleigh 42 D4
Purley
  London 28 C4
  W Berks 26 B4
Purlogue 48 B4
Purls Bridge 66 F4
Purse Caundle 12 C4

220 Pur–St D


Purslow 60 F3
Purston Jaglin 88 C5
Purton
  Glos 36 D3
  Glos 36 D3
  Wilts 37 F7
Purton Stoke 37 E7
Pury End 52 E5
Pusey 38 E3
Putley 49 F8
Putney 28 B3
Putsborough 20 E3
Puttenham
  Herts 40 C1
  Sur 27 E7
Puxton 23 C6
Pwll 33 D5
Pwllcrochan 44 E4
Pwll-glas 72 D5
Pwllgloyw 48 F2
Pwllheli 70 D4
Pwllmeyric 36 E2
Pwll-trap 32 C3
Pwll-y-glaw 34 E1
Pyecombe 17 C6
Pye Corner 35 F7
Pye Green 62 C3
Pyewipe 91 C6
Pyle 15 G5
Pyle = Y Pîl 34 F2
Pylle 23 F8
Pymoor 66 F4
Pyrford 27 D8
Pyrton 39 E6
Pytchley 53 B6
Pyworthy 8 D5


## Q


Quabbs 60 F2
Quadring 78 F5
Quainton 39 C7
Quarley 25 E7
Quarndon 76 E3
Quarrier's Homes 118 C3
Quarrington 78 E3
Quarrington Hill 111 F6
Quarry Bank 62 F3
Quarryford 121 C8
Quarryhill 151 C10
Quarrywood 152 B1
Quarter 119 D7
Quatford 61 E7
Quatt 61 F7
Quebec 110 E4
Quedgeley 37 C5
Queen Adelaide 67 F5
Queenborough 30 B3
Queen Camel 12 B3
Queen Charlton 23 C8
Queen Dart 10 C3
Queenhill 50 F3
Queen Oak 24 F2
Queensbury 94 F4
Queensferry
  Edin 120 B4
  Flint 73 C7
Queensferry Crossing 120 B4
Queen's Head 60 B3
Queen's Park
  Bedford 53 E8
  W Nhants 53 C5
Queenstown 92 F3
Queen Street
  Kent 29 E7
  Wilts 37 F7
Queenzieburn 119 B6
Quemerford 24 C5
Quendale 160 M5
Quendon 55 F6
Queniborough 64 C3
Quenington 37 D8
Quernmore 92 D5
Quethiock 5 C8
Quholm 159 G3
Quicks Green 26 B3
Quidenham 68 F3
Quidhampton
  Hants 26 D3
  Wilts 25 F6
Quilquox 153 E9
Quina Brook 74 F2
Quindry 159 J5
Quinton
  W Mid 62 F3
  W Nhants 53 D5
Quintrell Downs 4 C3
Quixhill 75 E8
Quoditch 9 E6
Quoig 127 B7
Quorndon 64 C2
Quothquan 120 F2
Quoyloo 159 F3
Quoyness 159 H3
Quoys
  Shetland 160 B8
  Shetland 160 G6


## R


Raasay House 149 E10
Rabbit's Cross 29 E8
Raby 73 B7
Rachan Mill 120 F4
Rachub 83 E6
Rackenford 10 C3
Rackham 16 C4
Rackheath 69 C5
Racks 107 B7
Rackwick
  Orkney 159 D5
  Orkney 159 J3
Radbourne 76 F2
Radcliffe
  Gtr Man 87 D5
  Northumb 117 D8
Radcliffe on Trent 77 F6
Radclive 52 F4
Radcot 38 E2
Raddery 151 F10
Radernie 129 D6
Radford Semele 51 C8
Radipole 12 F4
Radlett 40 E4
Radley 39 E5
Radmanthwaite 76 C5
Radmoor 61 B6
Radmore Green 74 D2
Radnage 39 E7
Radstock 23 D8
Radstone 52 E3
Radway 51 E8
Radway Green 74 D4
Radwell
  Bedford 53 D8
  Herts 54 F3
Radwinter 55 F7
Radyr 35 F5
Rafford 151 F13
Ragdale 64 C3
Raglan 35 D8
Ragnall 77 B8
Rahane 145 E11
Rainford 86 D2
Rainford Junction 86 D2
Rainham
  London 41 F8
  Medway 30 C2
Rainhill 86 E2
Rainhill Stoops 86 E3
Rainow 75 B6
Rainton 95 B6
Rainworth 77 D5
Raisbeck 99 D8
Raise 109 E7
Rait 128 B4
Raithby
  Lincs 79 C6
  Lincs 91 F7
Rake 16 B2
Rakewood 87 C7
Ram 46 E4
Ramasaig 148 D6
Rame
  Corn 3 C6
  Corn 6 E2
Rameldry Mill Bank 128 D5
Ram Lane 30 E3
Ramnageo 160 C8
Rampisham 12 D3
Rampside 92 C2
Rampton
  Cambs 54 C5
  Notts 77 B7
Ramsbottom 87 C5
Ramsbury 25 B7
Ramscraigs 158 H3
Ramsdean 15 B8
Ramsdell 26 D3
Ramsden 38 C3
Ramsden Bellhouse 42 E3
Ramsden Heath 42 E3
Ramsey
  Cambs 66 F2
  Essex 57 F6
  IoM 84 C4
Ramseycleuch 115 C5
Ramsey Forty Foot 66 F3
Ramsey Heights 66 F2
Ramsey Island 43 D5
Ramsey Mereside 66 F2
Ramsey St Mary's 66 F2
Ramsgate 31 C7
Ramsgill 94 B4
Ramshorn 75 E7
Ramsnest Common 27 F7
Ranais 155 E9
Ranby
  Lincs 78 B5
  Notts 89 F7
Rand 78 B4
Randwick 37 D5
Ranfurly 118 C3
Rangag 158 F3
Rangemore 63 B5
Rangeworthy 36 F3
Rankinston 112 C4
Ranmoor 88 F4
Ranmore Common 28 D2
Rannerdale 98 C3
Rannoch Station 131 D8
Ranochan 147 C11
Ranskill 89 F7
Ranton 62 B2
Ranworth 69 C6
Raploch 127 E6
Rapness 159 D6
Rascal Moor 96 F4
Rascarrel 106 E4
Rashiereive 141 B8
Raskelf 95 B7
Rassau 35 C5
Rastrick 88 B2
Ratagan 136 C2
Ratby 64 D2
Ratcliffe Culey 63 E7
Ratcliffe on Soar 63 B8
Ratcliffe on the Wreake 64 C3
Rathen 153 B10
Rathillet 129 B5
Rathmell 93 D8
Ratho 120 B4
Ratho Station 120 B4
Rathven 152 B4
Ratley 51 E8
Ratlinghope 60 E4
Rattar 158 C4
Ratten Row 92 E4
Rattery 6 C5
Rattlesden 56 D3
Rattray 134 E1
Raughton Head 108 E3
Raunds 53 B7
Ravenfield 89 E5
Ravenglass 98 E2
Raveningham 69 E6
Ravenscar 103 D7
Ravenscraig 118 B2
Ravensdale 84 C3
Ravensden 53 D8
Ravenseat 100 D3
Ravenshead 77 D5
Ravensmoor 74 D3
Ravensthorpe
  W Nhants 52 B4
  W Yorks 88 B3
Ravenstone
  Leics 63 C8
  M Keynes 53 D6
Ravenstonedale 100 D2
Ravenstown 92 B3
Ravenstruther 120 E2
Ravensworth 101 D6
Raw 103 D7
Rawcliffe
  E Yorks 89 B7
  York 95 D8
Rawcliffe Bridge 89 B7
Rawdon 94 F5
Rawmarsh 88 E5
Rawreth 42 E3
Rawridge 11 D7
Rawtenstall 87 B6
Raxton 153 E8
Raydon 56 F4
Raylees 117 E5
Rayleigh 42 E4
Rayne 42 B3
Rayners Lane 40 F4
Raynes Park 28 C3
Reach 55 C6
Read 93 F7
Reading 26 B5
Reading Street 19 B6
Reagill 99 C8
Rearquhar 151 B10
Rearsby 64 C3
Reaster 158 D4
Reawick 160 J5
Reay 157 C12
Rechullin 149 C13
Reculver 31 C6
Redberth 32 D1
Redbourn 40 C4
Redbourne 90 E3
Redbrook
  Mon 36 C2
  Wrex 74 E2
Redburn
  Highld 151 E8
  Highld 151 G12
  Northumb 109 C7
Redcar 102 B4
Redcastle
  Angus 135 D6
  Highld 151 G8
Redcliff Bay 23 B6
Red Dial 108 E2
Redding 120 B2
Reddingmuirhead 120 B2
Reddish 87 E6
Redditch 50 C5
Rede 56 D2
Redenhall 69 F5
Redesdale Camp 116 E4
Redesmouth 116 F4
Redford
  Aberds 135 B7
  Angus 135 E5
  Durham 110 F3
Redfordgreen 115 C6
Redgorton 128 B2
Redgrave 56 B4
Redhill
  Aberds 141 D6
  Aberds 153 E6
  N Som 23 C7
  Sur 28 D3
Red Hill 50 D3
Redhouse 145 G7
Redhouses 142 B4
Red Houses 17 I3
Redisham 69 F7
Redland
  Bristol 23 B7
  Orkney 159 F4
Redlingfield 57 B5
Red Lodge 55 B7
Redlynch
  Som 23 F9
  Wilts 14 B3
Redmarley D'Abitot 50 F2
Redmarshall 102 B1
Redmile 77 F7
Redmire 101 E5
Redmoor 5 C5
Rednal 60 B3
Redpath 121 F8
Redpoint 149 B12
Red Rail 36 B2
Red Rock 86 D3
Red Roses 32 C3
Red Row 117 E8
Redruth 3 B5
Red Street 74 D5
Redvales 87 D6
Red Wharf Bay 82 C5
Redwick
  Newport 35 F8
  S Glos 36 F2
Redworth 101 B7
Reed 54 F4
Reedham 69 D7
Reedness 89 B8
Reeds Beck 78 C5
Reepham
  Lincs 78 B3
  Norf 81 E6
Reeth 101 E5
Regaby 84 C4
Regoul 151 F11
Reiff 156 H2
Reigate 28 D3
Reighton 97 B7
Reighton Gap 97 B7
Reinigeadal 154 G7
Reiss 158 E5
Rejerrah 4 D2
Releath 3 C5
Relubbus 2 C4
Relugas 151 G12
Remenham 39 F7
Remenham Hill 39 F7
Remony 132 E4
Rempstone 64 B2
Rendcomb 37 D7
Rendham 57 C7
Rendlesham 57 D7
Renfrew 118 C5
Renhold 53 D8
Renishaw 76 B4
Rennington 117 C8
Renton 118 B3
Renwick 109 E5
Repps 69 C7
Repton 63 B7
Reraig 149 F13
Rescobie 135 D5
Resipole 147 E10
Resolis 151 E9
Resolven 34 D2
Reston 122 C4
Reswallie 135 D5
Retew 4 D4
Retford 89 F8
Rettendon 42 E3
Rettendon Place 42 E3
Revesby 79 C5
Revesby Bridge 79 C6
Rewe 10 E4
Rew Street 15 E5
Reydon 57 B8
Reydon Smear 57 B8
Reymerston 68 D3
Reynalton 32 D1
Reynoldston 33 E5
Rezare 5 B8
Rhaeadr Gwy = Rhayader 47 C8
Rhandirmwyn 47 E6
Rhayader = Rhaeadr Gwy 47 C8
Rhedyn 70 D3
Rhemore 147 F8
Rhencullen 84 C3
Rhes-y-cae 73 B5
Rhewl
  Denb 72 C5
  Denb 73 E5
Rhian 157 H8
Rhicarn 156 G3
Rhiconich 156 D5
Rhicullen 151 D9
Rhidorroch House 150 B4
Rhifail 157 E10
Rhigos 34 D3
Rhilochan 157 J10
Rhiroy 150 C4
Rhisga = Risca 35 E6
Rhiw 70 E3
Rhiwabon = Ruabon 73 E7
Rhiwbina 35 F5
Rhiwbryfdir 71 C7
Rhiwderin 35 F6
Rhiwlas
  Gwyn 72 F3
  Gwyn 83 E5
  Powys 73 F5
Rhodes 87 D6
Rhodesia 77 B5
Rhodes Minnis 31 E5
Rhodiad 44 C2
Rhondda 34 E3
Rhonehouse or Kelton Hill 106 D4
Rhoose = Y Rhws 22 C2
Rhôs
  Carms 46 F2
  Neath 33 D8
Rhosamman 33 C8
Rhosbeirio 82 B3
Rhoscefnhir 82 D5
Rhoscolyn 82 D2
Rhoscrowther 44 E4
Rhosesmor 73 C6
Rhos-fawr 70 D4
Rhosgadfan 82 F5
Rhosgoch 82 C4
Rhos-goch 48 E3
Rhos-hill 45 E3
Rhoshirwaun 70 E2
Rhoslan 71 C5
Rhoslefain 58 D2
Rhosllanerchrugog 73 E6
Rhosmaen 33 B7
Rhosmeirch 82 D4
Rhosneigr 82 D3
Rhosnesni 73 D7
Rhos-on-Sea 83 C8
Rhosrobin 73 D7
Rhossili 33 F5
Rhosson 44 C2
Rhostryfan 82 F4
Rhostyllen 73 E7
Rhosybol 82 C4
Rhos-y-brithdir 59 B8
Rhos-y-garth 46 B5
Rhos-y-gwaliau 72 F3
Rhos-y-llan 70 D3
Rhos-y-Madoc 73 E7
Rhos-y-meirch 48 C4
Rhu
  Argyll 145 E11
  Argyll 145 G7
Rhualt 72 B4
Rhuddall Heath 74 C2
Rhuddlan
  Ceredig 46 E3
  Denb 72 B4
Rhue 150 B3
Rhulen 48 E3
Rhunahaorine 143 D8
Rhuthun = Ruthin 72 D5
Rhyd
  Gwyn 71 C7
  Powys 59 D6
Rhydaman = Ammanford 33 C7
Rhydargaeau 33 B5
Rhydcymerau 46 F4
Rhydd 50 E3
Rhyd-Ddu 83 F5
Rhydding 33 E8
Rhydfudr 46 C4
Rhydlewis 46 E2
Rhydlios 70 D2
Rhydlydan 83 F8
Rhyd-moel-ddu 48 B2
Rhydness 48 E3
Rhydowen 46 E3
Rhyd-Rosser 46 C4
Rhydspence 48 E4
Rhydtalog 73 D6
Rhyd-uchaf 72 F3
Rhyd-wen 58 C4
Rhydwyn 82 C3
Rhyd-y-clafdy 70 D4
Rhydycroesau 73 F6
Rhydyfelin
  Ceredig 46 B4
  Rhondda 34 F4
Rhyd-y-foel 72 B3
Rhyd-y-fro 33 D8
Rhyd-y-gwin 33 D7
Rhydymain 58 B5
Rhyd-y-meirch 35 D7
Rhyd-y-meudwy 72 D5
Rhydymwyn 73 C6
Rhyd-y-pandy 33 D7
Rhyd-yr-onen 58 D3
Rhyd-y-sarn 71 C7
Rhyl = Y Rhyl 72 A4
Rhymney = Rhymni 35 D5
Rhymni = Rhymney 35 D5
Rhynd
  Fife 129 B6
  Perth 128 B3
Rhynie
  Aberds 140 B3
  Highld 151 D11
Ribbesford 50 B2
Ribblehead 93 B7
Ribbleton 93 F5
Ribchester 93 F6
Ribigill 157 D8
Riby 91 D5
Riby Cross Roads 91 D5
Riccall 96 F2
Riccarton 118 F4
Richards Castle 49 C6
Richings Park 27 B8
Richmond
  London 28 B2
  N Yorks 101 D6
Rickarton 141 F7
Rickinghall 56 B4
Rickleton 111 D5
Rickling 55 F5
Rickmansworth 40 E3
Riddings
  Cumb 108 B4
  Derbys 76 D4
Riddlecombe 9 C8
Riddlesden 94 E3
Riddrie 119 C6
Ridge
  Dorset 13 F7
  Hants 14 C4
  Wilts 24 F4
Ridgebourne 48 C2
Ridge Green 28 E4
Ridgehill 23 C7
Ridge Lane 63 E6
Ridgeway Cross 50 E2
Ridgewell 55 E8
Ridgewood 17 C8
Ridgmont 53 F7
Riding Mill 110 C3
Ridleywood 73 D8
Ridlington
  Norf 69 A6
  Rutland 64 D5
Ridsdale 116 F5
Riechip 133 E7
Riemore 133 E7
Rienachait 156 F3
Rievaulx 102 F3
Rift House 111 F7
Rigg 108 C2
Riggend 119 B7
Rigsby 79 B7
Rigside 119 F8
Riley Green 86 B4
Rileyhill 62 C5
Rilla Mill 5 B7
Rillington 96 B4
Rimington 93 E8
Rimpton 12 B4
Rimswell 91 B7
Rinaston 44 C4
Ringasta 160 M5
Ringford 106 D3
Ringinglow 88 F3
Ringland 68 C4
Ringles Cross 17 B8
Ringmer 17 C8
Ringmore 6 E4
Ringorm 152 D2
Ring's End 66 D3
Ringsfield 69 F7
Ringsfield Corner 69 F7
Ringshall
  Herts 40 C2
  Suff 56 D4
Ringshall Stocks 56 D4
Ringstead
  N Nhants 53 B7
  Norf 80 C3
Ringwood 14 D2
Ringwould 31 E7
Rinmore 140 C3
Rinnigill 159 J4
Rinsey 2 D4
Riof 154 D6
Ripe 18 D2
Ripley
  Derbys 76 D3
  Hants 14 E2
  N Yorks 95 C5
  Sur 27 D8
Riplingham 97 F5
Ripon 95 B6
Rippingale 65 B7
Ripple
  Kent 31 E7
  Worcs 50 F3
Ripponden 87 C8
Rireavach 150 B3
Risabus 142 D4
Risbury 49 D7
Risby 55 C8
Risca = Rhisga 35 E6
Rise 97 E7
Riseden 18 B3
Risegate 66 B2
Riseholme 78 B2
Riseley
  Bedford 53 C8
  Wokingham 26 C5
Rishangles 57 C5
Rishton 93 F7
Rishworth 87 C8
Rising Bridge 87 B5
Risley
  Derbys 76 F4
  Warr 86 E4
Risplith 94 C5
Rispond 156 C7
Rivar 25 C8
Rivenhall End 42 C4
River Bank 55 C6
Riverhead 29 D6
Rivington 86 C4
Roachill 10 B3
Roade 53 D5
Road Green 69 E5
Roadhead 108 B5
Roadmeetings 119 E8
Roadside 158 D3
Roadside of Catterline 135 B8
Roadside of Kinneff 135 B8
Roadwater 22 F2
Roag 149 D7
Roa Island 92 C2
Roath 22 B3
Roberton
  Borders 115 C7
  S Lanark 114 B2
Robertsbridge 18 C4
Roberttown 88 B2
Robeston Cross 44 E3
Robeston Wathen 32 C1
Robin Hood 88 B4
Robin Hood's Bay 103 D7
Roborough
  Devon 6 C3
  Devon 9 C7
Roby 86 E2
Roby Mill 86 D3
Rocester 75 F8
Roch 44 C3
Rochdale 87 C6
Roche 4 C4
Rochester
  Medway 29 C8
  Northumb 116 E4
Rochford 42 E4
Roch Gate 44 C3
Rock
  Corn 4 B4
  Northumb 117 B8
  Worcs 50 B2
  W Sus 16 C5
Rockbeare 10 E5
Rockbourne 14 C2
Rockcliffe
  Cumb 108 C3
  Dumfries 107 D5
Rock Ferry 85 F4
Rockfield
  Highld 151 C12
  Mon 36 C1
Rockford 14 D2
Rockhampton 36 E3
Rockingham 65 E5
Rockland All Saints 68 E2
Rockland St Mary 69 D6
Rockland St Peter 68 E2
Rockley 25 B6
Rockwell End 39 F7
Rockwell Green 11 B6
Rodborough 37 D5
Rodbourne
  Swindon 37 F8
  Wilts 37 F6
Rodbourne Cheney 37 F8
Rodd 48 C5
Roddam 117 B6
Rodden 12 F4
Rode 24 D3
Rodeheath 75 C5
Rode Heath 74 D5
Roden 61 C5
Rodhuish 22 F2
Rodington 61 C5
Rodley
  Glos 36 C4
  W Yorks 94 F5
Rodmarton 37 E6
Rodmell 17 D8
Rodmersham 30 C3
Rodney Stoke 23 D6
Rodsley 76 E2
Rodway 22 F4
Rodwell 12 G4
Roecliffe 95 C6
Roe Green 54 F4
Roehampton 28 B3
Roesound 160 G5
Roffey 28 F2
Rogart 157 J10
Rogart Station 157 J10
Rogate 16 B2
Rogerstone 35 F6
Roghadal 154 J5
Rogiet 36 F1
Rogue's Alley 66 D3
Roke 39 E6
Roker 111 D7
Rollesby 69 C7
Rolleston
  Leics 64 D4
  Notts 77 D7
Rolleston-on-Dove 63 B6
Rolston 97 E8
Rolvenden 18 B5
Rolvenden Layne 19 B5
Romaldkirk 100 B4
Romanby 102 E1
Romannobridge 120 E4
Romansleigh 10 B2
Romford 41 F8
Romiley 87 E7
Romsey 14 B4
Romsey Town 55 D5
Romsley
  Shrops 61 F7
Romsley *continued*
  Worcs 50 B4
Ronague 84 E2
Rookhope 110 E2
Rookley 15 F6
Rooks Bridge 23 D5
Roos 97 F8
Roosebeck 92 C2
Rootham's Green 54 D2
Rootpark 120 D2
Ropley 26 F4
Ropley Dean 26 F4
Ropsley 78 F2
Rora 153 C10
Rorandle 141 C5
Rorrington 60 D3
Roscroggan 3 B5
Rose 4 D2
Roseacre
  Kent 29 D8
  Lancs 92 F4
Rose Ash 10 B2
Rosebank 119 E8
Rosebrough 117 B7
Rosebush 32 B1
Rosecare 8 E3
Rosedale Abbey 103 E5
Roseden 117 B6
Rosefield 151 F1
Rose Green 16 E3
Rose Grove 93 F8
Rosehall 156 J7
Rosehaugh Mains 151 F9
Rosehearty 153 B9
Rosehill 74 F3
Rose Hill
  E Sus 17 C8
  Lancs 93 F8
  Suff 57 E5
Roseisle 152 B1
Roselands 18 E3
Rosemarket 44 E4
Rosemarkie 151 F10
Rosemary Lane 11 C6
Rosemount 134 E1
Rosenannon 4 C4
Rosewell 121 C5
Roseworth 102 B2
Roseworthy 2 C5
Rosgill 99 C7
Roshven 147 D10
Roskhill 149 D7
Roskill House 151 F9
Rosley 108 E3
Roslin 121 C5
Rosliston 63 C6
Rosneath 145 E11
Ross
  Dumfries 106 E3
  Northumb 123 F7
  Perth 127 B6
Rossett 73 D7
Rossett Green 95 D6
Rossie Ochill 128 C2
Rossie Priory 134 F2
Rossington 89 E7
Rosskeen 151 E9
Rossland 118 B4
Ross-on-Wye 36 B3
Roster 158 G4
Rostherne 86 F5
Rosthwaite 98 C4
Roston 75 E8
Rosyth 128 F3
Rothbury 117 D6
Rotherby 64 C3
Rotherfield 18 C2
Rotherfield Greys 39 F7
Rotherfield Peppard 39 F7
Rotherham 88 E5
Rothersthorpe 52 D5
Rotherwick 26 D5
Rothes 152 D2
Rothesay 145 G9
Rothiebrisbane 153 E7
Rothienorman 153 E7
Rothiesholm 159 F7
Rothley
  Leics 64 C2
  Northumb 117 F6
Rothley Shield East 117 E6
Rothmaise 153 E6
Rothwell
  Lincs 91 E5
  N Nhants 64 F5
  W Yorks 88 B4
Rothwell Haigh 88 B4
Rotsea 97 D6
Rottal 134 C3
Rotten End 57 C7
Rottingdean 17 D7
Rottington 98 C1
Roud 15 F6
Rougham
  Norf 80 E4
  Suff 56 C3
Rougham Green 56 C3
Roughburn 137 F6
Rough Close 75 F6
Rough Common 30 D5
Roughlee 93 E8
Roughley 62 E5
Roughsike 108 B5
Roughton
  Lincs 78 C5
  Norf 81 D8
  Shrops 61 E7
Roughton Moor 78 C5
Roundhay 95 F6
Roundstonefoot 114 D4
Roundstreet Common 16 B4
Roundway 24 C5
Rousdon 11 E7
Rous Lench 50 D5
Routenburn 118 C1
Routh 97 E6
Row
  Corn 5 B5
  Cumb 99 F6
Rowanburn 108 B4
Rowardennan 126 E2
Rowde 24 C4
Rowen 83 D7
Rowfoot 109 C6
Row Heath 43 C7
Rowhedge 43 B6
Rowhook 28 F2
Rowington 51 C7
Rowland 76 B2
Rowlands Castle 15 C8
Rowlands Gill 110 D4
Rowledge 27 E6
Rowlestone 35 B7
Rowley
  E Yorks 97 F5
  Shrops 60 D3
Rowley Hill 88 C2
Rowley Regis 62 F3
Rowly 27 E8
Rowney Green 50 B5
Rownhams 14 C4
Rowrah 98 C2
Rowsham 39 C8
Rowsley 76 C2
Rowstock 38 F4
Rowston 78 D3
Rowton
  Ches W 73 C8
  Shrops 60 C3
  Telford 61 C6
Roxburgh 122 F3
Roxby
  N Lincs 90 C3
  N Yorks 103 C5
Roxton 54 D2
Roxwell 42 D2
Royal Leamington Spa 51 C8
Royal Oak
  Darl 101 B7
  Lancs 86 D2
Royal Tunbridge Wells 18 B2
Royal Wootton Bassett 37 F7
Roybridge 137 F5
Roydhouse 88 C3
Roydon
  Essex 41 D7
  Norf 68 F3
  Norf 80 E3
Roydon Hamlet 41 D7
Royston
  Herts 54 E4
  S Yorks 88 C4
Royton 87 D7
Rozel 17 I3
Ruabon = Rhiwabon 73 E7
Ruaig 146 G3
Ruan Lanihorne 3 B7
Ruan Minor 3 E6
Ruarach 136 B2
Ruardean 36 C3
Ruardean Woodside 36 C3
Rubery 50 B4
Ruckcroft 108 E5
Ruckhall 49 F6
Ruckinge 19 B7
Ruckland 79 B6
Ruckley 60 D5
Rudbaxton 44 C4
Rudby 102 D2
Ruddington 77 F5
Rudford 36 B4
Rudge
  Shrops 62 E2
  Som 24 D3
Rudgeway 36 F3
Rudgwick 27 F8
Rudhall 36 B3
Rudheath 74 B3
Rudley Green 42 D4
Rudry 35 F5
Rudston 97 C6
Rudyard 75 D6
Rufford 86 C2
Rufforth 95 D8
Rugby 52 B3
Rugeley 62 C4
Ruglen 112 D2
Ruilick 151 G8
Ruishton 11 B7
Ruisigearraidh 154 J4
Ruislip 40 F3
Ruislip Common 40 F3
Rumbling Bridge 128 E2
Rumburgh 69 F6
Rumford 4 B3
Rumney 22 B4
Runcorn 86 F3
Runcton 16 D2
Runcton Holme 67 D6
Rundlestone 6 B3
Runfold 27 E6
Runhall 68 D3
Runham
  Norf 69 C7
  Norf 69 D8
Runnington 11 B6
Runsell Green 42 D3
Runswick Bay 103 C6
Runwell 42 E3
Ruscombe 27 B5
Rushall
  Hereford 49 F8
  Norf 68 F4
  Wilts 25 D6
  W Mid 62 D4
Rushbrooke 56 C2
Rushbury 60 E5
Rushden
  Herts 54 F4
  N Nhants 53 C7
Rushenden 30 B3
Rushford 68 F2
Rush Green 41 F8
Rush-head 153 D8
Rushlake Green 18 D3
Rushmere 69 F7
Rushmere St Andrew 57 E6
Rushmoor 27 E6
Rushock 50 B3
Rusholme 87 E6
Rushton
  Ches W 74 C2
  N Nhants 64 F5
  Shrops 61 D6
Rushton Spencer 75 C6
Rushwick 50 D3
Rushyford 101 B7
Ruskie 126 D5
Ruskington 78 D3
Rusland 99 F5
Rusper 28 F3
Ruspidge 36 C3
Russell's Water 39 F7
Russel's Green 57 B6
Rusthall 18 B2
Rustington 16 D4
Ruston 103 F7
Ruston Parva 97 C6
Ruswarp 103 D6
Rutherford 122 F2
Rutherglen 119 C6
Ruthernbridge 4 C5
Ruthin = Rhuthun 72 D5
Ruthrieston 141 D8
Ruthven
  Aberds 152 D5
  Angus 134 E2
  Highld 138 E3
  Highld 151 H11
Ruthven House 134 E3
Ruthvoes 4 C4
Ruthwell 107 C7
Ruyton-XI-Towns 60 B3
Ryal 110 B3
Ryal Fold 86 B4
Ryall 12 E2
Ryarsh 29 D7
Rydal 99 D5
Ryde 15 E6
Rye 19 C6
Ryecroft Gate 75 C6
Rye Foreign 19 C5
Rye Harbour 19 D6
Ryehill 91 B6
Rye Park 41 C6
Rye Street 50 F2
Ryhall 65 C7
Ryhill 88 C4
Ryhope 111 D7
Rylstone 94 D2
Ryme Intrinseca 12 C3
Ryther 95 F8
Ryton
  Glos 50 F2
  N Yorks 96 B3
  Shrops 61 D7
  T&W 110 C4
Ryton-on-Dunsmore 51 B8


## S


Sabden 93 F7
Sacombe 41 C6
Sacriston 110 E5
Sadberge 101 C8
Saddell 143 E8
Saddington 64 E3
Saddle Bow 67 C6
Saddlescombe 17 C6
Sadgill 99 D6
Saffron Walden 55 F6
Sageston 32 D1
Saham Hills 68 D2
Saham Toney 68 D2
Saighdinis 148 B3
Saighton 73 C8
St Abbs 122 C5
St Abb's Haven 122 C5
St Agnes
  Corn 4 D2
  Scilly 2 F3
St Albans 40 D4
St Allen 4 D3
St Andrews 129 C7
St Andrew's Major 22 B3
St Anne 16 I1
St Annes 85 B4
St Ann's 114 E3
St Ann's Chapel
  Corn 6 B2
  Devon 6 E4
St Anthony-in-Meneage 3 D6
St Anthony's Hill 18 E3
St Arvans 36 E2
St Asaph = Llanelwy 72 B4
St Athan 22 C2
St Aubin 17 I3
St Austell 4 D5
St Bees 98 C1
St Blazey 5 D5
St Boswells 121 F8
St Brelade 17 I3
St Breock 4 B4
St Breward 5 B5
St Briavels 36 D2
St Bride's 44 D3
St Brides Major 21 B7
St Bride's Netherwent 35 F8
St Brides-super-Ely 22 B2
St Brides Wentlooge 35 F6
St Budeaux 6 D2
Saintbury 51 F6
St Buryan 2 D3
St Catherine 24 B2
St Catherine's 125 E7
St Clears = Sanclêr 32 C3
St Cleer 5 C7
St Clement 3 B7
St Clements 17 I3
St Clether 8 F4
St Colmac 145 G9
St Columb Major 4 C4
St Columb Minor 4 C3
St Columb Road 4 D4
St Combs 153 B10
St Cross South Elmham 69 F5
St Cyrus 135 C7
St David's 127 B8
St David's = Tyddewi 44 C2
St Day 3 B6
St Dennis 4 D4
St Devereux 49 F6

St Dogmaels ....45 E3
St Dogwells ....44 C4
St Dominick ....6 C2
St Donat's ....21 E7
St Edith's ....24 C4
St Endellion ....4 B4
St Enoder ....4 D3
St Erme ....2 C4
St Erney ....5 D8
St Erth ....2 C4
St Ervan ....4 B3
St Eval ....4 C3
St Ewe ....3 B8
St Fagans ....22 B3
St Fergus ....153 C10
St Fillans ....127 B5
St Florence ....32 D1
St Genny's ....8 E3
St George ....72 B3
St George's ....22 B2
St Germans ....5 D8
St Giles ....78 D2
St Giles in the Wood ....9 C7
St Giles on the Heath ....9 E5
St Harmon ....47 B8
St Helena ....63 D6
St Helen Auckland ....101 B6
St Helens
 IoW ....15 F7
 Mers ....86 E3
St Helen's ....18 D5
St Helier
 Jersey ....17 I3
 London ....28 C3
St Hilary
 Corn ....2 C4
 V Glam ....22 B2
Saint Hill ....28 F4
St Illtyd ....35 D6
St Ippollytts ....40 B4
St Ishmael's ....44 E3
St Issey ....4 B4
St Ive ....5 C8
St Ives
 Cambs ....54 B4
 Corn ....2 B4
 Dorset ....14 D2
St James South Elmham ....69 F6
St Jidgey ....4 C4
St John ....6 D2
St John's
 IoM ....84 D2
 Jersey ....17 I3
 Sur ....27 D7
 Worcs ....50 D3
St John's Chapel ....109 F8
St John's Fen End ....66 C5
St John's Highway ....66 C5
St John's Town of Dalry ....113 F6
St Judes ....84 C3
St Just ....2 C2
St Just in Roseland ....3 C7
St Katherine's ....153 E7
St Keverne ....3 D6
St Kew ....4 B5
St Kew Highway ....4 B5
St Keyne ....5 C7
St Lawrence
 Corn ....4 B4
 Essex ....43 D5
 IoW ....15 G6
St Leonards
 Dorset ....14 D2
 E Sus ....18 E4
 S Lanark ....119 D6
St Leonard's ....40 D2
St Levan ....2 D2
St Lythans ....22 B3
St Mabyn ....4 B5
St Madoes ....128 B3
St Margarets ....41 C6
St Margaret's ....49 F5
St Margaret's at Cliffe ....31 E7
St Margaret's Hope ....159 J5
St Margaret South Elmham ....69 F6
St Mark's ....84 E2
St Martin ....5 D7
St Martins
 Corn ....3 D6
 Perth ....134 F1
St Martin's
 Jersey ....17 I3
 Shrops ....73 F7
St Mary Bourne ....26 D2
St Mary Church ....22 B3
St Mary Cray ....29 C5
St Mary Hill ....21 B8
St Mary Hoo ....30 B2
St Mary in the Marsh ....19 C7
St Mary's
 Jersey ....17 I3
 Orkney ....159 H5
St Mary's Bay ....19 C7
St Maughans ....36 C1
St Mawes ....3 C7
St Mawgan ....4 C3
St Mellion ....5 C8
St Mellons ....35 F6
St Merryn ....4 B3
St Mewan ....4 D4
St Michael Caerhays ....3 B8
St Michael Penkevil ....3 B7
St Michaels ....49 C7
St Michael's ....19 B5
St Michael's on Wyre ....92 E4
St Michael South Elmham ....69 F6
St Minver ....4 B4
St Monans ....129 D7
St Neot ....5 C6
St Neots ....54 C2
St Newlyn East ....4 D3

St Nicholas
 Pembs ....44 B3
 V Glam ....22 B2
St Nicholas at Wade ....31 C6
St Ninians ....127 E6
St Osyth ....43 C7
St Osyth Heath ....43 C7
St Ouens ....17 I3
St Owens Cross ....36 B2
St Paul's Cray ....29 C5
St Paul's Walden ....40 B4
St Peter Port ....16 I2
St Peter's
 Jersey ....17 I3
 Kent ....31 C7
St Petrox ....44 F4
St Pinnock ....5 C7
St Quivox ....112 B3
St Ruan ....3 E6
St Sampson ....16 I2
St Stephen ....4 D4
St Stephens
 Corn ....6 D2
 Herts ....40 D4
St Stephen's ....8 F5
St Teath ....4 C5
St Thomas ....10 E4
St Tudy ....5 B5
St Twynnells ....44 F4
St Veep ....5 D6
St Vigeans ....135 E6
St Wenn ....4 C4
St Weonards ....36 B1
Salcombe ....6 F5
Salcombe Regis ....11 F6
Salcott ....43 C5
Sale ....87 E5
Sale Green ....50 D4
Saleby ....79 B7
Salehurst ....18 C4
Salem
 Carms ....33 B7
 Ceredig ....58 F3
Salen
 Argyll ....147 G8
 Highld ....147 E9
Salesbury ....93 F6
Salford
 C Beds ....53 F7
 Gtr Man ....87 E6
 Oxon ....38 B2
Salford Priors ....51 D5
Salfords ....28 E3
Salhouse ....69 C6
Saline ....128 E2
Salisbury ....14 B2
Sallachan ....130 C3
Sallachy
 Highld ....150 H2
 Highld ....157 J8
Salle ....81 E7
Salmonby ....79 B6
Salmond's Muir ....135 F5
Salperton ....37 B7
Salph End ....53 D8
Salsburgh ....119 C8
Salt ....62 B3
Saltaire ....94 F4
Saltash ....6 D2
Saltburn ....157 K10
Saltburn-by-the-Sea ....102 B4
Saltby ....65 B5
Saltcoats
 Cumb ....98 E2
 N Ayrs ....118 E2
Saltdean ....17 D7
Salt End ....91 B5
Salter ....93 C6
Salterforth ....93 E8
Salterswall ....74 C3
Saltfleet ....91 E4
Saltfleetby All Saints ....91 E4
Saltfleetby St Clements ....91 E4
Saltfleetby St Peter ....91 F8
Saltford ....23 C8
Salthouse ....81 C6
Saltmarshe ....89 B8
Saltney ....73 C7
Salton ....96 B3
Saltwick ....110 B4
Saltwood ....19 B8
Salum ....146 G3
Salvington ....16 D5
Salwarpe ....50 C3
Salwayash ....12 E2
Sambourne ....51 C5
Sambrook ....61 B7
Samhla ....148 B2
Samlesbury ....93 F6
Samlesbury Bottoms ....86 B4
Sampford Arundel ....11 C6
Sampford Brett ....22 E2
Sampford Courtenay ....9 D8
Sampford Peverell ....10 C5
Sampford Spiney ....6 B3
Samuelston ....121 B7
Sanachan ....149 D13
Sanaigmore ....142 A3
Sanclêr
 =St Clears ....32 C3
Sancreed ....2 D3
Sancton ....96 F5
Sand
 Highld ....150 B2
 Shetland ....160 J5
Sandaig ....149 H12
Sandale ....108 E2
Sandal Magna ....88 C4
Sandbach ....74 C4
Sandbank ....145 E10
Sandbanks ....13 F8
Sandend ....152 B5
Sanderstead ....28 C4
Sandfields ....37 B6
Sandford

Sandford *continued*
 IoW ....15 F6
 N Som ....23 D6
 Shrops ....74 F2
 S Lanark ....119 E7
Sandfordhill ....153 D11
Sandford on Thames ....39 D5
Sandford Orcas ....12 B4
Sandford St Martin ....38 B4
Sandgate ....19 B8
Sandgreen ....106 D2
Sandhaven ....153 B9
Sandhead ....104 E4
Sandhills ....27 F7
Sandhoe ....110 C2
Sand Hole ....96 F4
Sandholme
 E Yorks ....96 F4
 Lincs ....79 F6
Sandhurst
 Brack ....27 C6
 Glos ....37 B5
 Kent ....18 C4
Sandhurst Cross ....18 C4
Sandhutton ....102 F1
Sand Hutton ....96 D2
Sandiacre ....76 F4
Sandilands
 Lincs ....91 F9
 S Lanark ....119 F8
Sandiway ....74 B3
Sandleheath ....14 C2
Sandling ....29 D8
Sandlow Green ....74 C4
Sandness ....160 H3
Sandon
 Essex ....42 D3
 Herts ....54 F4
 Staffs ....75 F6
Sandown ....15 F6
Sandplace ....5 D7
Sandridge
 Herts ....40 C4
 Wilts ....24 C4
Sandringham ....67 B6
Sandsend ....103 C6
Sandside House ....157 C12
Sandsound ....160 J5
Sandtoft ....89 D8
Sandway ....30 D2
Sandwell ....62 F4
Sandwich ....31 D7
Sandwick
 Cumb ....99 C6
 Orkney ....159 K5
 Shetland ....160 L6
Sandwith ....98 C1
Sandy
 Carms ....33 D5
 C Beds ....54 E2
Sandy Bank ....79 D5
Sandycroft ....73 C7
Sandyford
 Dumfries ....114 E5
 Stoke ....75 D5
Sandygate ....84 C3
Sandy Haven ....44 E3
Sandyhills ....107 D5
Sandylands ....92 C4
Sandy Lane
 Wilts ....24 C4
 Wrex ....73 E7
Sandypark ....10 F2
Sandysike ....108 C3
Sangobeg ....156 C7
Sangomore ....156 C7
Sanna ....146 E7
Sanndabhaig
 W Isles ....148 D3
 W Isles ....155 D9
Sannox ....143 D11
Sanquhar ....113 D7
Santon ....90 C3
Santon Bridge ....98 D3
Santon Downham ....67 F8
Sapcote ....63 E8
Sapey Common ....50 C2
Sapiston ....56 B3
Sapley ....54 B3
Sapperton
 Glos ....37 D6
 Lincs ....78 F3
Saracen's Head ....66 B3
Sarclet ....158 F5
Sardis ....33 D6
Sarn
 Bridgend ....34 F3
 Powys ....60 E2
Sarnau
 Carms ....32 C4
 Ceredig ....46 D2
 Gwyn ....72 F3
 Powys ....48 F2
 Powys ....60 C2
Sarn Bach ....70 E4
Sarnesfield ....49 D6
Sarn Meyllteyrn ....70 D3
Saron
 Carms ....33 C7
 Carms ....46 F2
 Denb ....72 C4
 Gwyn ....82 E5
 Gwyn ....82 F4
Sarratt ....40 E3
Sarre ....31 C6
Sarsden ....38 B2
Sarsgrum ....156 C6
Satley ....110 E4
Satron ....100 E4
Satterleigh ....9 B8
Satterthwaite ....99 E5
Satwell ....39 F7
Sauchen ....141 C5
Saucher ....134 F1
Sauchie ....127 E7
Sauchieburn ....135 C6
Saughall ....73 B7
Saughtree ....115 E8
Saul ....36 D4
Saundby ....89 F8
Saundersfoot ....32 D2
Saunderton ....39 D7
Saunton ....20 F3
Sausthorpe ....79 C6
Saval ....157 J8

Savary ....147 G9
Savile Park ....87 B8
Sawbridge ....52 C3
Sawbridgeworth ....41 C7
Sawdon ....103 F7
Sawley
 Derbys ....76 F4
 Lancs ....93 E7
 N Yorks ....94 C5
Sawston ....55 E5
Sawtry ....65 F8
Saxby
 Leics ....64 C5
 Lincs ....90 F4
Saxby All Saints ....90 C3
Saxelbye ....64 B4
Saxham Street ....56 C4
Saxilby ....77 B8
Saxlingham Green ....68 E5
Saxlingham Nethergate ....68 E5
Saxlingham Thorpe ....68 E5
Saxmundham ....57 C7
Saxondale ....77 F6
Saxon Street ....55 D7
Saxtead ....57 C6
Saxtead Green ....57 C6
Saxthorpe ....81 D7
Saxton ....95 F7
Sayers Common ....17 C6
Scackleton ....96 B2
Scadabhagh ....154 H6
Scaftworth ....89 E7
Scagglethorpe ....96 B4
Scaitcliffe ....87 B5
Scalasaig ....144 D2
Scalby
 E Yorks ....90 B2
 N Yorks ....103 E8
Scaldwell ....53 B5
Scaleby ....108 C4
Scaleby Hill ....108 C4
Scale Houses ....109 E5
Scales
 Cumb ....92 B2
 Cumb ....99 B5
 Lancs ....92 F4
Scalford ....64 B4
Scaling ....103 C5
Scallastle ....124 B2
Scalloway ....160 K6
Scalpay ....154 H7
Scalpay House ....149 F11
Scalpsie ....145 H9
Scamadale ....147 B10
Scamblesby ....79 B5
Scamodale ....130 B2
Scampston ....96 B4
Scampton ....78 B2
Scapa ....159 H5
Scapegoat Hill ....87 C8
Scar ....159 D7
Scarborough ....103 F8
Scarcliffe ....76 C4
Scarcroft ....95 E6
Scarcroft Hill ....95 E6
Scardroy ....150 F5
Scarff ....160 E4
Scarfskerry ....158 C4
Scargill ....101 C5
Scarinish ....146 G3
Scarisbrick ....85 C4
Scarning ....68 C2
Scarrington ....77 E7
Scartho ....91 D6
Scarwell ....159 F3
Scatness ....160 M5
Scatraig ....151 H10
Scawby ....90 D3
Scawsby ....89 D6
Scawton ....102 F3
Scayne's Hill ....17 B7
Scethrog ....35 B5
Scholar Green ....74 D5
Scholes
 W Yorks ....88 B2
 W Yorks ....88 D2
 W Yorks ....95 F6
School Green ....74 C3
Scleddau ....44 B4
Scofton ....89 F7
Scole ....56 B5
Scolpaig ....148 A2
Scone ....128 B3
Sconser ....149 E10
Scoonie ....129 D5
Scoor ....146 K7
Scopwick ....78 D3
Scoraig ....150 B3
Scorborough ....97 E6
Scorrier ....3 B6
Scorton
 Lancs ....92 E5
 N Yorks ....101 D7
Sco Ruston ....81 E8
Scotbheinn ....148 C3
Scotby ....108 D4
Scotch Corner ....101 D7
Scotforth ....92 D4
Scothern ....78 B3
Scotland Gate ....117 F8
Scotlandwell ....128 D3
Scotsburn ....151 D10
Scotscalder Station ....158 E2
Scotscraig ....129 B6
Scots' Gap ....117 F6
Scotston
 Aberds ....135 B7
 Perth ....133 E6
Scotstoun ....118 C5
Scotstown ....130 C2
Scotswood ....110 C4
Scottas ....149 H12
Scotter ....90 D2
Scotterthorpe ....90 D2
Scottlethorpe ....65 B7
Scotton
 Lincs ....90 E2
 N Yorks ....95 D6
 N Yorks ....101 E6
Scottow ....81 E8
Scoughall ....129 F8
Scoulag ....145 H10
Scoulton ....68 D2

Scourie ....156 E4
Scourie More ....156 E4
Scousburgh ....160 M5
Scrabster ....158 C2
Scrafield ....79 C6
Scrainwood ....117 D5
Scrane End ....79 E6
Scraptoft ....64 D3
Scratby ....69 C8
Scrayingham ....96 C3
Scredington ....78 E3
Scremby ....79 C7
Scremerston ....123 E6
Screveton ....77 E7
Scrivelsby ....79 C5
Scriven ....95 D6
Scrooby ....89 E7
Scropton ....75 F8
Scrub Hill ....78 D5
Scruton ....101 E7
Sculcoates ....97 F6
Sculthorpe ....80 D4
Scurlage ....33 F5
Seaborough ....12 D2
Seacombe ....85 E4
Seacroft
 Lincs ....79 C8
 W Yorks ....95 F6
Seadyke ....79 F6
Seafield
 S Ayrs ....112 B3
 W Loth ....120 C3
Seaford ....17 E8
Seaforth ....85 E4
Seagrave ....64 C3
Seaham ....111 E7
Seahouses ....123 F8
Seal ....29 D6
Sealand ....73 C7
Seale ....27 E6
Seamer
 N Yorks ....102 C2
 N Yorks ....103 F8
Seamill ....118 E2
Sea Palling ....69 B7
Searby ....90 D4
Seasalter ....30 C4
Seascale ....98 D2
Seathorne ....79 C8
Seathwaite
 Cumb ....98 C4
 Cumb ....98 E4
Seatoller ....98 C4
Seaton
 Corn ....5 D8
 Cumb ....107 F7
 Devon ....11 F7
 Durham ....111 D6
 E Yorks ....97 E7
 Northumb ....111 B6
 Rutland ....65 E6
Seaton Burn ....110 B5
Seaton Carew ....102 B3
Seaton Delaval ....111 B6
Seaton Ross ....96 E3
Seaton Sluice ....111 B6
Seatown
 Aberds ....152 B5
 Dorset ....12 E2
Seave Green ....102 D3
Seaview ....15 E7
Seaville ....107 D8
Seavington St Mary ....12 C2
Seavington St Michael ....12 C2
Sebastopol ....35 E6
Sebergham ....108 E3
Seckington ....63 D6
Second Coast ....150 B2
Sedbergh ....100 E1
Sedbusk ....100 E3
Sedgeberrow ....50 F5
Sedgebrook ....77 F8
Sedgefield ....102 B1
Sedgeford ....80 D3
Sedgehill ....13 B6
Sedgley ....62 E3
Sedgwick ....99 F7
Sedlescombe ....18 D4
Seend ....24 C4
Seend Cleeve ....24 C4
Seer Green ....40 E2
Seething ....69 E6
Sefton ....85 D4
Seghill ....111 B5
Seifton ....60 F4
Seighford ....62 B2
Seilebost ....154 H5
Seion ....82 E5
Seisdon ....62 E2
Seisiadar ....155 D10
Selattyn ....73 F6
Selborne ....26 F5
Selby ....96 F2
Selham ....16 B3
Selhurst ....28 C4
Selkirk ....115 B7
Sellack ....36 B2
Sellafirth ....160 D7
Sellibister ....159 D8
Sellindge ....19 B8
Sellindge Lees ....19 B8
Selling ....30 D4
Sells Green ....24 C4
Selly Oak ....62 F4
Selmeston ....18 E2
Selsdon ....28 C4
Selsey ....16 E2
Selsfield Common ....28 F4
Selsted ....31 E6
Selston ....76 D4
Selworthy ....21 E8
Semblister ....160 H5
Semer ....56 E3
Semington ....24 C3
Semley ....13 B6
Send ....27 D8
Send Marsh ....27 D8
Senghenydd ....35 E5
Sennen ....2 D2
Sennen Cove ....2 D2
Sennybridge
 =Pont Senni ....34 B3

Serlby ....89 F7
Sessay ....95 B7
Setchey ....67 C6
Setley ....14 D4
Setter
 Shetland ....160 E6
 Shetland ....160 H5
 Shetland ....160 J7
Settiscarth ....159 G4
Settle ....93 C8
Settrington ....96 B4
Sevenhampton ....37 B7
Sevenoaks ....29 D6
Sevenoaks Weald ....29 D6
Seven Kings ....41 F7
Seven Sisters ....34 D2
Severn Beach ....36 F2
Severnhampton ....38 E2
Severn Stoke ....50 E3
Sevington ....30 E4
Sewards End ....55 F6
Sewardstone ....41 E6
Sewardstonebury ....41 E6
Sewerby ....97 C7
Seworgan ....3 C6
Sewstern ....65 B5
Sezincote ....51 F6
Sgarasta Mhor ....154 H5
Sgiogarstaigh ....155 A10
Shabbington ....39 D6
Shackerstone ....63 D7
Shackleford ....27 E7
Shade ....87 B7
Shadforth ....111 E6
Shadingfield ....69 F7
Shadoxhurst ....19 B6
Shadsworth ....86 B5
Shadwell
 Norf ....68 F2
 W Yorks ....95 F6
Shaftenhoe End ....54 F5
Shaftesbury ....13 B6
Shafton ....88 C4
Shalbourne ....25 C8
Shalcombe ....14 F4
Shalden ....26 E4
Shaldon ....7 B7
Shalfleet ....14 F5
Shalford
 Essex ....42 B3
 Sur ....27 E8
Shalford Green ....42 B3
Shallowford ....21 E6
Shalmsford Street ....30 D4
Shalstone ....52 F4
Shamley Green ....27 E8
Shandon ....145 E11
Shandwick ....151 D11
Shangton ....64 E4
Shankhouse ....111 B5
Shanklin ....15 F6
Shanquhar ....152 E5
Shanzie ....134 D2
Shap ....99 C7
Shapwick
 Dorset ....13 D7
 Som ....23 F6
Shardlow ....76 F4
Shareshill ....62 D3
Sharlston ....88 C4
Sharlston Common ....88 C4
Sharnal Street ....30 B2
Sharnbrook ....53 D7
Sharnford ....63 E8
Sharoe Green ....92 F5
Sharow ....95 B6
Sharpenhoe ....53 F8
Sharperton ....117 D5
Sharpness ....36 D3
Sharp Street ....69 B6
Sharpthorne ....28 F4
Sharrington ....81 D6
Shatterford ....61 F7
Shaugh Prior ....6 C3
Shavington ....74 D4
Shaw
 Gtr Man ....87 D7
 W Berks ....26 C2
 Wilts ....24 C3
Shawbury ....61 B5
Shawdon Hall ....117 C6
Shawell ....64 F2
Shawford ....15 B5
Shawforth ....87 B6
Shaw Green ....86 C3
Shawhead ....107 B5
Shaw Mills ....95 C5
Shawton ....119 E6
Shawtonhill ....119 E6
Shear Cross ....24 E3
Shearington ....107 C7
Shearsby ....64 E3
Shebbear ....9 D6
Shebdon ....61 B7
Shebster ....157 C13
Sheddens ....119 D5
Shedfield ....15 C6
Sheen ....75 C8
Sheepscar ....95 F6
Sheepscombe ....37 C5
Sheepstor ....6 C3
Sheepwash ....9 D6
Sheepway ....23 B6
Sheepy Magna ....63 D7
Sheepy Parva ....63 D7
Sheering ....41 C8
Sheerness ....30 B3
Sheet ....15 B8
Sheffield Bottom ....26 C4
Sheffield Green ....17 B8
Shefford ....54 F2
Shefford Woodlands ....25 B8
Sheigra ....156 C4
Sheinton ....61 D6
Shelderton ....49 B6
Sheldon
 Derbys ....75 C8
 Devon ....11 D6
 W Mid ....63 F5
Sheldwich ....30 D4
Shelf ....88 B2
Shelfanger ....68 F4
Shelfield
 W Mid ....62 D4
 Warks ....51 C6

Shelford ....77 E6
Shellacres ....122 E4
Shelley
 Essex ....42 D1
 Suff ....56 F4
 W Yorks ....88 C3
Shellingford ....38 E3
Shellow Bowells ....42 D2
Shelsley Beauchamp ....50 C2
Shelsley Walsh ....50 C2
Shelthorpe ....64 C2
Shelton
 Bedford ....53 C8
 Norf ....68 E5
 Notts ....77 E7
 Shrops ....60 C4
Shelton Green ....68 E5
Shelve ....60 E3
Shelwick ....49 E7
Shenfield ....42 E2
Shenington ....51 E8
Shenley ....40 D4
Shenley Brook End ....53 F6
Shenleybury ....40 D4
Shenley Church End ....53 F6
Shenmore ....49 F5
Shennanton ....105 C7
Shenstone
 Staffs ....62 D5
 Worcs ....50 B3
Shenton ....63 D7
Shenval
 Highld ....137 B7
 Moray ....139 B8
Shepeau Stow ....66 C3
Shephall ....41 B5
Shepherd's Green ....39 F7
Shepherd's Port ....80 D2
Shepherdswell ....31 E6
Shepley ....88 D2
Shepperdine ....36 E3
Shepperton ....27 C8
Shepreth ....54 E4
Shepshed ....63 C8
Shepton Beauchamp ....12 C2
Shepton Mallet ....23 E8
Shepton Montague ....23 F8
Shepway ....29 D8
Sheraton ....111 F7
Sherborne
 Dorset ....12 C4
 Glos ....38 C1
Sherborne St John ....26 D4
Sherbourne ....51 C7
Sherburn
 Durham ....111 E6
 N Yorks ....97 B5
Sherburn Hill ....111 E6
Sherburn in Elmet ....95 F7
Shere ....27 E8
Shereford ....80 E4
Sherfield English ....14 B3
Sherfield on Loddon ....26 D4
Sherford ....7 E5
Sheriffhales ....61 C7
Sheriff Hutton ....96 C2
Sheringham ....81 C7
Sherington ....53 E6
Shernal Green ....50 C4
Shernborne ....80 D3
Sherrington ....24 F4
Sherston ....37 F5
Sherwood Green ....9 B7
Shettleston ....119 C6
Shevington ....86 D3
Shevington Moor ....86 C3
Shevington Vale ....86 D3
Sheviock ....5 D8
Shide ....15 F5
Shiel Bridge ....136 C2
Shieldaig
 Highld ....149 A13
 Highld ....149 C13
Shieldhill
 Dumfries ....114 B3
 Falk ....119 B8
 S Lanark ....120 E3
Shielfoot ....147 E9
Shielhill
 Angus ....134 D4
 Inverclyd ....118 B2
Shifford ....38 D3
Shifnal ....61 D7
Shilbottle ....117 D7
Shildon ....101 B7
Shillingford
 Devon ....10 B4
 Oxon ....39 E5
Shillingford St George ....10 F4
Shillingstone ....13 C6
Shillington ....54 F2
Shillmoor ....116 D4
Shilton
 Oxon ....38 D2
 Warks ....63 F8
Shilvington ....117 F7
Shimpling
 Norf ....68 F4
 Suff ....56 D2
Shimpling Street ....56 D2
Shincliffe ....111 E5
Shiney Row ....111 D6
Shinfield ....26 C5
Shingham ....67 D7
Shingle Street ....57 E7
Shinner's Bridge ....7 C5
Shinness ....157 H8
Shipbourne ....29 D6
Shipdham ....68 D2
Shipham ....23 D6
Shiphay ....7 C6
Shiplake ....27 B5
Shiplaw ....120 D5
Shipley
 Derbys ....76 E4
 Northumb ....117 C7
 Shrops ....62 E2
 W Sus ....16 B5
 W Yorks ....94 F4
Shipley Shiels ....116 E3

Shipmeadow ....69 F6
Shippea Hill Station ....67 F6
Shippon ....38 E4
Shipston-on-Stour ....51 E7
Shipton
 Glos ....37 C7
 N Yorks ....95 D8
 Shrops ....61 E5
Shipton Bellinger ....25 E7
Shipton Gorge ....12 E2
Shipton Green ....16 D2
Shipton Moyne ....37 F5
Shipton on Cherwell ....38 C4
Shipton Solers ....37 C7
Shiptonthorpe ....96 E4
Shipton-under-Wychwood ....38 C2
Shirburn ....39 E6
Shirdley Hill ....85 C4
Shirebrook ....76 C5
Shiregreen ....88 E4
Shirehampton ....23 B7
Shiremoor ....111 B6
Shirenewton ....36 E1
Shireoaks ....89 F6
Shirkoak ....19 B6
Shirl Heath ....49 D6
Shirland ....76 D3
Shirley
 Derbys ....76 E2
 London ....28 C4
 Soton ....14 C5
 W Mid ....51 B6
Shirrell Heath ....15 C6
Shirwell ....20 F4
Shirwell Cross ....20 F4
Shiskine ....143 F10
Shobdon ....49 C6
Shobnall ....63 B6
Shobrooke ....10 D3
Shoby ....64 C3
Shocklach ....73 E8
Shoeburyness ....43 F5
Sholden ....31 D7
Sholing ....14 C5
Shoot Hill ....60 C4
Shop
 Corn ....4 B3
 Corn ....8 C4
Shop Corner ....57 F6
Shoreditch ....41 F6
Shoreham ....29 C6
Shoreham-by-Sea ....17 D6
Shore Mill ....151 E10
Shoresdean ....123 E5
Shoreswood ....122 E5
Shoreton ....151 E9
Shorncote ....37 E7
Shorne ....29 B7
Shortacombe ....9 F7
Shortgate ....17 C8
Short Heath ....62 D3
Shortlanesend ....3 B7
Shortlees ....118 F4
Shortstown ....53 E8
Shorwell ....15 F5
Shoscombe ....24 D2
Shotatton ....60 B3
Shotesham ....69 E5
Shotgate ....42 E3
Shotley ....57 F6
Shotley Bridge ....110 D3
Shotleyfield ....110 D3
Shotley Gate ....57 F6
Shottenden ....30 D4
Shottermill ....27 F6
Shottery ....51 D6
Shotteswell ....52 E2
Shottisham ....57 E7
Shottle ....76 E3
Shottlegate ....76 E3
Shotton
 Durham ....111 F7
 Flint ....73 C7
 Northumb ....122 F4
Shotton Colliery ....111 E6
Shotts ....119 C8
Shotwick ....73 B7
Shouldham ....67 D6
Shouldham Thorpe ....67 D6
Shoulton ....50 D3
Shover's Green ....18 B3
Shraleybrook ....74 D4
Shrawardine ....60 C4
Shrawley ....50 C3
Shrewley Common ....51 C7
Shrewsbury ....60 C4
Shrewton ....25 E5
Shripney ....16 D3
Shrivenham ....38 F2
Shropham ....68 E2
Shrub End ....43 B5
Shucknall ....49 E7
Shudy Camps ....55 E7
Shulishadermor ....149 D9
Shurdington ....37 C6
Shurlock Row ....27 B6
Shurrery ....157 D13
Shurrery Lodge ....157 D13
Shurton ....22 E4
Shustoke ....63 E6
Shute
 Devon ....10 D3
 Devon ....11 E7
Shutford ....51 E8
Shuthonger ....50 F3
Shutlanger ....52 D5
Shuttington ....63 D6
Shuttlewood ....76 B4
Siabost bho Dheas ....154 C7
Siabost bho Thuath ....154 C7
Siadar ....155 B8
Siadar Iarach ....155 B8
Siadar Uarach ....155 B8
Sibbaldbie ....114 F4
Sibbertoft ....64 F3
Sibdon Carwood ....60 F4
Sibford Ferris ....51 F8
Sibford Gower ....51 F8
Sible Hedingham ....55 F8

Sibsey ....79 D6
Sibson
 Cambs ....65 E7
 Leics ....63 D7
Sibthorpe ....77 E7
Sibton ....57 C7
Sicklesmere ....56 C2
Sicklinghall ....95 E6
Sid ....11 F6
Sidbury
 Devon ....11 E6
 Shrops ....61 F6
Sidcot ....23 D6
Sidcup ....29 B5
Siddick ....107 F7
Siddington
 Ches E ....74 B5
 Glos ....37 E7
Sidemoor ....50 B4
Sidestrand ....81 D8
Sidford ....11 E6
Sidlesham ....16 E2
Sidley ....18 E4
Sidlow ....28 E3
Sidmouth ....11 F6
Sigford ....7 B5
Sigglesthorne ....97 E7
Sighthill ....120 B4
Sigingstone ....21 B8
Signet ....38 C2
Silchester ....26 C4
Sildinis ....155 F7
Sileby ....64 C2
Silecroft ....98 F3
Silfield ....68 E4
Silian ....46 D4
Silkstone ....88 D3
Silkstone Common ....88 D3
Silk Willoughby ....78 E3
Silloth ....107 D8
Sills ....116 D4
Sillyearn ....152 C5
Siloh ....47 F6
Silpho ....103 E7
Silsden ....94 E3
Silsoe ....53 F8
Silverburn ....120 C5
Silverdale
 Lancs ....92 B4
 Staffs ....74 E5
Silver End ....42 C4
Silvergate ....81 E7
Silverley's Green ....57 B6
Silverstone ....52 E4
Silverton ....10 D4
Silvington ....49 B8
Silwick ....160 J4
Simmondley ....87 E8
Simonburn ....109 B8
Simonsbath ....21 F6
Simonstone ....93 F7
Simprim ....122 E4
Simpson ....53 F6
Simpson Cross ....44 D3
Sinclair's Hill ....122 D4
Sinclairston ....112 C4
Sinderby ....101 F8
Sinderhope ....109 D8
Sindlesham ....27 C5
Singdean ....115 D8
Singleborough ....53 F5
Singleton
 Lancs ....92 F3
 W Sus ....16 C2
Singlewell ....29 B7
Sinkhurst Green ....30 E2
Sinnahard ....140 C3
Sinnington ....103 F5
Sinton Green ....50 C3
Sipson ....27 B8
Sirhowy ....35 C5
Sisland ....69 E6
Sissinghurst ....18 B4
Sisterpath ....122 E3
Siston ....23 B8
Sithney ....2 D5
Sittingbourne ....30 C2
Six Ashes ....61 F7
Sixhills ....91 F5
Six Hills ....64 B3
Six Mile Bottom ....55 D6
Sixpenny Handley ....13 C7
Sizewell ....57 C8
Skail ....157 E10
Skaill
 Orkney ....159 E5
 Orkney ....159 G3
 Orkney ....159 H6
Skares ....113 C5
Skateraw ....122 B3
Skaw ....160 G7
Skeabost ....149 D9
Skeabrae ....159 F3
Skeeby ....101 D7
Skeffington ....64 D4
Skeffling ....91 C7
Skegby ....76 C4
Skegness ....79 C8
Skelberry ....160 M5
Skelbo ....151 B10
Skelbrooke ....89 C6
Skeldyke ....79 F6
Skellingthorpe ....78 B2
Skellister ....160 H6
Skellow ....89 C6
Skelmanthorpe ....88 C3
Skelmersdale ....86 D2
Skelmonae ....153 E8
Skelmorlie ....118 C1
Skelmuir ....153 D9
Skelpick ....157 D10
Skelton
 Cumb ....108 F4
 E Yorks ....89 B8
 N Yorks ....101 D5
 Redcar ....102 C4
 York ....95 D8
Skelton-on-Ure ....95 C6
Skelwick ....159 D5
Skelwith Bridge ....99 D5
Skendleby ....79 C7
Skene House ....141 D6

Skenfrith 36 B1
Skerne 97 D6
Skeroblingarry 143 F8
Skerray 157 C9
Skerton 92 C4
Sketchley 63 E8
Sketty 33 E7
Skewen 33 E8
Skewsby 96 B2
Skeyton 81 E8
Skiag Bridge 156 G5
Skibo Castle 151 C10
Skidbrooke 91 E8
Skidbrooke North End 91 E8
Skidby 97 F6
Skilgate 10 B4
Skillington 65 B5
Skinburness 107 D8
Skinflats 127 F8
Skinidin 148 D7
Skinnet 157 C8
Skinningrove 103 B5
Skipness 145 H7
Skippool 92 E3
Skipsea 97 D6
Skipsea Brough 97 D7
Skipton 94 D2
Skipton-on-Swale 95 B6
Skipwith 96 F2
Skirbeck 79 E6
Skirbeck Quarter 79 E6
Skirlaugh 97 F7
Skirling 120 F3
Skirmett 39 F7
Skirpenbeck 96 D3
Skirwith 109 F6
Skirza 158 D5
Skulamus 149 F11
Skullomie 157 C9
Skyborry Green 48 B4
Skye of Curr 139 B5
Skyreholme 94 C3
Slackhall 87 F8
Slackhead 152 B4
Slad 37 D5
Slade
  Devon 20 E4
  Pembs 44 D4
Slade Green 29 B6
Slaggyford 109 D6
Slaidburn 93 D7
Slaithwaite 87 C8
Slaley 110 D2
Slamannan 119 B8
Slapton
  Bucks 40 B2
  Devon 7 E6
  W Nhants 52 E4
Slatepit Dale 76 C3
Slattocks 87 D6
Slaugham 17 B6
Slaughterford 24 B3
Slawston 64 E4
Sleaford
  Hants 27 F6
  Lincs 78 E3
Sleagill 99 C7
Sleapford 61 C6
Sledge Green 50 F3
Sledmere 96 C5
Sleightholme 100 C4
Sleights 103 D6
Slepe 13 E7
Slickly 158 D4
Sliddery 143 F10
Sligachan Hotel 149 F9
Slimbridge 36 D4
Slindon
  Staffs 74 F5
  W Sus 16 D3
Slinfold 28 F2
Sling 83 E6
Slingsby 96 B2
Slioch 152 E5
Slip End
  C Beds 40 C3
  Herts 54 F3
Slipton 53 B7
Slitting Mill 62 C4
Slochd 138 B4
Slockavullin 124 F4
Sloley 81 E8
Sloothby 79 B7
Slough 27 B7
Slough Green 17 B6
Sluggan 138 B4
Slumbay 149 E13
Slyfield 27 D7
Slyne 92 C4
Smailholm 122 F2
Smallbridge 87 C7
Smallburgh 69 B6
Smallburn
  Aberds 153 D10
  E Ayrs 113 B6
Small Dole 17 C6
Smalley 76 E4
Smallfield 28 E4
Small Hythe 19 B5
Smallridge 11 D8
Smannell 25 E8
Smardale 100 D2
Smarden 30 E2
Smarden Bell 30 E2
Smeatharpe 11 C6
Smeeth 19 B7
Smeeton Westerby 64 E3
Smercleit 148 G2
Smerral 158 G3
Smethwick 62 F4
Smirisary 147 D9
Smisby 63 C7
Smithfield 108 C4
Smith Green 92 D4
Smithincott 11 C5
Smith's Green 42 B1
Smithstown 149 A12
Smithton 151 G10
Smithy Green 74 B4
Smockington 63 F8
Smoogro 159 H4
Smythe's Green 43 C5

Snaigow House 133 E7
Snailbeach 60 D3
Snailwell 55 C7
Snainton 103 F7
Snaith 89 B7
Snape
  N Yorks 101 F7
  Suff 57 D7
Snape Green 85 C4
Snarestone 63 D7
Snarford 90 F4
Snargate 19 C6
Snave 19 C7
Snead 60 E3
Sneath Common 68 F4
Sneaton 103 D6
Sneatonthorpe 103 D7
Snelland 90 F4
Snelston 75 E8
Snettisham 80 D2
Snibston 63 C8
Sniseabhal 148 E2
Snitter 117 D6
Snitterby 90 E3
Snitterfield 51 D7
Snitton 49 B7
Snodhill 48 E5
Snodland 29 C7
Snowden Hill 88 D3
Snowdown 31 D6
Snowshill 51 F5
Snydale 88 C5
Soar
  Anglesey 82 D3
  Carms 33 B7
  Devon 6 F5
Soar-y-Mynydd 47 D6
Soberton 15 C7
Soberton Heath 15 C7
Sockbridge 99 B7
Sockburn 101 D8
Soham 55 B6
Soham Cotes 55 B6
Solas 148 A3
Soldon Cross 8 C5
Soldridge 26 F4
Sole Street
  Kent 29 C7
  Kent 30 E4
Solihull 51 B6
Sollers Dilwyn 49 D6
Sollers Hope 49 F8
Sollom 86 C2
Solva 44 C2
Somerby
  Leics 64 C4
  Lincs 90 D4
Somercotes 76 D4
Somerford 14 E2
Somerford Keynes 37 E7
Somerley 16 E2
Somerleyton 69 E7
Somersal Herbert 75 F8
Somersby 79 B6
Somersham
  Cambs 54 B4
  Suff 56 E4
Somerton
  Oxon 38 B4
  Som 12 B2
Sompting 17 D5
Sonning 27 B5
Sonning Common 39 F7
Sonning Eye 27 B5
Sontley 73 E7
Sopley 14 E2
Sopworth 37 F5
Sorbie 105 E8
Sordale 158 D3
Sorisdale 146 E5
Sorn 113 B5
Sornhill 118 F5
Sortat 158 D4
Sotby 78 B5
Sots Hole 78 C4
Sotterley 69 F7
Soudley 61 B7
Soughton 73 C6
Soulbury 40 B1
Soulby 100 C2
Souldern 52 F3
Souldrop 53 C7
Sound
  Ches E 74 E3
  Shetland 160 H5
  Shetland 160 J6
Sound Heath 74 E3
Soundwell 23 B8
Sourhope 116 B4
Sourin 159 E5
Sourton 9 E7
Soutergate 98 F4
South Acre 67 C8
Southall 40 F4
South Allington 7 F5
South Alloa 127 E7
Southam
  Glos 37 B6
  Warks 52 C2
South Ambersham 16 B3
Southampton 14 C5
South Anston 89 F6
South Ascot 27 C7
South Ballachulish 130 D4
South Balloch 112 E3
South Bank 102 B3
South Barrow 12 B4
South Beach 70 D4
South Benfleet 42 F3
South Bersted 16 D3
Southborough 29 E6
Southbourne
  BCP 14 E2
  W Sus 15 D8
South Brent 6 C4
South Brewham 24 F2
South Broomhill 117 E8
Southburgh 68 D2
South Burlington 69 D6
Southburn 97 D5
South Cadbury 12 B4
South Cairn 104 C3
South Carlton 78 B2
South Cave 96 F5

South Cerney 37 E7
South Chard 11 D8
South Charlton 117 B7
South Cheriton 12 B4
South Cliffe 96 F4
South Clifton 77 B8
South Cockerington 91 F7
South Cornelly 34 F2
Southcott 25 D6
Southcourt 39 C8
South Cove 69 F7
South Creagan 130 E3
South Creake 80 D4
South Croxton 64 C3
South Croydon 28 C4
South Dalton 97 E5
South Darenth 29 C6
Southdean 116 C2
Southdene 86 E2
South Duffield 96 F2
South Elkington 91 F6
South Elmsall 89 C5
Southend
  Argyll 143 H7
  W Berks 26 B3
  Wilts 25 B6
South End
  Bucks 40 B1
  Cumb 92 C2
  N Lincs 90 B5
Southend-on-Sea 42 F4
Southerndown 21 B7
Southerness 107 D6
South Erradale 149 A12
Southery 67 E6
South Fambridge 42 E4
South Fawley 38 F3
South Ferriby 90 B3
Southfield 111 B5
Southfleet 29 B7
South Garth 160 D7
South Garvan 130 B3
Southgate
  Ceredig 46 B4
  London 41 E5
  Norf 81 E7
  Swansea 33 F6
South Glendale 148 G2
South Godstone 28 E4
South Gorley 14 C2
South Green
  Essex 42 E2
  Kent 30 C2
South Hanningfield 42 E3
South Harting 15 C8
South Hatfield 41 D5
South Hayling 15 E8
South Hazelrigg 123 F6
South Heath 40 D2
South Heighton 17 D8
South Hetton 111 E6
South Hiendley 88 C4
South Hill 23 C8
South Hinksey 39 D5
South Hole 8 B4
South Holme 96 B2
South Holmwood 28 E2
South Hornchurch 41 F8
South Hykeham 78 C2
South Hylton 111 D6
Southill 54 E2
South Kelsey 90 E4
South Kessock 151 G9
South Killingholme 91 C5
South Kilvington 102 F1
South Kilworth 64 F3
South Kirkby 88 C5
South Kirkton 141 D6
South Kiscadale 143 F11
South Kyme 78 E4
South Lancing 17 D5
Southleigh 11 E7
South Leigh 38 D3
South Leverton 89 F8
South Littleton 51 E5
South Lopham 68 F3
South Luffenham 65 D6
South Malling 17 C8
South Marston 38 F1
South Middleton 117 B5
South Milford 95 F7
South Millbrex 153 D8
South Milton 6 E5
South Mimms 41 D5
Southminster 43 E5
South Molton 10 B2
South Moor 110 D4
South Moreton 39 F5
South Mundham 16 D2
South Muskham 77 D7
South Newbald 96 F5
South Newington 52 F2
South Newton 25 F5
South Normanton 76 D4
South Norwood 28 C4
South Nutfield 28 E4
South Ockendon 42 F1
Southoe 54 C2
Southolt 57 C5
South Ormsby 79 B6
Southorpe 65 D7
South Otterington 102 F1
South Owersby 90 E4
Southowram 88 B2
South Oxhey 40 E4
South Perrott 12 D2
South Petherton 12 C2
South Petherwin 9 E5
South Pickenham 67 D8
South Pool 85 C4
Southport 85 C4
South Port 125 C6
Southpunds 160 L6
South Radworthy 21 C7

South Rauceby 78 E3
South Raynham 80 E4
Southrepps 81 D8
South Reston 91 F8
Southrey 78 C4
Southrop 38 D1
Southrope 26 E4
South Runcton 67 D6
South Scarle 77 C8
Southsea 15 E7
South Shian 130 E3
South Shields 111 C6
South Shore 92 E3
South Somercotes 91 E8
South Stainley 95 C6
South Stainmore 100 C3
South Stifford 29 B7
Southstoke 24 C2
South Stoke
  Oxon 39 F5
  W Sus 16 D4
South Street
  E Sus 17 C7
  Kent 30 C5
  Kent 30 D4
South Tawton 9 E8
South Thoresby 79 B7
South Tidworth 25 E7
Southtown
  Norf 69 D8
  Orkney 159 J5
South Town 26 F4
South View 26 D4
Southwaite 108 E4
South Walsham 69 C6
Southwark 28 B4
South Warnborough 26 E5
Southwater 17 B5
Southwater Street 17 B5
South Weald 42 E1
Southwell
  Dorset 12 G4
  Notts 77 D6
South Weston 39 E7
South Wheatley
  Corn 8 E4
  Notts 89 F8
South Whiteness 160 J5
Southwick
  Hants 15 D7
  N Nhants 65 E7
  T&W 111 D6
  Wilts 24 D3
  W Sus 17 D6
South Widcombe 23 D7
South Wigston 64 E2
South Willingham 91 F5
South Wingfield 76 D3
South Witham 65 C6
Southwold 57 B9
South Wonston 26 F2
Southwood
  Norf 69 D6
  Som 23 F7
South Woodham Ferrers 42 E4
South Wootton 67 B6
South Wraxall 24 C3
South Zeal 9 E8
Soval Lodge 155 E8
Sowber Gate 102 F1
Sowerby
  N Yorks 102 F2
  W Yorks 87 B8
Sowerby Bridge 87 B8
Sowerby Row 108 F3
Sowood 87 C8
Sowton 10 E4
Soyal 151 B8
Spacey Houses 95 D6
Spa Common 81 D8
Spadeadam Farm 109 B5
Spalding 66 B2
Spaldington 96 F3
Spaldwick 54 B2
Spalford 77 C8
Spanby 78 F3
Sparham 68 C3
Spark Bridge 99 F5
Sparkford 12 B4
Sparkwell 6 D3
Sparrow Green 68 C2
Sparrowpit 87 F8
Sparsholt
  Hants 26 F2
  Oxon 38 F3
Spartylea 109 E8
Spaunton 103 F5
Spaxton 22 F4
Spean Bridge 136 F5
Spear Hill 16 C5
Speen
  Bucks 39 E8
  W Berks 26 C2
Speeton 97 B7
Speke 86 F2
Speldhurst 29 E6
Spellbrook 41 C7
Spelsbury 38 B3
Spelter 34 E2
Spencers Wood 26 C5
Spennithorne 101 F6
Spennymoor 111 F5
Spetchley 50 D3
Spetisbury 13 D7
Spexhall 69 F6
Spey Bay 152 B3
Speybridge 139 B6
Speyview 152 D2
Spilsby 79 C7
Spindlestone 123 F7
Spinkhill 76 B4
Spinningdale 151 C9
Spirthill 24 B4
Spital Hill 89 E7
Spital in the Street 90 F3
Spithurst 17 C8
Spittal
  Dumfries 105 D7
  E Loth 121 B7
  Highld 158 E3
  Northumb 123 D6
  Pembs 44 C4
  Stirling 126 F4
Spittal of Glenmuick 140 E2
Spittal of Glenshee 133 B8
Spixworth 68 C5
Splayne's Green 17 B8
Spofforth 95 D6
Spon End 51 B8
Spondon 76 F4
Spon Green 73 C6
Spooner Row 68 E3
Sporle 67 C8
Spott 122 B2
Spratton 52 B5
Spreakley 27 E6
Spreyton 9 E8
Spridlington 90 F4
Springburn 119 C6
Springfield
  Dumfries 108 C3
  Essex 42 D3
  Fife 128 C5
  Moray 151 F13
  W Mid 62 F4
Springhill 62 D3
Springholm 106 C5
Springkell 108 B2
Springside 118 F3
Springthorpe 90 F2
Spring Vale 88 D3
Spring Valley 84 E3
Springwell 111 D5
Sproatley 97 F7
Sproston Green 74 C4
Sprotbrough 89 D6
Sproughton 56 E5
Sprouston 122 F3
Sprowston 68 C5
Sproxton
  Leics 65 B5
  N Yorks 102 F4
Spurstow 74 D2

Spittal 30 E2
Standford 27 F6
Standingstone 107 F7
Standish 86 C3
Standlake 38 D3
Standon
  Hants 14 B5
  Herts 41 B6
  Staffs 74 F5
Stane 119 D8
Stanfield 80 E5
Stanford
  C Beds 54 E2
  Pembs 45 E4
Stanford Bishop 49 D8
Stanford Bridge 50 C2
Stanford Dingley 26 B3
Stanford in the Vale 38 E3
Stanford-le-Hope 42 F2
Stanford on Avon 52 B3
Stanford on Soar 64 B2
Stanford on Teme 50 C2
Stanford Rivers 41 D8
Stanfree 76 B4
Stanghow 102 C4
Stanground 66 E2
Stanhoe 80 D4
Stanhope
  Borders 114 B4
  Durham 110 F2
Stanion 65 F6
Stanley
  Derbys 76 E4
  Durham 110 D4
  Lancs 86 D2
  Perth 133 F8
  Staffs 75 D6
  W Yorks 88 B4
Stanley Common 76 E4
Stanley Gate 86 D2
Stanley Hill 49 E8
Stanlow 73 B8
Stanmer 17 D7
Stanmore
  Hants 15 B5
  London 40 E4
  W Berks 26 B2
Stannergate 134 F4
Stanningley 94 F5
Stannington
  Northumb 110 B5
  S Yorks 88 F4
Stansbatch 48 C5
Stansfield 55 D8
Stanstead 56 E2
Stanstead Abbotts 41 C6
Stansted 29 C7
Stansted Airport 42 B1
Stansted Mountfitchet 41 B8
Stanton
  Glos 51 F5
  Mon 35 B7
  Northumb 117 F7
  Staffs 75 E8
  Suff 56 B3
Stanton by Bridge 63 B7
Stanton-by-Dale 76 F4
Stanton Drew 23 C7
Stanton Fitzwarren 38 E1
Stanton Harcourt 38 D4
Stanton Hill 76 C4
Stanton in Peak 76 C2
Stanton Lacy 49 B6
Stanton Long 61 E5
Stanton-on-the-Wolds 77 F6
Stanton Prior 23 C8
Stanton St Bernard 25 C5
Stanton St John 39 D5
Stanton St Quintin 24 B4
Stanton Street 56 C3
Stanton under Bardon 63 C8
Stanton upon Hine Heath 61 B5
Stanton Wick 23 C8
Stanwardine in the Fields 60 B4
Stanwardine in the Wood 60 B4
Stanway
  Essex 43 B5
  Glos 51 F5
Stanway Green 57 B6
Stanwell 27 B8
Stanwell Moor 27 B8
Stanwick 53 B7
Stanwick-St-John 101 C6
Stanwix 108 D4
Stanydale 160 H4
Staoinebrig 148 E2
Stape 103 E5
Stapehill 13 D8
Stapeley 74 E3
Stapenhill 63 B6
Staple
  Kent 31 D6
  Som 22 E3
Staple Cross 18 C4
Staplefield 17 B6
Staple Fitzpaine 11 C7
Stapleford
  Cambs 55 D5
  Herts 41 C6
  Leics 64 C5
  Lincs 77 D8
  Notts 76 F4
  Wilts 25 F5
Stapleford Abbotts 41 E8
Stapleford Tawney 41 E8
Staplegrove 11 B7
Staplehay 11 B7
Staplehurst 29 E8
Staplers 15 F6
Stapleton
  Bristol 23 B8

Stapleton continued
  Cumb 108 B5
  Hereford 48 C5
  Leics 63 E8
  N Yorks 101 C7
  Shrops 60 D4
  Som 12 B2
Staple 11 C6
Staploe 54 C2
Staplow 49 E8
Star
  Fife 128 D5
  Pembs 45 F4
  Som 23 D6
Stara 159 F3
Starbeck 95 D6
Starbotton 94 B2
Starcross 10 F4
Starkholmes 76 D3
Starlings Green 55 F5
Starston 68 F5
Startforth 101 C5
Startley 37 F6
Stathe 11 B8
Stathern 77 F7
Station Town 111 F7
Staughton Green 54 C2
Staughton Highway 54 C2
Staunton
  Glos 36 B4
  Glos 36 C2
Staunton in the Vale 77 E8
Staunton on Arrow 49 C5
Staunton on Wye 49 E5
Staveley
  Cumb 99 E6
  Cumb 99 F5
  Derbys 76 B4
  N Yorks 95 C6
Staverton
  Devon 7 C5
  Glos 37 B5
  Warks 52 C2
  Wilts 24 C3
Staverton Bridge 37 B5
Stawell 23 F7
Staxigoe 158 E5
Staxton 97 B6
Staylittle 59 E5
Staynall 92 E3
Staythorpe 77 D7
Stean 94 C3
Stearsby 96 B2
Steart 22 E4
Stebbing 42 B2
Stebbing Green 42 B2
Stedham 16 B2
Steele Road 115 E8
Steen's Bridge 49 D7
Steep 15 B8
Steeple
  Dorset 13 F7
  Essex 43 D5
Steeple Ashton 24 D4
Steeple Aston 38 B4
Steeple Barton 38 B4
Steeple Bumpstead 55 E7
Steeple Claydon 39 B6
Steeple Gidding 65 F8
Steeple Langford 24 F5
Steeple Morden 54 E3
Steep Marsh 15 B8
Steeton 94 E3
Stein 148 C7
Steinmanhill 153 D7
Stelling Minnis 30 E5
Stemster 158 D3
Stemster House 158 D3
Stenalees 4 D5
Stenhousemuir 127 F7
Stenigot 91 F6
Stenness 160 F4
Stenscholl 149 B9
Stenso 159 F4
Stenson 63 B7
Stenton
  E Loth 122 B2
  Fife 128 E4
Stenwith 77 F8
Stepaside 32 D2
Stepping Hill 87 F7
Steppingley 53 F8
Stepps 119 C6
Sterndale Moor 75 C8
Sternfield 57 C7
Sterridge 20 E4
Stert 24 D5
Stetchworth 55 D7
Stevenage 41 B5
Stevenston 118 E2
Steventon
  Hants 26 E3
  Oxon 38 E4
Stevington 53 D7
Stewartby 53 E8
Stewarton
  Argyll 143 G7
  E Ayrs 118 E4
Stewkley 40 B1
Stewton 91 F7
Steyne Cross 15 F7
Steyning 17 C5
Steynton 44 E4
Stibb 8 C4
Stibbard 81 E5
Stibb Cross 9 C6
Stibb Green 25 C7
Stibbington 65 E7
Stichill 122 F3
Sticker 4 D4
Stickford 79 D6
Sticklepath 9 E8
Stickney 79 D6
Stiffkey 81 D5
Stifford's Bridge 50 E2
Stillingfleet 95 E8
Stillington
  N Yorks 95 C8
  Stockton 102 B1
Stilton 65 F8
Stinchcombe 36 E4
Stinsford 12 E5
Stirchley 61 D7

Stirkoke House 158 E5
Stirling
  Aberds 153 D11
  Stirling 127 E6
Stisted 42 B3
Stithians 3 C6
Stittenham 151 D9
Stivichall 51 B8
Stixwould 78 C4
Stoak 73 B8
Stobieside 119 F6
Stobo 120 F4
Stoborough 13 F7
Stoborough Green 13 F7
Stobshiel 121 C7
Stobswood 117 E8
Stock 42 E2
Stockbridge 25 F8
Stockbury 30 C2
Stockcross 26 C2
Stockdalewath 108 E3
Stockerston 64 E5
Stock Green 50 D4
Stockheath 15 D8
Stockiemuir 126 F4
Stockingford 63 E7
Stocking Pelham 41 B7
Stockland 11 D7
Stockland Bristol 22 E4
Stockleigh English 10 D3
Stockleigh Pomeroy 10 D3
Stockley 24 C5
Stocklinch 11 C8
Stockport 87 E6
Stocksbridge 88 E3
Stocksfield 110 C3
Stockton
  Hereford 49 C7
  Norf 69 E6
  Shrops 60 D2
  Shrops 61 E7
  Warks 52 C2
  Wilts 24 F4
Stockton Heath 86 F4
Stockton-on-Tees 102 C2
Stockton on Teme 50 C2
Stockton on the Forest 96 D2
Stock Wood 50 D5
Stodmarsh 31 C6
Stody 81 D6
Stoer 156 G3
Stoford
  Som 12 C3
  Wilts 25 F5
Stogumber 22 F2
Stogursey 22 E4
Stoke
  Devon 8 B4
  Hants 15 B8
  Hants 26 D2
  Medway 30 B2
  Suff 57 E5
Stoke Abbott 12 D2
Stoke Albany 64 F5
Stoke Ash 56 B5
Stoke Bardolph 77 E6
Stoke Bliss 49 C8
Stoke Bruerne 52 E5
Stoke by Clare 55 E8
Stoke-by-Nayland 56 F3
Stoke Canon 10 E4
Stoke Charity 26 F2
Stoke Climsland 5 B8
Stoke D'Abernon 28 D2
Stoke Doyle 65 F7
Stoke Dry 65 E5
Stoke Farthing 13 B8
Stoke Ferry 67 E7
Stoke Fleming 7 E6
Stokeford 13 F6
Stoke Gabriel 7 D6
Stoke Gifford 23 B8
Stoke Golding 63 E7
Stoke Goldington 53 E6
Stoke Green 40 F2
Stokeham 77 B7
Stoke Hammond 40 B1
Stoke Heath 61 B6
Stoke Holy Cross 68 D5
Stokeinteignhead 7 B7
Stoke Lacy 49 E8
Stoke Lyne 39 B5
Stoke Mandeville 39 C8
Stokenchurch 39 E7
Stokenham 7 E6
Stoke on Tern 61 B6
Stoke-on-Trent 75 E5
Stoke Orchard 37 B6
Stoke Poges 40 F2
Stoke Prior
  Hereford 49 D7
  Worcs 50 C4
Stoke Rivers 20 F5
Stoke Rochford 65 B6
Stoke Row 39 F6
Stoke St Gregory 11 B8
Stoke St Mary 11 B7
Stoke St Michael 23 E8
Stoke St Milborough 61 F5
Stokesay 60 F4
Stokesby 69 C7
Stokesley 102 D3
Stoke sub Hamdon 12 C2
Stoke Talmage 39 E6
Stoke Trister 12 B5
Stoke Wake 13 D5
Stolford 22 E4
Stondon Massey 42 D1
Stone
  Bucks 39 C7
  Glos 36 E3
  Kent 19 C6
  Kent 29 B6
  Staffs 75 F6
  S Yorks 89 F6
  Worcs 50 B3
Stone Allerton 23 D6

Stone Bridge Corner 66 D2
Stonebroom 76 D4
Stone Chair 88 B2
Stone Cross
  E Sus 18 E3
  Kent 31 D7
Stone-edge Batch 23 B6
Stoneferry 97 F7
Stonefield 119 D6
Stonegate
  E Sus 18 C4
  N Yorks 103 D5
Stonegrave 96 B2
Stonehaugh 109 B7
Stonehaven 141 F7
Stonehouse
  Glos 37 D5
  Northumb 109 D6
  S Lanark 119 E7
Stone House 100 F2
Stoneleigh 51 B8
Stonely 54 C2
Stoner Hill 15 B8
Stonesby 64 B5
Stonesfield 38 C3
Stone's Green 43 B7
Stone Street
  Kent 29 D6
  Suff 56 F3
  Suff 69 F6
Stonethwaite 98 C4
Stoneybreck 160 N8
Stoneyburn 120 C2
Stoney Cross 14 C3
Stoneygate
  Aberds 153 E10
  Leicester 64 D3
Stoneyhills 43 E5
Stoney Middleton 76 B2
Stoney Stanton 63 E8
Stoney Stoke 24 F2
Stoney Stratton 23 F8
Stoney Stretton 60 D3
Stoneywood
  Aberdeen 141 C7
  Falk 127 F6
Stonganess 160 C7
Stonham Aspal 56 D5
Stonnall 62 D4
Stonor 39 F7
Stonton Wyville 64 E4
Stony Cross 50 E2
Stonyfield 151 D9
Stony Stratford 53 E5
Stoodleigh 10 C4
Stopes 88 F3
Stopham 16 C4
Stopsley 40 B4
Stores Corner 57 E7
Storeton 85 F4
Stornoway 155 D9
Storridge 50 E2
Storrington 16 C4
Storrs 99 E5
Storth 99 F6
Storwood 96 E3
Stotfield 152 A2
Stotfold 54 F3
Stottesdon 61 F6
Stoughton
  Leics 64 D3
  Sur 27 D7
  W Sus 16 C2
Stoul 147 B10
Stoulton 50 E4
Stourbridge 62 F3
Stourpaine 13 D6
Stourport on Severn 50 B3
Stour Provost 13 B5
Stour Row 13 B6
Stourton
  Staffs 62 F2
  Warks 51 F7
  Wilts 24 F2
Stourton Caundle 12 C5
Stove
  Orkney 159 E7
  Shetland 160 L6
Stoven 69 F7
Stow
  Borders 121 E7
  Lincs 78 F3
  Lincs 90 F2
Stow Bardolph 67 D6
Stow Bedon 68 E2
Stowbridge 67 D6
Stow cum Quy 55 C6
Stowe 48 B5
Stowe-by-Chartley 62 B4
Stowe Green 36 D2
Stowell 12 B4
Stowford 9 E6
Stowlangtoft 56 C3
Stow Longa 54 B2
Stow Maries 42 E4
Stowmarket 56 D4
Stow-on-the-Wold 38 B1
Stowting 30 E5
Stowupland 56 D4
Straad 145 G9
Strachan 141 E5
Strachur 125 F6
Stradbroke 57 B6
Stradishall 55 D8
Stradsett 67 D6
Stragglethorpe 78 D2
Straid 112 E1
Straith 113 F8
Straiton
  Edin 121 C5
  S Ayrs 112 D3
Straloch
  Aberds 141 B7
  Perth 133 C7
Stramshall 75 F7
Strang 84 E3
Stranraer 104 C4
Stratfield Mortimer 26 C4
Stratfield Saye 26 C4
Stratfield Turgis 26 D4
Stratford 41 F6

Stratford St Andrew 57 C7
Stratford St Mary 56 F4
Stratford Sub Castle 25 F6
Stratford Tony 13 B8
Stratford-upon-Avon 51 D6
Strath
  Highld 149 A12
  Highld 158 E4
Strathan
  Highld 136 E2
  Highld 156 G3
  Highld 157 C8
Strathaven 119 E7
Strathblane 119 B5
Strathcanaird 156 J4
Strathcarron 150 G2
Strathcoil 124 B2
Strathdon 140 C2
Strathellie 153 B10
Strathkinness 129 C6
Strathmashie House 137 E8
Strathmiglo 128 C4
Strathmore Lodge 158 F3
Strathpeffer 150 F7
Strathrannoch 150 D6
Strathtay 133 D6
Strathvaich Lodge 150 D6
Strathwhillan 143 E11
Strathy 157 C11
Strathyre 126 C4
Stratton
  Corn 8 D4
  Dorset 12 E4
  Glos 37 D7
Stratton Audley 39 B6
Stratton on the Fosse 23 D8
Stratton St Margaret 38 F1
Stratton St Michael 68 E5
Stratton Strawless 81 E8
Stravithie 129 C7
Streat 17 C7
Streatham 28 B4
Streatley
  C Beds 40 B3
  W Berks 39 F5
Street
  Lancs 92 D5
  N Yorks 103 D5
  Som 23 F6
Street Dinas 73 F7
Street End
  Kent 30 D5
  W Sus 16 E2
Street Gate 110 D5
Streethay 62 C5
Streetlam 101 E8
Streetly 62 E4
Street Lydan 73 F8
Streetly End 55 E7
Strefford 60 F4
Strelley 76 E5
Strensall 96 C2
Stretcholt 22 E4
Strete 7 E6
Stretford 87 E6
Strethall 55 F5
Stretham 55 B6
Strettington 16 D2
Stretton
  Ches W 73 D8
  Derbys 76 C3
  Rutland 65 C6
  Staffs 62 C2
  Staffs 63 B6
  Warr 86 F4
Stretton Grandison 49 E8
Stretton-on-Dunsmore 52 B2
Stretton-on-Fosse 51 F7
Stretton Sugwas 49 E6
Stretton under Fosse 63 F8
Stretton Westwood 61 E5
Strichen 153 C9
Strines 87 F7
Stringston 22 E3
Strixton 53 C7
Stroat 36 E2
Stromeferry 149 E13
Stromemore 149 E13
Stromness 159 H3
Stronaba 136 F5
Stronachlachar 126 C3
Stronchreggan 130 B4
Stronchrubie 156 H5
Strone
  Argyll 145 E10
  Highld 136 F4
  Highld 137 B8
  Invclyd 118 B2
Stronmilchan 125 C7
Strontian 130 C2
Strood 29 C8
Strood Green
  Sur 28 E3
  W Sus 16 B4
  W Sus 28 F2
Stroud
  Glos 37 D5
  Hants 15 B8
Stroud Green 42 E4
Stroxton 78 F2
Struan
  Highld 149 E8
  Perth 133 C5
Strubby 91 F8
Strumpshaw 69 D6
Strutherhill 119 E7
Struy 150 H6
Stryt-issa 73 E6
Stuartfield 153 D9
Stubbington 15 D6
Stubbins 87 C5
Stubbs Cross 19 B6
Stubbs Green 69 E6
Stubb's Green 69 E5
Stubhampton 13 C7
Stub Place 98 E2
Stubton 77 E8
Stuckgowan 126 D2
Stuckton 14 C2
Stud Green 27 B6
Studham 40 C3
Studland 13 F8
Studley
  Warks 51 C5
  Wilts 24 B4
Studley Roger 95 B5
Stump Cross 55 E6
Stuntney 55 B6
Sturbridge 74 F5
Sturmer 55 E7
Sturminster Marshall 13 D7
Sturminster Newton 13 C5
Sturry 31 C5
Sturton 90 D3
Sturton by Stow 90 F2
Sturton le Steeple 89 F8
Stuston 56 B5
Stutton
  N Yorks 95 E7
  Suff 57 F5
Styal 87 F6
Styrrup 89 E7
Suainebost 155 A10
Suardail 155 D9
Succoth
  Aberds 152 E4
  Argyll 125 E8
Suckley 50 D2
Suckquoy 159 K5
Sudborough 65 F6
Sudbourne 57 D8
Sudbrook
  Lincs 78 E2
  Mon 36 F2
Sudbrooke 78 B3
Sudbury
  Derbys 75 F8
  London 40 F4
  Suff 56 E2
Suddie 151 F9
Sudgrove 37 D6
Suffield
  Norf 81 D8
  N Yorks 103 E7
Sugnall 74 F4
Suladale 149 C8
Sulaisiadar 155 D10
Sulby 84 C3
Sulgrave 52 E3
Sulham 26 B4
Sulhamstead 26 C4
Sulland 159 D6
Sullington 16 C4
Sullom 160 F5
Sullom Voe Oil Terminal 160 F5
Sully 22 C3
Sumburgh 160 N6
Summer Bridge 94 C5
Summercourt 4 D3
Summerfield 80 D3
Summergangs 97 F7
Summer-house 101 C7
Summerleaze 35 F8
Summersdale 16 D2
Summerseat 87 C5
Summertown 39 D5
Summit 87 D7
Sunbury-on-Thames 28 C2
Sundaywell 113 F8
Sunderland
  Argyll 142 B3
  Cumb 107 F8
  T&W 111 D6
Sunderland Bridge 111 F5
Sundhope 115 B6
Sundon Park 40 B3
Sundridge 29 D5
Sunipol 146 F6
Sunk Island 91 C6
Sunningdale 27 C7
Sunninghill 27 C7
Sunningwell 38 D4
Sunniside
  Durham 110 F4
  T&W 110 D5
Sunnyhurst 86 B4
Sunnylaw 127 E6
Sunnyside 28 F4
Sunton 25 D7
Surbiton 28 C2
Surby 84 E2
Surfleet 66 B2
Surfleet Seas End 66 B2
Surlingham 69 D6
Sustead 81 D7
Susworth 90 D2
Sutcombe 8 C5
Suton 68 E3
Sutors of Cromarty 151 E11
Sutterby 79 B6
Sutterton 79 F5
Sutton
  Cambs 54 B5
  C Beds 54 E3
  Kent 31 E7
  London 28 C3
  Mers 86 E3
  Norf 69 B6
  Notts 77 F7
  Notts 89 F7
  N Yorks 89 B5
  Oxon 38 D4
  Pboro 65 E7
  Shrops 61 F7
  Shrops 74 F3
  Som 23 F8
  Staffs 61 B7
  Suff 57 E7
  Sur 27 E8
  S Yorks 89 C6
  W Sus 16 C3
Sutton at Hone 29 B6
Sutton Bassett 64 E4
Sutton Benger 24 B4
Sutton Bonington 64 B2
Sutton Bridge 66 B4
Sutton Cheney 63 D8
Sutton Coldfield 62 E5
Sutton Courtenay 39 E5
Sutton Crosses 66 B4
Sutton Grange 95 B5
Sutton Green 27 D8
Sutton Howgrave 95 B6
Sutton in Ashfield 76 D4
Sutton-in-Craven 94 E3
Sutton Ings 97 F7
Sutton in the Elms 64 E2
Sutton Lane Ends 75 B6
Sutton Leach 86 E3
Sutton Maddock 61 D7
Sutton Mallet 23 F5
Sutton Mandeville 13 B7
Sutton Manor 86 E3
Sutton Montis 12 B4
Sutton on Hull 97 F7
Sutton on Sea 91 F9
Sutton-on-the-Forest 95 C8
Sutton on the Hill 76 F2
Sutton on Trent 77 C7
Sutton St Edmund 66 C3
Sutton St James 66 C3
Sutton St Nicholas 49 E7
Sutton Scarsdale 76 C4
Sutton Scotney 26 F2
Sutton under Brailes 51 F8
Sutton-under-Whitestonecliffe 102 F2
Sutton upon Derwent 96 E3
Sutton Valence 30 E2
Sutton Veny 24 E3
Sutton Waldron 13 C6
Sutton Weaver 74 B2
Sutton Wick 23 D7
Swaby 79 B6
Swadlincote 63 C7
Swaffham 67 D8
Swaffham Bulbeck 55 C6
Swaffham Prior 55 C6
Swafield 81 D8
Swainby 102 D2
Swainshill 49 E6
Swainsthorpe 68 D5
Swainswick 24 C2
Swalcliffe 51 F8
Swalecliffe 30 C5
Swallow 91 D5
Swallowcliffe 13 B7
Swallowfield 26 C5
Swallownest 89 F5
Swallows Cross 42 E2
Swanage 13 G8
Swanbister 159 H4
Swanbourne 39 B8
Swan Green
  Ches W 74 B4
  Suff 57 B6
Swanland 90 B3
Swanley 29 C6
Swanley Village 29 C6
Swanmore 15 C6
Swannington
  Leics 63 C8
  Norf 68 C4
Swanscombe 29 B7
Swansea = Abertawe 33 E7
Swanton Abbott 81 E8
Swanton Morley 68 C3
Swanton Novers 81 D6
Swanton Street 30 D2
Swanwick
  Derbys 76 D4
  Hants 15 D6
Swarby 78 E3
Swardeston 68 D5
Swarister 160 E7
Swarkestone 63 B7
Swarland 117 D7
Swarland Estate 117 D7
Swarthmoor 92 B2
Swathwick 76 C3
Swaton 78 F4
Swavesey 54 C4
Sway 14 E3
Swayfield 65 B6
Swaythling 14 C5
Sweet Green 49 C8
Sweetham 10 E3
Sweethouse 5 C5
Sweffling 57 C7
Swepstone 63 C7
Swerford 51 F8
Swettenham 74 C5
Swetton 94 B4
Swffryd 35 E6
Swiftsden 18 C4
Swilland 57 D5
Swillington 95 F6
Swimbridge 9 B8
Swimbridge Newland 20 F5
Swinbrook 38 C2
Swinderby 77 C8
Swindon
  Glos 37 B6
  Staffs 62 E2
  Swindon 38 F1
Swine 97 F7
Swinefleet 89 B8
Swineshead
  Bedford 53 C8
  Lincs 78 E5
Swineshead Bridge 78 E5
Swiney 158 G4
Swinford
  Leics 52 B3
  Oxon 38 D4
Swingate 76 E5
Swingfield Minnis 31 E6
Swingfield Street 31 E6
Swinhoe 117 B8
Swinhope 91 E6
Swining 160 G6
Swinithwaite 101 F5
Swinnow Moor 94 F5
Swinscoe 75 E8
Swinside Hall 116 C3
Swinstead 65 B7
Swinton
  Borders 122 E4
  Gtr Man 87 D5
  N Yorks 94 B3
  N Yorks 96 B3
  S Yorks 88 E5
Swintonmill 122 E4
Swithland 64 C2
Swordale 151 E8
Swordland 147 B10
Swordly 157 C10
Sworton Heath 86 F4
Swydd-ffynnon 47 C5
Swynnerton 75 F5
Swyre 12 F3
Sychtyn 59 D6
Syde 37 C6
Sydenham
  London 28 B4
  Oxon 39 D7
Sydenham Damerel 6 B2
Syderstone 80 D4
Sydling St Nicholas 12 E4
Sydmonton 26 D2
Syerston 77 E7
Syke 87 C6
Sykehouse 89 C7
Sykes 93 D6
Syleham 57 B6
Sylen 33 D6
Symbister 160 G7
Symington
  S Ayrs 118 F3
  S Lanark 120 F2
Symondsbury 12 E2
Symonds Yat 36 C2
Synod Inn 46 D3
Syre 157 E9
Syreford 37 B7
Syresham 52 E4
Syston
  Leics 64 C3
  Lincs 78 E2
Sytchampton 50 C3
Sywell 53 C6


## T


Taagan 150 E3
Tàbost 155 A10
Tabost 155 F8
Tackley 38 B4
Tacleit 154 D6
Tacolneston 68 E4
Tadcaster 95 E7
Taddington 75 B8
Taddiport 9 C6
Tadley 26 C4
Tadlow 54 E3
Tadmarton 51 F8
Tadworth 28 D3
Tafarnau-bach 35 C5
Tafarn-y-gelyn 73 C5
Taff's Well 35 F5
Tafolwern 59 D5
Tai 83 E7
Taibach 34 F1
Tai-bach 59 B8
Taigh a Ghearraidh 148 A2
Tai-mawr 72 E3
Tain
  Highld 151 C10
  Highld 158 D4
Tainant 73 E6
Tainlon 82 F4
Tairbeart = Tarbert 154 G6
Tai'r-Bull 34 B3
Tairgwaith 33 C8
Tai-Ucha 72 D4
Takeley 42 B1
Takeley Street 41 B8
Talachddu 48 F2
Talacre 85 F2
Talardd 59 B5
Talaton 11 E5
Talbenny 44 D3
Talbot Green 34 F4
Talbot Village 13 E8
Tale 11 D5
Talerddig 59 D6
Talgarreg 46 D3
Talgarth 48 F3
Talisker 149 E8
Talke 74 D5
Talkin 109 D5
Talladale 150 D2
Talla Linnfoots 114 B4
Tallarn Green 73 E8
Tallentire 107 F8
Talley 46 F5
Tallington 65 D7
Talmine 157 C8
Talog 32 B4
Talsarn 34 B1
Tal-sarn 46 D4
Talsarnau 71 D7
Talskiddy 4 C4
Talwrn
  Anglesey 82 D4
  Wrex 73 E6
Tal-y-bont
  Ceredig 58 F3
  Conwy 83 E7
  Gwyn 71 E6
  Gwyn 83 D6
Talybont-on-Usk 35 B5
Tal-y-cafn 83 D7
Talygarn 34 F4
Talyllyn 35 B5
Tal-y-llyn 58 D4
Talysarn 82 F4
Talywain 35 D6
Tal-y-wern 58 D5
Tame Bridge 102 D3
Tamerton Foliot 6 C2
Tamworth 63 D6
Tandem 88 C2
Tanden 19 B6
Tandridge 28 D4
Tanerdy 33 B5
Tanfield 110 D4
Tanfield Lea 110 D4
Tangasdal 148 J1
Tangiers 44 D4
Tangley 25 D8
Tanglwst 46 F2
Tangmere 16 D3
Tangwick 160 F4
Tan Hinon 59 F5
Tankersley 88 D4
Tankerton 30 C5
Tan-lan
  Conwy 83 E7
  Gwyn 71 C7
Tannach 158 F5
Tannachie 141 F6
Tannadice 134 D4
Tannington 57 C6
Tansley 76 D3
Tansley Knoll 76 C3
Tansor 65 E7
Tantobie 110 D4
Tanton 102 C3
Tanworth-in-Arden 51 B6
Tan-y-bwlch 71 C7
Tan-y-fron 72 C3
Tan-y-graig
  Anglesey 82 D5
  Gwyn 70 D4
Tanygrisiau 71 C7
Tan-y-groes 45 E4
Tan-y-pistyll 59 B7
Tan-yr-allt 82 F4
Tanyrhydiau 47 C6
Taobh a Chaolais 148 G2
Taobh a'Ghlinne 155 F8
Taobh a Thuath Loch Aineort 148 F2
Taobh a Tuath Loch Baghasdail 148 F2
Taobh Tuath 154 J4
Taplow 40 F2
Tapton 76 B3
Tarbat House 151 D10
Tarbert
  Argyll 143 C7
  Argyll 144 E5
  Argyll 145 G7
Tarbert = Tairbeart 154 G6
Tarbet
  Argyll 126 D2
  Highld 147 B10
  Highld 156 E4
Tarbock Green 86 F2
Tarbolton 112 B4
Tarbrax 120 D3
Tardebigge 50 C5
Tarfside 134 B4
Tarland 140 D3
Tarleton 86 B2
Tarlogie 151 C10
Tarlscough 86 C2
Tarlton 37 E6
Tarnbrook 93 D5
Tarporley 74 C2
Tarr 22 F3
Tarrant Crawford 13 D7
Tarrant Gunville 13 C7
Tarrant Hinton 13 C7
Tarrant Keyneston 13 D7
Tarrant Launceston 13 D7
Tarrant Monkton 13 D7
Tarrant Rawston 13 D7
Tarrant Rushton 13 D7
Tarrel 151 C11
Tarring Neville 17 D8
Tarrington 49 E8
Tarsappie 128 B3
Tarskavaig 149 H10
Tarves 153 E8
Tarvie
  Highld 150 F7
  Perth 133 C7
Tarvin 73 C8
Tasburgh 68 E5
Tasley 61 E6
Taston 38 B3
Tatenhill 63 B6
Tathall End 53 E6
Tatham 93 C6
Tathwell 91 F7
Tatling End 40 F3
Tatsfield 28 D5
Tattenhall 73 D8
Tattenhoe 53 F6
Tatterford 80 E4
Tattersett 80 D4
Tattershall 78 D5
Tattershall Bridge 78 D4
Tattershall Thorpe 78 D5
Tattingstone 56 F5
Tatworth 11 D8
Taunton 11 B7
Taverham 68 C4
Tavernspite 32 C2
Tavistock 6 B2
Taw Green 9 E8
Tawstock 9 B7
Taxal 75 B7
Tay Bridge 129 B6
Tayinloan 143 D7
Taymouth Castle 132 E4
Taynish 144 E6
Taynton
  Glos 36 B4
  Oxon 38 C2
Taynuilt 125 B6
Tayport 129 B6
Tayvallich 144 E6
Tealby 91 E5
Tealing 134 F4
Teangue 149 H11
Teanna Mhachair 148 B2
Tebay 99 D8
Tebworth 40 B2
Tedburn St Mary 10 E3
Teddington
  Glos 50 F4
  London 28 B2
Tedstone Delamere 49 D8
Tedstone Wafre 49 D8
Teeton 52 B4
Teffont Evias 24 F4
Teffont Magna 24 F4
Tegryn 45 F4
Teigh 65 C5
Teigncombe 9 F8
Teigngrace 7 B6
Teignmouth 7 B7
Telford 61 D6
Telham 18 D4
Tellisford 24 D3
Telscombe 17 D8
Telscombe Cliffs 17 D7
Templand 114 F3
Temple
  Corn 5 B6
  Glasgow 118 C5
  Midloth 121 D6
Temple Balsall 51 B7
Temple Bar
  Carms 33 C6
  Ceredig 46 D4
Temple Cloud 23 D8
Temple Combe 12 B5
Temple Ewell 31 E6
Temple Grafton 51 D6
Temple Guiting 37 B7
Templehall 128 E4
Temple Herdewyke 51 D8
Temple Hirst 89 B7
Temple Normanton 76 C4
Temple Sowerby 99 B8
Templeton
  Devon 10 C3
  Pembs 32 C2
Templeton Bridge 10 C3
Templetown 110 D4
Tempsford 54 D2
Tenbury Wells 49 C7
Tenby = Dinbych-y-Pysgod 32 D2
Tendring 43 B7
Tendring Green 43 B7
Ten Mile Bank 67 E6
Tenston 159 G3
Tenterden 19 B5
Terling 42 C3
Ternhill 74 F3
Terregles Banks 107 B6
Terrick 39 D8
Terrington 96 B2
Terrington St Clement 66 C5
Terrington St John 66 C5
Teston 29 D8
Testwood 14 C4
Tetbury 37 E5
Tetbury Upton 37 E5
Tetchill 73 F7
Tetcott 8 E5
Tetford 79 B6
Tetney 91 D7
Tetney Lock 91 D7
Tetsworth 39 D6
Tettenhall 62 E2
Teuchan 153 E10
Teversal 76 C4
Teversham 55 D5
Teviothead 115 D7
Tewel 141 F7
Tewin 41 C5
Tewkesbury 50 F3
Teynham 30 C3
Thackthwaite 98 B3
Thainston 135 B6
Thakeham 16 C5
Thame 39 D7
Thames Ditton 28 C2
Thames Haven 42 F3
Thamesmead 41 F7
Thanington 30 D5
Thankerton 120 F2
Tharston 68 E4
Thatcham 26 C3
Thatto Heath 86 E3
Thaxted 55 F7
The Aird 149 C9
Theakston 101 F8
Thealby 90 C2
Theale
  Som 23 E6
  W Berks 26 B4
The Arms 67 E8
Thearne 97 F6
The Bage 48 E4
The Balloch 127 C7
The Barony 159 F3
Theberton 57 C8
The Bog 60 E3
The Bourne 27 E6
The Braes 149 E10
The Broad 49 C6
The Butts 24 E2
The Camp
  Glos 37 D6
  Herts 40 D4
The Chequer 73 E8
The City 39 E7
The Common 25 F7
The Craigs 150 B7
The Cronk 84 C3
Theddingworth 64 F3
Theddlethorpe All Saints 91 F8
Theddlethorpe St Helen 91 F8
The Dell 69 E7
The Den 118 D3
The Eals 116 F3
The Eaves 36 D3
The Flatt 109 B5
The Four Alls 74 F3
The Garths 160 B8
The Green
  Cumb 98 F3
  Wilts 24 F3
The Grove 107 B6
The Hall 160 D8
The Haven 27 F8
The Heath
  Norf 81 E7
  Suff 56 F5
The Hill 98 F3
The Howe
  Cumb 99 F6
  IoM 84 F1
The Hundred 49 C7
Thelbridge Barton 10 C2
The Lee 40 D2
The Lhen 84 B3
Thelnetham 56 B4
Thelveton 68 F4
Thelwall 86 F4
The Marsh
  Powys 60 E3
  Wilts 37 F7
Themelthorpe 81 E6
The Middles 110 D5
The Moor 18 C4
The Mumbles = Y Mwmbwls 33 F7
The Murray 119 D6
The Neuk 141 E6
Thenford 52 E3
The Oval 24 C2
The Pole of Itlaw 153 C6
The Quarry 36 E4
Therfield 54 F4
The Rhos 32 C1
The Rock 61 D6
The Ryde 41 D5
The Sands 27 E6
The Stocks 19 C6
Thetford
  Lincs 65 C8
  Norf 67 F8
The Throat 27 C6
The Vauld 49 E7
The Wyke 61 D7
Theydon Bois 41 E7
Thickwood 24 B3
Thimbleby
  Lincs 78 C5
  N Yorks 102 E2
Thingwall 85 F3
Thirdpart 118 E1
Thirlby 102 F2
Thirlestane 121 E8
Thirn 101 F7
Thirsk 102 F2
Thirtleby 97 F7
Thistleton
  Lancs 92 F4
  Rutland 65 C6
Thistley Green 55 B7
Thixendale 96 C4
Thockrington 110 B2
Tholomas Drove 66 D3
Tholthorpe 95 C7
Thomas Chapel 32 D2
Thomas Close 108 E4
Thomastown 152 E5
Thompson 68 E2
Thomshill 152 C2
Thong 29 B7
Thongsbridge 88 D2
Thoralby 101 F5
Thoresway 91 E5
Thorganby
  Lincs 91 E6
  N Yorks 96 E2
Thorgill 103 E5
Thorington 57 B8
Thorington Street 56 F4
Thorlby 94 D2
Thorley 41 C7
Thorley Street
  Herts 41 C7
  IoW 14 F4
Thormanby 95 B7
Thornaby-on-Tees 102 C2
Thornage 81 D6
Thornborough
  Bucks 52 F5
  N Yorks 95 B5
Thornbury
  Devon 9 D6
  Hereford 49 D8
  S Glos 36 E3
  W Yorks 94 F4
Thornby 52 B4
Thorncliffe 75 D7
Thorncombe
  Dorset 11 D8
  Dorset 13 D6
Thorncombe Street 27 E8
Thorncote Green 54 E2
Thorncross 14 F5
Thorndon 56 C5
Thorndon Cross 9 E7
Thorne 89 C7
Thorner 95 E6
Thorne St Margaret 11 B5
Thorney
  Notts 77 B8
  Pboro 66 D2
Thorney Crofts 91 B6
Thorney Green 56 C4
Thorney Hill 14 E2
Thorney Toll 66 D3
Thornfalcon 11 B7
Thornford 12 C4
Thorngumbald 91 B6
Thornham 80 C3
Thornham Magna 56 B5
Thornham Parva 56 B5
Thornhaugh 65 D7
Thornhill
  Cardiff 35 F5
  Cumb 98 D2
  Derbys 88 F2
  Dumfries 113 E8
  Soton 15 C5
  Stirling 127 E5
  W Yorks 88 C3
Thornhill Edge 88 C3
Thornhill Lees 88 C3
Thornholme 97 C7
Thornley
  Durham 110 F4
  Durham 111 F6
Thornliebank 118 D5
Thorns 55 D8
Thornsett 87 F8
Thorns Green 87 F5
Thornthwaite
  Cumb 98 B4
  N Yorks 94 D4
Thornton
  Angus 134 E3
  Bucks 53 F5
  E Yorks 96 E3
  Fife 128 E4
  Lancs 92 E3
  Leics 63 D8
  Lincs 78 C5
  Mbro 102 C2
  Mers 85 D4
  Northumb 123 E5
  Pembs 44 E4
  W Yorks 94 F4
Thornton Curtis 90 C4
Thorntonhall 119 D5
Thornton Heath 28 C4
Thornton Hough 85 F4
Thornton in Craven 94 E2
Thornton-le-Beans 102 E1
Thornton-le-Clay 96 C2
Thornton-le-Dale 103 F6
Thornton le Moor 90 E4
Thornton-le-Moor 102 F1
Thornton-le-Moors 73 B8
Thornton-le-Street 102 F2
Thorntonloch 122 B3
Thorntonpark 122 E5
Thornton Rust 100 F4
Thornton Steward 101 F6
Thornton Watlass 101 F7
Thornwood Common 41 D7
Thornydykes 122 E2
Thoroton 77 E7
Thorp Arch 95 E7
Thorpe
  Derbys 75 D8
  E Yorks 97 E5
  Lincs 91 F8
  Norf 69 E7
  Notts 77 E7
  N Yorks 94 C3
  Sur 27 C8
Thorpe Abbotts 57 B5
Thorpe Acre 64 B2
Thorpe Arnold 64 B4
Thorpe Audlin 89 C5
Thorpe Bassett 96 B4
Thorpe Bay 43 F5
Thorpe by Water 65 E5
Thorpe Common 57 F6
Thorpe Constantine 63 D6
Thorpe Culvert 79 C7
Thorpe End 69 C5
Thorpe Fendykes 79 C7
Thorpe Green
  Essex 43 B7
  Suff 56 D3
Thorpe Hesley 88 E4
Thorpe in Balne 89 C6
Thorpe in the Fallows 90 F3
Thorpe Langton 64 E4
Thorpe Larches 102 B1
Thorpe-le-Soken 43 B7
Thorpe le Street 96 E4
Thorpe Malsor 53 B6
Thorpe Mandeville 52 E3
Thorpe Market 81 D8
Thorpe Marriot 68 C4
Thorpe Morieux 56 D3
Thorpeness 57 D8
Thorpe on the Hill 78 C2
Thorpe St Andrew 69 D5
Thorpe St Peter 79 C7
Thorpe Salvin 89 F6
Thorpe Satchville 64 C4
Thorpe Thewles 102 B2
Thorpe Tilney 78 D4
Thorpe Underwood 95 D7
Thorpe Waterville 65 F7
Thorpe Willoughby 95 F8
Thorrington 43 C6
Thorverton 10 D4
Thrandeston 56 B5
Thrapston 53 B7
Thrashbush 119 C7
Threapland
  Cumb 107 F8
  N Yorks 94 C2
Threapwood
  Ches W 73 E8
  Staffs 75 E7
Three Ashes 36 B2
Three Bridges 28 F3
Three Burrows 3 B6
Three Chimneys 18 B5
Three Cocks 48 F3
Three Crosses 33 E6
Three Cups Corner 18 C3
Threehammer Common 69 C6
Three Holes 66 D5
Threekingham 78 F3
Three Leg Cross 18 B3
Three Legged Cross 13 D8
Threemile Cross 26 C5
Threemilestone 3 B6
Threemiletown 120 B3
Three Oaks 18 D5
Threlkeld 99 B5
Threshfield 94 C2
Thrigby 69 C7
Thringarth 100 B4
Thringstone 63 C8
Thrintoft 101 E8
Thriplow 54 E5
Throckenholt 66 D3
Throcking 54 F4
Throckley 110 C4
Throckmorton 50 E4
Throphill 117 F7
Thropton 117 D6
Throsk 127 E7
Throwleigh 9 E8
Throwley 30 D3
Thrumpton 76 F5
Thrumster 158 F5
Thrunton 117 C6
Thrupp
  Glos 37 D5
  Oxon 38 C4
Thrushelton 9 F6
Thrussington 64 C3
Thruxton
  Hants 25 E7
  Hereford 49 F6
Thrybergh 89 E5
Thulston 76 F4
Thundergay 143 D9
Thundersley 42 F3
Thundridge 41 C6
Thurcaston 64 C2
Thurcroft 89 F5
Thurgarton
  Norf 81 D7
  Notts 77 E6
Thurgoland 88 D3
Thurlaston
  Leics 64 E2
  Warks 52 B2
Thurlbear 11 B7
Thurlby
  Lincs 65 C8
  Lincs 78 C2
Thurleigh 53 D8
Thurlestone 6 E4
Thurloxton 22 F4
Thurlstone 88 D3
Thurlton 69 E7
Thurlwood 74 D5
Thurmaston 64 D3
Thurnby 64 D3
Thurne 69 C7
Thurnham
  Kent 30 D2
  Lancs 92 D4
Thurning
  N Nhants 65 F7
  Norf 81 E6
Thurnscoe 89 D5
Thurnscoe East 89 D5
Thursby 108 D3
Thursford 81 D5
Thursley 27 F7
Thurso 158 D3
Thurso East 158 D3
Thurstaston 85 F3
Thurston 56 C3
Thurstonfield 108 D3
Thurstonland 88 C2
Thurton 69 D6
Thurvaston 76 F2
Thuxton 68 D3
Thwaite
  N Yorks 100 E3
  Suff 56 C5
Thwaites 94 E3
Thwaite St Mary 69 E6
Thwaites Brow 94 E3
Thwing 97 B6
Tibbermore 128 B2
Tibberton
  Glos 36 B4
  Telford 61 B6
  Worcs 50 D4
Tibenham 68 F4
Tibshelf 76 C4
Tibthorpe 97 D5
Ticehurst 18 B3
Tichborne 26 F3
Tickencote 65 D6
Tickenham 23 B6
Tickhill 89 E6
Ticklerton 60 E4
Ticknall 63 B7
Tickton 97 E6
Tidcombe 25 D7
Tiddington
  Oxon 39 D6
  Warks 51 D7
Tidebrook 18 C3
Tideford 5 D8
Tideford Cross 5 C8
Tidenham 36 E2
Tideswell 75 B8
Tidmarsh 26 B4
Tidmington 51 F7
Tidpit 13 C8
Tidworth 25 E7
Tiers Cross 44 D4
Tiffield 52 D4
Tifty 153 D7
Tigerton 135 C5
Tigh-na-Blair 127 C6
Tighnabruaich 145 F8
Tighnafiline 155 J13
Tigley 7 C5
Tilbrook 53 C8
Tilbury 29 B7
Tilbury Juxta Clare 55 E8
Tile Cross 63 F5
Tile Hill 51 B7
Tilehurst 26 B4
Tilford 27 E6
Tilgate 28 F3
Tilgate Forest Row 28 F3
Tillathrowie 152 E4
Tilley 60 B5
Tillicoultry 127 E8
Tillingham 43 D5
Tillington
  Hereford 49 E6
  W Sus 16 B3

Tillington
 Common......49 E6
Tillyarblet....135 C5
Tillybirloch...141 D5
Tillydrine....140 E5
Tillyfour.....140 C4
Tillyfourie...140 C5
Tillygarmond.140 E5
Tillygreig....141 B7
Tillykerrie...141 B7
Tilmanstone...31 D7
Tilney All Saints..67 C5
Tilney High End..67 C5
Tilney
 St Lawrence...66 C5
Tilshead......24 E5
Tilstock......74 F2
Tilston......73 D8
Tilstone Fearnall.74 C2
Tilsworth.....40 B2
Tilton on the Hill.64 D4
Timberland....78 D4
Timbersbrook..75 C5
Timberscombe..21 E8
Timble.......94 D4
Timperley....87 F5
Timsbury
 Bath.......23 D8
 Hants......14 B4
Timsgearraidh.154 D5
Timworth Green.56 C2
Tincleton....13 E5
Tindale......109 D6
Tingewick....52 F4
Tingley......88 B3
Tingrith.....53 F8
Tingwall.....159 F4
Tinhay.......9 F5
Tinshill.....95 F5
Tinsley......88 E5
Tintagel.....8 F2
Tintern Parva.36 D2
Tintinhull...12 C3
Tintwistle...87 E8
Tinwald......114 F3
Tinwell......65 D7
Tipperty.....141 B8
Tipsend......66 E5
Tipton......62 E3
Tipton St John..11 E5
Tiptree......42 C4
Tirabad......47 E7
Tiraghoil....146 J6
Tirley.......37 B5
Tirphil......35 D5
Tirril.......99 B7
Tir-y-dail...33 C7
Tisbury......13 B7
Tisman's
 Common.....27 F8
Tissington...75 D8
Titchberry...8 B4
Titchfield...15 D6
Titchmarsh...53 B8
Titchwell....80 C3
Tithby.......77 F6
Titley.......48 C5
Titlington...117 C7
Titsey.......28 D5
Tittensor....75 F5
Tittleshall..80 E4
Tiverton
 Ches W.....74 C2
 Devon......10 C4
Tivetshall
 St Margaret..68 F4
Tivetshall St Mary.68 F4
Tividale.....62 E3
Tivy Dale....88 D3
Tixall.......62 B3
Tixover......65 D6
Toab
 Orkney.....159 H6
 Shetland...160 M5
Toadmoor.....76 D3
Tobermory....147 F8
Toberonochy..124 E3
Tobha Mor....148 E2
Tobhtarol....154 D6
Tobson......154 D6
Tocher......153 E6
Tockenham....37 F7
Tockenham Wick.37 F7
Tockholes....86 B4
Tockington...36 F3
Tockwith.....95 D7
Todber......13 B6
Todding.....49 B6
Toddington
 C Beds.....40 B3
 Glos.......50 F5
Todenham....51 F7
Todhills....108 C3
Todlachie...141 C5
Todmorden...87 B7
Todrig......115 C7
Todwick.....89 F5
Toft
 Cambs......54 D4
 Lincs......65 C7
Toft Hill
 Durham.....101 B6
 Lincs......78 C5
Toft Monks...69 E7
Toft next Newton.90 F4
Toftrees.....80 E4
Tofts.......158 D5
Toftwood....68 C2
Togston.....117 D8
Tokavaig....149 G11
Tokers Green..26 B5
Tolastadh a
 Chaolais...154 D6
Tolastadh bho
 Thuath....155 C10
Tolland.....22 F3
Tollard Royal.13 C7
Toll Bar.....89 D6
Tollbar End..51 B8
Toll End.....62 E3
Toller Fratrum.12 E3
Toller Porcorum.12 E3
Tollerton
 Notts......77 F6

Tollerton continued
 N Yorks....95 C8
Tollesbury...43 C5
Tolleshunt
 D'Arcy.....43 C5
Tolleshunt Major.43 C5
Toll of Birness.153 E10
Tolm.......155 D9
Tolpuddle...13 E5
Tolvah......138 E4
Tolworth....28 C2
Tomatin.....138 B4
Tombreck....151 H9
Tomchrasky..137 C5
Tomdoun....136 D4
Tomich
 Highld.....137 B6
 Highld.....151 D9
Tomich House.151 G8
Tomintoul
 Aberds.....139 E7
 Moray......139 C7
Tomnaven....152 E4
Tomnavoulin.139 B8
Tondu.......34 F2
Tonfanau....58 D2
Tong
 Shrops.....61 D7
 W Yorks....94 F5
Tonge.......63 B8
Tongham.....27 E6
Tongland....106 D3
Tong Norton..61 D7
Tongue......157 D8
Tongue End...65 C8
Tongwynlais..35 F5
Tonna.......34 E1
Ton-Pentre..34 E3
Tonwell.....41 C6
Tonypandy...34 E3
Tonyrefail...34 F4
Toot Baldon..39 D5
Toothill....14 C4
Toot Hill....41 D8
Topcliffe...95 B7
Topcroft....69 E5
Topcroft Street.69 E5
Top of Hebers.87 D6
Toppesfield..55 F8
Toppings....86 C5
Topsham.....10 F4
Torbay......7 D7
Torbeg......143 F10
Torboll Farm.151 B10
Torbrex.....127 E6
Torbryan....7 C6
Torcross....7 E6
Tore.......151 F9
Torinturk...145 G7
Torksey.....77 B8
Torlum......148 C2
Torlundy....131 B5
Tormarton...24 B2
Tormisdale..142 C2
Tormitchell.112 E2
Tormore....143 E9
Tornagrain..151 G10
Tornahaish..139 D8
Tornaveen...140 D5
Torness....137 B8
Toronto....110 F4
Torpenhow...108 F2
Torphichen..120 B2
Torphins....140 D5
Torpoint....6 D2
Torquay.....7 C7
Torquhan....121 E7
Torran
 Argyll.....124 E4
 Highld.....149 D10
 Highld.....151 D10
Torrance....119 B6
Torrans....146 J7
Torranyard..118 E3
Torre.......7 C7
Torridon...150 F2
Torridon
 House.....149 C13
Torrin.....149 F10
Torrisdale
 =Newport..45 F2
Torrisdale-
 Square.....143 E8
Torrish.....157 H12
Torrisholme..92 C4
Torroble....157 J8
Torry
 Aberds.....141 D8
 Aberds.....152 E4
Torryburn...128 F2
Torterston..153 D10
Torthorwald.107 B7
Tortington...16 D4
Tortworth...36 E4
Torvaig.....149 D9
Torver......98 E4
Torwood....127 F7
Torworth....89 F7
Tosberry....8 B4
Toscaig....149 E12
Toseland....54 C3
Tosside.....93 D7
Tostock....56 C3
Totaig
 Highld.....148 C7
 Highld.....149 F13
Tote.......149 D9
Totegan....157 C11
Tothill.....91 F8
Totland.....14 F4
Totnes......7 C6
Toton......76 F5
Totronald...146 F4
Totscore....149 B8
Tottenham...41 E6
Tottenhill...67 C6
Tottenhill Row.67 C6
Totteridge..41 E5
Totternhoe..40 B2
Tottington..87 C5
Totton......14 C4
Touchen End..27 B6
Tournaig....155 J13
Toux.......153 C9
Tovil.......29 D8
Toward.....145 G10
Towcester...52 E4
Towednack...2 C3

Tower End.....67 C6
Towersey.....39 D7
Towie
 Aberds.....140 C3
 Aberds.....153 B8
Towiemore...152 D3
Tow Law......110 F4
Townend.....118 B4
Town End
 Cambs......66 E4
 Cumb.......99 F6
Towngate.....65 C8
Townhead
 Cumb.......108 F5
 Dumfries...106 E3
 S Ayrs.....112 D2
 S Yorks....88 D2
Townhead of
 Greenlaw...106 C4
Townhill....128 F3
Town Row.....18 B2
Townsend
 Bucks......39 D7
 Herts......40 D4
Townshend...2 C4
Town Yetholm.116 B4
Towthorpe....96 D2
Towton......95 F7
Towyn.......72 B3
Toxteth......85 F4
Toynton
 All Saints..79 C6
Toynton Fen Side.79 C6
Toynton St Peter.79 C7
Toy's Hill...29 D5
Trabboch....112 B4
Traboe......3 D6
Tradespark
 Highld.....151 F11
 Orkney.....159 H5
Trafford Park..87 E5
Trallong....34 B3
Tranent....121 B7
Tranmere....85 F4
Trantlebeg..157 D11
Trantlemore.157 D11
Tranwell....117 F7
Trapp.......33 C7
Traprain....121 B8
Traquair....121 F6
Trawden.....94 F2
Trawsfynydd.71 D8
Trealaw.....34 E4
Treales.....92 F4
Trearddur...149 C8
Treaslane...149 C8
Trebanog....82 D2
Trebanos....33 D8
Trebartha....5 B7
Trebarwith..8 F2
Trebetherick..4 B4
Treborough...21 F8
Trebudannon..4 C3
Trebullett...5 B8
Treburley....5 B8
Trebyan......5 C5
Trecastle...34 B2
Trecenydd...35 F5
Trecwn......44 B4
Trecynon....34 D3
Tredavoe....2 D3
Treddiog.....44 B4
Tredegar....35 D5
Tredegar =Newydd
 New Tredegar.35 D5
Tredington
 Glos.......37 B6
 Warks......51 E7
Tredinnick...4 B4
Tredomen....48 F3
Tredunnock..35 E7
Tredustan...48 F3
Treen.......2 D2
Treeton......88 F5
Trefaldwyn
 =Montgomery.60 E2
Trefasser....44 B3
Trefdraeth...82 D4
Trefdraeth
 =Newport...45 F2
Trefecca....48 F3
Trefechan...34 D3
Trefeglwys...59 E6
Trefenter....46 C5
Treffgarne...44 C4
Treffynnon
 =Holywell..73 B5
Trefgarn Owen.44 C3
Trefi.......44 B3
Trefil.......35 C5
Trefilan....46 D4
Treflach....60 B2
Trefnanney..60 C2
Trefnant....72 B4
Trefonen....60 B2
Trefor
 Anglesey...82 C3
 Gwyn.......70 C4
Treforest...34 F4
Trefriw.....83 E7
Tref-y-Clawdd
 =Knighton..48 B4
Trefynwy
 =Monmouth..36 C2
Tregadillett..8 F4
Tregaian....82 D4
Tregare.....36 C1
Tregaron....47 D5
Tregarth....83 E6
Tregeare....8 F4
Tregeiriog...73 F5
Tregele......82 B3
Tre-Gibbon..34 D3
Tregidden....3 D6
Treglemais..44 C3
Tregole......8 E3
Tregonetha...4 C4
Tregony......3 B8
Tregoss......4 C4
Tregoyd.....48 F4
Tregroes....46 E3
Tregurrian...4 C3
Tregynon....59 E7
Trehafod....34 E4
Treharris....34 E4
Treherbert...34 E3
Trekenner....5 B8

Treknow......8 F2
Trelan......3 E6
Trelash......8 E3
Trelassick...4 D3
Trelawnyd...72 B4
Trelech.....45 F4
Treleddyd-fawr.44 C2
Trelewis....35 E5
Treligga....8 F2
Trelights....4 B4
Trelill......4 B5
Trelissick...3 C7
Trellech....36 D2
Trellech Grange.36 D1
Trelogan....85 F2
Trelystan...60 D2
Tremadog....71 C6
Tremail......8 F3
Tremain.....45 E4
Tremaine....8 F4
Tremar......5 C7
Trematon....5 D8
Tremeirchion.72 B4
Trenance....4 C3
Trenarren....3 B9
Trench......61 C6
Treneglos....8 F4
Trenewan....5 D6
Trent......12 C3
Trentham....75 E5
Trentishoe..20 E5
Trent Vale...75 E5
Treoes......21 B8
Treorchy
 =Treorci...34 E3
Treorci
 =Treorchy..34 E3
Tre'r-ddôl...58 E3
Trerulefoot...5 D8
Tresaith....45 D4
Tresawle.....3 B7
Trescott....62 E2
Trescowe....2 C4
Tresham....36 E4
Tresillian...3 B7
Tresinwen...44 A4
Treskinnick Cross.8 E4
Tresmeer....8 F4
Tresparrett..8 E3
Tresparrett Posts.8 E3
Tressait....133 C5
Tresta
 Shetland...160 D8
 Shetland...160 H5
Treswell....77 B7
Tre-Taliesin.58 E3
Trethosa....4 D4
Trethurgy....4 D5
Tretio......44 C2
Tretire.....36 B2
Tretower....35 B5
Treuddyn....73 D6
Trevalga.....8 F2
Trevalyn....73 D7
Trevanson....4 B4
Trevarren....4 C3
Trevarrian...4 C3
Trevarrick...3 B8
Trevaughan..32 C2
Tre-vaughan.32 B4
Treveighan...5 B5
Trevellas....3 D6
Treverva....3 C6
Trevethin...35 D6
Trevigro....5 C8
Treviscoe....4 D4
Trevone......4 B3
Trewarmett...8 F2
Trewassa.....8 F3
Trewellard...2 C2
Trewen......8 F4
Trewennack...3 D5
Trewern....60 C2
Trewethern...4 B5
Trewidland...5 D7
Trewint......8 E3
Trewithian...3 C7
Trewoofe....2 D3
Trewoon......3 D8
Treworga....3 C7
Treworlas....3 C7
Tre-wyn.....35 B7
Treyarnon....4 B3
Treyford....16 C2
Trezaise.....4 D4
Triangle....87 B8
Trickett's Cross.13 D8
Triffleton...44 C4
Trimdon....111 F6
Trimdon
 Colliery...111 F6
Trimdon Grange.111 F6
Trimingham..81 D8
Trimley Lower
 Street.....57 F6
Trimley St Martin.57 F6
Trimley St Mary.57 F6
Trimpley....50 B2
Trimsaran...33 D5
Trimstone...20 E3
Trinafour...132 C4
Trinant.....35 D6
Tring.......40 C2
Tring Wharf..40 C2
Trinity
 Angus.....135 C6
 Jersey.....17 I3
Trisant.....47 B6
Trislaig...130 B4
Trispen......4 D3
Tritlington.117 E8
Trochry....133 E6
Trodigal...143 F7
Troed-rhiwdalar.47 D8
Troedyraur..46 E2
Troedyrhiw..34 D4
Tromode.....84 E3
Trondavoe..160 F5
Troon
 Corn.......3 C5
 S Ayrs.....118 F3
Trosaraidh..148 G2
Trossachs Hotel.126 D4
Troston....56 B2
Trottiscliffe.29 C7
Trotton....16 B2

Troutbeck
 Cumb.......99 B5
 Cumb.......99 D6
Troutbeck Bridge.99 D6
Trowbridge..24 D3
Trowell.....76 F4
Trow Green..36 D2
Trowley Bottom.40 C3
Trows......122 F2
Trowse Newton.68 D5
Trudoxhill...24 E2
Trull......11 B7
Trumaisgearraidh
 ...........148 A3
Trumpan....148 B7
Trumpet.....49 F8
Trumpington.54 D5
Trunch......81 D8
Trunnah.....92 E3
Truro......3 B7
Trusham.....10 F3
Trusley.....76 F2
Trusthorpe..91 F9
Trysull.....62 E2
Tubney......38 E4
Tuckenhay....7 D7
Tuckhill....61 F7
Tuckingmill..3 B5
Tuddenham
 St Martin..57 E5
Tuddenham...55 B8
Tudeley.....29 E7
Tudhoe.....111 F5
Tudorville..36 B2
Tudweiliog..70 D3
Tuesley.....27 E7
Tuffley.....37 C5
Tufton
 Hants......26 E2
 Pembs......32 B1
Tugby......64 D4
Tugford......61 F5
Tullibardine.127 C8
Tullibody..127 E7
Tullich
 Argyll.....125 D6
 Highld.....138 B2
Tullich Muir.151 D10
Tulliemet..133 D6
Tulloch
 Aberds.....135 B7
 Aberds.....153 E8
 Perth......128 B2
Tulloch Castle.151 E8
Tullochgorm.125 F5
Tulloes.....135 E5
Tullybannocher.127 B6
Tullybelton.133 F7
Tullyfergus.134 E2
Tullymurdoch.134 D1
Tullynessle..140 C4
Tumble......33 C6
Tumby Woodside.79 D5
Tummel Bridge.132 D4
Tunga......155 D9
Tunstall
 E Yorks....97 F9
 Kent.......30 C2
 Lancs......93 B6
 Norf.......69 D7
 N Yorks...101 E7
 Stoke......75 D5
 Suff.......57 D7
 T&W........111 D6
Tunstead
 Derbys.....75 B8
 Gtr Man....87 D8
 Norf.......81 E8
Tunworth...26 E4
Tupsley.....49 E7
Tupton.....76 C3
Turgis Green.26 D4
Turin......135 D5
Turkdean....37 C8
Tur Langton.64 E4
Turleigh....24 C3
Turn.......87 C6
Turnastone..49 F5
Turnberry..112 D2
Turnditch...76 E2
Turners Hill.28 F4
Turners Puddle.13 E6
Turnford....41 D6
Turnhouse..120 B4
Turnworth...13 D6
Turriff....153 C7
Turton Bottoms.86 C5
Turves......66 E3
Turvey......53 D7
Turville....39 E7
Turville Heath.39 E7
Turweston...52 F4
Tushielaw..115 C6
Tutbury.....63 B6
Tutnall.....50 B4
Tutshill....36 E2
Tuttington..81 E8
Tutts Clump.26 B3
Tuxford.....77 B7
Twatt
 Orkney.....159 F3
 Shetland...160 H5
Twechar....119 B7
Tweedmouth.123 D5
Tweedsmuir.114 B3
Twelve Heads..3 B6
Twelvewoods..5 C7
Twenham.....17 B8
Twenty......65 B8
Twerton.....24 C2
Twickenham..28 B2
Twigworth...37 B5
Twineham....17 C6
Twinhoe.....24 D2
Twinstead...56 F2
Twinstead Green.56 F2
Twiss Green..86 E4
Twiston.....93 E8
Twitchen
 Devon......21 F6
 Shrops.....49 B5
Two Bridges..6 B4
Two Dales...76 C2
Two Mills...73 B7
Twycross....63 D7
Twyford
 Bucks......39 B6
 Derbys.....63 B7

Twyford continued
 Hants......15 B5
 Leics......64 C4
 Lincs......65 B6
 Norf.......81 E6
 Wokingham..27 B5
Twyford Common.49 F7
Twynholm....106 D3
Twyning.....50 F4
Twyning Green.50 F4
Twynllanan..34 B1
Twyn-y-Sheriff.35 D8
Twywell.....53 B7
Tyberton....49 F5
Tyburn......62 E5
Tycroes.....33 C7
Tycrwyn.....59 C8
Tyddewi
 =St David's.44 C2
Tydd Gote....66 C4
Tydd St Giles.66 C4
Tydd St Mary.66 C4
Tyddyn-mawr..71 C6
Ty-draw.....83 F8
Tye Green
 Essex......41 D7
 Essex......42 B3
 Essex......55 F6
Ty-hen
 Carms......32 B4
 Gwyn.......70 D2
Tyldesley...86 D4
Tyler Hill...30 C5
Tylers Green.40 E2
Tylorstown..34 E4
Tylwch......59 F6
Ty-mawr.....82 C4
Ty Mawr Cwm..72 E3
Ty-nant
 Conwy......72 E3
 Gwyn.......59 B6
Tyncelyn....73 F5
Tyndrum....131 F7
Tyneham.....13 F6
Tynehead...121 D6
Tynemouth..111 C6
Tyne Tunnel.111 C6
Tynewydd...34 E3
Tyninghame.122 B2
Tynron.....113 E8
Tyn-y-celyn.73 F5
Tyn-y-coed..60 B2
Tyn-y-fedwen.72 F5
Tyn-y-ffridd.72 F5
Tynygongl...82 C5
Tynygraig....47 C5
Tyn-y-graig..48 D2
Ty'n-y-groes.83 D7
Ty'n-y-maes.83 E6
Tyn-y-pwll...82 C4
Ty'n-yr-eithin.47 C5
Tyrie......153 B9
Tyringham...53 E6
Tythecott....9 C6
Tythegston..21 B7
Tytherington
 Ches E.....75 B6
 S Glos.....36 F3
 Som........24 E2
 Wilts......24 E4
Tytherleigh..11 D8
Ty-uchaf.....59 B7
Tywardreath..5 D5
Tywyn
 Conwy......83 D7
 Gwyn.......58 D2

**U**

Uachdar....148 C2
Uags.......149 E12
Ubbeston Green.57 B7
Ubley.......23 D7
Uckerby....101 D7
Uckfield....17 B8
Uckington...37 B6
Uddingston.119 C6
Uddington..119 F8
Udimore....19 D5
Udny Green..141 B7
Udny Station.141 B8
Udston....119 C6
Udstonhead.119 E7
Uffcott.....25 B6
Uffculme....11 C5
Uffington
 Lincs......65 D7
 Oxon.......38 F3
 Shrops.....60 C5
Ufford
 Pboro......65 D7
 Suff.......57 D6
Ufton......51 C8
Ufton Nervet.26 C4
Ugadale....143 F8
Ugborough....6 D4
Uggeshall...69 F7
Ugglebarnby.103 D6
Ughill......88 E3
Ugley......41 B8
Ugley Green..41 B8
Ugthorpe...103 C5
Uidh.......148 J1
Uig
 Argyll.....145 E10
 Highld.....148 C6
 Highld.....149 B8
Uigen......154 D5
Uigshader..149 D9
Uisken.....146 K6
Ulbster....158 F5
Ulceby
 Lincs......79 B7
 N Lincs....90 C5
Ulceby Skitter.90 C5
Ulcombe....30 E2
Uldale.....108 F2
Uley.......36 D4
Ulgham.....117 E8
Ullapool...156 J3
Ullenhall...51 C6
Ullenwood...37 C6
Ulleskelf...95 E8
Ullesthorpe..64 F2

Ulley.......89 F5
Ullingswick.49 E7
Ullinish...149 E8
Ullock......98 B2
Ulnes Walton.86 C3
Ulpha......98 E3
Ulrome......97 D7
Ulsta......160 E6
Ulva House..146 H7
Ulverston...92 B2
Ulwell......13 F8
Umberleigh...9 B8
Unapool....156 F5
Unasary....148 F2
Underbarrow.99 E6
Undercliffe..94 F4
Underhoull..160 C7
Underriver..29 D6
Underwood...76 D4
Undy.......35 F8
Unifirth...160 H4
Union Cottage.141 E7
Union Mills..84 E3
Union Street.18 B4
Unstone.....76 B3
Unstone Green.76 B3
Unthank
 Cumb......108 F4
 Cumb......109 E6
Unthank End.108 F4
Upavon......25 D6
Up Cerne....12 D4
Upchurch....30 C2
Upcott......48 D5
Upend......55 D7
Up Exe......10 D4
Upgate......68 C4
Uphall.....120 B3
Uphall Station.120 B3
Upham......15 B6
Uphampton..50 C3
Up Hatherley.37 B6
Up Holland..86 D3
Uplawmoor..118 D4
Upleadon....36 B4
Upleatham..102 C4
Uplees......30 C3
Uploders....12 E3
Uplowman...10 C5
Uplyme......11 E8
Up Marden...15 C8
Upminster...42 F1
Up Nately...26 D4
Upnor......29 B8
Upottery....11 D7
Upper Affcot..60 F4
Upper
 Ardchronie.151 C9
Upper Arley..61 F7
Upper Arncott.39 C6
Upper Astrop..52 F3
Upper Badcall.156 E4
Upper Basildon.26 B3
Upper Beeding.17 C5
Upper Benefield.65 F6
Upper
 Bighouse..157 D11
Upper
 Boddington.52 D2
Upper Borth..58 F3
Upper Boyndlie.153 B9
Upper Brailes.51 F8
Upper Breakish.149 F11
Upper Breinton.49 E6
Upper
 Broadheath.50 D3
Upper Broughton.64 B3
Upper
 Bucklebury.26 C3
Upper
 Burnhaugh.141 E7
Upperby....108 D4
Upper Caldecote.54 E2
Upper Catesby.52 D3
Upper Chapel.48 E2
Upper Church
 Village....34 F4
Upper Chute..25 D7
Upper Clatford.25 E8
Upper Clynnog.71 C5
Upper
 Cumberworth.88 D3
Upper Cwmbran.35 E6
Upper Dallachy.152 B3
Upper Dean..53 C8
Upper Denby..88 D3
Upper Denton.109 C6
Upper Derraid.151 H13
Upper Dicker.18 E2
Upper Dovercourt.57 F6
Upper Druimfin.147 F8
Upper Dunsforth.95 C7
Upper Eathie.151 E10
Upper Elkstone.75 D7
Upper End....75 B8
Upper Farringdon.26 F5
Upper Framilode.36 C4
Upper
 Glenfintaig.137 F5
Upper Gornal..62 E3
Upper
 Gravenhurst.54 F2
Upper Green
 Mon........35 C7
 W Berks....25 C8
Upper Grove
 Common....36 B2
Upper Hackney.76 C2
Upper Halistra.148 C7
Upper Halling.29 C7
Upper
 Hambleton.65 D6
Upper Hardres
 Court......31 D5
Upper Hartfield.29 F5
Upper Haugh..88 E5
Upper Heath..61 F5
Upper Hellesdon.68 C5
Upper Helmsley.96 D2
Upper Hergest.48 D4
Upper Heyford
 Northants..52 D4
Upper Hill...49 D6

Upper Hopton..88 C2
Upper
 Horsebridge.18 D2
Upper Hulme..75 C7
Upper Inglesham.38 E2
Upper
 Inverbrough.151 H11
Upper Killay..33 E6
Upper
 Knockando..152 D1
Upper Lambourn.38 F3
Upper Leigh..75 F7
Upper Lenie.137 B8
Upper Lochton.141 E5
Upper Longdon.62 C4
Upper Lybster.158 G4
Upper Lydbrook.36 C3
Upper
 Maes-coed..48 F5
Upper Midway.63 B6
Upper Milovaig.148 D6
Upper Minety..37 E7
Upper Mitton..50 B3
Upper
 North Dean..39 E8
Upper Obney.133 F7
Upper Ollach.149 E10
Upper Padley..76 B2
Upper Pollicott.39 C7
Upper Poppleton.95 D8
Upper Quinton.51 E6
Upper Ratley..14 B4
Upper Rissington.38 C2
Upper Rochford.49 C8
Upper Sandaig.149 G12
Upper Sanday.159 H6
Upper Sapey..49 C8
Upper Saxondale.77 F6
Upper Seagry..37 F6
Upper Shelton.53 E7
Upper
 Sheringham.81 C7
Upper
 Skelmorlie.118 C2
Upper Slaughter.38 B1
Upper Soudley.36 C3
Uppersound..160 J6
Upper Stondale.54 F2
Upper Stowe..52 D4
Upper Stratton.38 F1
Upper Street
 Hants......14 C2
 Norf.......69 C6
 Norf.......69 C6
 Suff.......56 F5
Upper Strensham.50 F3
Upper Sundon.40 B3
Upper Swell..38 B1
Upper Tean...75 F7
Upperthong..88 D2
Upperthorpe.89 D8
Upperton....16 B3
Upper Tillyrie.128 C3
Upper Tooting.28 B3
Upper Tote..149 C10
Upper Town..23 C7
Upper
 Treverward..48 B4
Upper Tysoe..51 E8
Upper Upham..25 B7
Upper
 Wardington..52 E2
Upper Weald..53 F5
Upper Weedon.52 D4
Upper Wield..26 F4
Upper
 Winchendon.39 C7
Upper Witton..62 E4
Upper Woodend.141 C5
Upper Woodford.25 F6
Upper Wootton.26 D3
Upper Wyche..50 E2
Uppingham...65 E5
Uppington...61 D6
Upsall.....102 F2
Upshire....41 D7
Up Somborne.25 F8
Upstreet....31 C6
Up Sydling..12 D4
Upthorpe....56 B3
Upton
 Cambs......54 B2
 Ches W.....73 C8
 Corn.......8 A4
 Dorset.....12 F5
 Dorset.....13 E7
 Hants......14 C4
 Hants......25 D8
 Leics......63 E7
 Lincs......90 F2
 Mers.......85 F3
 Norf.......69 C6
 Notts......77 B7
 Notts......77 D7
 Oxon.......39 F5
 Pboro......65 D8
 Slough.....27 B7
Upton Bishop.36 B3
Upton Cheyney.23 C8
Upton Cressett.61 E6
Upton Cross..5 B7
Upton Grey..26 E4
Upton Hellions.10 D3
Upton Lovell.24 E4
Upton Magna..61 C5
Upton Noble..24 F2
Upton Pyne..10 E4
Upton
 St Leonard's.37 C5
Upton
 Scudamore..24 E3
Upton Snodsbury.50 D4
Upton upon
 Severn.....50 E3
Upton Warren.50 C4
Upware......55 B6
Upwell......66 D5
Upwey......12 F4
Upwood......66 F2

Uradale.....160 K6
Urafirth....160 F5
Urchfont....24 D5
Urdimarsh...49 E7
Ure........160 F4
Ure Bank....95 B6
Urgha......154 H6
Urishay Common.48 F5
Urlay Nook..102 C1
Urmston.....87 E5
Urpeth.....110 D5
Urquhart
 Highld.....151 F8
 Moray......152 B2
Urra.......102 D3
Urray......151 F8
Ushaw Moor..110 E5
Usk =Brynbuga.35 D7
Usselby.....90 E4
Usworth....111 D6
Utkinton....74 C2
Utley.......94 E3
Uton.......10 E3
Utterby.....91 E7
Uttoxeter...75 F7
Uwchmynydd..70 E2
Uxbridge....40 F3
Uyeasound..160 C7

**V**

Valley......82 D2
Valleyfield.106 D3
Valley Truckle.8 F2
Valsgarth..160 B8
Valtos.....149 B10
Van........59 F6
Vange......42 F3
Varteg......35 D6
Vatten.....149 D7
Vaul.......146 G3
Vaynor.....34 C4
Veensgarth..160 J6
Velindre....48 F3
Vellow......22 F2
Veness.....159 F6
Venn Green...9 C5
Vennington..60 D3
Venn Ottery..11 E5
Venny Tedburn.10 E3
Ventnor.....15 G6
Vernham Dean.25 D8
Vernham Street.25 D8
Vernolds
 Common....60 F4
Verwood.....13 D8
Veryan......3 C8
Vicarage....11 F7
Vickerstown.92 C1
Victoria
 Corn.......4 C4
 S Yorks....88 D2
Vidlin.....160 G6
Viewpark...119 C7
Vigo Village.29 C7
Vinehall Street.18 C4
Vine's Cross.18 D2
Viney Hill...36 D3
Virginia Water.27 C8
Virginstow...9 E5
Vobster.....24 E2
Voe
 Shetland...160 E6
 Shetland...160 G6
Vowchurch...49 F5
Voxter.....160 F5
Voy........159 G4

**W**

Wackerfield.101 B6
Wacton......68 E4
Wadbister..160 J6
Wadborough..50 E4
Waddesdon...39 C7
Waddingham..90 E3
Waddington
 Lancs......93 E7
 Lincs......78 C2
Wadebridge...4 B4
Wadeford....11 C8
Wadenhoe....65 F7
Wadesmill...41 C6
Wadhurst....18 B3
Wadshelf....76 B3
Wadsley.....88 E4
Wadsley Bridge.88 E4
Wadworth....89 E6
Waen
 Denb.......72 C3
 Denb.......72 C5
Waen Fach...60 C2
Waen Goleugoed.72 B4
Wag........157 G13
Wainfleet All
 Saints.....79 D7
Wainfleet Bank.79 D7
Wainfleet
 St Mary....79 D7
Wainfleet Tofts.79 D7
Wainhouse Corner.8 E3
Wainscott...29 B8
Wainstalls..87 B8
Waitby.....100 D2
Waithe......91 D6
Wakefield...88 B4
Wake Lady
 Green.....102 E4
Wakerley....65 E6
Wakes Colne..56 F3
Walberswick.57 B8
Walberton...16 D3
Walbottle..110 C4
Walcot
 Lincs......78 F4
 N Lincs....90 B2
 Shrops.....60 F3
 Swindon....38 F1
 Telford....61 C5
Walcote
 Leics......64 F2
 Warks......51 D6
Walcot Green.68 F4
Walcott
 Lincs......78 D4

Walcott *continued*
Norf 69 A6
Walden 101 F5
Walden Head 100 F4
Walden Stubbs 89 C6
Waldersey 66 D4
Walderslade 29 C8
Walderton 15 C8
Walditch 12 E2
Waldley 75 F8
Waldridge 111 D5
Waldringfield 57 E6
Waldringfield Heath 57 E6
Waldron 18 D2
Wales 89 F5
Walesby
Lincs 90 E5
Notts 77 B6
Walford
Hereford 36 B2
Hereford 49 B5
Shrops 60 B4
Walford Heath 60 C4
Walgherton 74 E3
Walgrave 53 B6
Walhampton 14 E4
Walkden 86 D5
Walker 111 C5
Walker Barn 75 B6
Walkerburn 121 F6
Walker Fold 93 E6
Walkeringham 89 E8
Walkerith 89 E8
Walkern 41 B5
Walker's Green 49 E7
Walkerville 101 E7
Walkford 14 E3
Walkhampton 6 C3
Walkington 97 F5
Walkley 88 F4
Walk Mill 93 F8
Wall
Northumb 110 C2
Staffs 62 D5
Wallaceton 113 F8
Wallacetown
S Ayrs 112 B3
S Ayrs 112 D2
Wallands Park 17 C8
Wallasey 85 E4
Wall Bank 60 E5
Wallcrouch 18 B3
Wall Heath 62 F2
Wallingford 39 F6
Wallington
Hants 15 D6
Herts 54 F3
London 28 C3
Wallis 32 B1
Walliswood 28 F2
Walls 160 J4
Wallsend 111 C5
Wallston 22 B3
Wall under Heywood 60 E5
Wallyford 121 B6
Walmer 31 D7
Walmer Bridge 86 B2
Walmersley 87 C6
Walmley 62 E5
Walpole 57 B7
Walpole Cross Keys 66 C5
Walpole Highway 66 C5
Walpole Marsh 66 C4
Walpole St Andrew 66 C5
Walpole St Peter 66 C5
Walsall 62 E4
Walsall Wood 62 D4
Walsden 87 B7
Walsgrave on Sowe 63 F7
Walsham le Willows 56 B3
Walshaw 87 C5
Walshford 95 D7
Walsoken 66 C4
Walston 120 E3
Walsworth 54 F3
Walters Ash 39 E8
Walterston 22 B2
Walterstone 35 B7
Waltham
Kent 30 E5
NE Lincs 91 D6
Waltham Abbey 41 D6
Waltham Chase 15 C6
Waltham Cross 41 D6
Waltham on the Wolds 64 B5
Waltham St Lawrence 27 B6
Walthamstow 41 F6
Walton
Cumb 108 C5
Derbys 76 C3
Leics 64 F2
Mers 85 E4
M Keynes 53 F6
Pboro 65 D8
Powys 48 D4
Som 23 F6
Staffs 75 F5
Suff 57 F6
Telford 61 C5
Warks 51 D7
W Yorks 88 C4
W Yorks 95 E7
Walton Cardiff 50 F4
Walton East 32 B1
Walton-in-Gordano 23 B6
Walton-le-Dale 86 B3
Walton-on-Thames 28 C2
Walton on the Hill
Staffs 62 B3
Sur 28 D3
Walton-on-the-Naze 43 B8
Walton on the Wolds 64 C2
Walton-on-Trent 63 C6
Walton West 44 D3
Walwen 73 B6
Walwick 110 B2
Walworth 101 C7
Walworth Gate 101 B7
Walwyn's Castle 44 D3
Wambrook 11 D7
Wanborough
Sur 27 E7
Swindon 38 F2
Wandsworth 28 B3
Wangford 57 B8
Wanlockhead 113 C8
Wansford
E Yorks 97 D6
Pboro 65 E7
Wanstead 41 F7
Wanstrow 24 E2
Wanswell 36 D3
Wantage 38 F3
Wapley 24 B2
Wappenbury 51 C8
Wappenham 52 E4
Warbleton 18 D3
Warblington 15 D8
Warborough 39 E5
Warboys 66 F3
Warbreck 92 F3
Warbstow 8 E4
Warburton 86 F5
Warcop 100 C2
Warden
Kent 30 B4
Northumb 110 C2
Ward End 62 F5
Ward Green 56 C4
Wardhill 159 F7
Wardington 52 E2
Wardlaw 115 C5
Wardle
Ches E 74 D3
Gtr Man 87 C7
Wardley 64 D5
Wardlow 75 B8
Wardy Hill 66 F4
Ware
Herts 41 C6
Kent 31 C6
Wareham 13 F7
Warehorne 19 B6
Warenford 117 B7
Waren Mill 123 F7
Warenton 123 F7
Wareside 41 C6
Waresley
Cambs 54 D3
Worcs 50 B3
Warfield 27 B6
Warfleet 7 D6
Wargrave 27 B5
Warham 80 C5
Warhill 87 E7
Wark
Northumb 109 B8
Northumb 122 F4
Warkleigh 9 B8
Warkton 53 B6
Warkworth
Northumb 117 D8
W Nhants 52 E2
Warlaby 101 E8
Warland 87 B7
Warleggan 5 C6
Warlingham 28 D4
Warmfield 88 B4
Warmingham 74 C4
Warmington
N Nhants 65 E7
Warks 52 E2
Warminster 24 E3
Warmlake 30 D2
Warmley 23 B8
Warmley Tower 23 B8
Warmonds Hill 53 C7
Warmsworth 89 D6
Warmwell 13 F5
Warndon 50 D3
Warnford 15 B7
Warnham 28 F2
Warninglid 17 B6
Warren
Ches E 75 B5
Pembs 44 F4
Warren Heath 57 E6
Warren Row 39 F8
Warren Street 30 D3
Warrington
M Keynes 53 D6
Warr 86 F4
Warsash 15 D5
Warslow 75 D7
Warter 96 D4
Warthermarske 94 B5
Warthill 96 D2
Wartling 18 E3
Wartnaby 64 B4
Warton
Lancs 86 B2
Lancs 92 B4
Northumb 117 D6
Warks 63 D6
Warwick 51 C7
Warwick Bridge 108 D4
Warwick on Eden 108 D4
Wasbister 159 E4
Wasdale Head 98 D3
Washaway 4 C5
Washbourne 7 D5
Wash Common 26 C2
Washfield 10 C4
Washfold 101 D5
Washford 22 E2
Washford Pyne 10 C3
Washingborough 78 B3
Washington
T&W 111 D6
W Sus 16 C5
Wasing 26 C3
Waskerley 110 E3
Wasperton 51 D7
Wasps Nest 78 C3
Wass 95 B8
Watchet 22 E2
Watchfield
Oxon 38 E2
Som 22 E5
Watchgate 99 E7
Watchhill 107 E8
Watcombe 7 C7
Watendlath 98 C4
Water
Devon 10 F2
Lancs 87 B6
Waterbeach 55 C5
Waterbeck 108 B2
Waterden 80 D4
Water End
E Yorks 96 F3
Herts 40 C3
Herts 41 D5
Waterfall 75 D7
Waterfoot
E Renf 119 D5
Lancs 87 B6
Waterford
Hants 14 E4
Herts 41 C6
Waterhead
Cumb 99 D5
Dumfries 114 E4
Waterheads 120 D5
Waterhouses
Durham 110 E4
Staffs 75 D7
Wateringbury 29 D7
Waterloo
BCP 13 E8
Gtr Man 87 D7
Highld 149 F11
Mers 85 E4
N Lanark 119 D8
Norf 68 C5
Perth 133 F7
Shrops 74 F2
Waterloo Port 82 E4
Waterlooville 15 D7
Watermeetings 114 C2
Watermillock 99 B6
Water Newton 65 E8
Water Orton 63 E5
Waterperry 39 D6
Waterrow 11 B5
Watersfield 16 C4
Waterside
Aberds 141 B9
Blackburn 86 B5
Cumb 108 E2
E Ayrs 112 D4
E Ayrs 118 E4
E Dunb 119 B6
E Renf 118 D5
Water's Nook 86 D4
Waterstock 39 D6
Waterston 44 E4
Water Stratford 52 F4
Waters Upton 61 C6
Water Yeat 98 F4
Watford
Herts 40 E4
W Nhants 52 C4
Watford Gap 62 D5
Wath
N Yorks 94 C4
N Yorks 95 B6
N Yorks 96 B2
Wath Brow 98 C2
Wath upon Dearne 88 D5
Watlington
Norf 67 C6
Oxon 39 E6
Watnall 76 E5
Watten 158 E4
Wattisfield 56 B4
Wattisham 56 D4
Wattlesborough Heath 60 C3
Watton
E Yorks 97 D6
Norf 68 D2
Watton at Stone 41 C6
Wattston 119 B7
Wattstown 34 E4
Wauchan 136 F2
Waulkmill Lodge 159 H4
Waun 59 D5
Waunarlwydd 33 E7
Waunclunda 47 F5
Waunfawr 82 F5
Waungron 33 D6
Waunlwyd 35 D5
Waun-y-clyn 33 D5
Wavendon 53 F7
Waverbridge 108 E2
Waverton
Ches W 73 C8
Cumb 108 E2
Wavertree 85 F4
Wawne 97 F6
Waxham 69 B7
Waxholme 91 B7
Way 31 C7
Wayfield 29 C8
Wayford 12 D2
Waymills 74 E2
Wayne Green 35 C8
Way Village 10 C3
Wdig = *Goodwick* 44 B4
Weachyburn 153 C6
Weald 38 D3
Wealdstone 40 F4
Weardley 95 E5
Weare 23 D6
Weare Giffard 9 B6
Wearhead 109 F8
Weasdale 100 D1
Weasenham All Saints 80 E4
Weasenham St Peter 80 E4
Weatherhill 28 E4
Weaverham 74 B3
Weaverthorpe 97 B5
Webheath 50 C5
Wedderlairs 153 E8
Wedderlie 122 D2
Weddington 63 E7
Wedhampton 25 D5
Wedmore 23 E6
Wednesbury 62 E3
Wednesfield 62 D3
Weedon 39 C8
Weedon Bec 52 D4
Weedon Lois 52 E4
Weeford 62 D5
Week 10 C2
Weeke 26 F2
Weekley 65 F5
Week St Mary 8 E4
Weel 97 F6
Weeley 43 B7
Weeley Heath 43 B7
Weem 133 E5
Weeping Cross 62 B3
Weethley Gate 51 D5
Weeting 67 F7
Weeton
E Yorks 91 B7
Lancs 92 F3
N Yorks 95 E5
Weetwood Hall 117 B6
Weir 87 B6
Weir Quay 6 C2
Welborne 68 D3
Welbourn 78 D2
Welburn
N Yorks 96 C3
N Yorks 102 F4
Welbury 102 D1
Welby 78 F2
Welches Dam 66 F4
Welcombe 8 C4
Weld Bank 86 C3
Weldon 117 E7
Welford
W Berks 26 B2
W Nhants 64 F3
Welford-on-Avon 51 D6
Welham
Leics 64 E4
Notts 89 F8
Welham Green 41 D5
Well
Hants 27 E5
Lincs 79 B7
N Yorks 101 F7
Welland 50 E2
Wellbank 134 F4
Welldale 107 C8
Well End 40 F1
Wellesbourne 51 D7
Well Heads 94 F3
Well Hill 29 C5
Welling 29 B5
Wellingborough 53 C6
Wellingham 80 E4
Wellingore 78 D2
Wellington
Cumb 98 D2
Hereford 49 E6
Som 11 B6
Telford 61 C6
Wellington Heath 50 E2
Wellington Hill 95 F6
Wellow
Bath 24 D2
IoW 14 F4
Notts 77 C6
Wellpond Green 41 B7
Wells 23 E7
Wellsborough 63 D7
Wells Green 74 D3
Wells-next-the-Sea 80 C5
Wellswood 7 C7
Well Town 10 D4
Wellwood 128 F2
Welney 66 E5
Welshampton 73 F8
Welsh Bicknor 36 C2
Welsh End 74 F2
Welsh Frankton 73 F7
Welsh Hook 44 C4
Welsh Newton 36 C1
Welshpool = *Y Trallwng* 60 D2
Welsh St Donats 22 B2
Welton
Cumb 108 E3
E Yorks 90 B3
Lincs 78 B3
W Nhants 52 C3
Welton Hill 90 F4
Welton le Marsh 79 C7
Welton le Wold 91 F6
Welwick 91 B7
Welwyn 41 C5
Welwyn Garden City 41 C5
Wem 60 B5
Wembdon 22 F4
Wembley 40 F4
Wembury 6 E3
Wembworthy 9 D8
Wemyss Bay 118 C1
Wenallt
Ceredig 47 B5
Gwyn 72 E3
Wendens Ambo 55 F6
Wendlebury 39 C5
Wendling 68 C2
Wendover 40 D1
Wendron 3 C5
Wendy 54 E4
Wenfordbridge 5 B5
Wenhaston 57 B8
Wennington
Cambs 54 B3
Lancs 93 B6
London 41 F8
Wensley
Derbys 76 C2
N Yorks 101 F5
Wentbridge 89 C5
Wentnor 60 E3
Wentworth
Cambs 55 B5
S Yorks 88 E4
Wenvoe 22 B3
Weobley 49 D6
Weobley Marsh 49 D6
Wereham 67 D6
Wergs 62 D2
Wern
Powys 59 C6
Powys 60 C2
Wernffrwd 33 E6
Wernyrheolydd 35 C7
Werrington
Corn 8 F5
Pboro 65 D8
Staffs 75 E6
Wervin 73 B8
Wesham 92 F4
Wessington 76 D3
Westacott 20 F4
West Acre 67 C7
West Adderbury 52 F2
West Allerdean 123 E5
West Alvington 6 E5
West Amesbury 25 E6
West Anstey 10 B3
West Ashby 79 B5
West Ashling 16 D2
West Ashton 24 D3
West Auckland 101 B6
West Ayton 103 F7
West Bagborough 22 F3
West Barkwith 91 F5
West Barnby 103 C6
West Barns 122 B2
West Barsham 80 D5
West Bay 12 E2
West Beckham 81 D7
West Bedfont 27 B8
West Benhar 119 C8
Westbere 31 C5
West Bergholt 43 B5
West Bexington 12 F3
West Bilney 67 C7
West Blatchington 17 D6
Westborough 77 E8
Westbourne
BCP 13 E8
Suff 56 E5
W Sus 15 D8
West Bowling 94 F4
West Bradford 93 E7
West Bradley 23 F7
West Bretton 88 C3
West Bridgford 77 F5
West Bromwich 62 E4
Westbrook 26 B2
West Buckland
Devon 21 F5
Som 11 B6
West Burrafirth 160 H4
West Burton
N Yorks 101 F5
W Sus 16 C3
Westbury
Bucks 52 F4
Shrops 60 D3
Wilts 24 D3
Westbury Leigh 24 D3
Westbury-on-Severn 36 C4
Westbury on Trym 23 B7
Westbury-sub-Mendip 23 E7
West Butterwick 90 D2
Westby 92 F3
West Byfleet 27 C8
West Caister 69 C8
West Calder 120 C3
West Camel 12 B3
West Challow 38 F3
West Chelborough 12 D3
West Chevington 117 E8
West Chiltington 16 C4
West Chiltington Common 16 C4
West Chinnock 12 C2
West Chisenbury 25 D6
West Clandon 27 D8
West Cliffe 31 E7
Westcliff-on-Sea 42 F4
West Clyne 157 J11
West Clyth 158 G4
West Coker 12 C3
Westcombe 23 F8
West Compton
Dorset 12 E3
Som 23 E7
Westcote 38 B2
Westcott
Bucks 39 C7
Devon 10 D5
Sur 28 E2
Westcott Barton 38 B4
West Cowick 89 B7
West Cranmore 23 E8
West Cross 33 F7
West Cullery 141 D6
West Curry 8 E4
West Curthwaite 108 E3
West Darlochan 143 F7
Westdean 18 F2
West Dean
Wilts 14 B3
W Sus 16 C2
West Deeping 65 D8
Westdene 17 D6
West Derby 85 E4
West Dereham 67 D6
West Didsbury 87 E6
West Ditchburn 117 B7
West Down 20 E4
West Drayton
London 27 B8
Notts 77 B7
West Ella 90 B4
West End
Bedford 53 D7
E Yorks 96 F5
E Yorks 97 F7
Hants 15 C5
Lancs 86 B5
Norf 68 D2
Norf 69 C8
N Som 23 C6
N Yorks 94 D4
Oxon 38 D4
S Lanark 120 E2
Suff 69 F7
Sur 27 C7
S Yorks 89 D7
Wilts 13 B7
Wilts 24 B4
W Sus 17 C6
West End Green 26 C4
Wester Aberchalder 137 B8
Wester Balgedie 128 D3
Wester Culbeuchly 153 B6
Westerdale
Highld 158 E3
N Yorks 102 D4
Wester Dechmont 120 C3
Wester Denoon 134 E3
Westerfield
Shetland 160 H5
Suff 57 E5
Wester Fintray 141 C7
Westergate 16 D3
Wester Gruinards 151 B8
Westerham 28 D5
Westerhope 110 C4
Wester Lealty 151 D9
Westerleigh 23 B9
Wester Milton 151 F12
Wester Newburn 129 D6
Wester Quarff 160 K6
Wester Skeld 160 J4
Westerton
Angus 135 D6
Durham 110 F5
W Sus 16 D2
Westerwick 160 J4
West Farleigh 29 D8
West Felton 60 B3
West Fenton 129 F6
West Ferry 134 F4
Westfield
Cumb 98 B1
E Sus 18 D5
Hereford 50 E2
Highld 158 D2
N Lanark 119 B7
Norf 68 D2
W Loth 120 B2
Westfields 12 D5
Westfields of Rattray 134 E1
West Firle 17 D8
Westgate
Durham 110 F2
N Lincs 89 D8
Norf 80 C4
Norf 81 C5
Westgate on Sea 31 B7
West Ginge 38 F4
West Grafton 25 C7
West Green 26 D5
West Greenskares 153 B7
West Grimstead 14 B3
West Grinstead 17 B5
West Haddlesey 89 B6
West Haddon 52 B4
West Hagbourne 39 F5
West Hagley 62 F3
Westhall
Aberds 141 B5
Suff 69 F7
West Hall 109 C5
West Hallam 76 E4
West Halton 90 B3
Westham
Dorset 12 G4
E Sus 18 E3
Som 23 E6
West Ham 41 F7
Westhampnett 16 D2
West Handley 76 B3
West Hanney 38 E4
West Hanningfield 42 E3
West Hardwick 88 C5
West Harnham 14 B2
West Harptree 23 D7
West Hatch 11 B7
Westhay 23 E6
Westhead 86 D2
West Head 67 D5
West Heath
Ches E 74 C5
Hants 26 D3
Hants 27 D6
West Helmsdale 157 H13
West Hendred 38 F4
West Heslerton 96 B5
Westhide 49 E7
Westhill
Aberds 141 D7
Highld 151 G10
West Hill
Devon 11 E5
E Yorks 97 C7
N Som 23 B6
West Hoathly 28 F4
West Holme 13 F6
Westhope
Hereford 49 D6
Shrops 60 F4
West Horndon 42 F2
Westhorpe
Lincs 78 F5
Suff 56 C4
West Horrington 23 E7
West Horsley 27 D8
West Horton 123 F6
West Hougham 31 E6
Westhoughton 86 D4
West Houlland 160 H4
Westhouse 93 B6
Westhouses 76 D4
Westhumble 28 D2
West Huntington 96 D2
West Hythe 19 B8
West Ilsley 38 F4
Westing 160 C7
West Itchenor 15 D8
West Keal 79 C6
West Kennett 25 C6
West Kilbride 118 E2
West Kingsdown 29 C6
West Kington 24 B3
West Kinharrachie 153 E9
West Kirby 85 F3
West Knapton 96 B4
West Knighton 12 F5
West Knoyle 24 F3
West Kyloe 123 E6
Westlake 6 D4
West Lambrook 12 C2
West Langdon 31 E7
West Langwell 157 J9
West Lavington
Wilts 24 D5
W Sus 16 B2
West Layton 101 D6
West Lea 111 E7
West Leake 64 B2
West Learmouth 122 F4
Westleigh
Devon 9 B6
Devon 11 C5
Gtr Man 86 D4
West Leigh 9 D8
Westleton 57 C8
West Lexham 67 C8
Westley
Shrops 60 D3
Suff 56 C2
Westley Waterless 55 D7
West Lilling 96 C2
Westlington 39 C7
Westlinton 108 C3
West Linton 120 D4
West Liss 15 B8
West Littleton 24 B2
West Looe 5 D7
West Luccombe 21 E7
West Lulworth 13 F6
West Lutton 96 C5
West Lydford 23 F7
West Lyng 11 B8
West Lynn 67 B6
West Malling 29 D7
West Malvern 50 E2
West Marden 15 C8
West Marina 18 E4
West Markham 77 B7
Westmarsh 31 C6
West Marsh 91 C6
West Marton 93 D8
West Meon 15 B7
West Mersea 43 C6
Westmeston 17 C7
Westmill 41 B6
West Milton 12 E3
Westminster 28 B4
West Minster 30 B3
West Molesey 28 C2
West Monkton 11 B7
West Moors 13 D8
West Morriston 122 E2
Westmuir 134 D3
West Muir 135 C5
Westness 159 F4
West Ness 96 B2
West Newham 110 B3
Westnewton
Cumb 107 E8
Northumb 122 F5
West Newton
E Yorks 97 F7
Norf 67 B6
West Norwood 28 B4
Westoe 111 C6
West Ogwell 7 B6
Weston
Bath 24 C2
Ches E 74 D4
Devon 11 F6
Dorset 12 G4
Halton 86 F3
Hants 15 B8
Herts 54 F3
Lincs 66 B2
Notts 77 C7
N Yorks 94 E4
Shrops 61 B5
Shrops 61 E5
Staffs 62 B3
W Berks 25 B8
W Nhants 52 E3
Weston Beggard 49 E7
Westonbirt 37 F5
Weston by Welland 64 E4
Weston Colville 55 D7
Westoncommon 60 B4
Weston Coyney 75 E6
Weston Favell 53 C5
Weston Green
Cambs 55 D7
Norf 68 C4
Weston Heath 61 C7
Weston Hills 66 B2
Westoning 53 F8
Weston-in-Gordano 23 B6
Weston Jones 61 B7
Weston Longville 68 C4
Weston Lullingfields 60 B4
Weston-on-the-Green 39 C5
Weston-on-Trent 63 B8
Weston Patrick 26 E4
Weston Rhyn 73 F6
Weston-sub-Edge 51 E6
Weston-super-Mare 22 C5
Weston Turville 40 C1
Weston under Lizard 62 C2
Weston under Penyard 36 B3
Weston under Wetherley 51 C8
Weston Underwood
Derbys 76 E2
M Keynes 53 D6
Westonzoyland 23 F5
West Orchard 13 C6
West Overton 25 C6
Westow 96 C3
West Park 111 F7
West Parley 13 E8
West Peckham 29 D7
West Pelton 110 D5
West Pennard 23 F7
West Pentire 4 C2
West Perry 54 C2
Westport
Argyll 143 F7
Som 11 C8
West Putford 9 C5
West Quantoxhead 22 E3
West Rainton 111 E6
West Rasen 90 F4
West Raynham 80 E4
West Retford 89 F7
Westrigg 120 C2
West Rounton 102 D2
West Row 55 B7
West Rudham 80 E4
West Runton 81 C7
Westruther 122 E2
Westry 66 E3
West Saltoun 121 C7
West Sandwick 160 E6
West Scrafton 101 F5
West Sleekburn 117 F8
West Somerton 69 C7
West Stafford 12 F5
West Stockwith 89 E8
West Stoke 16 D2
West Stonesdale 100 D3
West Stoughton 23 E6
West Stour 13 B5
West Stourmouth 31 C6
West Stow 56 B2
West Stowell 25 C6
West Strathan 157 C8
West Stratton 26 E3
West Street 30 D3
West Tanfield 95 B5
West Taphouse 5 C6
West Tarbert 145 G7
West Thirston 117 E7
West Thorney 15 D8
West Thurrock 29 B6
West Tilbury 29 B7
West Tisted 15 B7
West Tofts
Norf 67 E8
Perth 133 F8
West Torrington 90 F5
West Town
Hants 15 E8
N Som 23 C6
West Tytherley 14 B3
West Tytherton 24 B4
Westville 76 E5
West Walton 66 C4
West Walton Highway 66 C4
Westward 108 E2
Westward Ho! 9 B6
Westwell
Kent 30 E3
Oxon 38 D2
Westwell Leacon 30 E3
West Wellow 14 C3
West Wemyss 128 E5
Westwick
Cambs 54 C5
Durham 101 C5
Norf 81 E8
West Wick 23 C5
West Wickham
Cambs 55 E7
London 28 C4
West Williamston 32 D1
West Willoughby 78 E2
West Winch 67 C6
West Winterslow 25 F7
West Wittering 15 E8
West Witton 101 F5
Westwood
Devon 10 E5
Wilts 24 D3
West Woodburn 116 F4
West Woodhay 25 C8
West Woodlands 24 E2
Westwoodside 89 E8
West Worldham 26 F5
West Worlington 10 C2
West Worthing 16 D5
West Wratting 55 D7
West Wycombe 39 E8
West Wylam 110 C4
West Yell 160 E6
Wetheral 108 D4
Wetherby 95 E7
Wetherden 56 C4
Wetheringsett 56 C5
Wethersfield 55 F8
Wethersta 160 G5
Wetherup Street 56 C5
Wetley Rocks 75 E6
Wettenhall 74 C3
Wetton 75 D8
Wetwang 96 D5
Wetwood 74 F4
Wexcombe 25 D7
Wexham Street 40 F2
Weybourne 81 C7
Weybread 68 F5
Weybridge 27 C8
Weycroft 11 E8
Weydale 158 D3
Weyhill 25 E8
Weymouth 12 G4
Whaddon
Bucks 53 F6
Cambs 54 E4
Glos 37 C5
Wilts 14 B2
Whale 99 B7
Whaley 76 B5
Whaley Bridge 87 F8
Whaley Thorns 76 B5
Whaligoe 158 F5
Whalley 93 F7
Whalton 117 F7
Wham 93 C7
Whaplode 66 B3
Whaplode Drove 66 C3
Whaplode St Catherine 66 B3
Wharfe 93 C7
Wharles 92 F4
Wharncliffe Side 88 E3
Wharram le Street 96 C4
Wharton 74 C3
Wharton Green 74 C3
Whashton 101 D6
Whatcombe 13 D6
Whatcote 51 E8
Whatfield 56 E4
Whatley
Som 11 D8
Som 24 E2
Whatlington 18 D4
Whatstandwell 76 D3
Whatton 77 F7
Whauphill 105 E8
Whaw 100 D4
Wheatacre 69 E7
Wheatcroft 76 D3
Wheathampstead 40 C4
Wheathill 61 F6
Wheatley
Devon 10 E4
Hants 27 E5
Oxon 39 D5
S Yorks 89 D6
W Yorks 87 B8
Wheatley Hill 111 F6
Wheaton Aston 62 C2
Wheddon Cross 21 F8
Wheedlemont 140 B3
Wheelerstreet 27 E7
Wheelock 74 D4
Wheelock Heath 74 D4
Wheelton 86 B4
Wheen 134 B3
Wheldrake 96 E2
Whelford 38 E1
Whelpley Hill 40 D2
Whempstead 41 B6
Whenby 96 C2
Whepstead 56 D2
Wherstead 57 E5
Wherwell 25 E8
Wheston 75 B8
Whetsted 29 E7
Whetstone 64 E2
Whicham 98 F3
Whichford 51 F8
Whickham 110 C5
Whiddon Down 9 E8
Whigstreet 134 E4
Whilton 52 C4
Whimble 9 D5
Whim Farm 120 D5
Whimple 10 E5
Whimpwell Green 69 B6
Whinburgh 68 D3
Whinnieliggate 106 D4
Whinnyfold 153 E10
Whippingham 15 E6
Whipsnade 40 C3
Whipton 10 E4
Whirlow 88 F4
Whisby 78 C2
Whissendine 64 C5
Whissonsett 80 E5
Whistlefield
Argyll 145 D10
Argyll 145 D11
Whistley Green 27 B5
Whiston
Mers 86 E2
Staffs 62 C2
Staffs 75 E7
S Yorks 88 F5
W Nhants 53 C6
Whitbeck 98 F3
Whitbourne 50 D2
Whitburn
T&W 111 C7
W Loth 120 C2
Whitburn Colliery 111 C7
Whitby
Ches W 73 B7
N Yorks 103 C6
Whitbyheath 73 B7
Whitchurch
Bath 23 C8
Bucks 39 B7
Cardiff 35 F5
Devon 6 B2
Hants 26 E2
Hereford 36 C2
Oxon 26 B4
Pembs 44 C2
Shrops 74 E2
Whitchurch Canonicorum 11 E8
Whitchurch Hill 26 B4
Whitcombe 12 F5
Whitcott Keysett 60 F2
Whiteacen 152 D2
Whiteacre Heath 63 E6
Whitebridge 137 C7
Whitebrook 36 D2
Whiteburn 121 E8
Whitecairns 141 C8
Whitecastle 120 E3
Whitechapel 93 E5
Whitecleat 159 H6
White Coppice 86 C4
Whitecraig 121 B6
Whitecroft 36 D3
Whitecross
Corn 4 B4
Falk 120 B2
Staffs 62 B2
Whiteface 151 C10
Whitefarland 143 D9
Whitefaulds 112 D2
Whitefield
Gtr Man 87 D6
Perth 134 F1
Whiteford 141 B6
Whitegate 74 C3
Whitehall
Blackburn 86 B4
W Sus 16 B5
Whitehall Village 159 F7
Whitehaven 98 C1
Whitehill 27 F5
Whitehills
Aberds 153 B6
S Lanark 119 D6
Whitehough 87 F8
Whitehouse
Aberds 140 C5
Argyll 145 G7
Whiteinch 118 C5
Whitekirk 129 F7
White Lackington 12 E5
White Ladies Aston 50 D4

Whitelaw 119 E6
Whiteleas 111 C6
Whiteley Bank 15 F6
Whiteley Green 75 B6
Whiteley Village 27 C8
White Lund 92 C4
Whitemans Green 17 B7
White Mill 33 B5
Whitemire 151 F12
Whitemoor 4 D4
Whitemore 75 C5
Whitenap 14 B4
White Ness 160 J5
White Notley 42 C3
Whiteoak Green 38 C3
Whiteparish 14 B3
White Pit 79 B6
White Post 77 D6
Whiterashes 141 B7
White Rocks 35 B8
White Roding 42 C1
Whiterow 158 F5
Whiteshill 37 D5
Whiteside — Northumb 109 C7; W Loth 120 C2
Whitesmith 18 D2
Whitestaunton 11 C7
Whitestone — Devon 10 E3; Devon 20 E3; Warks 63 F7
Whitestones 153 C6
Whitestreet Green 56 F3
Whitewall Corner 96 B3
White Waltham 27 B6
Whiteway — Glos 37 C6; Glos 37 E6
Whitewell — Aberds 153 B9; Lancs 93 E6
Whitewell Bottom 87 B6
Whiteworks 6 B4
Whitfield — Kent 31 E7; Northumb 109 D7; S Glos 36 F3; W Nhants 52 F4
Whitford — Devon 11 E7; Flint 72 B5
Whitgift 90 B2
Whitgreave 62 B2
Whithorn 105 E8
Whiting Bay 143 F11
Whitkirk 95 F6
Whitland 32 C2
Whitletts 112 B3
Whitley — N Yorks 89 B6; Reading 26 B5; Wilts 24 C3
Whitley Bay 111 B6
Whitley Chapel 110 D2
Whitley Lower 88 C3
Whitley Row 29 D5
Whitlock's End 51 B6
Whitminster 36 D4
Whitmore 74 E5
Whitnage 10 C5
Whitnash 51 C8
Whitney-on-Wye 48 E4
Whitrigg — Cumb 108 D2; Cumb 108 F2
Whitsbury 14 C2
Whitsome 122 D4
Whitson 35 F7
Whitstable 30 C5
Whitstone 8 E4
Whittingham 117 C6
Whittingslow 60 F4
Whittington — Glos 37 B7; Lancs 93 B6; Norf 67 D7; Shrops 73 F7; Staffs 62 F7; Staffs 63 D5; Worcs 50 D3
Whittlebury 52 E4
Whittle-le-Woods 86 B3
Whittlesey 66 E2
Whittlesford 55 E5
Whittlestone Head 86 C4
Whitton — Borders 116 B3; N Lincs 90 B3; Northumb 117 D6; Powys 48 C4; Shrops 49 B7; Stockton 102 B1; Suff 56 E5
Whittonditch 25 B7
Whittonstall 110 D3
Whitway 26 D2
Whitwell — Derbys 76 B5; Herts 40 B4; IoW 15 G6; N Yorks 101 E7; Rutland 65 D6
Whitwell-on-the-Hill 96 C3
Whitwell Street 81 E7
Whitwick 63 C8
Whitwood 88 B5
Whitworth 87 C6
Whixall 74 F2
Whixley 95 D7
Whoberley 51 B8
Whorlton — Durham 101 C6; N Yorks 102 D2
Whygate 109 B7
Whyle 49 C7
Whyteleafe 28 D4
Wibdon 36 E2
Wibsey 88 A2

Wibtoft 63 F8
Wichenford 50 C2
Wichling 30 D3
Wick — BCP 14 E2; Devon 11 D6; Highld 158 E5; S Glos 24 B2; Shetland 160 K6; V Glam 21 B8; Wilts 14 B2; Worcs 50 E4; W Sus 16 D4
Wicken — Cambs 55 B6; W Nhants 52 F5
Wicken Bonhunt 55 F6
Wickenby 90 F4
Wicken Green Village 80 D4
Wickersley 89 E5
Wickford 42 E3
Wickham — Hants 15 C6; W Berks 25 B8
Wickham Bishops 42 C4
Wickhambreaux 31 D6
Wickhambrook 55 D8
Wickhamford 51 E5
Wickham Market 57 D7
Wickhampton 69 D7
Wickham St Paul 56 F2
Wickham Skeith 56 C4
Wickham Street — Suff 55 D8; Suff 56 C4
Wick Hill 27 C5
Wicklewood 68 D3
Wickmere 81 D7
Wick St Lawrence 23 C5
Wickwar 36 F4
Widdington 55 F6
Widdrington 117 E8
Widdrington Station 117 E8
Widecombe in the Moor 6 B5
Widegates 6 D2
Widemouth Bay 8 D4
Widewall 159 J5
Widford — Essex 42 D2; Herts 41 C7
Widham 37 F7
Widmer End 40 E1
Widmerpool 64 B3
Widnes 86 F3
Wigan 86 D3
Wiggaton 11 E6
Wiggenhall St Germans 67 C5
Wiggenhall St Mary Magdalen 67 C5
Wiggenhall St Mary the Virgin 67 C5
Wigginton — Herts 40 C2; Oxon 51 F8; Staffs 63 D6; York 95 D8
Wigglesworth 93 D8
Wiggonby 108 D2
Wiggonholt 16 C4
Wighill 95 E7
Wighton 80 D5
Wigley 14 C4
Wigmore — Hereford 49 C6; Medway 30 C2
Wigsley 77 B8
Wigsthorpe 65 F7
Wigston 64 E3
Wigthorpe 89 F6
Wigtoft 79 F5
Wigton 108 E2
Wigtown 105 D8
Wigtwizzle 88 E3
Wike 95 E6
Wike Well End 89 C7
Wilbarston 64 F5
Wilberfoss 96 D3
Wilberlee 87 C8
Wilburton 55 B5
Wilby — N Nhants 53 C6; Norf 68 F3; Suff 57 B6
Wilcot 25 C6
Wilcott 60 C3
Wilcrick 35 F8
Wilday Green 76 B3
Wildboarclough 75 C6
Wilden — Bedford 53 D8; Worcs 50 B3
Wildhern 25 D8
Wildhill 41 D5
Wildmoor 50 B4
Wildsworth 90 E2
Wilford 77 F5
Wilkesley 74 E3
Wilkhaven 151 C12
Wilkieston 120 C4
Willand 10 C5
Willaston — Ches E 74 D3; Ches W 73 B7
Willen 53 E6
Willenhall — W Mid 51 B8; W Mid 62 E3
Willerby — E Yorks 97 F6; N Yorks 97 B6
Willersey 51 F6
Willersley 48 E5
Willesborough 30 E4
Willesborough Lees 30 E4
Willesden 41 F5
Willett 22 F3
Willey — Shrops 61 E6; Warks 63 F8
Willey Green 27 D7

Williamscott 52 E2
Willian 54 F3
Willingale 42 D1
Willingdon 18 E2
Willingham 54 B5
Willingham by Stow 90 F2
Willington — Bedford 54 E2; Derbys 63 B6; Durham 110 F4; T&W 111 C6; Warks 51 F7
Willington Corner 74 C2
Willisham Tye 56 D4
Willitoft 96 F3
Williton 22 E2
Willoughbridge 74 E4
Willoughby — Lincs 79 B7; Warks 52 C3
Willoughby-on-the-Wolds 64 B3
Willoughby Waterleys 64 E2
Willoughton 90 E3
Willows Green 42 C3
Willsbridge 23 B8
Willsworthy 9 F7
Wilmcote 51 D6
Wilmington — Devon 11 E7; E Sus 18 E2; Kent 29 B6
Wilminstone 6 B2
Wilmslow 87 F6
Wilnecote 63 D6
Wilpshire 93 F6
Wilsden 94 F3
Wilsford — Lincs 78 E3; Wilts 25 D6; Wilts 25 F6
Wilsill 94 C4
Wilsley Pound 18 B4
Wilsom 26 F5
Wilson 63 B8
Wilsontown 120 D2
Wilstead 53 E8
Wilsthorpe 65 C7
Wilstone 40 C2
Wilton — Borders 115 C7; Cumb 98 C2; N Yorks 103 F6; Redcar 102 C3; Wilts 25 C7; Wilts 25 F5
Wimbish 55 F6
Wimbish Green 55 F7
Wimblebury 62 C4
Wimbledon 28 B3
Wimblington 66 E4
Wimborne Minster 13 E8
Wimborne St Giles 13 C8
Wimbotsham 67 D6
Wimpson 14 C4
Wimpstone 51 E7
Wincanton 12 B5
Wincham 74 B3
Winchburgh 120 B3
Winchcombe 37 B7
Winchelsea 19 D6
Winchelsea Beach 19 D6
Winchester 15 B5
Winchet Hill 29 E8
Winchfield 27 D5
Winchmore Hill — Bucks 40 E2; London 41 E6
Wincle 75 C6
Wincobank 88 E4
Windermere 99 E6
Winderton 51 E8
Windhill 151 G8
Windhouse 160 D6
Windlehurst 87 F7
Windlesham 27 C7
Windley 76 E3
Windmill Hill — E Sus 18 D3; Som 11 C8
Windrush 38 C1
Windsor — N Lincs 89 C8; Windsor 27 B7
Windsoredge 37 D5
Windygates 128 D5
Windyknowe 120 C2
Windywalls 122 F3
Wineham 17 B6
Winestead 91 B6
Winewall 94 E2
Winfarthing 68 F4
Winford — IoW 15 F6; N Som 23 C7
Winforton 48 E4
Winfrith Newburgh 13 F6
Wing — Bucks 40 B1; Rutland 65 D5
Wingate 111 F7
Wingates — Gtr Man 86 D4; Northumb 117 E7
Wingerworth 76 C3
Wingfield — C Beds 40 B2; Suff 57 B6; Wilts 24 D3
Wingham 31 D6
Wingmore 31 E5
Wingrave 40 C1
Winkburn 77 D7
Winkfield 27 B6
Winkfield Row 27 B6
Winkhill 75 D7
Winkleigh 9 D8
Winksley 95 B5
Winkton 14 E2
Winlaton 110 C4

Winless 158 E5
Winmarleigh 92 E4
Winnal 49 F6
Winnall 15 B5
Winnersh 27 B5
Winscales 98 B2
Winscombe 23 D6
Winsford — Ches W 74 C3; Som 21 F8
Winsham 11 D8
Winshill 63 B6
Winskill 109 F5
Winslade 26 E4
Winsley 24 C3
Winslow 39 B7
Winson 37 D7
Winson Green 62 F4
Winsor 14 C4
Winster — Cumb 99 E6; Derbys 76 C2
Winston — Durham 101 C6; Suff 57 C5
Winstone 37 D6
Winston Green 57 C5
Winswell 9 C6
Winterborne Clenston 13 D6
Winterborne Herringston 12 F4
Winterborne Houghton 13 D6
Winterborne Kingston 13 E6
Winterborne Monkton 12 F4
Winterborne Stickland 13 D6
Winterborne Whitechurch 13 D6
Winterborne Zelston 13 E6
Winterbourne — S Glos 36 F3; W Berks 26 B2
Winterbourne Abbas 12 F4
Winterbourne Bassett 25 B6
Winterbourne Dauntsey 25 F6
Winterbourne Down 23 B8
Winterbourne Earls 25 F6
Winterbourne Gunner 25 F6
Winterbourne Monkton 25 B6
Winterbourne Steepleton 12 F4
Winterbourne Stoke 25 E5
Winter Gardens 42 F3
Winteringham 90 B3
Winterley 74 D4
Wintersett 88 C4
Wintershill 15 C6
Winterton 90 C3
Winterton-on-Sea 69 C7
Winthorpe — Lincs 79 C8; Notts 77 D8
Winton — BCP 13 E8; Cumb 100 C2; N Yorks 102 E2
Wintringham 96 B4
Winwick — Cambs 65 F8; Warr 86 E4; W Nhants 52 B4
Wirksworth 76 D2
Wirksworth Moor 76 D3
Wirswall 74 E2
Wisbech 66 D4
Wisbech St Mary 66 D4
Wisborough Green 16 B4
Wiseton 89 F8
Wishaw — N Lanark 119 D7; Warks 63 E5
Wisley 27 D8
Wispington 78 B5
Wissenden 30 E3
Wissett 57 B7
Wistanstow 60 F4
Wistanswick 61 B6
Wistaston 74 D3
Wistaston Green 74 D3
Wiston — Pembs 32 C1; S Lanark 120 F2; W Sus 16 C5
Wistow — Cambs 66 F2; N Yorks 95 F8
Wiswell 93 F7
Witcham 66 F4
Witchampton 13 D7
Witchford 55 B6
Witham 42 C4
Witham Friary 24 E2
Witham on the Hill 65 C7
Withcall 91 F6
Withdean 17 D7
Witherenden Hill 18 C3
Witheridge 10 C3
Witherley 63 E7
Withern 91 F8
Withernsea 91 B7
Withernwick 97 E7
Withersdale Street 69 F5
Withersfield 55 E7
Witherslack 99 F6
Withiel 4 C4
Withiel Florey 21 F8
Withington — Glos 37 C7

Withington continued — Staffs 75 F7
Withington Green 74 B5
Withleigh 10 C4
Withnell 86 B4
Withybrook 63 F8
Withycombe 22 E2
Withycombe Raleigh 10 F5
Withyham 29 F5
Withypool 21 F7
Witley 27 F7
Witnesham 57 D5
Witney 38 C3
Wittering 65 D7
Wittersham 19 C5
Witton — Angus 135 B5; Worcs 50 C3
Witton Bridge 69 A6
Witton Gilbert 110 E5
Witton-le-Wear 110 F4
Witton Park 110 F4
Wiveliscombe 11 B5
Wivelrod 26 F4
Wivelsfield 17 B7
Wivelsfield Green 17 B7
Wivenhoe 43 B6
Wivenhoe Cross 43 B6
Wiveton 81 C6
Wix 43 B7
Wixford 51 D5
Wixhill 61 B5
Wixoe 55 E8
Woburn 53 F7
Woburn Sands 53 F7
Wokefield Park 26 C4
Woking 27 D8
Wokingham 27 C6
Wolborough 7 B6
Woldingham 28 D4
Wold Newton — E Yorks 97 B6; NE Lincs 91 E6
Wolfclyde 120 F3
Wolferton 67 B6
Wolfhill 134 F1
Wolf's Castle 44 C4
Wolfsdale 44 C4
Woll 115 B7
Wollaston — N Nhants 53 C7; Shrops 60 C3
Wollaton 76 F5
Wollerton 74 F3
Wollescote 62 F3
Wolsingham 110 F3
Wolstanton 75 E5
Wolston 52 B2
Wolvercote 38 D4
Wolverhampton 62 E3
Wolverley — Shrops 73 F8; Worcs 50 B3
Wolverton — Hants 26 D3; M Keynes 53 E6; Warks 51 C7
Wolverton Common 26 D3
Wolvesnewton 36 E1
Wolvey 63 F8
Wolviston 102 B2
Wombleton 102 F4
Wombourne 62 E2
Wombwell 88 D4
Womenswold 31 D6
Womersley 89 C6
Wonastow 36 C1
Wonersh 27 E8
Wonson 9 F8
Wonston 26 F2
Wooburn 40 F2
Wooburn Green 40 F2
Woodacott 9 D5
Woodale 94 B3
Woodbank 73 B7
Woodbastwick 69 C6
Woodbeck 77 B7
Woodborough — Notts 77 E6; Wilts 25 D6
Woodbridge — Dorset 12 C5; Suff 57 E6
Woodbury 10 F5
Woodbury Salterton 10 F5
Woodchester 37 D5
Woodchurch — Kent 19 B6; Mers 85 F3
Woodcombe 21 E8
Woodcote 39 F6
Woodcott 26 D2
Woodcroft 36 E2
Woodcutts 13 C7
Wood Dalling 81 E6
Woodditton 55 D7
Woodeaton 39 C5
Woodend — Cumb 98 E3; W Nhants 52 E4; W Sus 16 D2
Wood End — Herts 41 B6; Warks 51 B6; Warks 63 E6
Wood Enderby 79 C5
Woodend Green 52 F6
Woodfalls 14 B2
Woodfield — Oxon 39 B5; S Ayrs 112 B3
Wood Field 28 D2
Woodford — Corn 8 C4; Devon 7 D5; Glos 36 E3; Gtr Man 87 F6; London 41 E7; N Nhants 53 B7
Woodford Bridge 41 E7
Woodford Halse 52 D3
Woodgate — Norf 68 C3

Woodgate continued — W Sus 16 D3
Woodgreen 14 C2
Wood Green 41 E6
Woodhall — Herts 41 C5; Invclyd 118 B3; N Yorks 100 E4
Woodhall Spa 78 C4
Woodham 27 C8
Woodham Ferrers 42 E3
Woodham Mortimer 42 D4
Woodham Walter 42 D4
Woodhaven 129 B6
Wood Hayes 62 D3
Woodhead 153 E7
Woodhey 87 C5
Woodhill 61 F7
Woodhorn 117 F8
Woodhouse — Leics 64 C2; N Lincs 89 D8; S Yorks 88 F5; W Yorks 88 B4; W Yorks 95 F5
Woodhouse Eaves 64 C2
Woodhouselee 120 C5
Woodhouselees 108 B3
Woodhouse Park 87 F6
Woodhouses — Ches W 74 B2; Gtr Man 87 D7; Gtr Man 88 D4; Staffs 63 C5; Staffs 63 C6
Woodhurst 54 B4
Woodingdean 17 D7
Woodkirk 88 B3
Woodland — Devon 7 C5; Durham 101 B5
Woodlands — Aberds 141 E6; Dorset 13 D8; Hants 14 C4; Highld 151 E8; N Yorks 95 D6; S Yorks 89 D6
Woodlands Park 27 B6
Woodlands St Mary 25 B8
Wood Lanes 87 F7
Woodleigh 6 E5
Woodlesford 88 B4
Woodley — Gtr Man 87 E7; Wokingham 27 B5
Woodmancote — Glos 36 E4; Glos 37 B7; Glos 37 D7; W Sus 15 D8; W Sus 17 C6
Woodmancott 26 E3
Woodmansey 97 F6
Woodmansterne 28 D3
Woodminton 13 B8
Woodnesborough 31 D7
Wood Norton 81 E6
Woodnewton 65 E7
Woodplumpton 92 F5
Woodrising 68 D2
Woodseaves — Shrops 74 F3; Staffs 61 B7
Woodsend 25 B7
Woodsetts 89 F6
Woodsford 13 E5
Wood's Green 18 B3
Woodside — Aberdeen 141 D8; Aberds 153 D10; Brack 27 B7; Fife 129 D6; Hants 14 E4; Herts 41 D5; Perth 134 F2
Woodside of Arbeadie 141 E6
Woodstock — Oxon 38 C4; Pembs 32 B1
Wood Street — Norf 69 B6; Sur 27 D7
Woodthorpe — Derbys 76 B4; Leics 64 C2; Lincs 91 F8; York 95 E8
Woodton 69 E5
Woodtown — Devon 9 B6; Devon 9 B6
Woodvale 85 C4
Woodville 63 C7
Wood Walton 66 F2
Woodyates 13 C8
Woofferton 49 C7
Wookey 23 E7
Wookey Hole 23 E7
Wool 13 F6
Woolacombe 20 E3
Woolage Green 31 E6
Woolaston 36 E2
Woolavington 22 E5
Woolbeding 16 B2
Wooldale 88 D2
Wooler 117 B5
Woolfardisworthy — Devon 8 B5; Devon 10 D3
Woolfords Cottages 120 D3
Woolhampton 26 C3
Woolhope 49 F8
Woolhope Cockshoot 49 F8
Woolland 13 D5
Woollaton 9 C6
Woolley — Bath 24 C2; Cambs 54 B2; Corn 8 C4; Derbys 76 C3; W Yorks 88 C4
Woolmere Green 50 C4
Woolmer Green 41 C5

Woolpit 56 C3
Woolscott 52 C2
Woolsington 110 C4
Woolstanwood 74 D3
Woolstaston 60 E4
Woolsthorpe — Lincs 65 B6; Lincs 77 F8
Woolston — Devon 6 E5; Shrops 60 B3; Shrops 60 F4; Soton 14 C5; Warr 86 F4
Woolstone — M Keynes 53 F6; Oxon 38 F2
Woolton 86 F2
Woolton Hill 26 C2
Woolverstone 57 F5
Woolverton 24 D2
Woolwich 28 B5
Woolwich Ferry 28 B5
Woonton 49 D5
Wooperton 117 B6
Woore 74 E4
Wootten Green 57 B6
Wootton — Bedford 53 E8; Hants 14 E3; Hereford 48 D5; Kent 31 E6; N Lincs 90 C4; Oxon 38 C4; Oxon 38 D4; Shrops 49 B6; Shrops 60 B3; Staffs 62 B2; Staffs 75 E8; W Nhants 53 D5
Wootton Bridge 15 E6
Wootton Common 15 E6
Wootton Courtenay 21 E8
Wootton Fitzpaine 11 E8
Wootton Rivers 25 C6
Wootton St Lawrence 26 D3
Wootton Wawen 51 C6
Worcester 50 D3
Worcester Park 28 C3
Wordsley 62 F2
Worfield 61 E7
Work 159 G5
Workington 98 B1
Worlaby 90 C4
World's End 26 B2
Worle 23 C5
Worleston 74 D3
Worlingham 69 F7
Worlington 55 B7
Worlingworth 57 C6
Wormald Green 95 C6
Wormbridge 49 F6
Wormegay 67 C6
Wormelow Tump 49 F6
Wormhill 75 B8
Wormingford 56 F3
Worminghall 39 D6
Wormington 50 F5
Wormit 129 B5
Wormleighton 52 D2
Wormley — Herts 41 D6; Sur 27 F7
Wormley West End 41 D6
Wormshill 30 D2
Wormsley 49 E6
Worplesdon 27 D7
Worrall 88 E4
Worsbrough Common 88 D4
Worsbrough 88 D4
Worsley 86 D5
Worstead 69 B6
Worsthorne 93 F8
Worston 93 E7
Worswell 6 E3
Worth — Kent 31 D7; W Sus 28 F4
Wortham 56 B4
Worthen 60 D3
Worthenbury 73 E8
Worthing — Norf 68 C2; W Sus 16 D5
Worthington 63 B8
Worth Matravers 13 G7
Wortley — S Yorks 88 E4; W Yorks 95 F5
Worton — N Yorks 100 E4; Wilts 24 D4
Wortwell 69 F5
Wotherton 60 D2
Wotter 6 C3
Wotton 28 E2
Wotton-under-Edge 36 E4
Wotton Underwood 39 C6
Woughton on the Green 53 F6
Wouldham 29 C8
Wrabness 57 F5
Wrafton 20 F3
Wragby — Lincs 78 B4; W Yorks 88 C5
Wragholme 91 E7
Wramplingham 68 D4
Wrangbrook 89 C5
Wrangle 79 D7
Wrangle Bank 79 D7
Wrangle Lowgate 79 D7
Wrangway 11 C6
Wrantage 11 B8
Wrawby 90 D4

Wraxall — Dorset 12 D3; N Som 23 B6; Som 23 F8
Wray 93 C6
Wraysbury 27 B8
Wrayton 93 B6
Wrea Green 92 F3
Wreay — Cumb 99 B6; Cumb 108 E4
Wrecclesham 27 E6
Wrecsam = Wrexham 73 D7
Wrekenton 111 D5
Wrelton 103 F5
Wrenbury 74 E2
Wreningham 68 E4
Wrentham 69 F8
Wrenthorpe 88 B4
Wrentnall 60 D4
Wressle — E Yorks 96 F3; N Lincs 90 D3
Wrestlingworth 54 E3
Wretham 68 F2
Wretton 67 D6
Wrexham = Wrecsam 73 D7
Wrexham Industrial Estate 73 E7
Wribbenhall 50 B2
Wrightington Bar 86 C3
Wrinehill 74 E4
Wrington 23 C6
Writhlington 24 D2
Writtle 42 D2
Wrockwardine 61 C6
Wroot 89 D8
Wrotham 29 D7
Wrotham Heath 29 D7
Wroughton 37 F8
Wroxall — IoW 15 G6; Warks 51 B7
Wroxeter 61 D5
Wroxham 69 C6
Wroxton 52 E2
Wyaston 75 E8
Wyberton 79 E6
Wyboston 54 D2
Wybunbury 74 E4
Wychbold 50 C4
Wych Cross 28 F5
Wyck 27 F5
Wyck Rissington 38 B1
Wycoller 94 F2
Wycomb 64 B4
Wycombe Marsh 40 E2
Wyddial 54 F4
Wye 30 E4
Wyesham 36 C2
Wyfordby 64 C4
Wyke — Dorset 13 B5; Shrops 61 D6; Sur 27 D6; W Yorks 88 B2
Wyke Regis 12 G4
Wykeham — N Yorks 96 B4; N Yorks 103 F7
Wyken 63 F7
Wykey 60 B3
Wykin 63 E8
Wylam 110 C4
Wylde Green 62 E5
Wyllie 35 E5
Wylye 24 F5
Wymering 15 D7
Wymeswold 64 B3
Wymington 53 C7
Wymondham — Leics 65 C5; Norf 68 D4
Wyndham 34 E3
Wynford Eagle 12 E3
Wyng 159 J4
Wynyard Village 102 B2
Wyre Piddle 50 E4
Wysall 64 B3
Wythall 51 B5
Wytham 38 D4
Wythburn 99 C5
Wythenshawe 87 F6
Wythop Mill 98 B3
Wyton 54 B3
Wyverstone 56 C4
Wyverstone Street 56 C4
Wyville 65 B5
Wyvis Lodge 150 D7

**Y**
Yaddlethorpe 90 D2
Yafford 15 F5
Yafforth 101 E8
Yalding 29 D7
Yanworth 37 C7
Yapham 96 D3
Yapton 16 D3
Yarburgh 91 E7
Yarcombe 11 D7
Yard 22 F2
Yardley 62 F5
Yardley Gobion 53 E5
Yardley Hastings 53 D6
Yardro 48 D4
Yarkhill 49 E8
Yarlet 62 B3
Yarlington 12 B4
Yarlside 92 C2
Yarm 102 C2
Yarmouth 14 F4
Yarnbrook 24 D3
Yarnfield 75 F6
Yarnscombe 9 B7
Yarnton 38 C4
Yarpole 49 C6
Yarrow 115 B6
Yarrow Feus 115 B6
Yarsop 49 E6
Yarwell 65 E7
Yate 36 F4
Yateley 27 C6
Yatesbury 25 B5

Yattendon 26 B3
Yatton — Hereford 49 C6; N Som 23 C6; Som 23 F8
Yatton Keynell 24 B3
Yaverland 15 F7
Yaxham 68 C3
Yaxley — Cambs 65 E8; Suff 56 B5
Yazor 49 E6
Y Bala = Bala 72 F3
Y Barri = Barry 22 C3
Y Bont-Faen = Cowbridge 21 B8
Y Drenewydd = Newtown 59 E8
Yeading 40 F4
Yeadon 94 E5
Yealand Conyers 92 B5
Yealand Redmayne 92 B5
Yealmpton 6 D3
Yearby 102 B4
Yearsley 95 B8
Yeaton 60 C4
Yeaveley 75 E8
Yedingham 96 B4
Yeldon 53 C8
Yelford 38 D3
Yelland 20 F3
Yelling 54 C3
Yelvertoft 52 B3
Yelverton — Devon 6 C3; Norf 69 D5
Yenston 12 B5
Yeoford 10 E2
Yeolmbridge 8 F5
Yeo Mill 10 B3
Yeovil 12 C3
Yeovil Marsh 12 C3
Yeovilton 12 B3
Yerbeston 32 D1
Yesnaby 159 G3
Yetlington 117 D6
Yetminster 12 C3
Yettington 11 F5
Yetts o'Muckhart 128 D2
Y Felinheli 82 E5
Y Fenni = Abergavenny 35 C6
Y Fflint = Flint 73 B6
Y Ffôr 70 D4
Y-Ffrith 72 A4
Y Gelli Gandryll = Hay-on-Wye 48 E4
Yieldshields 119 D8
Yiewsley 40 F3
Y Mwmbwls = The Mumbles 33 F7
Ynysboeth 34 E4
Ynysddu 35 E5
Ynysgyfflog 58 C3
Ynyshir 34 E4
Ynyslas 58 E3
Ynys-meudwy 33 D8
Ynystawe 33 D7
Ynysybwl 34 E4
Yockenthwaite 94 B2
Yockleton 60 C3
Yokefleet 90 B2
Yoker 118 C5
Yonder Bognie 152 D5
York 95 D8
Yorkletts 30 C4
Yorkley 36 D3
York Town 27 C6
Yorton 60 B5
Youlgreave 76 C2
Youlstone 8 C4
Youlthorpe 96 D3
Youlton 95 C7
Young's End 42 C3
Young Wood 78 B4
Yoxall 62 C5
Yoxford 57 C7
Y Pîl = Pyle 34 F2
Yr Hôb = Hope 73 D7
Y Rhws = Rhoose 22 C2
Y Rhyl = Rhyl 72 A4
Yr Wyddgrug = Mold 73 C6
Ysbyty-Cynfyn 47 B6
Ysbyty Ifan 72 E2
Ysbyty Ystwyth 47 B6
Ysceifiog 73 B5
Yspitty 33 E6
Ystalyfera 34 D1
Ystrad 34 E3
Ystrad Aeron 46 D4
Ystradfellte 34 C3
Ystradffîn 47 E6
Ystradgynlais 34 C1
Ystradmeurig 47 C6
Ystrad-mynach 35 E5
Ystradowen — Carms 33 C8; V Glam 22 B2
Ystumtuen 47 B6
Ythanbank 153 E9
Ythanwells 153 E6
Ythsie 153 E8
Y Trallwng = Welshpool 60 D2
Y Waun = Chirk 73 F6

**Z**
Zeal Monachorum 10 D2
Zeals 24 F2
Zelah 4 D3
Zennor 2 C3